Data Structures and Algorithms in Java™

Fifth Edition

Data Structures and Algorithms in Java™

Fifth Edition

Michael T. Goodrich
Department of Computer Science
University of California, Irvine

Roberto Tamassia
Department of Computer Science
Brown University

John Wiley & Sons, Inc.

New York • Chichester • Weinheim • Brisbane • Singapore • Toronto

ASSOCIATE PUBLISHER	Beth Golub
MARKETING MANAGER	Chris Ruel
MARKETING ASSISTANT	Diana Smith
MEDIA EDITOR	Lauren Sapira
MEDIA ASSISTANT	Andre Legaspi
PRODUCTION MANAGER	Micheline Frederick
EDITORIAL ASSISTANT	Mike Berlin

This book was set in LATEX by the authors and printed and bound by R.R. Donnelley - Craw-fordsville. The cover was printed by Phoenix Color, Inc. Cover image is from Iconotec Royalty-Free/Inmagine Corporation LLC.

This book is printed on acid free paper. ∞

Trademark Acknowledgments: *Java is a trademark of Sun Microsystems, Inc. UNIX® is a registered trademark in the United States and other countries, licensed through X/Open Company, Ltd. PowerPoint® is a trademark of Microsoft Corporation. All other product names mentioned herein are the trademarks of their respective owners.*

Library of Congress Cataloging-in-Publication Data

Goodrich, Michael T.
    Data structures and algorithms in Java / Michael T. Goodrich, Roberto Tamassia. – 5th ed.
        p. cm.
    Includes bibliographical references and index.
    ISBN 978-0-470-38326-1 (cloth)
    1. Java (Computer program language) 2. Data structures (Computer science)
    3. Computer algorithms. I. Tamassia, Roberto, 1960- II. Title.

    QA76.73.J38G66 2010
    005.1–dc22

        2009048008

Printed in the United States of America

10 9 8 7 6 5 4 3

To Karen, Paul, Anna, and Jack
  – *Michael T. Goodrich*

To Isabel
  – *Roberto Tamassia*

Preface

This fifth edition of *Data Structures and Algorithms in Java* is designed to provide an introduction to data structures and algorithms, including their design, analysis, and implementation. In terms of curricula based on the ***IEEE/ACM 2001 Computing Curriculum***, this book is appropriate for use in the courses CS102 (I/O/B versions), CS103 (I/O/B versions), CS111 (A version), and CS112 (A/I/O/F/H versions). We discuss its use for such courses in more detail later in this preface.

The major changes in the fifth edition are the following:

- We added more examples and discussion of data structure and algorithm analysis.
- We enhanced consistency with the Java Collections Framework.
- We enhanced the discussion of algorithmic design techniques, like dynamic programming and the greedy method.
- We added new material on improved Java I/O methods.
- We created an ***international student version*** of the book, which contains content, such as Java internationalization and international units, more appropriate for readers outside of North America and Europe.
- We added a discussion of the difference between array variable-name assignment and array cloning.
- We included an expanded discussion of the Deque interface and LinkedList class in Java.
- We increased coverage of entry objects in the Java Collection Framework.
- We fully integrated all code fragment APIs to use generic types.
- We added discussions of the NavigatableMap interface, as well as their implementations in the Java Collections Framework using skip lists.
- We included a discussion of the Java TreeMap class.
- We provided discriptions of the sorting methods included in the Java library.
- We expanded and revised exercises, continuing our approach of dividing them into reinforcement, creativity, and project exercises.

This book is related to the following books:

- M.T. Goodrich, R. Tamassia, and D.M. Mount, *Data Structures and Algorithms in C++*, John Wiley & Sons, Inc. This book has a similar overall structure to the present book, but uses C++ as the underlying language (with some modest, but necessary pedagogical differences required by this approach).
- M.T. Goodrich and R. Tamassia, *Algorithm Design: Foundations, Analysis, and Internet Examples*, John Wiley & Sons, Inc. This is a textbook for a more advanced algorithms and data structures course, such as CS210 (T/W/C/S versions) in the IEEE/ACM 2001 curriculum.

Use as a Textbook

The design and analysis of efficient data structures has long been recognized as a vital subject in computing, for the study of data structures is part of the core of every collegiate computer science and computer engineering major program we are familiar with. Typically, the introductory courses are presented as a two- or three-course sequence. Elementary data structures are often briefly introduced in the first programming course or in an introduction to computer science course and this is followed by a more in-depth introduction to data structures in the courses that follow after this. Furthermore, this course sequence is typically followed at a later point in the curriculum by a more in-depth study of data structures and algorithms. We feel that the central role of data structure design and analysis in the curriculum is fully justified, given the importance of efficient data structures in most software systems, including the Web, operating systems, databases, compilers, and scientific simulation systems.

With the emergence of the object-oriented paradigm as the framework of choice for building robust and reusable software, we have tried to take a consistent object-oriented viewpoint throughout this text. One of the main ideas of the object-oriented approach is that data should be presented as being encapsulated with the methods that access and modify them. That is, rather than simply viewing data as a collection of bytes and addresses, we think of data objects as instances of an ***abstract data type*** (***ADT***), which includes a repertoire of methods for performing operations on data objects of this type. Likewise, object-oriented solutions are often organized utilizing common ***design patterns***, which facilitate software reuse and robustness. Thus, we present each data structure using ADTs and their respective implementations and we introduce important design patterns as means to organize those implementations into classes, methods, and objects.

For each ADT presented in this book, we provide an associated Java interface. Also, concrete data structures realizing the ADTs are discussed and we often give concrete Java classes implementing these interfaces. We also give Java implementations of fundamental algorithms, such as sorting and graph searching. Moreover, in addition to providing techniques for using data structures to implement ADTs, we also give sample applications of data structures, such as in HTML tag matching and a simple system to maintain a photo album. Due to space limitations, however, we sometimes show only code fragments of some implementations in this book and make additional source code available on the companion web site. The Java code implementing fundamental data structures in this book is organized into a single Java package, net.datastructures, which forms a coherent library of data structures and algorithms in Java specifically designed for educational purposes in a way that is complementary with the Java Collections Framework. The net.datastructures library is not required, however, to get full use from this book.

Online Resources

This book is accompanied by an extensive accompanying set of online resources, which can be found at the following web site:

www.wiley.com/college/goodrich

Students are encouraged to use this site along with the book, to help with exercises and increase understanding of the subject. Instructors are likewise welcome to use the site to help plan, organize, and present their course materials. Included on this Web site is a collection of educational aids that augment the topics of this book, for both students and instructors. Because of their added value, some of these online resources are password protected.

For the Student

For all readers, and especially for students, we include the following resources:

- All the Java source code presented in this book.
- PDF handouts of Powerpoint slides (four-per-page) provided to instructors.
- A database of hints to *all* exercises, indexed by problem number.
- An online study guide, which includes solutions to selected exercises.

The hints should be of considerable use to anyone needing a little help getting started on certain exercises, and the solutions should help anyone wishing to see completed exercises. Students who have purchased a new copy of this book will get password access to the hints and other password-protected online resources at no extra charge. Other readers can purchase password access for a nominal fee.

For the Instructor

For instructors using this book, we include the following additional teaching aids:

- Solutions to over two hundred of the book's exercises.
- A database of additional exercises, suitable for quizzes and exams.
- The complete net.datastructures package.
- Additional Java source code.
- Slides in Powerpoint and PDF (one-per-page) format.
- Self-contained special-topic supplements, including discussions on convex hulls, range trees, and orthogonal segment intersection.
- Ready-to-use, turn-key projects, complete with supporting Java code for graphical-user interfaces (GUIs), so that students can concentrate on data structure design, implementation, and usage, rather than GUI programming.

The slides are fully editable, so as to allow an instructor using this book full freedom in customizing his or her presentations. All the online resources are provided at no extra charge to any instructor adopting this book for his or her course.

A Resource for Teaching Data Structures and Algorithms

This book contains many Java-code and pseudo-code fragments, and hundreds of exercises, which are divided into roughly 40% reinforcement exercises, 40% creativity exercises, and 20% programming projects.

This book can be used for the CS2 course, as descirbed in the 1978 ACM Computer Science Curriculum, or in courses CS102 (I/O/B versions), CS103 (I/O/B versions), CS111 (A version), and/or CS112 (A/I/O/F/H versions), as described in the IEEE/ACM 2001 Computing Curriculum, with instructional units as outlined in Table 0.1.

Instructional Unit	Relevant Material
PL1. Overview of Programming Languages	Chapters 1 & 2
PL2. Virtual Machines	Sections 14.1.1, 14.1.2, & 14.1.3
PL3. Introduction to Language Translation	Section 1.9
PL4. Declarations and Types	Sections 1.1, 2.4, & 2.5
PL5. Abstraction Mechanisms	Sections 2.4, 5.1, 5.2, 5.3, 6.1.1, 6.2, 6.4, 6.3, 7.1, 7.3.1, 8.1, 9.1, 9.5, 11.4, & 13.1
PL6. Object-Oriented Programming	Chapters 1 & 2 and Sections 6.2.2, 6.3, 7.3.7, 8.1.2, & 13.3.1
PF1. Fundamental Programming Constructs	Chapters 1 & 2
PF2. Algorithms and Problem-Solving	Sections 1.9 & 4.2
PF3. Fundamental Data Structures	Sections 3.1, 5.1–3.2, 5.3, , 6.1–6.4, 7.1, 7.3, 8.1, 8.3, 9.1–9.4, 10.1, & 13.1
PF4. Recursion	Section 3.5
SE1. Software Design	Chapter 2 and Sections 6.2.2, 6.3, 7.3.7, 8.1.2, & 13.3.1
SE2. Using APIs	Sections 2.4, 5.1, 5.2, 5.3, 6.1.1, 6.2, 6.4, 6.3, 7.1, 7.3.1, 8.1, 9.1, 9.5, 11.4, & 13.1
AL1. Basic Algorithmic Analysis	Chapter 4
AL2. Algorithmic Strategies	Sections 11.1.1, 11.5.1, 12.3.1, 12.4.2, & 12.2
AL3. Fundamental Computing Algorithms	Sections 8.1.4, 8.2.2, 8.3.5, 9.2, & 9.3.1, and Chapters 11, 12, & 13
DS1. Functions, Relations, and Sets	Sections 4.1, 8.1, & 11.4
DS3. Proof Techniques	Sections 4.3, 6.1.4, 7.3.3, 8.3, 10.2, 10.3, 10.4, 10.5, 11.2.1, 11.3.1, 11.4.3, 13.1, 13.3.1, 13.4, & 13.5
DS4. Basics of Counting	Sections 2.2.3 & 11.1.5
DS5. Graphs and Trees	Chapters 7, 8, 10, & 13
DS6. Discrete Probability	Appendix A and Sections 9.2.2, 9.4.2, 11.2.1, & 11.5

Table 0.1: Material for Units in the IEEE/ACM 2001 Computing Curriculum.

Contents and Organization

The chapters for this course are organized to provide a pedagogical path that starts with the basics of Java programming and object-oriented design. We provide an early discussion of concrete structures, like arrays and linked lists, so as to provide a concrete footing to build upon when constructing other data structures. We then add foundational techniques like recursion and algorithm analysis, and, in the main portion of the book, we present fundamental data structures and algorithms, concluding with a discussion of memory management (that is, the architectural underpinnings of data structures). Specifically, the chapters for this book are organized as follows:

1. Java Primer
2. Object-Oriented Design
3. Indices, Nodes, and Recursion
4. Analysis Tools
5. Stacks, Queues, and Deques
6. List and Iterator ADTs
7. Trees
8. Heaps and Priority Queues
9. Hash Tables, Maps, and Skip Lists
10. Search Trees
11. Sorting, Sets, and Selection
12. Strings and Dynamic Programming
13. Graph Algorithms
14. Memory Management and B-Trees
A. Useful Mathematical Facts

A more detailed listing of the contents of this book can be found in the table of contents.

Prerequisites

We have written this book assuming that the reader comes to it with certain knowledge. We assume that the reader is at least vaguely familiar with a high-level programming language, such as C, C++, Python, or Java, and that he or she understands the main constructs from such a high-level language, including:

- Variables and expressions.
- Methods (also known as functions or procedures).
- Decision structures (such as if-statements and switch-statements).
- Iteration structures (for-loops and while-loops).

For readers who are familiar with these concepts, but not with how they are expressed in Java, we provide a primer on the Java language in Chapter 1. Still, this book is primarily a data structures book, not a Java book; hence, it does not provide a comprehensive treatment of Java. Nevertheless, we do not assume that the reader is necessarily familiar with object-oriented design or with linked structures, such as linked lists, for these topics are covered in the core chapters of this book.

In terms of mathematical background, we assume the reader is somewhat familiar with topics from high-school mathematics. Even so, in Chapter 4, we discuss the seven most-important functions for algorithm analysis. In fact, sections that use something other than one of these seven functions are considered optional, and are indicated with a star ($\star$). We give a summary of other useful mathematical facts, including elementary probability, in Appendix A.

About the Authors

Professors Goodrich and Tamassia are well-recognized researchers in algorithms and data structures, having published many papers in this field, with applications to Internet computing, information visualization, computer security, and geometric computing. They have served as principal investigators in several joint projects sponsored by the National Science Foundation, the Army Research Office, the Office of Naval Research, and the Defense Advanced Research Projects Agency. They are also active in educational technology research.

Michael Goodrich received his Ph.D. in Computer Science from Purdue University in 1987. He is currently a Chancellor's Professor in the Department of Computer Science at University of California, Irvine. Previously, he was a professor at Johns Hopkins University. He is an editor for a number of journals in computer science theory, computational geometry, and graph algorithms. He is an ACM Distinguished Scientist, a Fellow of the American Association for the Advancement of Science (AAAS), a Fulbright Scholar, and a Fellow of the IEEE. He is a recipient of the IEEE Computer Society Technical Achievement Award, the ACM Recognition of Service Award, and the Pond Award for Excellence in Undergraduate Teaching.

Roberto Tamassia received his Ph.D. in Electrical and Computer Engineering from the University of Illinois at Urbana-Champaign in 1988. He is the Plastech Professor of Computer Science and the Chair of the Department of Computer Science at Brown University. He is also the Director of Brown's Center for Geometric Computing. His research interests include information security, cryptography, analysis, design, and implementation of algorithms, graph drawing and computational geometry. He is an IEEE Fellow and a recipient of the Technical Achievement Award from the IEEE Computer Society, for pioneering the field of graph drawing. He is an editor of several journals in geometric and graph algorithms. He previously served on the editorial board of *IEEE Transactions on Computers.*

In addition to their research accomplishments, the authors also have extensive experience in the classroom. For example, Dr. Goodrich has taught data structures and algorithms courses, including Data Structures as a freshman-sophomore level course and Introduction to Algorithms as an upper level course. He has earned several teaching awards in this capacity. His teaching style is to involve the students in lively interactive classroom sessions that bring out the intuition and insights behind data structuring and algorithmic techniques. Dr. Tamassia has taught Data Structures and Algorithms as an introductory freshman-level course since 1988. One thing that has set his teaching style apart is his effective use of interactive hypermedia presentations integrated with the Web.

Acknowledgments

There are a number of individuals who have made contributions to this book.

We are grateful to all our research collaborators and teaching assistants, who provided feedback on early drafts of chapters and have helped us in developing exercises, software, and algorithm animation systems. In particular, we would like to thank Jeff Achter, Vesselin Arnaudov, James Baker, Ryan Baker, Benjamin Boer, Mike Boilen, Devin Borland, Lubomir Bourdev, Stina Bridgeman, Bryan Cantrill, Yi-Jen Chiang, Robert Cohen, David Ellis, David Emory, Jody Fanto, Ben Finkel, Peter Fröhlich, Ashim Garg, Natasha Gelfand, Mark Handy, Michael Horn, Greg Howard, Benoît Hudson, Jovanna Ignatowicz, Seth Padowitz, Babis Papamanthou, James Piechota, Dan Polivy, Seth Proctor, Susannah Raub, Haru Sakai, Andy Schwerin, Michael Shapiro, Mike Shim, Michael Shin, Galina Shubina, Amy Simpson, Christian Straub, Ye Sun, Nikos Triandopoulos, Luca Vismara, Danfeng Yao, Jason Ye, and Eric Zamore. Lubomir Bourdev, Mike Demmer, Mark Handy, Michael Horn, and Scott Speigler developed a basic Java tutorial, which ultimately led to Chapter 1, Java Primer. Special thanks go to Eric Zamore, who contributed to the development of the Java code examples in this book and to the initial design, implementation, and testing of the net.datastructures library of data structures and algorithms in Java. We are also grateful to Vesselin Arnaudov and Mike Shim for testing the current version of net.datastructures, and to Jeffrey Bosboom for additional Java code examples and updates. Comments from students and instructors who have used previous editions of this book have helped shape this edition.

There have been a number of friends and colleagues whose comments have lead to improvements in the text. We are particularly thankful to Karen Goodrich, Art Moorshead, David Mount, Scott Smith, and Ioannis Tollis for their insightful comments. In addition, contributions by David Mount to Section 3.5 and to several figures are gratefully acknowledged.

We are also truly indebted to the outside reviewers and readers for their copious comments, emails, and constructive criticism, which were extremely useful in writing this edition. We specifically thank the following reviewers for their comments and suggestions: Divy Agarwal, University of California, Santa Barbara; Terry Andres, University of Manitoba; Bobby Blumofe, University of Texas, Austin; Michael Clancy, University of California, Berkeley; Larry Davis, University of Maryland; Scott Drysdale, Dartmouth College; Arup Guha, University of Central Florida; Chris Ingram, University of Waterloo; Stan Kwasny, Washington University; Calvin Lin, University of Texas at Austin; John Mark Mercer, McGill University; Laurent Michel, University of Connecticut; Leonard Myers, California Polytechnic State University, San Luis Obispo; David Naumann, Stevens Institute of Technology; Robert Pastel, Michigan Technological University; Bina Ramamurthy, SUNY Buffalo; Ken Slonneger, University of Iowa; C.V. Ravishankar, University of Michigan; Val Tannen, University of Pennsylvania; Paul Van Arragon, Messiah College; and Christopher Wilson, University of Oregon.

We are grateful to our editor, Beth Golub, for her enthusiastic support of this project. The team at Wiley has been great. Many thanks go to Mike Berlin, Lilian Brady, Regina Brooks, Paul Crockett, Richard DeLorenzo, Simon Durkin, Micheline Frederick, Lisa Gee, Katherine Hepburn, Rachael Leblond, Andre Legaspi, Madelyn Lesure, Frank Lyman, Hope Miller, Bridget Morrisey, Chris Ruel, Ken Santor, Lauren Sapira, Dan Sayre, Diana Smith, Bruce Spatz, Dawn Stanley, Jeri Warner, and Bill Zobrist.

The computing systems and excellent technical support staff in the departments of computer science at Brown University and University of California, Irvine gave us reliable working environments. This manuscript was prepared primarily with the LaTeX typesetting package.

Finally, we would like to warmly thank Isabel Cruz, Karen Goodrich, Giuseppe Di Battista, Franco Preparata, Ioannis Tollis, and our parents for providing advice, encouragement, and support at various stages of the preparation of this book. We also thank them for reminding us that there are things in life beyond writing books.

Michael T. Goodrich
Roberto Tamassia

Contents

Chapter

1

Java Primer

Contents

1.1 Getting Started: Classes, Types, and Objects

Building data structures and algorithms requires that we communicate detailed instructions to a computer, and an excellent way to perform such communication is using a high-level computer language, such as Java. In this chapter, we give a brief overview of the Java programming language, assuming the reader is somewhat familiar with an existing high-level language, and we continue this discussion in the next chapter, focusing on object-oriented design principles. This book does not provide a complete description of the Java language, however. There are major aspects of the language that are not directly relevant to data structure design, which are not included here. We begin our Java primer with a program that prints "Hello Universe!" on the screen, which is shown in a dissected form in Figure 1.1.

Figure 1.1: A "Hello Universe!" program.

The main "actors" in a Java program are *objects*. Objects store data and provide methods for accessing and modifying this data. Every object is an instance of a *class*, which defines the *type* of the object, as well as the kinds of operations that it performs. The critical *members* of a class in Java are the following (classes can also contain inner class definitions, but let us defer discussing this concept for now):

- Data of Java objects are stored in *instance variables* (also called *fields*). Therefore, if an object from some class is to store data, its class must specify instance variables to do the storage. Instance variables can either come from base types (such as integers, floating-point numbers, or Booleans) or they can refer to objects of other classes.
- The operations that can act on data, expressing the "messages" objects respond to, are called *methods*. These consist of constructors, procedures, and functions. They define the behavior of objects from that class.

How Classes Are Declared

An *object* is a specific combination of data and the methods that can process and communicate that data. Classes define the *types* for objects; hence, objects are sometimes referred to as instances of their defining class, because they take on the name of that class as their type.

An example definition of a Java class is shown in Code Fragment 1.1.

```java
public class Counter {
  protected int count; // a simple integer instance variable
  /** The default constructor for a Counter object */
  Counter() { count = 0; }
  /** An accessor method to get the current count */
  public int getCount() { return count; }
  /** A modifier method for incrementing the count */
  public void incrementCount() { count++; }
  /** A modifier method for decrementing the count */
  public void decrementCount() {count--; }
}
```

Code Fragment 1.1: A Counter class for a simple counter, which can be accessed, incremented, and decremented.

In this example, notice that the class definition is delimited by braces, that is, we use a "{" to mark its beginning and a "}" to mark its end. In Java, any set of statements between the braces "{" and "}" define a program *block*.

As with the Universe class, the Counter class is public, which means that any other class can create and use a Counter object. The Counter has one instance variable—an integer called count. This variable is initialized to 0 in the constructor method, Counter, which is called when we want to create a new Counter object (this method always has the same name as the class it belongs to). This class also has one accessor method, getCount, which returns the current value of the counter. Finally, this class has two update methods—a method, incrementCount, which increments the counter, and a method, decrementCount, which decrements the counter. Admittedly, this is a pretty boring class, but at least it shows us the syntax and structure of a Java class. It also shows us that a Java class does not have to have a main method (but such a class can do nothing by itself).

The name of a class, method, or variable in Java is called an *identifier*, which can be any string of characters as long as it begins with a letter and consists of letters, numbers, and underscore characters (where "letter" and "number" can be from any written language defined in the Unicode character set). We list the exceptions to this general rule for Java identifiers in Table 1.1.

Reserved Words			
abstract	else	interface	switch
boolean	extends	long	synchronized
break	false	native	this
byte	final	new	throw
case	finally	null	throws
catch	float	package	transient
char	for	private	true
class	goto	protected	try
const	if	public	void
continue	implements	return	volatile
default	import	short	while
do	instanceof	static	
double	int	super	

Table 1.1: A listing of the reserved words in Java. These names cannot be used as method or variable names.

Class Modifiers

Class modifiers are optional keywords that precede the **class** keyword. We have already seen examples that use the **public** keyword. In general, the different class modifiers and their meaning is as follows:

- The **abstract** class modifier describes a class that has abstract methods. Abstract methods are declared with the **abstract** keyword and are empty (that is, they have no block defining a body of code for this method). A class that has nothing but abstract methods and no instance variables is more properly called an interface (see Section 2.4), so an **abstract** class usually has a mixture of abstract methods and actual methods. (We discuss abstract classes and their uses in Section 2.4.)

- The **final** class modifier describes a class that can have no subclasses. (We discuss this concept in the next chapter.)

- The **public** class modifier describes a class that can be instantiated or extended by anything in the same package or by anything that *imports* the class. (This is explained in more detail in Section 1.8.) Public classes are declared in their own separate file called *classname*.java, where "*classname*" is the name of the class.

- If the **public** class modifier is not used, the class is considered *friendly*. This means that it can be used and instantiated by all classes in the same *package*. This is the default class modifier.

1.1.1   Base Types

The types of objects are determined by the class they come from. For the sake of efficiency and simplicity, Java also has the following *base types* (also called *primitive types*), which are not objects:

boolean	Boolean value: true or false
char	16-bit Unicode character
byte	8-bit signed two's complement integer
short	16-bit signed two's complement integer
int	32-bit signed two's complement integer
long	64-bit signed two's complement integer
float	32-bit floating-point number (IEEE 754-1985)
double	64-bit floating-point number (IEEE 754-1985)

A variable having one of these types simply stores a value of that type, rather than a reference to some object. Integer constants, like 14 or 195, are of type **int**, unless followed immediately by an 'L' or 'l', in which case they are of type **long**. Floating-point constants, like 3.1415 or 2.158*e*5, are of type **double**, unless followed immediately by an 'F' or 'f', in which case they are of type **float**. We show a simple class in Code Fragment 1.2 that defines a number of base types as local variables for the main method.

```java
public class Base {
  public static void main (String[] args) {
    boolean flag = true;
    char ch = 'A';
    byte b = 12;
    short s = 24;
    int i = 257;
    long l = 890L;              // note the use of "L" here
    float f = 3.1415F;          // note the use of "F" here
    double d = 2.1828;
    System.out.println ("flag = " + flag); // the "+" is string concatenation
    System.out.println ("ch = " + ch);
    System.out.println ("b = " + b);
    System.out.println ("s = " + s);
    System.out.println ("i = " + i);
    System.out.println ("l = " + l);
    System.out.println ("f = " + f);
    System.out.println ("d = " + d);
  }
}
```

Code Fragment 1.2: A Base class showing example uses of base types.

Comments

Note that these examples use comments, which are annotations provided for human readers and are not processed by the Java compiler. Java allows for two kinds of comments—block comments and inline comments—which define text ignored by the compiler. Java uses a "/*" to begin a block comment and a "*/" to close it. Of particular note is a comment that begins with "/**" since such comments have a special format that allows a program, called Javadoc, to read these comments and automatically generate software documentation. We discuss the syntax and interpretation of Javadoc comments in Section 1.9.3.

In addition to block comments, Java uses a "//" to begin inline comments and it ignores everything else on the rest of such a line. By the way, all comments shown in this book will be colored blue, so that they are not confused with executable code. For example:

```
/*
 * This is a block comment.
 */
// This is an inline comment.
```

Output from the Base Class

Output from an execution of the Base class (main method) is shown in Figure 1.2.

```
flag = true
ch = A
b = 12
s = 24
i = 257
l = 890
f = 3.1415
d = 2.1828
```

Figure 1.2: Output from the Base class.

Even though they themselves do not refer to objects, base-type variables are useful in the context of objects, for they can be used for the instance variables (or fields) inside an object. For example, the Counter class (Code Fragment 1.1) had a single instance variable that was of type **int**. Another nice feature of base types in Java is that base-type instance variables are always given an initial value when an object containing them is created (either zero, false, or a **null** character, depending on the type).

1.1.2 Objects

In Java, a new object is created by using the **new** operator. The **new** operator creates a new object from a specified class and returns a *reference* to that object. In order to create a new object of a certain type, we must immediately follow our use of the **new** operator by a call to a constructor for that type of object. We can use any constructor that is included in the class definition, including the default constructor (which has no arguments between the parentheses). In Figure 1.3, we show a number of dissected example uses of the **new** operator, both to simply create new objects and to assign the reference to these objects to a variable.

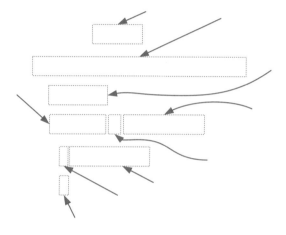

Figure 1.3: Example uses of the **new** operator.

Calling the **new** operator on a class type causes three events to occur:

- A new object is dynamically allocated in memory, and all instance variables are initialized to standard default values. The default values are **null** for object variables and 0 for all base types except **boolean** variables (which are **false** by default).
- The constructor for the new object is called with the parameters specified. The constructor fills in meaningful values for the instance variables and performs any additional computations that must be done to create this object.
- After the constructor returns, the **new** operator returns a reference (that is, a memory address) to the newly created object. If the expression is in the form of an assignment statement, then this address is stored in the object variable, so the object variable *refers* to this newly created object.

Number Objects

We sometimes want to store numbers as objects, but base type numbers are not themselves objects, as we have noted. To get around this obstacle, Java defines a wrapper class for each numeric base type. We call these classes *number classes*. In Table 1.2, we show the numeric base types and their corresponding number class, along with examples of how number objects are created and accessed. Since Java SE 5, a creation operation is performed automatically any time we pass a base number to a method expecting a corresponding object. Likewise, the corresponding access method is performed automatically any time we want to assign the value of a corresponding Number object to a base number type.

Base Type	*Class Name*	*Creation Example*	*Access Example*
byte	Byte	n = new Byte((byte)34);	n.byteValue()
short	Short	n = new Short((short)100);	n.shortValue()
int	Integer	n = new Integer(1045);	n.intValue()
long	Long	n = new Long(10849L);	n.longValue()
float	Float	n = new Float(3.934F);	n.floatValue()
double	Double	n = new Double(3.934);	n.doubleValue()

Table 1.2: Java number classes. Each class is given with its corresponding base type and example expressions for creating and accessing such objects. For each row, we assume the variable n is declared with the corresponding class name.

String Objects

A string is a sequence of characters that comes from some *alphabet* (the set of all possible *characters*). Each character c that makes up a string s can be referenced by its index in the string, which is equal to the number of characters that come before c in s (so the first character is at index 0). In Java, the alphabet used to define strings is the Unicode international character set, a 16-bit character encoding that covers most used written languages. Other programming languages tend to use the smaller ASCII character set (which is a proper subset of the Unicode alphabet based on a 7-bit encoding). In addition, Java defines a special built-in class of objects called String objects.

For example, a string P could be

"hogs and dogs",

which has length 13 and could have come from someone's Web page. In this case, the character at index 2 is 'g' and the character at index 5 is 'a'. Alternately, P could be the string "CGTAATAGTTAATCCG", which has length 16 and could have come from a scientific application for DNA sequencing, where the alphabet is $\{G, C, A, T\}$.

Concatenation

String processing involves dealing with strings. The primary operation for combining strings is called **concatenation**, which takes a string P and a string Q combines them into a new string, denoted $P + Q$, which consists of all the characters of P followed by all the characters of Q. In Java, the "+" operation works exactly like this when acting on two strings. Thus, it is legal (and even useful) in Java to write an assignment statement like

```
String s = "dino" + "saur";
```

This statement defines a variable s that references objects of the String class, and assigns it the string "dinosaur". (We will discuss assignment statements and expressions such as that above in more detail later in this chapter.) Every object in Java is assumed to have a built-in method toString() that returns a string associated with the object. This description of the String class should be sufficient for most uses. We discuss the String class and its "relative" the StringBuffer class in more detail in Section 12.1.

Object References

As mentioned above, creating a new object involves the use of the **new** operator to allocate the object's memory space and use the object's constructor to initialize this space. The location, or **address**, of this space is then typically assigned to a **reference** variable. Therefore, a reference variable can be viewed as a "pointer" to some object. It is as if the variable is a holder for a remote control that can be used to control the newly created object (the device). That is, the variable has a way of pointing at the object and asking it to do things or give us access to its data. We illustrate this concept in Figure 1.4.

Figure 1.4: Illustrating the relationship between objects and object reference variables. When we assign an object reference (that is, memory address) to a reference variable, it is as if we are storing that object's remote control at that variable.

The Dot Operator

Every object reference variable must refer to some object, unless it is **null**, in which case it points to nothing. Using the remote control analogy, a **null** reference is a remote control holder that is empty. Initially, unless we assign an object variable to point to something, it is **null**.

There can, in fact, be many references to the same object, and each reference to a specific object can be used to call methods on that object. Such a situation would correspond to our having many remote controls that all work on the same device. Any of the remotes can be used to make a change to the device (like changing a channel on a television). Note that if one remote control is used to change the device, then the (single) object pointed to by all the remotes changes. Likewise, if we use one object reference variable to change the state of the object, then its state changes for all the references to it. This behavior comes from the fact that there are many references, but they all point to the same object.

One of the primary uses of an object reference variable is to access the members of the class for this object, an instance of its class. That is, an object reference variable is useful for accessing the methods and instance variables associated with an object. This access is performed with the dot (".") operator. We call a method associated with an object by using the reference variable name, following that by the dot operator and then the method name and its parameters.

This calls the method with the specified name for the object referred to by this object reference. It can optionally be passed multiple parameters. If there are several methods with this same name defined for this object, then the Java run-time system uses the one that matches the number of parameters and most closely matches their respective types. A method's name combined with the number and types of its parameters is called a method's *signature*, for it takes all of these parts to determine the actual method to perform for a certain method call. Consider the following examples:

```
oven.cookDinner();
oven.cookDinner(food);
oven.cookDinner(food,seasoning);
```

Each of these method calls is actually referring to a different method with the same name defined in the class that oven belongs to. Note, however, that the signature of a method in Java does not include the type that the method returns, so Java does not allow two methods with the same signature to return different types.

Instance Variables

Java classes can define ***instance variables***, which are also called ***fields***. These variables represent the data associated with the objects of a class. Instance variables must have a ***type***, which can either be a ***base type*** (such as **int, float, double**) or a ***reference type*** (as in our remote control analogy), that is, a class, such as String, an interface (see Section 2.4), or an array (see Section 1.5). A base-type instance variable stores the value of that base type, whereas an instance variable declared with a class name stores a ***reference*** to an object of that class.

Continuing our analogy of visualizing object references as remote controls, instance variables are like device parameters that can be read or set from the remote control (such as the volume and channel controls on a television remote control). Given a reference variable v, which points to some object o, we can access any of the instance variables for o that the access rules allow. For example, **public** instance variables are accessible by everyone. Using the dot operator we can ***get*** the value of any such instance variable, i, just by using $v.i$ in an arithmetic expression. Likewise, we can ***set*** the value of any such instance variable, i, by writing $v.i$ on the left-hand side of the assignment operator ("="). (See Figure 1.5.) For example, if gnome refers to a Gnome object that has public instance variables name and age, then the following statements are allowed:

```
gnome.name = "Professor Smythe";
gnome.age = 132;
```

Also, an object reference does not have to only be a reference variable. It can also be any expression that returns an object reference.

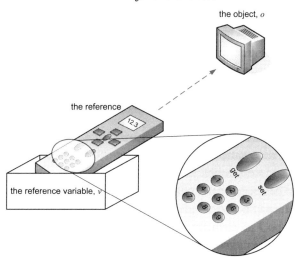

Figure 1.5: Illustrating the way an object reference can be used to get and set instance variables in an object (assuming we are allowed access to those variables).

Variable Modifiers

In some cases, we may not be allowed to directly access some of the instance variables for an object. For example, an instance variable declared as **private** in some class is only accessible by the methods defined inside that class. Such instance variables are similar to device parameters that cannot be accessed directly from a remote control. For example, some devices have internal parameters that can only be read or assigned by a factory technician (and a user is not allowed to change those parameters without violating the device's warranty).

When we declare an instance variable, we can optionally define such a variable modifier, and follow that by the variable's type and the identifier we are going to use for that variable. Additionally, we can optionally assign an initial value to the variable (using the assignment operator ("="). The rules for a variable name are the same as any other Java identifier. The variable type parameter can be either a base type, indicating that this variable stores values of this type, or a class name, indicating that this variable is a *reference* to an object from this class. Finally, the optional initial value we might assign to an instance variable must match the variable's type. For example, we could define a Gnome class, which contains several definitions of instance variables, shown in in Code Fragment 1.3.

The *scope* (or visibility) of instance variables can be controlled through the use of the following *variable modifiers*:

- **public**: Anyone can access public instance variables.
- **protected**: Only methods of the same package or of its subclasses can access protected instance variables.
- **private**: Only methods of the same class (not methods of a subclass) can access private instance variables.
- If none of the above modifiers are used, the instance variable is considered friendly. Friendly instance variables can be accessed by any class in the same package. Packages are discussed in more detail in Section 1.8.

In addition to scope variable modifiers, there are also the following usage modifiers:

- **static**: The **static** keyword is used to declare a variable that is associated with the class, not with individual instances of that class. Static variables are used to store "global" information about a class (for example, a static variable could be used to maintain the total number of Gnome objects created). Static variables exist even if no instance of their class is created.
- **final**: A final instance variable is one that *must* be assigned an initial value, and then can never be assigned a new value after that. If it is a base type, then it is a constant (like the MAX_HEIGHT constant in the Gnome class). If an object variable is **final**, then it will always refer to the same object (even if that object changes its internal state).

```
public class Gnome {
  // Instance variables:
  public String name;
  public int age;
  public Gnome gnomeBuddy;
  private boolean magical = false;
  protected double height = 2.6;
  public static final int MAX_HEIGHT = 3; // maximum height
  // Constructors:
  Gnome(String nm, int ag, Gnome bud, double hgt) { // fully parameterized
    name = nm;
    age = ag;
    gnomeBuddy = bud;
    height = hgt;
  }
  Gnome() { // Default constructor
    name = "Rumple";
    age = 204;
    gnomeBuddy = null;
    height = 2.1;
  }
  // Methods:
  public static void makeKing (Gnome h) {
    h.name = "King " + h.getRealName();
    h.magical = true;  // Only the Gnome class can reference this field.
  }
  public void makeMeKing () {
    name = "King " + getRealName();
    magical = true;
  }
  public boolean isMagical() { return magical; }
  public void setHeight(int newHeight) { height = newHeight; }
  public String getName() { return "I won't tell!"; }
  public String getRealName() { return name; }
  public void renameGnome(String s) { name = s; }
}
```

Code Fragment 1.3: The Gnome class.

Note the uses of instance variables in the Gnome example. The variables age, magical, and height are base types, the variable name is a reference to an instance of the built-in class String, and the variable gnomeBuddy is a reference to an object of the class we are now defining. Our declaration of the instance variable MAX_HEIGHT in the Gnome class is taking advantage of these two modifiers to define a "variable" that has a fixed constant value. Indeed, constant values associated with a class should always be declared to be both **static** and **final**.

1.1.3   Enum Types

Since SE 5, Java supports enumerated types, called *enums*. These are types that are only allowed to take on values that come from a specified set of names. They are declared inside of a class as follows:

modifier **enum** *name* { *value_name*$_0$, *value_name*$_1$, ..., *value_name*$_{n-1}$ };

where the *modifier* can be blank, **public, protected**, or **private**. The name of this enum, *name*, can be any legal Java identifier. Each of the value identifiers, *value_name*$_i$, is the name of a possible value that variables of this enum type can take on. Each of these name values can also be any legal Java identifier, but the Java convention is that these should usually be capitalized words. For example, the following enumerated type definition might be useful in a program that must deal with dates:

public enum Day { MON, TUE, WED, THU, FRI, SAT, SUN };

Once defined, we can use an enum type, such as this, to define other variables, much like a class name. But since Java knows all the value names for an enumerated type, if we use an enum type in a string expression, Java will automatically use its name. Enum types also have a few built-in methods, including a method valueOf, which returns the enum value that is the same as a given string. We show an example use of an enum type in Code Fragment 1.4.

```java
public class DayTripper {
  public enum Day {MON, TUE, WED, THU, FRI, SAT, SUN};
  public static void main(String[] args) {
    Day d = Day.MON;
    System.out.println("Initially d is " + d);
    d = Day.WED;
    System.out.println("Then it is " + d);
    Day t = Day.valueOf("WED");
    System.out.println("I say d and t are the same: " + (d == t));
  }
}
```

The output from this program is:

```
Initially d is MON
Then it is WED
I say d and t are the same: true
```

Code Fragment 1.4: An example use of an enum type.

1.2 Methods

Methods in Java are conceptually similar to functions and procedures in other high-level languages. In general, they are "chunks" of code that can be called on a particular object (from some class). Methods can accept parameters as arguments, and their behavior depends on the object they belong to and the values of any parameters that are passed. Every method in Java is specified in the body of some class. A method definition has two parts: the *signature*, which defines the name and parameters for a method, and the *body*, which defines what the method does.

A method allows a programmer to send a message to an object. The method signature specifies how such a message should look and the method body specifies what the object will do when it receives such a message.

Declaring Methods

The syntax for defining a method is as follows:

> *modifiers type name*($type_0$ $parameter_0$, ..., $type_{n-1}$ $parameter_{n-1}$) {
>   // method body . . .
> }

Each of the pieces of this declaration have important uses, which we describe in detail in this section. The *modifiers* part includes the same kinds of scope modifiers that can be used for variables, such as **public**, **protected**, and **static**, with similar meanings. The *type* part of the declaration defines the return type of the method. The *name* is the name of the method, which can be any valid Java identifier. The list of parameters and their types declares the local variables that correspond to the values that are to be passed as arguments to this method. Each type declaration $type_i$ can be any Java type name and each $parameter_i$ can be any Java identifier. This list of parameters and their types can be empty, which signifies that there are no values to be passed to this method when it is invoked. These parameter variables, as well as the instance variables of the class, can be used inside the body of the method. Likewise, other methods of this class can be called from inside the body of a method.

When a method of a class is called, it is invoked on a specific instance of that class and can change the state of that object (except for a **static** method, which is associated with the class itself). For example, invoking the following method on a particular gnome changes its name.

```
public void renameGnome (String s) {
   name = s;   // Reassign the name instance variable of this gnome.
}
```

Method Modifiers

As with instance variables, method modifiers can restrict the scope of a method:

- **public**: Anyone can call public methods.
- **protected**: Only methods of the same package or of subclasses can call a protected method.
- **private**: Only methods of the same class (not methods of a subclass) can call a private method.
- If none of the modifiers above are used, then the method is friendly. Friendly methods can only be called by objects of classes in the same package.

The above modifiers may be followed by additional modifiers:

- **abstract**: A method declared as **abstract** has no code. The signature of such a method is followed by a semicolon with no method body. For example:

```
public abstract void setHeight (double newHeight);
```

  Abstract methods may only appear within an abstract class. We discuss the usefulness of this construct in Section 2.4.
- **final**: This is a method that cannot be overridden by a subclass.
- **static**: This is a method that is associated with the class itself, and not with a particular instance of the class. Static methods can also be used to change the state of static variables associated with a class (provided these variables are not declared to be **final**).

Return Types

A method definition must specify the type of value the method will return. If the method does not return a value, then the keyword **void** must be used. If the return type is **void**, the method is called a *procedure*; otherwise, it is called a *function*. To return a value in Java, a method must use the **return** keyword (and the type returned must match the return type of the method). Here is an example of a method (from inside the Gnome class) that is a function:

```
public boolean isMagical () {
    return magical;
}
```

As soon as a **return** is performed in a Java function, the method ends.

Java functions can return only one value. To return multiple values in Java, we should instead combine all the values we want to return in a *compound object*, whose instance variables include all the values we want to return, and then return a reference to that compound object. In addition, we can change the internal state of an object that is passed to a method as another way of "returning" multiple results.

Parameters

A method's parameters are defined in a comma-separated list enclosed in parentheses after the name of the method. A parameter consists of two parts, the parameter type and the parameter name. If a method has no parameters, then only an empty pair of parentheses is used.

All parameters in Java are passed *by value*, that is, any time we pass a parameter to a method, a copy of that parameter is made for use within the method body. So if we pass an **int** variable to a method, then that variable's integer value is copied. The method can change the copy but not the original. If we pass an object reference as a parameter to a method, then the reference is copied as well. Remember that we can have many different variables that all refer to the same object. Changing the internal reference inside a method will not change the reference that was passed in. For example, if we pass a Gnome reference g to a method that calls this parameter h, then this method can change the reference h to point to a different object, but g will still refer to the same object as before. Of course, the method can use the reference h to change the internal state of the object, and this will change g's object as well (since g and h are currently referring to the same object).

Constructors

A *constructor* is a special kind of method that is used to initialize newly created objects. Java has a special way to declare the constructor and a special way to invoke the constructor. First, let's look at the syntax for declaring a constructor:

```
modifiers name(type_0 parameter_0, ..., type_{n-1} parameter_{n-1}) {
    // constructor body . . .
}
```

Thus, its syntax is essentially the same as that of any other method, but there are some important differences. The name of the constructor, *name*, must be the same as the name of the class it constructs. So, if the class is called Fish, the constructor must be called Fish as well. In addition, we don't specify a return type for a constructor—its return type is implicitly the same as its name (which is also the name of the class). Constructor modifiers, shown above as *modifiers*, follow the same rules as normal methods, except that an **abstract**, **static**, or **final** constructor is not allowed.

Here is an example:

```
public Fish (int w, String n) {
    weight = w;
    name = n;
}
```

Constructor Definition and Invocation

The body of a constructor is like a normal method's body, with a couple of minor exceptions. The first difference involves a concept known as constructor chaining, which is a topic discussed in Section 2.2.3 and is not critical at this point.

The second difference between a constructor body and that of a regular method is that **return** statements are not allowed in a constructor body. A constructor's body is intended to be used to initialize the data associated with objects of this class so that they may be in a stable initial state when first created.

Constructors are invoked in a unique way: they ***must*** be called using the **new** operator. So, upon invocation, a new instance of this class is automatically created and its constructor is then called to initialize its instance variables and perform other setup tasks. For example, consider the following constructor invocation (which is also a declaration for the myFish variable):

```
Fish myFish = new Fish (7, "Wally");
```

A class can have many constructors, but each must have a different ***signature***, that is, each must be distinguished by the type and number of the parameters it takes.

The main Method

Some Java classes are meant to be used by other classes, others are meant to be stand-alone programs. Classes that define stand-alone programs must contain one other special kind of method for a class—the main method. When we want to execute a stand-alone Java program, we reference the name of the class that defines this program by issuing the following command (in a Windows, Linux, or UNIX shell):

```
java Aquarium
```

In this case, the Java run-time system looks for a compiled version of the Aquarium class, and then invokes the special main method in that class. This method must be declared as follows:

```
public static void main(String[] args) {
    // main method body . . .
}
```

The arguments passed as the parameter args to the main method are the command-line arguments given when the program is called. The args variable is an array of String objects, that is, a collection of indexed strings, with the first string being args[0], the second being args[1], and so on. (We say more about arrays in Section 1.5.)

Calling a Java Program from the Command Line

Java programs can be called from the command line using the java command, followed by the name of the Java class whose main method we want to run, plus any optional arguments. For example, we may have defined the Aquarium program to take an optional argument that specifies the number of fish in the aquarium. We could then invoke the program by typing the following in a shell window:

java Aquarium 45

to specify that we want an aquarium with 45 fish in it. In this case, args[0] would refer to the string "45". One nice feature of the main method in a class definition is that it allows each class to define a stand-alone program, and one of the uses for this method is to test all the other methods in a class. Thus, thorough use of the main method is an effective tool for debugging collections of Java classes.

Statement Blocks and Local Variables

The body of a method is a ***statement block***, which is a sequence of statements and declarations to be performed between the braces "{" and "}". Method bodies and other statement blocks can themselves have statement blocks nested inside of them. In addition to statements that perform some action, like calling the method of some object, statement blocks can contain declarations of *local variables*. These variables are declared inside the statement body, usually at the beginning (but between the braces "{" and "}"). Local variables are similar to instance variables, but they only exist while the statement block is being executed. As soon as control flow exits out of that block, all local variables inside it can no longer be referenced. A local variable can either be a ***base type*** (such as **int**, **float**, **double**) or a *reference* to an instance of some class. Single statements and declarations in Java are always terminated by a semicolon, that is, a ";".

There are two ways of declaring local variables:

type name;
type name = *initial_value*;

The first declaration simply defines the identifier, *name*, to be of the specified type. The second declaration defines the identifier, its type, and also initializes this variable to the specified value. Here are some examples of local variable declarations:

```
{
  double r;
  Point p1 = new Point (3, 4);
  Point p2 = new Point (8, 2);
  int i = 512;
  double e = 2.71828;
}
```

1.3   Expressions

Variables and constants are used in *expressions* to define new values and to modify variables. In this section, we discuss how expressions work in Java in more detail. Expressions involve the use of *literals*, *variables*, and *operators*. Since we have already discussed variables, let us briefly focus on literals and then discuss operators in some detail.

1.3.1   Literals

A *literal* is any "constant" value that can be used in an assignment or other expression. Java allows the following kinds of literals:

- The **null** object reference (this is the only object literal, and it is allowed to be any reference type).

- Boolean: **true** and **false**.

- Integer: The default for an integer like 176, or -52 is that it is of type **int**, which is a 32-bit integer. A long integer literal must end with an "L" or "l," for example, 176L or -52l, and defines a 64-bit integer.

- Floating Point: The default for floating-point numbers, such as 3.1415 and 135.23, is that they are **double**. To specify that a literal is a **float**, it must end with an "F" or "f." Floating-point literals in exponential notation are also allowed, such as 3.14E2 or .19e10; the base is assumed to be 10.

- Character: In Java, character constants are assumed to be taken from the Unicode alphabet. Typically, a character is defined as an individual symbol enclosed in single quotes. For example, 'a' and '?' are character constants. In addition, Java defines the following special character constants:

'\n'	(newline)	'\t'	(tab)
'\b'	(backspace)	'\r'	(return)
'\f'	(form feed)	'\\'	(backslash)
'\''	(single quote)	'\"'	(double quote).

- String Literal: A string literal is a sequence of characters enclosed in double quotes, for example, the following is a string literal:

```
"dogs cannot climb trees"
```

1.3.2 Operators

Java expressions involve composing literals and variables with operators. We survey the operators in Java in this section.

The Assignment Operator

The standard assignment operator in Java is "=". It is used to assign a value to an instance variable or local variable. Its syntax is as follows:

variable = *expression*

where *variable* refers to a variable that is allowed to be referenced by the statement block containing this expression. The value of an assignment operation is the value of the expression that was assigned. Thus, if i and j are both declared as type **int**, it is correct to have an assignment statement like the following:

i = j = 25; // works because '=' operators are evaluated right-to-left

Arithmetic Operators

The following are binary arithmetic operators in Java:

+	addition
−	subtraction
*	multiplication
/	division
%	the modulo operator

This last operator, modulo, is also known as the "remainder" operator, because it is the remainder left after an integer division. We often use "mod" to denote the modulo operator, and we define it formally as

$$n \bmod m = r,$$

such that

$$n = mq + r,$$

for an integer q and $0 \leq r < m$.

Java also provides a unary minus (−), which can be placed in front of an arithmetic expression to invert its sign. Parentheses can be used in any expression to define the order of evaluation. Java also uses a fairly intuitive operator precedence rule to determine the order of evaluation when parentheses are not used. Unlike C++, Java does not allow operator overloading.

Increment and Decrement Operators

Like C and C++, Java provides increment and decrement operators. Specifically, it provides the plus-one increment (++) and decrement (−−) operators. If such an operator is used in front of a variable reference, then 1 is added to (or subtracted from) the variable and its value is read into the expression. If it is used after a variable reference, then the value is first read and then the variable is incremented or decremented by 1. So, for example, the code fragment

```
int i = 8;
int j = i++;
int k = ++i;
int m = i−−;
int n = 9 + i++;
```

assigns 8 to j, 10 to k, 10 to m, 18 to n, and leaves *i* with value 10.

Logical Operators

Java allows for the standard comparison operators between numbers:

<	less than
<=	less than or equal to
==	equal to
!=	not equal to
>=	greater than or equal to
>	greater than

The operators == and != can also be used for object references. The type of the result of a comparison is a **boolean**.

Operators that operate on **boolean** values are the following:

!	not (prefix)
&&	conditional and
||	conditional or

The Boolean operators && and || will not evaluate the second operand (to the right) in their expression if it is not needed to determine the value of the expression. This feature is useful, for example, for constructing Boolean expressions where we first test that a certain condition holds (such as a reference not being **null**), and then test a condition that could have otherwise generated an error condition had the prior test not succeeded.

Bitwise Operators

Java also provides the following bitwise operators for integers and Booleans:

~	bitwise complement (prefix unary operator)
&	bitwise and
|	bitwise or
^	bitwise exclusive-or
<<	shift bits left, filling in with zeros
>>	shift bits right, filling in with sign bit
>>>	shift bits right, filling in with zeros

Operational Assignment Operators

Besides the standard assignment operator (=), Java also provides a number of other assignment operators that have operational side effects. These other kinds of operators are of the following form:

variable op = expression

where *op* is any binary operator. The above expression is equivalent to

variable = variable op expression

except that if *variable* contains an expression (for example, an array index), the expression is evaluated only once. Thus, the code fragment

```
a[5] = 10;
i = 5;
a[i++] += 2;
```

leaves a[5] with value 12 and i with value 6.

String Concatenation

Strings can be composed using the ***concatenation*** operator (+), so that the code

```
String rug = "carpet";
String dog = "spot";
String mess = rug + dog;
String answer = mess + " will cost me " + 5 + " hours!";
```

would have the effect of making answer refer to the string

```
"carpetspot will cost me 5 hours!"
```

This example also shows how Java converts nonstring constants into strings, when they are involved in a string concatenation operation.

Operator Precedence

Operators in Java are given preferences, or precedence, that determine the order in which operations are performed when the absence of parentheses brings up evaluation ambiguities. For example, we need a way of deciding if the expression, "5+2*3," has value 21 or 11 (Java says it is 11).

We show the precedence of the operators in Java (which, incidentally, is the same as in C) in Table 1.3.

Operator Precedence		
	Type	**Symbols**
1	postfix ops prefix ops cast	*exp* ++ *exp* −− ++*exp* −−*exp* +*exp* −*exp* ∼*exp* !*exp* (*type*) *exp*
2	mult./div.	* / %
3	add./subt.	+ −
4	shift	<< >> >>>
5	comparison	< <= > >= **instanceof**
6	equality	== !=
7	bitwise-and	&
8	bitwise-xor	ˆ
9	bitwise-or		
10	and	&&
11	or	||
12	conditional	*boolean_expression? value_if_true: value_if_false*
13	assignment	= += −= *= /= %= >>= <<= >>>= &= ˆ= |=

Table 1.3: The Java precedence rules. Operators in Java are evaluated according to the ordering above if parentheses are not used to determine the order of evaluation. Operators on the same line are evaluated in left-to-right order (except for assignment and prefix operations, which are evaluated right-to-left), subject to the conditional evaluation rule for Boolean **and** and **or** operations. The operations are listed from highest to lowest precedence (we use *exp* to denote an atomic or parenthesized expression). Without parenthesization, higher precedence operators are performed before lower precedence operators.

We have now discussed almost all of the operators listed in Table 1.3. A notable exception is the conditional operator, which involves evaluating a Boolean expression and then taking on the appropriate value depending on whether this Boolean expression is true or false. (We discuss the use of the **instanceof** operator in the next chapter.)

1.3.3   Casting and Autoboxing/Unboxing in Expressions

Casting is an operation that allows us to change the type of a value. In essence, we can take a value of one type and *cast* it into an equivalent value of another type. Casting can be useful for doing certain numerical and input/output operations.

The syntax for casting an expression to a desired type is as follows:

(type) exp

where *type* is the type that we would like the expression *exp* to have. There are two fundamental types of casting that can be done in Java. We can either cast with respect to the base numerical types or we can cast with respect to objects. Here, we discuss how to perform casting of numerical and string types, and we discuss object casting in Section 2.5.1. For instance, it might be helpful to cast an **int** to a **double** in order to perform operations like division.

Ordinary Casting

When casting from a **double** to an **int**, we may lose precision. This means that the resulting double value will be rounded down. But we can cast an **int** to a **double** without this worry. For example, consider the following:

```
double d1 = 3.2;
double d2 = 3.9999;
int i1 = (int)d1;        // i1 has value 3
int i2 = (int)d2;        // i2 has value 3
double d3 = (double)i2;  // d3 has value 3.0
```

Casting with Operators

Certain binary operators, like division, will have different results depending on the variable types they are used with. We must take care to make sure operations perform their computations on values of the intended type. When used with integers, division does not keep track of the fractional part, for example. When used with doubles, division keeps this part, as is illustrated in the following example:

```
int i1 = 3;
int i2 = 6;
dresult = (double)i1 / (double)i2;   // dresult has value 0.5
dresult = i1 / i2;                    // dresult has value 0.0
```

Notice that when i1 and i2 were cast to doubles, regular division for real numbers was performed. When i1 and i2 were not cast, the " /" operator performed an integer division and the result of i1 / i2 was the **int** 0. Then, Java did an *implicit cast* to assign an **int** value to the **double** result. We discuss implicit casting next.

Implicit Casting and Autoboxing/Unboxing

There are cases where Java will perform an ***implicit cast***, according to the type of the assignment variable, provided there is no loss of precision. For example:

```
int iresult, i = 3;
double dresult, d = 3.2;
dresult = i / d;          // dresult is 0.9375. i was cast to a double
iresult = i / d;          // loss of precision -> this is a compilation error
iresult = (int) i / d;    // iresult is 0, since the fractional part is lost
```

Note that since Java will not perform implicit casts where precision is lost, the explicit cast in the last line above is required.

Since Java SE 5, there is a new kind of implicit cast, for going between Number objects, like Integer and Float, and their related base types, like **int** and **float**. Any time a Number object is expected as a parameter to a method, the corresponding base type can be passed. In this case, Java will perform an implicit cast, called ***autoboxing***, which will convert the base type to its corresponding Number object. Likewise, any time a base type is expected in an expression involving a Number reference, that Number object is changed to the corresponding base type, in an operation called ***unboxing***.

There are a few caveats regarding autoboxing and unboxing, however. One is that if a Number reference is **null**, then trying to unbox it will generate an error, called **NullPointerException**. Second, the operator, "==", is used both to test the equality of base type values as well as whether two Number references are pointing to the same object. So when testing for equality, try to avoid the implicit casts done by autoboxing and unboxing. Finally, implicit casts, of any kind, take time, so we should try to minimize our reliance on them if performance is an issue.

Incidentally, there is one situation in Java when only implicit casting is allowed, and that is in string concatenation. Any time a string is concatenated with any object or base type, that object or base type is automatically converted to a string. Explicit casting of an object or base type to a string is not allowed, however. Thus, the following assignments are incorrect:

```
String s = (String) 4.5;              // this is wrong!
String t = "Value = " + (String) 13;  // this is wrong!
String u = 22;                        // this is wrong!
```

To perform a conversion to a string, we must use the appropriate toString method or perform an implicit cast via the concatenation operation.

Thus, the following statements are correct:

```
String s = "" + 4.5;              // correct, but poor style
String t = "Value = " + 13;       // this is good
String u = Integer.toString(22);  // this is good
```

1.4 Control Flow

Control flow in Java is similar to that of other high-level languages. We review the basic structure and syntax of control flow in Java in this section, including method returns, **if** statements, **switch** statements, loops, and restricted forms of "jumps" (the **break** and **continue** statements).

1.4.1 The If and Switch Statements

In Java, conditionals work similarly to the way they work in other languages. They provide a way to make a decision and then execute one or more different statement blocks based on the outcome of that decision.

The If Statement

The syntax of a simple **if** statement is as follows:

> **if** (*boolean_exp*)
>   *true_statement*
> **else**
>   *false_statement*

where *boolean_exp* is a Boolean expression and *true_statement* and *false_statement* are each either a single statment or a block of statements enclosed in braces ("{" and "}"). Note that, unlike some similar languages, the value tested by an **if** statement in Java must be a Boolean expression. In particular, it is definitely not an integer expression. Nevertheless, as in other similar languages, the **else** part (and its associated statement) in a Java **if** statement is optional. There is also a way to group a number of Boolean tests, as follows:

> **if** (*first_boolean_exp*)
>   *true_statement*
> **else if** (*second_boolean_exp*)
>   *second_true_statement* .
> **else**
>   *false_statement*

If the first Boolean expression is false, the second Boolean expression will be tested, and so on. An **if** statement can have an arbitrary number of **else if** parts. To be safe when defining complicated **if** statements, use braces to enclose all the statement bodies.

For example, the following is a correct **if** statement.

```
if (snowLevel < 2) {
    goToClass();
    comeHome();
}
else if (snowLevel < 5) {
    goSledding();
    haveSnowballFight();
}
else
    stayAtHome();
```

Switch Statements

Java provides for multiple-value control flow using the **switch** statement, which is especially useful with enum types. The following is an indicative example (based on a variable d of the Day enum type of Section 1.1.3).

```
switch (d) {
  case MON:
    System.out.println("This is tough.");
    break;
  case TUE:
    System.out.println("This is getting better.");
    break;
  case WED:
    System.out.println("Half way there.");
    break;
  case THU:
    System.out.println("I can see the light.");
    break;
  case FRI:
    System.out.println("Now we are talking.");
    break;
  default:
    System.out.println("Day off!");
    break;
}
```

The **switch** statement evaluates an integer or enum expression and causes control flow to jump to the code location labeled with the value of this expression. If there is no matching label, then control flow jumps to the location labeled "**default**." This is the only explicit jump performed by the **switch** statement, however, so flow of control "falls through" to other cases if the code for each case is not ended with a **break** statement (which causes control flow to jump to the next line after the **switch** statement).

1.4.2 Loops

Another important control flow mechanism in a programming language is looping. Java provides for three types of loops.

While Loops

The simplest kind of loop in Java is a **while** loop. Such a loop tests that a certain condition is satisfied and will perform the body of the loop each time this condition is evaluated to be **true**. The syntax for such a conditional test before a loop body is executed is as follows:

> **while** (*boolean_exp*)
>   *loop_statement*

At the beginning of each iteration, the loop tests the expression, *boolean_exp*, and then executes the loop body, *loop_statement*, only if this Boolean expression evaluates to **true**. The loop body statement can also be a block of statements.

Consider, for example, a gnome that is trying to water all of the carrots in his carrot patch, which he does as long as his watering can is not empty. Since his can might be empty to begin with, we would write the code to perform this task as follows:

```
public void waterCarrots () {
    Carrot current = garden.findNextCarrot ();

    while (!waterCan.isEmpty ()) {
        water (current, waterCan);
        current = garden.findNextCarrot ();
    }
}
```

Recall that "!" in Java is the "not" operator.

For Loops

Another kind of loop is the **for** loop. In their simplest form, **for** loops provide for repeated code based on an integer index. In Java, we can do that and much more. The functionality of a **for** loop is significantly more flexible. In particular, the usage of a **for** loop is split into four sections: the initialization, the condition, the increment, and the body.

Defining a For Loop

Here is the syntax for a Java **for** loop:

>**for** (*initialization*; *condition*; *increment*)
>   *loop_statement*

where each of the sections *initialization*, *condition*, and *increment* can be empty.

In the *initialization* section, we can declare an index variable that will only exist in the scope of the **for** loop. For example, if we want a loop that indexes on a counter, and we have no need for the counter variable outside of the **for** loop, then declaring something like the following

>**for** (**int** counter = 0; *condition*; *increment*)
>   *loop_statement*

will declare a variable counter whose scope is the loop body only.

In the *condition* section, we specify the repeat (while) condition of the loop. This must be a Boolean expression. The body of the **for** loop will be executed each time the *condition* is **true** when evaluated at the beginning of a potential iteration. As soon as *condition* evaluates to **false**, then the loop body is not executed, and, instead, the program executes the next statement after the **for** loop.

In the *increment* section, we declare the incrementing statement for the loop. The incrementing statement can be any legal statement, allowing for significant flexibility in coding. Thus, the syntax of a **for** loop is equivalent to the following:

>*initialization*;
>**while** (*condition*) {
>   *loop_statement*;
>   *increment*;
>}

except that, in Java, a **while** loop cannot have an empty Boolean condition, whereas a **for** loop can. The following example shows a simple **for** loop in Java:

```java
public void eatApples (Apples apples) {
    numApples = apples.getNumApples ();
    for (int x = 0; x < numApples; x++) {
        eatApple (apples.getApple (x));
        spitOutCore ();
    }
}
```

In the Java example above, the loop variable x was declared as **int** x = 0. Before each iteration, the loop tests the condition " x < numApples" and executes the loop body only if this is true. Finally, at the end of each iteration the loop uses the statement x++ to increment the loop variable x before again testing the condition.

Incidentally, since SE 5, Java also includes a for-each loop, which we discuss in Section 6.3.2.

Do-While Loops

Java has yet another kind of loop besides the **for** loop and the standard **while** loop—the **do-while** loop. The former loops tests a condition before performing an iteration of the loop body, the **do-while** loop tests a condition after the loop body. The syntax for a **do-while** loop is as shown below:

> **do**
>   *loop_statement*
> **while** (*boolean_exp*)

Again, the loop body statement, *loop_statement*, can be a single statement or a block of statements, and the conditional, *boolean_exp*, must be a Boolean expression. In a **do-while** loop, we repeat the loop body for as long as the condition is true each time it is evaluated.

Consider, for example, that we want to prompt the user for input and then do something useful with that input. (We discuss Java input and output in more detail in Section 1.6.) A possible condition, in this case, for exiting the loop is when the user enters an empty string. However, even in this case, we may want to handle that input and inform the user that he or she has quit. The following example illustrates this case:

```java
public void getUserInput() {
    String input;
    do {
        input = getInputString();
        handleInput(input);
    } while (input.length()>0);
}
```

Notice the exit condition for the above example. Specifically, it is written to be consistent with the rule in Java that **do-while** loops exit when the condition is ***not*** true (unlike the repeat-until construct used in other languages).

1.4.3 Explicit Control-Flow Statements

Java also provides statements that allow for explicit change in the flow of control of a program.

Returning from a Method

If a Java method is declared with a return type of **void**, then flow of control returns when it reaches the last line of code in the method or when it encounters a **return** statement with no argument. If a method is declared with a return type, however, the method is a function and it must exit by returning the function's value as an argument to a **return** statement. The following (correct) example illustrates returning from a function:

```java
// Check for a specific birthday
public boolean checkBDay (int date) {
    if (date == Birthdays.MIKES_BDAY) {
        return true;
    }
    return false;
}
```

It follows that the **return** statement *must* be the last statement executed in a function, as the rest of the code will never be reached.

Note that there is a significant difference between a statement being the last line of code that is *executed* in a method and the last line of code in the method itself. In the example above, the line **return true;** is clearly not the last line of code that is written in the function, but it may be the last line that is executed (if the condition involving date is **true**). Such a statement explicitly interrupts the flow of control in the method. There are two other such explicit control-flow statements, which are used in conjunction with loops and switch statements.

The break Statement

The typical use of a **break** statement has the following simple syntax:

```java
break;
```

It is used to "break" out of the innermost **switch, for, while,** or **do-while** statement body. When it is executed, a break statement causes the flow of control to jump to the next line after the loop or **switch** to the body containing the **break**.

The **break** statement can also be used in a labeled form to jump out of an outer-nested loop or **switch** statement. In this case, it has the syntax

break *label*;

where *label* is a Java identifier that is used to label a loop or **switch** statement. Such a label can only appear at the beginning of the declaration of a loop. There are no other kinds of "go to" statements in Java.

We illustrate the use of a label with a **break** statement in the following simple example:

```
public static boolean hasZeroEntry (int[][] a) {
    boolean foundFlag = false;

zeroSearch:
    for (int i=0; i<a.length; i++) {
        for (int j=0; j<a[i].length; j++) {
            if (a[i][j] == 0) {
                foundFlag = true;
                break zeroSearch;
            }
        }
    }
    return foundFlag;
}
```

The example above also uses arrays, which are covered in the next section (and in Section 3.1).

The continue Statement

The other statement to explicitly change the flow of control in a Java program is the **continue** statement, which has the following syntax:

continue *label*;

where *label* is an optional Java identifier that is used to label a loop. As mentioned above, there are no explicit "go to" statements in Java. Likewise, the **continue** statement can only be used inside loops (**for, while,** and **do-while**). The **continue** statement causes the execution to skip over the remaining steps of the loop body in the current iteration (but then continue the loop if its condition is satisfied).

1.5 Arrays

A common programming task is to keep track of a numbered group of related objects. For example, we may want a video game to keep track of the top ten scores for that game. Rather than use ten different variables for this task, we would prefer to use a single name for the group and use index numbers to refer to the high scores in that group. Similarly, we may want a medical information system to keep track of the patients currently assigned to beds in a certain hospital. Again, we would rather not have to introduce 200 variables in our program just because the hospital has 200 beds.

In such cases, we can save programming effort by using an **array**, which is a numbered collection of variables all of the same type. Each variable, or **cell**, in an array has an **index**, which uniquely refers to the value stored in that cell. The cells of an array a are numbered 0, 1, 2, and so on. We illustrate an array of high scores for a video game in Figure 1.6.

Figure 1.6: An illustration of an array of ten (**int**) high scores for a video game.

Such an organization is quite useful, for it allows us to do some interesting computations. For example, the following method adds up all the numbers in an array of integers:

```java
/** Adds all the numbers in an integer array. */
public static int sum(int[] a) {
int total = 0;
for (int i=0; i < a.length; i++) // note the use of the length variable
   total += a[i];
return total;
}
```

This example takes advantage of a nice feature of Java, which allows us to find the number of cells an array stores, that is, its **length**. In Java, an array a is a special kind of object and the length of a is stored in an instance variable, length. That is, we never need to guess the length of an array in Java, the length of an array can be accessed as follows:

      array_name.length

where *array_name* is the name of the array. Thus, the cells of an array a are numbered 0, 1, 2, and so on, up to $a.\text{length} - 1$.

Array Elements and Capacities

Each object stored in an array is called an ***element*** of that array. Element number 0 is $a[0]$, element number 1 is $a[1]$, element number 2 is $a[2]$, and so on. Since the length of an array determines the maximum number of things that can be stored in the array, we will sometimes refer to the length of an array as its ***capacity***. We show another simple use of an array in the following code fragment, which counts the number of times a certain number appears in an array:

```java
/** Counts the number of times an integer appears in an array. */
public static int findCount(int[] a, int k) {
  int count = 0;
  for (int i=0; i < a.length; i++) {
    if (a[i] == k)     // check if the current element equals k
      count++;
  }
  return count;
}
```

Out of Bounds Errors

It is a dangerous mistake to attempt to index into an array a using a number outside the range from 0 to $a.length - 1$. Such a reference is said to be ***out of bounds***. Out of bounds references have been exploited numerous times by hackers using a method called the ***buffer overflow attack*** to compromise the security of computer systems written in languages other than Java. As a safety feature, array indices are always checked in Java to see if they are ever out of bounds. If an array index is out of bounds, the run-time Java environment signals an error condition. The name of this condition is the ArrayIndexOutOfBoundsException. This check helps Java avoid a number of security problems (including buffer overflow attacks) that other languages must cope with.

We can avoid out-of-bounds errors by making sure that we alway index into an array, a, using an integer value between 0 and a.length. One shorthand way we can do this is by carefully using the early termination feature of Boolean operations in Java. For example, a statement like the following will never generate an index out-of-bounds error:

```java
if ((i >= 0) && (i < a.length) && (a[i] > 2) )
  x = a[i];
```

for the comparison "a[i] > 2" will only be performed if the first two comparisons succeed.

1.5.1   Declaring Arrays

One way to declare and initialize an array is as follows:

element_type[] *array_name* = {*init_val_0*,*init_val_1*,...,*init_val_N-1*};

The *element_type* can be any Java base type or class name, and *array_name* can be
any value Java identifier. The initial values must be of the same type as the array.
For example, consider the following declaration of an array that is initialized to
contain the first ten prime numbers:

```
int[] primes = {2, 3, 5, 7, 11, 13, 17, 19, 23, 29};
```

In addition to creating an array and defining all its initial values when we declare it,
we can declare an array variable without initializing it. The form of this declaration
is as follows:

element_type[] *array_name*;

An array created in this way is initialized with all zeros if the array type is a number
type. Arrays of objects are initialized to all **null** references. Once we have declared
an array in this way, we can create the collection of cells for an array later using the
following syntax:

new *element_type*[*length*]

where *length* is a positive integer denoting the length of the array created. Typically
this expression appears in an assignment statement with an array name on the left-
hand side of the assignment operator. So, for example, the following statement
defines an array variable named a, and later assigns it an array of 10 cells, each of
type **double**, which it then initializes:

```
double[] a;

// ... various steps ...

a = new double[10];
for (int k=0; k < a.length; k++) {
  a[k] = 1.0;
}
```

The cells of this new array, "a," are indexed using the integer set $\{0,1,2,\ldots,9\}$
(recall that arrays in Java always start indexing at 0), and, like every array in Java,
all the cells in this array are of the same type—**double**.

1.5.2 Arrays are Objects

Arrays in Java are special kinds of objects. In fact, this is the reason we can use the **new** operator to create a new instance of an array. An array can be used just like any general object in Java, but we have a special syntax (using square brackets, "[" and "]") to refer to its members. An array in Java can do everything that a general object can. Since an array is an object, though, the name of an array in Java is actually a reference to the place in memory where the array is stored. Thus, there is nothing too special about using the dot operator and the instance variable, length, to refer to the length of an array, for example, as "a.length." The name, a, in this case is just a reference, or pointer, to the underlying array object.

The fact that arrays in Java are objects has an important implication when it comes to using array names in assignment statements. For when we write something like

$$b = a;$$

in a Java program, we really mean that b and a now both refer to the same array. So, if we then write something like

$$b[3] = 5;$$

then we will also be setting the number a[3] to 5. We illustrate this crucial point in Figure 1.7.

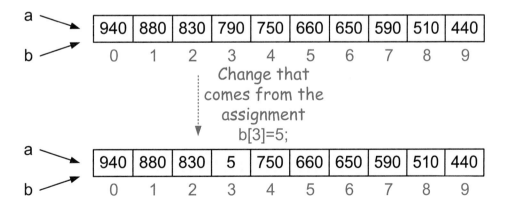

Figure 1.7: An illustration of an assignment of array objects. We show the result of setting "$b[3] = 5;$" after previously setting "$b = a;$".

Cloning an Array

If instead, we wanted to create an exact copy of the array, a, and assign that array to the array variable, b, we should write

  b = a.clone();

which copies all of the cells of a into a new array and assigns b to point to that new array. In fact, the clone method is a built-in method of every Java object, which makes an exact copy of that object. In this case, if we then write

  b[3] = 5;

then the new (copied) array will have its cell at index 3 assigned the value 5, but a[3] will remain unchanged. We illustrate this point in Figure 1.8.

Figure 1.8: An illustration of cloning of array objects. We show the result of setting "b[3] = 5;" after previously setting "b = a.clone();".

We should stress that the cells of an array are copied when we clone it. If the cells are a base type, like **int**, their values are copied. But if the cells are object references, then those references are copied. This means that there are now two ways to reference such an object. We explore the consequences of this fact in Exercise R-1.3.

1.6   Simple Input and Output

Java provides a rich set of classes and methods for performing input and output within a program. There are classes in Java for doing graphical user interface design, complete with pop-up windows and pull-down menus, as well as methods for the display and input of text and numbers. Java also provides methods for dealing with graphical objects, images, sounds, Web pages, and mouse events (such as clicks, mouse overs, and dragging). Moreover, many of these input and output methods can be used in either stand-alone programs or in applets.

Unfortunately, going into the details on how all of the methods work for constructing sophisticated graphical user interfaces is beyond the scope of this book. Still, for the sake of completeness, we describe how simple input and output can be done in Java in this section.

Simple input and output in Java occurs within the Java console window. Depending on the Java environment we are using, this window is either a special pop-up window that can be used for displaying and inputting text, or a window used to issue commands to the operating system (such windows are referred to as shell windows, DOS windows, or terminal windows).

Simple Output Methods

Java provides a built-in static object, called System.out, that performs output to the "standard output" device. Most operating system shells allow users to redirect standard output to files or even as input to other programs, but the default output is to the Java console window. The System.out object is an instance of the java.io.PrintStream class. This class defines methods for a buffered output stream, meaning that characters are put in a temporary location, called a **buffer**, which is then emptied when the console window is ready to print characters.

Specifically, the java.io.PrintStream class provides the following methods for performing simple output (we use *base_type* here to refer to any of the possible base types):

print(Object *o*): Print the object *o* using its toString method.

print(String *s*): Print the string *s*.

print(*base_type b*): Print the base type value *b*.

println(String *s*): Print the string *s*, followed by the newline character.

An Output Example

Consider, for example, the following code fragment:

```
System.out.print("Java values: ");
System.out.print(3.1415);
System.out.print(',');
System.out.print(15);
System.out.println(" (double,char,int).");
```

When executed, this fragment will output the following in the Java console window:

```
Java values: 3.1415,15 (double,char,int).
```

Simple Input Using the java.util.Scanner Class

Just as there is a special object for performing output to the Java console window, there is also a special object, called System.in, for performing input from the Java console window. Technically, the input is actually coming from the "standard input" device, which by default is the computer keyboard echoing its characters in the Java console. The System.in object is an object associated with the standard input device. A simple way of reading input with this object is to use it to create a Scanner object, using the expression

         new Scanner(System.in)

The Scanner class has a number of convenient methods that read from the given input stream. For example, the following program uses a Scanner object to process input:

```
import java.io.*;
import java.util.Scanner;
public class InputExample {
  public static void main(String args[]) throws IOException {
    Scanner s = new Scanner(System.in);
    System.out.print("Enter your age in years: ");
    double age = s.nextDouble();
    System.out.print("Enter your maximum heart rate: ");
    double rate = s.nextDouble();
    double fb = (rate - age) * 0.65;
    System.out.println("Your target fat burning heart rate is " + fb + ".");
  }
}
```

When executed, this program could produce the following on the Java console:

```
Enter your age in years: 21
Enter your maximum heart rate: 220
Your target fat burning heart rate is 129.35.
```

java.util.Scanner Methods

The Scanner class reads the input stream and divides it into *tokens*, which are strings of characters separated by *delimiters*. A delimiter is a special separating string, and the default delimiter is whitespace. That is, tokens are separated by strings of spaces, tabs, and newlines, by default. Tokens can either be read immediately as strings or a Scanner object can convert a token to a base type, if the token is in the right syntax. Specifically, the Scanner class includes the following methods for dealing with tokens:

hasNext(): Return **true** if and only if there is another token in the input stream.

next(): Return the next token string in the input stream; generate an error if there are no more tokens left.

hasNext*Type*(): Return **true** if and only if there is another token in the input stream and it can be interpreted as the corresponding base type, *Type*, where *Type* can be Boolean, Byte, Double, Float, Int, Long, or Short.

next*Type*(): Return the next token in the input stream, returned as the base type corresponding to *Type*; generate an error if there are no more tokens left or if the next token cannot be interpreted as a base type corresponding to *Type*.

Additionally, Scanner objects can process input line by line, ignoring delimiters, and even look for patterns within lines while doing so. The methods for processing input in this way include the following:

hasNextLine(): Returns **true** if and only if the input stream has another line of text.

nextLine(): Advances the input past the current line ending and returns the input that was skipped.

findInLine(String s): Attempts to find a string matching the (regular expression) pattern s in the current line. If the pattern is found, it is returned and the scanner advances to the first character after this match. If the pattern is not found, the scanner returns **null** and doesn't advance.

These methods can be used with those above, as well as in the following:

```
Scanner input = new Scanner(System.in);
System.out.print("Please enter an integer: ");
while (!input.hasNextInt()) {
  input.nextLine();
  System.out.print("That's not an integer; please enter an integer: ");
}
int i = input.nextInt();
```

Console Input and Output

Sometimes we want to make sure input and output is occurring with the Java console, and not allow input or output elsewhere. Although the default location for the input stream for System.in is from the Java console, this input can also be redirected to come from a file or another program. Likewise, even though the default location for the output stream for System.out is to the Java console, this output can also be redirected to go into a file or to another program.

Fortunately, since SE 6, Java provides a mechanism to perform exclusive input and output with the Java console. This mechanism is through the System.console() method, which returns an object of type Console. If the program that calls this method is associated with a Java console, then this object represents that console. If the program that calls this method is not associated with a Java console, however, then System.console() returns **null**.

The input stream associated with a Console object, c, is returned by the method, c.reader(), and its output stream is returned by the method, c.writer(). These objects can be used just as one would use System.in and System.out, respectively, except that the output stream that is returned by c.writer() does not get flushed to the console until it encounters a println or printf method, or is explicitly flushed using the method c.flush(). Thus, to get the same input-output behavior as our previous simple example, but now restricted so that we are interacting strictly with the Java console, we would have to use a program like the following:

```
import java.io.*;
import java.util.Scanner;
public class InputExample2 {
  public static void main(String args[]) throws IOException {
    Console c = System.console();
    if (c == null) return; // no console
    Scanner s = new Scanner(c.reader());
    PrintWriter pr = c.writer();
    pr.print("Enter your age in years: ");
    c.flush();
    double age = s.nextDouble();
    pr.print("Enter your maximum heart rate: ");
    c.flush();
    double rate = s.nextDouble();
    double fb = (rate - age) * 0.65;
    pr.println("Your target fat burning heart rate is " + fb + ".");
  }
}
```

1.7 An Example Program

In this section, we describe a simple example Java program that illustrates many of the constructs defined above. Our example consists of two classes, one, CreditCard, that defines credit card objects, and another, Test, that tests the functionality of CreditCard class. The credit card objects defined by the CreditCard class are simplified versions of traditional credit cards. They have identifying numbers, identifying information about their owners and their issuing bank, and information about their current balance and credit limit. They do not charge interest or late payments, however, but they do restrict charges that would cause a card's balance to go over its spending limit.

The CreditCard Class

We show the CreditCard class in Code Fragment 1.5. Note that the CreditCard class defines five instance variables, all of which are private to the class, and it provides a simple constructor that initializes these instance variables.

It also defines five ***accessor methods*** that provide access to the current values of these instance variables. Of course, we could have alternatively defined the instance variables as being public, which would have made the accessor methods moot. The disadvantage with this direct approach, however, is that it allows users to modify an object's instance variables directly, whereas in many cases such as this, we prefer to restrict the modification of instance variables to special ***update methods***. We include two such update methods, chargeIt and makePayment in Code Fragment 1.5.

In addition, it is often convenient to include ***action methods***, which define specific actions for that object's behavior. To demonstrate, we have defined such an action method, the printCard method, as a static method, which is also included in Code Fragment 1.5.

The Test Class

We test the CreditCard class in a Test class. Note the use of an array, wallet, of CreditCard objects here, and how we are using iteration to make charges and payments. We show the complete code for the Test class in Code Fragment 1.6. For simplicity's sake, the Test class does not do any fancy graphical output, but simply sends its output to the Java console. We show this output in Code Fragment 1.7. Note the difference between the way we utilize the nonstatic chargeIt and makePayment methods and the static printCard method.

```java
public class CreditCard {
  // Instance variables:
  private String number;
  private String name;
  private String bank;
  private double balance;
  private int limit;
  // Constructor:
  CreditCard(String no, String nm, String bk, double bal, int lim) {
    number = no;
    name = nm;
    bank = bk;
    balance = bal;
    limit = lim;
  }
  // Accessor methods:
  public String getNumber() { return number; }
  public String getName() { return name; }
  public String getBank() { return bank; }
  public double getBalance() { return balance; }
  public int getLimit() { return limit; }
  // Action methods:
  public boolean chargeIt(double price) { // Make a charge
    if (price + balance > (double) limit)
      return false; // There is not enough money left to charge it
    balance += price;
    return true; // The charge goes through in this case
  }
  public void makePayment(double payment) { // Make a payment
    balance -= payment;
  }
  public static void printCard(CreditCard c) { // Print a card's information
    System.out.println("Number = " + c.getNumber());
    System.out.println("Name = " + c.getName());
    System.out.println("Bank = " + c.getBank());
    System.out.println("Balance = " + c.getBalance()); // Implicit cast
    System.out.println("Limit = " + c.getLimit()); // Implicit cast
  }
}
```

Code Fragment 1.5: The CreditCard class.

```
public class Test {
  public static void main(String[] args) {
    CreditCard wallet[] = new CreditCard[10];
    wallet[0] = new CreditCard("5391 0375 9387 5309",
                        "John Bowman", "California Savings", 0.0, 2500);
    wallet[1] = new CreditCard("3485 0399 3395 1954",
                        "John Bowman", "California Federal", 0.0, 3500);
    wallet[2] = new CreditCard("6011 4902 3294 2994",
                        "John Bowman", "California Finance", 0.0, 5000);
    for (int i=1; i<=16; i++) {
      wallet[0].chargeIt((double)i);
      wallet[1].chargeIt(2.0*i);         // implicit cast
      wallet[2].chargeIt((double)3*i);   // explicit cast
    }
    for (int i=0; i<3; i++) {
      CreditCard.printCard(wallet[i]);
      while (wallet[i].getBalance() > 100.0) {
        wallet[i].makePayment(100.0);
        System.out.println("New balance = " + wallet[i].getBalance());
      }
    }
  }
}
```

Code Fragment 1.6: The Test class.

```
Number = 5391 0375 9387 5309
Name = John Bowman
Bank = California Savings
Balance = 136.0
Limit = 2500
New balance = 36.0
Number = 3485 0399 3395 1954
Name = John Bowman
Bank = California Federal
Balance = 272.0
Limit = 3500
New balance = 172.0
New balance = 72.0
Number = 6011 4902 3294 2994
Name = John Bowman
Bank = California Finance
Balance = 408.0
Limit = 5000
New balance = 308.0
New balance = 208.0
New balance = 108.0
New balance = 8.0
```

Code Fragment 1.7: Output from the Test class.

1.8   Nested Classes and Packages

The Java language takes a general and useful approach to the organization of classes into programs. Every stand-alone public class defined in Java must be given in a separate file. The file name is the name of the class with a *.java* extension. So a class, **public class** SmartBoard, is defined in a file, *SmartBoard.java*. In this section, we describe two ways that Java allows multiple classes to be organized in meaningful ways.

Nested Classes

Java allows class definitions to be placed inside, that is, **nested** inside the definitions of other classes. This is a useful construct, which we will exploit several times in this book in the implementation of data structures. The main use for such nested classes is to define a class that is strongly affiliated with another class. For example, a text editor class may wish to define a related cursor class. Defining the cursor class as a nested class inside the definition of the text editor class keeps these two highly related classes together in the same file. Moreover, it also allows each of them to access nonpublic methods of the other. One technical point regarding nested classes is that the nested class should be declared as **static**. This declaration implies that the nested class is associated with the outer class, not an instance of the outer class, that is, a specific object.

Packages

A set of classes, all defined in a common subdirectory, can be a Java **package**. Every file in a package starts with the line:

> **package** *package_name*;

The subdirectory containing the package must be named the same as the package. We can also define a package in a single file that contains several class definitions, but when it is compiled, all the classes will be compiled into separate files in the same subdirectory.

In Java, we can use classes that are defined in other packages by prefixing class names with dots (that is, using the '.' character) that correspond to the other packages' directory structures.

```
public boolean Temperature(TA.Measures.Thermometer thermometer,
                           int temperature) {
    // . . .
}
```

The function Temperature takes a class Thermometer as a parameter. Thermometer is defined in the TA package in a subpackage called Measures. The dots in TA.Measures.Thermometer correspond directly to the directory structure in the TA package.

All the extra typing needed to refer to a class outside of the current package can get tiring. In Java, we can use the **import** keyword to include external classes or entire packages in the current file. To import an individual class from a specific package, we type the following at the beginning of the file:

> **import** *packageName.classNames*;

For example, we could type

```
package Project;
import TA.Measures.Thermometer;
import TA.Measures.Scale;
```

at the beginning of a Project package to indicate that we are importing the classes named TA.Measures.Thermometer and TA.Measures.Scale. The Java run-time environment will now search these classes to match identifiers to classes, methods, and instance variables that we use in our program.

We can also import an entire package, by using the following syntax:

> **import** ⟨packageName⟩.*;

For example:

```
package student;
import TA.Measures.*;
public boolean Temperature(Thermometer thermometer, int temperature) {
    // . . .
}
```

In the case where two packages have classes of the same name, we ***must*** specifically reference the package that contains a class. For example, suppose both the package Gnomes and package Cooking have a class named Mushroom.

If we provide an **import** statement for both packages, then we must specify which class we mean as follows:

```
Gnomes.Mushroom shroom = new Gnomes.Mushroom ("purple");
Cooking.Mushroom topping = new Cooking.Mushroom ();
```

If we do not specify the package (that is, in the previous example we just use a variable of type Mushroom), the compiler will give an "ambiguous class" error.

To sum up the structure of a Java program, we can have instance variables and methods inside a class, and classes inside a package.

1.9   Writing a Java Program

The process of writing a Java program involves three fundamental steps:

1. Design
2. Coding
3. Testing and Debugging.

We briefly discuss each of these steps in this section.

1.9.1   Design

The design step is perhaps the most important step in the process of writing a program. For it is in the design step that we decide how to divide the workings of our program into classes, we decide how these classes will interact, what data each will store, and what actions each will perform. Indeed, one of the main challenges that beginning Java programmers face is deciding what classes to define to do the work of their program. While general prescriptions are hard to come by, there are some general rules of thumb that we can apply when determining how to define our classes:

- *Responsibilities*: Divide the work into different *actors*, each with a different responsibility. Try to describe responsibilities using action verbs. These actors will form the classes for the program.

- *Independence*: Define the work for each class to be as independent from other classes as possible. Subdivide responsibilities between classes so that each class has autonomy over some aspect of the program. Give data (as instance variables) to the class that has jurisdiction over the actions that require access to this data.

- *Behaviors*: So that the consequences of each action performed by a class will be well understood by other classes that interact with it, define the behaviors for each class carefully and precisely. These behaviors will define the methods that this class performs. The set of behaviors for a class is sometimes referred to as a *protocol*, for we expect the behaviors for a class to hold together as a cohesive unit.

Defining the classes, together with their instance variables and methods, determines the design of a Java program. A good programmer will naturally develop greater skill in performing these tasks over time, as experience teaches him or her to notice patterns in the requirements of a program that match patterns that he or she has seen before.

1.9.2 Pseudo-Code

Programmers are often asked to describe algorithms in a way that is intended for human eyes only, prior to writing actual code. Such descriptions are called ***pseudo-code***. Pseudo-code is not a computer program, but is more structured than usual prose. Pseudo-code is a mixture of natural language and high-level programming constructs that describe the main ideas behind a generic implementation of a data structure or algorithm. There really is no precise definition of the ***pseudo-code*** language, however, because of its reliance on natural language. At the same time, to help achieve clarity, pseudo-code mixes natural language with standard programming language constructs. The programming language constructs we choose are those consistent with modern high-level languages such as C, C++, and Java.

These constructs include the following:

- ***Expressions:*** We use standard mathematical symbols to express numeric and Boolean expressions. We use the left arrow sign ($\leftarrow$) as the assignment operator in assignment statements (equivalent to the $=$ operator in Java) and we use the equal sign ($=$) as the equality relation in Boolean expressions (equivalent to the "$==$" relation in Java).
- ***Method declarations:*** **Algorithm** name($param1, param2, \ldots$) declares a new method "name" and its parameters.
- ***Decision structures:*** **if** condition **then** true-actions [**else** false-actions]. We use indentation to indicate what actions should be included in the true-actions and false-actions.
- ***While-loops:*** **while** condition **do** actions. We use indentation to indicate what actions should be included in the loop actions.
- ***Repeat-loops:*** **repeat** actions **until** condition. We use indentation to indicate what actions should be included in the loop actions.
- ***For-loops:*** **for** variable-increment-definition **do** actions. We use indentation to indicate what actions should be included among the loop actions.
- ***Array indexing:*** $A[i]$ represents the ith cell in the array A. The cells of an n-celled array A are indexed from $A[0]$ to $A[n-1]$ (consistent with Java).
- ***Method calls:*** object.method(args) (object is optional if it is understood).
- ***Method returns:*** **return** value. This operation returns the value specified to the method that called this one.
- ***Comments:*** { Comment goes here. }. We enclose comments in braces.

When we write pseudo-code, we must keep in mind that we are writing for a human reader, not a computer. Thus, we should strive to communicate high-level ideas, not low-level implementation details. At the same time, we should not gloss over important steps. Like many forms of human communication, finding the right balance is an important skill that is refined through practice.

1.9.3 Coding

As mentioned above, one of the key steps in coding up an object-oriented program is coding up the descriptions of classes and their respective data and methods. In order to accelerate the development of this skill, we discuss various ***design patterns*** for designing object-oriented programs (see Section 2.1.3) at various points throughout this text. These patterns provide templates for defining classes and the interactions between these classes.

Many programmers do their initial coding not on a computer, but by using ***CRC cards***. Class-Responsibility-Collaborator (CRC) cards are simple index cards that subdivide the work required of a program. The main idea behind this tool is to have each card represent a component, which will ultimately become a class in our program. We write the name of each component on the top of an index card. On the left-hand side of the card, we begin writing the responsibilities for this component. On the right-hand side, we list the collaborators for this component, that is, the other components that this component will have to interact with to perform its duties. The design process iterates through an action/actor cycle, where we first identify an action (that is, a responsibility), and we then determine an actor (that is, a component) that is best suited to perform that action. The design is complete when we have assigned all actions to actors.

By the way, in using index cards to begin our coding, we are assuming that each component will have a small set of responsibilities and collaborators. This assumption is no accident, for it helps keep our programs manageable.

An alternative to CRC cards is the use of UML (Unified Modeling Language) diagrams to express the organization of a Program, and the use of pseudo-code to describe the algorithms. UML diagrams are a standard visual notation to express object-oriented software designs. Several computer-aided tools are available to build UML diagrams. Describing algorithms in pseudo-code, on the other hand, is a technique that we utilize throughout this book.

Once we have decided on the classes for our program and their responsibilities, we are ready to begin the actual coding on a computer. We create the actual code for the classes in our program by using either an independent text editor (such as emacs, WordPad, or vi), or the editor embedded in an ***integrated development environment*** (IDE), such as Eclipse or Borland JBuilder.

Once we have completed coding for a class (or package), we compile this file into working code by invoking a compiler. If we are not using an IDE, then we compile our program by calling a program, such as `javac`, on our file. If we are using an IDE, then we compile our program by clicking the appropriate compilation button. If we are fortunate, and our program has no syntax errors, then this compilation process will create files with a ".`class`" extension.

If our program contains syntax errors, then these will be identified, and we will have to go back into our editor to fix the offending lines of code. Once we have eliminated all syntax errors, and created the appropriate compiled code, we can run our program by either invoking a command, such as "java" (outside an IDE), or by clicking on the appropriate "run" button (within an IDE). When a Java program is run in this way, the run-time environment locates the directories containing the named class and any other classes that are referenced from this class according to a special operating system environment variable. This variable is named "CLASS-PATH," and the order of directories to search in is given as a list of directories, which are separated by colons in Unix/Linux or semicolons in DOS/Windows. An example CLASSPATH assignment in the DOS/Windows operating system could be the following:

```
SET CLASSPATH=.;C:\java;C:\Program Files\Java\
```

Whereas an example CLASSPATH assignment in the Unix/Linux operating system could be the following:

```
setenv  CLASSPATH ".:/usr/local/java/lib:/usr/netscape/classes"
```

In both cases, the dot (".") refers to the current directory in which the run-time environment is invoked.

Javadoc

In order to encourage good use of block comments and the automatic production of documentation, the Java programming environment comes with a documentation production program called *javadoc*. This program takes a collection of Java source files that have been commented using certain keywords, called *tags*, and it produces a series of HTML documents that describe the classes, methods, variables, and constants contained in these files. For space reasons, we have not used javadoc-style comments in all the example programs included in this book, but we include a javadoc example in Code Fragment 1.8 as well as other examples at the Web site that accompanies this book.

Each javadoc comment is a block comment that starts with "/**" and ends with "*/," and each line between these two can begin with a single asterisk, "*," which is ignored. The block comment is assumed to start with a descriptive sentence, followed by a blank line, which is followed by special lines that begin with javadoc tags. A block comment that comes just before a class definition, instance variable declaration, or method definition, is processed by javadoc into a comment about that class, variable, or method.

Code Fragment 1.8: An example class definition using javadoc-style comments. Note that this class includes two instance variables, one constructor, and two accessor methods.

The primary javadoc tags are the following:

- `@author` *text*: Identifies each author (one per line) for a class.

- `@exception` *exception-name description*: Identifies an error condition that is signaled by this method (see Section 2.3).

- `@param` *parameter-name description*: Identifies a parameter accepted by this method.

- `@return` *description*: Describes the return type and its range of values for a method.

There are other tags as well; the interested reader is referred to on-line documentation for javadoc for further discussion.

Readability and Style

Programs should be made easy to read and understand. Good programmers should therefore be mindful of their coding style, and develop a style that communicates the important aspects of a program's design for both humans and computers.

Much has been written about good coding style, with some of the main principles being the following:

- Use meaningful names for identifiers. Try to choose names that can be read aloud, and choose names that reflect the action, responsibility, or data each identifier is naming. The tradition in most Java circles is to capitalize the first letter of each word in an identifier, except for the first word in an identifier for a variable or method. So, in this tradition, "Date," "Vector," "DeviceManager" would identify classes, and 'isFull(),' "insertItem()," "studentName," and "studentHeight" would respectively identify methods and variables.

- Use named constants or enum types instead of literals. Readability, robustness, and modifiability are enhanced if we include a series of definitions of named constant values in a class definition. These can then be used within this class and others to refer to special values for this class. The tradition in Java is to fully capitalize such constants, as shown below:

```
public class Student {
  public static final int MIN_CREDITS = 12;  // min. credits in a term
  public static final int MAX_CREDITS = 24;  // max. credits in a term
  public static final int FRESHMAN = 1;   // code for freshman
  public static final int SOPHOMORE = 2;  // code for sophomore
  public static final int JUNIOR = 3;     // code for junior
  public static final int SENIOR = 4;     // code for senior

  // Instance variables, constructors, and method definitions go here...
}
```

- Indent statement blocks. Typically programmers indent each statement block by 4 spaces; in this book we typically use 2 spaces, however, to avoid having our code overrun the book's margins.
- Organize each class in the following order:
  1. Constants
  2. Instance variables
  3. Constructors
  4. Methods.

We note that some Java programmers prefer to put instance variable definitions last. We put them earlier so that we can read each class sequentially and understand the data each method is working with.

- Use comments that add meaning to a program and explain ambiguous or confusing constructs. In-line comments are good for quick explanations and do not need to be sentences. Block comments are good for explaining the purpose of a method and complex code sections.

1.9.4 Testing and Debugging

Testing is the process of experimentally checking the correctness of a program, while debugging is the process of tracking the execution of a program and discovering the errors in it. Testing and debugging are often the most time-consuming activity in the development of a program.

Testing

A careful testing plan is an essential part of writing a program. While verifying the correctness of a program over all possible inputs is usually infeasible, we should aim at executing the program on a representative subset of inputs. At the very minimum, we should make sure that every method in the program is tested at least once (method coverage). Even better, each code statement in the program should be executed at least once (statement coverage).

Programs often tend to fail on *special cases* of the input. Such cases need to be carefully identified and tested. For example, when testing a method that sorts (that is, puts in order) an array of integers, we should consider the following inputs:

- The array has zero length (no elements).
- The array has one element.
- All the elements of the array are the same.
- The array is already sorted.
- The array is reverse sorted.

In addition to special inputs to the program, we should also consider special conditions for the structures used by the program. For example, if we use an array to store data, we should make sure that boundary cases, such as inserting/removing at the beginning or end of the subarray holding data, are properly handled.

While it is essential to use hand-crafted test suites, it is also advantageous to run the program on a large collection of randomly generated inputs. The Random class in the java.util package provides several methods to generate random numbers.

There is a hierarchy among the classes and methods of a program induced by the caller-callee relationship. Namely, a method A is above a method B in the hierarchy if A calls B. There are two main testing strategies, *top-down* and *bottom-up*, which differ in the order in which methods are tested.

Bottom-up testing proceeds from lower-level methods to higher-level methods. Namely, bottom-level methods, which do not invoke other methods, are tested first, followed by methods that call only bottom-level methods, and so on. This strategy ensures that errors found in a method are not likely to be caused by lower-level methods nested within it.

Top-down testing proceeds from the top to the bottom of the method hierarchy. It is typically used in conjunction with *stubbing*, a boot-strapping technique that replaces a lower-level method with a *stub*, a replacement for the method that simulates the output of the original method. For example, if method A calls method B to get the first line of a file, when testing A we can replace B with a stub that returns a fixed string.

Debugging

The simplest debugging technique consists of using *print statements* (using method System.out.println(*string*)) to track the values of variables during the execution of the program. A problem with this approach is that the print statements need to be eventually removed or commented out before the software is finally released.

A better approach is to run the program within a *debugger*, which is a specialized environment for controlling and monitoring the execution of a program. The basic functionality provided by a debugger is the insertion of *breakpoints* within the code. When the program is executed within the debugger, it stops at each breakpoint. While the program is stopped, the current value of variables can be inspected. In addition to fixed breakpoints, advanced debuggers allow for specification of ***conditional breakpoints***, which are triggered only if a given expression is satisfied.

The standard Java tools include a basic debugger called jdb, which is command-line oriented. IDEs for Java programming provide advanced debugging environments with graphical user interfaces.

1.10 Exercises

For help with exercises, please visit the web site, www.wiley.com/college/goodrich.

Reinforcement

R-1.1 What we would have to change in the CreditCard class in order to guarantee that all its output is done exclusively to the Java console?

R-1.2 Write a pseudo-code description of a method for finding the smallest and largest numbers in an array of integers and compare that to a Java method that would do the same thing.

R-1.3 Suppose that we create an array A of GameEntry objects, which has an integer scores field, and we clone A and store the result in an array B. If we then immediately set $A[4]$.score equal to 550, what is the score value of the GameEntry object referenced by $B[4]$?

R-1.4 Modify the CreditCard class from Code Fragment 1.5 to charge interest on each payment.

R-1.5 Modify the CreditCard class from Code Fragment 1.5 to charge a late fee for any payment that is past its due date.

R-1.6 Modify the CreditCard class from Code Fragment 1.5 to include *modifier methods*, which allow a user to modify internal variables in a CreditCard class in a controlled manner.

R-1.7 Modify the declaration of the first **for** loop in the Test class in Code Fragment 1.6 so that its charges will eventually cause exactly one of the three credit cards to go over its credit limit. Which credit card is it?

R-1.8 Write a short Java function, inputAllBaseTypes, that inputs a different value of each base type from the standard input device and prints it back to the standard output device.

R-1.9 Write a Java class, Flower, that has three instance variables of type **String**, **int**, and **float**, which respectively represent the name of the flower, its number of pedals, and price. Your class must include a constructor method that initializes each variable to an appropriate value, and your class should include methods for setting the value of each type, and getting the value of each type.

R-1.10 Write a short Java function, isMultiple, that takes two **long** values, n and m, and returns true if and only if n is a multiple of m, that is, $n = mi$ for some integer i.

R-1.11 Write a short Java function, isEven, that takes an **int** i and returns true if and only if i is even. Your function cannot use the multiplication, modulus, or division operators, however.

R-1.12 Write a short Java function that takes an integer n and returns the sum of all the integers smaller than n.

R-1.13 Write a short Java function that takes an integer n and returns the sum of all the odd integers smaller than n.

Creativity

C-1.1 Write a pseudo-code description of a method that reverses an array of n integers, so that the numbers are listed in the opposite order than they were before, and compare this method to an equivalent Java method for doing the same thing.

C-1.2 Write a short Java function that takes an array of **int** values and determines if there is a pair of numbers in the array whose product is even.

C-1.3 Write a Java method that takes an array of **float** values and determines if all the numbers are different from each other (that is, they are distinct).

C-1.4 Write a Java method that takes an array containing the set of all integers in the range 1 to 52 and shuffles it into random order. Your method should output each possible order with equal probability.

C-1.5 Write a short Java program that outputs all possible strings formed by using the characters 'c', 'a', 't', 'd', 'o', and 'g' exactly once.

C-1.6 Write a short Java program that takes all the lines input to standard input and writes them to standard output in reverse order. That is, each line is output in the correct order, but the ordering of the lines is reversed.

C-1.7 Write a short Java program that takes two arrays a and b of length n storing **int** values, and returns the dot product of a and b. That is, it returns an array c of length n such that $c[i] = a[i] \cdot b[i]$, for $i = 0, \ldots, n-1$.

Projects

P-1.1 Write a Java program that can simulate a simple calculator, using the Java console as the exclusive input and output device. That is, each input to the calculator, be it a number, like 12.34 or 1034, or an operator, like + or =, can be done on a separate line. After each such input, you should output to the Java console what would be displayed on your calculator.

P-1.2 A common punishment for school children is to write out a sentence multiple times. Write a Java stand-alone program that will write out the following sentence one hundred times: "I will never spam my friends again." Your program should number each of the sentences and it should make eight different random-looking typos.

P-1.3 (For those who know Java graphical user interface methods) Define a GraphicalTest class that tests the functionality of the CreditCard class from Code Fragment 1.5 using text fields and buttons.

P-1.4 The *birthday paradox* says that the probability that two people in a room will have the same birthday is more than half, provided n, the number of people in the room, is more than 23. This property is not really a paradox, but many people find it surprising. Design a Java program that can test this paradox by a series of experiments on randomly generated birthdays, which test this paradox for $n = 5, 10, 15, 20, \ldots, 100$.

Chapter Notes

For more detailed information about the Java programming language, we refer the reader to some of the fine books about Java, including the books by Arnold, Gosling and Holmes [7], Flanagan [32], Horstmann [49], and Horstmann and Cornell [50, 51], as well as Sun's Java Web site (http://www.java.sun.com).

Chapter

2

Object-Oriented Design

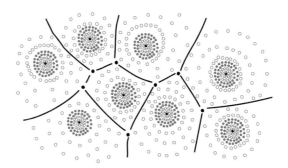

Contents

2.1   Goals, Principles, and Patterns

As the name implies, the main "actors" in the object-oriented design paradigm are called *objects*. An object comes from a *class*, which is a specification of the data *fields*, also called *instance variables*, that the object contains, as well as the *methods* (operations) that the object can execute. Each class presents to the outside world a concise and consistent view of the objects that are instances of this class, without going into too much unnecessary detail or giving others access to the inner workings of the objects. This view of computing is intended to fulfill several goals and incorporate several design principles, which we discuss in this chapter.

2.1.1   Object-Oriented Design Goals

Software implementations should achieve *robustness*, *adaptability*, and *reusability*. (See Figure 2.1.)

Robustness   Adaptability   Reusability

Figure 2.1: Goals of object-oriented design.

Robustness

Every good programmer wants to develop software that is correct, which means that a program produces the right output for all the anticipated inputs in the program's application. In addition, we want software to be *robust*, that is, capable of handling unexpected inputs that are not explicitly defined for its application. For example, if a program is expecting a positive integer (for example, representing the price of an item) and instead is given a negative integer, then the program should be able to recover gracefully from this error. More importantly, in *life-critical applications*, where a software error can lead to injury or loss of life, software that is not robust could be deadly. This point was driven home in the late 1980s in accidents involving Therac-25, a radiation-therapy machine, which severely overdosed six patients between 1985 and 1987, some of whom died from complications resulting from their radiation overdose. All six accidents were traced to software errors.

Adaptability

Modern software applications, such as Web browsers and Internet search engines, typically involve large programs that are used for many years. Software, therefore, needs to be able to evolve over time in response to changing conditions in its environment. Thus, another important goal of quality software is that it achieves *adaptability* (also called *evolvability*). Related to this concept is *portability*, which is the ability of software to run with minimal change on different hardware and operating system platforms. An advantage of writing software in Java is the portability provided by the language itself.

Reusability

Going hand in hand with adaptability is the desire that software be reusable, that is, the same code should be usable as a component of different systems in various applications. Developing quality software can be an expensive enterprise, and its cost can be offset somewhat if the software is designed in a way that makes it easily reusable in future applications. Such reuse should be done with care, however, for one of the major sources of software errors in the Therac-25 came from inappropriate reuse of Therac-20 software (which was not object-oriented and not designed for the hardware platform used with the Therac-25).

2.1.2 Object-Oriented Design Principles

Chief among the principles of the object-oriented approach, which are intended to facilitate the goals outlined above, are the following (see Figure 2.2):

- Abstraction
- Encapsulation
- Modularity.

Abstraction   Encapsulation   Modularity

Figure 2.2: Principles of object-oriented design.

Abstraction

The notion of *abstraction* is to distill a complicated system down to its most fundamental parts and describe these parts in a simple, precise language. Typically, describing the parts of a system involves naming them and explaining their functionality. Applying the abstraction paradigm to the design of data structures gives rise to *abstract data types* (ADTs). An ADT is a mathematical model of a data structure that specifies the type of data stored, the operations supported on them, and the types of parameters of the operations. An ADT specifies *what* each operation does, but not *how* it does it. In Java, an ADT can be expressed by an *interface*, which is simply a list of method declarations, where each method has an empty body. (We say more about Java interfaces in Section 2.4.)

An ADT is realized by a concrete data structure, which is modeled in Java by a *class*. A class defines the data being stored and the operations supported by the objects that are instances of the class. Also, unlike interfaces, classes specify *how* the operations are performed in the body of each method. A Java class is said to *implement an interface* if its methods include all the methods declared in the interface, thus providing a body for them. However, a class can have more methods than those of the interface.

Encapsulation

Another important principle of object-oriented design is the concept of *encapsulation*, which states that different components of a software system should not reveal the internal details of their respective implementations. One of the main advantages of encapsulation is that it gives the programmer freedom in implementing the details of a system. The only constraint on the programmer is to maintain the abstract interface that outsiders see.

Modularity

In addition to abstraction and encapsulation, a fundamental principle of object-oriented design is *modularity*. Modern software systems typically consist of several different components that must interact correctly in order for the entire system to work properly. Keeping these interactions straight requires that these different components be well organized. In object-oriented design, this code structuring approach centers around the concept of *modularity*. Modularity refers to an organizing principle for code in which different components of a software system are divided into separate functional units.

Hierarchical Organization

The structure imposed by modularity helps to enable software reusability. If software modules are written in an abstract way to solve general problems, then modules can be reused when instances of these same general problems arise in other contexts.

For example, the structural definition of a wall is the same from house to house, typically being defined in terms of vertical studs, spaced at fixed-distance intervals, etc. Thus, an organized architect can reuse his or her wall definitions from one house to another. In reusing such a definition, some parts may require redefinition, for example, a wall in a commercial building may be similar to that of a house, but the electrical system and stud material might be different.

A natural way to organize various structural components of a software package is in a *hierarchical* fashion, which groups similar abstract definitions together in a level-by-level manner that goes from specific to more general as one traverses up the hierarchy. A common use of such hierarchies is in an organizational chart, where each link going up can be read as "is a," as in "a ranch is a house is a building." This kind of hierarchy is useful in software design, for it groups together common functionality at the most general level, and views specialized behavior as an extension of the general one.

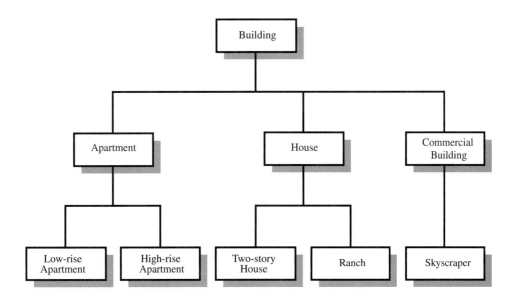

Figure 2.3: An example of an "is a" hierarchy involving architectural buildings.

2.1.3   Design Patterns

One of the advantages of object-oriented design is that it facilitates reusable, robust, and adaptable software. Designing good code takes more than simply understanding object-oriented methodologies, however. It requires the effective use of object-oriented design techniques.

Computing researchers and practitioners have developed a variety of organizational concepts and methodologies for designing quality object-oriented software that is concise, correct, and reusable. Of special relevance to this book is the concept of a ***design pattern***, which describes a solution to a "typical" software design problem. A pattern provides a general template for a solution that can be applied in many different situations. It describes the main elements of a solution in an abstract way that can be specialized for a specific problem at hand. It consists of a name, which identifies the pattern, a context, which describes the scenarios for which this pattern can be applied, a template, which describes how the pattern is applied, and a result, which describes and analyzes what the pattern produces.

We present several design patterns in this book, and we show how they can be consistently applied to implementations of data structures and algorithms. These design patterns fall into two groups—patterns for solving algorithm design problems and patterns for solving software engineering problems. Some of the algorithm design patterns we discuss include the following:

- Recursion (Section 3.5)
- Amortization (Section 6.1.4)
- Divide-and-conquer (Section 11.1.1)
- Prune-and-search, also known as decrease-and-conquer (Section 11.5.1)
- Brute force (Section 12.3.1)
- The greedy method (Section 12.4.2)
- Dynamic programming (Section 12.2).

Likewise, some of the software engineering design patterns we discuss include:

- Position (Section 6.2.2)
- Adapter (Section 6.1.2)
- Iterator (Section 6.3)
- Template method (Sections 7.3.7, 11.4, and 13.3.2)
- Composition (Section 8.1.2)
- Comparator (Section 8.1.2)
- Decorator (Section 13.3.1).

Rather than explain each of these concepts here, however, we introduce them throughout the text as noted above. For each pattern, be it for algorithm engineering or software engineering, we explain its general use and we illustrate it with at least one concrete example.

2.2 Inheritance and Polymorphism

To take advantage of hierarchical relationships, which are common in software projects, the object-oriented design approach provides ways of reusing code.

2.2.1 Inheritance

The object-oriented paradigm provides a modular and hierarchical organizing structure for reusing code, through a technique called ***inheritance***. This technique allows the design of general classes that can be specialized to more particular classes, with the specialized classes reusing the code from the general class. The general class, which is also known as a ***base class*** or ***superclass***, can define standard instance variables and methods that apply in a multitude of situations. A class that ***specializes***, or ***extends***, or ***inherits from***, a superclass need not give new implementations for the general methods, for it inherits them. It should only define those methods that are specialized for this particular ***subclass***.

Example 2.1: *Consider a class* S *that defines objects with a field,* x, *and three methods,* a(), b(), *and* c(). *Suppose we were to define a class* T *that extends* S *and includes an additional field,* y, *and two methods,* d() *and* e(). *The class* T *would then* **inherit** *the instance variable* x *and the methods* a(), b(), *and* c() *from* S. *We illustrate the relationships between the class* S *and the class* T *in a* **class inheritance diagram** *in Figure 2.4. Each box in such a diagram denotes a class, with its name, fields (or instance variables), and methods included as subrectangles.*

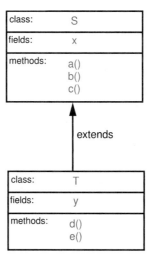

Figure 2.4: A class inheritance diagram. Each box denotes a class, with its name, fields, and methods, and an arrow between boxes denotes an inheritance relation.

Object Creation and Referencing

When an object o is created, memory is allocated for its data fields, and these same fields are initialized to specific beginning values. Typically, one associates the new object o with a variable, which serves as a "link" to object o, and is said to *reference* o. When we wish to access object o (for the purpose of getting at its fields or executing its methods), we can either request the execution of one of o's methods (defined by the class that o belongs to), or look up one of the fields of o. Indeed, the primary way that an object p interacts with another object o is for p to send a "message" to o that invokes one of o's methods, for example, for o to print a description of itself, for o to convert itself to a string, or for o to return the value of one of its data fields. The secondary way that p can interact with o is for p to access one of o's fields directly, but only if o has given other objects like p permission to do so. For example, an instance of the Java class Integer stores, as an instance variable, an integer, and it provides several operations for accessing this data, including methods for converting it into other number types, for converting it to a string of digits, and for converting strings of digits to a number. It does not allow for direct access of its instance variable, however, for such details are hidden.

Dynamic Dispatch

When a program wishes to invoke a certain method a() of some object o, it sends a message to o, which is usually denoted, using the dot-operator syntax (Section 1.3.2), as "o.a()." In the compiled version of this program, the code corresponding to this invocation directs the run-time environment to examine o's class T to determine if the class T supports an a() method, and, if so, to execute it. Specifically, the run-time environment examines the class T to see if it defines an a() method itself. If it does, then this method is executed. If T does not define an a() method, then the run-time environment examines the superclass S of T. If S defines a(), then this method is executed. If S does not define a(), on the other hand, then the run-time environment repeats the search at the superclass of S. This search continues up the hierarchy of classes until it either finds an a() method, which is then executed, or it reaches a topmost class (for example, the Object class in Java) without an a() method, which generates a run-time error. The algorithm that processes the message o.a() to find the specific method to invoke is called the *dynamic dispatch* (or *dynamic binding*) algorithm, which provides an effective mechanism for locating reused software. It also allows for another powerful technique of object-oriented programming—*polymorphism*.

2.2.2 Polymorphism

Literally, "polymorphism" means "many forms." In the context of object-oriented design, it refers to the ability of an object variable to take different forms. Object-oriented languages, such as Java, address objects using reference variables. The reference variable o must define which class of objects it is allowed to refer to, in terms of some class S. But this implies that o can also refer to any object belonging to a class T that extends S. Now consider what happens if S defines an a() method and T also defines an a() method. The dynamic dispatch algorithm for method invocation always starts its search from the most restrictive class that applies. When o refers to an object from class T, then it will use T's a() method when asked for o.a(), not S's. In this case, T is said to **override** method a() from S. Alternatively, when o refers to an object from class S (that is not also a T object), it will execute S's a() method when asked for o.a(). Polymorphism such as this is useful because the caller of o.a() does not have to know whether the object o refers to an instance of T or S in order to get the a() method to execute correctly. Thus, the object variable o can be **polymorphic**, or take many forms, depending on the specific class of the objects it is referring to. This kind of functionality allows a specialized class T to extend a class S, inherit the standard methods from S, and redefine other methods from S to account for specific properties of objects of T.

Some object-oriented languages, such as Java, also provide a useful technique related to polymorphism, which is called method **overloading**. Overloading occurs when a single class T has multiple methods with the same name, provided each one has a different **signature**. The signature of a method is a combination of its name and the type and number of arguments that are passed to it. Thus, even though multiple methods in a class can have the same name, they can be distinguished by a compiler, provided they have different signatures, that is, are different in actuality. In languages that allow for method overloading, the run-time environment determines which actual method to invoke for a specific method call by searching up the class hierarchy to find the first method with a signature matching the method being invoked. For example, suppose a class T, which defines a method a(), extends a class U, which defines a method a(x, y). If an object o from class T receives the message "o.a(x, y)," then it is U's version of method a that is invoked (with the two parameters x and y). Thus, true polymorphism applies only to methods that have the same signature, but are defined in different classes.

Inheritance, polymorphism, and method overloading support the development of reusable software. We can define classes that inherit the standard instance variables and methods and can then define new more-specific instance variables and methods that deal with special aspects of objects of the new class.

2.2.3   Using Inheritance in Java

There are two primary ways of using inheritance of classes in Java, *specialization* and *extension*.

Specialization

In using specialization we are specializing a general class to particular subclasses. Such subclasses typically possess an "is a" relationship to their superclass. A subclass then inherits all the methods of the superclass. For each inherited method, if that method operates correctly independent of whether it is operating for a specialization, no additional work is needed. If, on the other hand, a general method of the superclass would not work correctly on the subclass, then we should override the method to have the correct functionality for the subclass. For example, we could have a general class, Dog, which has a method drink and a method sniff. Specializing this class to a Bloodhound class would probably not require that we override the drink method, as all dogs drink pretty much the same way. But it could require that we override the sniff method, as a Bloodhound has a much more sensitive sense of smell than a standard dog. In this way, the Bloodhound class specializes the methods of its superclass, Dog.

Extension

In using extension, on the other hand, we utilize inheritance to reuse the code written for methods of the superclass, but we then add new methods that are not present in the superclass, so as to extend its functionality. For example, returning to our Dog class, we might wish to create a subclass, BorderCollie, which inherits all the standard methods of the Dog class, but then adds a new method, herd, since Border Collies have a herding instinct that is not present in standard dogs. By adding the new method, we are extending the functionality of a standard dog.

In Java, each class can extend exactly one other class. Even if a class definition makes no explicit use of the **extends** clause, it still inherits from exactly one other class, which in this case is class java.lang.Object. Because of this property, Java is said to allow only for *single inheritance* among classes.

Types of Method Overriding

Inside the declaration of a new class, Java uses two kinds of method overriding, *refinement* and *replacement*. In the replacement type of overriding, a method completely replaces the method of the superclass that it is overriding (as in the sniff method of Bloodhound mentioned above). In Java, all regular methods of a class utilize this type of overriding behavior.

In the refinement type of overriding, however, a method does not replace the method of its superclass, but instead adds additional code to that of its superclass. In Java, all constructors utilize the refinement type of overriding, a scheme called **constructor chaining**. Namely, a constructor begins its execution by calling a constructor of the superclass. This call can be made explicitly or implicitly. To call a constructor of the superclass explicitly, we use the keyword **super** to refer to the superclass. (For example, super() calls the constructor of the superclass with no arguments.) If no explicit call is made in the body of a constructor, however, the compiler automatically inserts, as the first line of the constructor, a call to super(). (There is an exception to this general rule, which is discussed in the next section.) Summarizing, in Java, constructors use the refinement type of method overriding whereas regular methods use replacement.

The Keyword **this**

Sometimes, in a Java class, it is convenient to reference the current instance of that class. Java provides a keyword, called **this**, for such a reference. Reference **this** is useful, for example, if we would like to pass the current object as a parameter to some method. Another application of **this** is to reference a field inside the current object that has a name clash with a variable defined in the current block, as shown in the program given in Code Fragment 2.1.

```java
public class ThisTester {
  public int dog = 2; // instance variable
  public void clobber() {
    int dog = 5;        // a different dog!
    System.out.println("The dog local variable = " + dog);
    System.out.println("The dog field = " + this.dog);
    }
  public static void main(String args[]) {
    ThisTester t = new ThisTester();
    t.clobber();
  }
}
```

Code Fragment 2.1: Sample program illustrating the use of reference **this** to disambiguate between a field of the current object and a local variable with the same name.

When this program is executed, it prints the following:

```
The dog local variable = 5
The dog field = 2
```

An Illustration of Inheritance in Java

To make some of the notions above about inheritance and polymorphism more concrete, let us consider some simple examples in Java.

In particular, we consider a series of several classes for stepping through and printing out numeric progressions. A numeric progression is a sequence of numbers, where each number depends on one or more of the previous numbers. For example, an *arithmetic progression* determines the next number by addition and a *geometric progression* determines the next number by multiplication. In any case, a progression requires a way of defining its first value and it needs a way of identifying the current value as well.

We begin by defining a class, Progression, shown in Code Fragment 2.2, which defines the standard fields and methods of a numeric progression. Specifically, it defines the following two long-integer fields:

- first: first value of the progression;
- cur: current value of the progression;

and the following three methods:

> firstValue(): Reset the progression to the first value, and return that value.
>
> nextValue(): Step the progression to the next value and return that value.
>
> printProgression(n): Reset the progression and print the first n values of the progression.

We say that the method printProgression has no output in the sense that it does not return any value, whereas the methods firstValue and nextValue both return long-integer values. That is, firstValue and nextValue are functions, and printProgression is a procedure.

The Progression class also includes a method Progression(), which is a *constructor*. Recall that constructors set up all the instance variables at the time an object of this class is created. The Progression class is meant to be a general superclass from which specialized classes inherit, so this constructor is code that will be included in the constructors for each class that extends the Progression class.

```java
/**
 * A class for numeric progressions.
 */
public class Progression {

  /** First value of the progression.  */
  protected long first;

  /** Current value of the progression. */
  protected long cur;

  /** Default constructor. */
  Progression() {
    cur = first = 0;
  }

  /** Resets the progression to the first value.
   *
   * @return first value
   */
  protected long firstValue() {
    cur = first;
    return cur;
  }

  /** Advances the progression to the next value.
   *
   * @return next value of the progression
   */
  protected long nextValue() {
    return ++cur; // default next value
  }

  /** Prints the first n values of the progression.
   *
   * @param n number of values to print
   */
  public void printProgression(int n) {
    System.out.print(firstValue());
    for (int i = 2; i <= n; i++)
      System.out.print(" " + nextValue());
    System.out.println(); // ends the line
  }
}
```

Code Fragment 2.2: General numeric progression class.

An Arithmetic Progression Class

Next, we consider the class ArithProgression, which we present in Code Fragment 2.3. This class defines an arithmetic progression, where the next value is determined by adding a fixed increment, inc, to the previous value. ArithProgression inherits fields first and cur and methods firstValue() and printProgression(n) from the Progression class. It adds a new field, inc, to store the increment, and two constructors for setting the increment. Finally, it overrides the nextValue() method to conform to the way we get the next value for an arithmetic progression.

Polymorphism is at work here. When a Progression reference is pointing to an ArithProgression object, then it is the ArithProgression methods firstValue() and nextValue() that will be used. This polymorphism is also true inside the inherited version of printProgression(n), because the calls to the firstValue() and nextValue() methods here are implicit for the "current" object (called this in Java), which in this case will be of the ArithProgression class.

Example Constructors and the Keyword **this**

In the definition of the ArithProgression class, we have added two constructors, a default one, which takes no parameters, and a parametric one, which takes an integer parameter as the increment for the progression. The default constructor actually calls the parametric one, using the keyword **this** and passing 1 as the value of the increment parameter. These two constructors illustrate method overloading (where a method name can have multiple versions inside the same class), since a method is actually specified by its name, the class of the object that calls it, and the types of arguments that are passed to it—its signature. In this case, the overloading is for constructors (a default constructor and a parametric constructor).

The call **this**(1) to the parametric constructor as the first statement of the default constructor triggers an exception to the general constructor chaining rule discussed in Section 2.2.3. Namely, whenever the first statement of a constructor C' calls another constructor C'' of the same class using the **this** reference, the superclass constructor is not implicitly called for C'. Note that a superclass constructor will eventually be called along the chain, either explicitly or implicitly. In particular, for our ArithProgression class, the default constructor of the superclass (Progression) is implicitly called as the first statement of the parametric constructor of ArithProgression.

We discuss constructors in more detail in Section 1.2.

```
/**
 * Arithmetic progression.
 */
class ArithProgression extends Progression {

  /** Increment. */
  protected long inc;

  // Inherits variables first and cur.

  /** Default constructor setting a unit increment. */
  ArithProgression() {
    this(1);
  }

  /** Parametric constructor providing the increment. */
  ArithProgression(long increment) {
    inc = increment;
  }

  /** Advances the progression by adding the increment to the current value.
   *
   * @return next value of the progression
   */
  protected long nextValue() {
    cur += inc;
    return cur;
  }

  // Inherits methods firstValue() and printProgression(int).
}
```

Code Fragment 2.3: Class for arithmetic progressions, which inherits from the general progression class shown in Code Fragment 2.2.

A Geometric Progression Class

Let us next define a class, GeomProgression, shown in Code Fragment 2.4, which steps through and prints out a geometric progression, where the next value is determined by multiplying the previous value by a fixed base, base. A geometric progression is like a general progression, except for the way we determine the next value. Hence, GeomProgression is declared as a subclass of the Progression class. As with the ArithProgression class, the GeomProgression class inherits the fields first and cur, and the methods firstValue and printProgression from Progression.

```java
/**
 * Geometric Progression
 */
class GeomProgression extends Progression {

  /** Base. */
  protected long base;

  // Inherits variables first and cur.

  /** Default constructor setting base 2. */
  GeomProgression() {
    this(2);
  }

  /** Parametric constructor providing the base.
   *
   * @param b base of the progression.
   */
  GeomProgression(long b) {
    base = b;
    first = 1;
    cur = first;
  }

  /** Advances the progression by multiplying the base with the current value.
   *
   * @return next value of the progression
   */
  protected long nextValue() {
    cur *= base;
    return cur;
  }

  // Inherits methods firstValue() and printProgression(int).
}
```

Code Fragment 2.4: Class for geometric progressions.

A Fibonacci Progression Class

As a further example, we define a FibonacciProgression class that represents another kind of progression, the ***Fibonacci progression***, where the next value is defined as the sum of the current and previous values. We show class FibonacciProgression in Code Fragment 2.5. Note our use of a parameterized constructor in the FibonacciProgression class to provide a different way of starting the progression.

```java
/**
 * Fibonacci progression.
 */
class FibonacciProgression extends Progression {
  /** Previous value. */
  long prev;
  // Inherits variables first and cur.

  /** Default constructor setting 0 and 1 as the first two values. */
  FibonacciProgression() {
    this(0, 1);
  }
  /** Parametric constructor providing the first and second values.
   *
   * @param value1 first value.
   * @param value2 second value.
   */
  FibonacciProgression(long value1, long value2) {
      first = value1;
      prev = value2 − value1; // fictitious value preceding the first
  }

  /** Advances the progression by adding the previous value to the current value.
   *
   * @return next value of the progression
   */
  protected long nextValue() {
    long temp = prev;
    prev = cur;
    cur += temp;
    return cur;
  }
  // Inherits methods firstValue() and printProgression(int).
}
```

Code Fragment 2.5: Class for the Fibonacci progression.

In order to visualize how the three different progression classes are derived from the general Progression class, we give their inheritance diagram in Figure 2.5.

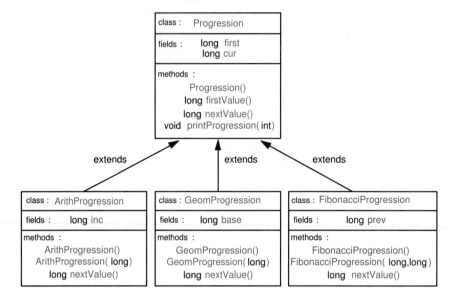

Figure 2.5: Inheritance diagram for class Progression and its subclasses.

To complete our example, we define a class TestProgression, shown in Code Fragment 2.6, which performs a simple test of each of the three classes. In this class, variable prog is polymorphic during the execution of the main method, since it references objects of class ArithProgression, GeomProgression, and FibonacciProgression in turn. When the main method of the TestProgression class is invoked by the Java run-time system, the output shown in Code Fragment 2.7 is produced.

The example presented in this section is admittedly small, but it provides a simple illustration of inheritance in Java. The Progression class, its subclasses, and the tester program have a number of shortcomings, however, which might not be immediately apparent. One problem is that the geometric and Fibonacci progressions grow quickly, and there is no provision for handling the inevitable overflow of the long integers involved. For example, since $3^{40} > 2^{63}$, a geometric progression with base $b = 3$ will overflow a long integer after 40 iterations. Likewise, the 94th Fibonacci number is greater than 2^{63}; hence, the Fibonacci progression will overflow a long integer after 94 iterations. Another problem is that we may not allow arbitrary starting values for a Fibonacci progression. For example, do we allow a Fibonacci progression starting with 0 and -1? Dealing with input errors or error conditions that occur during the running of a Java program requires that we have some mechanism for handling them. We discuss this topic next.

```
/** Test program for the progression classes */
class TestProgression {
  public static void main(String[] args) {
    Progression prog;
    // test ArithProgression
    System.out.println("Arithmetic progression with default increment:");
    prog = new ArithProgression();
    prog.printProgression(10);
    System.out.println("Arithmetic progression with increment 5:");
    prog = new ArithProgression(5);
    prog.printProgression(10);
    // test GeomProgression
    System.out.println("Geometric progression with default base:");
    prog = new GeomProgression();
    prog.printProgression(10);
    System.out.println("Geometric progression with base 3:");
    prog = new GeomProgression(3);
    prog.printProgression(10);
    // test FibonacciProgression
    System.out.println("Fibonacci progression with default start values:");
    prog = new FibonacciProgression();
    prog.printProgression(10);
    System.out.println("Fibonacci progression with start values 4 and 6:");
    prog = new FibonacciProgression(4,6);
    prog.printProgression(10);
  }
}
```

Code Fragment 2.6: Program for testing the progression classes.

Arithmetic progression with default increment:
0 1 2 3 4 5 6 7 8 9
Arithmetic progression with increment 5:
0 5 10 15 20 25 30 35 40 45
Geometric progression with default base:
1 2 4 8 16 32 64 128 256 512
Geometric progression with base 3:
1 3 9 27 81 243 729 2187 6561 19683
Fibonacci progression with default start values:
0 1 1 2 3 5 8 13 21 34
Fibonacci progression with start values 4 and 6:
4 6 10 16 26 42 68 110 178 288

Code Fragment 2.7: Output of the TestProgression program shown in Code Fragment 2.6.

2.3   Exceptions

Exceptions are unexpected events that occur during the execution of a program. An exception can be the result of an error condition or simply an unanticipated input. In any case, in an object-oriented language, such as Java, exceptions can be thought of as being objects themselves.

2.3.1   Throwing Exceptions

In Java, exceptions are objects that are ***thrown*** by code that encounters some sort of unexpected condition. They can also be thrown by the Java run-time environment should it encounter an unexpected condition, like running out of memory. A thrown exception is ***caught*** by other code that "handles" the exception somehow, or the program is terminated unexpectedly. (We will say more about catching exceptions shortly.)

Exceptions originate when a piece of Java code finds some sort of problem during execution and ***throws*** an exception object. It is convenient to give a descriptive name to the class of the exception object. For instance, if we try to delete the tenth element from a sequence that has only five elements, the code may throw a BoundaryViolationException. This action could be done, for example, using the following code fragment:

```
if (insertIndex >= A.length) {
  throw new
    BoundaryViolationException("No element at index " + insertIndex);
}
```

It is often convenient to instantiate an exception object at the time the exception has to be thrown. Thus, a **throw** statement is typically written as follows:

throw new *exception_type*(*param*$_0$, *param*$_1$, ..., *param*$_{n-1}$);

where *exception_type* is the type of the exception and the *param$_i$*'s form the list of parameters for a constructor for this exception.

Exceptions are also thrown by the Java run-time environment itself. For example, the counterpart to the example above is ArrayIndexOutOfBoundsException. If we have a six-element array and ask for the ninth element, then this exception will be thrown by the Java run-time system.

The Throws Clause

When a method is declared, it is appropriate to specify the exceptions it might throw. This convention has both a functional and courteous purpose. For one, it lets users know what to expect. It also lets the Java compiler know which exceptions to prepare for. The following is an example of such a method definition:

```
public void goShopping() throws ShoppingListTooSmallException,
                              OutOfMoneyException {
  // method body . . .
}
```

By specifying all the exceptions that might be thrown by a method, we prepare others to be able to handle all of the exceptional cases that might arise from using this method. Another benefit of declaring exceptions is that we do not need to catch those exceptions in our method. Sometimes this is appropriate in the case where other code is responsible for causing the circumstances leading up to the exception.

The following illustrates an exception that is "passed through":

```
public void getReadyForClass() throws ShoppingListTooSmallException,
                                  OutOfMoneyException {
  goShopping();      // I don't have to try or catch the exceptions
                     // which goShopping() might throw because
                     // getReadyForClass() will just pass these along.
  makeCookiesForTA();
}
```

A function can declare that it throws as many exceptions as it likes. Such a listing can be simplified somewhat if all exceptions that can be thrown are subclasses of the same exception. In this case, we only have to declare that a method throws the appropriate superclass.

Kinds of Throwables

Java defines classes Exception and Error as subclasses of Throwable, which denotes any object that can be thrown and caught. Also, it defines class RuntimeException as a subclass of Exception. The Error class is used for abnormal conditions occurring in the run-time environment, such as running out of memory. Errors can be caught, but they probably should not be, because they usually signal problems that cannot be handled gracefully. An error message or a sudden program termination is about as much grace as we can expect. The Exception class is the root of the exception hierarchy. Specialized exceptions (for example, BoundaryViolationException) should be defined by subclassing from either Exception or RuntimeException. Note that exceptions that are not subclasses of RuntimeException must be declared in the **throws** clause of any method that can throw them.

2.3.2 Catching Exceptions

When an exception is thrown, it must be *caught* or the program will terminate. In any particular method, an exception in that method can be passed through to the calling method or it can be caught in that method. When an exception is caught, it can be analyzed and dealt with. The general methodology for dealing with exceptions is to "*try*" to execute some fragment of code that might throw an exception. If it does throw an exception, then that exception is *caught* by having the flow of control jump to a predefined **catch** block that contains the code dealing with the exception.

The general syntax for a *try-catch block* in Java is as follows:

try
> *main_block_of_statements*

catch (*exception_type*$_1$ *variable*$_1$)
> *block_of_statements*$_1$

catch (*exception_type*$_2$ *variable*$_2$)
> *block_of_statements*$_2$

> . . .

finally
> *block_of_statements*$_n$

where there must be at least one **catch** part, but the **finally** part is optional. Each *exception_type*$_i$ is the type of some exception, and each *variable*$_i$ is a valid Java variable name.

The Java run-time environment begins performing a **try-catch** block such as this by executing the block of statements, *main_block_of_statements*. If this execution generates no exceptions, then the flow of control continues with the first statement after the last line of the entire **try-catch** block, unless it includes an optional **finally** part. The **finally** part, if it exists, is executed regardless of whether any exceptions are thrown or caught. Thus, in this case, if no exception is thrown, execution progresses through the **try-catch** block, jumps to the **finally** part, and then continues with the first statement after the last line of the **try-catch** block.

If, on the other hand, the block, *main_block_of_statements*, generates an exception, then execution in the **try-catch** block terminates at that point and execution jumps to the **catch** block whose *exception_type* most closely matches the exception thrown. The *variable* for this catch statement references the exception object itself, which can be used in the block of the matching **catch** statement. Once execution of that **catch** block completes, control flow is passed to the optional **finally** block, if it exists, or immediately to the first statement after the last line of the entire **try-catch** block if there is no **finally** block. Otherwise, if there is no **catch** block matching the exception thrown, then control is passed to the optional **finally** block, if it exists, and then the exception is thrown back to the calling method.

Consider the following example code fragment:

```
int index = Integer.MAX_VALUE; // 2.14 Billion
try                            // This code might have a problem...
  {
    String toBuy = shoppingList[index];
  }
catch (ArrayIndexOutOfBoundsException aioobx)
  {
    System.out.println("The index "+index+" is outside the array.");
  }
```

If this code does not catch a thrown exception, the flow of control will immediately exit the method and return to the code that called our method. There, the Java run-time environment will look again for a catch block. If there is no catch block in the code that called this method, the flow of control will jump to the code that called this, and so on. Eventually, if no code catches the exception, the Java run-time system (the origin of our program's flow of control) will catch the exception. At this point, an error message and a stack trace is printed to the screen and the program is terminated.

The following is an actual run-time error message:

```
java.lang.NullPointerException: Returned a null locator
    at java.awt.Component.handleEvent(Component.java:900)
    at java.awt.Component.postEvent(Component.java:838)
    at java.awt.Component.postEvent(Component.java:845)
    at sun.awt.motif.MButtonPeer.action(MButtonPeer.java:39)
    at java.lang.Thread.run(Thread.java)
```

Once an exception is caught, there are several things a programmer might want to do. One possibility is to print out an error message and terminate the program. There are also some interesting cases in which the best way to handle an exception is to ignore it (this can be done by having an empty **catch** block).

Ignoring an exception is usually done, for example, when the programmer does not care whether there was an exception or not. Another legitimate way of handling exceptions is to create and throw another exception, possibly one that specifies the exceptional condition more precisely. The following is an example of this approach:

```
catch (ArrayIndexOutOfBoundsException aioobx) {
    throw new ShoppingListTooSmallException(
             "Product index is not in the shopping list");
}
```

Perhaps the best way to handle an exception (although this is not always possible) is to find the problem, fix it, and continue execution.

2.4   Interfaces and Abstract Classes

In order for two objects to interact, they must "know" about the various messages that each will accept, that is, the methods each object supports. To enforce this "knowledge," the object-oriented design paradigm asks that classes specify the ***application programming interface*** (API), or simply ***interface***, that their objects present to other objects. In the ***ADT-based*** approach (see Section 2.1.2) to data structures followed in this book, an interface defining an ADT is specified as a type definition and a collection of methods for this type, with the arguments for each method being of specified types. This specification is, in turn, enforced by the compiler or run-time system, which requires that the types of parameters that are actually passed to methods rigidly conform with the type specified in the interface. This requirement is known as ***strong typing***. Having to define interfaces and then having those definitions enforced by strong typing admittedly places a burden on the programmer, but this burden is offset by the rewards it provides, for it enforces the encapsulation principle and often catches programming errors that would otherwise go unnoticed.

2.4.1   Implementing Interfaces

The main structural element in Java that enforces an API is the ***interface***. An interface is a collection of method declarations with no data and no bodies. That is, the methods of an interface are always empty (that is, they are simply method signatures). When a class implements an interface, it must implement all of the methods declared in the interface. In this way, interfaces enforce requirements that an implementing class has methods with certain specified signatures.

Suppose, for example, that we want to create an inventory of antiques we own, categorized as objects of various types and with various properties. We might, for instance, wish to identify some of our objects as sellable, in which case they could implement the Sellable interface shown in Code Fragment 2.8.

We can then define a concrete class, Photograph, shown in Code Fragment 2.9, that implements the Sellable interface, indicating that we would be willing to sell any of our Photograph objects. This class defines an object that implements each of the methods of the Sellable interface, as required. In addition, it adds a method, isColor, which is specialized for Photograph objects.

Another kind of object in our collection might be something we could transport. For such objects, we define the interface shown in Code Fragment 2.10.

```
/** Interface for objects that can be sold. */
public interface Sellable {

  /** description of the object */
  public String description();

  /** list price in cents */
  public int listPrice();

  /** lowest price in cents we will accept */
  public int lowestPrice();
}
```

Code Fragment 2.8: Interface Sellable.

```
/** Class for photographs that can be sold */
public class Photograph implements Sellable {
  private String descript;    // description of this photo
  private int price;          // the price we are setting
  private boolean color;      // true if photo is in color

  public Photograph(String desc, int p, boolean c) { // constructor
    descript = desc;
    price = p;
    color = c;
  }

  public String description() { return descript; }
  public int listPrice() { return price; }
  public int lowestPrice() { return price/2; }
  public boolean isColor() { return color; }
}
```

Code Fragment 2.9: Class Photograph implementing the Sellable interface.

```
/** Interface for objects that can be transported. */
public interface Transportable {
  /** weight in grams */
  public int weight();
  /** whether the object is hazardous */
  public boolean isHazardous();
}
```

Code Fragment 2.10: Interface Transportable.

We could then define the class BoxedItem, shown in Code Fragment 2.11, for miscellaneous antiques that we can sell, pack, and ship. Thus, the class BoxedItem implements the methods of the Sellable interface and the Transportable interface, while also adding specialized methods to set an insured value for a boxed shipment and to set the dimensions of a box for shipment.

```java
/** Class for objects that can be sold, packed, and shipped. */
public class BoxedItem implements Sellable, Transportable {
    private String descript;        // description of this item
    private int price;              // list price in cents
    private int weight;             // weight in grams
    private boolean haz;            // true if object is hazardous
    private int height=0;           // box height in centimeters
    private int width=0;            // box width in centimeters
    private int depth=0;            // box depth in centimeters
    /** Constructor */
    public BoxedItem(String desc, int p, int w, boolean h) {
        descript = desc;
        price = p;
        weight = w;
        haz = h;
    }
    public String description() { return descript; }
    public int listPrice() { return price; }
    public int lowestPrice() { return price/2; }
    public int weight() { return weight; }
    public boolean isHazardous() { return haz; }
    public int insuredValue() { return price*2; }
    public void setBox(int h, int w, int d) {
        height = h;
        width = w;
        depth = d;
    }
}
```

Code Fragment 2.11: Class BoxedItem.

The class BoxedItem shows another feature of classes and interfaces in Java, as well—a class can implement multiple interfaces—which allows us a great deal of flexibility when defining classes that should conform to multiple APIs. For, while a class in Java can extend only one other class, it can nevertheless implement many interfaces.

2.4.2 Multiple Inheritance in Interfaces

The ability of extending from more than one class is known as ***multiple inheritance***. In Java, multiple inheritance is allowed for interfaces but not for classes. The reason for this rule is that the methods of an interface never have bodies, while methods in a class always do. Thus, if Java were to allow for multiple inheritance for classes, there could be a confusion if a class tried to extend from two classes that contained methods with the same signatures. This confusion does not exist for interfaces, however, since their methods are empty. So, since no confusion is involved, and there are times when multiple inheritance of interfaces is useful, Java allows for interfaces to use multiple inheritance.

One use for multiple inheritance of interfaces is to approximate a multiple inheritance technique called the ***mixin***. Unlike Java, some object-oriented languages, such as Smalltalk and C++, allow for multiple inheritance of concrete classes, not just interfaces. In such languages, it is common to define classes, called ***mixin*** classes, that are never intended to be created as stand-alone objects, but are instead meant to provide additional functionality to existing classes. Such inheritance is not allowed in Java, however, so programmers must approximate it with interfaces. In particular, we can use multiple inheritance of interfaces as a mechanism for "mixing" the methods from two or more unrelated interfaces to define an interface that combines their functionality, possibly adding more methods of its own. Returning to our example of the antique objects, we could define an interface for insurable items as follows:

```java
public interface InsurableItem extends Transportable, Sellable {
  /** Returns insured Value in cents */
  public int insuredValue();
}
```

This interface mixes the methods of the Transportable interface with the methods of the Sellable interface, and adds an extra method, insuredValue. Such an interface could allow us to define the BoxedItem alternately as follows:

```java
public class BoxedItem2 implements InsurableItem {

  // ... same code as class BoxedItem
}
```

In this case, note that the method insuredValue is not optional, whereas it was optional in the declaration of BoxedItem given previously.

Java interfaces that approximate the mixin include java.lang.Cloneable, which adds a copy feature to a class, java.lang.Comparable, which adds a comparability feature to a class (imposing a natural order on its instances), and java.util.Observer, which adds an update feature to a class that wishes to be notified when certain "observable" objects change state.

2.4.3   Abstract Classes and Strong Typing

An abstract class is a class that contains empty method declarations (that is, declarations of methods without bodies) as well as concrete definitions of methods and/or instance variables. Thus, an abstract class lies between an interface and a complete concrete class. Like an interface, an abstract class may not be instantiated, that is, no object can be created from an abstract class. A subclass of an abstract class must provide an implementation for the abstract methods of its superclass, unless it is itself abstract. But, like a concrete class, an abstract class A can extend another abstract class, and abstract and concrete classes can further extend A, as well. Ultimately, we must define a new class that is not abstract and extends (subclasses) the abstract superclass, and this new class must fill in code for all abstract methods. Thus, an abstract class uses the specification style of inheritance, but also allows for the specialization and extension styles as well (see Section 2.2.3).

The java.lang.Number Class

It turns out that we have already seen an example of an abstract class. Namely, the Java number classes (shown in Table 1.2) specialize an abstract class called java.lang.Number. Each concrete number class, such as java.lang.Integer and java.lang.Double, extends the java.lang.Number class and fills in the details for the abstract methods of the superclass. In particular, the methods intValue, floatValue, doubleValue, and longValue are all abstract in java.lang.Number. Each concrete number class must specify the details of these methods.

Strong Typing

In Java, an object can be viewed as being of various types. The primary type of an object o is the class C specified at the time o was instantiated. In addition, o is of type S for each superclass S of C and is of type I for each interface I implemented by C.

However, a variable can be declared as being of only one type (either a class or an interface), which determines how the variable is used and how certain methods will act on it. Similarly, a method has a unique return type. In general, an expression has a unique type.

By enforcing that all variables be typed and that methods declare the types they expect and return, Java uses the technique of ***strong typing*** to help prevent bugs. But with rigid requirements on types, it is sometimes necessary to change, or convert, a type into another type. Such conversions may have to be specified by an explicit ***cast*** operator. We have already discussed (Section 1.3.3) how conversions and casting work for base types. Next, we discuss how they work for reference variables.

2.5 Casting and Generics

In this section, we discuss casting among reference variables, as well as a technique, called generics, which allow us to avoid explicit casting in many cases.

2.5.1 Casting

We begin our discussion with methods for type conversions for objects.

Widening Conversions

A *widening conversion* occurs when a type T is converted into a "wider" type U. The following are common cases of widening conversions:

- T and U are class types and U is a superclass of T
- T and U are interface types and U is a superinterface of T
- T is a class that implements interface U.

Widening conversions are automatically performed to store the result of an expression into a variable, without the need for an explicit cast. Thus, we can directly assign the result of an expression of type T into a variable v of type U when the conversion from T to U is a widening conversion. The example code fragment below shows that an expression of type Integer (a newly constructed Integer object) can be assigned to a variable of type Number.

```
Integer i = new Integer(3);
Number n = i;      // widening conversion from Integer to Number
```

The correctness of a widening conversion can be checked by the compiler and its validity does not require testing by the Java run-time environment during program execution.

Narrowing Conversions

A *narrowing conversion* occurs when a type T is converted into a "narrower" type S. The following are common cases of narrowing conversions:

- T and S are class types and S is a subclass of T
- T and S are interface types and S is a subinterface of T
- T is an interface implemented by class S.

In general, a narrowing conversion of reference types requires an explicit cast. Also, the correctness of a narrowing conversion may not be verifiable by the compiler. Thus, its validity should be tested by the Java run-time environment during program execution.

The example code fragment below shows how to use a cast to perform a narrowing conversion from type Number to type Integer.

```
Number n = new Integer(2); // widening conversion from Integer to Number
Integer i = (Integer) n;    // narrowing conversion from Number to Integer
```

In the first statement, a new object of class Integer is created and assigned to a variable n of type Number. Thus, a widening conversion occurs in this assignment and no cast is required. In the second statement, we assign n to a variable i of type Integer using a cast. This assignment is possible because n refers to an object of type Integer. However, since variable n is of type Number, a narrowing conversion occurs and the cast is necessary.

Casting Exceptions

In Java, we can cast an object reference o of type T into a type S, provided the object o is referring to is actually of type S. If, on the other hand, object o is not also of type S, then attempting to cast o to type S will throw an exception called ClassCastException. We illustrate this rule in the following code fragment:

```
Number n;
Integer i;
n = new Integer(3);
i = (Integer) n;      // This is legal
n = new Double(3.1415);
i = (Integer) n;      // This is illegal!
```

To avoid problems such as this and to avoid peppering our code with **try-catch** blocks every time we perform a cast, Java provides a way to make sure an object cast will be correct. Namely, it provides an operator, **instanceof**, that allows us to test whether an object variable is referring to an object of a certain class (or implementing a certain interface). The syntax for using this operator is *object_reference* **instanceof** *reference_type*, where *object_reference* is an expression that evaluates to an object reference and *reference_type* is the name of some existing class, interface, or enum (Section 1.1.3). If *object_reference* is indeed an instance of *reference_type*, then the expression above returns **true**. Otherwise, it returns **false**. Thus, we can avoid a ClassCastException from being thrown in the code fragment above by modifying it as follows:

```
Number n;
Integer i;
n = new Integer(3);
if (n instanceof Integer)
   i = (Integer) n;      // This is legal
n = new Double(3.1415);
if (n instanceof Integer)
   i = (Integer) n;      // This will not be attempted
```

Casting with Interfaces

Interfaces allow us to enforce that objects implement certain methods, but using interface variables with concrete objects sometimes requires casting. Suppose we declare a Person interface as shown in Code Fragment 2.12. Note that method equalTo of the Person interface takes one parameter of type Person. Thus, we can pass an object of any class implementing the Person interface to this method.

```java
public interface Person {
  public boolean equalTo (Person other); // is this the same person?
  public String getName(); // get this person's name
  public int getAge(); // get this person's age
}
```

Code Fragment 2.12: Interface Person.

We show in Code Fragment 2.13 a class, Student, that implements Person. The method equalTo assumes that the argument (declared of type Person) is also of type Student and performs a narrowing conversion from type Person (an interface) to type Student (a class) using a cast. The conversion is allowed in this case, because it is a narrowing conversion from class T to interface U, where we have an object taken from T such that T extends S (or $T = S$) and S implements U.

```java
public class Student implements Person {
  String id;
  String name;
  int age;
  public Student (String i, String n, int a) { // simple constructor
    id = i;
    name = n;
    age = a;
  }
  protected int studyHours() { return age/2; } // just a guess
  public String getID () { return id; } // ID of the student
  public String getName() { return name; } // from Person interface
  public int getAge() { return age; } // from Person interface
  public boolean equalTo (Person other) { // from Person interface
    Student otherStudent = (Student) other; // cast Person to Student
    return (id.equals (otherStudent.getID())); // compare IDs
  }
  public String toString() { // for printing
    return "Student(ID: " + id +
      ", Name: " + name +
      ", Age: " + age + ")";
  }
}
```

Code Fragment 2.13: Class Student implementing interface Person.

Because of the assumption above in the implementation of method equalTo, we have to make sure that an application using objects of class Student will not attempt the comparison of Student objects with other types of objects, or otherwise, the cast in method equalTo will fail. For example, if our application manages a directory of Student objects and uses no other types of Person objects, the assumption will be satisfied.

The ability of performing narrowing conversions from interface types to class types allows us to write general kinds of data structures that only make minimal assumptions about the elements they store. In Code Fragment 2.14, we sketch how to build a directory storing pairs of objects implementing the Person interface. The remove method performs a search on the directory contents and removes the specified person pair, if it exists, and, like the findOther method, it uses the equalTo method to do this.

```
public class PersonPairDirectory {
  // ... instance variables would go here ...
  public PersonPairDirectory() {/* default constructor goes here */}
  public void insert (Person person, Person other) {/* insert code goes here */}
  public Person findOther (Person person) { return null; } // stub for find
  public void remove (Person person, Person other) {/* remove code goes here */}
}
```

Code Fragment 2.14: Sketch of class PersonPairDirectory.

Now, suppose we have filled a directory, myDirectory, with pairs of Student objects that represent roommate pairs. In order to find the roommate of a given Student object, smart_one, we may try to do the following (which is ***wrong***):

```
Student cute_one = myDirectory.findOther(smart_one);     // wrong!
```

The statement above causes an "explicit-cast-required" compilation error. The problem here is that we are trying to perform a narrowing conversion without an explicit cast. Namely, the value returned by method findOther is of type Person while the variable cute_one, to which it is assigned, is of the narrower type Student, a class implementing interface Person. Thus, we use a cast to convert type Person to type Student, as follows:

```
Student cute_one = (Student) myDirectory.findOther(smart_one);
```

Casting the value of type Person returned by method findOther to type Student works fine as long as we are sure that the call to myDirectory.findOther is really giving us a Student object. In general, interfaces can be a valuable tool for the design of general data structures, which can then be specialized by other programmers through the use of casting.

2.5.2   Generics

Starting with 5.0, Java includes a *generics framework* for using abstract types in a way that avoids many explicit casts. A *generic type* is a type that is not defined at compilation time, but becomes fully specified at run time. The generics framework allows us to define a class in terms of a set of *formal type parameters*, which could be used, for example, to abstract the types of some internal variables of the class. Angle brackets are used to enclose the list of formal type parameters. Although any valid identifier can be used for a formal type parameter, single-letter uppercase names are conventionally used. Given a class that has been defined with such parameterized types, we instantiate an object of this class by using *actual type parameters* to indicate the concrete types to be used.

In Code Fragment 2.15, we show a class Pair storing key-value pairs, where the types of the key and value are specified by parameters K and V, respectively. The main method creates two instances of this class, one for a String-Integer pair (for example, to store a dimension and its value), and the other for a Student-Double pair (for example, to store the grade given to a student).

```java
public class Pair<K, V> {
  K key;
  V value;
  public void set(K k, V v) {
    key = k;
    value = v;
  }
  public K getKey() { return key; }
  public V getValue() { return value; }
  public String toString() {
    return "[" + getKey() + ", " + getValue() + "]";
  }
  public static void main (String[] args) {
    Pair<String,Integer> pair1 = new Pair<String,Integer>();
    pair1.set(new String("height"), new Integer(36));
    System.out.println(pair1);
    Pair<Student,Double> pair2 = new Pair<Student,Double>();
    pair2.set(new Student("A5976","Sue",19), new Double(9.5));
    System.out.println(pair2);
  }
}
```

Code Fragment 2.15: Example using the Student class from Code Fragment 2.13.

The output of the execution of this method is shown below:

```
[height, 36]
[Student(ID: A5976, Name: Sue, Age: 19), 9.5]
```

In the previous example, the actual type parameter can be an arbitrary type. To restrict the type of an actual parameter, we can use an **extends** clause, as shown below, where class PersonPairDirectoryGeneric is defined in terms of a generic type parameter P, partially specified by stating that it extends class Person.

```
public class PersonPairDirectoryGeneric<P extends Person> {
    // ... instance variables would go here ...
    public PersonPairDirectoryGeneric() { /* default constructor goes here */ }
    public void insert (P person, P other) { /* insert code goes here */ }
    public P findOther (P person) { return null; } // stub for find
    public void remove (P person, P other) { /* remove code goes here */ }
}
```

This class should be compared with class PersonPairDirectory in Code Fragment 2.14. Given the class above, we can declare a variable referring to an instance of PersonPairDirectoryGeneric, that stores pairs of objects of type Student:

```
PersonPairDirectoryGeneric<Student> myStudentDirectory;
```

For such an instance, method findOther returns a value of type Student. Thus, the following statement, which does not use a cast, is correct:

```
Student cute_one = myStudentDirectory.findOther(smart_one);
```

The generics framework allows us to define generic versions of methods. In this case, we can include the generic definition among the method modifiers. For example, we show below the definition of a method that can compare the keys from any two Pair objects, provided that their keys implement the Comparable interface:

```
public static <K extends Comparable,V,L,W> int
        comparePairs(Pair<K,V> p, Pair<L,W> q) {
    return p.getKey().compareTo(q.getKey()); // p's key implements compareTo
}
```

There is an important caveat related to generic types, namely, that the elements stored in an array cannot be a type variable or a parameterized type. Java allows for an array to be defined with a parameterized type, but it doesn't allow a parameterized type to be used to create a new array. Fortunately, it allows for an array defined with a parameterized type to be initialized with a newly created, nonparametric array. Even so, this latter mechanism causes the Java compiler to issue a warning, because it is not 100% type-safe. We illustrate this point in the following:

```
public static void main(String[] args) {
    Pair<String,Integer>[] a = new Pair[10]; // right, but gives a warning
    Pair<String,Integer>[] b = new Pair<String,Integer>[10]; // wrong!!
    a[0] = new Pair<String,Integer>(); // this is completely right
    a[0].set("Dog",10);        // this and the next statement are right too
    System.out.println("First pair is "+a[0].getKey()+", "+a[0].getValue());
}
```

2.6   Exercises

For help with exercises, please visit the web site, www.wiley.com/college/goodrich.

Reinforcement

R-2.1   What are some potential efficiency disadvantages of having very deep inheritance trees, that is, a large set of classes, A, B, C, and so on, such that B extends A, C extends B, D extends C, etc.?

R-2.2   What are some potential efficiency disadvantages of having very shallow inheritance trees, that is, a large set of classes, A, B, C, and so on, such that all of these classes extend a single class, Z?

R-2.3   Can two interfaces mutually extend each other? Why or why not?

R-2.4   Give three examples of life-critical software applications.

R-2.5   Give an example of a software application where adaptability can mean the difference between a prolonged sales lifetime and bankruptcy.

R-2.6   Describe a component from a text-editor GUI (other than an "edit" menu) and the methods that it encapsulates.

R-2.7   Draw a class inheritance diagram for the following set of classes:
- Class Goat extends Object and adds an instance variable tail and methods milk() and jump().
- Class Pig extends Object and adds an instance variable nose and methods eat() and wallow().
- Class Horse extends Object and adds instance variables height and color, and methods run() and jump().
- Class Racer extends Horse and adds a method race().
- Class Equestrian extends Horse and adds an instance variable weight and methods trot() and isTrained().

R-2.8   Give a short fragment of Java code that uses the progression classes from Section 2.2.3 to find the 8th value of a Fibonacci progression that starts with 2 and 2 as its first two values.

R-2.9   If we choose inc = 128, how many calls to the nextValue method from the ArithProgression class of Section 2.2.3 can we make before we cause a long-integer overflow?

R-2.10 Suppose we have an instance variable p that is declared of type Progression, using the classes of Section 2.2.3. Suppose further that p actually refers to an instance of the class GeomProgression that was created with the default constructor. If we cast p to type Progression and call p.firstValue(), what will be returned? Why?

R-2.11 Consider the inheritance of classes from Exercise R-2.7, and let *d* be an object variable of type Horse. If *d* refers to an actual object of type Equestrian, can it be cast to the class Racer? Why or why not?

R-2.12 Consider the following code fragment, taken from some package:

```java
public class Maryland extends State {
  Maryland() { /* null constructor */ }
  public void printMe() { System.out.println("Read it."); }
  public static void main(String[] args) {
    Region mid = new State();
    State md = new Maryland();
    Object obj = new Place();
    Place usa = new Region();
    md.printMe();
    mid.printMe();
    ((Place) obj).printMe();
    obj = md;
    ((Maryland) obj).printMe();
    obj = usa;
    ((Place) obj).printMe();
    usa = md;
    ((Place) usa).printMe();
  }
}
class State extends Region {
  State() { /* null constructor */ }
  public void printMe() { System.out.println("Ship it."); }
}
class Region extends Place {
  Region() { /* null constructor */ }
  public void printMe() { System.out.println("Box it."); }
}
class Place extends Object {
  Place() { /* null constructor */ }
  public void printMe() { System.out.println("Buy it."); }
}
```

What is the output from calling the main() method of the Maryland class?

R-2.13 Give an example of a Java code fragment that performs an array reference that is possibly out of bounds, and if it is out of bounds, the program catches that exception and prints the following error message:
"Don't try buffer overflow attacks in Java!"

R-2.14 Write a short Java method that counts the number of vowels in a given character string.

R-2.15 Write a short Java method that removes all the punctuation from a string s storing a sentence. For example, this operation would transform the string `"Let's try, Mike."` to `"Lets try Mike"`.

R-2.16 Write a short program that takes as input three integers, a, b, and c, from the Java console and determines if they can be used in a correct arithmetic formula (in the given order), like "$a+b=c$," "$a=b-c$," or "$a*b=c$."

R-2.17 Write a short Java program that creates a Pair class that can store two objects declared as generic types. Demonstrate this program by creating and printing Pair objects that contain five different kinds of pairs, such as <Integer,String> and <Float,Long>.

R-2.18 Generic parameters are not included in the signature of a method declaration, so you cannot have different methods in the same class that have different generic parameters but otherwise have the same names and the types and number of their parameters. How can you change the signatures of the conflicting methods to get around this restriction?

Creativity

C-2.1 Give an example of a Java program that outputs its source code when it is run. Such a program is called a *quine*.

C-2.2 Suppose you are on the design team for a new e-book reader. What are the primary classes and methods that the Java software for your reader will need? You should include an inheritance diagram for this code, but you don't need to write any actual code. Your software architecture should at least include ways for customers to buy new books, view their list of purchased book, and read their purchased books.

C-2.3 Most modern Java compilers have optimizers that can detect simple cases when it is logically impossible for certain statements in a program to ever be executed. In such cases, the compiler warns the programmer about the useless code. Write a short Java method that contains code for which it is provably impossible for that code to ever be executed, but your favorite Java compiler does not detect this fact.

C-2.4 Explain why the Java dynamic dispatch algorithm, which looks for the method to invoke for a call o.a(), will never get into an infinite loop.

C-2.5 Write a Java class that extends the Progression class so that each value in the progression is the absolute value of the difference between the previous two values. You should include a default constructor that starts with 2 and 200 as the first two values and a parametric constructor that starts with a specified pair of numbers as the first two values.

C-2.6   Write a Java class that extends the Progression class so that each value in the progression is the square root of the previous value. (Note that you can no longer represent each value with an integer.) You should include a default constructor that has 65,536 as the first value and a parametric constructor that starts with a specified (**double**) number as the first value.

C-2.7   Rewrite all the classes in the Progression hierarchy so that all values are from the BigInteger class, in order to avoid overflows all together.

C-2.8   Write a program that consists of three classes, *A*, *B*, and *C*, such that *B* extends *A* and *C* extends *B*. Each class should define an instance variable named "x" (that is, each has its own variable named x). Describe a way for a method in *C* to access and set *A*'s version of x to a given value, without changing *B* or *C*'s version.

C-2.9   Write a set of Java classes that can simulate an Internet application, where one party, Alice, is periodically creating a set of packets that she wants to send to Bob. An Internet process is continually checking if Alice has any packets to send, and if so, it delivers them to Bob's computer, and Bob is periodically checking if his computer has a packet from Alice, and, if so, he reads and deletes it.

C-2.10 Write a Java program that can input any polynomial in standard algebraic notation and outputs the first derivative of that polynomial.

Projects

P-2.1   Write a Java program to simulate an ecosystem containing two types of creatures, **bears** and **fish**. The ecosystem consists of a river, which is modeled as a relatively large array. Each cell of the array should contain an Animal object, which can be a Bear object, a Fish object, or **null**. In each time step, bears and fish attempt to move into adjacent array cells or they can stay where they are, at random. If two animals of the same type are about to collide in the same cell, then they stay where they are, but they create a new instance of that type of animal, which is placed in a random empty (i.e., previously **null**) cell in the array. If a bear and a fish collide, however, then the fish dies (i.e., it disappears). Use actual object creation, via the **new** operator, to model the creation of new objects, and provide a visualization of the array after each time step.

P-2.2   Write a simulator as in the previous project, but add a Boolean gender field and a floating-point strength field to each Animal object. Now, if two animals of the same type try to collide, then they only create a new instance of that type of animal if they are of different genders. Otherwise, if two animals of the same type and gender try to collide, then only the one of larger strength survives.

P-2.3 Write a Java program that simulates a system that supports the functions of an e-book reader. You should include methods for users of your system to "buy" new books, view their list of purchased books, and read their purchased books. Your system should use actual books, which have expired copyrights and are available on the Internet, to populate your set of available books for users of your system to "purchase" and read.

P-2.4 Write a Java program that has a Polygon interface, which has abstract methods, area(), and perimeter(). Implement classes for Triangle, Quadrilateral, Pentagon, Hexagon, and Octagon, which implement this interface, with the obvious meanings for the area() and perimeter() methods. Also implement classes, IsoscelesTriangle, EquilateralTriangle, Rectangle, and Square, which have the appropriate inheritance relationships. Finally, write a simple user interface, which allows users to create polygons of the various types, input their geometric dimensions, and then output their area and perimeter. For extra effort, allow users to input polygons by specifying their vertex coordinates and be able to test if two such polygons are similar.

P-2.5 Write a Java program that inputs a document and then outputs a bar-chart plot of the frequencies of each alphabet character that appears in that document.

P-2.6 Fill in code for the PersonPairDirectory class of Code Fragment 2.14, assuming person pairs are stored in an array with capacity 1,000. The directory should keep track of how many person pairs are actually in it.

P-2.7 Write a Java program that can take a positive integer greater than 2 as input and write out the number of times one must repeatedly divide this number by 2 before getting a value less than 2.

P-2.8 Write a Java program that can "make change." Your program should take two numbers as input, one that is a monetary amount charged and the other that is a monetary amount given. It should then return the number of each kind of bill and coin to give back as change for the difference between the amount given and the amount charged. The values assigned to the bills and coins can be based on the monetary system of any current or former government. Try to design your program so that it returns the fewest number of bills and coins as possible.

P-2.9 Write a Java program that inputs a list of words, separated by whitespace, and outputs how many times each word appears in the list. You need not worry about efficiency at this point, however, as this topic is something that will be addressed later in this book.

Chapter Notes

For a broad overview of developments in computer science and engineering, we refer the reader to *The Computer Science and Engineering Handbook* [92]. For more information about the Therac-25 incident, please see the paper by Leveson and Turner [66].

The reader interested in studying object-oriented programming further, is referred to the books by Booch [15], Budd [18], and Liskov and Guttag [69]. Liskov and Guttag [69] also provide a nice discussion of abstract data types, as does the survey paper by Cardelli and Wegner [20] and the book chapter by Demurjian [27] in the *The Computer Science and Engineering Handbook* [92]. Design patterns are described in the book by Gamma, *et al.* [36]. The class inheritance diagram notation we use is derived from the book by Gamma, *et al.*

Chapter

3

Indices, Nodes, and Recursion

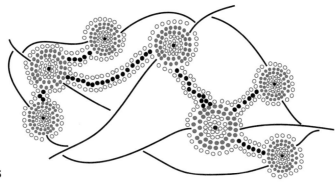

Contents

3.1   Using Arrays

In this section, we explore a few applications of arrays—the concrete data structures introduced in Section 1.5 that access their entries using integer indices.

3.1.1   Storing Game Entries in an Array

The first application we study is for storing entries in an array; in particular, high score entries for a video game. Storing objects in arrays is a common use for arrays, and we could just as easily have chosen to store records for patients in a hospital or the names of players on a football team. Nevertheless, let us focus on storing high score entries, which is a simple application that is already rich enough to present some important data structuring concepts.

Let us begin by thinking about what we want to include in an object representing a high score entry. Obviously, one component to include is an integer representing the score itself, which we will call score. Another useful thing to include is the name of the person earning this score, which we will simply call name. We could go on from here, adding fields representing the date the score was earned or game statistics that led to that score. Let us keep our example simple, however, and just have two fields, score and name. We show a Java class, GameEntry, representing a game entry in Code Fragment 3.1.

```java
public class GameEntry {
  protected String name;    // name of the person earning this score
  protected int score;      // the score value
  /** Constructor to create a game entry */
  public GameEntry(String n, int s) {
    name = n;
    score = s;
  }
  /** Retrieves the name field */
  public String getName() { return name; }
  /** Retrieves the score field */
  public int getScore() { return score; }
  /** Returns a string representation of this entry */
  public String toString() {
    return "(" + name + ", " + score + ")";
  }
}
```

Code Fragment 3.1: Java code for a simple GameEntry class. Note that we include methods for returning the name and score for a game entry object, as well as a method for returning a string representation of this entry.

A Class for High Scores

Suppose we have some high scores that we want to store in an array named entries. The number of scores we want to store could be 10, 20, or 50, so let us use a symbolic name, maxEntries, which represents the number of scores we want to store. We must set this variable to a specific value, of course, but by using this variable throughout our code, we can make it easy to change its value later if we need to. We can then define the array, entries, to be an array of length maxEntries. Initially, this array stores only **null** entries, but as users play our video game, we will fill in the entries array with references to new GameEntry objects. So we will eventually have to define methods for updating the GameEntry references in the entries array.

The way we keep the entries array organized is simple—we store our set of GameEntry objects ordered by their integer score values, highest to lowest. If the number of GameEntry objects is less than maxEntries, then we let the end of the entries array store **null** references. This approach prevents having any empty cells, or "holes," in the continuous series of cells of array entries that store the game entries from index 0 onward. We illustrate an instance of the data structure in Figure 3.1 and we give Java code for such a data structure in Code Fragment 3.2. In an exercise (C-3.3), we explore how game entry addition might be simplified for the case when we don't need to preserve relative orders.

Figure 3.1: An illustration of an array of length ten storing references to six GameEntry objects in the cells from index 0 to 5, with the rest being **null** references.

```
/** Class for storing high scores in an array in non-decreasing order. */
public class Scores {
  public static final int maxEntries = 10; // number of high scores we keep
  protected int numEntries;        // number of actual entries
  protected GameEntry[] entries;   // array of game entries (names & scores)
  /** Default constructor */
  public Scores() {
    entries = new GameEntry[maxEntries];
    numEntries = 0;
  }
  /** Returns a string representation of the high scores list */
  public String toString() {
    String s = "[";
    for (int i = 0; i < numEntries; i++) {
      if (i > 0) s += ", "; // separate entries by commas
      s += entries[i];
    }
    return s + "]";
  }
  // ... methods for updating the set of high scores go here ...
}
```

Code Fragment 3.2: Class for maintaining a set of scores as GameEntry objects.

Note that we include a method, toString(), which produces a string representation of the high scores in the entries array. This method is quite useful for debugging purposes. In this case, the string will be a comma-separated listing of the GameEntry objects in the entries array. We produce this listing with a simple **for**-loop, which adds a comma just before each entry that comes after the first one. With such a string representation, we can print out the state of the entries array during debugging, for testing how things look before and after we make updates.

Insertion

One of the most common updates we might want to make to the entries array of high scores is to add a new game entry. So suppose we want to insert a new GameEntry object, e. In particular, let us consider how we might perform the following update operation on an instance of the Scores class:

> add(e): Insert game entry e into the collection of high scores. If the collection is full, then e is added only if its score is higher than the lowest score in the set, and in this case, e replaces the entry with the lowest score.

The main challenge in implementing this operation is figuring out where e should go in the entries array and making room for e.

Visualizing Game Entry Insertion

To visualize this insertion process, imagine that we store remote controls representing references to the nonnull GameEntry objects in array entries, listed left-to-right from the one with highest score to the one with the lowest.

Given the new game entry, e, we need to figure out where it belongs. We start this search at the end of the entries array. If the last reference in this array is not **null** and its score is bigger than e's score, then we can stop immediately. For, in this case, e is not a high score—it doesn't belong in the entries array at all. Otherwise, we know that e belongs in the array, and we also know that the last thing in the entries array no longer belongs there. Next, we go to the second to the last reference in the array. If this reference is **null** or it points to a GameEntry object whose score is less than e's, this reference needs to be moved one cell to the right in the entries array. Moreover, if we move this reference, then we need to repeat this comparison with the next one, provided we haven't reached the beginning of the entries array. We continue comparing and shifting references to game entries until we either reach the beginning of the entries array or we compare e's score with a game entry with a higher score. In either case, we will have identified the place where e belongs. (See Figure 3.2.)

Figure 3.2: Preparing to add a new GameEntry object to the entries array. In order to make room for the new reference, we have to shift the references to game entries with smaller scores than the new one to the right by one cell.

Once we have identified the place in the entries array where the new game entry, e, belongs, we add a reference to e at this position. That is, continuing our visualization of object references as remote controls, we add a remote control designed especially for e to this location in the entries array. (See Figure 3.3.)

Figure 3.3: Adding a reference to a new GameEntry object to the entries array. The reference can now be inserted at index 2, since we have shifted all references to GameEntry objects with scores less than the new one to the right.

The details of our algorithm for adding the new game entry *e* to the entries array are similar to this informal description, and are given in Java in Code Fragment 3.3. Note that we use a loop to move references out of the way. The number of times we perform this loop depends on the number of references we have to move to make room for a reference to the new game entry. If there are 0, 1, or even just a few references to move over, this add method will be pretty fast. But if there are a lot to move, then this method could be fairly slow. Also note that if the array is full and we perform an add on it, then we will either remove the reference to the current last game entry or we will fail to add a reference to the new game entry, *e*.

```java
/** Attempt to add a new score to the collection (if it is high enough) */
public void add(GameEntry e) {
  int newScore = e.getScore();
  // is the new entry e really a high score?
  if (numEntries == maxEntries) { // the array is full
    if (newScore <= entries[numEntries−1].getScore())
      return;  // the new entry, e, is not a high score in this case
  }
  else // the array is not full
    numEntries++;
  // Locate the place that the new (high score) entry e belongs
  int i = numEntries−1;
  for ( ; (i >= 1) && (newScore > entries[i−1].getScore()); i−−)
    entries[i] = entries[i − 1];        // move entry i one to the right
  entries[i] = e;                       // add the new score to entries
}
```

Code Fragment 3.3: Java code for inserting a GameEntry object.

Object Removal

Suppose some hot shot plays our video game and gets his or her name on our high score list. In this case, we might want to have a method that lets us remove a game entry from the list of high scores. Therefore, let us consider how we might remove a reference to a GameEntry object from the entries array. That is, let us consider how we might implement the following operation:

remove(i): Remove and return the game entry e at index i in the entries array. If index i is outside the bounds of the entries array, then this method throws an exception; otherwise, the entries array will be updated to remove the object at index i and all objects previously stored at indices higher than i are "moved over" to fill in for the removed object.

Our implementation for remove will be much like performing our algorithm for object addition, but in reverse. Again, we can visualize the entries array as an array of remote controls pointing to GameEntry objects. To remove the reference to the object at index i, we start at index i and move all the references at indices higher than i one cell to the left. (See Figure 3.4.)

Figure 3.4: An illustration of a removal at index 3 in an array storing references to GameEntry objects.

Some Subtle Points About Entry Removal

The details for doing the remove operation contain a few subtle points. The first is that, in order to remove and return the game entry (let's call it *e*) at index *i* in our array, we must first save *e* in a temporary variable. We will use this variable to return *e* when we are done removing it. The second subtle point is that, in moving references higher than *i* one cell to the left, we don't go all the way to the end of the array—we stop at the second to last reference. We stop just before the end, because the last reference does not have any reference to its right (hence, there is no reference to move into the last place in the entries array). For the last reference in the entries array, it is enough that we simply null it out. We conclude by returning a reference to the removed entry (which no longer has any reference pointing to it in the entries array). See Code Fragment 3.4.

```java
/** Remove and return the high score at index i */
public GameEntry remove(int i) throws IndexOutOfBoundsException {
  if ((i < 0) || (i >= numEntries))
    throw new IndexOutOfBoundsException("Invalid index: " + i);
  GameEntry temp = entries[i]; // temporarily save the object to be removed
  for (int j = i; j < numEntries − 1; j++) // count up from i (not down)
    entries[j] = entries[j+1];        // move one cell to the left
  entries[numEntries −1 ] = null;      // null out the old last score
  numEntries−−;
  return temp;              // return the removed object
}
```

Code Fragment 3.4: Java code for performing the remove operation.

These methods for adding and removing objects in an array of high scores are simple. Nevertheless, they form the basis of techniques that are used repeatedly to build more sophisticated data structures. These other structures may be more general than the array structure above, of course, and often they will have a lot more operations that they can perform than just add and remove. But studying the concrete array data structure, as we are doing now, is a great starting point to understanding these other structures, since every data structure has to be implemented using concrete means.

In fact, later in this book, we will study a Java Collections Class, ArrayList, which is more general than the array structure we are studying here. The ArrayList has methods to do a lot of the things we will want to do with an array, while also eliminating the error that occurs when adding an object to a full array. The ArrayList eliminates this error by automatically copying the objects into a larger array if necessary. Rather than discuss this process here, however, we will say more about how this is done when we discuss the ArrayList in detail.

3.1.2 Sorting an Array

In the previous subsection, we worked hard to show how we can add or remove objects at a certain index i in an array while keeping the previous order of the objects intact. In this section, we study a way of starting with an array with objects that are out of order and putting them in order. This is known as the ***sorting*** problem.

A Simple Insertion-Sort Algorithm

We study several sorting algorithms in this book, most of which appear in Chapter 11. As a warmup, we describe a nice, simple sorting algorithm called ***insertion-sort*** in this section. In this case, we describe a specific version of the algorithm where the input is an array of comparable elements. We consider more general kinds of sorting algorithms later in this book.

This simple insertion-sort algorithm goes as follows. We start with the first element in the array. One element by itself is already sorted. Then we consider the next element in the array. If it is smaller than the first, we swap them. Next we consider the third element in the array. We swap it leftward until it is in its proper order with the first two elements. We then consider the fourth element, and swap it leftward until it is in the proper order with the first three. We continue in this manner with the fifth element, the sixth, and so on, until the whole array is sorted. Mixing this informal description with programming constructs, we can express the insertion-sort algorithm as shown in Code Fragment 3.5.

Algorithm InsertionSort(A):
 Input: An array A of n comparable elements
 Output: The array A with elements rearranged in nondecreasing order
 for $i \leftarrow 1$ to $n-1$ **do**
  Insert $A[i]$ at its proper location in $A[0], A[1], \ldots, A[i-1]$.

Code Fragment 3.5: High-level description of the insertion-sort algorithm.

This is a simple, high-level description of insertion-sort. It also demonstrates why this algorithm is called "insertion-sort"—because each iteration of the algorithm inserts the next element into the current sorted part of the array, which was previously the subarray in front of that element. Before we can code this description up, however, we need to work out more of the details of how we do this insertion task.

Diving into those details a bit more, let us rewrite our description so that we now use two nested loops. The outer loop will consider each element in the array in turn and the inner loop will move that element to its proper location with the (sorted) subarray of elements that are to its left.

Refining the Details for Insertion-Sort

Refining the details, then, we can describe our algorithm as shown in Code Fragment 3.6.

Algorithm InsertionSort(A):

    Input: An array A of n comparable elements

    Output: The array A with elements rearranged in nondecreasing order

    for $i \leftarrow 1$ to $n-1$ **do**

        $\{$Insert $A[i]$ at its proper location in $A[0], A[1], \ldots, A[i-1]\}$

        $cur \leftarrow A[i]$

        $j \leftarrow i-1$

        while $j \geq 0$ and $a[j] > cur$ **do**

            $A[j+1] \leftarrow A[j]$

            $j \leftarrow j-1$

        $A[j+1] \leftarrow cur$ $\{cur$ is now in the right place$\}$

Code Fragment 3.6: Intermediate-level description of the insertion-sort algorithm.

This description is much closer to actual code, since it is a better explanation of how to insert the element $A[i]$ into the subarray that comes before it. It still uses an informal description of moving elements if they are out of order, but this is not a terribly difficult thing to do.

A Java Description of Insertion-Sort

Now we are ready to give Java code for this simple version of the insertion-sort algorithm. We give such a description in Code Fragment 3.7 for the special case when A is an array of characters, a.

```java
/** Insertion sort of an array of characters into non-decreasing order */
public static void insertionSort(char[] a) {
    int n = a.length;
    for (int i = 1; i < n; i++) {        // index from the second character in a
        char cur = a[i];                 // the current character to be inserted
        int j = i - 1;                   // start comparing with cell left of i
        while ((j >= 0) && (a[j] > cur)) // while a[j] is out of order with cur
            a[j + 1] = a[j--];           // move a[j] right and decrement j
        a[j + 1]=cur;                    // this is the proper place for cur
    }
}
```

Code Fragment 3.7: Java code for performing insertion-sort on an array of characters.

We illustrate an example run of the insertion-sort algorithm in Figure 3.5.

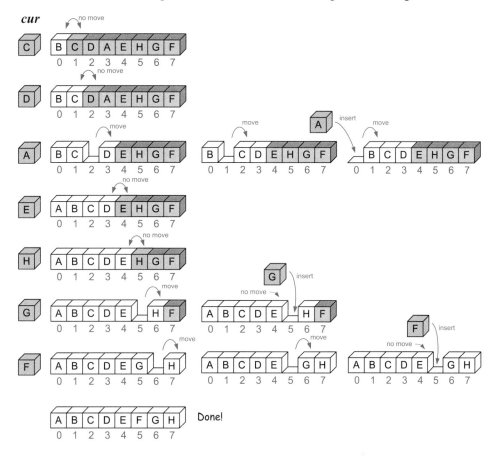

Figure 3.5: Execution of the insertion-sort algorithm on an array of eight characters. We show the completed (sorted) part of the array in white, and we color the next element that is being inserted into the sorted part of the array with light blue. We also highlight that character on the left, since it is stored in the *cur* variable. Each row corresponds to an iteration of the outer loop, and each copy of the array in a row corresponds to an iteration of the inner loop. Each comparison is shown with an arc. In addition, we indicate whether that comparison resulted in a move or not.

An interesting thing happens in the insertion-sort algorithm if the array is already sorted. In this case, the inner loop does only one comparison, determines that there is no swap needed, and returns back to the outer loop. That is, we perform only one iteration of the inner loop for each iteration of the outer loop. Thus, in this case, we perform a minimum number of comparisons. Of course, we might have to do a lot more work than this if the input array is extremely out of order. In fact, we will have to do the most work if the input array is in decreasing order.

3.1.3   java.util Methods for Arrays and Random Numbers

Because arrays are so important, Java provides a number of built-in methods for performing common tasks on arrays, which appear as static methods in the java.util.Arrays class. That is, they are associated with the class, java.util.Arrays itself, and not with a particular instance of this class. Describing a few of these methods will have to wait, however, until later in this book (when we discuss the concepts these methods are based on). Nevertheless, we discuss some java.util.Arrays methods here.

Some Simple Methods of java.util.Arrays

We list some simple methods of the class java.util.Arrays below:

equals(A, B): Returns true if and only if the array A and the array B are equal. Two arrays are considered equal if they have the same number of elements and every corresponding pair of elements in the two arrays are equal. That is, A and B have the same elements in the same order.

fill(A, x): Stores element x into every cell of array A, provided the type of array A is defined so that it is allowed to store the value x.

copyOf(A, n): Returns an array of size n such that the first k elements of this array are copied from A, where $k = \min\{n, A.\text{length}\}$. If $n > A.\text{length}$, then the last $n - A.\text{length}$ elements in this array will be padded with default values, e.g., 0 for an array of **int** and **null** for an array of objects.

copyOfRange(A, s, t): Returns an array of size $t - s$ such that the elements of this array are copied in order from $A[s]$ to $A[t-1]$, where $s < t$, with padding as with copyOf() if $t > A.\text{length}$.

sort(A): Sorts the array A based on a natural ordering of its elements, which must be comparable. This methods uses the quick-sort algorithm discussed in Section 11.2.

toString(A): Returns a String representation of the array A, which is a comma-separated list of the elements of A, ordered as they appear in A, beginning with [and ending with]. The string representation of an element $A[i]$ is obtained using String.valueOf($A[i]$), which returns the string "null" for a **null** object and otherwise calls $A[i]$.toString().

For example, the following string would be returned by the method toString called on an array of integers $A = [4, 5, 2, 3, 5, 7, 10]$:

[4, 5, 2, 3, 5, 7, 10]

Pseudo-Random Number Generation

Another feature built into Java, which is often useful when testing programs dealing with arrays, is the ability to generate pseudo-random numbers, that is, numbers that are statistically random (but not necessarily truly random). In particular, Java has a built-in class, java.util.Random, whose instances are ***pseudo-random number generators***, that is, objects that compute a sequence of numbers that are statistically random. These sequences are not actually random, however, in that it is possible to predict the next number in the sequence given the past list of numbers. Indeed, a popular pseudo-random number generator is to generate the next number, next, from the current number, cur, according to the formula (in Java syntax):

next = (a*cur + b) % n;

where a, b, and n are appropriately chosen integers. Something along these lines is, in fact, the method used by java.util.Random objects, with $n = 2^{48}$. It turns out that such a sequence can be proven to be statistically uniform, which is usually good enough for most applications requiring random numbers, such as games. For applications, such as computer security settings, where one needs unpredictable random sequences, this kind of formula should not be used. Instead, one should ideally sample from a source that is actually random, such as radio static coming from outer space.

Since the next number in a pseudo-random generator is determined by the previous number(s), such a generator always needs a place to start, which is called its *seed*. The sequence of numbers generated for a given seed will always be the same. The seed for an instance of the java.util.Random class can be set in its constructor or with its setSeed() method.

One common trick to get a different sequence each time a program is run is to use a seed that will be different for each run. For example, we could use some timed input from a user or we could set the seed to the current time in milliseconds since January 1, 1970 (provided by method System.currentTimeMillis).

Methods of the java.util.Random class include the following:

nextBoolean(): Returns the next pseudo-random **boolean** value.

nextFloat(): Returns the next pseudo-random **float** value, between 0.0 and 1.0.

nextInt(): Returns the next pseudo-random **int** value.

nextInt(n): Returns the next pseudo-random **int** value in the range $[0, n)$.

setSeed(s): Sets the seed of this pseudo-random number generator to the **long** s.

An Illustrative Example

We provide a short (but complete) illustrative program in Code Fragment 3.8.

```java
import java.util.Arrays;
import java.util.Random;
/** Program showing some array uses. */
public class ArrayTest {
  public static void main(String[] args) {
    int num[] = new int[10];
    Random rand = new Random(); // a pseudo-random number generator
    rand.setSeed(System.currentTimeMillis()); // use current time as a seed
    // fill the num array with pseudo-random numbers from 0 to 99, inclusive
    for (int i = 0; i < num.length; i++)
      num[i] = rand.nextInt(100); // the next pseudo-random number
    int[] old = (int[]) num.clone();      // cloning the num array
    System.out.println("arrays equal before sort: " + Arrays.equals(old,num));
    Arrays.sort(num); // sorting the num array (old is unchanged)
    System.out.println("arrays equal after sort: " + Arrays.equals(old,num));
    System.out.println("old = " + Arrays.toString(old));
    System.out.println("num = " + Arrays.toString(num));
  }
}
```

Code Fragment 3.8: A simple test of some built-in methods in java.util.Arrays.

We show a sample output of this program below:

```
arrays equal before sort: true
arrays equal after sort: false
old = [41,38,48,12,28,46,33,19,10,58]
num = [10,12,19,28,33,38,41,46,48,58]
```

In another run, we got the following output:

```
arrays equal before sort: true
arrays equal after sort: false
old = [87,49,70,2,59,37,63,37,95,1]
num = [1,2,37,37,49,59,63,70,87,95]
```

By using a pseudo-random number generator to determine program values, we get a different input to our program each time we run it. This feature is, in fact, what makes pseudo-random number generators useful for testing code, particularly when dealing with arrays. Even so, we should not use random test runs as a replacement for reasoning about our code, as we might miss important special cases in test runs. Note, for example, that there is a slight chance that the old and num arrays will be equal even after num is sorted, namely, if num is already sorted. The odds of this occurring are less than one in four million, so it's unlikely to happen during even a few thousand test runs; hence, we need to reason that this is possible.

3.1.4 Simple Cryptography with Character Arrays

One of the primary applications of arrays is the representation of strings of characters. That is, string objects are usually stored internally as an array of characters. Even if strings may be represented in some other way, there is a natural relationship between strings and character arrays—both use indices to refer to their characters. Because of this relationship, Java makes it easy for us to create string objects from character arrays and vice versa. Specifically, to create an object of class String from a character array A, we simply use the expression,

new String(A)

that is, one of the constructors for the String class takes a character array as its argument and returns a string having the same characters in the same order as the array. For example, the string we would construct from the array $A = [a, c, a, t]$ is acat. Likewise, given a string S, we can create a character array representation of S by using the expression,

S.toCharArray()

that is, the String class has a method, toCharArray, which returns an array (of type **char**[]) with the same characters as S. For example, if we call toCharArray on the string adog, we would get the array $B = [a, d, o, g]$.

The Caesar Cipher

One area where being able to switch from string to character array and back again is useful is in *cryptography*, the science of secret messages and their applications. This field studies ways of performing *encryption*, which takes a message, called the *plaintext*, and converts it into a scrambled message, called the *ciphertext*. Likewise, cryptography also studies corresponding ways of performing *decryption*, which takes a ciphertext and turns it back into its original plaintext.

Arguably the earliest encryption scheme is the *Caesar cipher*, which is named after Julius Caesar, who used this scheme to protect important military messages. (All of Caesar's messages were written in Latin, of course, which already makes them unreadable for most of us!) The Caesar cipher is a simple way to obscure a message written in a language that forms words with an alphabet.

The Caesar cipher involves replacing each letter in a message with the letter that is three letters after it in the alphabet for that language. So, in an English message, we would replace each A with D, each B with E, each C with F, and so on. We continue this approach all the way up to W, which is replaced with Z. Then, we let the substitution pattern *wrap around*, so that we replace X with A, Y with B, and Z with C.

Using Characters as Array Indices

If we were to number our letters like array indices, so that A is 0, B is 1, C is 2, and so on, then we can write the Caesar cipher as a simple formula:

Replace each letter i with the letter $(i+3)$ mod 26,

where mod is the **modulus** operator, which returns the remainder after performing an integer division. This operator is denoted % in Java, and it is exactly the operator we need to easily perform the wrap around at the end of the alphabet. For 26 mod 26 is 0, 27 mod 26 is 1, and 28 mod 26 is 2. The decryption algorithm for the Caesar cipher is just the opposite—we replace each letter with the one three places before it, with wrap around for A, B, and C.

We can capture this replacement rule using arrays for encryption and decryption. Since every character in Java is actually stored as a number—its Unicode value—we can use letters as array indices. For an uppercase character c, for example, we can use c as an array index by taking the Unicode value for c and subtracting A. Of course, this only works for uppercase letters, so we will require our secret messages to be uppercase. We can then use an array, encrypt, that represents the encryption replacement rule, so that encrypt$[i]$ is the letter that replaces letter number i (which is $c - $ A for an uppercase character c in Unicode). This usage is illustrated in Figure 3.6. Likewise, an array, decrypt, can represent the decryption replacement rule, so that decrypt$[i]$ is the letter that replaces letter number i.

encrypt array:

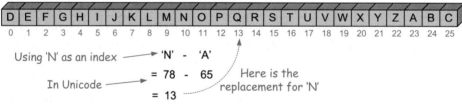

Figure 3.6: Illustrating the use of uppercase characters as array indices, in this case to perform the replacement rule for Caesar cipher encryption.

In Code Fragment 3.9, we give a simple, complete Java class for performing the Caesar cipher, which uses the approach above and also makes use of conversions between strings and character arrays. When we run this program (to perform a simple test), we get the following output:

```
Encryption order = DEFGHIJKLMNOPQRSTUVWXYZABC
Decryption order = XYZABCDEFGHIJKLMNOPQRSTUVW
WKH HDJOH LV LQ SODB; PHHW DW MRH'V.
THE EAGLE IS IN PLAY; MEET AT JOE'S.
```

```
/** Class for doing encryption and decryption using the Caesar Cipher. */
public class Caesar {
  public static final int ALPHASIZE = 26; // English alphabet (uppercase only)
  public static final char[] alpha = {'A','B','C','D','E','F','G','H', 'I',
    'J','K','L','M', 'N','O','P','Q','R','S','T','U','V','W','X','Y','Z'};
  protected char[] encrypt = new char[ALPHASIZE]; // Encryption array
  protected char[] decrypt = new char[ALPHASIZE]; // Decryption array
  /** Constructor that initializes the encryption and decryption arrays */
  public Caesar() {
    for (int i=0; i<ALPHASIZE; i++)
      encrypt[i] = alpha[(i + 3) % ALPHASIZE]; // rotate alphabet by 3 places
    for (int i=0; i<ALPHASIZE; i++)
      decrypt[encrypt[i] - 'A'] = alpha[i]; // decrypt is reverse of encrypt
  }
  /** Encryption method */
  public String encrypt(String secret) {
    char[] mess = secret.toCharArray();   // the message array
    for (int i=0; i<mess.length; i++)     // encryption loop
      if (Character.isUpperCase(mess[i]))  // we have a letter to change
        mess[i] = encrypt[mess[i] - 'A']; // use letter as an index
    return new String(mess);
  }
  /** Decryption method */
  public String decrypt(String secret) {
    char[] mess = secret.toCharArray();   // the message array
    for (int i=0; i<mess.length; i++)     // decryption loop
      if (Character.isUpperCase(mess[i]))  // we have a letter to change
        mess[i] = decrypt[mess[i] - 'A']; // use letter as an index
    return new String(mess);
  }
  /** Simple main method for testing the Caesar cipher */
  public static void main(String[] args) {
    Caesar cipher = new Caesar();         // Create a Caesar cipher object
    System.out.println("Encryption order = " + new String(cipher.encrypt));
    System.out.println("Decryption order = " + new String(cipher.decrypt));
    String secret = "THE EAGLE IS IN PLAY; MEET AT JOE'S.";
    secret = cipher.encrypt(secret);
    System.out.println(secret);            // the ciphertext
    secret = cipher.decrypt(secret);
    System.out.println(secret);            // should be plaintext again
  }
}
```

Code Fragment 3.9: A simple, complete Java class for the Caesar cipher.

3.1.5   Two-Dimensional Arrays and Positional Games

Many computer games, be they strategy games, simulation games, or first-person conflict games, use a two-dimensional "board." Programs that deal with such *positional games* need a way of representing objects in a two-dimensional space. A natural way to do this is with a *two-dimensional array*, where we use two indices, say i and j, to refer to the cells in the array. The first index usually refers to a row number and the second to a column number. Given such an array we can then maintain two-dimensional game boards, as well as perform other kinds of computations involving data that is stored in rows and columns.

Arrays in Java are one-dimensional; we use a single index to access each cell of an array. Nevertheless, there is a way we can define two-dimensional arrays in Java—we can create a two-dimensional array as an array of arrays. That is, we can define a two-dimensional array to be an array with each of its cells being another array. Such a two-dimensional array is sometimes also called a *matrix*. In Java, we declare a two-dimensional array as follows:

int[][] Y = **new int**[8][10];

This statement creates a two-dimensional "array of arrays," Y, which is 8×10, having 8 rows and 10 columns. That is, Y is an array of length 8 such that each element of Y is an array of length 10 of integers. (See Figure 3.7.) The following would then be valid uses of array Y and **int** variables i and j:

Y[i][i+1] = Y[i][i] + 3;
i = Y.length;   // i is 8
j = Y[4].length;   // j is 10

Two-dimensional arrays have many applications to numerical analysis. Rather than going into the details of such applications, however, we explore an application of two-dimensional arrays for implementing a simple positional game.

	0	1	2	3	4	5	6	7	8	9
0	22	18	709	5	33	10	4	56	82	440
1	45	32	830	120	750	660	13	77	20	105
2	4	880	45	66	61	28	650	7	510	67
3	940	12	36	3	20	100	306	590	0	500
4	50	65	42	49	88	25	70	126	83	288
5	398	233	5	83	59	232	49	8	365	90
6	33	58	632	87	94	5	59	204	120	829
7	62	394	3	4	102	140	183	390	16	26

Figure 3.7: Illustration of a two-dimensional integer array, Y, which has 8 rows and 10 columns. The value of Y[3][5] is 100 and the value of Y[6][2] is 632.

Tic-Tac-Toe

As most school children know, **Tic-Tac-Toe** is a game played in a three-by-three board. Two players—X and O—alternate in placing their respective marks in the cells of this board, starting with player X. If either player succeeds in getting three of his or her marks in a row, column, or diagonal, then that player wins.

This is admittedly not a sophisticated positional game, and it's not even that much fun to play, since a good player O can always force a tie. Tic-Tac-Toe's saving grace is that it is a nice, simple example showing how two-dimensional arrays can be used for positional games. Software for more sophisticated positional games, such as checkers, chess, or the popular simulation games, are all based on the same approach we illustrate here for using a two-dimensional array for Tic-Tac-Toe. (See Exercise P-7.12.)

The basic idea is to use a two-dimensional array, board, to maintain the game board. Cells in this array store values that indicate if that cell is empty or stores an X or O. That is, board is a three-by-three matrix, whose middle row consists of the cells board[1][0], board[1][1], and board[1][2]. In our case, we choose to make the cells in the board array be integers, with a 0 indicating an empty cell, a 1 indicating an X, and a -1 indicating O. This encoding allows us to have a simple way of testing if a given board configuration is a win for X or O, namely, if the values of a row, column, or diagonal add up to -3 or 3. We illustrate this approach in Figure 3.8.

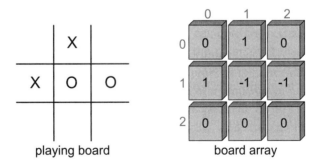

playing board   board array

Figure 3.8: An illustration of a Tic-Tac-Toe board and the two-dimensional integer array, board, representing it.

We give a complete Java class for maintaining a Tic-Tac-Toe board for two players in Code Fragments 3.10 and 3.11. We show a sample output in Figure 3.9. Note that this code is just for maintaining the Tic-Tac-Toe board and register-ing moves; it doesn't perform any strategy or allow someone to play Tic-Tac-Toe against the computer. The details of such a program are beyond the scope of this chapter, but it might nonetheless make a good course project (see Exercise P-7.12).

```java
/** Simulation of a Tic-Tac-Toe game (does not do strategy). */
public class TicTacToe {
  protected static final int X = 1, O = -1; // players
  protected static final int EMPTY = 0;      // empty cell
  protected int board[][] = new int[3][3];   // game board
  protected int player;                      // current player
  /** Constructor */
  public TicTacToe() { clearBoard(); }
  /** Clears the board */
  public void clearBoard() {
    for (int i = 0; i < 3; i++)
      for (int j = 0; j < 3; j++)
        board[i][j] = EMPTY;        // every cell should be empty
    player = X;                     // the first player is 'X'
  }
  /** Puts an X or O mark at position i,j */
  public void putMark(int i, int j) throws IllegalArgumentException {
    if ((i < 0) || (i > 2) || (j < 0) || (j > 2))
      throw new IllegalArgumentException("Invalid board position");
    if (board[i][j] != EMPTY)
      throw new IllegalArgumentException("Board position occupied");
    board[i][j] = player;     // place the mark for the current player
    player = - player;        // switch players (uses fact that O = - X)
  }
  /** Checks whether the board configuration is a win for the given player */
  public boolean isWin(int mark) {
    return ((board[0][0] + board[0][1] + board[0][2] == mark*3) // row 0
         || (board[1][0] + board[1][1] + board[1][2] == mark*3) // row 1
         || (board[2][0] + board[2][1] + board[2][2] == mark*3) // row 2
         || (board[0][0] + board[1][0] + board[2][0] == mark*3) // column 0
         || (board[0][1] + board[1][1] + board[2][1] == mark*3) // column 1
         || (board[0][2] + board[1][2] + board[2][2] == mark*3) // column 2
         || (board[0][0] + board[1][1] + board[2][2] == mark*3) // diagonal
         || (board[2][0] + board[1][1] + board[0][2] == mark*3)); // diagonal
  }
  /** Returns the winning player or 0 to indicate a tie */
  public int winner() {
    if (isWin(X))
      return(X);
    else if (isWin(O))
      return(O);
    else
      return(0);
  }
```

Code Fragment 3.10: A simple, complete Java class for playing Tic-Tac-Toe between two players. (Continues in Code Fragment 3.11.)

```java
/** Returns a simple character string showing the current board */
public String toString() {
  String s = "";
  for (int i=0; i<3; i++) {
    for (int j=0; j<3; j++) {
      switch (board[i][j]) {
      case X: s += "X"; break;
      case O: s += "O"; break;
      case EMPTY: s += " "; break;
      }
      if (j < 2) s += "|";              // column boundary
    }
    if (i < 2) s += "\n-----\n";        // row boundary
  }
  return s;
}
/** Test run of a simple game */
public static void main(String[] args) {
  TicTacToe game = new TicTacToe();
  /* X moves: */            /* O moves: */
  game.putMark(1,1);        game.putMark(0,2);
  game.putMark(2,2);        game.putMark(0,0);
  game.putMark(0,1);        game.putMark(2,1);
  game.putMark(1,2);        game.putMark(1,0);
  game.putMark(2,0);
  System.out.println(game.toString());
  int winningPlayer = game.winner();
  if (winningPlayer != 0)
    System.out.println(winningPlayer + " wins");
  else
    System.out.println("Tie");
}
}
```

Code Fragment 3.11: A simple, complete Java class for playing Tic-Tac-Toe between two players. (Continued from Code Fragment 3.10.)

```
O|X|O
-----
O|X|X
-----
X|O|X
Tie
```

Figure 3.9: Sample output of a Tic-Tac-Toe game.

Going Deeper

The fact that two-dimensional arrays in Java are really one-dimensional arrays nested inside a common one-dimensional array raises an interesting issue with respect to how we think about compound objects. In particular, it brings up the question of where a **compound object**, which is an object—like a two-dimensional array—that is made up of other objects, begins and ends.

As we mentioned in Section 1.5, an array reference in Java points to an array **object**. Thus, if we have a two-dimensional array, A, and another two-dimensional array, B, that has the same entries as A, we probably want to think that A is equal to B. But the one-dimensional arrays that make up the rows of A and B are stored in different memory locations, even though they have the same internal content. Therefore, a call to the method java.util.Arrays.equals(A, B) will return **false** in this case. The reason for this behavior is that this equals() method tests for **shallow equality**, that is, it tests only whether the corresponding elements in A and B are equal to each other using only a simple notion of equality. This **simple equality** rule says that two base type variables are equal if they have the same value and two object references are equal if they both refer to the same object. Fortunately, if we want to have a **deep equality** test for arrays of objects, like two-dimensional arrays, the java.util.Arrays class provides the following method:

deepEquals(A, B): Returns whether A and B are **deeply equal**. A and B are deeply equal if they have the same number of elements and the two elements $A[i]$ and $B[i]$ in each pair of corresponding elements are themselves equal in the simple sense, are arrays of the same primitive type such that Arrays.equals($A[i], B[i]$) would return **true**, or are arrays of object references such that $A[i]$ and $B[i]$ are deeply equal.

In addition to deep equality, we also desire a deep method for converting a two-dimensional array or an array of object references into a string. Such a method is in fact provided by the java.util.Arrays class:

deepToString(A): Returns a string representing the contents of A. To convert an element $A[i]$ to a string, if $A[i]$ is an array reference, Arrays.deepToString($A[i]$) is called, else the standard method String.valueOf($A[i]$) is used.

We may also want to have a corresponding deepCopyOf method for making an identical copy of a two-dimensional array, but, as of this writing, no such method exists in the java.util.Arrays class. Thus, if we want to make an identical, but different, copy of a two-dimensional array, A, we need to make a call to $A[i]$.clone() or java.util.Arrays.copyOf($A[i], A[i].length$) for each row, $A[i]$, of A, in turn.

3.2 Singly Linked Lists

In the previous section, we presented the array data structure and discussed some of its applications. Arrays are nice and simple for storing things in a certain order, but they have drawbacks. They are not very adaptable, for one, since we have to fix the size N of an array in advance, and we have to use integer indices to access its contents, for another.

There are other ways to store a sequence of elements, however, that do not have these drawbacks. In this section, we explore an important alternate implementation, which is known as the singly linked list.

A *linked list*, in its simplest form, is a collection of *nodes* that together form a linear ordering. The ordering is determined as in the children's game "Follow the Leader," in that each node is an object that stores a reference to an element and a reference, called next, to another node. (See Figure 3.10.)

Figure 3.10: Example of a singly linked list whose elements are strings indicating airport codes. The next pointers of each node are shown as arrows. The **null** object is denoted as $\emptyset$.

It might seem strange to have a node reference another node, but such a scheme easily works. The next reference inside a node can be viewed as a *link* or *pointer* to another node. Likewise, moving from one node to another by following a next reference is known as *link hopping* or *pointer hopping*. The first and last node of a linked list usually are called the *head* and *tail* of the list, respectively. Thus, we can link hop through the list starting at the head and ending at the tail. We can identify the tail as the node having a null next reference, which indicates the end of the list. A linked list defined in this way is known as a *singly linked list*.

Like an array, a singly linked list keeps its elements in a certain order. This order is determined by the chain of next links going from each node to its successor in the list. Unlike an array, a singly linked list does not have a predetermined fixed size, and uses space proportional to the number of its elements. Likewise, we do not keep track of any index numbers for the nodes in a linked list. So we cannot tell just by examining a node if it is the second, fifth, or twentieth node in the list.

Implementing a Singly Linked List

To implement a singly linked list, we define a Node class, as shown in Code Fragment 3.12, which specifies the type of objects stored at the nodes of the list. Here we assume elements are character strings. In Chapter 5, we describe how to define nodes that can store arbitrary types of elements. Given the Node class, we can define a class, SLinkedList, shown in Code Fragment 3.13, defining the actual linked list. This class keeps a reference to the head node and a variable counting the total number of nodes.

```
/** Node of a singly linked list of strings. */
public class Node {
  private String element;        // we assume elements are character strings
  private Node next;
  /** Creates a node with the given element and next node. */
  public Node(String s, Node n) {
    element = s;
    next = n;
  }
  /** Returns the element of this node. */
  public String getElement() { return element; }
  /** Returns the next node of this node. */
  public Node getNext() { return next; }
  // Modifier methods:
  /** Sets the element of this node. */
  public void setElement(String newElem) { element = newElem; }
  /** Sets the next node of this node. */
  public void setNext(Node newNext) { next = newNext; }
}
```

Code Fragment 3.12: Implementation of a node of a singly linked list.

```
/** Singly linked list .*/
public class SLinkedList {
  protected Node head;          // head node of the list
  protected long size;          // number of nodes in the list
  /** Default constructor that creates an empty list */
  public SLinkedList() {
    head = null;
    size = 0;
  }
  // ... update and search methods would go here ...
}
```

Code Fragment 3.13: Partial implementation of the class for a singly linked list.

3.2.1 Insertion in a Singly Linked List

When using a singly linked list, we can easily insert an element at the head of the list, as shown in Figure 3.11 and Code Fragment 3.14. The main idea is that we create a new node, set its next link to refer to the same object as head, and then set head to point to the new node.

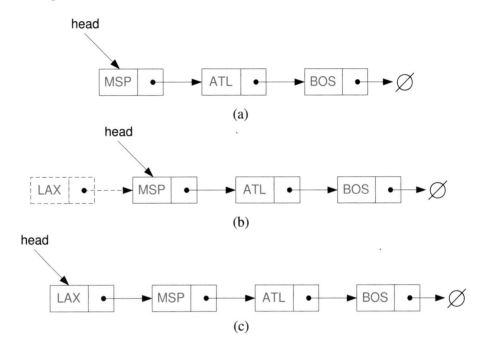

Figure 3.11: Insertion of an element at the head of a singly linked list: (a) before the insertion; (b) creation of a new node; (c) after the insertion.

Algorithm addFirst(v):

    v.setNext(head)   {make v point to the old head node}
    head $\leftarrow v$ {make variable head point to new node}
    size $\leftarrow$ size $+ 1$ {increment the node count}

Code Fragment 3.14: Inserting a new node v at the beginning of a singly linked list. Note that this method works even if the list is empty. Note that we set the next pointer for the new node v ***before*** we make variable head point to v.

Inserting an Element at the Tail of a Singly Linked List

We can also easily insert an element at the tail of the list, provided we keep a reference to the tail node, as shown in Figure 3.12. In this case, we create a new node, assign its next reference to point to the **null** object, set the next reference of the tail to point to this new object, and then assign the tail reference itself to this new node. We give the details in Code Fragment 3.15.

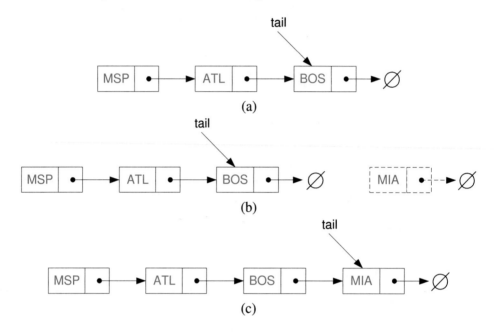

Figure 3.12: Insertion at the tail of a singly linked list: (a) before the insertion; (b) creation of a new node; (c) after the insertion. Note that we set the next link for the tail in (b) before we assign the tail variable to point to the new node in (c).

Algorithm addLast(v):

    v.setNext(**null**)   {make new node v point to null object}
    tail.setNext(v)   {make old tail node point to new node}
    tail $\leftarrow v$ {make variable tail point to new node.}
    size $\leftarrow$ size $+\,1$ {increment the node count}

Code Fragment 3.15: Inserting a new node at the end of a singly linked list. This method works also if the list is empty. Note that we set the next pointer for the old tail node *before* we make variable tail point to the new node.

3.2.2 Removing an Element in a Singly Linked List

The reverse operation of inserting a new element at the head of a linked list is to remove an element at the head. This operation is illustrated in Figure 3.13 and given in detail in Code Fragment 3.16.

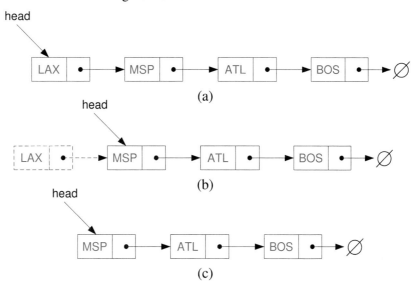

Figure 3.13: Removal of an element at the head of a singly linked list: (a) before the removal; (b) "linking out" the old new node; (c) after the removal.

Algorithm removeFirst():
    if head = **null then**
        Indicate an error: the list is empty.
    $t \leftarrow$ head
    head $\leftarrow$ head.getNext()   {make head point to next node (or null)}
    t.setNext(**null**)   {null out the next pointer of the removed node}
    size $\leftarrow$ size $- 1$ {decrement the node count}

Code Fragment 3.16: Removing the node at the beginning of a singly linked list.

Unfortunately, we cannot easily delete the tail node of a singly linked list. Even if we have a tail reference directly to the last node of the list, we must be able to access the node *before* the last node in order to remove the last node. But we cannot reach the node before the tail by following next links from the tail. The only way to access this node is to start from the head of the list and search all the way through the list. But such a sequence of link hopping operations could take a long time.

3.3   Doubly Linked Lists

As we saw in the previous section, removing an element at the tail of a singly linked list is not easy. Indeed, it is time consuming to remove any node other than the head in a singly linked list, since we do not have a quick way of accessing the node in front of the one we want to remove. Indeed, there are many applications where we do not have quick access to such a predecessor node. For such applications, it would be nice to have a way of going both directions in a linked list.

There is a type of linked list that allows us to go in both directions—forward and reverse—in a linked list. It is the ***doubly linked*** list. Such lists allow for a great variety of quick update operations, including insertion and removal at both ends, and in the middle. A node in a doubly linked list stores two references—a next link, which points to the next node in the list, and a prev link, which points to the previous node in the list.

A Java implementation of a node of a doubly linked list is shown in Code Fragment 3.17, where we assume that elements are character strings. In Chapter 5, we discuss how to define nodes for arbitrary element types.

```java
/** Node of a doubly linked list of strings */
public class DNode {
  protected String element;    // String element stored by a node
  protected DNode next, prev;  // Pointers to next and previous nodes
  /** Constructor that creates a node with given fields */
  public DNode(String e, DNode p, DNode n) {
    element = e;
    prev = p;
    next = n;
  }
  /** Returns the element of this node */
  public String getElement() { return element; }
  /** Returns the previous node of this node */
  public DNode getPrev() { return prev; }
  /** Returns the next node of this node */
  public DNode getNext() { return next; }
  /** Sets the element of this node */
  public void setElement(String newElem) { element = newElem; }
  /** Sets the previous node of this node */
  public void setPrev(DNode newPrev) { prev = newPrev; }
  /** Sets the next node of this node */
  public void setNext(DNode newNext) { next = newNext; }
}
```

Code Fragment 3.17: Java class DNode representing a node of a doubly linked list that stores a character string.

Header and Trailer Sentinels

To simplify programming, it is convenient to add special nodes at both ends of a doubly linked list: a ***header*** node just before the head of the list, and a ***trailer*** node just after the tail of the list. These "dummy" or ***sentinel*** nodes do not store any elements. The header has a valid next reference but a null prev reference, while the trailer has a valid prev reference but a null next reference. A doubly linked list with these sentinels is shown in Figure 3.14. Note that a linked list object would simply need to store references to these two sentinels and a size counter that keeps track of the number of elements (not counting sentinels) in the list.

Figure 3.14: A doubly linked list with sentinels, header and trailer, marking the ends of the list. An empty list would have these sentinels pointing to each other. We do not show the null prev pointer for the header nor do we show the null next pointer for the trailer.

Inserting or removing elements at either end of a doubly linked list is straight-forward to do. Indeed, the prev links eliminate the need to traverse the list to get to the node just before the tail. We show the removal at the tail of a doubly linked list in Figure 3.15 and the details for this operation in Code Fragment 3.18.

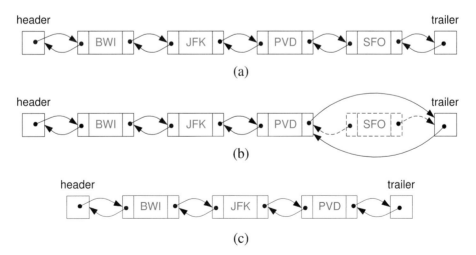

Figure 3.15: Removing the node at the end of a a doubly linked list with header and trailer sentinels: (a) before deleting at the tail; (b) deleting at the tail; (c) after the deletion.

Algorithm removeLast():

    if size $= 0$ **then**

        Indicate an error: the list is empty

    $v \leftarrow$ trailer.getPrev()   {last node}

    $u \leftarrow v$.getPrev()   {node before the last node}

    trailer.setPrev(u)

    u.setNext(trailer)

    v.setPrev(**null**)

    v.setNext(**null**)

    size $=$ size $- 1$

Code Fragment 3.18: Removing the last node of a doubly linked list. Variable size keeps track of the current number of elements in the list. Note that this method works also if the list has size one.

Likewise, we can easily perform an insertion of a new element at the beginning of a doubly linked list, as shown in Figure 3.16 and Code Fragment 3.19.

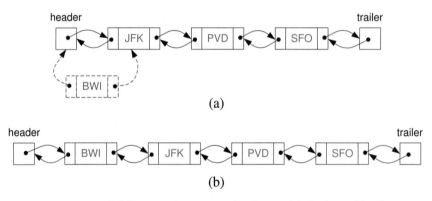

Figure 3.16: Adding an element at the front: (a) during; (b) after.

Algorithm addFirst(v):

    $w \leftarrow$ header.getNext()   {first node}

    v.setNext(w)

    v.setPrev(header)

    w.setPrev(v)

    header.setNext(v)

    size $=$ size $+ 1$

Code Fragment 3.19: Inserting a new node v at the beginning of a doubly linked list. Variable size keeps track of the current number of elements in the list. Note that this method works also on an empty list.

3.3.1 Insertion in the Middle of a Doubly Linked List

Doubly linked lists are useful for more than just inserting and removing elements at the head and tail of the list, however. They also are convenient for maintaining a list of elements while allowing for insertion and removal in the middle of the list. Given a node v of a doubly linked list (which could be possibly the header but not the trailer), we can easily insert a new node z immediately after v. Specifically, let w the be node following v. We execute the following steps:

1. Make z's prev link refer to v
2. Make z's next link refer to w
3. Make w's prev link refer to z
4. Make v's next link refer to z.

This method is given in detail in Code Fragment 3.20, and is illustrated in Figure 3.17. Recalling our use of header and trailer sentinels, note that this algorithm works even if v is the tail node (the node just before the trailer).

Algorithm addAfter(v, z):

$\quad w \leftarrow v.\text{getNext}()$ {node after v}
$\quad z.\text{setPrev}(v)$ {link z to its predecessor, v}
$\quad z.\text{setNext}(w)$ {link z to its successor, w}
$\quad w.\text{setPrev}(z)$ {link w to its new predecessor, z}
$\quad v.\text{setNext}(z)$ {link v to its new successor, z}
$\quad \text{size} \leftarrow \text{size} + 1$

Code Fragment 3.20: Inserting a new node z after a given node v in a doubly linked list.

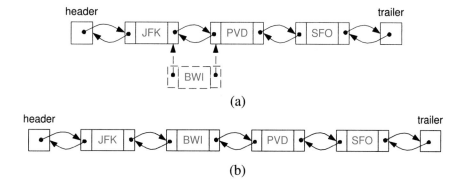

Figure 3.17: Adding a new node after the node storing JFK: (a) creating a new node with element BWI and linking it in; (b) after the insertion.

3.3.2   Removal in the Middle of a Doubly Linked List

Likewise, it is easy to remove a node v in the middle of a doubly linked list. We access the nodes u and w on either side of v using v's getPrev and getNext methods (these nodes must exist, since we are using sentinels). To remove node v, we simply have u and w point to each other instead of to v. We refer to this operation as the ***linking out*** of v. We also null out v's prev and next pointers so as not to retain old references in the list. This algorithm is given in Code Fragment 3.21 and is illustrated in Figure 3.18.

Algorithm remove(v):

$u \leftarrow v.\text{getPrev}()$ {node before v}
$w \leftarrow v.\text{getNext}()$ {node after v}
$w.\text{setPrev}(u)$ {link out v}
$u.\text{setNext}(w)$
$v.\text{setPrev}(\textbf{null})$ {null out the fields of v}
$v.\text{setNext}(\textbf{null})$
size $\leftarrow$ size $- 1$ {decrement the node count}

Code Fragment 3.21: Removing a node v in a doubly linked list. This method works even if v is the first, last, or only nonsentinel node.

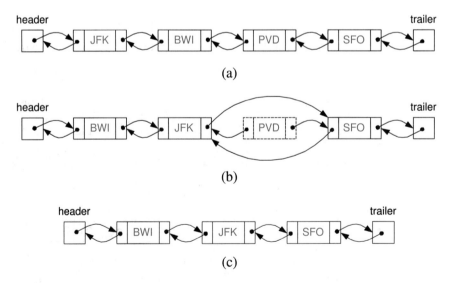

Figure 3.18: Removing the node storing PVD: (a) before the removal; (b) linking out the old node; (c) after the removal (and garbage collection).

3.3.3 An Implementation of a Doubly Linked List

In Code Fragments 3.22–3.24, we show an implementation of a doubly linked list with nodes that store character string elements.

```java
/** Doubly linked list with nodes of type DNode storing strings. */
public class DList {
  protected int size;                    // number of elements
  protected DNode header, trailer;       // sentinels
  /** Constructor that creates an empty list */
  public DList() {
    size = 0;
    header = new DNode(null, null, null);   // create header
    trailer = new DNode(null, header, null);  // create trailer
    header.setNext(trailer);        // make header and trailer point to each other
  }
  /** Returns the number of elements in the list */
  public int size() { return size; }
  /** Returns whether the list is empty */
  public boolean isEmpty() { return (size == 0); }
  /** Returns the first node of the list */
  public DNode getFirst() throws IllegalStateException {
    if (isEmpty()) throw new IllegalStateException("List is empty");
    return header.getNext();
  }
  /** Returns the last node of the list */
  public DNode getLast() throws IllegalStateException {
    if (isEmpty()) throw new IllegalStateException("List is empty");
    return trailer.getPrev();
  }
  /** Returns the node before the given node v. An error occurs if v
   * is the header */
  public DNode getPrev(DNode v) throws IllegalArgumentException {
    if (v == header) throw new IllegalArgumentException
      ("Cannot move back past the header of the list");
    return v.getPrev();
  }
  /** Returns the node after the given node v. An error occurs if v
   * is the trailer */
  public DNode getNext(DNode v) throws IllegalArgumentException {
    if (v == trailer) throw new IllegalArgumentException
      ("Cannot move forward past the trailer of the list");
    return v.getNext();
  }
}
```

Code Fragment 3.22: Java class DList for a doubly linked list whose nodes are objects of class DNode (see Code Fragment 3.17) storing character strings. (Continues in Code Fragment 3.23.)

```java
/** Inserts the given node z before the given node v. An error
  * occurs if v is the header */
public void addBefore(DNode v, DNode z) throws IllegalArgumentException {
  DNode u = getPrev(v);     // may throw an IllegalArgumentException
  z.setPrev(u);
  z.setNext(v);
  v.setPrev(z);
  u.setNext(z);
  size++;
}
/** Inserts the given node z after the given node v. An error occurs
  * if v is the trailer */
public void addAfter(DNode v, DNode z) {
  DNode w = getNext(v);     // may throw an IllegalArgumentException
  z.setPrev(v);
  z.setNext(w);
  w.setPrev(z);
  v.setNext(z);
  size++;
}
/** Inserts the given node at the head of the list */
public void addFirst(DNode v) {
  addAfter(header, v);
}
/** Inserts the given node at the tail of the list */
public void addLast(DNode v) {
  addBefore(trailer, v);
}
/** Removes the given node v from the list. An error occurs if v is
  * the header or trailer */
public void remove(DNode v) {
  DNode u = getPrev(v);     // may throw an IllegalArgumentException
  DNode w = getNext(v);     // may throw an IllegalArgumentException
  // unlink the node from the list
  w.setPrev(u);
  u.setNext(w);
  v.setPrev(null);
  v.setNext(null);
  size--;
}
```

Code Fragment 3.23: Java class DList for a doubly linked list. (Continues in Code Fragment 3.24.)

```
/** Returns whether a given node has a previous node */
public boolean hasPrev(DNode v) { return v != header; }
/** Returns whether a given node has a next node */
public boolean hasNext(DNode v) { return v != trailer; }
/** Returns a string representation of the list */
public String toString() {
  String s = "[";
  DNode v = header.getNext();
  while (v != trailer) {
    s += v.getElement();
    v = v.getNext();
    if (v != trailer)
      s += ",";
  }
  s += "]";
  return s;
  }
}
```

Code Fragment 3.24: A doubly linked list class. (Continued from Code Fragment 3.23.)

We make the following observations about class DList above.

- Object of class DNode, which store String elements, are used for all the nodes of the list, including the header and trailer sentinels.
- We can use class DList for a doubly linked list of String objects only. To build a linked list of other types of objects, we can use a generic declaration, which we discuss in Chapter 5.
- Methods getFirst and getLast provide direct access to the first and last nodes in the list.
- Methods getPrev and getNext allow to traverse the list.
- Methods hasPrev and hasNext detect the boundaries of the list.
- Methods addFirst and addLast add a new node at the beginning or end of the list.
- Methods addBefore and addAfter add a new node before or after an existing node.
- Having only a single removal method, remove, is not actually a restriction, since we can remove at the beginning or end of a doubly linked list L by executing L.remove(L.getFirst()) or L.remove(L.getLast()), respectively.
- Method toString for converting an entire list into a string is useful for testing and debugging purposes.

3.4   Circularly Linked Lists and Linked-List Sorting

In this section, we study some applications and extensions of linked lists.

3.4.1   Circularly Linked Lists and Duck, Duck, Goose

The children's game, "***Duck, Duck, Goose***," is played in many cultures. Children in Minnesota play a version called "Duck, Duck, Grey Duck" (but please don't ask us why.) In Indiana, this game is called "The Mosh Pot." And children in the Czech Republic and Ghana play sing-song versions known respectively as "Pesek" and "Antoakyire." A variation on the singly linked list, called the circularly linked list, is used for a number of applications involving circle games, like "Duck, Duck, Goose." We discuss this type of list and the circle-game application next.

A ***circularly linked list*** has the same kind of nodes as a singly linked list. That is, each node in a circularly linked list has a next pointer and a reference to an element. But there is no head or tail in a circularly linked list. For instead of having the last node's next pointer be **null**, in a circularly linked list, it points back to the first node. Thus, there is no first or last node. If we traverse the nodes of a circularly linked list from any node by following **next** pointers, we will cycle through the nodes.

Even though a circularly linked list has no beginning or end, we nevertheless need some node to be marked as a special node, which we call the ***cursor***. The cursor node allows us to have a place to start from if we ever need to traverse a circularly linked list. And if we remember this starting point, then we can also know when we are done—we are done with a traversal of a circularly linked list when we return to the node that was the cursor node when we started.

We can then define some simple update methods for a circularly linked list:

      add(v): Insert a new node v immediately after the cursor; if the list is empty, then v becomes the cursor and its next pointer points to itself.

    remove(): Remove and return the node v immediately after the cursor (not the cursor itself, unless it is the only node); if the list becomes empty, the cursor is set to **null**.

    advance(): Advance the cursor to the next node in the list.

In Code Fragment 3.25, we show a Java implementation of a circularly linked list, which uses the Node class from Code Fragment 3.12 and also includes a toString method for producing a string representation of the list.

```java
/** Circular linked list with nodes of type Node storing strings. */
public class CircleList {
  protected Node cursor;        // the current cursor
  protected int size;           // the number of nodes in the list
  /** Constructor that creates and empty list */
  public CircleList() { cursor = null; size = 0; }
  /** Returns the current size */
  public int size() { return size; }
  /** Returns the cursor */
  public Node getCursor() { return cursor; }
  /** Moves the cursor forward */
  public void advance() { cursor = cursor.getNext(); }
  /** Adds a node after the cursor */
  public void add(Node newNode) {
    if (cursor == null) {   // list is empty
      newNode.setNext(newNode);
      cursor = newNode;
    }
    else {
      newNode.setNext(cursor.getNext());
      cursor.setNext(newNode);
    }
    size++;
  }
  /** Removes the node after the cursor */
  public Node remove() {
    Node oldNode = cursor.getNext(); // the node being removed
    if (oldNode == cursor)
      cursor = null; // list is becoming empty
    else {
      cursor.setNext(oldNode.getNext());       // link out the old node
      oldNode.setNext(null);
    }
    size--;
    return oldNode;
  }
  /** Returns a string representation of the list, starting from the cursor */
  public String toString() {
    if (cursor == null) return "[]";
    String s = "[..." + cursor.getElement();
    Node oldCursor = cursor;
    for (advance(); oldCursor != cursor; advance())
      s += ", " + cursor.getElement();
    return s + "...]";
  }
}
```

Code Fragment 3.25: A circularly linked list class with simple nodes.

Some Observations about the CircleList Class

There are a few observations we can make about the CircleList class. It is a simple program that can provide enough functionality to simulate circle games, like Duck, Duck, Goose, as we will soon show. It is not a robust program, however. In particular, if a circle list is empty, then calling advance or remove on that list will cause an exception. (Which one?) Exercise R-3.8 deals with this exception-generating behavior and ways of handling this empty-list condition better.

Duck, Duck, Goose

In the children's game, Duck, Duck, Goose, a group of children sit in a circle. One of them is elected "it" and that person walks around the outside of the circle. The person who is "it" pats each child on the head, saying "Duck" each time, until reaching a child that the "it" person identifies as "Goose." At this point there is a mad scramble, as the "Goose" and the "it" person race around the circle. Who ever returns to the Goose's former place first gets to remain in the circle. The loser of this race is the "it" person for the next round of play. This game continues like this until the children get bored or an adult tells them it's snack time, at which point the game ends. (See Figure 3.19.)

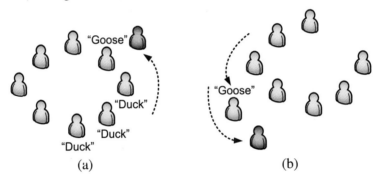

Figure 3.19: The Duck, Duck, Goose game: (a) choosing the "Goose;" (b) the race to the "Goose's" place between the "Goose" and the "it" person.

Simulating this game is an ideal application of a circularly linked list. The children can represent nodes in the list. The "it" person can be identified as the person sitting after the cursor, and can be removed from the circle to simulate the marching around. We can advance the cursor with each "Duck" the "it" person identifies, which we can simulate with a random decision. Once a "Goose" is identified, we can remove this node from the list, make a random choice to simulate whether the "Goose" or the "it" person wins the race, and insert the winner back into the list. We can then advance the cursor and insert the "it" person back in to repeat the process (or be done if this is the last time we play the game).

Using a Circularly Linked List to Simulate Duck, Duck, Goose

We give Java code for a simulation of Duck, Duck, Goose in Code Fragment 3.26.

```java
/** Simulation of Duck, Duck, Goose with a circularly linked list. */
public static void main(String[] args) {
  CircleList C = new CircleList();
  int N = 3; // number of iterations of the game
  Node it;    // the player who is "it"
  Node goose; // the goose
  Random rand = new Random();
  rand.setSeed(System.currentTimeMillis()); // use current time as seed
  // The players...
  String[] names = {"Bob","Jen","Pam","Tom","Ron","Vic","Sue","Joe"};
  for (int i = 0; i< names.length; i++) {
    C.add(new Node(names[i], null));
    C.advance();
  }
  for (int i = 0; i < N; i++) {     // play Duck, Duck, Goose N times
    System.out.println("Playing Duck, Duck, Goose for " + C.toString());
    it = C.remove();
    System.out.println(it.getElement() + " is it.");
    while (rand.nextBoolean() || rand.nextBoolean()) { // march around circle
      C.advance(); // advance with probability 3/4
      System.out.println(C.getCursor().getElement() + " is a duck.");
    }
    goose = C.remove();
    System.out.println(goose.getElement() + " is the goose!");
    if (rand.nextBoolean()) {
      System.out.println("The goose won!");
      C.add(goose); // add the goose back in its old place
      C.advance(); // now the cursor is on the goose
      C.add(it);    // The "it" person will be it again in next round
    }
    else {
      System.out.println("The goose lost!");
      C.add(it);       // add who's "it" back at the goose's place
      C.advance(); // now the cursor is on the "it" person
      C.add(goose); // The goose will be "it" in the next round
    }
  }
  System.out.println("Final circle is " + C.toString());
}
```

Code Fragment 3.26: The main method from a program that uses a circularly linked list to simulate the Duck, Duck, Goose children's game.

Some Sample Output

We show an example output from a run of the Duck, Duck, Goose program in Figure 3.20.

```
Playing Duck, Duck, Goose for [...Joe, Bob, Jen, Pam, Tom, Ron, Vic, Sue...]
Bob is it.
Jen is a duck.
Pam is a duck.
Tom is a duck.
Ron is the goose!
The goose won!
Playing Duck, Duck, Goose for [...Ron, Bob, Vic, Sue, Joe, Jen, Pam, Tom...]
Bob is it.
Vic is the goose!
The goose won!
Playing Duck, Duck, Goose for [...Vic, Bob, Sue, Joe, Jen, Pam, Tom, Ron...]
Bob is it.
Sue is a duck.
Joe is a duck.
Jen is a duck.
Pam is a duck.
Tom is a duck.
Ron is a duck.
Vic is a duck.
Sue is the goose!
The goose lost!
Final circle is [...Bob, Sue, Joe, Jen, Pam, Tom, Ron, Vic...]
```

Figure 3.20: Sample output from the Duck, Duck, Goose program.

Note that each iteration in this particular execution of this program produces a different outcome, due to the different initial configurations and the use of random choices to identify ducks and geese. Likewise, whether the "Duck" or the "Goose" wins the race is also different, depending on random choices. This execution shows a situation where the next child after the "it" person is immediately identified as the "Goose," as well a situation where the "it" person walks all the way around the group of children before identifying the "Goose." Such situations also illustrate the usefulness of using a circularly linked list to simulate circular games like Duck, Duck, Goose.

3.4.2 Sorting a Linked List

In Code Fragment 3.27, we show the ***insertion-sort*** algorithm (Section 3.1.2) for a doubly linked list. A Java implementation is given in Code Fragment 3.28.

Algorithm InsertionSort(*L*):

   Input: A doubly linked list *L* of comparable elements

   Output: The list *L* with elements rearranged in nondecreasing order

   if *L*.size() $<=$ 1 **then**

     return

   end ← *L*.getFirst()

   while *end* is not the last node in *L* **do**

     pivot ← *end*.getNext()

     Remove *pivot* from *L*

     ins ← *end*

     while *ins* is not the header and *ins*'s element is greater than *pivot*'s **do**

       ins ← *ins*.getPrev()

     Add *pivot* just after *ins* in *L*

     if *ins* = *end* **then** {We just added *pivot* after *end* in this case}

       end ← *end*.getNext()

Code Fragment 3.27: High-level, pseudo-code description of insertion-sort on a doubly linked list.

```java
/** Insertion-sort for a doubly linked list of class DList.   */
public static void sort(DList L) {
  if (L.size() <= 1) return; // L is already sorted in this case
  DNode pivot;       // pivot node
  DNode ins;         // insertion point
  DNode end = L.getFirst(); // end of run
  while (end != L.getLast()) {
    pivot = end.getNext();   // get the next pivot node
    L.remove(pivot);         // remove it
    ins = end;               // start searching from the end of the sorted run
    while (L.hasPrev(ins) &&
          ins.getElement().compareTo(pivot.getElement()) > 0)
      ins = ins.getPrev();   // move left
    L.addAfter(ins,pivot);   // add the pivot back, after insertion point
    if (ins == end)          // we just added pivot after end in this case
      end = end.getNext();   // so increment the end marker
  }
}
```

Code Fragment 3.28: Java implementation of the insertion-sort algorithm on a doubly linked list represented by class DList (see Code Fragments 3.22–3.24).

3.5 Recursion

We have seen that repetition can be achieved by writing loops, such as **for** loops and **while** loops. Another way to achieve repetition is through ***recursion***, which occurs when a function refers to itself in its own definition. We have seen examples of methods calling other methods, so it should come as no surprise that most modern programming languages, including Java, allow a method to call itself. Indeed, we didn't take note of it then, but the deepEquals() and deepToString() methods, described in Section 3.1.5, are defined recursively. In this section, we will see why this capability provides an elegant and powerful alternative for performing repetitive tasks.

The Factorial Function

To illustrate recursion, let us begin with a simple example of computing the value of the ***factorial function***. The factorial of a positive integer n, denoted $n!$, is defined as the product of the integers from 1 to n. If $n = 0$, then $n!$ is defined as 1 by convention. More formally, for any integer $n \geq 0$,

$$n! = \begin{cases} 1 & \text{if } n = 0 \\ n \cdot (n-1) \cdot (n-2) \cdots 3 \cdot 2 \cdot 1 & \text{if } n \geq 1. \end{cases}$$

For example, $5! = 5 \cdot 4 \cdot 3 \cdot 2 \cdot 1 = 120$. To make the connection with methods clearer, we use the notation factorial(n) to denote $n!$.

The factorial function can be defined in a manner that suggests a recursive formulation. To see this, observe that

$$\text{factorial}(5) = 5 \cdot (4 \cdot 3 \cdot 2 \cdot 1) = 5 \cdot \text{factorial}(4).$$

Thus, we can define factorial(5) in terms of factorial(4). In general, for a positive integer n, we can define factorial(n) to be $n \cdot$ factorial$(n-1)$. This leads to the following ***recursive definition***

$$\text{factorial}(n) = \begin{cases} 1 & \text{if } n = 0 \\ n \cdot \text{factorial}(n-1) & \text{if } n \geq 1. \end{cases}$$

This definition is typical of many recursive definitions. First, it contains one or more ***base cases***, which are defined nonrecursively in terms of fixed quantities. In this case, $n = 0$ is the base case. It also contains one or more ***recursive cases***, which are defined by appealing to the definition of the function being defined. Observe that there is no circularity in this definition, because each time the function is invoked, its argument is smaller by one.

A Recursive Implementation of the Factorial Function

Let us consider a Java implementation of the factorial function shown in Code Fragment 3.29 under the name recursiveFactorial(). Notice that no looping was needed here. The repeated recursive invocations of the function take the place of looping.

```java
public static int recursiveFactorial(int n) {    // recursive factorial function
    if (n == 0) return 1;                         // basis case
    else return n * recursiveFactorial(n−1);      // recursive case
}
```

Code Fragment 3.29: A recursive implementation of the factorial function.

We can illustrate the execution of a recursive function definition by means of a *recursion trace*. Each entry of the trace corresponds to a recursive call. Each new recursive function call is indicated by an arrow to the newly called function. When the function returns, an arrow showing this return is drawn and the return value may be indicated with this arrow. An example of a trace is shown in Figure 3.21.

What is the advantage of using recursion? Although the recursive implementation of the factorial function is somewhat simpler than the iterative version, in this case there is no compelling reason for preferring recursion over iteration. For some problems, however, a recursive implementation can be significantly simpler and easier to understand than an iterative implementation. Such an example follows.

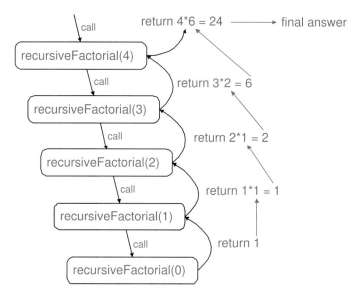

Figure 3.21: A recursion trace for the call recursiveFactorial(4).

Drawing an English Ruler

As a more complex example of the use of recursion, consider how to draw the markings of a typical English ruler. Such a ruler is broken into intervals, and each interval consists of a set of *ticks*, placed at intervals of 1/2 inch, 1/4 inch, and so on. As the size of the interval decreases by half, the tick length decreases by one. (See Figure 3.22.)

```
    ---- 0                 ----- 0              --- 0
    -                      -                    -
    --                     --                   --
    -                      -                    -
    ---                    ---                  --- 1
    -                      -                    -
    --                     --                   --
    -                      -                    -
    ---- 1                 ----                 --- 2
    -                      -                    -
    --                     --                   --
    -                      -                    -
    ---                    ---                  --- 3
    -                      -
    --                     --
    -                      -
    ---- 2                 ----- 1

     (a)                    (b)                  (c)
```

Figure 3.22: Three sample outputs of an English ruler drawing: (a) a 2-inch ruler with major tick length 4; (b) a 1-inch ruler with major tick length 5; (c) a 3-inch ruler with major tick length 3.

Each fraction of an inch also has a numeric label. The longest tick length is called the *major tick length*. We will not worry about actual distances, however, and just print one tick per line.

A Recursive Approach to Ruler Drawing

Our approach to drawing such a ruler consists of three methods. The main method drawRuler() draws the entire ruler. Its arguments are the total number of inches in the ruler, nInches, and the major tick length, majorLength. The utility method drawOneTick() draws a single tick of the given length. It can also be given an optional integer label, which is printed if it is nonnegative.

The interesting work is done by the recursive method drawTicks(), which draws the sequence of ticks within some interval. Its only argument is the tick length associated with the interval's central tick. Consider the English ruler with major tick length 5 shown in Figure 3.22(b). Ignoring the lines containing 0 and 1, let us consider how to draw the sequence of ticks lying between these lines. The central tick (at 1/2 inch) has length 4. Observe that the two patterns of ticks above and below this central tick are identical, and each has a central tick of length 3. In general, an interval with a central tick length $L \geq 1$ is composed of the following:

- An interval with a central tick length $L - 1$
- A single tick of length L
- A interval with a central tick length $L - 1$.

With each recursive call, the length decreases by one. When the length drops to zero, we simply return. As a result, this recursive process will always terminate. This suggests a recursive process, in which the first and last steps are performed by calling the drawTicks($L - 1$) recursively. The middle step is performed by calling the method drawOneTick(L). This recursive formulation is shown in Code Fragment 3.30. As in the factorial example, the code has a base case (when $L = 0$). In this instance we make two recursive calls to the method.

```java
                                                    // draw a tick with no label
public static void drawOneTick(int tickLength) { drawOneTick(tickLength, −1); }
                                                    // draw one tick
public static void drawOneTick(int tickLength, int tickLabel) {
  for (int i = 0; i < tickLength; i++)
    System.out.print("-");
  if (tickLabel >= 0) System.out.print(" " + tickLabel);
  System.out.print("\n");
}
public static void drawTicks(int tickLength) { // draw ticks of given length
  if (tickLength > 0) {                          // stop when length drops to 0
    drawTicks(tickLength−1);                     // recursively draw left ticks
    drawOneTick(tickLength);                     // draw center tick
    drawTicks(tickLength−1);                     // recursively draw right ticks
  }
}
public static void drawRuler(int nInches, int majorLength) { // draw ruler
  drawOneTick(majorLength, 0);                   // draw tick 0 and its label
  for (int i = 1; i <= nInches; i++) {
    drawTicks(majorLength−1);                    // draw ticks for this inch
    drawOneTick(majorLength, i);                 // draw tick i and its label
  }
}
```

Code Fragment 3.30: A recursive implementation of a method that draws a ruler.

Illustrating Ruler Drawing using a Recursion Trace

The recursive execution of the recursive drawTicks method, defined above, can be visualized using a recursion trace.

The trace for drawTicks is more complicated than in the factorial example, however, because each instance makes two recursive calls. To illustrate this, we will show the recursion trace in a form that is reminiscent of an outline for a document. See Figure 3.23.

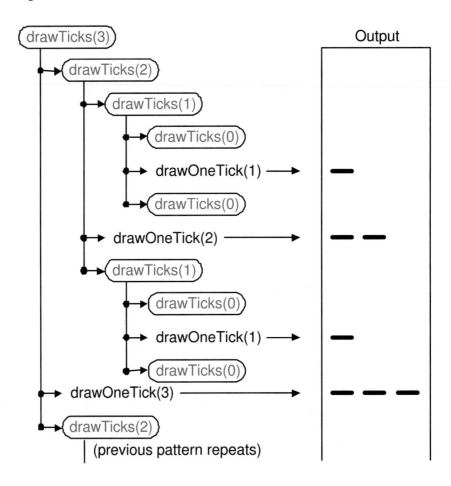

Figure 3.23: A partial recursion trace for the call drawTicks(3). The second pattern of calls for drawTicks(2) is not shown, but it is identical to the first.

Throughout this book we will see many other examples of how recursion can be used in the design of data structures and algorithms.

Further Illustrations of Recursion

As we discussed above, ***recursion*** is the concept of defining a method that makes a call to itself. Whenever a method calls itself, we refer to this as a ***recursive*** call. We also consider a method M to be recursive if it calls another method that ultimately leads to a call back to M.

The main benefit of a recursive approach to algorithm design is that it allows us to take advantage of the repetitive structure present in many problems. By making our algorithm description exploit this repetitive structure in a recursive way, we can often avoid complex case analyses and nested loops. This approach can lead to more readable algorithm descriptions, while still being quite efficient.

In addition, recursion is a useful way for defining objects that have a repeated similar structural form, such as in the following examples.

Example 3.1: *Modern operating systems define file-system directories (which are also sometimes called "folders") in a recursive way. Namely, a file system consists of a top-level directory, and the contents of this directory consists of files and other directories, which in turn can contain files and other directories, and so on. The base directories in the file system contain only files, but by using this recursive definition, the operating system allows for directories to be nested arbitrarily deep (as long as there is enough space in memory).*

Example 3.2: *Much of the syntax in modern programming languages is defined in a recursive way. For example, we can define an argument list in Java using the following notation:*

> *argument-list:*
>> *argument*
>> *argument-list , argument*

In other words, an argument list consists of either (i) an argument or (ii) an argument list followed by a comma and an argument. That is, an argument list consists of a comma-separated list of arguments. Similarly, arithmetic expressions can be defined recursively in terms of primitives (like variables and constants) and arithmetic expressions.

Example 3.3: *There are many examples of recursion in art and nature. One of the most classic examples of recursion used in art is in the Russian Matryoshka dolls. Each doll is made of solid wood or is hollow and contains another Matryoshka doll inside it.*

3.5.1 Linear Recursion

The simplest form of recursion is *linear recursion*, where a method is defined so that it makes at most one recursive call each time it is invoked. This type of recursion is useful when we view an algorithmic problem in terms of a first or last element plus a remaining set that has the same structure as the original set.

Summing the Elements of an Array Recursively

Suppose, for example, we are given an array, A, of n integers that we want to sum together. We can solve this summation problem using linear recursion by observing that the sum of all n integers in A is equal to $A[0]$, if $n = 1$, or the sum of the first $n-1$ integers in A plus the last element in A. In particular, we can solve this summation problem using the recursive algorithm described in Code Fragment 3.31.

Algorithm LinearSum(A, n):
    Input: A integer array A and an integer $n \geq 1$, such that A has at least n elements
    Output: The sum of the first n integers in A
    if $n = 1$ **then**
        return $A[0]$
    else
        return LinearSum($A, n-1$) $+ A[n-1]$

Code Fragment 3.31: Summing the elements in an array using linear recursion.

This example also illustrates an important property that a recursive method should always possess—the method terminates. We ensure this by writing a nonrecursive statement for the case $n = 1$. In addition, we always perform the recursive call on a smaller value of the parameter ($n-1$) than that which we are given (n), so that, at some point (at the "bottom" of the recursion), we will perform the nonrecursive part of the computation (returning $A[0]$). In general, an algorithm that uses linear recursion typically has the following form:

- *Test for base cases.* We begin by testing for a set of base cases (there should be at least one). These base cases should be defined so that every possible chain of recursive calls will eventually reach a base case, and the handling of each base case should not use recursion.

- *Recur.* After testing for base cases, we then perform a single recursive call. This recursive step may involve a test that decides which of several possible recursive calls to make, but it should ultimately choose to make just one of these calls each time we perform this step. Moreover, we should define each possible recursive call so that it makes progress towards a base case.

Analyzing Recursive Algorithms using Recursion Traces

We can analyze a recursive algorithm by using a visual tool known as a ***recursion trace***. We used recursion traces, for example, to analyze and visualize the recursive factorial function of Section 3.5, and we will similarly use recursion traces for the recursive sorting algorithms of Sections 11.1 and 11.2.

To draw a recursion trace, we create a box for each instance of the method and label it with the parameters of the method. Also, we visualize a recursive call by drawing an arrow from the box of the calling method to the box of the called method. For example, we illustrate the recursion trace of the LinearSum algorithm of Code Fragment 3.31 in Figure 3.24. We label each box in this trace with the parameters used to make this call. Each time we make a recursive call, we draw a line to the box representing the recursive call. We can also use this diagram to visualize stepping through the algorithm, since it proceeds by going from the call for n to the call for $n-1$, to the call for $n-2$, and so on, all the way down to the call for 1. When the final call finishes, it returns its value back to the call for 2, which adds in its value, and returns this partial sum to the call for 3, and so on, until the call for $n-1$ returns its partial sum to the call for n.

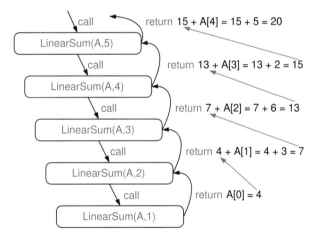

Figure 3.24: Recursion trace for an execution of LinearSum(A, n) with input parameters $A = \{4, 3, 6, 2, 5\}$ and $n = 5$.

From Figure 3.24, it should be clear that for an input array of size n, Algorithm LinearSum makes n calls. Hence, it will take an amount of time that is roughly proportional to n, since it spends a constant amount of time performing the nonrecursive part of each call. Moreover, we can also see that the memory space used by the algorithm (in addition to the array A) is also roughly proportional to n, since we need a constant amount of memory space for each of the n boxes in the trace at the time we make the final recursive call (for $n = 1$).

Reversing an Array by Recursion

Next, let us consider the problem of reversing the n elements of an array, A, so that the first element becomes the last, the second element becomes second to the last, and so on. We can solve this problem using linear recursion, by observing that the reversal of an array can be achieved by swapping the first and last elements and then recursively reversing the remaining elements in the array. We describe the details of this algorithm in Code Fragment 3.32, using the convention that the first time we call this algorithm we do so as ReverseArray($A, 0, n-1$).

Algorithm ReverseArray(A, i, j):
    Input: An array A and nonnegative integer indices i and j
    Output: The reversal of the elements in A starting at index i and ending at j
    if $i < j$ **then**
        Swap $A[i]$ and $A[j]$
        ReverseArray($A, i+1, j-1$)
    return

Code Fragment 3.32: Reversing the elements of an array using linear recursion.

Note that, in this algorithm, we actually have two base cases, namely, when $i = j$ and when $i > j$. Moreover, in either case, we simply terminate the algorithm, since a sequence with zero elements or one element is trivially equal to its reversal. Furthermore, note that in the recursive step we are guaranteed to make progress towards one of these two base cases. If n is odd, we will eventually reach the $i = j$ case, and if n is even, we will eventually reach the $i > j$ case. The above argument immediately implies that the recursive algorithm of Code Fragment 3.32 is guaranteed to terminate.

Defining Problems in Ways that Facilitate Recursion

To design a recursive algorithm for a given problem, it is useful to think of the different ways we can subdivide this problem to define problems that have the same general structure as the original problem. This process sometimes means we need to redefine the original problem to facilitate similar-looking subproblems. For example, with the ReverseArray algorithm, we added the parameters i and j so that a recursive call to reverse the inner part of the array A would have the same structure (and same syntax) as the call to reverse all of A. Then, rather than initially calling the algorithm as ReverseArray(A), we call it initially as ReverseArray($A, 0, n-1$). In general, if one has difficulty finding the repetitive structure needed to design a recursive algorithm, it is sometimes useful to work out the problem on a few concrete examples to see how the subproblems should be defined.

Tail Recursion

Using recursion can often be a useful tool for designing algorithms that have elegant, short definitions. But this usefulness does come at a modest cost. When we use a recursive algorithm to solve a problem, we have to use some of the memory locations in our computer to keep track of the state of each active recursive call. When computer memory is at a premium, then, it is useful in some cases to be able to derive nonrecursive algorithms from recursive ones.

We can use the stack data structure, discussed in Section 5.1, to convert a recursive algorithm into a nonrecursive algorithm, but there are some instances when we can do this conversion more easily and efficiently. Specifically, we can easily convert algorithms that use ***tail recursion***. An algorithm uses tail recursion if it uses linear recursion and the algorithm makes a recursive call as its very last operation. For example, the algorithm of Code Fragment 3.32 uses tail recursion to reverse the elements of an array.

It is not enough that the last statement in the method definition includes a recursive call, however. In order for a method to use tail recursion, the recursive call must be absolutely the last thing the method does (unless we are in a base case, of course). For example, the algorithm of Code Fragment 3.31 does not use tail recursion, even though its last statement includes a recursive call. This recursive call is not actually the last thing the method does. After it receives the value returned from the recursive call, it adds this value to $A[n-1]$ and returns this sum. That is, the last thing this algorithm does is an add, not a recursive call.

When an algorithm uses tail recursion, we can convert the recursive algorithm into a nonrecursive one, by iterating through the recursive calls rather than calling them explicitly. We illustrate this type of conversion by revisiting the problem of reversing the elements of an array. In Code Fragment 3.33, we give a nonrecursive algorithm that performs this task by iterating through the recursive calls of the algorithm of Code Fragment 3.32. We initially call this algorithm as IterativeReverseArray$(A, 0, n-1)$.

Algorithm IterativeReverseArray(A, i, j):
    Input: An array A and nonnegative integer indices i and j
    Output: The reversal of the elements in A starting at index i and ending at j
    while $i < j$ **do**
      Swap $A[i]$ and $A[j]$
      $i \leftarrow i + 1$
      $j \leftarrow j - 1$
    return

Code Fragment 3.33: Reversing the elements of an array using iteration.

3.5.2 Binary Recursion

When an algorithm makes two recursive calls, we say that it uses **binary recursion**. These calls can, for example, be used to solve two similar halves of some problem, as we did in Section 3.5 for drawing an English ruler. As another application of binary recursion, let us revisit the problem of summing the n elements of an integer array A. In this case, we can sum the elements in A by: (*i*) recursively summing the elements in the first half of A; (*ii*) recursively summing the elements in the second half of A; and (*iii*) adding these two values together. We give the details in the algorithm of Code Fragment 3.34, which we initially call as BinarySum($A, 0, n$).

Algorithm BinarySum(A, i, n):

　　Input: An array A and integers i and n

　　Output: The sum of the n integers in A starting at index i

　　if $n = 1$ **then**

　　　　return $A[i]$

　　return BinarySum($A, i, \lceil n/2 \rceil$) + BinarySum($A, i + \lceil n/2 \rceil, \lfloor n/2 \rfloor$)

Code Fragment 3.34: Summing the elements in an array using binary recursion.

To analyze Algorithm BinarySum, we consider, for simplicity, the case where n is a power of two. The general case of arbitrary n is considered in Exercise R-4.5. Figure 3.25 shows the recursion trace of an execution of method BinarySum($0, 8$). We label each box with the values of parameters i and n, which represent the starting index and length of the sequence of elements to be summed, respectively. Notice that the arrows in the trace go from a box labeled (i, n) to another box labeled $(i, n/2)$ or $(i + n/2, n/2)$. That is, the value of parameter n is halved at each recursive call. Thus, the depth of the recursion, that is, the maximum number of method instances that are active at the same time, is $1 + \log_2 n$. Thus, Algorithm Binary-Sum uses an amount of additional space roughly proportional to this value. This is a big improvement over the space needed by the LinearSum method of Code Fragment 3.31. The running time of Algorithm BinarySum is still roughly proportional to n, however, since each box is visited in constant time when stepping through our algorithm and there are $2n - 1$ boxes.

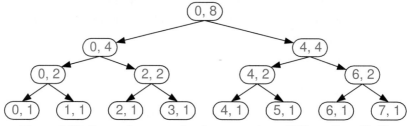

Figure 3.25: Recursion trace for the execution of BinarySum($0, 8$).

Computing Fibonacci Numbers via Binary Recursion

Let us consider the problem of computing the kth Fibonacci number. Recall from Section 2.2.3, that the Fibonacci numbers are recursively defined as follows:

$$
\begin{aligned}
F_0 &= 0 \\
F_1 &= 1 \\
F_i &= F_{i-1} + F_{i-2} \quad \text{for } i > 1.
\end{aligned}
$$

By directly applying this definition, Algorithm BinaryFib, shown in Code Fragment 3.35, computes the sequence of Fibonacci numbers using binary recursion.

Algorithm BinaryFib(k):

    Input: Nonnegative integer k

    Output: The kth Fibonacci number F_k

    if $k \leq 1$ **then**

        return k

    else

        return BinaryFib($k-1$) + BinaryFib($k-2$)

Code Fragment 3.35: Computing the kth Fibonacci number using binary recursion.

Unfortunately, in spite of the Fibonacci definition looking like a binary recursion, using this technique is inefficient in this case. In fact, it takes an exponential number of calls to compute the kth Fibonacci number in this way. Specifically, let n_k denote the number of calls performed in the execution of BinaryFib(k). Then, we have the following values for the n_k's:

$$
\begin{aligned}
n_0 &= 1 \\
n_1 &= 1 \\
n_2 &= n_1 + n_0 + 1 = 1 + 1 + 1 = 3 \\
n_3 &= n_2 + n_1 + 1 = 3 + 1 + 1 = 5 \\
n_4 &= n_3 + n_2 + 1 = 5 + 3 + 1 = 9 \\
n_5 &= n_4 + n_3 + 1 = 9 + 5 + 1 = 15 \\
n_6 &= n_5 + n_4 + 1 = 15 + 9 + 1 = 25 \\
n_7 &= n_6 + n_5 + 1 = 25 + 15 + 1 = 41 \\
n_8 &= n_7 + n_6 + 1 = 41 + 25 + 1 = 67.
\end{aligned}
$$

If we follow the pattern forward, we see that the number of calls more than doubles for each two consecutive indices. That is, n_4 is more than twice n_2, n_5 is more than twice n_3, n_6 is more than twice n_4, and so on. Thus, $n_k > 2^{k/2}$, which means that BinaryFib(k) makes a number of calls that are exponential in k. In other words, using binary recursion to compute Fibonacci numbers is very inefficient.

Computing Fibonacci Numbers via Linear Recursion

The main problem with the approach above, based on binary recursion, is that the computation of Fibonacci numbers is really a linearly recursive problem. It is not a good candidate for using binary recursion. We simply got tempted into using binary recursion because of the way the kth Fibonacci number, F_k, depends on the two previous values, F_{k-1} and F_{k-2}. But we can compute F_k much more efficiently using linear recursion.

In order to use linear recursion, however, we need to slightly redefine the problem. One way to accomplish this conversion is to define a recursive function that computes a pair of consecutive Fibonacci numbers (F_k, F_{k-1}) using the convention $F_{-1} = 0$. Then we can use the linearly recursive algorithm shown in Code Fragment 3.36.

Algorithm LinearFibonacci(k):
    Input: A nonnegative integer k
    Output: Pair of Fibonacci numbers (F_k, F_{k-1})
    if $k \leq 1$ **then**
        return $(k, 0)$
    else
        $(i, j) \leftarrow$ LinearFibonacci($k - 1$)
        return $(i + j, i)$

Code Fragment 3.36: Computing the kth Fibonacci number using linear recursion.

The algorithm given in Code Fragment 3.36 shows that using linear recursion to compute Fibonacci numbers is much more efficient than using binary recursion. Since each recursive call to LinearFibonacci decreases the argument k by 1, the original call LinearFibonacci(k) results in a series of $k - 1$ additional calls. That is, computing the kth Fibonacci number via linear recursion requires k method calls. This performance is significantly faster than the exponential time needed by the algorithm based on binary recursion, which was given in Code Fragment 3.35. Therefore, when using binary recursion, we should first try to fully partition the problem in two (as we did for summing the elements of an array) or, we should be sure that overlapping recursive calls are really necessary.

Usually, we can eliminate overlapping recursive calls by using more memory to keep track of previous values. In fact, this approach is a central part of a technique called ***dynamic programming***, which is related to recursion and is discussed in Section 12.2.

3.5.3 Multiple Recursion

Generalizing from binary recursion, we use ***multiple recursion*** when a method may make multiple recursive calls, with that number potentially being more than two. One of the most common applications of this type of recursion is used when we want to enumerate various configurations in order to solve a combinatorial puzzle. For example, the following are all instances of ***summation puzzles***:

$$
\begin{aligned}
pot + pan &= bib \\
dog + cat &= pig \\
boy + girl &= baby
\end{aligned}
$$

To solve such a puzzle, we need to assign a unique digit (that is, $0, 1, \ldots, 9$) to each letter in the equation, in order to make the equation true. Typically, we solve such a puzzle by using our human observations of the particular puzzle we are trying to solve to eliminate configurations (that is, possible partial assignments of digits to letters) until we can work though the feasible configurations left, testing for the correctness of each one.

If the number of possible configurations is not too large, however, we can use a computer to simply enumerate all the possibilities and test each one, without employing any human observations. In addition, such an algorithm can use multiple recursion to work through the configurations in a systematic way. We show pseudo-code for such an algorithm in Code Fragment 3.37. To keep the description general enough to be used with other puzzles, the algorithm enumerates and tests all k-length sequences without repetitions of the elements of a given set U. We build the sequences of k elements by the following steps:

1. Recursively generating the sequences of $k - 1$ elements

2. Appending to each such sequence an element not already contained in it.

Throughout the execution of the algorithm, we use the set U to keep track of the elements not contained in the current sequence, so that an element e has not been used yet if and only if e is in U.

Another way to look at the algorithm of Code Fragment 3.37 is that it enumerates every possible size-k ordered subset of U, and tests each subset for being a possible solution to our puzzle.

For summation puzzles, $U = \{0, 1, 2, 3, 4, 5, 6, 7, 8, 9\}$ and each position in the sequence corresponds to a given letter. For example, the first position could stand for b, the second for o, the third for y, and so on.

Algorithm PuzzleSolve(k, S, U):

   Input: An integer k, sequence S, and set U

   Output: An enumeration of all k-length extensions to S using elements in U
      without repetitions

   for each e in U **do**

      Remove e from U {e is now being used}

      Add e to the end of S

      if $k = 1$ **then**

         Test whether S is a configuration that solves the puzzle

         if S solves the puzzle **then**

            return "Solution found: " S

      else

         PuzzleSolve($k - 1, S, U$)

      Add e back to U {e is now unused}

      Remove e from the end of S

Code Fragment 3.37: Solving a combinatorial puzzle by enumerating and testing
all possible configurations.

In Figure 3.26, we show a recursion trace of a call to PuzzleSolve($3, S, U$),
where S is empty and $U = \{a, b, c\}$. During the execution, all the permutations
of the three characters are generated and tested. Note that the initial call makes
three recursive calls, each of which in turn makes two more. If we had executed
PuzzleSolve($3, S, U$) on a set U consisting of four elements, the initial call would
have made four recursive calls, each of which would have a trace looking like the
one in Figure 3.26.

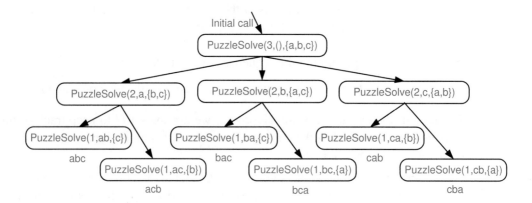

Figure 3.26: Recursion trace for an execution of PuzzleSolve($3, S, U$), where S is
empty and $U = \{a, b, c\}$. This execution generates and tests all permutations of a, b,
and c. We show the permutations generated directly below their respective boxes.

3.6 Exercises

For help with exercises, please visit the web site, www.wiley.com/college/goodrich.

Reinforcement

R-3.1 What is the difference between a deep equality test between two Java arrays, A and B, if they are one-dimensional arrays of type **int**? What if the arrays are two-dimensional arrays of type **int**?

R-3.2 Give three different examples of a single Java statement that copies the contents of one array, a, of **int** entries into another array, b, of **int** entries.

R-3.3 The add and remove methods of Code Fragments 3.3 and 3.4 do not keep track of the number, n, of nonnull entries in the array, a. Instead, the unused cells point to the **null** object. Show how to change these methods so that they keep track of the actual size of a in an instance variable n.

R-3.4 Give the next five pseudo-random numbers using the generator described in this chapter, with $a = 12$, $b = 5$, and $n = 100$, using the seed 92.

R-3.5 Describe a way to use recursion to add all the elements in a $n \times n$ (two-dimensional) array of integers.

R-3.6 Explain how to modify the Caesar cipher program (Code Fragment 3.9) so that it performs ROT13 encryption and decryption, which uses 13 as the alphabet shift amount. How can you further simplify the code so that the body of the decrypt method is only a single line?

R-3.7 Explain the changes that would have to be made to the program of Code Fragment 3.9 so that it could perform the Caesar cipher for messages that are written in an alphabet-based language other than English, such as Greek, Russian, or Hebrew.

R-3.8 What is the exception that is thrown when advance or remove is called on an empty list, from Code Fragment 3.25? Explain how to modify these methods so that they give a more instructive exception name for this condition.

R-3.9 Give a recursive definition of a singly linked list.

R-3.10 Describe a method for inserting an element at the beginning of a singly linked list. Assume that the list does *not* have a sentinel header node, and instead uses a variable head to reference the first node in the list.

R-3.11 Give an algorithm for finding the penultimate node in a singly linked list where the last element is indicated by a null next reference.

R-3.12 Describe a nonrecursive method for finding, by link hopping, the middle node of a doubly linked list with header and trailer sentinels. (Note: This method must only use link hopping; it cannot use a counter.) What is the running time of this method?

R-3.13 Describe a recursive algorithm for finding the maximum element in an array A of n elements. What is your running time and space usage?

R-3.14 Draw the recursion trace for the execution of method ReverseArray$(A,0,4)$ (Code Fragment 3.32) on array $A = \{4,3,6,2,5\}$.

R-3.15 Draw the recursion trace for the execution of method PuzzleSolve$(3,S,U)$ (Code Fragment 3.37), where S is empty and $U = \{a,b,c,d\}$.

R-3.16 Write a short Java method that repeatedly selects and removes a random entry from an array until the array holds no more entries.

R-3.17 Write a short Java method to count the number of nodes in a circularly linked list.

Creativity

C-3.1 Give examples of values for a and b in the pseudo-random generator given in this chapter such that the result is not very random looking, for n = 1000.

C-3.2 Suppose you are given an array, A, containing 100 integers that were put into A using the method r.nextInt(10), where r is an object of type java.util.Random. Let x denote the product of the integers in A. There is a single number that x will equal with probability at least 0.99. What is that number and what is a formula describing the probability that x is equal to that number?

C-3.3 Give Java code for performing add(e) and remove(i) methods for game entries, stored in an array a, as in Code Fragments 3.3 and 3.4, except this time, don't maintain the game entries in order. Assume that we still need to keep n entries stored in indices 0 to $n-1$. Try to implement the add and remove methods without using any loops, so that the number of steps they perform does not depend on n.

C-3.4 Let A be an array of size $n \geq 2$ containing integers from 1 to $n-1$, inclusive, with exactly one repeated. Describe a fast algorithm for finding the integer in A that is repeated.

C-3.5 Let B be an array of size $n \geq 6$ containing integers from 1 to $n-5$, inclusive, with exactly five repeated. Describe a good algorithm for finding the five integers in B that are repeated.

C-3.6 Suppose you are designing a multi-player game that has $n \geq 1000$ players, numbered 1 to n, interacting in an enchanted forest. The winner of this game is the first player who can meet all the other players at least once (ties are allowed). Assuming that there is a method meet(i,j), which is called each time a player i meets a player j (with $i \neq j$), describe a way to keep track of the pairs of meeting players and who is the winner.

C-3.7 Give a recursive algorithm to compute the product of two positive integers, m and n, using only addition and subtraction.

C-3.8 Describe a fast recursive algorithm for reversing a singly linked list L, so that the ordering of the nodes becomes opposite of what it was before.

C-3.9 Describe a good algorithm for concatenating two singly linked lists L and M, with header sentinels, into a single list L' that contains all the nodes of L followed by all the nodes of M.

C-3.10 Give a fast algorithm for concatenating two doubly linked lists L and M, with header and trailer sentinel nodes, into a single list L'.

C-3.11 Describe in detail how to swap two nodes x and y (and not just their contents) in a singly linked list L given references only to x and y. Repeat this exercise for the case when L is a doubly linked list. Which algorithm takes more time?

C-3.12 Describe in detail an algorithm for reversing a singly linked list L using only a constant amount of additional space and not using any recursion.

C-3.13 In the ***Towers of Hanoi*** puzzle, we are given a platform with three pegs, a, b, and c, sticking out of it. On peg a is a stack of n disks, each larger than the next, so that the smallest is on the top and the largest is on the bottom. The puzzle is to move all the disks from peg a to peg c, moving one disk at a time, so that we never place a larger disk on top of a smaller one. See Figure 3.27 for an example of the case $n = 4$. Describe a recursive algorithm for solving the Towers of Hanoi puzzle for arbitrary n. (Hint: Consider first the subproblem of moving all but the nth disk from peg a to another peg using the third as "temporary storage.")

Figure 3.27: An illustration of the Towers of Hanoi puzzle.

C-3.14 Describe a recursive method for converting a string of digits into the integer it represents. For example, `"13531"` represents the integer $13,531$.

C-3.15 Describe a recursive algorithm that counts the number of nodes in a singly linked list.

C-3.16 Write a recursive Java program that will output all the subsets of a set of n elements (without repeating any subsets).

C-3.17 Write a short recursive Java method that finds the minimum and maximum values in an array of **int** values without using any loops.

C-3.18 Describe a recursive algorithm that will check if an array A of integers contains an integer $A[i]$ that is the sum of two integers that appear earlier in A, that is, such that $A[i] = A[j] + A[k]$ for $j, k < i$.

C-3.19 Write a short recursive Java method that will rearrange an array of **int** values so that all the even values appear before all the odd values.

C-3.20 Write a short recursive Java method that takes a character string s and outputs its reverse. So for example, the reverse of `"pots&pans"` would be `"snap&stop"`.

C-3.21 Write a short recursive Java method that determines if a string s is a palindrome, that is, it is equal to its reverse. For example, `"racecar"` and `"gohangasalamiimalasagnahog"` are palindromes.

C-3.22 Use recursion to write a Java method for determining if a string s has more vowels than consonants.

C-3.23 Suppose you are given two circularly linked lists, L and M, that is, two lists of nodes such that each node has a nonnull next node. Describe a fast algorithm for telling if L and M are really the same list of nodes, but with different (cursor) starting points.

C-3.24 Given a circularly linked list L containing an even number of nodes, describe how to split L into two circularly linked lists of half the size.

C-3.25 Give the details for implementing a deepCopyOf method in Java for making an identical copy of a two-dimensional array.

Projects

P-3.1 Write a Java method that takes two three-dimensional integer arrays and adds them componentwise.

P-3.2 Write a Java program for a matrix class that can add and multiply arbitrary two-dimensional arrays of integers.

P-3.3 Perform the previous project, but use generic types so that the matrices involved can contain arbitrary number types.

P-3.4 Write a class that maintains the top 10 scores for a game application, implementing the add and remove methods of Section 3.1.1, but using a singly linked list instead of an array.

P-3.5 Perform the previous project, but use a doubly linked list. Moreover, your implementation of remove(i) should make the fewest number of pointer hops to get to the game entry at index i.

P-3.6 Perform the previous project, but use a linked list that is both circularly linked and doubly linked.

P-3.7 Write a program for solving summation puzzles by enumerating and testing all possible configurations. Using your program, solve the three puzzles given in Section 3.5.3.

P-3.8 Write a program that can perform encryption and decryption using an arbitrary substitution cipher. In this case, the encryption array is a random shuffling of the letters in the alphabet. Your program should generate a random encryption array, its corresponding decryption array, and use these to encode and decode a message.

P-3.9 Write a program that can perform the Caesar cipher for English messages that include both upper and lowercase characters.

P-3.10 Write a program that can solve instances of the Tower of Hanoi problem (from Exercise C-3.13).

Chapter Notes

The fundamental data structures of arrays and linked lists, as well as recursion, discussed in this chapter, belong to the folklore of computer science. They were first chronicled in the computer science literature by Knuth in his seminal book on *Fundamental Algorithms* [62].

Chapter

4

Analysis Tools

Contents

4.1 The Seven Functions Used in This Book

In this section, we briefly discuss the seven most important functions used in the analysis of algorithms. We will use only these seven simple functions for almost all the analysis we do in this book. In fact, a section that uses a function other than one of these seven will be marked with a star ($\star$) to indicate that it is optional. In addition to these seven fundamental functions, Appendix A contains a list of other useful mathematical facts that apply in the context of data structure and algorithm analysis.

4.1.1 The Constant Function

The simplest function we can think of is the **constant function**. This is the function,

$$f(n) = c,$$

for some fixed constant c, such as $c = 5$, $c = 27$, or $c = 2^{10}$. That is, for any argument n, the constant function $f(n)$ assigns the value c. In other words, it doesn't matter what the value of n is, $f(n)$ will always be equal to the constant value c.

Since we are most interested in integer functions, the most fundamental constant function is $g(n) = 1$, and this is the typical constant function we use in this book. Note that any other constant function, $f(n) = c$, can be written as a constant c times $g(n)$. That is, $f(n) = cg(n)$ in this case.

As simple as it is, the constant function is useful in algorithm analysis, because it characterizes the number of steps needed to do a basic operation on a computer, like adding two numbers, assigning a value to some variable, or comparing two numbers.

4.1.2 The Logarithm Function

One of the interesting and sometimes even surprising aspects of the analysis of data structures and algorithms is the ubiquitous presence of the **logarithm function**, $f(n) = \log_b n$, for some constant $b > 1$. This function is defined as follows:

$$x = \log_b n \quad \text{if and only if} \quad b^x = n.$$

By definition, $\log_b 1 = 0$. The value b is known as the **base** of the logarithm.

Computing the logarithm function exactly for any integer n involves the use of calculus, but we can use an approximation that is good enough for our purposes without calculus. In particular, we can easily compute the smallest integer greater than or equal to $\log_a n$, for this number is equal to the number of times we can divide n by a until we get a number less than or equal to 1. For example, this evaluation of $\log_3 27$ is 3, since $27/3/3/3 = 1$. Likewise, this evaluation of $\log_4 64$ is 3, since $64/4/4/4 = 1$, and this approximation to $\log_2 12$ is 4, since $12/2/2/2/2 = 0.75 \leq 1$. This base-two approximation arises in algorithm analysis, actually, since a common operation in many algorithms is to repeatedly divide an input in half.

Indeed, since computers store integers in binary, the most common base for the logarithm function in computer science is 2. In fact, this base is so common that we will typically leave it off when it is 2. That is, for us,

$$\log n = \log_2 n.$$

We note that most handheld calculators have a button marked LOG, but this is typically for calculating the logarithm base-10, not base-two.

There are some important rules for logarithms, similar to the exponent rules.

Proposition 4.1 (Logarithm Rules): *Given real numbers $a > 0$, $b > 1$, $c > 0$ and $d > 1$, we have:*

1. $\log_b ac = \log_b a + \log_b c$
2. $\log_b a/c = \log_b a - \log_b c$
3. $\log_b a^c = c \log_b a$
4. $\log_b a = (\log_d a) / \log_d b$
5. $b^{\log_d a} = a^{\log_d b}$.

Also, as a notational shorthand, we use $\log^c n$ to denote the function $(\log n)^c$. Rather than show how we could derive each of the identities above which all follow from the definition of logarithms and exponents, let us illustrate these identities with a few examples instead.

Example 4.2: *We demonstrate below some interesting applications of the logarithm rules from Proposition 4.1 (using the usual convention that the base of a logarithm is 2 if it is omitted).*

- $\log(2n) = \log 2 + \log n = 1 + \log n$, *by rule 1*
- $\log(n/2) = \log n - \log 2 = \log n - 1$, *by rule 2*
- $\log n^3 = 3 \log n$, *by rule 3*
- $\log 2^n = n \log 2 = n \cdot 1 = n$, *by rule 3*
- $\log_4 n = (\log n)/\log 4 = (\log n)/2$, *by rule 4*
- $2^{\log n} = n^{\log 2} = n^1 = n$, *by rule 5.*

As a practical matter, we note that rule 4 gives us a way to compute the base-two logarithm on a calculator that has a base-10 logarithm button, LOG, for

$$\log_2 n = \text{LOG } n / \text{LOG } 2.$$

4.1.3   The Linear Function

Another simple yet important function is the ***linear function***,

$$f(n) = n.$$

That is, given an input value n, the linear function f assigns the value n itself.

This function arises in algorithm analysis any time we have to do a single basic operation for each of n elements. For example, comparing a number x to each element of an array of size n will require n comparisons. The linear function also represents the best running time we can hope to achieve for any algorithm that processes a collection of n objects that are not already in the computer's memory, since reading in the n objects itself requires n operations.

4.1.4   The N-Log-N Function

The next function we discuss in this section is the ***n-log-n function***,

$$f(n) = n \log n,$$

that is, the function that assigns to an input n the value of n times the logarithm base-two of n. This function grows a little faster than the linear function and a lot slower than the quadratic function. Thus, as we will show on several occasions, if we can improve the running time of solving some problem from quadratic to n-log-n, we will have an algorithm that runs much faster in general.

4.1.5   The Quadratic Function

Another function that appears quite often in algorithm analysis is the ***quadratic function***,

$$f(n) = n^2.$$

That is, given an input value n, the function f assigns the product of n with itself (in other words, "n squared").

The main reason why the quadratic function appears in the analysis of algorithms is that there are many algorithms that have nested loops, where the inner loop performs a linear number of operations and the outer loop is performed a linear number of times. Thus, in such cases, the algorithm performs $n \cdot n = n^2$ operations.

Nested Loops and the Quadratic Function

The quadratic function can also arise in the context of nested loops where the first iteration of a loop uses one operation, the second uses two operations, the third uses three operations, and so on. That is, the number of operations is

$$1 + 2 + 3 + \cdots + (n-2) + (n-1) + n.$$

In other words, this is the total number of operations that will be performed by the nested loop if the number of operations performed inside the loop increases by one with each iteration of the outer loop. This quantity also has an interesting history.

In 1787, a German schoolteacher decided to keep his 9- and 10-year-old pupils occupied by adding up the integers from 1 to 100. But almost immediately one of the children claimed to have the answer! The teacher was suspicious, for the student had only the answer on his slate. But the answer was correct—5,050—and the student, Carl Gauss, grew up to be one of the greatest mathematicians of his time. It is widely suspected that young Gauss used the following identity.

Proposition 4.3: *For any integer $n \geq 1$, we have:*

$$1 + 2 + 3 + \cdots + (n-2) + (n-1) + n = \frac{n(n+1)}{2}.$$

We give two "visual" justifications of Proposition 4.3 in Figure 4.1.

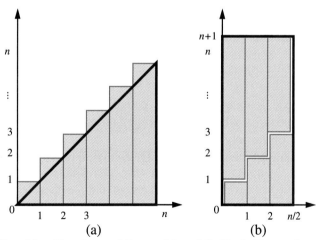

(a)   (b)

Figure 4.1: Visual justifications of Proposition 4.3. Both illustrations visualize the identity in terms of the total area covered by n unit-width rectangles with heights $1, 2, \ldots, n$. In (a) the rectangles are shown to cover a big triangle of area $n^2/2$ (base n and height n) plus n small triangles of area $1/2$ each (base 1 and height 1). In (b), which applies only when n is even, the rectangles are shown to cover a big rectangle of base $n/2$ and height $n+1$.

The lesson to be learned from Proposition 4.3 is that if we perform an algorithm with nested loops such that the operations in the inner loop increase by one each time, then the total number of operations is quadratic in the number of times, n, we perform the outer loop. In particular, the number of operations is $n^2/2 + n/2$, in this case, which is a little more than a constant factor $(1/2)$ times the quadratic function n^2. In other words, such an algorithm is only slightly better than an algorithm that uses n operations each time the inner loop is performed. This observation might at first seem nonintuitive, but it is nevertheless true, as shown in Figure 4.1.

4.1.6   The Cubic Function and Other Polynomials

Continuing our discussion of functions that are powers of the input, we consider the ***cubic function***,

$$f(n) = n^3,$$

which assigns to an input value n the product of n with itself three times. This function appears less frequently in the context of algorithm analysis than the constant, linear, and quadratic functions previously mentioned, but it does appear from time to time.

Polynomials

Interestingly, the functions we have listed so far can be viewed as all being part of a larger class of functions, the ***polynomials***.

A ***polynomial*** function is a function of the form,

$$f(n) = a_0 + a_1 n + a_2 n^2 + a_3 n^3 + \cdots + a_d n^d,$$

where $a_0, a_1, \ldots, a_d$ are constants, called the ***coefficients*** of the polynomial, and $a_d \neq 0$. Integer d, which indicates the highest power in the polynomial, is called the ***degree*** of the polynomial.

For example, the following functions are all polynomials:

- $f(n) = 2 + 5n + n^2$
- $f(n) = 1 + n^3$
- $f(n) = 1$
- $f(n) = n$
- $f(n) = n^2$.

Therefore, we could argue that this book presents just four important functions used in algorithm analysis, but we will stick to saying that there are seven, since the constant, linear, and quadratic functions are too important to be lumped in with other polynomials. Running times that are polynomials with degree, d, are generally better than polynomial running times with large degree.

Summations

A notation that appears again and again in the analysis of data structures and algorithms is the ***summation***, which is defined as follows:

$$\sum_{i=a}^{b} f(i) = f(a) + f(a+1) + f(a+2) + \cdots + f(b),$$

where a and b are integers and $a \leq b$. Summations arise in data structure and algorithm analysis because the running times of loops naturally give rise to summations.
Using a summation, we can rewrite the formula of Proposition 4.3 as

$$\sum_{i=1}^{n} i = \frac{n(n+1)}{2}.$$

Likewise, we can write a polynomial $f(n)$ of degree d with coefficients $a_0, \ldots, a_d$ as

$$f(n) = \sum_{i=0}^{d} a_i n^i.$$

Thus, the summation notation gives us a shorthand way of expressing sums of increasing terms that have a regular structure.

4.1.7 The Exponential Function

Another function used in the analysis of algorithms is the ***exponential function***,

$$f(n) = b^n,$$

where b is a positive constant, called the ***base***, and the argument n is the ***exponent***. That is, function $f(n)$ assigns to the input argument n the value obtained by multiplying the base b by itself n times. In algorithm analysis, the most common base for the exponential function is $b = 2$. For instance, if we have a loop that starts by performing one operation and then doubles the number of operations performed with each iteration, then the number of operations performed in the nth iteration is 2^n. In addition, an integer word containing n bits can represent all the nonnegative integers less than 2^n. Thus, the exponential function with base 2 is quite common. The exponential function will also be referred to as ***exponent function***.

We sometimes have other exponents besides n, however; hence, it is useful for us to know a few handy rules for working with exponents. In particular, the following ***exponent rules*** are quite helpful.

Proposition 4.4 (Exponent Rules): *Given positive integers a, b, and c, we have*

1. $(b^a)^c = b^{ac}$
2. $b^a b^c = b^{a+c}$
3. $b^a / b^c = b^{a-c}$.

For example, we have the following:

- $256 = 16^2 = (2^4)^2 = 2^{4 \cdot 2} = 2^8 = 256$ (Exponent Rule 1)
- $243 = 3^5 = 3^{2+3} = 3^2 3^3 = 9 \cdot 27 = 243$ (Exponent Rule 2)
- $16 = 1024/64 = 2^{10}/2^6 = 2^{10-6} = 2^4 = 16$ (Exponent Rule 3).

We can extend the exponential function to exponents that are fractions or real numbers and to negative exponents, as follows. Given a positive integer k, we define $b^{1/k}$ to be kth root of b, that is, the number r such that $r^k = b$. For example, $25^{1/2} = 5$, since $5^2 = 25$. Likewise, $27^{1/3} = 3$ and $16^{1/4} = 2$. This approach allows us to define any power whose exponent can be expressed as a fraction, for $b^{a/c} = (b^a)^{1/c}$, by Exponent Rule 1. For example, $9^{3/2} = (9^3)^{1/2} = 729^{1/2} = 27$. Thus, $b^{a/c}$ is really just the cth root of the integral exponent b^a.

We can further extend the exponential function to define b^x for any real number x, by computing a series of numbers of the form $b^{a/c}$ for fractions a/c that get progressively closer and closer to x. Any real number x can be approximated arbitrarily close by a fraction a/c; hence, we can use the fraction a/c as the exponent of b to get arbitrarily close to b^x. So, for example, the number 2^{π} is well defined. Finally, given a negative exponent d, we define $b^d = 1/b^{-d}$, which corresponds to applying Exponent Rule 3 with $a = 0$ and $c = -d$.

Geometric Sums

Suppose we have a loop where each iteration takes a multiplicative factor longer than the previous one. This loop can be analyzed using the following proposition.

Proposition 4.5: *For any integer $n \geq 0$ and any real number a such that $a > 0$ and $a \neq 1$, consider the summation*

$$\sum_{i=0}^{n} a^i = 1 + a + a^2 + \cdots + a^n$$

(remembering that $a^0 = 1$ if $a > 0$). This summation is equal to

$$\frac{a^{n+1} - 1}{a - 1}.$$

Summations as shown in Proposition 4.5 are called **geometric** summations, because each term is geometrically larger than the previous one if $a > 1$. For example, everyone working in computing should know that

$$1 + 2 + 4 + 8 + \cdots + 2^{n-1} = 2^n - 1,$$

for this is the largest integer that can be represented in binary notation using n bits.

4.1.8 Comparing Growth Rates

To sum up, Table 4.1 shows, in order, each of the seven common functions used in algorithm analysis.

constant	logarithm	linear	n-log-n	quadratic	cubic	exponential
1	$\log n$	n	$n \log n$	n^2	n^3	a^n

Table 4.1: Classes of functions. Here we assume that $a > 1$ is a constant.

Ideally, we would like data structure operations to run in times proportional to the constant or logarithm function, and we would like our algorithms to run in linear or n-log-n time. Algorithms with quadratic or cubic running times are less practical, but algorithms with exponential running times are infeasible for all but the smallest sized inputs. Plots of the seven functions are shown in Figure 4.2.

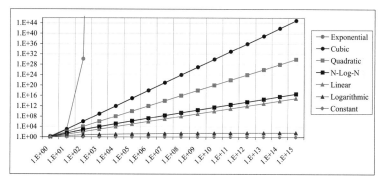

Figure 4.2: Growth rates for the seven fundamental functions used in algorithm analysis. We use base $a = 2$ for the exponential function. The functions are plotted in a log-log chart, to compare the growth rates primarily as slopes. Even so, the exponential function grows too fast to display all its values on the chart. Also, we use the scientific notation for numbers, where, $a\text{E}+b$ denotes $a10^b$.

The Ceiling and Floor Functions

One additional comment concerning the functions above is in order. The value of a logarithm is typically not an integer, yet the running time of an algorithm is usually expressed by means of an integer quantity, such as the number of operations performed. Thus, the analysis of an algorithm may sometimes involve the use of the *floor function* and *ceiling function*, which are defined respectively as follows:

- $\lfloor x \rfloor$ = the largest integer less than or equal to x.
- $\lceil x \rceil$ = the smallest integer greater than or equal to x.

4.2   Analysis of Algorithms

In a classic story, the famous mathematician Archimedes was asked to determine if a golden crown commissioned by the king was indeed pure gold, and not part silver, as an informant had claimed. Archimedes discovered a way to perform this analysis while stepping into a (Greek) bath. He noted that water spilled out of the bath in proportion to the amount of him that went in. Realizing the implications of this fact, he immediately got out of the bath and ran naked through the city shouting, "Eureka, eureka!," for he had discovered an analysis tool (displacement), which, when combined with a simple scale, could determine if the king's new crown was good or not. That is, Archimedes could dip the crown and an equal-weight amount of gold into a bowl of water to see if they both displaced the same amount. This discovery was unfortunate for the goldsmith, however, for when Archimedes did his analysis, the crown displaced more water than an equal-weight lump of pure gold, indicating that the crown was not, in fact, pure gold.

In this book, we are interested in the design of "good" data structures and algorithms. Simply put, a *data structure* is a systematic way of organizing and accessing data, and an *algorithm* is a step-by-step procedure for performing some task in a finite amount of time. These concepts are central to computing, but to be able to classify some data structures and algorithms as "good," we must have precise ways of analyzing them.

The primary analysis tool we will use in this book involves characterizing the running times of algorithms and data structure operations, with space usage also being of interest. Running time is a natural measure of "goodness," since time is a precious resource—computer solutions should run as fast as possible.

In general, the running time of an algorithm or data structure method increases with the input size, although it may also vary for different inputs of the same size. Also, the running time is affected by the hardware environment (as reflected in the processor, clock rate, memory, disk, etc.) and software environment (as reflected in the operating system, programming language, compiler, interpreter, etc.) in which the algorithm is implemented, compiled, and executed. All other factors being equal, the running time of the same algorithm on the same input data will be smaller if the computer has, say, a much faster processor or if the implementation is done in a program compiled into native machine code instead of an interpreted implementation run on a virtual machine. Nevertheless, in spite of the possible variations that come from different environmental factors, we would like to focus on the relationship between the running time of an algorithm and the size of its input.

We are interested in characterizing an algorithm's running time as a function of the input size. But what is the proper way of measuring it?

4.2.1 Experimental Studies

If an algorithm has been implemented, we can study its running time by executing it on various test inputs and recording the actual time spent in each execution. Fortunately, such measurements can be taken in an accurate manner by using system calls that are built into the language or operating system (for example, by using the System.currentTimeMillis() method or calling the run-time environment with profiling enabled). Such tests assign a specific running time to a specific input size, but we are interested in determining the general dependence of running time on the size of the input. In order to determine this dependence, we should perform several experiments on many different test inputs of various sizes. Then we can visualize the results of such experiments by plotting the performance of each run of the algorithm as a point with x-coordinate equal to the input size, n, and y-coordinate equal to the running time, t. (See Figure 4.3.) From this visualization and the data that supports it, we can perform a statistical analysis that seeks to fit the best function of the input size to the experimental data. To be meaningful, this analysis requires that we choose good sample inputs and test enough of them to be able to make sound statistical claims about the algorithm's running time.

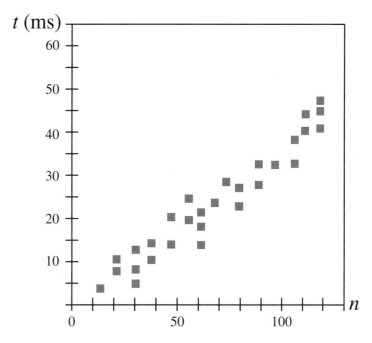

Figure 4.3: Results of an experimental study on the running time of an algorithm. A dot with coordinates (n,t) indicates that on an input of size n, the running time of the algorithm is t milliseconds (ms).

While experimental studies of running times are useful, they have three major limitations:

- Experiments can be done only on a limited set of test inputs; hence, they leave out the running times of inputs not included in the experiment (and these inputs may be important).
- We will have difficulty comparing the experimental running times of two algorithms unless the experiments were performed in the same hardware and software environments.
- We have to fully implement and execute an algorithm in order to study its running time experimentally.

This last requirement is obvious, but it is probably the most time consuming aspect of performing an experimental analysis of an algorithm. The other limitations impose serious hurdles too, of course. Thus, we would ideally like to have an analysis tool that allows us to avoid performing experiments.

In the rest of this chapter, we develop a general way of analyzing the running times of algorithms that:

- Takes into account all possible inputs
- Allows us to evaluate the relative efficiency of any two algorithms in a way that is independent from the hardware and software environment
- Can be performed by studying a high-level description of the algorithm without actually implementing it or running experiments on it.

This methodology aims at associating, with each algorithm, a function $f(n)$ that characterizes the running time of the algorithm as a function of the input size n. Typical functions that will be encountered include the seven functions mentioned earlier in this chapter.

4.2.2   Primitive Operations

As noted above, experimental analysis is valuable, but it has its limitations. If we wish to analyze a particular algorithm without performing experiments on its running time, we can perform an analysis directly on the high-level pseudo-code instead. We define a set of ***primitive operations*** such as the following:

- Assigning a value to a variable
- Calling a method
- Performing an arithmetic operation (for example, adding two numbers)
- Comparing two numbers
- Indexing into an array
- Following an object reference
- Returning from a method.

Counting Primitive Operations

Specifically, a primitive operation corresponds to a low-level instruction with an execution time that is constant. Instead of trying to determine the specific execution time of each primitive operation, we will simply **count** how many primitive operations are executed, and use this number t as a measure of the running time of the algorithm.

This operation count will correlate to an actual running time in a specific computer, for each primitive operation corresponds to a constant-time instruction, and there are only a fixed number of primitive operations. The implicit assumption in this approach is that the running times of different primitive operations will be fairly similar. Thus, the number, t, of primitive operations an algorithm performs will be proportional to the actual running time of that algorithm.

An algorithm may run faster on some inputs than it does on others of the same size. Thus, we may wish to express the running time of an algorithm as the function of the input size obtained by taking the average over all possible inputs of the same size. Unfortunately, such an **average-case** analysis is typically quite challenging. It requires us to define a probability distribution on the set of inputs, which is often a difficult task. Figure 4.4 schematically shows how, depending on the input distribution, the running time of an algorithm can be anywhere between the worst-case time and the best-case time. For example, what if inputs are really only of types "A" or "D"?

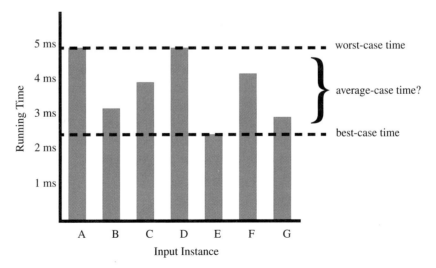

Figure 4.4: The difference between best-case and worst-case time. Each bar represents the running time of some algorithm on a different possible input.

Chapter 4. Analysis Tools

Focusing on the Worst Case

An average-case analysis usually requires that we calculate expected running times based on a given input distribution, which usually involves sophisticated probability theory. Therefore, for the remainder of this book, unless we specify otherwise, we will characterize running times in terms of the *worst case*, as a function of the input size, n, of the algorithm.

Worst-case analysis is much easier than average-case analysis, as it requires only the ability to identify the worst-case input, which is often simple. Also, this approach typically leads to better algorithms. Making the standard of success for an algorithm to perform well in the worst case necessarily requires that it will do well on *every* input. That is, designing for the worst case leads to stronger algorithmic "muscles," much like a track star who always practices by running up an incline.

4.2.3 Asymptotic Notation

In general, each basic step in a pseudo-code description or a high-level language implementation corresponds to a small number of primitive operations (except for method calls, of course). Thus, we can perform a simple analysis of an algorithm written in pseudo-code that estimates the number of primitive operations executed up to a constant factor, by pseudo-code steps (but we must be careful, since a single line of pseudo-code may denote a number of steps in some cases).

In algorithm analysis, we focus on the growth rate of the running time as a function of the input size n, taking a "big-picture" approach. It is often enough just to know that the running time of an algorithm such as arrayMax, shown in Code Fragment 4.1, *grows proportionally to* n, with its true running time being n times a constant factor that depends on the specific computer.

We analyze algorithms using a mathematical notation for functions that disregards constant factors. Namely, we characterize the running times of algorithms by using functions that map the size of the input, n, to values that correspond to the main factor that determines the growth rate in terms of n. This approach allows us to focus on the "big-picture" aspects of an algorithm's running time.

Algorithm arrayMax(A, n):
   Input: An array A storing $n \geq 1$ integers.
   Output: The maximum element in A.
   currMax $\leftarrow A[0]$
   for $i \leftarrow 1$ **to** $n - 1$ **do**
     if *currMax* $< A[i]$ **then**
       currMax $\leftarrow A[i]$
   return *currMax*

Code Fragment 4.1: Algorithm arrayMax.

The "Big-Oh" Notation

Let $f(n)$ and $g(n)$ be functions mapping nonnegative integers to real numbers. We say that $f(n)$ is $O(g(n))$ if there is a real constant $c > 0$ and an integer constant $n_0 \geq 1$ such that

$$f(n) \leq cg(n), \quad \text{for} \quad n \geq n_0.$$

This definition is often referred to as the "big-Oh" notation, for it is sometimes pronounced as "$f(n)$ is **big-Oh** of $g(n)$." Alternatively, we can also say "$f(n)$ is *order of* $g(n)$." (This definition is illustrated in Figure 4.5.)

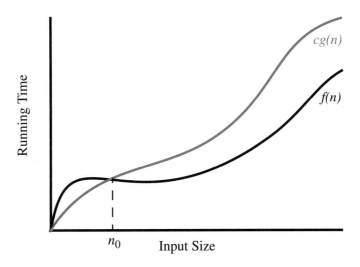

Figure 4.5: Illustrating the "big-Oh" notation. The function $f(n)$ is $O(g(n))$, since $f(n) \leq c \cdot g(n)$ when $n \geq n_0$.

Example 4.6: *The function $8n - 2$ is $O(n)$.*

Justification: By the big-Oh definition, we need to find a real constant $c > 0$ and an integer constant $n_0 \geq 1$ such that $8n - 2 \leq cn$ for every integer $n \geq n_0$. It is easy to see that a possible choice is $c = 8$ and $n_0 = 1$. Indeed, this is one of infinitely many choices available because any real number greater than or equal to 8 will work for c, and any integer greater than or equal to 1 will work for n_0. ∎

The big-Oh notation allows us to say that a function $f(n)$ is "less than or equal to" another function $g(n)$ up to a constant factor and in the *asymptotic* sense as n grows toward infinity. This ability comes from the fact that the definition uses "$\leq$" to compare $f(n)$ to a $g(n)$ times a constant, c, for the asymptotic cases when $n \geq n_0$.

Characterizing Running Times using the Big-Oh Notation

The big-Oh notation is used widely to characterize running times and space bounds in terms of some parameter n, which varies from problem to problem, but is always defined as a chosen measure of the "size" of the problem. For example, if we are interested in finding the largest element in an array of integers, as in the arrayMax algorithm, we should let n denote the number of elements of the array. Using the big-Oh notation, we can write the following mathematically precise statement on the running time of algorithm arrayMax for **any** computer.

Proposition 4.7: *The Algorithm* arrayMax, *for computing the maximum element in an array of n integers, runs in $O(n)$ time.*

Justification: The number of primitive operations executed by algorithm array-Max in each iteration is a constant. Hence, since each primitive operation runs in constant time, we can say that the running time of algorithm arrayMax on an input of size n is at most a constant times n, that is, we may conclude that the running time of algorithm arrayMax is $O(n)$.   ∎

Some Properties of the Big-Oh Notation

The big-Oh notation allows us to ignore constant factors and lower order terms and focus on the main components of a function that affect its growth.

Example 4.8: $5n^4 + 3n^3 + 2n^2 + 4n + 1$ *is* $O(n^4)$.

Justification: Note that $5n^4 + 3n^3 + 2n^2 + 4n + 1 \leq (5+3+2+4+1)n^4 = cn^4$, for $c = 15$, when $n \geq n_0 = 1$.   ∎

In fact, we can characterize the growth rate of any polynomial function.

Proposition 4.9: *If $f(n)$ is a polynomial of degree d, that is,*

$$f(n) = a_0 + a_1 n + \cdots + a_d n^d,$$

and $a_d > 0$, then $f(n)$ is $O(n^d)$.

Justification: Note that, for $n \geq 1$, we have $1 \leq n \leq n^2 \leq \cdots \leq n^d$; hence,

$$a_0 + a_1 n + a_2 n^2 + \cdots + a_d n^d \leq (a_0 + a_1 + a_2 + \cdots + a_d)n^d.$$

Therefore, we can show $f(n)$ is $O(n^d)$ by defining $c = a_0 + a_1 + \cdots + a_d$ and $n_0 = 1$.   ∎

Thus, the highest-degree term in a polynomial is the term that determines the asymptotic growth rate of that polynomial. We consider some additional properties of the big-Oh notation in the exercises. Let us consider some further examples here, however, focusing on combinations of the seven fundamental functions used in algorithm design.

Example 4.10: $5n^2 + 3n\log n + 2n + 5$ is $O(n^2)$.

Justification: $5n^2 + 3n\log n + 2n + 5 \leq (5+3+2+5)n^2 = cn^2$, for $c = 15$, when $n \geq n_0 = 2$ (note that $n\log n$ is zero for $n = 1$). ■

Example 4.11: $20n^3 + 10n\log n + 5$ is $O(n^3)$.

Justification: $20n^3 + 10n\log n + 5 \leq 35n^3$, for $n \geq 1$. ■

Example 4.12: $3\log n + 2$ is $O(\log n)$.

Justification: $3\log n + 2 \leq 5\log n$, for $n \geq 2$. Note that $\log n$ is zero for $n = 1$. That is why we use $n \geq n_0 = 2$ in this case. ■

Example 4.13: 2^{n+2} is $O(2^n)$.

Justification: $2^{n+2} = 2^n 2^2 = 4 \cdot 2^n$; hence, we can take $c = 4$ and $n_0 = 1$ in this case. ■

Example 4.14: $2n + 100\log n$ is $O(n)$.

Justification: $2n + 100\log n \leq 102n$, for $n \geq n_0 = 2$; hence, we can take $c = 102$ in this case. ■

Characterizing Functions in Simplest Terms

In general, we should use the big-Oh notation to characterize a function as closely as possible. While it is true that the function $f(n) = 4n^3 + 3n^2$ is $O(n^5)$ or even $O(n^4)$, it is more accurate to say that $f(n)$ is $O(n^3)$. Consider, by way of analogy, a scenario where a hungry traveler driving along a long country road happens upon a local farmer walking home from a market. If the traveler asks the farmer how much longer he must drive before he can find some food, it may be truthful for the farmer to say, "certainly no longer than 12 hours," but it is much more accurate (and helpful) for him to say, "you can find a market just a few minutes drive up this road." Thus, even with the big-Oh notation, we should strive as much as possible to tell the whole truth.

It is also considered poor taste to include constant factors and lower order terms in the big-Oh notation. For example, it is not fashionable to say that the function $2n^2$ is $O(4n^2 + 6n\log n)$, although this is completely correct. We should strive instead to describe the function in the big-Oh in *simplest terms*.

The seven functions listed in Section 4.1 are the most common functions used in conjunction with the big-Oh notation to characterize the running times and space usage of algorithms. Indeed, we typically use the names of these functions to refer to the running times of the algorithms they characterize. So, for example, we would say that an algorithm that runs in worst-case time $4n^2 + n\log n$ is a ***quadratic-time*** algorithm, since it runs in $O(n^2)$ time. Likewise, an algorithm running in time at most $5n + 20\log n + 4$ would be called a ***linear-time*** algorithm.

Big-Omega

Just as the big-Oh notation provides an asymptotic way of saying that a function is "less than or equal to" another function, the following notations provide an asymptotic way of saying that a function grows at a rate that is "greater than or equal to" that of another.

Let $f(n)$ and $g(n)$ be functions mapping nonnegative integers to real numbers. We say that $f(n)$ is $\Omega(g(n))$ (pronounced "$f(n)$ is big-Omega of $g(n)$") if $g(n)$ is $O(f(n))$, that is, there is a real constant $c > 0$ and an integer constant $n_0 \geq 1$ such that

$$f(n) \geq cg(n), \quad \text{for} \quad n \geq n_0.$$

This definition allows us to say asymptotically that one function is greater than or equal to another, up to a constant factor.

Example 4.15: $3n \log n + 2n$ is $\Omega(n \log n)$.

Justification: $3n \log n + 2n \geq 3n \log n$, for $n \geq 2$. ∎

Big-Theta

In addition, there is a notation that allows us to say that two functions grow at the same rate, up to constant factors. We say that $f(n)$ is $\Theta(g(n))$ (pronounced "$f(n)$ is big-Theta of $g(n)$") if $f(n)$ is $O(g(n))$ and $f(n)$ is $\Omega(g(n))$, that is, there are real constants $c' > 0$ and $c'' > 0$, and an integer constant $n_0 \geq 1$ such that

$$c'g(n) \leq f(n) \leq c''g(n), \quad \text{for} \quad n \geq n_0.$$

Example 4.16: $3n \log n + 4n + 5 \log n$ is $\Theta(n \log n)$.

Justification: $3n \log n \leq 3n \log n + 4n + 5 \log n \leq (3 + 4 + 5)n \log n$ for $n \geq 2$. ∎

4.2.4 Asymptotic Analysis

Suppose two algorithms solving the same problem are available: an algorithm A, which has a running time of $O(n)$, and an algorithm B, which has a running time of $O(n^2)$. Which algorithm is better? We know that n is $O(n^2)$, which implies that algorithm A is **asymptotically better** than algorithm B, although for a small value of n, B may have a lower running time than A.

We can use the big-Oh notation to order classes of functions by asymptotic growth rate. Our seven functions are ordered by increasing growth rate in the sequence below, that is, if a function $f(n)$ precedes a function $g(n)$ in the sequence, then $f(n)$ is $O(g(n))$:

$$1 \quad \log n \quad n \quad n \log n \quad n^2 \quad n^3 \quad 2^n.$$

We illustrate the growth rates of some important functions in Table 4.2.

n	$\log n$	n	$n \log n$	n^2	n^3	2^n
8	3	8	24	64	512	256
16	4	16	64	256	4,096	65,536
32	5	32	160	1,024	32,768	4,294,967,296
64	6	64	384	4,096	262,144	1.84×10^{19}
128	7	128	896	16,384	2,097,152	3.40×10^{38}
256	8	256	2,048	65,536	16,777,216	1.15×10^{77}
512	9	512	4,608	262,144	134,217,728	1.34×10^{154}

Table 4.2: Selected values of fundamental functions in algorithm analysis.

We further illustrate the importance of the asymptotic viewpoint in Table 4.3. This table explores the maximum size allowed for an input instance that is processed by an algorithm in 1 second, 1 minute, and 1 hour. It shows the importance of good algorithm design, because an asymptotically slow algorithm is beaten in the long run by an asymptotically faster algorithm, even if the constant factor for the asymptotically faster algorithm is worse.

Running	Maximum Problem Size (n)		
Time (μs)	1 second	1 minute	1 hour
$400n$	2,500	150,000	9,000,000
$2n^2$	707	5,477	42,426
2^n	19	25	31

Table 4.3: Maximum size of a problem that can be solved in 1 second, 1 minute, and 1 hour, for various running times measured in microseconds.

The importance of good algorithm design goes beyond just what can be solved effectively on a given computer, however. As shown in Table 4.4, even if we achieve a dramatic speed-up in hardware, we still cannot overcome the handicap of an asymptotically slow algorithm. This table shows the new maximum problem size achievable for any fixed amount of time, assuming algorithms with the given running times are now run on a computer 256 times faster than the previous one.

Running Time	New Maximum Problem Size
$400n$	$256m$
$2n^2$	$16m$
2^n	$m + 8$

Table 4.4: Increase in the maximum size of a problem that can be solved in a fixed amount of time, by using a computer that is 256 times faster than the previous one. Each entry is a function of m, the previous maximum problem size.

4.2.5   Using the Big-Oh Notation

Having made the case of using the big-Oh notation for analyzing algorithms, let us briefly discuss a few issues concerning its use. It is considered poor taste, in general, to say "$f(n) \leq O(g(n))$," since the big-Oh already denotes the "less-than-or-equal-to" concept. Likewise, although common, it is not fully correct to say "$f(n) = O(g(n))$" (with the usual understanding of the "=" relation), since there is no way to make sense of the statement "$O(g(n)) = f(n)$." In addition, it is completely wrong to say "$f(n) \geq O(g(n))$" or "$f(n) > O(g(n))$," since the $g(n)$ in the big-Oh expresses an upper bound on $f(n)$. It is best to say,

"$f(n)$ **is** $O(g(n))$."

For the more mathematically inclined, it is also correct to say,

"$f(n) \in O(g(n))$,"

for the big-Oh notation is, technically speaking, denoting a whole collection of functions. In this book, we will stick to presenting big-Oh statements as "$f(n)$ **is** $O(g(n))$." Even with this interpretation, there is considerable freedom in how we can use arithmetic operations with the big-Oh notation, and with this freedom comes a certain amount of responsibility.

Some Words of Caution

A few words of caution about asymptotic notation are in order at this point. First, note that the use of the big-Oh and related notations can be somewhat misleading should the constant factors they "hide" be very large. For example, while it is true that the function $10^{100}n$ is $O(n)$, if this is the running time of an algorithm being compared to one whose running time is $10n \log n$, we should prefer the $O(n \log n)$ time algorithm, even though the linear-time algorithm is asymptotically faster. This preference is because the constant factor, 10^{100}, which is called "one googol," is believed by many astronomers to be an upper bound on the number of atoms in the observable universe. So we are unlikely to ever have a real-world problem that has this number as its input size. Thus, even when using the big-Oh notation, we should at least be somewhat mindful of the constant factors and lower order terms we are "hiding."

The observation above raises the issue of what constitutes a "fast" algorithm. Generally speaking, any algorithm running in $O(n \log n)$ time (with a reasonable constant factor) should be considered efficient. Even an $O(n^2)$ time method may be fast enough in some contexts, that is, when n is small. But an algorithm running in $O(2^n)$ time should almost never be considered efficient.

Exponential Running Times

There is a famous story about the inventor of the game of chess. He asked only that his king pay him 1 grain of rice for the first square on the board, 2 grains for the second, 4 grains for the third, 8 for the fourth, and so on. It is an interesting test of programming skills to write a program to compute exactly the number of grains of rice the king would have to pay. In fact, any Java program written to compute this number in a single integer value will cause an integer overflow to occur (although the run-time machine will probably not complain). To represent this number exactly as an integer requires using a BigInteger class.

If we must draw a line between efficient and inefficient algorithms, therefore, it is natural to make this distinction be that between those algorithms running in polynomial time and those running in exponential time. That is, make the distinction between algorithms with a running time that is $O(n^c)$, for some constant $c > 1$, and those with a running time that is $O(b^n)$, for some constant $b > 1$. Like so many notions we have discussed in this section, this too should be taken with a "grain of salt," for an algorithm running in $O(n^{100})$ time should probably not be considered "efficient." Even so, the distinction between polynomial-time and exponential-time algorithms is considered a robust measure of tractability.

To summarize, the asymptotic notations of big-Oh, big-Omega, and big-Theta provide a convenient language for us to analyze data structures and algorithms. As mentioned earlier, these notations provide convenience because they let us concentrate on the "big picture" rather than low-level details.

Two Examples of Asymptotic Algorithm Analysis

We conclude this section by analyzing two algorithms that solve the same problem but have rather different running times. The problem we are interested in is the one of computing the so-called *prefix averages* of a sequence of numbers. Namely, given an array X storing n numbers, we want to compute an array A such that $A[i]$ is the average of elements $X[0], \ldots, X[i]$, for $i = 0, \ldots, n-1$, that is,

$$A[i] = \frac{\sum_{j=0}^{i} X[j]}{i+1}.$$

Computing prefix averages has many applications in economics and statistics. For example, given the year-by-year returns of a mutual fund, an investor will typically want to see the fund's average annual returns for the last year, the last three years, the last five years, and the last ten years. Likewise, given a stream of daily Web usage logs, a Web site manager may wish to track average usage trends over various time periods.

A Quadratic-Time Algorithm

Our first algorithm for the prefix averages problem, called prefixAverages1, is shown in Code Fragment 4.2. It computes every element of A separately, following the definition.

Algorithm prefixAverages1(X):
  Input: An n-element array X of numbers.
  Output: An n-element array A of numbers such that $A[i]$ is
    the average of elements $X[0], \ldots, X[i]$.
  Let A be an array of n numbers.
  for $i \leftarrow 0$ **to** $n-1$ **do**
    $a \leftarrow 0$
    for $j \leftarrow 0$ **to** i **do**
      $a \leftarrow a + X[j]$
    $A[i] \leftarrow a/(i+1)$
  return array A

Code Fragment 4.2: Algorithm prefixAverages1.

Let us analyze the prefixAverages1 algorithm.

- Initializing and returning array A at the beginning and end can be done with a constant number of primitive operations per element, and takes $O(n)$ time.

- There are two nested **for** loops, which are controlled by counters i and j, respectively. The body of the outer loop, controlled by counter i, is executed n times, for $i = 0, \ldots, n-1$. Thus, statements $a = 0$ and $A[i] = a/(i+1)$ are executed n times each. This implies that these two statements, plus the incrementing and testing of counter i, contribute a number of primitive operations proportional to n, that is, $O(n)$ time.

- The body of the inner loop, which is controlled by counter j, is executed $i+1$ times, depending on the current value of the outer loop counter i. Thus, statement $a = a + X[j]$ in the inner loop is executed $1 + 2 + 3 + \cdots + n$ times. By recalling Proposition 4.3, we know that $1 + 2 + 3 + \cdots + n = n(n+1)/2$, which implies that the statement in the inner loop contributes $O(n^2)$ time. A similar argument can be done for the primitive operations associated with the incrementing and testing counter j, which also take $O(n^2)$ time.

The running time of algorithm prefixAverages1 is given by the sum of three terms. The first and the second term are $O(n)$, and the third term is $O(n^2)$. By a simple application of Proposition 4.9, the running time of prefixAverages1 is $O(n^2)$.

A Linear-Time Algorithm

In order to compute prefix averages more efficiently, we can observe that two consecutive averages $A[i-1]$ and $A[i]$ are similar:

$$
\begin{aligned}
A[i-1] &= (X[0]+X[1]+\cdots+X[i-1])/i \\
A[i] &= (X[0]+X[1]+\cdots+X[i-1]+X[i])/(i+1).
\end{aligned}
$$

If we denote with S_i the **prefix sum** $X[0]+X[1]+\cdots+X[i]$, we can compute the prefix averages as $A[i] = S_i/(i+1)$. It is easy to keep track of the current prefix sum while scanning array X with a loop. We are now ready to present Algorithm prefixAverages2 in Code Fragment 4.3.

Algorithm prefixAverages2(X):
    Input: An n-element array X of numbers.
    Output: An n-element array A of numbers such that $A[i]$ is
        the average of elements $X[0], \ldots, X[i]$.
    Let A be an array of n numbers.
    $s \leftarrow 0$
    for $i \leftarrow 0$ **to** $n-1$ **do**
        $s \leftarrow s + X[i]$
        $A[i] \leftarrow s/(i+1)$
    return array A

Code Fragment 4.3: Algorithm prefixAverages2.

The analysis of the running time of algorithm prefixAverages2 follows:

- Initializing and returning array A at the beginning and end can be done with a constant number of primitive operations per element, and takes $O(n)$ time.

- Initializing variable s at the beginning takes $O(1)$ time.

- There is a single **for** loop, which is controlled by counter i. The body of the loop is executed n times, for $i = 0, \ldots, n-1$. Thus, statements $s = s + X[i]$ and $A[i] = s/(i+1)$ are executed n times each. This implies that these two statements plus the incrementing and testing of counter i contribute a number of primitive operations proportional to n, that is, $O(n)$ time.

The running time of algorithm prefixAverages2 is given by the sum of three terms. The first and the third term are $O(n)$, and the second term is $O(1)$. By a simple application of Proposition 4.9, the running time of prefixAverages2 is $O(n)$, which is much better than the quadratic-time algorithm prefixAverages1.

4.2.6   A Recursive Algorithm for Computing Powers

As a more interesting example of algorithm analysis, let us consider the problem of raising a number x to an arbitrary nonnegative integer, n. That is, we wish to compute the ***power function*** $p(x,n)$, defined as $p(x,n) = x^n$. This function has an immediate recursive definition based on linear recursion:

$$p(x,n) = \begin{cases} 1 & \text{if } n = 0 \\ x \cdot p(x, n-1) & \text{otherwise.} \end{cases}$$

This definition leads immediately to a recursive algorithm that uses $O(n)$ method calls to compute $p(x,n)$. We can compute the power function much faster than this, however, by using the following alternative definition, also based on linear recursion, which employs a squaring technique:

$$p(x,n) = \begin{cases} 1 & \text{if } n = 0 \\ x \cdot p(x, (n-1)/2)^2 & \text{if } n > 0 \text{ is odd} \\ p(x, n/2)^2 & \text{if } n > 0 \text{ is even.} \end{cases}$$

To illustrate how this definition works, consider the following examples:

$$\begin{aligned} 2^4 &= 2^{(4/2)2} = (2^{4/2})^2 = (2^2)^2 = 4^2 = 16 \\ 2^5 &= 2^{1+(4/2)2} = 2(2^{4/2})^2 = 2(2^2)^2 = 2(4^2) = 32 \\ 2^6 &= 2^{(6/2)2} = (2^{6/2})^2 = (2^3)^2 = 8^2 = 64 \\ 2^7 &= 2^{1+(6/2)2} = 2(2^{6/2})^2 = 2(2^3)^2 = 2(8^2) = 128. \end{aligned}$$

This definition suggests the algorithm of Code Fragment 4.4.

Algorithm Power(x,n):

  Input: A number x and integer $n \geq 0$
  Output: The value x^n

  if $n = 0$ **then**
      return 1
  if n is odd **then**
      $y \leftarrow$ Power$(x, (n-1)/2)$
      return $x \cdot y \cdot y$
  else
      $y \leftarrow$ Power$(x, n/2)$
      return $y \cdot y$

Code Fragment 4.4: Computing the power function using linear recursion.

To analyze the running time of the algorithm, we observe that each recursive call of method Power(x,n) divides the exponent, n, by two. Thus, there are $O(\log n)$ recursive calls, not $O(n)$. That is, by using linear recursion and the squaring technique, we reduce the running time for the computation of the power function from $O(n)$ to $O(\log n)$, which is a big improvement.

4.2.7 Some More Examples of Algorithm Analysis

Now that we have the big-oh notation for doing algorithm analysis, let us give some more examples of simple algorithms that can have their running times characterized using this notation. Moreover, in keeping with our earlier promise, we illustrate below how each of the seven functions given earlier in this chapter can be used to characterize the running time of an example algorithm.

A Constant-Time Method

To illustrate a constant-time algorithm, consider the following Java method, which returns the *capacity* of an array, that is, the number of cells in the array that are capable of storing elements:

```java
public static int capacity(int[] arr) {
    return arr.length;   // the capacity of an array is its length
}
```

This is a very simple algorithm, because the capacity of an array is the same as its length, and there is a direct way in Java for returning the length of an array. Moreover, this value is stored as an instance variable for the array object, so it takes only a constant-time lookup to return this value. Thus, the capacity method runs in $O(1)$ time; that is, the running time of this method is independent of the value of n, the size of the array.

Revisiting the Method for Finding the Maximum in an Array

For our next example, let us reconsider a simple problem studied earlier—finding the largest value in an array of integers—which can be done in Java as follows:

```java
public static int findMax(int[] arr) {
    int max = arr[0]; // start with the first integer in arr
    for (int i=1; i < arr.length; i++)
        if (max < arr[i])
            max = arr[i];  // update the current maximum
    return max; // the current maximum is now the global maximum
}
```

This method, which amounts to a Java implementation of the arrayMax method of Section 4.2.3, compares each of the n elements in the input array to a current maximum, and each time it finds an element larger than the current maximum, it updates the current maximum to be this value. Thus, it spends a constant amount of time for each of the n elements in the array; hence, as with the pseudo-code version of the arrayMax algorithm, the running time of this algorithm is $O(n)$.

Further Analysis of the Maximum-Finding Algorithm

A more interesting question, with respect to the above maximum-finding algorithm, is to ask how many times we update the current maximum value. Note that this statement is executed only if we encounter a value of the array that is larger than our current maximum. In the worst case, this condition could be true each time we perform the test. For instance, this situation would occur if the input array is given to us in sorted order. Thus, in the worst-case, the statement max = arr[i] is performed $n-1$ times, hence $O(n)$ times.

But what if the input array is given to us in random order, with all orders equally likely; what would be the expected number of times we updated the maximum value in this case? To answer this question, note that we update the current maximum in the ith iteration only if the ith element in the array is bigger than all the elements that precede it. But if the array is given to us in random order, the probability that the ith element is larger than all elements that precede it is $1/i$; hence, the expected number of times we update the maximum in this case is $H_n = \sum_{i=1}^{n} 1/i$, which is known as the nth **Harmonic number**. It turns out (see Proposition A.16) that H_n is $O(\log n)$. Therefore, the expected number of times the maximum is updated when the above maximum-finding algorithm is run on a random array is $O(\log n)$.

Three-Way Set Disjointness

Suppose we are given three sets, A, B, and C, with these sets stored in three different integer arrays, a, b, and c, respectively. The **three-way set disjointness** problem is to determine if these three sets are disjoint, that is, whether there is no element x such that $x \in A$, $x \in B$, and $x \in C$. A simple Java method to determine this property is given below:

```
public static boolean areDisjoint(int[] a, int[] b, int[] c) {
  for (int i=0; i < a.length; i++)
    for (int j=0; j < b.length; j++)
      for (int k=0; k < c.length; k++)
        if ((a[i] == b[j]) && (b[j] == c[k])) return false;
  return true;  // there is no element common to a, b, and c
}
```

This simple algorithm loops through each possible triple of indices i, j, and k to check if the respective elements indexed in a, b, and c are equal. Thus, if each of these arrays is of size n, then the worst-case running time of this method is $O(n^3)$. Moreover, the worst case is achieved when the sets are disjoint, since in this case we go through all n^3 triples of valid indices, i, j, and k. Such a running time would generally not be considered very efficient, but, fortunately, there is a better way to solve this problem, which we explore in Exercise C-4.3.

Recursion Run Amok

The next few example algorithms we study are for solving the ***element uniqueness problem***, in which we are given a range, $i, i+1, \ldots, j$, of indices for an array, A, and we want to determine if the elements of this range, $A[i], A[i+1], \ldots, A[j]$, are all unique, that is, there is no repeated element in this group of array entries. The first algorithm we give for solving the element uniqueness problem is a recursive one. But it uses recursion in a very inefficient manner, as shown in the following Java implementation.

```java
// Are all the entries in an array of int values unique from start to end?
public static boolean isUnique(int[] arr, int start, int end) {
    if (start >= end) return true;   // the range is too small for repeats
    // check if first part of arr is recursively unique
    if (!isUnique(arr, start, end−1)) return false;
    // check if second part of arr is recursively unique
    if (!isUnique(arr, start+1, end)) return false;
    return (arr[start] != arr[end]);   // check if first and last are different
}
```

To analyze this recursive algorithm, let us first determine how much time we spend outside of recursive calls in any invocation of this method. Note, in particular, that there are no loops—just comparisons, arithmetic operations, array element references, and method returns. Thus, the nonrecursive part of each method invocation runs in constant time, that is, $O(1)$ time; hence, to determine the worst-case running time of this method we only need to determine the worst-case total number of calls we make to the isUnique method.

Let n denote the number of entries under consideration, that is, let

$$n = \text{end} - \text{start} + 1.$$

If $n = 1$, then the running time of the isUnique is $O(1)$, since there are no recursive calls for this case. To characterize the running time of the general case, the important observation to make is that in order to solve a problem of size n, the isUnique method makes two recursive calls on problems of size $n - 1$. Thus, in the worst case, a call for a range of size n makes two calls on ranges of size $n - 1$, which each make two calls on ranges of size $n - 2$, which each make two calls on ranges of size $n - 3$, and so on. Thus, in the worst case, the total number of method calls is given by the geometric summation

$$1 + 2 + 4 + \cdots + 2^{n-1},$$

which is equal to $2^n - 1$ by Proposition 4.5. Thus, the worst-case running time of method isUnique is $O(2^n)$. This is an incredibly inefficient method for solving the element uniqueness problem. Its inefficiency comes not from the fact that it uses recursion—it comes from the fact that it uses recursion poorly, which is something we address in Exercise C-4.2.

An Iterative Method for Solving the Element Uniqueness Problem

We can do much better than the above exponential-time method by using the following iterative algorithm:

```
public static boolean isUniqueLoop(int[] arr, int start, int end) {
  if (start >= end) return true; // the range is too small for repeats
  for (int i=start; i < end; i++)
    for (int j=i+1; j <= end; j++)
      if (arr[i] == arr[j]) return false;
  return true;
}
```

This method solves the element uniqueness problem by looping through all distinct pairs of indices, i and j, and checking if any of them indexes a pair of elements that are equal to each other. It does this using two nested **for** loops, such that the first iteration of the outer loop causes $n - 1$ iterations of the inner loop, the second iteration of the outer loop causes $n - 2$ iterations of the inner loop, the third iteration of the outer loop causes $n - 3$ iterations of the inner loop, and so on. Thus, the worst-case running time of this method is proportional to

$$1+2+3+\cdots+(n-1),$$

which is $O(n^2)$ as we have seen earlier in this chapter (Proposition 4.3).

Using Sorting as a Problem-Solving Tool

An even better algorithm for the element uniqueness problem is based on using sorting as a problem-solving tool. In this case, by sorting an array of elements, we are guaranteed that any duplicate elements will be placed next to each other. Thus, to determine if there are any duplicates in the array, all we need to do is perform a single pass over the sorted array, looking for consecutive duplicates. A Java implementation of this algorithm is as follows:

```
public static boolean isUniqueSort(int[] arr, int start, int end) {
  if (start >= end) return true; // the range is too small for repeats
  int[] buf = arr.clone(); // duplicate arr so that sorting doesn't change it
  Arrays.sort(buf);   // sort the copy of arr, putting duplicates together
  for (int i=start; i < end; i++)
    if (buf[i] == buf[i+1]) return false;
  return true;
}
```

Method Arrays.sort uses the quick-sort algorithm, which runs in $O(n \log n)$ time (Section 11.2). Thus, the entire algorithm isUniqueSort runs in $O(n \log n)$ time because all the other steps run in $O(n)$ time. Incidentally, we can solve the element uniqueness problem even faster than $O(n \log n)$ time, at least in terms of its average-case running time, by using the hash table data structure we explore in Section 9.2.

4.3   Simple Justification Techniques

Sometimes, we will want to make claims about an algorithm, such as showing that it is correct or that it runs fast. In order to rigorously make such claims, we must use mathematical language, and in order to back up such claims, we must justify or ***prove*** our statements. Fortunately, there are several simple ways to do this.

4.3.1   By Example

Some claims are of the generic form, "There is an element x in a set S that has property P." To justify such a claim, we only need to produce a particular x in S that has property P. Likewise, some hard-to-believe claims are of the generic form, "Every element x in a set S has property P." To justify that such a claim is false, we only need to produce a particular x from S that does not have property P. Such an instance is called a ***counterexample***.

Example 4.17: *Professor Amongus claims that every number of the form $2^i - 1$ is a prime, when i is an integer greater than 1. Professor Amongus is wrong.*

Justification: To prove Professor Amongus is wrong, we find a counter-example. Fortunately, we need not look too far, for $2^4 - 1 = 15 = 3 \cdot 5$.   ■

4.3.2   The "Contra" Attack

Another set of justification techniques involves the use of the negative. The two primary such methods are the use of the ***contrapositive*** and the ***contradiction***. The use of the contrapositive method is like looking through a negative mirror. To justify the statement "if p is true, then q is true" we establish that "if q is not true, then p is not true" instead. Logically, these two statements are the same, but the latter, which is called the ***contrapositive*** of the first, may be easier to think about.

Example 4.18: *Let a and b be integers. If ab is even, then a is even or b is even.*

Justification: To justify this claim, consider the contrapositive, "If a is odd and b is odd, then ab is odd." So, suppose $a = 2i + 1$ and $b = 2j + 1$, for some integers i and j. Then $ab = 4ij + 2i + 2j + 1 = 2(2ij + i + j) + 1$; hence, ab is odd.   ■

Besides showing a use of the contrapositive justification technique, the previous example also contains an application of ***DeMorgan's Law***. This law helps us deal with negations, for it states that the negation of a statement of the form "p or q" is "not p and not q." Likewise, it states that the negation of a statement of the form "p and q" is "not p or not q."

Contradiction

Another negative justification technique is justification by ***contradiction***, which also often involves using DeMorgan's Law. In applying the justification by contradiction technique, we establish that a statement q is true by first supposing that q is false and then showing that this assumption leads to a contradiction (such as $2 \neq 2$ or $1 > 3$). By reaching such a contradiction, we show that no consistent situation exists with q being false, so q must be true. Of course, in order to reach this conclusion, we must be sure our situation is consistent before we assume q is false.

Example 4.19: *Let a and b be integers. If ab is odd, then a is odd and b is odd.*

Justification: Let ab be odd. We wish to show that a is odd and b is odd. So, with the hope of leading to a contradiction, let us assume the opposite, namely, suppose a is even or b is even. In fact, without loss of generality, we can assume that a is even (since the case for b is symmetric). Then $a = 2i$ for some integer i. Hence, $ab = (2i)b = 2(ib)$, that is, ab is even. But this is a contradiction: ab cannot simultaneously be odd and even. Therefore a is odd and b is odd.   ∎

4.3.3   Induction and Loop Invariants

Most of the claims we make about a running time or a space bound involve an integer parameter n (usually denoting an intuitive notion of the "size" of the problem). Moreover, most of these claims are equivalent to saying some statement $q(n)$ is true "for all $n \geq 1$." Since this is making a claim about an infinite set of numbers, we cannot justify this exhaustively in a direct fashion.

Induction

We can often justify claims such as those above as true, however, by using the technique of ***induction***. This technique amounts to showing that, for any particular $n \geq 1$, there is a finite sequence of implications that starts with something known to be true and ultimately leads to showing that $q(n)$ is true. Specifically, we begin a justification by induction by showing that $q(n)$ is true for $n = 1$ (and possibly some other values $n = 2, 3, \ldots, k$, for some constant k). Then we justify that the inductive "step" is true for $n > k$, namely, we show "if $q(i)$ is true for $i < n$, then $q(n)$ is true." The combination of these two pieces completes the justification by induction.

Proposition 4.20: *Consider the Fibonacci function $F(n)$, where we define $F(1) = 1$, $F(2) = 2$, and $F(n) = F(n-1) + F(n-2)$ for $n > 2$. (See Section 2.2.3.) We claim that $F(n) < 2^n$.*

Justification: We will show our claim is right by induction.
Base cases: $(n \leq 2)$. $F(1) = 1 < 2 = 2^1$ and $F(2) = 2 < 4 = 2^2$.
Induction step: $(n > 2)$. Suppose our claim is true for $n' < n$. Consider $F(n)$. Since $n > 2$, $F(n) = F(n-1) + F(n-2)$. Moreover, since $n-1 < n$ and $n-2 < n$, we can apply the inductive assumption (sometimes called the "inductive hypothesis") to imply that $F(n) < 2^{n-1} + 2^{n-2}$, since

$$2^{n-1} + 2^{n-2} < 2^{n-1} + 2^{n-1} = 2 \cdot 2^{n-1} = 2^n.$$

■

Let us do another inductive argument, this time for a fact we have seen before.

Proposition 4.21: *(which is the same as Proposition 4.3)*

$$\sum_{i=1}^{n} i = \frac{n(n+1)}{2}.$$

Justification: We will justify this equality by induction.
Base case: $n = 1$. Trivial, for $1 = n(n+1)/2$, if $n = 1$.
Induction step: $n \geq 2$. Assume the claim is true for $n' < n$. Consider n.

$$\sum_{i=1}^{n} i = n + \sum_{i=1}^{n-1} i.$$

By the induction hypothesis, then

$$\sum_{i=1}^{n} i = n + \frac{(n-1)n}{2},$$

which we can simplify as

$$n + \frac{(n-1)n}{2} = \frac{2n + n^2 - n}{2} = \frac{n^2 + n}{2} = \frac{n(n+1)}{2}.$$

■

We may sometimes feel overwhelmed by the task of justifying something true for *all* $n \geq 1$. We should remember, however, the concreteness of the inductive technique. It shows that, for any particular n, there is a finite step-by-step sequence of implications that starts with something true and leads to the truth about n. In short, the inductive argument is a formula for building a sequence of direct justifications.

Loop Invariants

The final justification technique we discuss in this section is the **loop invariant**. To prove some statement S about a loop is correct, define S in terms of a series of smaller statements $S_0, S_1, \ldots, S_k$, where:

1. The **initial** claim, S_0, is true before the loop begins.
2. If S_{i-1} is true before iteration i, then S_i will be true after iteration i.
3. The final statement, S_k, implies the statement S that we wish to be true.

Let us give a simple example of using a loop-invariant argument to justify the correctness of an algorithm. In particular, let us consider using a loop invariant to justify the correctness of arrayFind, shown in Code Fragment 4.5, for finding an element x in an array A.

Algorithm arrayFind(x, A):
    Input: An element x and an n-element array, A.
    Output: The index i such that $x = A[i]$ or -1 if no element of A is equal to x.
    $i \leftarrow 0$
    while $i < n$ **do**
      if $x = A[i]$ **then**
        return i
      else
        $i \leftarrow i + 1$
    return -1

Code Fragment 4.5: Algorithm arrayFind for finding a given element in an array.

To show that arrayFind is correct, we inductively define a series of statements, S_i, that lead to the correctness of our algorithm. Specifically, we claim the following is true at the beginning of iteration i of the **while** loop:

    S_i: x is not equal to any of the first i elements of A.

This claim is true at the beginning of the first iteration of the loop, since there are no elements among the first 0 in A (this kind of a trivially true claim is said to hold **vacuously**). In iteration i, we compare element x to element $A[i]$ and return the index i if these two elements are equal, which is clearly correct and completes the algorithm in this case. If the two elements x and $A[i]$ are not equal, then we have found one more element not equal to x and we increment the index i. Thus, the claim S_i will be true for this new value of i; hence, it is true at the beginning of the next iteration. If the while-loop terminates without ever returning an index in A, then we have $i = n$. That is, S_n is true—there are no elements of A equal to x. Therefore, the algorithm correctly returns -1 to indicate that x is not in A.

4.4 Exercises

For help with exercises, please visit the web site, www.wiley.com/college/goodrich.

Reinforcement

R-4.1 There is a well-known city (which will go nameless here) whose inhabitants have the reputation of enjoying a meal only if that meal is the best they have ever experienced in their life. Otherwise, they hate it. Assuming meal quality is distributed uniformly across a person's life, what is the expected number of times inhabitants of this city are happy with their meals?

R-4.2 Give a pseudo-code description of the $O(n)$-time algorithm for computing the power function $p(x,n)$. Also, draw the recursion trace of this algorithm for the computation of $p(2,5)$.

R-4.3 Give a Java description of Algorithm Power for computing the power function $p(x,n)$ (Code Fragment 4.4).

R-4.4 Draw the recursion trace of the Power algorithm (Code Fragment 4.4, which computes the power function $p(x,n)$) for computing $p(2,9)$.

R-4.5 Analyze the running time of Algorithm BinarySum (Code Fragment 3.34) for arbitrary values of the input parameter n.

R-4.6 Graph the functions $8n$, $4n\log n$, $2n^2$, n^3, and 2^n using a logarithmic scale for the x- and y-axes , that is, if the function value $f(n)$ is y, plot this as a point with x-coordinate at $\log n$ and y-coordinate at $\log y$.

R-4.7 The number of operations executed by algorithms A and B is $8n\log n$ and $2n^2$, respectively. Determine n_0 such that A is better than B for $n \geq n_0$.

R-4.8 The number of operations executed by algorithms A and B is $40n^2$ and $2n^3$, respectively. Determine n_0 such that A is better than B for $n \geq n_0$.

R-4.9 Give an example of a function that is plotted the same on a log-log scale as it is on a standard scale.

R-4.10 Explain why the plot of the function n^c is a straight line with slope c on a log-log scale.

R-4.11 What is the sum of all the even numbers from 0 to $2n$, for any positive integer n?

R-4.12 Show that the following two statements are equivalent:
(a) The running time of algorithm A is always $O(f(n))$.
(b) In the worst case, the running time of algorithm A is $O(f(n))$.

R-4.13 Order the following functions by asymptotic growth rate.

$$4n \log n + 2n \quad 2^{10} \quad 2^{\log n}$$
$$3n + 100 \log n \quad 4n \quad 2^n$$
$$n^2 + 10n \quad n^3 \quad n \log n$$

R-4.14 Show that if $d(n)$ is $O(f(n))$, then $ad(n)$ is $O(f(n))$, for any constant $a > 0$.

R-4.15 Show that if $d(n)$ is $O(f(n))$ and $e(n)$ is $O(g(n))$, then the product $d(n)e(n)$ is $O(f(n)g(n))$.

R-4.16 Give a big-Oh characterization, in terms of n, of the running time of the Ex1 method shown in Code Fragment 4.6.

R-4.17 Give a big-Oh characterization, in terms of n, of the running time of the Ex2 method shown in Code Fragment 4.6.

R-4.18 Give a big-Oh characterization, in terms of n, of the running time of the Ex3 method shown in Code Fragment 4.6.

R-4.19 Give a big-Oh characterization, in terms of n, of the running time of the Ex4 method shown in Code Fragment 4.6.

R-4.20 Give a big-Oh characterization, in terms of n, of the running time of the Ex5 method shown in Code Fragment 4.6.

R-4.21 Bill has an algorithm, find2D, to find an element x in an $n \times n$ array A. The algorithm find2D iterates over the rows of A, and calls the algorithm arrayFind, of Code Fragment 4.5, on each row, until x is found or it has searched all rows of A. What is the worst-case running time of find2D in terms of n? What is the worst-case running time of find2D in terms of N, where N is the total size of A? Would it be correct to say that Find2D is a linear-time algorithm? Why or why not?

R-4.22 For each function $f(n)$ and time t in the following table, determine the largest size n of a problem P that can be solved in time t if the algorithm for solving P takes $f(n)$ microseconds (one entry is already completed).

	1 Second	1 Hour	1 Month	1 Century
$\log n$	$\approx 10^{300000}$			
n				
$n \log n$				
n^2				
2^n				

R-4.23 Show that if $d(n)$ is $O(f(n))$ and $e(n)$ is $O(g(n))$, then $d(n) + e(n)$ is $O(f(n) + g(n))$.

Algorithm Ex1(A):
   Input: An array A storing $n \geq 1$ integers.
   Output: The sum of the elements in A.
  $s \leftarrow A[0]$
  for $i \leftarrow 1$ **to** $n-1$ **do**
    $s \leftarrow s + A[i]$
  return s

Algorithm Ex2(A):
   Input: An array A storing $n \geq 1$ integers.
   Output: The sum of the elements at even cells in A.
  $s \leftarrow A[0]$
  for $i \leftarrow 2$ **to** $n-1$ **by** increments of 2 **do**
    $s \leftarrow s + A[i]$
  return s

Algorithm Ex3(A):
   Input: An array A storing $n \geq 1$ integers.
   Output: The sum of the prefix sums in A.
  $s \leftarrow 0$
  for $i \leftarrow 0$ **to** $n-1$ **do**
    $s \leftarrow s + A[0]$
    for $j \leftarrow 1$ **to** i **do**
      $s \leftarrow s + A[j]$
  return s

Algorithm Ex4(A):
   Input: An array A storing $n \geq 1$ integers.
   Output: The sum of the prefix sums in A.
  $s \leftarrow A[0]$
  $t \leftarrow s$
  for $i \leftarrow 1$ **to** $n-1$ **do**
    $s \leftarrow s + A[i]$
    $t \leftarrow t + s$
  return t

Algorithm Ex5(A, B):
   Input: Arrays A and B each storing $n \geq 1$ integers.
   Output: The number of elements in B equal to the sum of prefix sums in A.
  $c \leftarrow 0$
  for $i \leftarrow 0$ **to** $n-1$ **do**
    $s \leftarrow 0$
    for $j \leftarrow 0$ **to** $n-1$ **do**
      $s \leftarrow s + A[0]$
      for $k \leftarrow 1$ **to** j **do**
        $s \leftarrow s + A[k]$
    if $B[i] = s$ **then**
      $c \leftarrow c + 1$
  return c

Code Fragment 4.6: Some algorithms.

R-4.24 Show that if $d(n)$ is $O(f(n))$ and $e(n)$ is $O(g(n))$, then $d(n) - e(n)$ is **not necessarily** $O(f(n) - g(n))$.

R-4.25 Show that if $d(n)$ is $O(f(n))$ and $f(n)$ is $O(g(n))$, then $d(n)$ is $O(g(n))$.

R-4.26 Show that $O(\max\{f(n), g(n)\}) = O(f(n) + g(n))$.

R-4.27 Show that $f(n)$ is $O(g(n))$ if and only if $g(n)$ is $\Omega(f(n))$.

R-4.28 Show that if $p(n)$ is a polynomial in n, then $\log p(n)$ is $O(\log n)$.

R-4.29 Show that $(n+1)^5$ is $O(n^5)$.

R-4.30 Show that 2^{n+1} is $O(2^n)$.

R-4.31 Show that n is $O(n \log n)$.

R-4.32 Show that n^2 is $\Omega(n \log n)$.

R-4.33 Show that $n \log n$ is $\Omega(n)$.

R-4.34 Show that $\lceil f(n) \rceil$ is $O(f(n))$, if $f(n)$ is a positive nondecreasing function that is always greater than 1.

R-4.35 Algorithm A executes an $O(\log n)$-time computation for each entry of an n-element array. What is the worst-case running time of Algorithm A?

R-4.36 Given an n-element array X, Algorithm B chooses $\log n$ elements in X at random and executes an $O(n)$-time calculation for each. What is the worst-case running time of Algorithm B?

R-4.37 Given an n-element array X of integers, Algorithm C executes an $O(n)$-time computation for each even number in X, and an $O(\log n)$-time computation for each odd number in X. What are the best-case and worst-case running times of Algorithm C?

R-4.38 Given an n-element array X, Algorithm D calls Algorithm E on each element $X[i]$. Algorithm E runs in $O(i)$ time when it is called on element $X[i]$. What is the worst-case running time of Algorithm D?

R-4.39 Al and Bob are arguing about their algorithms. Al claims his $O(n \log n)$-time method is *always* faster than Bob's $O(n^2)$-time method. To settle the issue, they perform a set of experiments. To Al's dismay, they find that if $n < 100$, the $O(n^2)$-time algorithm runs faster, and only when $n \geq 100$ is the $O(n \log n)$-time one better. Explain how this is possible.

Creativity

C-4.1 Describe a recursive algorithm to compute the integer part of the base-two logarithm of n using only addition and integer division.

C-4.2 Describe an efficient recursive method for solving the element uniqueness problem, which runs in time that is at most $O(n^2)$ in the worst case without using sorting.

C-4.3 Assuming it is possible to sort n numbers in $O(n \log n)$ time, show that it is possible to solve the three-way set disjointness problem in $O(n \log n)$ time.

C-4.4 Describe an efficient algorithm for finding the ten largest elements in an array of size n. What is the running time of your algorithm?

C-4.5 Suppose you are given an n-element array A containing distinct integers that are listed in increasing order. Given a number k, describe a recursive algorithm to find two integers in A that sum to k, if such a pair exists. What is the running time of your algorithm?

C-4.6 Given an n-element unsorted array A of n integers and an integer k, describe a recursive algorithm for rearranging the elements in A so that all elements less than or equal to k come before any elements larger than k. What is the running time of your algorithm?

C-4.7 Communication security is extremely important in computer networks, and one way many network protocols achieve security is to encrypt messages. Typical *cryptographic* schemes for the secure transmission of messages over such networks are based on the fact that no efficient algorithms are known for factoring large integers. Hence, if we can represent a secret message by a large prime number p, we can transmit, over the network, the number $r = p \cdot q$, where $q > p$ is another large prime number that acts as the *encryption key*. An eavesdropper who obtains the transmitted number r on the network would have to factor r in order to figure out the secret message p.

Using factoring to figure out a message is very difficult without knowing the encryption key q. To understand why, consider the following naive factoring algorithm:

> **for** $p = 2, \cdots, r-1$ **do**
>   **if** p divides r **then**
>   **return** "The secret message is p!"

  a. Suppose that the eavesdropper uses the above algorithm and has a computer that can carry out in 1 microsecond (1 millionth of a second) a division between two integers of up to 100 bits each. Give an estimate of the time that it will take in the worst case to decipher the secret message p if the transmitted message r has 100 bits.

  b. What is the worst-case time complexity of the above algorithm? Since the input to the algorithm is just one large number r, assume that the input size n is the number of bytes needed to store r, that is, $n = \lfloor (\log_2 r)/8 \rfloor + 1$, and that each division takes time $O(n)$.

C-4.8 Give an example of a positive function $f(n)$ such that $f(n)$ is neither $O(n)$ nor $\Omega(n)$.

C-4.9   Show that $\sum_{i=1}^{n} i^2$ is $O(n^3)$.

C-4.10   Show that $\sum_{i=1}^{n} i/2^i < 2$.   (Hint: Try to bound this sum term by term with a geometric progression.)

C-4.11   Show that $\log_b f(n)$ is $\Theta(\log f(n))$ if $b > 1$ is a constant.

C-4.12   Describe a method for finding both the minimum and maximum of n numbers using fewer than $3n/2$ comparisons.   (Hint: First construct a group of candidate minimums and a group of candidate maximums.)

C-4.13   Bob built a Web site and gave the URL only to his n friends, which he numbered from 1 to n. He told friend number i that he/she can visit the Web site at most i times. Now Bob has a counter, C, keeping track of the total number of visits to the site (but not the identities of who visits). What is the minimum value for C such that Bob should know that one of his friends has visited his/her maximum allowed number of times?

C-4.14   Al says he can prove that all sheep in a flock are the same color:

Base case: One sheep. It is clearly the same color as itself.

Induction step: A flock of n sheep. Take a sheep, a, out. The remaining $n - 1$ are all the same color by induction. Now put sheep a back in and take out a different sheep, b. By induction, the $n - 1$ sheep (now with a) are all the same color. Therefore, all the sheep in the flock are the same color.

What is wrong with Al's "justification"?

C-4.15   Consider the following "justification" that the Fibonacci function, $F(n)$ (see Proposition 4.20) is $O(n)$:

Base case $(n \leq 2)$: $F(1) = 1$ and $F(2) = 2$.

Induction step $(n > 2)$: Assume claim true for $n' < n$. Consider n. $F(n) = F(n-1) + F(n-2)$. By induction, $F(n-1)$ is $O(n-1)$ and $F(n-2)$ is $O(n-2)$. Then, $F(n)$ is $O((n-1) + (n-2))$, by the identity presented in Exercise R-4.23. Therefore, $F(n)$ is $O(n)$.

What is wrong with this "justification"?

C-4.16   Let $p(x)$ be a polynomial of degree n, that is, $p(x) = \sum_{i=0}^{n} a_i x^i$.

(a) Describe a simple $O(n^2)$ time method for computing $p(x)$.

(b) Now consider a rewriting of $p(x)$ as

$$p(x) = a_0 + x(a_1 + x(a_2 + x(a_3 + \cdots + x(a_{n-1} + xa_n)\cdots))),$$

which is known as ***Horner's method***. Using the big-Oh notation, characterize the number of arithmetic operations this method executes.

C-4.17   Consider the Fibonacci function, $F(n)$ (see Proposition 4.20). Show by induction that $F(n)$ is $\Omega((3/2)^n)$.

C-4.18 Given a set $A = \{a_1, a_2, \ldots, a_n\}$ of n integers, describe, in pseudo-code, an efficient method for computing each of partial sums $s_k = \sum_{i=1}^{k} a_i$, for $k = 1, 2, \ldots, n$. What is the running time of this method?

C-4.19 Draw a visual justification of Proposition 4.3 analogous to that of Figure 4.1(b) for the case when n is odd.

C-4.20 An array A contains $n - 1$ unique integers in the range $[0, n-1]$, that is, there is one number from this range that is not in A. Design an $O(n)$-time algorithm for finding that number. You are only allowed to use $O(1)$ additional space besides the array A itself.

C-4.21 Let S be a set of n lines in the plane such that no two are parallel and no three meet in the same point. Show, by induction, that the lines in S determine $\Theta(n^2)$ intersection points.

C-4.22 Show that the summation $\sum_{i=1}^{n} \lceil \log_2 i \rceil$ is $O(n \log n)$.

C-4.23 An evil king has n bottles of wine, and a spy has just poisoned one of them. Unfortunately, they don't know which one it is. The poison is very deadly; just one drop diluted even a billion to one will still kill. Even so, it takes a full month for the poison to take effect. Design a scheme for determining exactly which one of the wine bottles was poisoned in just one month's time while expending $O(\log n)$ taste testers.

C-4.24 An array A contains n integers taken from the interval $[0, 4n]$, with repetitions allowed. Describe an efficient algorithm for determining an integer value k that occurs the most often in A. What is the running time of your algorithm?

C-4.25 Describe, in pseudo-code, a method for multiplying an $n \times m$ matrix A and an $m \times p$ matrix B. Recall that the product $C = AB$ is defined so that $C[i][j] = \sum_{k=1}^{m} A[i][k] \cdot B[k][j]$. What is the running time of your method?

C-4.26 Suppose each row of an $n \times n$ array A consists of 1's and 0's such that, in any row i of A, all the 1's come before any 0's. Also suppose that the number of 1's in row i is at least the number in row $i+1$, for $i = 0, 1, \ldots, n-2$. Assuming A is already in memory, describe a method running in $O(n)$ time (not $O(n^2)$) for counting the number of 1's in A.

C-4.27 Describe a recursive method for computing the nth **Harmonic number**, $H_n = \sum_{i=1}^{n} 1/i$.

Projects

P-4.1 Implement prefixAverages1 and prefixAverages2 from Section 4.2.5, and perform an experimental analysis of their running times. Visualize their running times as a function of the input size with a log-log chart.

P-4.2 Perform a careful experimental analysis that compares the relative running times of the methods shown in Code Fragments 4.6.

P-4.3 Perform an experimental analysis to test the hypothesis that the Java library method, java.util.Arrays.sort, runs in $O(n \log n)$ time on average.

P-4.4 Perform an experimental analysis to determine the largest value of n for each of the three algorithms given in the chapter for solving the element uniqueness problem such that the given algorithm runs in one minute or less.

Chapter Notes

The big-Oh notation has prompted several comments about its proper use [17, 45, 61]. Knuth [62, 61] defines it using the notation $f(n) = O(g(n))$, but says this "equality" is only "one way." We have chosen to take a more standard view of equality and view the big-Oh notation as a set, following Brassard [17]. The reader interested in studying average-case analysis is referred to the book chapter by Vitter and Flajolet [97]. We found the story about Archimedes in [77]. For some additional mathematical tools, please refer to Appendix A.

Chapter 5

Stacks, Queues, and Deques

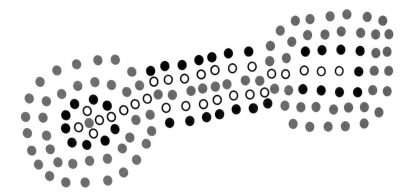

Contents

5.1   Stacks

A ***stack*** is a collection of objects that are inserted and removed according to the
last-in first-out (***LIFO***) principle. Objects can be inserted into a stack at any time,
but only the most recently inserted (that is, "last") object can be removed at any
time. The name "stack" is derived from the metaphor of a stack of plates in a
spring-loaded, cafeteria plate dispenser. In this case, the fundamental operations
involve the "pushing" and "popping" of plates on the stack. When we need a new
plate from the dispenser, we "pop" the top plate off the stack, and when we add
a plate, we "push" it down on the stack to become the new top plate. Perhaps an
even more amusing metaphor would be a PEZ® candy dispenser, which stores mint
candies in a spring-loaded container that "pops" out the top-most candy in the stack
when the top of the dispenser is lifted. (See Figure 5.1.) Stacks are a fundamental
data structure. They are used in many applications, including the following.

Figure 5.1: A schematic drawing of a PEZ® dispenser; a physical implementation
of the stack ADT. (PEZ® is a registered trademark of PEZ Candy, Inc.)

Example 5.1: *Internet Web browsers store the addresses of recently visited sites
on a stack. Each time a user visits a new site, that site's address is "pushed" onto the
stack of addresses. The browser then allows the user to "pop" back to previously
visited sites using the "back" button.*

Example 5.2: *Text editors usually provide an "undo" mechanism that cancels recent editing operations and reverts to former states of a document. This undo operation can be accomplished by keeping text changes in a stack.*

5.1.1 The Stack Abstract Data Type

Stacks are the simplest of all data structures, yet they are also among the most important, as they are used in a host of different applications that include many more sophisticated data structures. Formally, a stack is an abstract data type (ADT) that supports the following two methods:

> push(e): Insert element e, to be the top of the stack.
>
> pop(): Remove from the stack and return the top element on the stack; an error occurs if the stack is empty.

Additionally, let us also define the following methods:

> size(): Return the number of elements in the stack.
>
> isEmpty(): Return a Boolean indicating if the stack is empty.
>
> top(): Return the top element in the stack, without removing it; an error occurs if the stack is empty.

Example 5.3: *The following table shows a series of stack operations and their effects on an initially empty stack S of integers.*

Operation	Output	Stack Contents
push(5)	–	(5)
push(3)	–	(5,3)
pop()	3	(5)
push(7)	–	(5,7)
pop()	7	(5)
top()	5	(5)
pop()	5	()
pop()	"error"	()
isEmpty()	true	()
push(9)	–	(9)
push(7)	–	(9,7)
push(3)	–	(9,7,3)
push(5)	–	(9,7,3,5)
size()	4	(9,7,3,5)
pop()	5	(9,7,3)
push(8)	–	(9,7,3,8)
pop()	8	(9,7,3)
pop()	3	(9,7)

A Stack Interface in Java

Because of its importance, the stack data structure is included as a "built-in" class in the java.util package of Java. Class java.util.Stack is a data structure that stores generic Java objects and includes, among others, the methods push(), pop(), peek() (equivalent to top()), size(), and empty() (equivalent to isEmpty()). Methods pop() and peek() throw exception EmptyStackException if they are called on an empty stack. While it is convenient to just use the built-in class java.util.Stack, it is instructive to learn how to design and implement a stack "from scratch."

Implementing an abstract data type in Java involves two steps. The first step is the definition of a Java *Application Programming Interface* (API), or simply *interface*, which describes the names of the methods that the ADT supports and how they are to be declared and used.

In addition, we must define exceptions for any error conditions that can arise. For instance, the error condition that occurs when calling method pop() or top() on an empty stack is signaled by throwing an exception of type EmptyStackException, which is defined in Code Fragment 5.1.

```
/**
 * Runtime exception thrown when one tries to perform operation top or
 * pop on an empty stack.
 */

public class EmptyStackException extends RuntimeException {
  public EmptyStackException(String err) {
    super(err);
  }
}
```

Code Fragment 5.1: Exception thrown by methods pop() and top() of the Stack interface when called on an empty stack.

A complete Java interface for the stack ADT is given in Code Fragment 5.2. Note that this interface is very general since it specifies that elements of any given class (and its subclasses) can be inserted into the stack. It achieves this generality by using the concept of *generics* (Section 2.5.2).

For a given ADT to be of any use, we need to provide a concrete class that implements the methods of the interface associated with that ADT. We give a simple implementation of the Stack interface in the following subsection.

```
/**
 * Interface for a stack: a collection of objects that are inserted
 * and removed according to the last-in first-out principle.  This
 * interface includes the main methods of java.util.Stack.
 *
 * @author Roberto Tamassia
 * @author Michael Goodrich
 * @see EmptyStackException
 */
public interface Stack<E> {
  /**
   * Return the number of elements in the stack.
   * @return number of elements in the stack.
   */
  public int size();
  /**
   * Return whether the stack is empty.
   * @return true if the stack is empty, false otherwise.
   */
  public boolean isEmpty();
  /**
   * Inspect the element at the top of the stack.
   * @return top element in the stack.
   * @exception EmptyStackException if the stack is empty.
   */
  public E top()
    throws EmptyStackException;
  /**
   * Insert an element at the top of the stack.
   * @param element to be inserted.
   */
  public void push (E element);
  /**
   * Remove the top element from the stack.
   * @return element removed.
   * @exception EmptyStackException if the stack is empty.
   */
  public E pop()
    throws EmptyStackException;
}
```

Code Fragment 5.2: Interface Stack documented with comments in Javadoc style (Section 1.9.3). Note also the use of the generic parameterized type, E, which implies that a stack can contain elements of any specified class.

5.1.2 A Simple Array-Based Stack Implementation

We can implement a stack by storing its elements in an array. Specifically, the stack in this implementation consists of an N-element array S plus an integer variable t that gives the the index of the top element in array S. (See Figure 5.2.)

Figure 5.2: Implementing a stack with an array S. The top element in the stack is stored in the cell $S[t]$.

Recalling that arrays start at index 0 in Java, we initialize t to -1, and we use this value for t to identify an empty stack. Likewise, we can use t to determine the number of elements $(t + 1)$. We also introduce a new exception, called FullStackException, to signal the error that arises if we try to insert a new element into a full array. Exception FullStackException is specific to this implementation and is not defined in the stack ADT, however. We give the details of the array-based stack implementation in Code Fragment 5.3.

Algorithm size():
  return $t + 1$
Algorithm isEmpty():
  return $(t < 0)$
Algorithm top():
  if isEmpty() **then**
    throw a EmptyStackException
  return $S[t]$
Algorithm push(e):
  if size() $= N$ **then**
    throw a FullStackException
  $t \leftarrow t + 1$
  $S[t] \leftarrow e$
Algorithm pop():
  if isEmpty() **then**
    throw a EmptyStackException
  $e \leftarrow S[t]$.
  $S[t] \leftarrow$ **null**
  $t \leftarrow t - 1$
  return e

Code Fragment 5.3: Implementing a stack using an array of a given size, N.

Analyzing the Array-Based Stack Implementation

The correctness of the methods in the array-based implementation follows immediately from the definition of the methods themselves. There is, nevertheless, a
mildly interesting point here involving the implementation of the pop method.

Note that we could have avoided resetting the old $S[t]$ to **null** and we would still
have a correct method. There is a trade-off in being able to avoid this assignment
should we be thinking about implementing these algorithms in Java, however. The
trade-off involves the Java *garbage collection* mechanism that searches memory for
objects that are no longer referenced by active objects, and reclaims their space for
future use. (For more details, see Section 14.1.3.) Let $e = S[t]$ be the top element
before the pop method is called. By making $S[t]$ a null reference, we indicate that
the stack no longer needs to hold a reference to object e. Indeed, if there are no
other active references to e, then the memory space taken by e will be reclaimed by
the garbage collector.

Table 5.1 shows the running times for methods in a realization of a stack by an
array. Each of the stack methods in the array realization executes a constant number
of statements involving arithmetic operations, comparisons, and assignments. In
addition, pop also calls isEmpty, which itself runs in constant time. Thus, in this
implementation of the stack ADT, each method runs in constant time, that is, they
each run in $O(1)$ time.

Method	Time
size	$O(1)$
isEmpty	$O(1)$
top	$O(1)$
push	$O(1)$
pop	$O(1)$

Table 5.1: Performance of a stack realized by an array. The space usage is $O(N)$,
where N is the size of the array, determined at the time the stack is instantiated.
Note that the space usage is independent from the number $n \le N$ of elements that
are actually in the stack.

A concrete Java implementation of the pseudo-code of Code Fragment 5.3,
with Java class ArrayStack implementing the Stack interface, is given in Code
Fragments 5.4 and 5.5. Unfortunately, due to space considerations, we omit most
Javadoc comments for this and most other Java code fragments presented in the
remainder of this book. Note that we use a symbolic name, CAPACITY, to specify
the capacity of the array. This allows us to specify the capacity of the array in one
place in our code and have that value reflected throughout.

```java
/**
 * Implementation of the stack ADT using a fixed-length array. An
 * exception is thrown if a push operation is attempted when the size
 * of the stack is equal to the length of the array.  This class
 * includes the main methods of the built-in class java.util.Stack.
 */
public class ArrayStack<E> implements Stack<E> {
  protected int capacity;        // The actual capacity of the stack array
  public static final int CAPACITY = 1000; // default array capacity
  protected E S[];               // Generic array used to implement the stack
  protected int top = -1;        // index for the top of the stack
  public ArrayStack() {
    this(CAPACITY); // default capacity
  }
  public ArrayStack(int cap) {
    capacity = cap;
    S = (E[]) new Object[capacity]; // compiler may give warning, but this is ok
  }
  public int size() {
    return (top + 1);
  }
  public boolean isEmpty() {
    return (top < 0);
  }
  public void push(E element) throws FullStackException {
    if (size() == capacity)
      throw new FullStackException("Stack is full.");
    S[++top] = element;
  }
  public E top() throws EmptyStackException {
    if (isEmpty())
      throw new EmptyStackException("Stack is empty.");
    return S[top];
    }
  public E pop() throws EmptyStackException {
    E element;
    if (isEmpty())
      throw new EmptyStackException("Stack is empty.");
    element = S[top];
    S[top--] = null; // dereference S[top] for garbage collection.
    return element;
  }
```

Code Fragment 5.4: Array-based Java implementation of the Stack interface. (Continues in Code Fragment 5.5.)

```
public String toString() {
  String s;
  s = "[";
  if (size() > 0) s+= S[0];
  if (size() > 1)
    for (int i = 1; i <= size()−1; i++) {
      s += ", " + S[i];
    }
  return s + "]";
}
// Prints status information about a recent operation and the stack.
public void status(String op, Object element) {
  System.out.print("-----> " + op); // print this operation
  System.out.println(", returns " + element); // what was returned
  System.out.print("result: size = " + size() + ", isEmpty = " + isEmpty());
  System.out.println(", stack: " + this);    // contents of the stack
}
/**
 * Test our program by performing a series of operations on stacks,
 * printing the operations performed, the returned elements and the
 * contents of the stack involved, after each operation.
 */
public static void main(String[] args) {
  Object o;
  ArrayStack<Integer> A = new ArrayStack<Integer>();
  A.status("new ArrayStack<Integer> A", null);
  A.push(7);
  A.status("A.push(7)", null);
  o = A.pop();
  A.status("A.pop()", o);
  A.push(9);
  A.status("A.push(9)", null);
  o = A.pop();
  A.status("A.pop()", o);
  ArrayStack<String> B = new ArrayStack<String>();
  B.status("new ArrayStack<String> B", null);
  B.push("Bob");
  B.status("B.push(\"Bob\")", null);
  B.push("Alice");
  B.status("B.push(\"Alice\")", null);
  o = B.pop();
  B.status("B.pop()", o);
  B.push("Eve");
  B.status("B.push(\"Eve\")", null);
  }
}
```

Code Fragment 5.5: Array-based Stack. (Continued from Code Fragment 5.4.)

Example Output

Below, we show the output from the above ArrayStack program. Note that, through the use of generic types, we are able to create an ArrayStack A for storing integers and another ArrayStack B that stores character strings.

```
------> new ArrayStack<Integer> A, returns null
result: size = 0, isEmpty = true, stack: []
------> A.push(7), returns null
result: size = 1, isEmpty = false, stack: [7]
------> A.pop(), returns 7
result: size = 0, isEmpty = true, stack: []
------> A.push(9), returns null
result: size = 1, isEmpty = false, stack: [9]
------> A.pop(), returns 9
result: size = 0, isEmpty = true, stack: []
------> new ArrayStack<String> B, returns null
result: size = 0, isEmpty = true, stack: []
------> B.push("Bob"), returns null
result: size = 1, isEmpty = false, stack: [Bob]
------> B.push("Alice"), returns null
result: size = 2, isEmpty = false, stack: [Bob, Alice]
------> B.pop(), returns Alice
result: size = 1, isEmpty = false, stack: [Bob]
------> B.push("Eve"), returns null
result: size = 2, isEmpty = false, stack: [Bob, Eve]
```

A Drawback with the Array-Based Stack Implementation

The array implementation of a stack is simple and efficient. Nevertheless, this implementation has one negative aspect—it must assume a fixed upper bound, CAPACITY, on the ultimate size of the stack. In Code Fragment 5.4, we chose the capacity value 1,000 more or less arbitrarily. An application may actually need much less space than this, which would waste memory. Alternatively, an application may need more space than this, which would cause our stack implementation to generate an exception as soon as a client program tries to push its 1,001st object on the stack. Thus, even with its simplicity and efficiency, the array-based stack implementation is not necessarily ideal.

Fortunately, there is another implementation, which we discuss next, that does not have a size limitation and use space proportional to the actual number of elements stored in the stack. Still, in cases where we have a good estimate on the number of items needing to go in the stack, the array-based implementation is hard to beat. Stacks serve a vital role in a number of computing applications, so it is helpful to have a fast stack ADT implementation such as the simple array-based implementation.

5.1.3 Implementing a Stack with a Generic Linked List

In this section, we explore using a singly linked list to implement the stack ADT. In designing such an implementation, we need to decide if the top of the stack is at the head or at the tail of the list. There is clearly a best choice here, however, since we can insert and delete elements in constant time only at the head. Thus, it is more efficient to have the top of the stack at the head of our list. Also, in order to perform operation size in constant time, we keep track of the current number of elements in an instance variable.

Rather than use a linked list that can only store objects of a certain type, as we showed in Section 3.2, we would like, in this case, to implement a generic stack using a *generic* linked list. Thus, we need to use a generic kind of node to implement this linked list. We show such a Node class in Code Fragment 5.6.

```java
public class Node<E> {
  // Instance variables:
  private E element;
  private Node<E> next;
  /** Creates a node with null references to its element and next node. */
  public Node() {
    this(null, null);
  }
  /** Creates a node with the given element and next node. */
  public Node(E e, Node<E> n) {
    element = e;
    next = n;
  }
  // Accessor methods:
  public E getElement() {
    return element;
  }
  public Node<E> getNext() {
    return next;
  }
  // Modifier methods:
  public void setElement(E newElem) {
    element = newElem;
  }
  public void setNext(Node<E> newNext) {
    next = newNext;
  }
}
```

Code Fragment 5.6: Class Node, which implements a generic node for a singly linked list.

A Generic NodeStack Class

A Java implementation of a stack, by means of a generic singly linked list, is given in Code Fragment 5.7. All the methods of the Stack interface are executed in constant time. In addition to being time efficient, this linked list implementation has a space requirement that is $O(n)$, where n is the current number of elements in the stack. Thus, this implementation does not require that a new exception be created to handle size overflow problems. We use an instance variable top to refer to the head of the list (which points to the **null** object if the list is empty). When we push a new element e on the stack, we simply create a new node v for e, reference e from v, and insert v at the head of the list. Likewise, when we pop an element from the stack, we simply remove the node at the head of the list and return its element. Thus, we perform all insertions and removals of elements at the head of the list.

```java
public class NodeStack<E> implements Stack<E> {
  protected Node<E> top;      // reference to the head node
  protected int size;           // number of elements in the stack
  public NodeStack() { // constructs an empty stack
    top = null;
    size = 0;
  }
  public int size() { return size; }
  public boolean isEmpty() {
    if (top == null) return true;
    return false;
  }
  public void push(E elem) {
    Node<E> v = new Node<E>(elem, top); // create and link-in a new node
    top = v;
    size++;
  }
  public E top() throws EmptyStackException {
    if (isEmpty()) throw new EmptyStackException("Stack is empty.");
    return top.getElement();
  }
  public E pop() throws EmptyStackException {
    if (isEmpty()) throw new EmptyStackException("Stack is empty.");
    E temp = top.getElement();
    top = top.getNext();        // link-out the former top node
    size--;
    return temp;
  }
}
```

Code Fragment 5.7: Class NodeStack, which implements the Stack interface using a singly linked list, whose nodes are objects of class Node from Code Fragment 5.6.

5.1.4   Reversing an Array Using a Stack

We can use a stack to reverse the elements in an array, thereby producing a nonre-cursive algorithm for the array-reversal problem introduced in Section 3.5.1. The basic idea is simply to push all the elements of the array in order into a stack and then fill the array back up again by popping the elements off of the stack. In Code Fragment 5.8, we give a Java implementation of this algorithm. Incidentally, this method also illustrates how we can use generic types in a simple application that uses a generic stack. In particular, when the elements are popped off the stack in this example, they are automatically returned as elements of the E type; hence, they can be immediately returned to the input array. We show an example use of this method in Code Fragment 5.9.

```java
/** A nonrecursive generic method for reversing an array */
public static <E> void reverse(E[] a) {
  Stack<E> S = new ArrayStack<E>(a.length);
  for (int i=0; i < a.length; i++)
    S.push(a[i]);
  for (int i=0; i < a.length; i++)
    a[i] = S.pop();
}
```

Code Fragment 5.8: A generic method that reverses the elements in an array of type E objects, using a stack declared using the Stack<E> interface.

```java
/** Tester routine for reversing arrays */
public static void main(String args[]) {
  Integer[] a = {4, 8, 15, 16, 23, 42}; // autoboxing allows this
  String[] s = {"Jack", "Kate", "Hurley", "Jin", "Boone"};
  System.out.println("a = " + Arrays.toString(a));
  System.out.println("s = " + Arrays.toString(s));
  System.out.println("Reversing...");
  reverse(a);
  reverse(s);
  System.out.println("a = " + Arrays.toString(a));
  System.out.println("s = " + Arrays.toString(s));
}
```

The output from this method is the following:
```
a = [4, 8, 15, 16, 23, 42]
s = [Jack, Kate, Hurley, Jin, Michael]
Reversing...
a = [42, 23, 16, 15, 8, 4]
s = [Michael, Jin, Hurley, Kate, Jack]
```

Code Fragment 5.9: A test of the reverse method using two arrays.

5.1.5   Matching Parentheses and HTML Tags

In this subsection, we explore two related applications of stacks, the first of which is for matching parentheses and grouping symbols in arithmetic expressions.

Arithmetic expressions can contain various pairs of grouping symbols, such as

- Parentheses: "(" and ")"
- Braces: "{" and "}"
- Brackets: "[" and "]"
- Floor function symbols: "⌊" and "⌋"
- Ceiling function symbols: "⌈" and "⌉,"

and each opening symbol must match with its corresponding closing symbol. For example, a left bracket, "[," must match with a corresponding right bracket, "]," as in the following expression:

$$[(5+x)-(y+z)].$$

The following examples further illustrate this concept:

- Correct: ()(()){([()])}
- Correct: ((()(()){([()])}))
- Incorrect:)(()){([()])}
- Incorrect: ({[])}
- Incorrect: (.

We leave the precise definition of matching of grouping symbols to Exercise R-5.7.

An Algorithm for Parentheses Matching

An important problem in processing arithmetic expressions is to make sure their grouping symbols match up correctly. We can use a stack S to perform the matching of grouping symbols in an arithmetic expression with a single left-to-right scan. The algorithm tests that left and right symbols match up and also that the left and right symbols are both of the same type.

Suppose we are given a sequence $X = x_0 x_1 x_2 \ldots x_{n-1}$, where each x_i is a **token** that can be a grouping symbol, a variable name, an arithmetic operator, or a number. The basic idea behind checking that the grouping symbols in S match correctly, is to process the tokens in X in order. Each time we encounter an opening symbol, we push that symbol onto S, and each time we encounter a closing symbol, we pop the top symbol from the stack S (assuming S is not empty) and we check that these two symbols are of the same type. If the stack is empty after we have processed the whole sequence, then the symbols in X match. Assuming that the push and pop operations are implemented to run in constant time, this algorithm runs in $O(n)$, that is, linear, time. We give a pseudo-code description of this algorithm in Code Fragment 5.10.

Algorithm ParenMatch(X,n):

> *Input:* An array X of n tokens, each of which is either a grouping symbol, a variable, an arithmetic operator, or a number
>
> *Output:* **true** if and only if all the grouping symbols in X match
>
> Let S be an empty stack
> **for** $i \leftarrow 0$ to $n-1$ **do**
> > **if** $X[i]$ is an opening grouping symbol **then**
> > > S.push($X[i]$)
> >
> > **else if** $X[i]$ is a closing grouping symbol **then**
> > > **if** S.isEmpty() **then**
> > > > **return false**   {nothing to match with}
> > >
> > > **if** S.pop() does not match the type of $X[i]$ **then**
> > > > **return false**   {wrong type}
> >
> **if** S.isEmpty() **then**
> > **return true**   {every symbol matched}
> **else**
> > **return false**   {some symbols were never matched}

Code Fragment 5.10: Algorithm for matching grouping symbols in an arithmetic expression.

Matching Tags in an HTML Document

Another application in which matching is important is in the validation of HTML documents. HTML is the standard format for hyperlinked documents on the Internet. In an HTML document, portions of text are delimited by *HTML tags*. A simple opening HTML tag has the form "<name>" and the corresponding closing tag has the form "</name>." Commonly used HTML tags include

- body: document body
- h1: section header
- center: center justify
- p: paragraph
- ol: numbered (ordered) list
- li: list item.

Ideally, an HTML document should have matching tags, although most browsers tolerate a certain number of mismatching tags.

We show a sample HTML document and a possible rendering in Figure 5.3.

```
<body>
<center>
<h1> The Little Boat </h1>
</center>
<p> The storm tossed the little
boat like a cheap sneaker in an
old washing machine.  The three
drunken fishermen were used to
such treatment, of course, but
not the tree salesman, who even as
a stowaway now felt that he
had overpaid for the voyage. </p>
<ol>
<li> Will the salesman die? </li>
<li> What color is the boat? </li>
<li> And what about Naomi? </li>
</ol>
</body>
```

The Little Boat

The storm tossed the little boat like a cheap sneaker in an old washing machine. The three drunken fishermen were used to such treatment, of course, but not the tree salesman, who even as a stowaway now felt that he had overpaid for the voyage.

1. Will the salesman die?
2. What color is the boat?
3. And what about Naomi?

(a)   (b)

Figure 5.3: Illustrating HTML tags. (a) An HTML document; (b) its rendering.

Fortunately, more or less the same algorithm as in Code Fragment 5.10 can be used to match the tags in an HTML document. In Code Fragments 5.11 and 5.12, we give a Java program for matching tags in an HTML document read from standard input. For simplicity, we assume that all tags are the simple opening or closing tags defined above and that no tags are formed incorrectly.

```java
import java.io.*;
import java.util.Scanner;
import net.datastructures.*;
/** Simplified test of matching tags in an HTML document. */
public class HTML {
  /** Strip the first and last characters off a <tag> string. */
  public static String stripEnds(String t) {
    if (t.length() <= 2) return null;  // this is a degenerate tag
    return t.substring(1,t.length()−1);
  }
  /** Test if a stripped tag string is empty or a true opening tag. */
  public static boolean isOpeningTag(String tag) {
    return (tag.length() == 0) || (tag.charAt(0) != '/');
  }
}
```

Code Fragment 5.11: A complete Java program for testing if an HTML document has fully matching tags. (Continues in Code Fragment 5.12.)

```
/** Test if stripped tag1 matches closing tag2 (first character is '/'). */
public static boolean areMatchingTags(String tag1, String tag2) {
  return tag1.equals(tag2.substring(1)); // test against name after '/'
}
/** Test if every opening tag has a matching closing tag. */
public static boolean isHTMLMatched(String[] tag) {
  Stack<String> S = new NodeStack<String>(); // Stack for matching tags
  for (int i = 0; (i < tag.length) && (tag[i] != null); i++) {
    if (isOpeningTag(tag[i]))
      S.push(tag[i]); // opening tag; push it on the stack
    else {
      if (S.isEmpty())
        return false;          // nothing to match
      if (!areMatchingTags(S.pop(), tag[i]))
        return false;          // wrong match
    }
  }
  if (S.isEmpty()) return true; // we matched everything
  return false; // we have some tags that never were matched
}
public final static int CAPACITY = 1000; // Tag array size
/* Parse an HTML document into an array of html tags */
public static String[] parseHTML(Scanner s) {
  String[] tag = new String[CAPACITY]; // our tag array (initially all null)
  int count = 0;                        // tag counter
  String token;                         // token returned by the scanner s
  while (s.hasNextLine()) {
    while ((token = s.findInLine("<[^>]*>")) != null) // find the next tag
      tag[count++] = stripEnds(token); // strip the ends off this tag
    s.nextLine(); // go to the next line
  }
  return tag; // our array of (stripped) tags
}
public static void main(String[] args) throws IOException { // tester
  if (isHTMLMatched(parseHTML(new Scanner(System.in))))
    System.out.println("The input file is a matched HTML document.");
  else
    System.out.println("The input file is not a matched HTML document.");
}
}
```

Code Fragment 5.12: Java program for testing for matching tags in an HTML document. (Continued from 5.11.) Method isHTMLMatched uses a stack to store the names of the opening tags seen so far, similar to how the stack was used in Code Fragment 5.10. Method parseHTML uses a Scanner s to extract the tags from the HTML document, using the pattern "<[^ >]*>," which denotes a string that starts with '<', followed by zero or more characters that are not '>', followed by a '>'.

5.2 Queues

Another fundamental data structure is the **queue**. It is a close "cousin" of the stack, as a queue is a collection of objects that are inserted and removed according to the **first-in first-out** (**FIFO**) principle. That is, elements can be inserted at any time, but only the element that has been in the queue the longest can be removed at any time.

We usually say that elements enter a queue at the **rear** and are removed from the **front**. The metaphor for this terminology is a line of people waiting to get on an amusement park ride. People waiting for such a ride enter at the rear of the line and get on the ride from the front of the line.

5.2.1 The Queue Abstract Data Type

Formally, the queue abstract data type defines a collection that keeps objects in a sequence, where element access and deletion are restricted to the first element in the sequence, which is called the **front** of the queue, and element insertion is restricted to the end of the sequence, which is called the **rear** of the queue. This restriction enforces the rule that items are inserted and deleted in a queue according to the first-in first-out (FIFO) principle.

The **queue** abstract data type (ADT) supports the following two fundamental methods:

enqueue(e): Insert element e at the rear of the queue.

dequeue(): Remove and return from the queue the object at the front; an error occurs if the queue is empty.

Additionally, similar to the case with the stack ADT, the queue ADT includes the following supporting methods:

size(): Return the number of objects in the queue.

isEmpty(): Return a Boolean value that indicates whether the queue is empty.

front(): Return, but do not remove, the front object in the queue; an error occurs if the queue is empty.

Example 5.4: *The following table shows a series of queue operations and their effects on an initially empty queue Q of integer objects. For simplicity, we use integers instead of integer objects as arguments of the operations.*

Operation	Output	front ← Q ← rear
enqueue(5)	–	(5)
enqueue(3)	–	(5,3)
dequeue()	5	(3)
enqueue(7)	–	(3,7)
dequeue()	3	(7)
front()	7	(7)
dequeue()	7	()
isEmpty()	true	()
enqueue(9)	–	(9)
size()	1	(9)

There are several possible applications for queues. Stores, theaters, reservation centers, and other similar services typically process customer requests according to the FIFO principle. A queue would therefore be a logical choice for a data structure to handle calls to the reservation center of the box office of a theater.

The java.util.Queue Interface in Java

Java provides a type of queue interface, java.util.Queue, which has functionality similar to the traditional queue ADT, given above, but the documentation for the java.util.Queue interface does not insist that it support only the FIFO principle. When supporting the FIFO principle, the methods of the java.util.Queue interface have the equivalences with the queue ADT shown in Table 5.2.

Queue ADT	Interface java.util.Queue
size()	size()
isEmpty()	isEmpty()
enqueue(e)	add(e) or offer(e)
dequeue()	remove() or poll()
front()	peek() or element()

Table 5.2: Methods of the queue ADT and corresponding methods of the interface java.util.Queue, when supporting the FIFO principle.

Concrete classes in Java that implement the java.util.Queue interface to support the FIFO principle include the following:

- java.util.concurrent.ArrayBlockingQueue
- java.util.concurrent.ConcurrentLinkedQueue
- java.util.concurrent.LinkedBlockingQueue

A FIFO Queue Interface in Java

A Java interface for the queue ADT is given in Code Fragment 5.13.

This generic interface specifies that objects of arbitrary object types can be inserted into the queue, and it uses a generic identifier, E, to refer to this arbitrary type. Thus, we don't have to use explicit casting when removing elements.

```java
public interface Queue<E> {
  /**
   * Returns the number of elements in the queue.
   * @return number of elements in the queue.
   */
  public int size();
  /**
   * Returns whether the queue is empty.
   * @return true if the queue is empty, false otherwise.
   */
  public boolean isEmpty();
  /**
   * Inspects the element at the front of the queue.
   * @return element at the front of the queue.
   * @exception EmptyQueueException if the queue is empty.
   */
  public E front() throws EmptyQueueException;
  /**
   * Inserts an element at the rear of the queue.
   * @param element new element to be inserted.
   */
  public void enqueue (E element);
  /**
   * Removes the element at the front of the queue.
   * @return element removed.
   * @exception EmptyQueueException if the queue is empty.
   */
  public E dequeue() throws EmptyQueueException;
}
```

Code Fragment 5.13: A Java interface, Queue, documented with comments in Javadoc style, which implements the queue ADT, with a standard FIFO protocol for insertions and removals.

Note that the size and isEmpty methods have the same meaning as their counterparts in the stack ADT. These two methods, as well as the front method, are known as *accessor* methods, for they return a value and do not change the contents of the data structure.

5.2.2 A Simple Array-Based Queue Implementation

Let us now consider how we could implement a queue using an array, Q, of fixed capacity, to store its elements. Since the main rule with the queue ADT is that we insert and delete objects according to the FIFO principle, we must decide how we are going to keep track of the front and rear of the queue. One possibility is to adapt the approach we used for the stack implementation, letting $Q[0]$ be the front of the queue and then letting the queue grow from there. This is not an efficient solution, however, for it requires that we move all the elements forward one array cell each time we perform a dequeue operation. Such an implementation would therefore take $O(n)$ time to perform the dequeue method, where n is the current number of objects in the queue. To avoid moving objects once they are placed in Q, we define two variables, f and r, which have the following meanings:

- f is an index to the cell of Q storing the first element of the queue (which is the next candidate to be removed by a dequeue operation), unless the queue is empty (in which case $f = r$).
- r is an index to the next available array cell in Q.

Initially, we assign $f = r = 0$, which indicates that the queue is empty. Now, when we remove an element from the front of the queue, we increment f to index the next cell. Likewise, when we add an element, we store it in cell $Q[r]$ and increment r to index the next available cell in Q. This scheme allows us to implement methods front, enqueue, and dequeue in constant time, that is, $O(1)$ time. However, there is still a problem with this approach.

Consider, for example, what happens if we repeatedly enqueue and dequeue a single element N different times. We would have $f = r = N$. If we were then to try to insert the element just one more time, we would get an array-out-of-bounds error, even though there is plenty of room in the array in this case. To be able to utilize all of the array Q, we let the f and r indices "wrap around" the end of Q. That is, we now view Q as a "circular array" that goes from $Q[0]$ to $Q[N-1]$ and then back to $Q[0]$ again. (See Figure 5.4.)

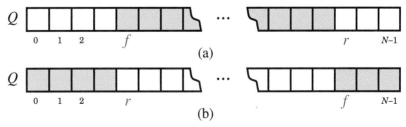

Figure 5.4: Using array Q in a circular fashion: (a) the "normal" configuration with $f \leq r$; (b) the "wrapped around" configuration with $r < f$.

Using the Modulo Operator to Implement a Circular Array

Implementing this circular view of Q is actually pretty easy. Each time we increment f or r, we compute this increment as "$(f+1)$ mod N" or "$(r+1)$ mod N," respectively.

Recall that operator "mod" is the ***modulo*** operator, which is computed by taking the remainder after an integral division. For example, 14 divided by 4 is 3 with remainder 2, so 14 mod 4 = 2. Specifically, given integers x and y such that $x \geq 0$ and $y > 0$, we have $x \bmod y = x - \lfloor x/y \rfloor y$. That is, if $r = x \bmod y$, then there is a nonnegative integer q, such that $x = qy + r$. Java uses "%" to denote the modulo operator. By using the modulo operator, we can view Q as a circular array and implement each queue method in a constant amount of time (that is, $O(1)$ time). We describe how to use this approach to implement a queue in Code Fragment 5.14.

Algorithm size():
    return $(N - f + r)$ mod N

Algorithm isEmpty():
    return $(f = r)$

Algorithm front():
    if isEmpty() **then**
       throw a EmptyQueueException
    return $Q[f]$

Algorithm dequeue():
    if isEmpty() **then**
       throw a EmptyQueueException
    $temp \leftarrow Q[f]$
    $Q[f] \leftarrow$ **null**
    $f \leftarrow (f+1)$ mod N
    return $temp$

Algorithm enqueue(e):
    if size() $= N - 1$ **then**
       throw a FullQueueException
    $Q[r] \leftarrow e$
    $r \leftarrow (r+1)$ mod N

Code Fragment 5.14: Implementation of a queue using a circular array. The implementation uses the modulo operator to "wrap" indices around the end of the array and it also includes two instance variables, f and r, which index the front of the queue and first empty cell after the rear of the queue respectively.

The implementation above contains an important detail, which might be missed at first. Consider the situation that occurs if we enqueue N objects into Q without dequeuing any of them. We would have $f = r$, which is the same condition that occurs when the queue is empty. Thus, we would not be able to tell the difference between a full queue and an empty one in this case. Fortunately, this is not a big problem, and a number of ways for dealing with it exist.

The solution we describe here is to insist that Q can never hold more than $N - 1$ objects. This simple rule for handling a full queue takes care of the final problem with our implementation, and leads to the pseudo-coded descriptions of the queue methods given in Code Fragment 5.14. Note our introduction of an implementation-specific exception, called FullQueueException, to signal that no more elements can be inserted in the queue. Also note the way we compute the size of the queue by means of the expression $(N - f + r) \bmod N$, which gives the correct result both in the "normal" configuration (when $f \leq r$) and in the "wrapped around" configuration (when $r < f$). The Java implementation of a queue by means of an array is similar to that of a stack, and is left as an exercise (P-5.10).

Table 5.3 shows the running times of methods in a realization of a queue by an array. As with our array-based stack implementation, each of the queue methods in the array realization executes a constant number of statements involving arithmetic operations, comparisons, and assignments. Thus, each method in this implementation runs in $O(1)$ time.

Method	Time
size	$O(1)$
isEmpty	$O(1)$
front	$O(1)$
enqueue	$O(1)$
dequeue	$O(1)$

Table 5.3: Performance of a queue realized by an array. The space usage is $O(N)$, where N is the size of the array, determined at the time the queue is created. Note that the space usage is independent from the number $n < N$ of elements that are actually in the queue.

As with the array-based stack implementation, the only real disadvantage of the array-based queue implementation is that we artificially set the capacity of the queue to be some fixed value. In a real application, we may actually need more or less queue capacity than this, but if we have a good capacity estimate, then the array-based implementation is quite efficient.

5.2.3   Implementing a Queue with a Generic Linked List

We can efficiently implement the queue ADT using a generic singly linked list. For
efficiency reasons, we choose the front of the queue to be at the head of the list, and
the rear of the queue to be at the tail of the list. In this way, we remove from the
head and insert at the tail. (Why would it be bad to insert at the head and remove at
the tail?) Note that we need to maintain references to both the head and tail nodes
of the list. Rather than go into every detail of this implementation, we simply give
a Java implementation for the fundamental queue methods in Code Fragment 5.15.

```java
public void enqueue(E elem) {
    Node<E> node = new Node<E>();
    node.setElement(elem);
    node.setNext(null); // node will be new tail node
    if (size == 0)
        head = node; // special case of a previously empty queue
    else
        tail.setNext(node); // add node at the tail of the list
    tail = node; // update the reference to the tail node
    size++;
}

    ...

public E dequeue() throws EmptyQueueException {
    if (size == 0)
        throw new EmptyQueueException("Queue is empty.");
    E tmp = head.getElement();
    head = head.getNext();
    size--;
    if (size == 0)
        tail = null; // the queue is now empty
    return tmp;
}
```

Code Fragment 5.15: Methods enqueue and dequeue in the implementation of the
queue ADT by means of a singly linked list, using nodes from class Node of Code
Fragment 5.6.

Each of the methods of the singly linked list implementation of the queue ADT
runs in $O(1)$ time. We also avoid the need to specify a maximum size for the queue,
as was done in the array-based queue implementation, but this benefit comes at the
expense of increasing the amount of space used per element. Still, the methods in
the singly linked list queue implementation are more complicated than we might
like, for we must take extra care in how we deal with special cases where the queue
is empty before an enqueue or where the queue becomes empty after a dequeue.

5.2.4   Round Robin Schedulers

A popular use of the queue data structure is to implement a ***round robin*** scheduler, where we iterate through a collection of elements in a circular fashion and "service" each element by performing a given action on it. Such a schedule is used, for example, to fairly allocate a resource that must be shared by a collection of clients. For instance, we can use a round robin scheduler to allocate a slice of CPU time to various applications running concurrently on a computer.

We can implement a round robin scheduler using a queue, Q, by repeatedly performing the following steps (see Figure 5.5):

1. $e \leftarrow Q.\text{dequeue}()$
2. Service element e
3. $Q.\text{enqueue}(e)$

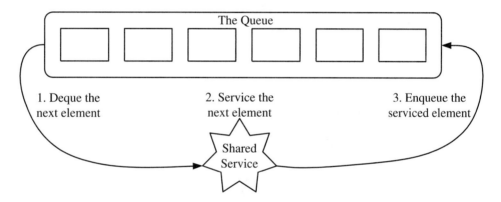

Figure 5.5: The three iterative steps for using a queue to implement a round robin scheduler.

The Josephus Problem

In the children's game "hot potato," a group of n children sit in a circle passing an object, called the "potato," around the circle. The potato begins with a starting child in the circle, and the children continue passing the potato until a leader rings a bell, at which point the child holding the potato must leave the game after handing the potato to the next child in the circle. After the selected child leaves, the other children close up the circle. This process is then continued until there is only one child remaining, who is declared the winner. If the leader always uses the strategy of ringing the bell after the potato has been passed k times, for some fixed value k, then determining the winner for a given list of children is known as the ***Josephus problem***.

Solving the Josephus Problem Using a Queue

We can solve the Josephus problem for a collection of n elements using a queue, by associating the potato with the element at the front of the queue and storing elements in the queue according to their order around the circle. Thus, passing the potato is equivalent to dequeuing an element and immediately enqueuing it again. After this process has been performed k times, we remove the front element by dequeuing it from the queue and discarding it. We show a complete Java program for solving the Josephus problem using this approach in Code Fragment 5.16, which describes a solution that runs in $O(nk)$ time. (We can solve this problem faster using techniques beyond the scope of this book.)

```java
import net.datastructures.*;
public class Josephus {
  /** Solution of the Josephus problem using a queue. */
  public static <E> E Josephus(Queue<E> Q, int k) {
    if (Q.isEmpty()) return null;
    while (Q.size() > 1) {
      System.out.println(" Queue: " + Q + " k = " + k);
      for (int i=0; i < k; i++)
        Q.enqueue(Q.dequeue()); // move the front element to the end
      E e = Q.dequeue(); // remove the front element from the collection
      System.out.println("    " + e + " is out");
    }
    return Q.dequeue(); // the winner
  }
  /** Build a queue from an array of objects */
  public static <E> Queue<E> buildQueue(E a[]) {
    Queue<E> Q = new NodeQueue<E>();
    for (int i=0; i<a.length; i++)
      Q.enqueue(a[i]);
    return Q;
  }
  /** Tester method */
  public static void main(String[] args) {
    String[] a1 = {"Alice", "Bob", "Cindy", "Doug", "Ed", "Fred"};
    String[] a2 = {"Gene", "Hope", "Irene", "Jack", "Kim", "Lance"};
    String[] a3 = {"Mike", "Roberto"};
    System.out.println("First winner is " + Josephus(buildQueue(a1), 3));
    System.out.println("Second winner is " + Josephus(buildQueue(a2), 10));
    System.out.println("Third winner is " + Josephus(buildQueue(a3), 7));
  }
}
```

Code Fragment 5.16: A complete Java program for solving the Josephus problem using a queue. Class NodeQueue is shown in Code Fragment 5.15.

5.3 Double-Ended Queues

Consider now a queue-like data structure that supports insertion and deletion at both the front and the rear of the queue. Such an extension of a queue is called a ***double-ended queue***, or ***deque***, which is usually pronounced "deck" to avoid confusion with the dequeue method of the regular queue ADT, which is pronounced like the abbreviation "D.Q."

5.3.1 The Deque Abstract Data Type

The deque abstract data type is richer than both the stack and the queue ADTs. The fundamental methods of the deque ADT are as follows:

addFirst(e): Insert a new element e at the head of the deque.

addLast(e): Insert a new element e at the tail of the deque.

removeFirst(): Remove and return the first element of the deque; an error occurs if the deque is empty.

removeLast(): Remove and return the last element of the deque; an error occurs if the deque is empty.

Additionally, the deque ADT may also include the following support methods:

getFirst(): Return the first element of the deque; an error occurs if the deque is empty.

getLast(): Return the last element of the deque; an error occurs if the deque is empty.

size(): Return the number of elements of the deque.

isEmpty(): Determine if the deque is empty.

Example 5.5: *The following table shows a series of operations and their effects on an initially empty deque D of integer objects. For simplicity, we use integers instead of integer objects as arguments of the operations.*

Operation	Output	D
addFirst(3)	–	(3)
addFirst(5)	–	(5,3)
removeFirst()	5	(3)
addLast(7)	–	(3,7)
removeFirst()	3	(7)
removeLast()	7	()
removeFirst()	"error"	()
isEmpty()	true	()

5.3.2 Implementing a Deque

Since the deque requires insertion and removal at both ends of a list, using a singly linked list to implement a deque would be inefficient. We can use a doubly linked list, however, to implement a deque efficiently.

As discussed in Section 3.3, inserting or removing elements at either end of a doubly linked list is straightforward to do in $O(1)$ time, if we use sentinel nodes for the header and trailer, which is an implementation we support.

For an insertion of a new element e, we can have access to the node p before the place e should go and the node q after the place e should go. To insert a new element between the two nodes p and q (either or both of which could be sentinels), we create a new node t, have t's prev and next links respectively refer to p and q, and then have p's next link refer to t, and have q's prev link refer to t.

Likewise, to remove an element stored at a node t, we can access the nodes p and q on either side of t (and these nodes must exist, since we are using sentinels). To remove node t between nodes p and q, we simply have p and q point to each other instead of t. We need not change any of the fields in t, for now t can be reclaimed by the garbage collector, since no one is pointing to t.

Performance and Linked List Implementation Details

Table 5.4 shows the running times of methods for a deque implemented with a doubly linked list. Note that every method runs in $O(1)$ time.

Method	Time
size, isEmpty	$O(1)$
getFirst, getLast	$O(1)$
addFirst, addLast	$O(1)$
removeFirst, removeLast	$O(1)$

Table 5.4: Performance of a deque realized by a doubly linked list.

Thus, a doubly linked list can be used to implement each method of the deque ADT in constant time. We leave the complete details of implementing the deque ADT efficiently in Java as an exercise (see P-5.3). Nevertheless, we show a Deque interface in Code Fragment 5.17 and a partial implementation of this interface in Code Fragment 5.18.

```
/**
 * Interface for a deque: a collection of objects that are inserted
 * and removed at both ends; a subset of java.util.LinkedList methods.
 *
 * @author Roberto Tamassia
 * @author Michael Goodrich
 */

public interface Deque<E> {
  /**
   * Returns the number of elements in the deque.
   */
  public int size();
  /**
   * Returns whether the deque is empty.
   */
  public boolean isEmpty();
  /**
   * Returns the first element; an exception is thrown if deque is empty.
   */
  public E getFirst() throws EmptyDequeException;
  /**
   * Returns the last element; an exception is thrown if deque is empty.
   */
  public E getLast() throws EmptyDequeException;
  /**
   * Inserts an element to be the first in the deque.
   */
  public void addFirst (E element);
  /**
   * Inserts an element to be the last in the deque.
   */
  public void addLast (E element);
  /**
   * Removes the first element; an exception is thrown if deque is empty.
   */
  public E removeFirst() throws EmptyDequeException;
  /**
   * Removes the last element; an exception is thrown if deque is empty.
   */
  public E removeLast() throws EmptyDequeException;
}
```

Code Fragment 5.17: Interface Deque documented with comments in Javadoc style (Section 1.9.3). Note also the use of the generic parameterized type, E, which implies that a deque can contain elements of any specified class.

```java
public class NodeDeque<E> implements Deque<E> {
  protected DLNode<E> header, trailer; // sentinels
  protected int size;    // number of elements
  public NodeDeque() { // initialize an empty deque
    header = new DLNode<E>();
    trailer = new DLNode<E>();
    header.setNext(trailer);   // make header point to trailer
    trailer.setPrev(header);   // make trailer point to header
    size = 0;
  }
  public int size() {
    return size;
  }
  public boolean isEmpty() {
    if (size == 0)
      return true;
    return false;
  }
  public E getFirst() throws EmptyDequeException {
    if (isEmpty())
      throw new EmptyDequeException("Deque is empty.");
    return header.getNext().getElement();
  }
  public void addFirst(E o) {
    DLNode<E> second = header.getNext();
    DLNode<E> first = new DLNode<E>(o, header, second);
    second.setPrev(first);
    header.setNext(first);
    size++;
  }
  public E removeLast() throws EmptyDequeException {
    if (isEmpty())
      throw new EmptyDequeException("Deque is empty.");
    DLNode<E> last = trailer.getPrev();
    E o = last.getElement();
    DLNode<E> secondtolast = last.getPrev();
    trailer.setPrev(secondtolast);
    secondtolast.setNext(trailer);
    size--;
    return o;
  }
}
```

Code Fragment 5.18: Class NodeDeque implementing the Deque interface, except that we have not shown the class DLNode, which is a generic doubly linked list node, nor have we shown methods getLast, addLast, and removeFirst.

5.3.3 Deques in the Java Collections Framework

Incidentally, all of the methods of the deque ADT, as described above, are included in the java.util.Deque interface. In the case of the update methods, which add or remove elements from the ends of the deque, the corresponding methods in the java.util.Deque interface are defined so that they throw an exception when used erroneously. Thus, the addFirst(e) method throws an exception if we try to add an element to a deque that is implemented in such a way that it is currently full and unable to accept additional elements, and the same is true for the addLast(e) method. Likewise, the removeFirst() method throws an exception if we attempt to remove an element from an empty deque, and the same is true for removeLast().

In addition to the above update methods, which fail in bad situations, there are also corresponding methods in the java.util.Deque interface that are defined to behave more gracefully in bad situations. In particular, these alternative methods are useful in applications, such as producer-consumer scenarios that use a fixed-size buffer, where it is normal for us to try to insert items in a full deque or try to remove elements from an empty deque. These methods are as follows:

offerFirst(e): Inserts e at the head of the deque unless the deque is full, in which case this method returns **false**; if the method succeeds, it returns **true**.

offerLast(e): Inserts e at the tail of the deque unless the deque is full, in which case this method returns **false**; if the method succeeds, it returns **true**.

pollFirst(): Removes and returns the first element of the deque; if the deque is empty, this method returns **null**.

pollLast(): Removes and returns the last element of the deque; if the deque is empty, this method returns **null**.

peekFirst(): Returns, but does not remove, the first element of the deque; if the deque is empty, this method returns **null**.

peekLast(): Returns, but does not remove, the last element of the deque; if the deque is empty, this method returns **null**.

There are several concrete classes in Java that implement the java.util.Deque interface. These include the following:

- java.util.ArrayDeque
- java.util.concurrent.LinkedBlockingDeque
- java.util.LinkedList

So, if we need to use a deque and would rather not implement one from scratch, we can simply use the built-in class java.util.LinkedList.

5.4 Exercises

For help with exercises, please visit the web site, www.wiley.com/college/goodrich.

Reinforcement

R-5.1 Describe how to implement a capacity-limited Stack, which uses the methods of a capacity-limited Deque to perform the methods of the stack ADT in ways that do not throw exceptions when we attempt to perform a push on a full stack or a pop on an empty stack.

R-5.2 Describe how to implement a capacity-limited queue, which uses the methods of a capacity-limited Deque to perform the methods of the queue ADT in ways that do not throw exceptions when we attempt to perform a enqueue on a full queue or a dequeue on an empty queue.

R-5.3 Suppose an initially empty stack S has performed a total of 25 push operations, 12 top operations, and 10 pop operations, 3 of which generated EmptyStackExceptions, which were caught and ignored. What is the current size of S?

R-5.4 If we implemented the stack S from the previous problem with an array, as described in this chapter, then what is the current value of the top instance variable?

R-5.5 Describe the output of the following series of stack operations: push(5), push(3), pop(), push(2), push(8), pop(), pop(), push(9), push(1), pop(), push(7), push(6), pop(), pop(), push(4), pop(), pop().

R-5.6 Give a recursive method for removing all the elements in a stack.

R-5.7 Give a precise and complete definition of the concept of matching for grouping symbols in an arithmetic expression.

R-5.8 Describe the output for the following sequence of queue operations: enqueue(5), enqueue(3), dequeue(), enqueue(2), enqueue(8), dequeue(), dequeue(), enqueue(9), enqueue(1), dequeue(), enqueue(7), enqueue(6), dequeue(), dequeue(), enqueue(4), dequeue(), dequeue().

R-5.9 Suppose an initially-empty queue Q has performed a total of 32 enqueue operations, 10 front operations, and 15 dequeue operations, 5 of which generated EmptyQueueExceptions, which were caught and ignored. What is the current size of Q?

R-5.10 If the queue of the previous problem was implemented with an array of capacity $N = 30$, as described in the chapter, and it never generated a FullQueueException, what would be the current values of f and r?

R-5.11 Describe the output for the following sequence of deque ADT operations: addFirst(3), addLast(8), addLast(9), addFirst(5), removeFirst(), removeLast(), first(), addLast(7), removeFirst(), last(), removeLast().

R-5.12 Suppose you have a deque D containing the numbers $(1,2,3,4,5,6,7,8)$, in this order. Suppose further that you have an initially empty queue Q. Give a pseudo-code description of a method that uses only D and Q (and no other variables or objects) and results in D storing the elements $(1,2,3,5,4,6,7,8)$, in this order.

R-5.13 Repeat the previous problem using the deque D and an initially empty stack S.

Creativity

C-5.1 Explain how you can implement all the methods of the Deque ADT using two stacks.

C-5.2 Suppose you have a stack S containing n elements and a queue Q that is initially empty. Describe how you can use Q to scan S to see if it contains a certain element x, with the additional constraint that your algorithm must return the elements back to S in their original order. You may not use an array or linked list—only S and Q and a constant number of reference variables.

C-5.3 Give a pseudo-code description for an array-based implementation of the double-ended queue ADT. What is the running time for each operation?

C-5.4 Suppose Alice has picked three distinct integers and placed them into a stack S in random order. Write a short, straightline piece of pseudo-code (with no loops or recursion) that uses only one comparison and only one variable x, yet guarantees with probability $2/3$ that at the end of this code the variable x will store the largest of Alice's three integers. Argue why your method is correct.

C-5.5 Describe how to implement the stack ADT using two queues. What is the running time of the push() and pop() methods in this case?

C-5.6 Suppose we have an $n \times n$ two-dimensional array A that we want to use to store integers, but we don't want to spend the $O(n^2)$ work to initialize it to all 0's (the way Java does), because we know in advance that we are only going to use up to n of these cells in our algorithm, which itself runs in $O(n)$ time (not counting the time to initialize A). Show how to use an array-based stack S storing (i,j,k) integer triples to allow us to use the array A without initializing it and still implement our algorithm in $O(n)$ time, even though the initial values in the cells of A might be total garbage.

C-5.7 Describe a nonrecursive algorithm for enumerating all permutations of the numbers $\{1, 2, \ldots, n\}$.

C-5.8 *Postfix notation* is an unambiguous way of writing an arithmetic expression without parentheses. It is defined so that if "$(exp_1)\mathbf{op}(exp_2)$" is a normal fully parenthesized expression whose operation is **op**, then the postfix version of this is "$pexp_1 \, pexp_2 \, \mathbf{op}$", where $pexp_1$ is the postfix version of exp_1 and $pexp_2$ is the postfix version of exp_2. The postfix version of a single number or variable is just that number or variable. So, for example, the postfix version of "$((5+2)*(8-3))/4$" is "$5\,2+8\,3-*4\,/$". Describe a nonrecursive way of evaluating an expression in postfix notation.

C-5.9 Suppose you have two nonempty stacks S and T and a deque D. Describe how to use D so that S stores all the elements of T below all of its original elements, with both sets of elements still in their original order.

C-5.10 Alice has three array-based stacks, A, B, and C, such that A has capacity 100, B has capacity 5, and C has capacity 3. Initially, A is full, and B and C are empty. Unfortunately, the person who programmed the class for these stacks made the push and pop methods private. The only method Alice can use is a static method, transfer(S, T), which transfers (by iteratively applying the private pop and push methods) elements from stack S to stack T until either S becomes empty or T becomes full. So, for example, starting from our initial configuration and performing transfer(A, C) results in A now holding 97 elements and C holding 3. Describe a sequence of transfer operations that starts from the initial configuration and results in B holding 4 elements at the end.

C-5.11 Alice has two queues, S and T, which can store integers. Bob gives Alice 50 odd integers and 50 even integers and insists that she stores all 100 integers in S and T. They then play a game where Bob picks S or T at random and then applies the round-robin scheduler, described in the chapter, to the chosen queue a random number of times. If the number left out of the queue at the end of this game is odd, Bob wins. Otherwise, Alice wins. How can Alice allocate integers to queues to optimize her chances of winning? What is her chance of winning?

C-5.12 Suppose Bob has four cows that he wants to take across a bridge, but only one yoke, which can hold up to two cows, side by side, tied to the yoke. The yoke is too heavy for him to carry across the bridge, but he can tie (and untie) cows to it in no time at all. Of his four cows, Mazie can cross the bridge in 2 minutes, Daisy can cross it in 4 minutes, Crazy can cross it in 10 minutes, and Lazy can cross it in 20 minutes. Of course, when two cows are tied to the yoke, they must go at the speed of the slower cow. Describe how Bob can get all his cows across the bridge in 34 minutes.

C-5.13 Show how to use a stack S and a queue Q to generate all possible subsets of an n-element set T nonrecursively.

Projects

P-5.1 Give an implementation of the Deque ADT using an array, so that each of the update methods run in $O(1)$ time.

P-5.2 Design an ADT for a two-color, double-stack ADT that consists of two stacks—one "red" and one "blue"—and has as its operations color-coded versions of the regular stack ADT operations. For example, this ADT should allow for both a red push operation and a blue push operation. Give an efficient implementation of this ADT using a single array whose capacity is set at some value N that is assumed to always be larger than the sizes of the red and blue stacks combined.

P-5.3 Implement the deque ADT with a doubly linked list.

P-5.4 Implement a capacity-limited version of the deque ADT, as given in Section 5.3.3, with an array used in a circular fashion.

P-5.5 Implement the Stack and Queue interfaces with a unique class that extends class NodeDeque (Code Fragment 5.18).

P-5.6 When a share of common stock of some company is sold, the *capital gain* (or, sometimes, loss) is the difference between the share's selling price and the price originally paid to buy it. This rule is easy to understand for a single share, but if we sell multiple shares of stock bought over a long period of time, then we must identify the shares actually being sold. A standard accounting principle for identifying which shares of a stock were sold in such a case is to use a FIFO protocol—the shares sold are the ones that have been held the longest (indeed, this is the default method built into several personal finance software packages). For example, suppose we buy 100 shares at $20 each on day 1, 20 shares at $24 on day 2, 200 shares at $36 on day 3, and then sell 150 shares on day 4 at $30 each. Then applying the FIFO protocol means that of the 150 shares sold, 100 were bought on day 1, 20 were bought on day 2, and 30 were bought on day 3. The capital gain in this case would therefore be $100 \cdot 10 + 20 \cdot 6 + 30 \cdot (-6)$, or $940. Write a program that takes as input a sequence of transactions of the form "buy x share(s) at $\$y$ each" or "sell x share(s) at $\$y$ each," assuming that the transactions occur on consecutive days and the values x and y are integers. Given this input sequence, the output should be the total capital gain (or loss) for the entire sequence, using the FIFO protocol to identify shares.

P-5.7 Implement the stack ADT with a doubly linked list.

P-5.8 Implement the stack ADT using the Java ArrayList class (without using the built-in Java Stack class).

P-5.9 Implement a program that can input an expression in postfix notation (see Exercise C-5.8) and output its value.

P-5.10 Implement the queue ADT using an array.

P-5.11 Implement the entire queue ADT using a singly linked list.

Chapter Notes

We were introduced to the approach of defining data structures first in terms of their ADTs and then in terms of concrete implementations by the classic books by Aho, Hopcroft, and Ullman [4, 5], which incidentally is where we first saw a problem similar to Exercise C-5.6. Exercises C-5.10, C-5.11, and C-5.12 are similar to interview questions said to be from a well-known software company. For further study of abstract data types, see Liskov and Guttag [69], Cardelli and Wegner [20], or Demurjian [27].

Chapter
6

List and Iterator ADTs

Contents

6.1 Array Lists

Suppose we have a collection S of n elements stored in a certain linear order, so that we can refer to the elements in S as first, second, third, and so on. Such a collection is generically referred to as a *list* or *sequence*. We can uniquely refer to each element e in S using an integer in the range $[0, n-1]$ that is equal to the number of elements of S that precede e in S. The *index* of an element e in S is the number of elements that are before e in S. Hence, the first element in S has index 0 and the last element has index $n-1$. Also, if an element of S has index i, its previous element (if it exists) has index $i-1$, and its next element (if it exists) has index $i+1$. This concept of index is related to that of the *rank* of an element in a list, which is usually defined to be one more than its index; so the first element is at rank 1, the second is at rank 2, and so on.

A sequence that supports access to its elements by their indices is called an *array list* (or *vector*, using an older term). Since our index definition is more consistent with the way arrays are indexed in Java and other programming languages (such as C and C++), we will be referring to the place where an element is stored in an array list as its "index," not its "rank" (although we may use r to denote this index, if the letter "i" is being used as a **for**-loop counter).

This index concept is a simple yet powerful notion, since it can be used to specify where to insert a new element into a list or where to remove an old element.

6.1.1 The Array List Abstract Data Type

As an ADT, an *array list* S has the following methods (besides the standard size() and isEmpty() methods):

get(i): Return the element of S with index i; an error condition occurs if $i < 0$ or $i > $ size() $- 1$.

set(i,e): Replace with e and return the element at index i; an error condition occurs if $i < 0$ or $i > $ size() $- 1$.

add(i,e): Insert a new element e into S to have index i; an error condition occurs if $i < 0$ or $i > $ size().

remove(i): Remove from S the element at index i; an error condition occurs if $i < 0$ or $i > $ size() $- 1$.

We do *not* insist that an array should be used to implement an array list, so that the element at index 0 is stored at index 0 in the array, although that is one (very natural) possibility. The index definition offers us a way to refer to the "place" where an element is stored in a sequence without having to worry about the exact implementation of that sequence. The index of an element may change whenever the sequence is updated, however, as we illustrate in the following example.

Example 6.1: *We show below some operations on an initially empty array list S.*

Operation	*Output*	*S*
add(0,7)	–	(7)
add(0,4)	–	(4,7)
get(1)	7	(4,7)
add(2,2)	–	(4,7,2)
get(3)	"error"	(4,7,2)
remove(1)	7	(4,2)
add(1,5)	–	(4,5,2)
add(1,3)	–	(4,3,5,2)
add(4,9)	–	(4,3,5,2,9)
get(2)	5	(4,3,5,2,9)
set(3,8)	2	(4,3,5,8,9)

6.1.2 The Adapter Pattern

Classes are often written to provide similar functionality to other classes. The *adapter* design pattern applies to any context where we want to modify an existing class so that its methods match those of a related, but different, class or interface. One general way for applying the adapter pattern is to define the new class in such a way that it contains an instance of the old class as a hidden field, and implement each method of the new class using methods of this hidden instance variable. The result of applying the adapter pattern is that a new class that performs almost the same functions as a previous class, but in a more convenient way, has been created.

With respect to our discussion of the array list ADT, we note that this ADT is sufficient to define an adapter class for the deque ADT, as shown in Table 6.1. (See also Exercise C-6.9.)

Deque Method	*Realization with Array-List Methods*
size(), isEmpty()	size(), isEmpty()
getFirst()	get(0)
getLast()	get(size() − 1)
addFirst(e)	add(0, e)
addLast(e)	add(size(), e)
removeFirst()	remove(0)
removeLast()	remove(size() − 1)

Table 6.1: Realization of a deque by means of an array list.

6.1.3   A Simple Array-Based Implementation

An obvious choice for implementing the array list ADT is to use an array A, where $A[i]$ stores (a reference to) the element with index i. We choose the size N of array A sufficiently large, and we maintain the number of elements in an instance variable, $n < N$.

The details of this implementation of the array list ADT are simple. To implement the get(i) operation, for example, we just return $A[i]$. Implementations of methods add(i,e) and remove(i) are given in Code Fragment 6.1. An important (and time-consuming) part of this implementation involves the shifting of elements up or down to keep the occupied cells in the array contiguous. These shifting operations are required to maintain our rule of always storing an element whose list index is i at index i in the array A. (See Figure 6.1 and also Exercise R-6.15.)

Algorithm add(i,e):
  for $j = n-1, n-2, \ldots, i$ **do**
    $A[j+1] \leftarrow A[j]$ {make room for the new element}
  $A[i] \leftarrow e$
  $n \leftarrow n+1$

Algorithm remove(i):
  $e \leftarrow A[i]$ {e is a temporary variable}
  for $j = i, i+1, \ldots, n-2$ **do**
    $A[j] \leftarrow A[j+1]$ {fill in for the removed element}
  $n \leftarrow n-1$
  return e

Code Fragment 6.1: Methods add(i,e) and remove(i) in the array implementation of the array list ADT. We denote, with n, the instance variable storing the number of elements in the array list.

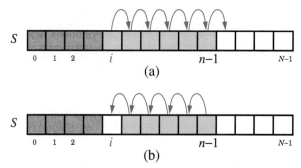

Figure 6.1: Array-based implementation of an array list S that is storing n elements: (a) shifting up for an insertion at index i; (b) shifting down for a removal at index i.

The Performance of a Simple Array-Based Implementation

Table 6.2 shows the worst-case running times of the methods of an array list with n elements realized by means of an array. Methods isEmpty, size, get and set clearly run in $O(1)$ time, but the insertion and removal methods can take much longer than this. In particular, add(i, e) runs in time $O(n)$. Indeed, the worst case for this operation occurs when $i = 0$, since all the existing n elements have to be shifted forward. A similar argument applies to method remove(i), which runs in $O(n)$ time, because we have to shift backward $n - 1$ elements in the worst case $(i = 0)$. In fact, assuming that each possible index is equally likely to be passed as an argument to these operations, their average running time is $O(n)$, for we will have to shift $n/2$ elements on average.

Method	Time
size()	$O(1)$
isEmpty()	$O(1)$
get(i)	$O(1)$
set(i, e)	$O(1)$
add(i, e)	$O(n)$
remove(i)	$O(n)$

Table 6.2: Performance of an array list with n elements realized by an array. The space usage is $O(N)$, where N is the size of the array.

Looking more closely at add(i, e) and remove(i), we note that they each run in time $O(n - i + 1)$, for only those elements at index i and higher have to be shifted up or down. Thus, inserting or removing an item at the end of an array list, using the methods add(n, e) and remove$(n - 1)$, respectively take $O(1)$ time each. Moreover, this observation has an interesting consequence for the adaptation of the array list ADT to the deque ADT given in Section 6.1.1. If the array list ADT in this case is implemented by means of an array as described above, then methods addLast and removeLast of the deque each run in $O(1)$ time. However, methods addFirst and removeFirst of the deque each run in $O(n)$ time.

Actually, with a little effort, we can produce an array-based implementation of the array list ADT that achieves $O(1)$ time for insertions and removals at index 0, as well as insertions and removals at the end of the array list. Achieving this requires that we give up on our rule that an element at index i is stored in the array at index i, however, as we would have to use a circular array approach like the one we used in Section 5.2 to implement a queue. We leave the details of this implementation for an exercise (C-6.10).

6.1.4   A Simple Interface and the java.util.ArrayList Class

To prepare for constructing a Java implementation of the array list ADT, we show, in Code Fragment 6.2, a Java interface, IndexList, that captures the main methods from the array list ADT. In this case, we use a IndexOutOfBoundsException to signal an invalid index argument.

```
public interface IndexList<E> {
  /** Returns the number of elements in this list. */
  public int size();
  /** Returns whether the list is empty. */
  public boolean isEmpty();
  /** Inserts an element e to be at index i, shifting all elements after this. */
  public void add(int i, E e)
    throws IndexOutOfBoundsException;
  /** Returns the element at index i, without removing it. */
  public E get(int i)
    throws IndexOutOfBoundsException;
  /** Removes and returns the element at index i, shifting the elements after this. */
  public E remove(int i)
    throws IndexOutOfBoundsException;
  /** Replaces the element at index i with e, returning the previous element at i. */
  public E set(int i, E e)
    throws IndexOutOfBoundsException;
}
```

Code Fragment 6.2: The IndexList interface for the array list ADT.

The java.util.ArrayList Class

Java provides a class, java.util.ArrayList, that implements all the methods that we give above for our array list ADT. That is, it includes all of the methods included in Code Fragment 6.2 for the IndexList interface. Moreover, the java.util.ArrayList class has features in addition to those of our simplified array list ADT. For example, the class java.util.ArrayList also includes a method, clear(), which removes all the elements from the array list, and a method, toArray(), which returns an array containing all the elements of the array list in the same order. In addition, the class java.util.ArrayList also has methods for searching the list, including a method indexOf(e), which returns the index of the first occurrence of an element equal to e in the array list, and a method lastIndexOf(e), which returns the index of the last occurrence of an element equal to e in the array list. Both of these methods return the (invalid) index value −1 if an element equal to e is not found.

6.1.5 Implementing an Array List Using Extendable Arrays

In addition to implementing the methods of the IndexList interface (and some other useful methods), the class java.util.ArrayList provides an an interesting feature that overcomes a weakness in the simple array implementation.

Specifically, a major weakness of the simple array implementation for the array list ADT given in Section 6.1.3, is that it requires advance specification of a fixed capacity, N, for the total number of elements that may be stored in the array list. If the actual number of elements, n, of the array list is much smaller than N, then this implementation will waste space. Worse, if n increases past N, then this implementation will crash.

Instead, the java.util.ArrayList uses an interesting extendable-array technique so that we never have to worry about array overflows when using this class.

As with the java.util.ArrayList class, let us provide a means to grow the array A that stores the elements of an array list S. Of course, in Java (and other programming languages), we cannot actually grow the array A; its capacity is fixed at some number N, as we have already observed. Instead, when an **overflow** occurs, that is, when $n = N$ and we make a call to the method add, we perform the following additional steps:

1. Allocate a new array B of capacity $2N$
2. Let $B[i] \leftarrow A[i]$, for $i = 0, \ldots, N - 1$
3. Let $A \leftarrow B$, that is, we use B as the array supporting S
4. Insert the new element in A.

This array replacement strategy is known as an **extendable array**, for it can be viewed as extending the end of the underlying array to make room for more elements. (See Figure 6.2.) Intuitively, this strategy is much like that of the hermit crab, which moves into a larger shell when it outgrows its previous one.

      (a)   (b)   (c)

Figure 6.2: An illustration of the three steps for "growing" an extendable array: (a) create new array B; (b) copy elements from A to B; (c) reassign reference A to the new array. Not shown is the future garbage collection of the old array.

Implementing the IndexList Interface with an Extendable Array

We give portions of a Java implementation of the array list ADT using an extend-able array in Code Fragment 6.3. This class only provides means for the array to grow. Exercise C-6.2 explores an implementation that can also shrink.

```
/** Realization of an indexed list by means of an array, which is doubled
  * when the size of the indexed list exceeds the capacity of the array.
  */
public class ArrayIndexList<E> implements IndexList<E> {
  private E[] A;            // array storing the elements of the indexed list
  private int capacity = 16; // initial length of array A
  private int size = 0;     // number of elements stored in the indexed list
  /** Creates the indexed list with initial capacity 16. */
  public ArrayIndexList() {
    A = (E[]) new Object[capacity]; // the compiler may warn, but this is ok
  }
  /** Inserts an element at the given index. */
  public void add(int r, E e)
    throws IndexOutOfBoundsException {
    checkIndex(r, size() + 1);
    if (size == capacity) {          // an overflow
      capacity *= 2;
      E[] B =(E[]) new Object[capacity];
      for (int i=0; i<size; i++)
        B[i] = A[i];
      A = B;
    }
    for (int i=size-1; i>=r; i--)     // shift elements up
      A[i+1] = A[i];
    A[r] = e;
    size++;
  }
  /** Removes the element stored at the given index. */
  public E remove(int r)
    throws IndexOutOfBoundsException {
    checkIndex(r, size());
    E temp = A[r];
    for (int i=r; i<size-1; i++)      // shift elements down
      A[i] = A[i+1];
    size--;
    return temp;
  }
```

Code Fragment 6.3: Portions of class ArrayIndexList realizing the array list ADT by means of an extendable array. Method checkIndex(r, n) (not shown) checks whether an index r is in the range $[0, n-1]$.

An Amortized Analysis of Extendable Arrays

This array replacement strategy might at first seem slow, for performing a single array replacement required by some element insertion can take $O(n)$ time. Still, notice that after we perform an array replacement, our new array allows us to add n new elements to the array list before the array must be replaced again. This simple fact allows us to show that performing a series of operations on an initially empty array list is efficient in terms of its total running time. As a shorthand notation, let us refer to the insertion of an element to be the last element in an array list as a *push* operation. (See Figure 6.3.)

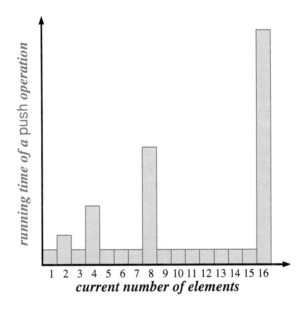

Figure 6.3: Running times of a series of push operations on a java.util.ArrayList of initial size 1.

Using an algorithmic design pattern called *amortization*, we can show that performing a sequence of such push operations on an array list implemented with an extendable array is actually quite efficient. To perform an *amortized analysis*, we use an accounting technique where we view the computer as a coin-operated appliance that requires the payment of one *cyber-dollar* for a constant amount of computing time. When an operation is executed, we should have enough cyber-dollars available in our current "bank account" to pay for that operation's running time. Thus, the total amount of cyber-dollars spent for any computation will be proportional to the total time spent on that computation. The beauty of using this analysis method is that we can overcharge some operations in order to save up cyber-dollars to pay for others.

Proposition 6.2: *Let S be an array list implemented by means of an extendable array with initial length one. The total time to perform a series of n push operations in S, starting from S being empty is $O(n)$.*

Justification: Let us assume that one cyber-dollar is enough to pay for the execution of each push operation in S, excluding the time spent for growing the array. Also, let us assume that growing the array from size k to size $2k$ requires k cyber-dollars for the time spent copying the elements. We shall charge each push operation three cyber-dollars. Thus, we overcharge each push operation that does not cause an overflow by two cyber-dollars. Think of the two cyber-dollars profited in an insertion that does not grow the array as being "stored" at the element inserted. An overflow occurs when the array list S has 2^i elements, for some integer $i \geq 0$, and the size of the array used by the array list representing S is 2^i. Thus, doubling the size of the array will require 2^i cyber-dollars. Fortunately, these cyber-dollars can be found at the elements stored in cells 2^{i-1} through $2^i - 1$. (See Figure 6.4.) Note that the previous overflow occurred when the number of elements became larger than 2^{i-1} for the first time, and thus the cyber-dollars stored in cells 2^{i-1} through $2^i - 1$ were not previously spent. Therefore, we have a valid amortization scheme in which each operation is charged three cyber-dollars and all the computing time is paid for. That is, we can pay for the execution of n push operations using $3n$ cyber-dollars. In other words, the amortized running time of each push operation is $O(1)$; hence, the total running time of n push operations is $O(n)$. ∎

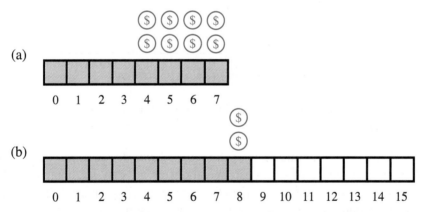

Figure 6.4: Illustration of a series of push operations on an array list: (a) an 8-cell array is full, with two cyber-dollars "stored" at cells 4 through 7; (b) a push operation causes an overflow and a doubling of capacity. Copying the eight old elements to the new array is paid for by the cyber-dollars already stored in the table. Inserting the new element is paid for by one of the cyber-dollars charged to the push operation, and the two cyber-dollars profited are stored at cell 8.

6.2 Node Lists

Using an index is not the only means of referring to the place where an element appears in a sequence. If we have a sequence S implemented with a (singly or doubly) linked list, then it could possibly be more natural and efficient to use a node instead of an index as a means of identifying where to access and update S. In this section, we define the node list ADT, which abstracts the concrete linked list data structure (Sections 3.2 and 3.3) using a related position ADT that abstracts the notion of "place" in a node list.

6.2.1 Node-Based Operations

Let S be a (singly or doubly) linked list. We would like to define methods for S that take nodes as parameters and provide nodes as return types. Such methods could provide significant speedups over index-based methods, because finding the index of an element in a linked list requires searching through the list incrementally from its beginning or end, counting elements as we go.

For instance, we could define a hypothetical method remove(v) that removes the element of S stored at node v of the list. Using a node as a parameter allows us to remove an element in $O(1)$ time by simply going directly to the place where that node is stored and then "linking out" this node through an update of the *next* and *prev* links of its neighbors. Similarly, we could insert, in $O(1)$ time, a new element e into S with an operation such as addAfter(v, e), which specifies the node v after which the node of the new element should be inserted. In this case, we simply "link in" the new node.

Defining methods of a list ADT by adding such node-based operations raises the issue of how much information we should be exposing about the implementation of our list. Certainly, it is desirable for us to be able to use either a singly or doubly linked list without revealing this detail to a user. Likewise, we do not wish to allow a user to modify the internal structure of a list without our knowledge. Such modification would be possible, however, if we provided a reference to a node in our list in a form that allowed the user to access internal data in that node (such as a *next* or *prev* field).

To abstract and unify the different ways of storing elements in the various implementations of a list, we introduce the concept of **position**, which formalizes the intuitive notion of "place" of an element relative to others in the list.

6.2.2   Positions

So as to safely expand the set of operations for lists, we abstract a notion of "position" that allows us to enjoy the efficiency of doubly or singly linked list implementations without violating object-oriented design principles. In this framework, we view a list as a collection of elements that stores each element at a position and that keeps these positions arranged in a linear order. A position is itself an abstract data type that supports the following simple method:

element(): Return the element stored at this position.

A position is always defined *relatively*, that is, in terms of its neighbors. In a list, a position p will always be "after" some position q and "before" some position s (unless p is the first or last position). A position p, which is associated with some element e in a list S, does not change, even if the index of e changes in S, unless we explicitly remove e (and, hence, destroy position p). Moreover, the position p does not change even if we replace or swap the element e stored at p with another element. These facts about positions allow us to define a set of position-based list methods that take position objects as parameters and also provide position objects as return values.

6.2.3   The Node List Abstract Data Type

Using the concept of position to encapsulate the idea of "node" in a list, we can define another type of sequence ADT called the *node list* ADT. This ADT supports the following methods for a list S:

first(): Return the position of the first element of S; an error occurs if S is empty.

last(): Return the position of the last element of S; an error occurs if S is empty.

prev(p): Return the position of the element of S preceding the one at position p; an error occurs if p is the first position.

next(p): Return the position of the element of S following the one at position p; an error occurs if p is the last position.

The above methods allow us to refer to relative positions in a list, starting at the beginning or end, and to move incrementally up or down the list. These positions can intuitively be thought of as nodes in the list, but note that there are no specific references to node objects. Moreover, if we provide a position as an argument to a list method, then that position must represent a valid position in that list.

Node List Update Methods

In addition to the above methods and the generic methods size and isEmpty, we also include the following update methods for the node list ADT, which take position objects as parameters and/or provide position objects as return values.

set(p,e): Replace the element at position p with e, returning the element formerly at position p.

addFirst(e): Insert a new element e into S as the first element.

addLast(e): Insert a new element e into S as the last element.

addBefore(p,e): Insert a new element e into S before position p.

addAfter(p,e): Insert a new element e into S after position p.

remove(p): Remove and return the element at position p in S, invalidating this position in S.

The node list ADT allows us to view an ordered collection of objects in terms of their places, without worrying about the exact way those places are represented. (See Figure 6.5.)

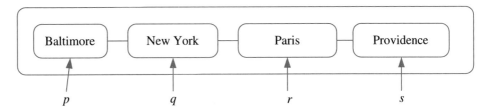

Figure 6.5: A node list. The positions in the current order are p, q, r, and s.

There may at first seem to be redundancy in the above repertory of operations for the node list ADT, since we can perform operation addFirst(e) with addBefore(first$()$, e), and operation addLast(e) with addAfter(getLast$()$, e). But these substitutions can only be done for a nonempty list.

Note that an error condition occurs if a position passed as argument to one of the list operations is invalid. Reasons for a position p to be invalid include:

- $p =$ **null**
- p was previously deleted from the list
- p is a position of a different list
- p is the first position of the list and we call prev(p)
- p is the last position of the list and we call next(p).

We illustrate the operations of the node list ADT in the following example.

Example 6.3: *We show below a series of operations for an initially empty list node S. We use variables p_1, p_2, and so on, to denote different positions, and we show the object currently stored at such a position in parentheses.*

Operation	Output	S
addFirst(8)	–	(8)
first()	$p_1(8)$	(8)
addAfter(p_1,5)	–	(8,5)
next(p_1)	$p_2(5)$	(8,5)
addBefore(p_2,3)	–	(8,3,5)
prev(p_2)	$p_3(3)$	(8,3,5)
addFirst(9)	–	(9,8,3,5)
last()	$p_2(5)$	(9,8,3,5)
remove(first())	9	(8,3,5)
set(p_3,7)	3	(8,7,5)
addAfter(first(),2)	–	(8,2,7,5)

The node list ADT, with its built-in notion of position, is useful in a number of settings. For example, a program that simulates a game of cards could model each person's hand as a node list. Since most people keep cards of the same suit together, inserting and removing cards from a person's hand could be implemented using the methods of the node list ADT, with the positions being determined by a natural ordering of the suits. Likewise, a simple text editor embeds the notion of positional insertion and removal, since such editors typically perform all updates relative to a *cursor*, which represents the current position in the list of characters of text being edited.

A Java interface representing the position ADT is given in Code Fragment 6.4.

```
public interface Position<E> {
  /** Return the element stored at this position. */
  E element();
}
```

Code Fragment 6.4: Java interface for the position ADT.

An interface for the node list ADT, called PositionList, is given in Code Fragment 6.5. This interface uses the following exceptions to indicate error conditions.

BoundaryViolationException: Thrown if an attempt is made at accessing an element whose position is outside the range of positions of the list (for example, calling method next on the last position of the sequence).

InvalidPositionException: Thrown if a position provided as argument is not valid (for example, it is a null reference or it has no associated list).

```
public interface PositionList<E> {
  /** Returns the number of elements in this list. */
  public int size();
  /** Returns whether the list is empty. */
  public boolean isEmpty();
  /** Returns the first node in the list. */
  public Position<E> first();
  /** Returns the last node in the list. */
  public Position<E> last();
  /** Returns the node after a given node in the list. */
  public Position<E> next(Position<E> p)
    throws InvalidPositionException, BoundaryViolationException;
  /** Returns the node before a given node in the list. */
  public Position<E> prev(Position<E> p)
    throws InvalidPositionException, BoundaryViolationException;
  /** Inserts an element at the front of the list, returning new position. */
  public void addFirst(E e);
  /** Inserts and element at the back of the list, returning new position. */
  public void addLast(E e);
  /** Inserts an element after the given node in the list. */
  public void addAfter(Position<E> p, E e)
    throws InvalidPositionException;
  /** Inserts an element before the given node in the list. */
  public void addBefore(Position<E> p, E e)
    throws InvalidPositionException;
  /** Removes a node from the list, returning the element stored there. */
  public E remove(Position<E> p) throws InvalidPositionException;
  /** Replaces the element stored at the given node, returning old element. */
  public E set(Position<E> p, E e) throws InvalidPositionException;
}
```

Code Fragment 6.5: Java interface for the node list ADT.

Yet Another Deque Adapter

With respect to our discussion of the node list ADT, we note that this ADT is sufficient to define an adapter class for the deque ADT, as shown in Table 6.3.

Deque Method	*Realization with Node-List Methods*
size(), isEmpty()	size(), isEmpty()
getFirst()	first().element()
getLast()	last().element()
addFirst(e)	addFirst(e)
addLast(e)	addLast(e)
removeFirst()	remove(first())
removeLast()	remove(last())

Table 6.3: Realization of a deque by means of a node list.

6.2.4   Doubly Linked List Implementation

Suppose we would like to implement the node list ADT using a doubly linked list (Section 3.3). We can simply make the nodes of the linked list implement the position ADT. That is, we have each node implement the Position interface and therefore define a method, element(), which returns the element stored at the node. Thus, the nodes themselves act as positions. They are viewed internally by the linked list as nodes, but from the outside, they are viewed only as positions. In the internal view, we can give each node *v* instance variables prev and next that respectively refer to the predecessor and successor nodes of *v* (which could in fact be header or trailer sentinel nodes marking the beginning and end of the list). Instead of using variables prev and next directly, we define methods getPrev, setPrev, getNext, and setNext of a node to access and modify these variables.

In Code Fragment 6.6, we show a Java class DNode for the nodes of a doubly linked list implementing the position ADT. This class is similar to class DNode shown in Code Fragment 3.17, except that now our nodes store a generic element instead of a character string. Note that the prev and next instance variables in the DNode class below are private references to other DNode objects.

```
public class DNode<E> implements Position<E> {
    private DNode<E> prev, next; // References to the nodes before and after
    private E element;    // Element stored in this position
    /** Constructor */
    public DNode(DNode<E> newPrev, DNode<E> newNext, E elem) {
      prev = newPrev;
      next = newNext;
      element = elem;
    }
    // Method from interface Position
    public E element() throws InvalidPositionException {
      if ((prev == null) && (next == null))
        throw new InvalidPositionException("Position is not in a list!");
      return element;
    }
    // Accessor methods
    public DNode<E> getNext() { return next; }
    public DNode<E> getPrev() { return prev; }
    // Update methods
    public void setNext(DNode<E> newNext) { next = newNext; }
    public void setPrev(DNode<E> newPrev) { prev = newPrev; }
    public void setElement(E newElement) { element = newElement; }
}
```

Code Fragment 6.6: Class DNode realizing a node of a doubly linked list and implementing the Position interface (ADT).

Given a position p in S, we can "unwrap" p to reveal the underlying node v. This is accomplished by ***casting*** the position to a node. Once we have node v, we can, for example, implement method prev(p) with v.getPrev (unless the node returned by v.getPrev is the header, in which case we signal an error). Therefore, positions in a doubly linked list implementation can be supported in an object-oriented way without any additional time or space overhead.

Consider how we might implement the addAfter(p, e) method, for inserting an element e after position p. Similar to the discussion in Section 3.3.1, we create a new node v to hold the element e, link v into its place in the list, and then update the next and prev references of v's two new neighbors. This method is given in Code Fragment 6.7, and is illustrated (again) in Figure 6.6. Recalling the use of sentinels (Section 3.3), note that this algorithm works even if p is the last real position.

Algorithm addAfter(p, e):
    Create a new node v
    v.setElement(e)
    v.setPrev(p)   {link v to its predecessor}
    v.setNext(p.getNext())   {link v to its successor}
    (p.getNext()).setPrev(v)   {link p's old successor to v}
    p.setNext(v)   {link p to its new successor, v}

Code Fragment 6.7: Inserting an element e after a position p in a linked list.

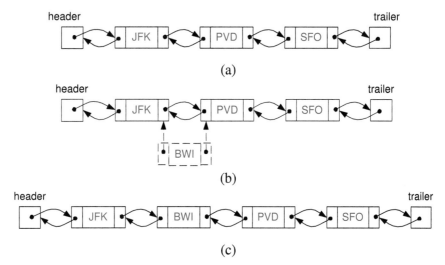

Figure 6.6: Adding a new node after the position for "JFK": (a) before the insertion; (b) creating node v with element "BWI" and linking it in; (c) after the insertion.

The algorithms for methods addBefore, addFirst, and addLast are similar to that for method addAfter. We leave their details as an exercise (R-6.8).

Next, consider the remove(p) method, which removes the element e stored at position p. Similar to the discussion in Section 3.3.2, to perform this operation, we link the two neighbors of p to refer to one another as new neighbors—linking out p. Note that after p is linked out, no nodes will be pointing to p; hence, the garbage collector can reclaim the space for p. This algorithm is given in Code Fragment 6.8 and is illustrated in Figure 6.7. Recalling our use of header and trailer sentinels, note that this algorithm works even if p is the first, last, or only real position in the list.

Algorithm remove(p):

  $t \leftarrow p$.element()   {a temporary variable to hold the return value}
  (p.getPrev()).setNext(p.getNext())   {linking out p}
  (p.getNext()).setPrev(p.getPrev())
  p.setPrev(**null**)   {invalidating the position p}
  p.setNext(**null**)
  return t

Code Fragment 6.8: Removing an element e stored at a position p in a linked list.

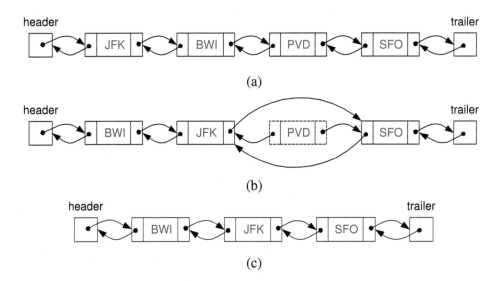

Figure 6.7: Removing the object stored at the position for "PVD": (a) before the removal; (b) linking out the old node; (c) after the removal (and garbage collection).

In conclusion, using a doubly linked list, we can perform all the methods of the node list ADT in $O(1)$ time. Thus, a doubly linked list is an efficient implementation of the node list ADT.

A Node List Implementation in Java

Portions of the Java class NodePositionList, which implements the node list ADT using a doubly linked list, are shown in Code Fragments 6.9–6.11. Code Fragment 6.9 shows NodePositionList's instance variables, its constructor, and a method, checkPosition, which performs safety checks and "unwraps" a position, casting it back to a DNode. Code Fragment 6.10 shows additional accessor and update methods. Code Fragment 6.11 shows additional update methods.

```java
public class NodePositionList<E> implements PositionList<E> {
  protected int numElts;                  // Number of elements in the list
  protected DNode<E> header, trailer;  // Special sentinels
  /** Constructor that creates an empty list; O(1) time */
  public NodePositionList() {
    numElts = 0;
    header = new DNode<E>(null, null, null); // create header
    trailer = new DNode<E>(header, null, null); // create trailer
    header.setNext(trailer);       // make header and trailer point to each other
  }
  /** Checks if position is valid for this list and converts it to
    *  DNode if it is valid; O(1) time */
  protected DNode<E> checkPosition(Position<E> p)
    throws InvalidPositionException {
    if (p == null)
      throw new InvalidPositionException
        ("Null position passed to NodeList");
    if (p == header)
        throw new InvalidPositionException
          ("The header node is not a valid position");
    if (p == trailer)
        throw new InvalidPositionException
          ("The trailer node is not a valid position");
    try {
      DNode<E> temp = (DNode<E>) p;
      if ((temp.getPrev() == null) || (temp.getNext() == null))
        throw new InvalidPositionException
          ("Position does not belong to a valid NodeList");
      return temp;
    } catch (ClassCastException e) {
      throw new InvalidPositionException
        ("Position is of wrong type for this list");
    }
  }
}
```

Code Fragment 6.9: Portions of the NodePositionList class implementing the node list ADT with a doubly linked list. (Continues in Code Fragments 6.10 and 6.11.)

```java
/** Returns the number of elements in the list; O(1) time */
public int size() { return numElts; }
/** Returns whether the list is empty; O(1) time */
public boolean isEmpty() { return (numElts == 0); }
/** Returns the first position in the list; O(1) time */
public Position<E> first()
    throws EmptyListException {
  if (isEmpty())
    throw new EmptyListException("List is empty");
  return header.getNext();
}
/** Returns the position before the given one; O(1) time */
public Position<E> prev(Position<E> p)
    throws InvalidPositionException, BoundaryViolationException {
  DNode<E> v = checkPosition(p);
  DNode<E> prev = v.getPrev();
  if (prev == header)
    throw new BoundaryViolationException
      ("Cannot advance past the beginning of the list");
  return prev;
}
/** Insert the given element before the given position;
  * O(1) time */
public void addBefore(Position<E> p, E element)
    throws InvalidPositionException {
  DNode<E> v = checkPosition(p);
  numElts++;
  DNode<E> newNode = new DNode<E>(v.getPrev(), v, element);
  v.getPrev().setNext(newNode);
  v.setPrev(newNode);
}
```

Code Fragment 6.10: Portions of the NodePositionList class implementing the node list ADT with a doubly linked list. (Continued from Code Fragment 6.9. Continues in Code Fragment 6.11.)

```
/** Insert the given element at the beginning of the list, returning
  * the new position; O(1) time */
public void addFirst(E element) {
  numElts++;
  DNode<E> newNode = new DNode<E>(header, header.getNext(), element);
  header.getNext().setPrev(newNode);
  header.setNext(newNode);
}
/**Remove the given position from the list; O(1) time */
public E remove(Position<E> p)
     throws InvalidPositionException {
  DNode<E> v = checkPosition(p);
  numElts--;
  DNode<E> vPrev = v.getPrev();
  DNode<E> vNext = v.getNext();
  vPrev.setNext(vNext);
  vNext.setPrev(vPrev);
  E vElem = v.element();
  // unlink the position from the list and make it invalid
  v.setNext(null);
  v.setPrev(null);
  return vElem;
}
/** Replace the element at the given position with the new element
  * and return the old element; O(1) time */
public E set(Position<E> p, E element)
     throws InvalidPositionException {
  DNode<E> v = checkPosition(p);
  E oldElt = v.element();
  v.setElement(element);
  return oldElt;
}
```

Code Fragment 6.11: Portions of the NodePositionList class implementing the node list ADT with a doubly linked list. (Continued from Code Fragments 6.10 and 6.11.) Note that the mechanism used to invalidate a position in the remove method is consistent with one of the checks performed in the checkPosition convenience function.

6.3   Iterators

A typical computation on an array list or a node list is to march through its elements in order, one at a time, for example, to look for a specific element.

6.3.1   The Iterator and Iterable Abstract Data Types

An *iterator* is a software design pattern that abstracts the process of scanning through a collection of elements one element at a time. An iterator consists of a list S, a current element in S, and a way of stepping to the next element in S and making it the current element. Thus, an iterator extends the concept of the position ADT we introduced in Section 6.2. In fact, a position can be thought of as an iterator that doesn't go anywhere. An iterator encapsulates the concepts of "place" and "next" in a collection of objects.

We define the *iterator* ADT as supporting the following two methods:

> hasNext(): Test whether there are elements left in the iterator.

> next(): Return the next element in the iterator.

Note that the iterator ADT has the *cursor* notion of the "current" element in a traversal of a list. The first element in an iterator is returned by the first call to the method next, assuming of course that the iterator contains at least one element.

An iterator provides a unified scheme to access all the elements of a collection of objects in a way that is independent from the specific organization of the collection. An iterator for an array list or node list should return the elements according to their linear ordering.

Simple Iterators in Java

Java provides an iterator through its java.util.Iterator interface. We note that the java.util.Scanner class (Section 1.6) implements this interface. This interface supports an additional (optional) method to remove the previously returned element from the collection. This functionality (removing elements through an iterator) is somewhat controversial from an object-oriented viewpoint, however, and it is not surprising that its implementation by classes is optional. Incidentally, Java also provides the java.util.Enumeration interface, which is historically older than the iterator interface and uses names hasMoreElements() and nextElement().

The Iterable Abstract Data Type

In order to provide a unified generic mechanism for scanning through a data structure, ADTs storing collections of objects should support the following method:

iterator(): Return an iterator of the elements in the collection.

This method is supported by the java.util.ArrayList class. In fact, this method is so important, that there is a whole interface, java.lang.Iterable, which has only this method in it. This method can make it simple for us to specify computations that need to loop through the elements of a list. To guarantee that a node list supports the above methods, for example, we could add this method to the PositionList interface, as shown in Code Fragment 6.12. In this case, we would also want to state that PositionList extends Iterable. Therefore, let us assume that our array lists and node lists lists support the iterator() method.

```
public interface PositionList<E> extends Iterable<E> {
  // ...all the other methods of the list ADT ...
  /** Returns an iterator of all the elements in the list. */
  public Iterator<E> iterator();
}
```

Code Fragment 6.12: Adding the iterator method to the PositionList interface.

Given such a PositionList definition, we could use an iterator returned by the iterator() method to create a string representation of a node list, as shown in Code Fragment 6.13.

```
/** Returns a textual representation of a given node list */
public static <E> String toString(PositionList<E> l) {
  Iterator<E> it = l.iterator();
  String s = "[";
  while (it.hasNext()) {
    s += it.next();   // implicit cast of the next element to String
    if (it.hasNext())
      s += ", ";
  }
  s += "]";
  return s;
}
```

Code Fragment 6.13: Example of a Java iterator used to convert a node list to a string.

6.3.2   The Java For-Each Loop

Since looping through the elements returned by an iterator is such a common construct, Java provides a shorthand notation for such loops, called the *for-each loop*. The syntax for such a loop is as follows:

for (*Type   name* : *expression*)
    loop_statement

where *expression* evaluates to a collection that implements the java.lang.Iterable interface, *Type* is the type of object returned by the iterator for this class, and *name* is the name of a variable that will take on the values of elements from this iterator in the *loop_statement*. This notation is really just shorthand for the following:

for (Iterator<*Type*> it = *expression*.iterator(); it.hasNext();) {
    Type   name = it.next();
    loop_statement
}

For example, if we had a list, values, of Integer objects, and values implements java.lang.Iterable, then we can add up all the integers in values as follows:

```
List<Integer> values;
// ... statements that create a new values list and fill it with Integers...
int sum = 0;
for (Integer i : values)
  sum += i; // unboxing allows this
```

We would read the above loop as, "for each Integer i in values, do the loop body (in this case, add i to sum)."

In addition to the above form of for-each loop, Java also allows a for-each loop to be defined for the case when *expression* is an array of type *Type*, which, in this case, can be either a base type or an object type. For example, we can total up the integers in an array, v, which stores the first ten positive integers, as follows:

```
int[] v = {1, 2, 3, 4, 5, 6, 7, 8, 9, 10};
int total = 0;
for (int i : v)
  total += i;
```

6.3.3 Implementing Iterators

One way to implement an iterator for a collection of elements is to make a "snapshot" of it and iterate over that. This approach would involve storing the collection in a separate data structure that supports sequential access to its elements. For example, we could insert all the elements of the collection into a queue, in which case method hasNext() would correspond to !isEmpty() and next() would correspond to dequeue(). With this approach, the method iterator() takes $O(n)$ time for a collection of size n. Since this copying overhead is relatively costly, we prefer, in most cases, to have iterators operate on the collection itself, not a copy.

In implementing this direct approach, we need only to keep track of where in the collection the iterator's cursor points. Thus, creating a new iterator in this case simply involves creating an iterator object that represents a cursor placed just before the first element of the collection. Likewise, performing the next() method involves returning the next element, if it exists, and moving the cursor just past this element's position. Thus, in this approach, creating an iterator takes $O(1)$ time, as do each of the iterator's methods. We show a class implementing such an iterator in Code Fragment 6.14, and we show in Code Fragment 6.15 how this iterator could be used to implement the iterator() method in the NodePositionList class.

```java
public class ElementIterator<E> implements Iterator<E> {
  protected PositionList<E> list; // the underlying list
  protected Position<E> cursor; // the next position
  /** Creates an element iterator over the given list. */
  public ElementIterator(PositionList<E> L) {
    list = L;
    cursor = (list.isEmpty())? null : list.first();
  }
  public boolean hasNext() { return (cursor != null); }
  public E next() throws NoSuchElementException {
    if (cursor == null)
      throw new NoSuchElementException("No next element");
    E toReturn = cursor.element();
    cursor = (cursor == list.last())? null : list.next(cursor);
    return toReturn;
  }
}
```

Code Fragment 6.14: An element iterator class for a PositionList.

```java
/** Returns an iterator of all the elements in the list. */
public Iterator<E> iterator() { return new ElementIterator<E>(this); }
```

Code Fragment 6.15: The iterator() method of class NodePositionList.

Position Iterators

For ADTs that support the notion of position, such as with the list ADT, we can also provide the following method:

> positions(): Return an Iterable object (like an array list or node list) containing the positions in the collection as elements.

An iterator returned by this method allows us to loop through the positions of a list. To guarantee that a node list supports this method, we could add it to the PositionList interface, as shown in Code Fragment 6.16. Then we could, for example, add an implementation of this method to the NodePositionList, as shown in Code Fragment 6.17. This method uses the NodePositionList class itself to create a list that contains the positions of the original list as its elements. Returning this list of positions as our Iterable object allows us to then call iterator() on this object to get an iterator of positions from the original list.

```
public interface PositionList<E> extends Iterable<E> {
  // ...all the other methods of the list ADT ...
  /** Returns an iterable collection of all the nodes in the list. */
  public Iterable<Position<E>> positions();
}
```

Code Fragment 6.16: Adding iterator methods to the PositionList interface.

```
/** Returns an iterable collection of all the nodes in the list. */
public Iterable<Position<E>> positions() {  // create a list of posiitons
  PositionList<Position<E>> P = new NodePositionList<Position<E>>();
  if (!isEmpty()) {
    Position<E> p = first();
    while (true) {
      P.addLast(p); // add position p as the last element of list P
      if (p == last())
        break;
      p = next(p);
    }
  }
  return P; // return P as our Iterable object
}
```

Code Fragment 6.17: The positions() method of class NodePositionList.

The iterator returned by iterator() and other Iterable objects defines a restricted type of iterator that allows only one pass through the elements. More powerful iterators can also be defined, however, which allows us to move forward and backward over a certain ordering of the elements.

6.3.4 List Iterators in Java

The java.util.LinkedList class does not expose a position concept to users in its API. Instead, the preferred way to access and update a LinkedList object in Java, without using indices, is to use a ListIterator that is generated by the linked list, using a listIterator() method. Such an iterator provides forward and backward traversal methods as well as local update methods. It views its current position as being before the first element, between two elements, or after the last element. That is, it uses a list **cursor**, much like a screen cursor is viewed as being located between two characters on a screen. Specifically, the java.util.ListIterator interface includes the following methods:

add(*e*):	Add the element *e* at the current position of the iterator.
hasNext():	True if and only if there is an element after the current position of the iterator.
hasPrevious():	True if and only if there is an element before the current position of the iterator.
previous():	Return the element *e* before the current position and sets the current position to be before *e*.
next():	Return the element *e* after the current position and sets the current position to be after *e*.
nextIndex():	Return the index of the next element.
previousIndex():	Return the index of the previous element.
set(*e*):	Replace the element returned by the previous next or previous operation with *e*.
remove():	Remove the element returned by the previous next or previous operation.

It is risky to use multiple iterators over the same list while modifying its contents. If insertions, deletions, or replacements are required at multiple "places" in a list, it is safer to use positions to specify these locations. But the java.util.LinkedList class does not expose its position objects to the user. So, to avoid the risks of modifying a list that has created multiple iterators (by calls to its iterator() method), java.util.Iterator objects have a "fail-fast" feature that immediately invalidates such an iterator if its underlying collection is modified unexpectedly. For example, if a java.util.LinkedList object L has returned five different iterators and one of them modifies L, then the other four all become immediately invalid. That is, Java allows many list iterators to be traversing a linked list L at the same time, but if one of them modifies L (using an add, set, or remove method), then all the other iterators for L become invalid. Likewise, if L is modified by one of its own update methods, then all existing iterators for L immediately become invalid.

6.4   List ADTs and the Collections Framework

In this section, we discuss general list ADTs, which combine methods of the deque, array list, and node list ADTs, and how they fit into the Java Collections Framework.

6.4.1   Lists in the Java Collections Framework

Java provides a package of data structure interfaces and classes, which together define the *Java Collections Framework*. This package, java.util, includes versions of several of the data structures discussed in this book, some of which we have already discussed and others of which we discuss later in this book. The root interface in the Java collections framework is the Collection interface. This is a general interface for any data structure that contains a collection of elements, such as a list. It extends java.lang.Iterable; hence, it includes an iterator() method, which returns an iterator of the elements in this collection. It is a superinterface for other interfaces in the Java Collections Framework that can hold elements, including the java.util interfaces Deque, List, and Queue, which are discussed above. In addition, it also has a subinterface that defines another type of collection, Set, which we discuss in Section 11.4, and it has several important related interfaces, including the Iterator and ListIterator interfaces discussed above, as well as the Map interface discussed in Section 9.1.

    The Java Collections Framework also includes several concrete list-based classes implementing various combinations of list-based interfaces. These include the following java.util classes:

ArrayBlockingQueue: An array implementation of the Queue interface that allows for a capacity limit.

ArrayDeque: An implementation of the Deque interface that uses an array, which can grow or shrink, as needed.

ArrayList: An implementation of the List interface that uses an array, which can grow or shrink, as needed.

ConcurrentLinkedQueue: A linked list FIFO queue implementation of the Queue interface that is thread safe.

LinkedBlockingDeque: A linked list implementation of the Deque interface that allows for a capacity limit.

LinkedBlockingQueue: A linked list implementation of the Queue interface that allows for a capacity limit.

LinkedList: A linked list implementation of the List interface.

Stack: An implementation of the stack ADT.

Collections are Iterable

Each of the above list-based classes in the Java Collections Framework implements the java.lang.Iterable interface; hence, it includes an iterator() method and can be used in a for-each loop. In addition, any class implementing the java.util.List interface, such as the ArrayList and LinkedList classes, also includes a listIterator() method, as well. As we observed above, such interfaces are useful for looping through the elements of a collection or list.

List-Based Algorithms in the Java Collections Framework

In addition to the list-based classes that are provided in the Java Collections Framework, there are a number of simple algorithms that it provides as well. These algorithms are implemented as static methods in the java.util.Collections class and they include the following methods:

disjoint(C, D): Returns a Boolean value indicating whether the collections C and D are disjoint.

fill(L, e): Replaces each of the elements in the list L with the same element, e.

frequency(C, e): Returns the number of elements in the collection C that are equal to e.

max(C): Returns the maximum element in the collection C, based on the natural ordering of its elements.

min(C): Returns the minimum element in the collection C, based on the natural ordering of its elements.

replaceAll(L, e, f): Replaces each element in L that is equal to e with the same element, f.

reverse(L): Reverses the ordering of elements in the list L.

rotate(L, d): Rotates the elements in the list L by the distance d (which can be negative), in a circular fashion.

shuffle(L): Pseudo-randomly permutes the ordering of the elements in the list L.

sort(L): Sorts the list L, using the natural ordering of the elements in L.

Converting Lists into Arrays

Lists are a beautiful concept and they can be applied in a number of different contexts, but there are some instances where it would be useful if we could treat a list like an array. Fortunately, the java.util.Collection interface includes the following helpful methods for generating an array that has the same elements as the given collection:

> toArray(): Returns an array of elements of type Object containing all the elements in this collection.

> toArray(A): Returns an array of elements of the same element type as A containing all the elements in this collection.

If the collection is a list, then the returned array must have its elements stored in the same ordering as that of the original list. Thus, if we have a useful array-based method that we want to use on a list or other type of collection, then we can do so by simply using that collection's toArray() method to to produce an array representation of that collection. For instance, if we want to print out a list of arrays, arrList, performing the following won't work:

```
System.out.println("arrList = " + arrList.toString()); // WRONG!
```

Instead, we should do something like this:

```
System.out.println("arrList = " + Arrays.deepToString(arrList.toArray()));
```

Converting Arrays into Lists

In a similar vein, it is often useful to be able to convert an array into an equivalent list. Fortunately, the java.util.Arrays class includes the following method:

> asList(A): Returns a list representation of the array A, with the same element type as the elements of A.

The list returned by this method uses the array A as its internal representation for the list. So this list is guaranteed to be an array-based list and any changes made to it will automatically be reflected in A. Because of these types of side effects, use of the asList method should always be done with caution, so as to avoid unintended consequences. But, used with care, this method can often save us a lot of work. For instance, the following code fragment could be used to randomly shuffle an array of integers, arr:

```
Integer[] arr = {1, 2, 3, 4, 5, 6, 7, 8}; // allowed by autoboxing
List<Integer> listArr= Arrays.asList(arr);
Collections.shuffle(listArr);      // this has side effect of shuffling arr
```

The java.util.List Interface and Its Implementations

Java provides functionality similar to our array list and node lists ADT in the java.util.List interface, which is implemented with an array in java.util.ArrayList and with a linked list in java.util.LinkedList. There are some trade-offs between these two implementations, which we explore in more detail in the next section. Moreover, Java uses iterators to achieve a functionality similar to what our node list ADT derives from positions. Table 6.4 shows corresponding methods between our (array and node) list ADTs and the java.util interfaces List and ListIterator interfaces, with notes about their implementations in the java.util classes ArrayList and LinkedList.

List ADT Method	java.util.List Method	ListIterator Method	Notes
size()	size()		$O(1)$ time
isEmpty()	isEmpty()		$O(1)$ time
get(i)	get(i)		A is $O(1)$, L is $O(\min\{i, n-i\})$
first()	listIterator()		first element is next
last()	listIterator(size())		last element is previous
prev(p)		previous()	$O(1)$ time
next(p)		next()	$O(1)$ time
set(p,e)		set(e)	$O(1)$ time
set(i,e)	set(i,e)		A is $O(1)$, L is $O(\min\{i, n-i\})$
add(i,e)	add(i,e)		$O(n)$ time
remove(i)	remove(i)		A is $O(1)$, L is $O(\min\{i, n-i\})$
addFirst(e)	add($0,e$)		A is $O(n)$, L is $O(1)$
addFirst(e)	addFirst(e)		only exists in L, $O(1)$
addLast(e)	add(e)		$O(1)$ time
addLast(e)	addLast(e)		only exists in L, $O(1)$
addAfter(p,e)		add(e)	insertion is at cursor; A is $O(n)$, L is $O(1)$
addBefore(p,e)		add(e)	insertion is at cursor; A is $O(n)$, L is $O(1)$
remove(p)		remove()	deletion is at cursor; A is $O(n)$, L is $O(1)$

Table 6.4: Correspondences between methods in the array list and node list ADTs and the java.util interfaces List and ListIterator. We use A and L as abbreviations for java.util.ArrayList and java.util.LinkedList (or their running times).

6.4.2   Sequences

A *sequence* is an ADT that supports all of the methods of the deque ADT (Section 5.3), the array list ADT (Section 6.1), and the node list ADT (Section 6.2). That is, it provides explicit access to the elements in the list either by their indices or by their positions. Moreover, since it provides this dual access capability, we also include, in the sequence ADT, the following two "bridging" methods that provide connections between indices and positions:

> atIndex(i): Return the position of the element with index i; an error condition occurs if $i < 0$ or $i > \text{size}() - 1$.

> indexOf(p): Return the index of the element at position p.

Multiple Inheritance in the Sequence ADT

The definition of the sequence ADT as including all the methods from three different ADTs is an example of *multiple inheritance* (Section 2.4.2). That is, the sequence ADT inherits methods from three "super" abstract data types. In other words, its methods include the union of the methods of these super ADTs. See Code Fragment 6.18 for a Java specification of the sequence ADT as a Java interface.

```
/**
 * An interface for a sequence, a data structure supporting all
 * operations of a deque, indexed list and position list.
 */
public interface Sequence<E>
     extends Deque<E>, IndexList<E>, PositionList<E> {
  /** Returns the position containing the element at the given index. */
  public Position<E> atIndex(int r) throws BoundaryViolationException;
  /** Returns the index of the element stored at the given position. */
  public int indexOf(Position<E> p) throws InvalidPositionException;
}
```

Code Fragment 6.18: The Sequence interface defined via multiple inheritance. It includes all the methods of the Deque, IndexList, and PositionList interfaces (defined for any generic type E), and adds two more methods.

In essence, the sequence ADT combines the functionality of the java.util.List and java.util.ListIterator interfaces.

Implementing a Sequence with a Linked List

Suppose we implement a sequence with a doubly linked list, which, as the documentation for the java.util.LinkedList class makes clear, is the implementation for this class. With this implementation, all of the position-based update methods run in $O(1)$ time each (just like the list iterator update methods in java.util.LinkedList). Likewise, all of the methods of the deque ADT also run in $O(1)$ time each, since they merely involve updating or querying the list at its ends. But the methods from the array list ADT (which are also included in the java.util.LinkedList class) are not well-suited to an implementation of a sequence with a doubly linked list.

Efficiency Trade-Offs with a Linked-List-Based Sequence

Since a linked list does not allow for indexed access to its elements, performing the operation get(i), to return the element at a given index i, requires that we perform link "hopping" from one of the ends of the list, counting up or down, until we locate the node storing the element with index i. As a slight optimization, we observe that we can start this hopping from the closer end of the list, thus achieving a running time that is

$$O(\min(i+1, n-i)),$$

where n is the number of elements in the list. The worst case for this kind of search occurs when

$$r = \lfloor n/2 \rfloor.$$

Thus, the running time is still $O(n)$.

The index-based update operations add(i,e) and remove(i) also must perform link hopping to locate the node storing the element with index i, and then insert or delete a node. The running times of these implementations of add(i,e) and remove(i) are likewise

$$O(\min(i+1, n-i+1)),$$

which is $O(n)$. One advantage of this approach is that,

$$\text{if } i = 0 \text{ or } i = n-1,$$

as is the case in the adaptation of the array list ADT to the deque ADT given in Section 6.1.1, then add and remove run in $O(1)$ time. Thus, in general, using array-list methods with a sequence implemented with a linked list is inefficient.

Implementing a Sequence with an Array

Suppose instead we implement a sequence S by storing each element e of S in a cell $A[i]$ of an array A. We can define a position object p to hold an index i and a reference to array A, as instance variables, in this case. We can then implement method element(p) simply by returning $A[i]$. A major drawback with this approach, however, is that the cells in A have no way to reference their corresponding positions. Thus, after performing an addFirst operation, we have no way of informing the existing positions in S that their indices each went up by 1 (remember that positions in a sequence are always defined relative to their neighboring positions, not their indices). Hence, if we are going to implement a general sequence with an array, we need a different approach.

Consider an alternate solution, then, in which, instead of storing the elements of S in array A, we store a new kind of position object in each cell of A, and we store elements in positions. The new position object p holds the index i and the element e associated with p.

With this data structure, illustrated in Figure 6.8, we can easily scan through the array to update the index variable i for each position whose index changes because of an insertion or deletion.

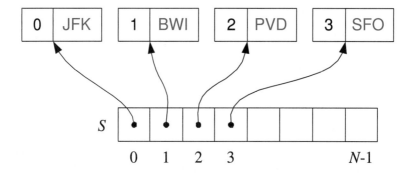

Figure 6.8: An array-based implementation of the sequence ADT.

Efficiency Trade-Offs with an Array-Based Sequence

In this array implementation of a sequence, the addFirst, addBefore, addAfter, and remove methods take $O(n)$ time, because we have to shift position objects to make room for the new position or to fill in the hole created by the removal of the old position (just as in the insert and remove methods based on index). All the other position-based methods take $O(1)$ time.

6.5 Case Study: The Move-to-Front Heuristic

Suppose we would like to maintain a collection of elements while keeping track of the number of times each element is accessed. Keeping such access counts allows us to know which elements are among the "top ten" most popular, for instance. Examples of such scenarios include a Web browser that keeps track of the most popular Web addresses (or URLs) a user visits or a photo album program that maintains a list of the most popular images a user views. In addition, a favorites list could be used in a graphical user interface (GUI) to keep track of the most popular buttons used in a pull-down menu, and then present the user with condensed pull-downs containing the most popular options.

Therefore, in this section, we consider how we can implement a *favorite list* ADT, which supports the size() and isEmpty() methods as well as the following:

> access(*e*): Access the element *e*, incrementing its access count, and adding it to the favorites list if it is not already present.

> remove(*e*): Remove element *e* from the favorites list, provided it is already there.

> top(*k*): Return an iterable collection of the *k* most accessed elements.

6.5.1 Using a Sorted List and a Nested Class

The first implementation of a favorite list that we consider (in Code Fragments 6.19 and 6.20) is to build a class, FavoriteList, storing references to accessed objects in a linked list ordered by nonincreasing access counts. This class also uses a feature of Java that allows us to define a related class nested inside an enclosing class definition. Such a *nested class* must be declared **static**, to indicate that this definition is related to the enclosing class, not any specific instance of that class. Using nested classes allows us to define "helper" or "support" classes that can be protected from outside use.

In this case, the nested class, Entry, stores, for each element *e* in our list, a pair (c, v), where *c* is the access count for *e* and *v* is a *value* reference to the element *e* itself. Each time an element is accessed, we find it in the linked list (adding it if it is not already there) and increment its access count. Removing an element amounts to finding it and taking it out of our linked list. Returning the *k* most accessed elements simply involves our copying the entry values into an output list according to their order in the internal linked list.

```java
/** List of favorite elements, with their access counts. */
public class FavoriteList<E> {
  protected PositionList<Entry<E>> fList;   // List of entries
  /** Constructor; O(1) time */
  public FavoriteList() { fList = new NodePositionList<Entry<E>>(); }
  /** Returns the number of elements in the list; O(1) time */
  public int size() { return fList.size(); }
  /** Returns whether the list is empty; O(1) time */
  public boolean isEmpty() { return fList.isEmpty(); }
  /** Removes a given element, provided it is in the list; O(n) time */
  public void remove(E obj) {
    Position<Entry<E>> p = find(obj); // search for obj
    if (p != null)
      fList.remove(p);              // remove the entry
  }
  /** Increments the access count for the given element and inserts it
   * if it is not already present; O(n) time */
  public void access(E obj) {
    Position<Entry<E>> p = find(obj); // find the position of obj
    if (p != null)
      p.element().incrementCount();   // increment access count
    else {
      fList.addLast(new Entry<E>(obj)); // add the new entry at the end
      p = fList.last();
    }
    moveUp(p);          // moves the entry to its final position
  }
  /** Finds the position of a given element, or returns null; O(n) time */
  protected Position<Entry<E>> find(E obj) {
    for (Position<Entry<E>> p: fList.positions())
      if (value(p).equals(obj))
        return p;       // fount at position p
    return null;        // not found
  }
  /** Moves up an entry to its correct position in the list; O(n) time */
  protected void moveUp(Position<Entry<E>> cur) {
    Entry<E> e = cur.element();
    int c = count(cur);
    while (cur != fList.first()) {
      Position<Entry<E>> prev = fList.prev(cur);    // previous position
      if (c <= count(prev)) break;     // entry is at correct position
      fList.set(cur, prev.element());       // move down previous entry
      cur = prev;
    }
    fList.set(cur, e);    // store the entry in its final position
  }
}
```

Code Fragment 6.19: Class FavoritesList. (Continues in Code Fragment 6.20.)

```
/** Returns the k most accessed elements, for a given k; O(k) time */
public Iterable<E> top(int k) {
  if (k < 0 || k > size())
    throw new IllegalArgumentException("Invalid argument");
  PositionList<E> T = new NodePositionList<E>(); // top-k list
  int i = 0;  // counter of the entries added to the list
  for (Entry<E> e: fList) {
    if (i++ >= k)
      break;         // all the k entries have been added
    T.addLast(e.value());    // add one entry to the list
  }
  return T;
}
/** String representation of the favorite list */
public String toString() { return fList.toString(); }
/** Helper method that extracts the value of the entry at a given position */
protected E value(Position<Entry<E>> p) { return ( p.element()).value(); }
/** Helper method that extracts the counter of the entry at a given position */
protected int count(Position<Entry<E>> p) { return ( p.element()).count(); }
/** Inner class storing elements and their access counts. */
protected static class Entry<E> {
  private E value;    // element
  private int count;  // access count
  /** Constructor */
  Entry(E v) { count = 1; value = v; }
  /** Returns the element */
  public E value() { return value; }
  /** Returns the access count */
  public int count() { return count; }
  /** Increments the access count */
  public int incrementCount() { return ++count; }
  /** String representation of the entry as [count,value] */
  public String toString() { return "[" + count + "," + value + "]"; }
}
} // End of FavoriteList class
```

Code Fragment 6.20: Class FavoriteList, including a nested class, Entry, for representing elements and their access count. (Continued from Code Fragment 6.19.)

6.5.2   Using a List with the Move-to-Front Heuristic

The previous implementation of a favorite list performs the access(e) method in time proportional to the index of e in the favorite list. That is, if e is the kth most popular element in the favorite list, then accessing it takes $O(k)$ time. In many real-life access sequences, including those formed by the visits that users make to Web pages, it is common that, once an element is accessed, it is likely to be accessed again in the near future. Such scenarios are said to possess *locality of reference*.

A *heuristic*, or rule of thumb, that attempts to take advantage of the locality of reference that is present in an access sequence is the *move-to-front heuristic*. To apply this heuristic, each time we access an element we move it all the way to the front of the list. Our hope, of course, is that this element will then be accessed again in the near future. Consider, for example, a scenario in which we have n elements and the following series of n^2 accesses:

- element 1 is accessed n times
- element 2 is accessed n times
- ...
- element n is accessed n times.

If we store the elements sorted by their access counts, inserting each element the first time it is accessed, then

- each access to element 1 runs in $O(1)$ time
- each access to element 2 runs in $O(2)$ time
- ...
- each access to element n runs in $O(n)$ time.

Thus, the total time for performing the series of accesses is proportional to

$$n + 2n + 3n + \cdots + n \cdot n = n(1 + 2 + 3 + \cdots + n) = n \cdot \frac{n(n+1)}{2},$$

which is $O(n^3)$.

On the other hand, if we use the move-to-front heuristic, inserting each element the first time it is accessed, then

- each access to element 1 takes $O(1)$ time
- each access to element 2 takes $O(1)$ time
- ...
- each access to element n runs in $O(1)$ time.

So the running time for performing all the accesses in this case is $O(n^2)$. Thus, the move-to-front implementation has faster access times for this scenario. This benefit comes at a cost, however.

Implementing the Move-to-Front Heuristic in Java

In Code Fragment 6.21, we give an implementation of a favorite list using the move-to-front heuristic. We implement the move-to-front approach in this case by defining a new class, FavoriteListMTF, which extends the FavoriteList class and then overrides the definitions of the moveUp and top methods. The moveUp method in this case simply removes the accessed element from its present position in the linked list and then inserts this element back in this list at the front. The top method, on the other hand, is more complicated.

The Trade-Offs with the Move-to-Front Heuristic

Now that we are no longer maintaining the favorite list as a list of entries ordered by their value's access counts, when we are asked to find the k most accessed elements, we need to search for them. In particular, we can implement method top(k) as follows:

1. We copy the entries of our favorite list into another list, C, and we create an empty list, T.

2. We scan list C k times. In each scan, we find an entry of C with the largest access count, remove this entry from C, and insert its value at the end of T.

3. We return list T.

This implementation of method top takes $O(kn)$ time. Thus, when k is a constant, method top runs in $O(n)$ time. This occurs, for example, when we want to get the "top ten" list. However, if k is proportional to n, then top runs in $O(n^2)$ time. This occurs, for example, when we want a "top 25%" list.

Still, the move-to-front approach is just a heuristic, or rule of thumb, for there are access sequences where using the move-to-front approach is slower than simply keeping the favorite list ordered by access counts. In addition, it trades off the potential speed of performing accesses that possess locality of reference, for a slower reporting of the top elements.

6.5.3 Possible Uses of a Favorites List

In Code Fragment 6.22, we use an example application of our favorite list implementations to solve the problem of maintaining the most popular URLs in a simulated sequence of Web page accesses. This program accesses a set of URLs in decreasing order and then pops up a window showing the most popular Web page accessed in the simulation.

```java
public class FavoriteListMTF<E> extends FavoriteList<E> {
  /** Default constructor */
  public FavoriteListMTF() { }
  /** Moves up an entry to the first position; O(1) time */
  protected void moveUp(Position<Entry<E>> pos) {
    fList.addFirst(fList.remove(pos));
  }
  /** Returns the k most accessed elements, for a given k; O(kn) time */
  public Iterable<E> top(int k) {
    if (k < 0 || k > size())
      throw new IllegalArgumentException("Invalid argument");
    PositionList<E> T = new NodePositionList<E>(); // top-k list
    if (!isEmpty()) {
      // copy entries into temporary list C
      PositionList<Entry<E>> C = new NodePositionList<Entry<E>>();
      for (Entry<E> e: fList)
        C.addLast(e);
      // find the top k elements, one at a time
      for (int i = 0; i < k; i++) {
        Position<Entry<E>> maxPos = null; // position of top entry
        int maxCount = -1;                // access count of top entry
        for (Position<Entry<E>> p: C.positions()) {
          // examine all entries of C
          int c = count(p);
          if (c > maxCount) { // found an entry with higher access count
            maxCount = c;
            maxPos = p;
          }
        }
        T.addLast(value(maxPos));     // add top entry to list T
        C.remove(maxPos);             // remove top entry from list C
      }
    }
    return T;
  }
}
```

Code Fragment 6.21: Class FavoriteListMTF implementing the move-to-front heuristic. This class extends FavoriteList (Code Fragments 6.19 and 6.20) and overrides methods moveUp and top.

```java
import java.io.*;
import javax.swing.*;
import java.awt.*;
import java.net.*;
import java.util.Random;
/** Example program for the FavoriteList and FavoriteListMTF classes */
public class FavoriteTester {
  public static void main(String[] args) {
    String[] urlArray = {"http://wiley.com", "http://datastructures.net",
                "http://algorithmdesign.net", "http://www.brown.edu",
                "http://uci.edu" };
    FavoriteList<String> L1 = new FavoriteList<String>();
    FavoriteListMTF<String> L2 = new FavoriteListMTF<String>();
    int n = 20; // number of access operations
    // Simulation scenario: access n times a random URL
    Random rand = new Random();
    for (int k = 0; k < n; k++) {
      System.out.println("-------------------------------------------------");
      int i = rand.nextInt(urlArray.length);    // random index
      String url = urlArray[i];                  // random URL
      System.out.println("Accessing: " + url);
      L1.access(url);
      System.out.println("L1 = " + L1);
      L2.access(url);
      System.out.println("L2 = " + L2);
    }
    int t = L1.size()/2;
    System.out.println("----------------------------------------------");
    System.out.println("Top " + t + " in L1 = " + L1.top(t));
    System.out.println("Top " + t + " in L2 = " + L2.top(t));
    // Pop up a browser window displaying the most popular URL in L1
    try {
      String popular = L1.top(1).iterator().next(); // most popular URL in L1
      JEditorPane jep = new JEditorPane(popular);
      jep.setEditable(false);
      JFrame frame = new JFrame(popular);
      frame.getContentPane().add(new JScrollPane(jep), BorderLayout.CENTER);
      frame.setSize(640, 480);
      frame.setVisible(true);
    } catch (IOException e) { // ignore I/O exceptions
    }
  }
}
```

Code Fragment 6.22: Illustrating the use of the FavoritesList and FavoriteListMTF classes for counting Web page access counts. This simulation randomly accesses several Web pages and then displays the most popular page.

6.6 Exercises

For help with exercises, please visit the web site, www.wiley.com/college/goodrich.

Reinforcement

R-6.1 Give a Java code fragment for reversing an array, using a list.

R-6.2 Give a Java code fragment for randomly shuffling an array, using a list.

R-6.3 Give Java code for circularly rotating an array by distance d.

R-6.4 Draw a representation of an initially empty array list A after performing the following sequence of operations: add(0,4), add(0,3), add(0,2), add(2,1), add(1,5), add(1,6), add(3,7), add(0,8).

R-6.5 Give a justification of the running times shown in Table 6.2 for the methods of an array list implemented with a (nonexpanding) array.

R-6.6 Give an adapter class to support the Stack interface using the methods of the array list ADT.

R-6.7 Redo the justification of Proposition 6.2 assuming that the the cost of growing the array from size k to size $2k$ is $3k$ cyber-dollars. How much should each push operation be charged to make the amortization work?

R-6.8 Give pseudo-code descriptions of algorithms for performing the methods addBefore(p,e), addFirst(e), and addLast(e) of the node list ADT, assuming the list is implemented using a doubly linked list.

R-6.9 Draw pictures illustrating each of the major steps in the algorithms given in the previous exercise.

R-6.10 Provide the details of an array implementation of the node list ADT, including how to perform the methods addBefore and addAfter.

R-6.11 Provide Java code fragments for the methods of the PositionList interface of Code Fragment 6.5 that are not included in Code Fragments 6.9–6.11.

R-6.12 Describe a nonrecursive method for reversing a node list represented with a doubly linked list using a single pass through the list.

R-6.13 Given the set of element $\{a,b,c,d,e,f\}$ stored in a list, show the final state of the list, assuming we use the move-to-front heuristic and access the elements according to the following sequence: $(a,b,c,d,e,f,a,c,f,b,d,e)$.

R-6.14 Suppose that we have made kn total accesses to the elements in a list L of n elements, for some integer $k \geq 1$. What are the minimum and maximum number of elements that have been accessed fewer than k times?

R-6.15 Give pseudo-code describing how to implement all the operations in the array list ADT using an array whose elements are stored in a contiguous fashion. What is the running time of each method?

R-6.16 Using the Sequence interface methods, describe a recursive method for determining if a sequence S of n integers contains a given integer k. Your method should not contain any loops. How much space does your method use in addition to the space used for S?

R-6.17 Briefly describe how to perform a new sequence method makeFirst(p) that moves an element of a sequence S at position p to be the first element in S while keeping the relative ordering of the remaining elements in S unchanged. That is, makeFirst(p) performs a move-to-front. Your method should run in $O(1)$ time if S is implemented with a doubly linked list.

R-6.18 Describe how to use an array list and an **int** field to implement an iterator. Include pseudo-code fragments describing hasNext() and next().

R-6.19 Describe how to create an iterator for a node list that returns every other element in the list.

R-6.20 Suppose we are maintaining a collection C of elements such that, each time we add a new element to the collection, we copy the contents of C into a new array list of just the right size. What is the running time of adding n elements to an initially empty collection C in this case?

R-6.21 Describe an implementation of the methods addLast and addBefore realized by using only methods in the set {isEmpty, checkPosition, first, last, prev, next, addAfter, addFirst}.

R-6.22 Let L be maintained to be a list of n items ordered by decreasing access count. Describe a series of $O(n^2)$ accesses that will reverse L.

R-6.23 Let L be a list of n items maintained according to the move-to-front heuristic. Describe a series of $O(n)$ accesses that will reverse L.

R-6.24 Give a short Java code fragment for sorting a list by converting it to an array and using the java.util.Arrays.sort method.

Creativity

C-6.1 Give pseudo-code for the methods of a class, ShrinkingArrayList, that extends the class ArrayIndexList shown in Code Fragment 6.3 and adds a method, shrinkToFit(), which replaces the underlying array with one whose capacity is equal to the number of elements currently in the list.

C-6.2 Describe the changes needed to the extendable array implementation given in Code Fragment 6.3 in order to have it shrink by half the size, N, of the array any time the number of elements in the array list goes below $N/4$.

C-6.3 Show that, using an extendable array that grows and shrinks as in the previous exercise, the following series of $2n$ operations takes $O(n)$ time: (i) n push operations on an array list with initial capacity $N = 1$; (ii) n pop (removal of the last element) operations.

C-6.4 Describe a method for performing a *card shuffle* of an array of $2n$ elements, by converting it into two lists. A card shuffle is a permutation where a list L is cut into two lists, L_1 and L_2, where L_1 is the first half of L and L_2 is the second half of L, and then these two lists are merged into one by taking the first element in L_1, then the first element in L_2, followed by the second element in L_1, the second element in L_2, and so on.

C-6.5 Show how to improve the implementation of method add in Code Fragment 6.3 so that, in case of an overflow, elements are copied into their final place in the new array, that is, no shifting should be done.

C-6.6 Consider an implementation of the array list ADT using an extendable array, but instead of copying the elements into an array of double the size (that is, from N to $2N$) when its capacity is reached, we copy the elements into an array with $\lceil N/4 \rceil$ additional cells, going from capacity N to $N + \lceil N/4 \rceil$. Show that performing a sequence of n push operations (that is, insertions at the end) still runs in $O(n)$ time in this case.

C-6.7 The NodePositionList implementation given in Code Fragments 6.9–6.11 does not do any error checks to test if a given position p is actually a member of this particular list. For example, if p is a position in list S and we call T.addAfter(p,e) on a different list T, then we actually will add the element to S just after p. Describe how to change the NodePositionList implementation in an efficient manner to disallow such misuses.

C-6.8 Suppose we want to extend the Sequence abstract data type with methods indexOfElement(e) and positionOfElement(e), which respectively return the index and the position of the (first occurrence of) element e in the sequence. Show how to implement these methods by expressing them in terms of other methods of the Sequence interface.

C-6.9 Give an adaptation of the array list ADT to the deque ADT that is different from that given in Table 6.1.

C-6.10 Give a pseudo-code description for an array-based implementation of the array list ADT that achieves $O(1)$ time for insertions and removals at index 0, as well as insertions and removals at the end of the array list. Your implementation should also provide for a constant-time get method.

C-6.11 Describe an efficient way of putting an array list representing a deck of n cards into random order. You may use a function, randomInteger(n), which returns a random number between 0 and $n - 1$, inclusive. Your method should guarantee that every possible ordering is equally likely. What is the running time of your method?

C-6.12 Describe an efficient method for maintaining a favorites list L such that every element in L has been accessed at least once in the last n accesses, where n is the size of L.

C-6.13 Suppose we have an n-element list L maintained according to the move-to-front heuristic. Describe a sequence of n^2 accesses that is guaranteed to take $\Omega(n^3)$ time to perform on L.

C-6.14 Design a circular node list ADT that abstracts a circularly linked list in the same way that the node list ADT abstracts a doubly linked list.

C-6.15 Describe how to implement an iterator for a circularly linked list. Since hasNext() will always return **true** in this case, describe how to perform hasNewNext(), which returns **true** if and only if the next node in the list has not previously had its element returned by this iterator.

C-6.16 Describe a scheme for creating list iterators that *fail fast*, that is, they all become invalid as soon as the underlying list changes.

C-6.17 An array is *sparse* if most of its entries are **null**. A list L can be used to implement such an array, A, efficiently. In particular, for each nonnull cell $A[i]$, we can store an entry (i, e) in L, where e is the element stored at $A[i]$. This approach allows us to represent A using $O(m)$ storage, where m is the number of nonnull entries in A. Describe and analyze efficient ways of performing the methods of the array list ADT on such a representation.

C-6.18 There is a simple, but inefficient, algorithm, called *bubble-sort*, for sorting a sequence S of n comparable elements. This algorithm scans the sequence $n - 1$ times, where, in each scan, the algorithm compares the current element with the next one and swaps them if they are out of order. Give a pseudo-code description of bubble-sort that is as efficient as possible assuming S is implemented with a doubly linked list. What is the running time of this algorithm?

C-6.19 Answer Exercise C-6.18 assuming S is implemented with an array list.

C-6.20 A useful operation in databases is the *natural join*. If we view a database as a list of ordered pairs of objects, then the natural join of databases A and B is the list of all ordered triples (x, y, z) such that the pair (x, y) is in A and the pair (y, z) is in B. Describe and analyze an efficient algorithm for computing the natural join of a list A of n pairs and a list B of m pairs.

C-6.21 When Bob wants to send Alice a message M on the Internet, he breaks M into n *data packets*, numbers the packets consecutively, and injects them into the network. When the packets arrive at Alice's computer, they may be out of order, so Alice must assemble the sequence of n packets in order before she can be sure she has the entire message. Describe an efficient scheme for Alice to do this. What is the running time of this algorithm?

C-6.22 Given a list L of n positive integers, each represented with $k = \lceil \log n \rceil + 1$ bits, describe an $O(n)$-time method for finding a k-bit integer not in L.

C-6.23 Argue why any solution to the previous problem must run in $\Omega(n)$ time.

C-6.24 Given a list L of n arbitrary integers, design an $O(n)$-time method for finding an integer that cannot be formed as the sum of two integers in L.

C-6.25 Isabel has an interesting way of summing up the values in an array A of n integers, where n is a power of two. She creates an array B of half the size of A and sets $B[i] = A[2i] + A[2i+1]$, for $i = 0, 1, \ldots, (n/2) - 1$. If B has size 1, then she outputs $B[0]$. Otherwise, she replaces A with B, and repeats the process. What is the running time of her algorithm?

Projects

P-6.1 Implement an adapter class that allows one to perform all of the relevant list-based methods of the java.util.Collections class on arrays.

P-6.2 Implement the array list ADT by means of an extendable array used in a circular fashion, so that insertions and deletions at the beginning and end of the array list run in constant time.

P-6.3 Implement the array list ADT using a doubly linked list. Show experimentally that this implementation is worse than the array-based approach.

P-6.4 Write a simple text editor, which stores and displays a string of characters using the list ADT, together with a cursor object that highlights a position in this string. Your editor should support the following operations:
  - left: Move cursor left one character (do nothing if at text end).
  - right: Move cursor right one character (do nothing if at text end).
  - cut: Delete the character right of the cursor (do nothing at text end).
  - paste c: Insert the character c just after the cursor.

P-6.5 Implement a ***phased favorites list***. A phase consists of N accesses in the list, for a given parameter N. During a phase, the list should maintain itself so that elements are ordered by decreasing access counts during that phase. At the end of a phase, it should clear all the access counts and start the next phase. Test this implementation's efficiency.

P-6.6 Write a complete adapter class that implements the sequence ADT using a java.util.ArrayList object.

P-6.7 Implement the favorites list application using an array list.

Chapter Notes

The concept of viewing data structures as collections (and other principles of object-oriented design) can be found in object-oriented design books by Booch [15], Budd [18], Golberg and Robson [38], and Liskov and Guttag [69]. Lists and iterators are pervasive concepts in the Java Collections Framework. Our node list ADT is derived from the "position" abstraction introduced by Aho, Hopcroft, and Ullman [5], and the list ADT of Wood [100]. Implementations of lists via arrays and linked lists are discussed by Knuth [62].

Chapter

7

Trees

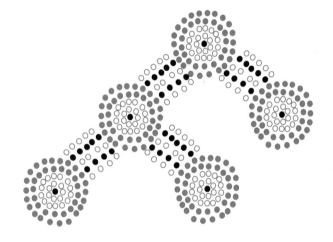

Contents

7.1   General Trees

Productivity experts say that breakthroughs come by thinking "nonlinearly." In this chapter, we discuss one of the most important nonlinear data structures in computing—***trees***. Tree structures are indeed a breakthrough in data organization, for they allow us to implement a host of algorithms much faster than when using linear data structures, such as list. Trees also provide a natural organization for data, and consequently have become ubiquitous structures in file systems, graphical user interfaces, databases, Web sites, and other computer systems.

It is not always clear what productivity experts mean by "nonlinear" thinking, but when we say that trees are "nonlinear," we are referring to an organizational relationship that is richer than the simple "before" and "after" relationships between objects in sequences. The relationships in a tree are ***hierarchical***, with some objects being "above" and some "below" others. Actually, the main terminology for tree data structures comes from family trees, with the terms "parent," "child," "ancestor," and "descendent" being the most common words used to describe relationships. We show an example of a family tree in Figure 7.1.

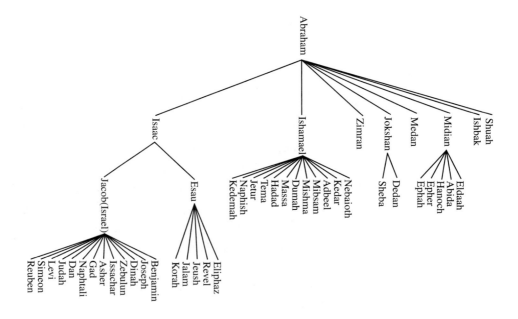

Figure 7.1: A family tree showing some descendents of Abraham, as recorded in Genesis, chapters 25–36.

7.1.1 Tree Definitions and Properties

A *tree* is an abstract data type that stores elements hierarchically. With the exception of the top element, each element in a tree has a *parent* element and zero or more *children* elements. A tree is usually visualized by placing elements inside ovals or rectangles, and by drawing the connections between parents and children with straight lines. (See Figure 7.2.) We typically call the top element the *root* of the tree, but it is drawn as the highest element, with the other elements being connected below (just the opposite of a botanical tree).

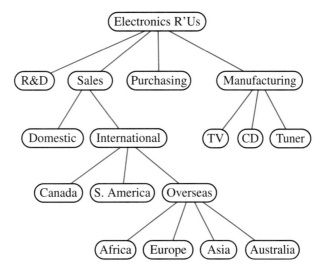

Figure 7.2: A tree with 17 nodes representing the organization of a fictitious corporation. The root stores *Electronics R'Us*. The children of the root store *R&D*, *Sales*, *Purchasing*, and *Manufacturing*. The internal nodes store *Sales*, *International*, *Overseas*, *Electronics R'Us*, and *Manufacturing*.

Formal Tree Definition

Formally, we define a *tree* T as a set of *nodes* storing elements such that the nodes have a *parent-child* relationship, that satisfies the following properties:

- If T is nonempty, it has a special node, called the *root* of T, that has no parent.
- Each node v of T different from the root has a unique *parent* node w; every node with parent w is a *child* of w.

Note that according to our definition, a tree can be empty, meaning that it doesn't have any nodes. This convention also allows us to define a tree recursively, such that a tree T is either empty or consists of a node r, called the root of T, and a (possibly empty) set of trees whose roots are the children of r.

Other Node Relationships

Two nodes that are children of the same parent are **siblings**. A node v is **external** if v has no children. A node v is **internal** if it has one or more children. External nodes are also known as **leaves**.

Example 7.1: *In most operating systems, files are organized hierarchically into nested directories (also called folders), which are presented to the user in the form of a tree. (See Figure 7.3.) More specifically, the internal nodes of the tree are associated with directories and the external nodes are associated with regular files. In the UNIX and Linux operating systems, the root of the tree is appropriately called the "root directory," and is represented by the symbol "/."*

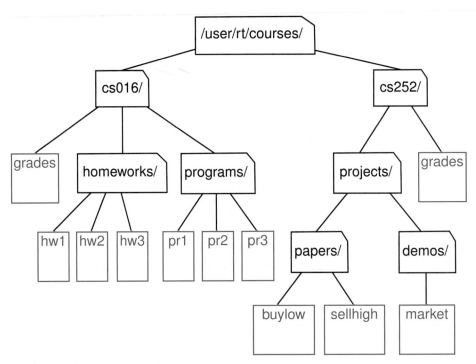

Figure 7.3: Tree representing a portion of a file system.

A node u is an **ancestor** of a node v if $u = v$ or u is an ancestor of the parent of v. Conversely, we say that a node v is a **descendent** of a node u if u is an ancestor of v. For example, in Figure 7.3, cs252/ is an ancestor of papers/, and pr3 is a descendent of cs016/. The **subtree** of T **rooted** at a node v is the tree consisting of all the descendents of v in T (including v itself). In Figure 7.3, the subtree rooted at cs016/ consists of the nodes cs016/, grades, homeworks/, programs/, hw1, hw2, hw3, pr1, pr2, and pr3.

Edges and Paths in Trees

An *edge* of tree T is a pair of nodes (u, v) such that u is the parent of v, or vice versa. A *path* of T is a sequence of nodes such that any two consecutive nodes in the sequence form an edge. For example, the tree in Figure 7.3 contains the path (cs252/, projects/, demos/, market).

Example 7.2: *The inheritance relation between classes in a Java program forms a tree. The root,* java.lang.Object, *is an ancestor of all other classes. Each class, C, is a descendent of this root and is the root of a subtree of the classes that extend C. Thus, there is a path from C to the root,* java.lang.Object, *in this inheritance tree.*

Ordered Trees

A tree is *ordered* if there is a linear ordering defined for the children of each node; that is, we can identify the children of a node as being the first, second, third, and so on. Such an ordering is usually visualized by arranging siblings left to right, according to their ordering. Ordered trees typically indicate the linear order among siblings by listing them in the correct order.

Example 7.3: *The components of a structured document, such as a book, are hierarchically organized as a tree whose internal nodes are parts, chapters, and sections, and whose external nodes are paragraphs, tables, figures, and so on. (See Figure 7.4.) The root of the tree corresponds to the book itself. We could, in fact, consider expanding the tree further to show paragraphs consisting of sentences, sentences consisting of words, and words consisting of characters. Such a tree is an example of an ordered tree, because there is a well-defined ordering among the children of each node.*

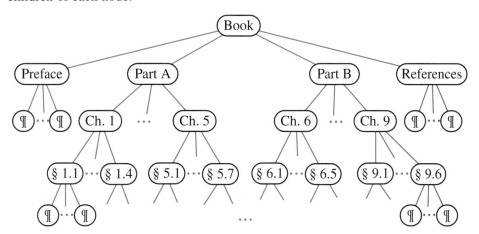

Figure 7.4: An ordered tree associated with a book.

7.1.2 The Tree Abstract Data Type

The tree ADT stores elements at positions, which, as with positions in a list, are defined relative to neighboring positions. The *positions* in a tree are its *nodes*, and neighboring positions satisfy the parent-child relationships that define a valid tree. Therefore, we use the terms "position" and "node" interchangeably for trees. As with a list position, a position object for a tree supports the method:

> element(): Return the object stored at this position.

The real power of node positions in a tree, however, comes from the *accessor methods* of the tree ADT that return and accept positions, such as the following:

> root(): Return the tree's root; an error occurs if the tree is empty.

> parent(v): Return the parent of v; an error occurs if v is the root.

> children(v): Return an iterable collection containing the children of node v.

If a tree T is ordered, then the iterable collection, children(v), stores the children of v in order. If v is an external node, then children(v) is empty.

In addition to the above fundamental accessor methods, we also include the following *query methods*:

> isInternal(v): Test whether node v is internal.

> isExternal(v): Test whether node v is external.

> isRoot(v): Test whether node v is the root.

These methods make programming with trees easier and more readable, since we can use them in the conditionals of **if** statements and **while** loops, rather than using a nonintuitive conditional.

There are also a number of *generic methods* a tree should probably support that are not necessarily related to its tree structure, including the following:

> size(): Return the number of nodes in the tree.

> isEmpty(): Test whether the tree has any nodes or not.

> iterator(): Return an iterator of all the elements stored at nodes of the tree.

> positions(): Return an iterable collection of all the nodes of the tree.

> replace(v, e): Replace with e and return the element stored at node v.

Any method that takes a position as an argument should generate an error condition if that position is invalid. We do not define any specialized update methods for trees here. Instead, we prefer to describe different tree update methods in conjunction with specific applications of trees in subsequent chapters. In fact, we can imagine several kinds of tree update operations beyond those given in this book.

7.1.3 Implementing a Tree

The Java interface shown in Code Fragment 7.1 represents the tree ADT. Error conditions are handled as follows: Each method that can take a position as an argument, may throw an InvalidPositionException, to indicate that the position is invalid. Method parent throws a BoundaryViolationException if it is called on the root. Method root throws an EmptyTreeException if it is called on an empty tree.

```java
/**
 * An interface for a tree where nodes can have an arbitrary number of children.
 */
public interface Tree<E> {
  /** Returns the number of nodes in the tree. */
  public int size();
  /** Returns whether the tree is empty. */
  public boolean isEmpty();
  /** Returns an iterator of the elements stored in the tree. */
  public Iterator<E> iterator();
  /** Returns an iterable collection of the the nodes. */
  public Iterable<Position<E>> positions();
  /** Replaces the element stored at a given node. */
  public E replace(Position<E> v, E e)
    throws InvalidPositionException;
  /** Returns the root of the tree. */
  public Position<E> root() throws EmptyTreeException;
  /** Returns the parent of a given node. */
  public Position<E> parent(Position<E> v)
    throws InvalidPositionException, BoundaryViolationException;
  /** Returns an iterable collection of the children of a given node. */
  public Iterable<Position<E>> children(Position<E> v)
    throws InvalidPositionException;
  /** Returns whether a given node is internal. */
  public boolean isInternal(Position<E> v)
    throws InvalidPositionException;
  /** Returns whether a given node is external. */
  public boolean isExternal(Position<E> v)
    throws InvalidPositionException;
  /** Returns whether a given node is the root of the tree. */
  public boolean isRoot(Position<E> v)
    throws InvalidPositionException;
}
```

Code Fragment 7.1: Java interface Tree representing the tree ADT. Additional update methods may be added, depending on the application. We do not include such methods in the interface, however.

A Linked Structure for General Trees

A natural way to realize a tree T is to use a ***linked structure***, where we represent each node v of T by a position object (see Figure 7.5a) with the following fields: A reference to the element stored at v, a link to the parent of v, and a some kind of collection (for example, a list or array) to store links to the children of v. If v is the root of T, then the parent field of v is null. Also, we store a reference to the root of T and the number of nodes of T in internal variables. This structure is schematically illustrated in Figure 7.5b.

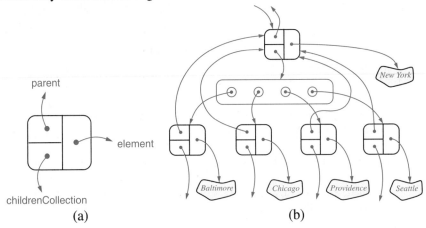

(a)   (b)

Figure 7.5: The linked structure for a general tree: (a) the position object associated with a node; (b) the portion of the data structure associated with a node and its children.

Table 7.1 summarizes the performance of the implementation of a general tree using a linked structure. The analysis is left as an exercise (C-7.27), but we note that, by using a collection to store the children of each node v, we can implement children(v) simply by returning a reference to this collection.

Operation	Time
size, isEmpty	$O(1)$
iterator, positions	$O(n)$
replace	$O(1)$
root, parent	$O(1)$
children(v)	$O(c_v)$
isInternal, isExternal, isRoot	$O(1)$

Table 7.1: Running times of the methods of an n-node general tree implemented with a linked structure. We let c_v denote the number of children of a node v. The space usage is $O(n)$.

7.2 Tree Traversal Algorithms

In this section, we present algorithms for performing traversal computations on a tree by accessing it through the tree ADT methods.

7.2.1 Depth and Height

Let v be a node of a tree T. The ***depth*** of v is the number of ancestors of v, excluding v itself. For example, in the tree of Figure 7.2, the node storing *International* has depth 2. Note that this definition implies that the depth of the root of T is 0.

The depth of a node v can also be recursively defined as follows:

- If v is the root, then the depth of v is 0
- Otherwise, the depth of v is one plus the depth of the parent of v.

Based on this definition, we present a simple, recursive algorithm, depth, in Code Fragment 7.2, for computing the depth of a node v in T. This method calls itself recursively on the parent of v, and adds 1 to the value returned. A simple Java implementation of this algorithm is shown in Code Fragment 7.3.

Algorithm depth(T,v):
    if v is the root of T **then**
        return 0
    else
        return $1 +$ depth(T,w), where w is the parent of v in T

Code Fragment 7.2: Algorithm for computing the depth of a node v in a tree T.

```java
public static <E> int depth (Tree<E> T, Position<E> v) {
  if (T.isRoot(v))
    return 0;
  else
    return 1 + depth(T, T.parent(v));
}
```

Code Fragment 7.3: Method depth written in Java.

The running time of algorithm depth(T,v) is $O(d_v)$, where d_v denotes the depth of the node v in the tree T, because the algorithm performs a constant-time recursive step for each ancestor of v. Thus, algorithm depth(T,v) runs in $O(n)$ worst-case time, where n is the total number of nodes of T, since a node of T may have depth $n-1$ in the worst case. Although such a running time is a function of the input size, it is more accurate to characterize the running time in terms of the parameter d_v, since this parameter can be much smaller than n.

Height

The **height** of a node v in a tree T is also defined recursively:

- If v is an external node, then the height of v is 0
- Otherwise, the height of v is one plus the maximum height of a child of v.

The **height** of a nonempty tree T is the height of the root of T. For example, the tree of Figure 7.2 has height 4. In addition, height can also be viewed as follows.

Proposition 7.4: *The height of a nonempty tree T is equal to the maximum depth of an external node of T.*

We leave the justification of this fact to an exercise (R-7.7). We present an algorithm, height1, shown in Code Fragment 7.4 and implemented in Java in Code Fragment 7.5, for computing the height of a nonempty tree T based on the proposition above and the algorithm depth from Code Fragment 7.2.

Algorithm height1(T):
   $h \leftarrow 0$
   for each vertex v in T **do**
      if v is an external node in T **then**
         $h \leftarrow \max(h, \text{depth}(T, v))$
   return h

Code Fragment 7.4: Algorithm height1 for computing the height of a nonempty tree T. Note that this algorithm calls algorithm depth (Code Fragment 7.2).

```java
public static <E> int height1 (Tree<E> T) {
    int h = 0;
    for (Position<E> v : T.positions()) {
        if (T.isExternal(v))
            h = Math.max(h, depth(T, v));
    }
    return h;
}
```

Code Fragment 7.5: Method height1 written in Java. Note the use of the max method of class java.lang.Math.

Unfortunately, algorithm height1 is not very efficient. Since height1 calls algorithm depth(v) on each external node v of T, the running time of height1 is given by $O(n + \sum_v (1 + d_v))$, where n is the number of nodes of T, d_v is the depth of node v, and E is the set of external nodes of T. In the worst case, the sum $\sum_v (1 + d_v)$ is proportional to n^2. (See Exercise C-7.8.) Thus, algorithm height1 runs in $O(n^2)$ time.

Algorithm height2, shown in Code Fragment 7.6 and implemented in Java in Code Fragment 7.7, computes the height of tree T in a more efficient manner by using the recursive definition of height.

Algorithm height2(T, v):

    if v is an external node in T **then**

        return 0

    else

        $h \leftarrow 0$

        for each child w of v in T **do**

            $h \leftarrow \max(h, \text{height2}(T, w))$

        return $1 + h$

Code Fragment 7.6: Algorithm height2 for computing the height of the subtree of tree T rooted at a node v.

```java
public static <E> int height2 (Tree<E> T, Position<E> v) {
  if (T.isExternal(v)) return 0;
  int h = 0;
  for (Position<E> w : T.children(v))
    h = Math.max(h, height2(T, w));
  return 1 + h;
}
```

Code Fragment 7.7: Method height2 written in Java.

Algorithm height2 is more efficient than height1 (from Code Fragment 7.4). The algorithm is recursive, and, if it is initially called on the root of T, it will eventually be called on each node of T. Thus, we can determine the running time of this method by summing, over all the nodes, the amount of time spent at each node (on the nonrecursive part). Processing each node in children(v) takes $O(c_v)$ time, where c_v denotes the number of children of node v. Also, the **while** loop has c_v iterations and each iteration of the loop takes $O(1)$ time plus the time for the recursive call on a child of v. Thus, algorithm height2 spends $O(1 + c_v)$ time at each node v, and its running time is $O(\sum_v (1 + c_v))$. In order to complete the analysis, we make use of the following property.

Proposition 7.5: *Let T be a tree with n nodes, and let c_v denote the number of children of a node v of T. Then, summing over the vertices in T, $\sum_v c_v = n - 1$.*

Justification: Each node of T, with the exception of the root, is a child of another node, and thus contributes one unit to the above sum. ∎

By Proposition 7.5, the running time of algorithm height2, when called on the root of T, is $O(n)$, where n is the number of nodes of T.

7.2.2 Preorder Traversal

A *traversal* of a tree T is a systematic way of accessing, or "visiting," all the nodes of T. In this section, we present a basic traversal scheme for trees, called preorder traversal. In the next section, we will study another basic traversal scheme, called postorder traversal.

In a *preorder traversal* of a tree T, the root of T is visited first and then the subtrees rooted at its children are traversed recursively. If the tree is ordered, then the subtrees are traversed according to the order of the children. The specific action associated with the "visit" of a node v depends on the application of this traversal, and could involve anything from incrementing a counter to performing some complex computation for v. The pseudo-code for the preorder traversal of the subtree rooted at a node v is shown in Code Fragment 7.8. We initially call this algorithm with preorder(T, T.root()).

Algorithm preorder(T, v):

    perform the "visit" action for node v

    for each child w of v in T **do**

        preorder(T, w)   {recursively traverse the subtree rooted at w}

Code Fragment 7.8: Algorithm preorder for performing the preorder traversal of the subtree of a tree T rooted at a node v.

The preorder traversal algorithm is useful for producing a linear ordering of the nodes of a tree where parents must always come before their children in the ordering. Such orderings have several different applications. We explore a simple instance of such an application in the next example.

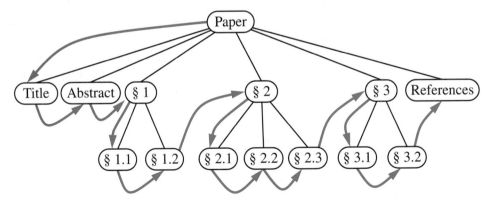

Figure 7.6: Preorder traversal of an ordered tree, where the children of each node are ordered from left to right.

Example 7.6: *The preorder traversal of the tree associated with a document, as in Example 7.3, examines an entire document sequentially, from beginning to end. If the external nodes are removed before the traversal, then the traversal examines the table of contents of the document. (See Figure 7.6.)*

The preorder traversal is also an efficient way to access all the nodes of a tree. To justify this, let us consider the running time of the preorder traversal of a tree T with n nodes under the assumption that visiting a node takes $O(1)$ time. The analysis of the preorder traversal algorithm is actually similar to that of algorithm height2 (Code Fragment 7.7), given in Section 7.2.1. At each node v, the nonrecursive part of the preorder traversal algorithm requires time $O(1 + c_v)$, where c_v is the number of children of v. Thus, by Proposition 7.5, the overall running time of the preorder traversal of T is $O(n)$.

Algorithm toStringPreorder(T, v), implemented in Java in Code Fragment 7.9, performs a preorder printing of the subtree of a node v of T, that is, it performs the preorder traversal of the subtree rooted at v and prints the element stored at a node when the node is visited. Recall that, for an ordered tree T, method T.children(v) returns an iterable collection that accesses the children of v in order.

```java
public static <E> String toStringPreorder(Tree<E> T, Position<E> v) {
    String s = v.element().toString(); // the main "visit" action
    for (Position<E> w : T.children(v))
        s += ", " + toStringPreorder(T, w);
    return s;
}
```

Code Fragment 7.9: Method toStringPreorder(T, v) that performs a preorder printing of the elements in the subtree of node v of T.

There is an interesting application of the preorder traversal algorithm that produces a string representation of an entire tree. Let us assume again that for each element e stored in tree T, calling e.toString() returns a string associated with e. The ***parenthetic string representation*** $P(T)$ of tree T is recursively defined as follows. If T consists of a single node v, then

$$P(T) = v.\text{element}().\text{toString}().$$

Otherwise,

$$P(T) = v.\text{element}().\text{toString}() + \text{"("} + P(T_1) + \text{","} + \cdots + \text{","} + P(T_k) + \text{")"},$$

where v is the root of T and $T_1, T_2, \ldots, T_k$ are the subtrees rooted at the children of v, which are given in order if T is an ordered tree.

Note that the above definition of $P(T)$ is recursive. Also, we are using "+" here to denote string concatenation. The parenthetic representation of the tree of Figure 7.2 is shown in Figure 7.7.

> *Electronics R'Us (R&D*
>   *Sales (Domestic*
>   *International (Canada S.America*
>   *Overseas (Africa Europe Asia Australia)))*
>   *Purchasing*
>   *Manufacturing (TV CD Tuner))*

Figure 7.7: Parenthetic representation of the tree of Figure 7.2. Indentation, line breaks and spaces have been added for clarity.

Note that, technically speaking, there are some computations that occur between and after the recursive calls at a node's children in the above algorithm. We still consider this algorithm to be a preorder traversal, however, since the primary action of printing a node's contents occurs prior to the recursive calls.

The Java method parentheticRepresentation, shown in Code Fragment 7.10, is a variation of method toStringPreorder (Code Fragment 7.9). It implements the definition given above to output a parenthetic string representation of a tree T. As with the method toStringPreorder, the method parentheticRepresentation makes use of the toString method that is defined for every Java object. In fact, we can view this method as a kind of toString() method for tree objects.

```java
public static <E> String parentheticRepresentation(Tree<E> T, Position<E> v) {
  String s = v.element().toString(); // main visit action
  if (T.isInternal(v)) {
    Boolean firstTime = true;
    for (Position<E> w : T.children(v))
      if (firstTime) {
        s += " ( " + parentheticRepresentation(T, w); // the first child
        firstTime = false;
      }
      else s += ", " + parentheticRepresentation(T, w); // subsequent child
    s += " )"; // close parenthesis
  }
  return s;
}
```

Code Fragment 7.10: Algorithm parentheticRepresentation. Note the use of the + operator to concatenate two strings.

We explore a modification to Code Fragment 7.10 in Exercise R-7.10, to display a tree in a fashion more closely matching that given in Figure 7.7.

7.2.3 Postorder Traversal

Another important tree traversal algorithm is the ***postorder traversal***. This algorithm can be viewed as the opposite of the preorder traversal, because it recursively traverses the subtrees rooted at the children of the root first, and then visits the root. It is similar to the preorder traversal, however, in that we use it to solve a particular problem by specializing an action associated with the "visit" of a node v. Still, as with the preorder traversal, if the tree is ordered, we make recursive calls for the children of a node v according to their specified order. Pseudo-code for the postorder traversal is given in Code Fragment 7.11.

Algorithm postorder(T, v):
    for each child w of v in T **do**
        postorder(T, w) {recursively traverse the subtree rooted at w}
    perform the "visit" action for node v

Code Fragment 7.11: Algorithm postorder for performing the postorder traversal of the subtree of a tree T rooted at a node v.

The name of the postorder traversal comes from the fact that this traversal method will visit a node v after it has visited all the other nodes in the subtree rooted at v. (See Figure 7.8.)

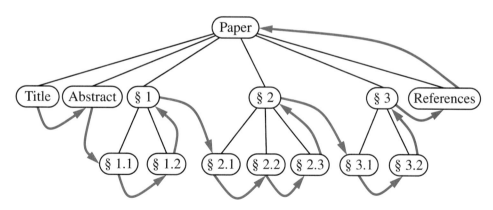

Figure 7.8: Postorder traversal of the ordered tree of Figure 7.6.

The analysis of the running time of a postorder traversal is analogous to that of a preorder traversal. (See Section 7.2.2.) The total time spent in the nonrecursive portions of the algorithm is proportional to the time spent visiting the children of each node in the tree. Thus, a postorder traversal of a tree T with n nodes takes $O(n)$ time, assuming that visiting each node takes $O(1)$ time. That is, the postorder traversal runs in linear time.

As an example of postorder traversal, we show a Java method toStringPostorder in Code Fragment 7.12, which performs a postorder traversal of a tree T. This method prints the element stored at a node when it is visited.

```java
public static <E> String toStringPostorder(Tree<E> T, Position<E> v) {
    String s = "";
    for (Position<E> w : T.children(v))
        s += toStringPostorder(T, w) + " ";
    s += v.element();          // main visit action
    return s;
}
```

Code Fragment 7.12: Method toStringPostorder(T, v) that performs a postorder printing of the elements in the subtree of node v of T. The method implicitly calls toString on elements, when they are involved in a string concatenation operation.

The postorder traversal method is useful for solving problems where we wish to compute some property for each node v in a tree, but computing that property for v requires that we have already computed that same property for v's children. Such an application is illustrated in the following example.

Example 7.7: *Consider a file system tree T, where external nodes represent files and internal nodes represent directories (Example 7.1). Suppose we want to compute the disk space used by a directory, which is recursively given by the sum of:*

- *The size of the directory itself*
- *The sizes of the files in the directory*
- *The space used by the children directories.*

(See Figure 7.9.) This computation can be done with a postorder traversal of tree T. After the subtrees of an internal node v have been traversed, we compute the space used by v by adding the sizes of the directory v itself and of the files contained in v to the space used by each internal child of v, which was computed by the recursive postorder traversals of the children of v.

A Recursive Java Method for Computing Disk Space

Motivated by Example 7.7, Java method diskSpace, shown in Code Fragment 7.13, performs a postorder traversal of a file-system tree T, printing the name and disk space used by the directory associated with each internal node of T. When called on the root of tree T, diskSpace runs in time $O(n)$, where n is the number of nodes of T, provided the auxiliary methods name and size take $O(1)$ time.

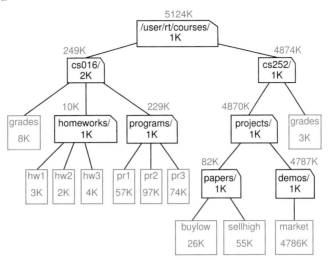

Figure 7.9: The tree of Figure 7.3 representing a file system, showing the name and size of the associated file/directory inside each node, and the disk space used by the associated directory above each internal node.

```
public static <E> int diskSpace (Tree<E> T, Position<E> v) {
    int s = size(v);              // start with the size of the node itself
    for (Position<E> w : T.children(v))
        // add the recursively computed space used by the children of v
        s += diskSpace(T, w);
    if (T.isInternal(v)) {
        // print name and disk space used
        System.out.print(name(v) + ": " + s);
    }
    return s;
}
```

Code Fragment 7.13: Method diskSpace prints the name and disk space used by the directory associated with each internal node of a file-system tree. This method calls the auxiliary methods name and size, which should be defined to return the name and size of the file/directory associated with a node.

Other Kinds of Traversals

Although the preorder and postorder traversals are common ways of visiting the nodes of a tree, we can also imagine other traversals. For example, we could traverse a tree so that we visit all the nodes at depth d before we visit the nodes at depth $d+1$. Consecutively numbering the nodes of a tree T as we visit them in this traversal is called the ***level numbering*** of the nodes of T (see Section 7.3.5).

7.3 Binary Trees

A ***binary tree*** is an ordered tree with the following properties:

1. Every node has at most two children.
2. Each child node is labeled as being either a ***left child*** or a ***right child***.
3. A left child precedes a right child in the ordering of children of a node.

The subtree rooted at a left or right child of an internal node v is called a ***left subtree*** or ***right subtree***, respectively, of v. A binary tree is ***proper*** if each node has either zero or two children. Some people also refer to such trees as being ***full*** binary trees. Thus, in a proper binary tree, every internal node has exactly two children. A binary tree that is not proper is ***improper***.

Example 7.8: *An important class of binary trees arises in contexts where we wish to represent a number of different outcomes that can result from answering a series of yes-or-no questions. Each internal node is associated with a question. Starting at the root, we go to the left or right child of the current node, depending on whether the answer to the question is "Yes" or "No." With each decision, we follow an edge from a parent to a child, eventually tracing a path in the tree from the root to an external node. Such binary trees are known as* **decision trees,** *because each external node v in such a tree represents a decision of what to do if the questions associated with v's ancestors are answered in a way that leads to v. A decision tree is a proper binary tree. Figure 7.10 illustrates a decision tree that provides recommendations to a prospective investor.*

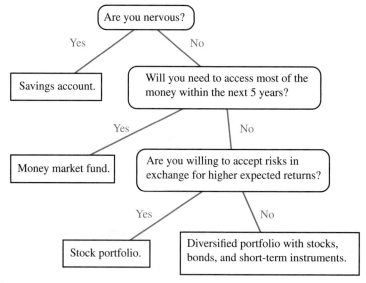

Figure 7.10: A decision tree providing investment advice.

Example 7.9: *An arithmetic expression can be represented by a binary tree whose external nodes are associated with variables or constants, and whose internal nodes are associated with one of the operators +, −, ×, and /. (See Figure 7.11.) Each node in such a tree has a value associated with it.*

- *If a node is external, then its value is that of its variable or constant.*
- *If a node is internal, then its value is defined by applying its operation to the values of its children.*

An arithmetic expression tree is a proper binary tree, since each operator +, −, ×, and / takes exactly two operands. Of course, if we were to allow for unary operators, like negation (−), as in "−x," then we could have an improper binary tree.

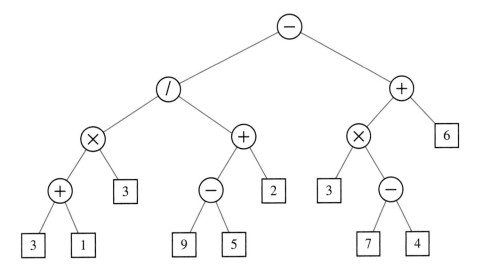

Figure 7.11: A binary tree representing an arithmetic expression. This tree represents the expression $((((3+1) \times 3)/((9-5)+2)) - ((3 \times (7-4))+6))$. The value associated with the internal node labeled "/" is 2.

A Recursive Binary Tree Definition

Incidentally, we can also define a binary tree in a recursive way such that a binary tree is either empty or consists of:

- A node r, called the root of T and storing an element
- A binary tree, called the left subtree of T
- A binary tree, called the right subtree of T.

We discuss some of the specialized topics for binary trees below.

7.3.1 The Binary Tree ADT

As an abstract data type, a binary tree is a specialization of a tree that supports three additional accessor methods:

left(v): Return the left child of v; an error condition occurs if v has no left child.

right(v): Return the right child of v; an error condition occurs if v has no right child.

hasLeft(v): Test whether v has a left child.

hasRight(v): Test whether v has a right child.

Just as in Section 7.1.2 for the tree ADT, we do not define specialized update methods for binary trees here. Instead, we will consider some possible update methods when we describe specific implementations and applications of binary trees.

7.3.2 A Binary Tree Interface in Java

We model a binary tree as an abstract data type that extends the tree ADT and adds the three specialized methods for a binary tree. In Code Fragment 7.14, we show the simple Java interface we can define using this approach. By the way, since binary trees are ordered trees, the iterable collection returned by method children(v) (inherited from the Tree interface) stores the left child of v before the right child of v.

```
/**
 * An interface for a binary tree, where each node can have zero, one,
 * or two children.
 */
public interface BinaryTree<E> extends Tree<E> {
  /** Returns the left child of a node. */
  public Position<E> left(Position<E> v)
    throws InvalidPositionException, BoundaryViolationException;
  /** Returns the right child of a node. */
  public Position<E> right(Position<E> v)
    throws InvalidPositionException, BoundaryViolationException;
  /** Returns whether a node has a left child. */
  public boolean hasLeft(Position<E> v) throws InvalidPositionException;
  /** Returns whether a node has a right child. */
  public boolean hasRight(Position<E> v) throws InvalidPositionException;
}
```

Code Fragment 7.14: Java interface BinaryTree for the binary tree ADT. Interface BinaryTree extends interface Tree (Code Fragment 7.1).

7.3.3 Properties of Binary Trees

Binary trees have several interesting properties dealing with relationships between their heights and number of nodes. We denote the set of all nodes of a tree T at the same depth d as the **level** d of T. In a binary tree, level 0 has at most one node (the root), level 1 has at most two nodes (the children of the root), level 2 has at most four nodes, and so on. (See Figure 7.12.) In general, level d has at most 2^d nodes.

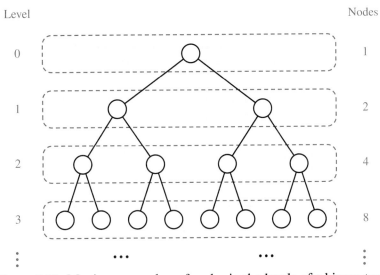

Level   Nodes

0   1

1   2

2   4

3   8

Figure 7.12: Maximum number of nodes in the levels of a binary tree.

We can see that the maximum number of nodes on the levels of a binary tree grows exponentially as we go down the tree. From this simple observation, we can derive the following properties relating the height of a binary T with its number of nodes. A detailed justification of these properties is left as an exercise (R-7.16).

Proposition 7.10: *Let T be a nonempty binary tree, and let n, n_E, n_I and h denote the number of nodes, number of external nodes, number of internal nodes, and height of T, respectively. Then T has the following properties:*

1. $h + 1 \le n \le 2^{h+1} - 1$
2. $1 \le n_E \le 2^h$
3. $h \le n_I \le 2^h - 1$
4. $\log(n+1) - 1 \le h \le n - 1.$

Also, if T is proper, then T has the following properties:

1. $2h + 1 \le n \le 2^{h+1} - 1$
2. $h + 1 \le n_E \le 2^h$
3. $h \le n_I \le 2^h - 1$
4. $\log(n+1) - 1 \le h \le (n-1)/2.$

Relating Internal Nodes to External Nodes in a Proper Binary Tree

In addition to the binary tree properties above, we also have the following relationship between the number of internal nodes and external nodes in a proper binary tree.

Proposition 7.11: *In a nonempty proper binary tree T, with n_E external nodes and n_I internal nodes, we have $n_E = n_I + 1$.*

Justification: We justify this proposition by removing nodes from T and dividing them up into two "piles", an internal-node pile and an external-node pile, until T becomes empty. The piles are initially empty. At the end, the external-node pile will have one more node than the internal-node pile. We consider two cases:

Case 1: If T has only one node v, we remove v and place it on the external-node pile. Thus, the external-node pile has one node and the internal-node pile is empty.

Case 2: Otherwise (T has more than one node), we remove from T an (arbitrary) external node w and its parent v, which is an internal node. We place w on the external-node pile and v on the internal-node pile. If v has a parent u, then we reconnect u with the former sibling z of w, as shown in Figure 7.13. This operation, removes one internal node and one external node, and leaves the tree being a proper binary tree.

Repeating this operation, we eventually are left with a final tree consisting of a single node. Note that the same number of external and internal nodes have been removed and placed on their respective piles by the sequence of operations leading to this final tree. Now, we remove the node of the final tree and we place it on the external-node pile. Thus, the the external-node pile has one more node than the internal-node pile. ∎

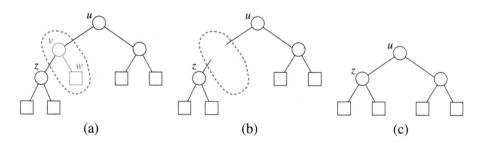

(a)   (b)   (c)

Figure 7.13: Operation that removes an external node and its parent node, used in the justification of Proposition 7.11.

Note that the above relationship does not hold, in general, for improper binary trees and nonbinary trees, although there are other interesting relationships that can hold, as we explore in an exercise (C-7.9).

7.3.4 A Linked Structure for Binary Trees

As with a general tree, a natural way to realize a binary tree T is to use a ***linked structure***, where we represent each node v of T by a position object (see Figure 7.14a) with fields providing references to the element stored at v and to the position objects associated with the children and parent of v. If v is the root of T, then the parent field of v is null. If v has no left child, then the left field of v is null. If v has no right child, then the right field of v is null. Also, we store the number of nodes of T in a variable, called size. We show the linked structure representation of a binary tree in Figure 7.14b.

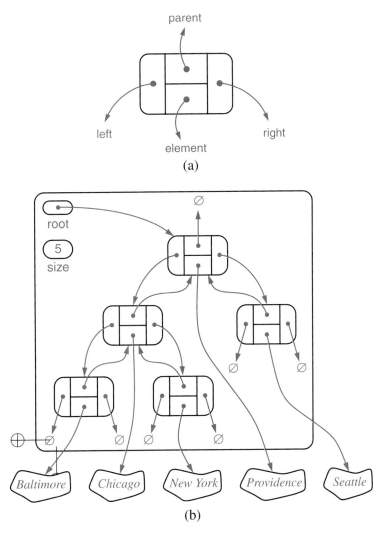

Figure 7.14: A node (a) and a linked structure (b) for representing a binary tree.

Java Implementation of a Binary Tree Node

We use a Java interface BTPosition (not shown) to represent a node of a binary tree. This interfaces extends Position, thus inheriting method element, and has additional methods for setting the element stored at the node (setElement) and for setting and returning the left child (setLeft and getLeft), right child (setRight and getRight), and parent (setParent and getParent) of the node. Class BTNode (Code Fragment 7.15) implements interface BTPosition by an object with fields element, left, right, and parent, which, for a node v, reference the element at v, the left child of v, the right child of v, and the parent of v, respectively.

```
/**
 * Class implementing a node of a binary tree by storing references to
 * an element, a parent node, a left node, and a right node.
 */
public class BTNode<E> implements BTPosition<E> {
  private E element; // element stored at this node
  private BTPosition<E> left, right, parent; // adjacent nodes
  /** Main constructor */
  public BTNode(E element, BTPosition<E> parent,
                BTPosition<E> left, BTPosition<E> right) {
    setElement(element);
    setParent(parent);
    setLeft(left);
    setRight(right);
  }
  /** Returns the element stored at this position */
  public E element() { return element; }
  /** Sets the element stored at this position */
  public void setElement(E o) { element=o; }
  /** Returns the left child of this position */
  public BTPosition<E> getLeft() { return left; }
  /** Sets the left child of this position */
  public void setLeft(BTPosition<E> v) { left=v; }
  /** Returns the right child of this position */
  public BTPosition<E> getRight() { return right; }
  /** Sets the right child of this position */
  public void setRight(BTPosition<E> v) { right=v; }
  /** Returns the parent of this position */
  public BTPosition<E> getParent() { return parent; }
  /** Sets the parent of this position */
  public void setParent(BTPosition<E> v) { parent=v; }
}
```

Code Fragment 7.15: Auxiliary class BTNode for implementing binary tree nodes.

Java Implementation of the Linked Binary Tree Structure

In Code Fragments 7.16–7.20, we show portions of class LinkedBinaryTree that implements the BinaryTree interface (Code Fragment 7.14) using a linked data structure. This class stores the size of the tree and a reference to the BTNode object associated with the root of the tree in internal variables. In addition to the BinaryTree interface methods, LinkedBinaryTree has various other methods, including accessor method sibling(v), which returns the sibling of a node v, and the following update methods:

addRoot(e): Create and return a new node r storing element e and make r the root of the tree; an error occurs if the tree is not empty.

insertLeft(v, e): Create and return a new node w storing element e, add w as the the left child of v and return w; an error occurs if v already has a left child.

insertRight(v, e): Create and return a new node z storing element e, add z as the the right child of v and return z; an error occurs if v already has a right child.

remove(v): Remove node v, replace it with its child, if any, and return the element stored at v; an error occurs if v has two children.

attach(v, T_1, T_2): Attach T_1 and T_2, respectively, as the left and right subtrees of the external node v; an error condition occurs if v is not external.

Class LinkedBinaryTree has a constructor with no arguments that returns an empty binary tree. Starting from this empty tree, we can build any binary tree by creating the first node with method addRoot and repeatedly applying the insertLeft and insertRight methods and/or the attach method. Likewise, we can dismantle any binary tree T using the remove operation, ultimately reducing such a tree T to an empty binary tree.

When a position v is passed as an argument to one of the methods of class LinkedBinaryTree, its validity is checked by calling an auxiliary helper method, checkPosition(v). A list of the nodes visited in a preorder traversal of the tree is constructed by recursive method preorderPositions. Error conditions are indicated by throwing exceptions InvalidPositionException, BoundaryViolationException, EmptyTreeException, and NonEmptyTreeException.

```java
/**
 * An implementation of the BinaryTree interface by means of a linked structure.
 */
public class LinkedBinaryTree<E> implements BinaryTree<E> {
  protected BTPosition<E> root;  // reference to the root
  protected int size;            // number of nodes
  /** Creates an empty binary tree. */
  public LinkedBinaryTree() {
    root = null;  // start with an empty tree
    size = 0;
  }
  /** Returns the number of nodes in the tree. */
  public int size() {
    return size;
  }
  /** Returns whether a node is internal. */
  public boolean isInternal(Position<E> v) throws InvalidPositionException {
    checkPosition(v);            // auxiliary method
    return (hasLeft(v) || hasRight(v));
  }
  /** Returns whether a node is the root. */
  public boolean isRoot(Position<E> v) throws InvalidPositionException {
    checkPosition(v);
    return (v == root());
  }
  /** Returns whether a node has a left child. */
  public boolean hasLeft(Position<E> v) throws InvalidPositionException {
    BTPosition<E> vv = checkPosition(v);
    return (vv.getLeft() != null);
  }
  /** Returns the root of the tree. */
  public Position<E> root() throws EmptyTreeException {
    if (root == null)
      throw new EmptyTreeException("The tree is empty");
    return root;
  }
  /** Returns the left child of a node. */
  public Position<E> left(Position<E> v)
    throws InvalidPositionException, BoundaryViolationException {
    BTPosition<E> vv = checkPosition(v);
    Position<E> leftPos = vv.getLeft();
    if (leftPos == null)
      throw new BoundaryViolationException("No left child");
    return leftPos;
  }
```

Code Fragment 7.16: Portions of the LinkedBinaryTree class, which implements the BinaryTree interface. (Continues in Code Fragment 7.17.)

```
/** Returns the parent of a node. */
public Position<E> parent(Position<E> v)
  throws InvalidPositionException, BoundaryViolationException {
  BTPosition<E> vv = checkPosition(v);
  Position<E> parentPos = vv.getParent();
  if (parentPos == null)
    throw new BoundaryViolationException("No parent");
  return parentPos;
}
/** Returns an iterable collection of the children of a node. */
public Iterable<Position<E>> children(Position<E> v)
  throws InvalidPositionException {
  PositionList<Position<E>> children = new NodePositionList<Position<E>>();
  if (hasLeft(v))
    children.addLast(left(v));
  if (hasRight(v))
    children.addLast(right(v));
  return children;
}
/** Returns an iterable collection of the tree nodes. */
public Iterable<Position<E>> positions() {
  PositionList<Position<E>> positions = new NodePositionList<Position<E>>();
  if(size != 0)
    preorderPositions(root(), positions);    // assign positions in preorder
  return positions;
}
/** Returns an iterator of the elements stored at the nodes */
public Iterator<E> iterator() {
  Iterable<Position<E>> positions = positions();
  PositionList<E> elements = new NodePositionList<E>();
  for (Position<E> pos: positions)
    elements.addLast(pos.element());
  return elements.iterator();   // An iterator of elements
}
/** Replaces the element at a node. */
public E replace(Position<E> v, E o)
  throws InvalidPositionException {
  BTPosition<E> vv = checkPosition(v);
  E temp = v.element();
  vv.setElement(o);
  return temp;
}
```

Code Fragment 7.17: Portions of the LinkedBinaryTree class, which implements the BinaryTree interface. (Continues in Code Fragment 7.18.)

```
// Additional accessor method
/** Return the sibling of a node */
public Position<E> sibling(Position<E> v)
  throws InvalidPositionException, BoundaryViolationException {
    BTPosition<E> vv = checkPosition(v);
    BTPosition<E> parentPos = vv.getParent();
    if (parentPos != null) {
      BTPosition<E> sibPos;
      BTPosition<E> leftPos = parentPos.getLeft();
      if (leftPos == vv)
        sibPos = parentPos.getRight();
      else
        sibPos = parentPos.getLeft();
      if (sibPos != null)
        return sibPos;
    }
    throw new BoundaryViolationException("No sibling");
}
// Additional update methods
/** Adds a root node to an empty tree */
public Position<E> addRoot(E e) throws NonEmptyTreeException {
  if(!isEmpty())
    throw new NonEmptyTreeException("Tree already has a root");
  size = 1;
  root = createNode(e,null,null,null);
  return root;
}
/** Inserts a left child at a given node. */
public Position<E> insertLeft(Position<E> v, E e)
  throws InvalidPositionException {
  BTPosition<E> vv = checkPosition(v);
  Position<E> leftPos = vv.getLeft();
  if (leftPos != null)
    throw new InvalidPositionException("Node already has a left child");
  BTPosition<E> ww = createNode(e, vv, null, null);
  vv.setLeft(ww);
  size++;
  return ww;
}
```

Code Fragment 7.18: Portions of the LinkedBinaryTree class, which implements the BinaryTree interface. (Continues in Code Fragment 7.19.)

```
/** Removes a node with zero or one child. */
public E remove(Position<E> v)
  throws InvalidPositionException {
  BTPosition<E> vv = checkPosition(v);
  BTPosition<E> leftPos = vv.getLeft();
  BTPosition<E> rightPos = vv.getRight();
  if (leftPos != null && rightPos != null)
    throw new InvalidPositionException("Cannot remove node with two children");
  BTPosition<E> ww;   // the only child of v, if any
  if (leftPos != null)
    ww = leftPos;
  else if (rightPos != null)
    ww = rightPos;
  else               // v is a leaf
    ww = null;
  if (vv == root) {  // v is the root
    if (ww != null)
      ww.setParent(null);
    root = ww;
  }
  else {             // v is not the root
    BTPosition<E> uu = vv.getParent();
    if (vv == uu.getLeft())
      uu.setLeft(ww);
    else
      uu.setRight(ww);
    if(ww != null)
      ww.setParent(uu);
  }
  size−−;
  return v.element();
}
```

Code Fragment 7.19: Portions of the LinkedBinaryTree class, which implements the BinaryTree interface. (Continues in Code Fragment 7.20.)

```
/** Attaches two trees to be subtrees of an external node. */
public void attach(Position<E> v, BinaryTree<E> T1, BinaryTree<E> T2)
  throws InvalidPositionException {
  BTPosition<E> vv = checkPosition(v);
  if (isInternal(v))
    throw new InvalidPositionException("Cannot attach from internal node");
  int newSize = size + T1.size() + T2.size();
  if (!T1.isEmpty()) {
    BTPosition<E> r1 = checkPosition(T1.root());
    vv.setLeft(r1);
    r1.setParent(vv);          // T1 should be invalidated
  }
  if (!T2.isEmpty()) {
    BTPosition<E> r2 = checkPosition(T2.root());
    vv.setRight(r2);
    r2.setParent(vv);          // T2 should be invalidated
  }
  size = newSize;
}
/** If v is a good binary tree node, cast to BTPosition, else throw exception */
protected BTPosition<E> checkPosition(Position<E> v)
  throws InvalidPositionException {
  if (v == null || !(v instanceof BTPosition))
    throw new InvalidPositionException("The position is invalid");
  return (BTPosition<E>) v;
}
/** Creates a new binary tree node */
protected BTPosition<E> createNode(E element, BTPosition<E> parent,
                        BTPosition<E> left, BTPosition<E> right) {
  return new BTNode<E>(element,parent,left,right); }
/** Creates a list storing the the nodes in the subtree of a node,
  * ordered according to the preorder traversal of the subtree. */
protected void preorderPositions(Position<E> v, PositionList<Position<E>> pos)
  throws InvalidPositionException {
  pos.addLast(v);
  if (hasLeft(v))
    preorderPositions(left(v), pos);    // recurse on left child
  if (hasRight(v))
    preorderPositions(right(v), pos);   // recurse on right child
}
```

Code Fragment 7.20: Portions of the LinkedBinaryTree class, which implements the BinaryTree interface. (Continued from Code Fragment 7.19.)

Performance of the LinkedBinaryTree Implementation

Let us now analyze the running times of the methods of class LinkedBinaryTree, which uses a linked structure representation:

- Methods size() and isEmpty() use an instance variable storing the number of nodes of T, and each take $O(1)$ time.

- The accessor methods root, left, right, sibling and parent take $O(1)$ time.

- Method replace(v, e) takes $O(1)$ time.

- Methods iterator() and positions() are implemented by performing a pre-order traversal of the tree (using the auxiliary method preorderPositions). The nodes visited by the traversal are stored in a position list implemented by class NodePositionList (Section 6.2.4) and the output iterator is generated with method iterator() of class NodePositionList. Methods iterator() and positions() take $O(n)$ time and methods hasNext() and next() of the returned iterators run in $O(1)$ time.

- Method children uses a similar approach to construct the returned iterable collection, but it runs in $O(1)$ time, since there are at most two children for any node in a binary tree.

- The update methods insertLeft, insertRight, attach, and remove all run in $O(1)$ time, as they involve constant-time manipulation of a constant number of nodes.

Considering the space required by this data structure for a tree with n nodes, note that there is an object of class BTNode (Code Fragment 7.15) for every node of tree T. Thus, the overall space requirement is $O(n)$. Table 7.2 summarizes the performance of the linked structure implementation of a binary tree.

Operation	Time
size, isEmpty	$O(1)$
iterator, positions	$O(n)$
replace	$O(1)$
root, parent, children, left, right, sibling	$O(1)$
hasLeft, hasRight, isInternal, isExternal, isRoot	$O(1)$
insertLeft, insertRight, attach, remove	$O(1)$

Table 7.2: Running times for the methods of an n-node binary tree implemented with a linked structure. Methods hasNext() and next() of the iterators returned by iterator(), positions().iterator(), and children(v).iterator() run in $O(1)$ time. The space usage is $O(n)$.

7.3.5 An Array-List Representation of a Binary Tree

An alternative representation of a binary tree T is based on a way of numbering the nodes of T. For every node v of T, let $p(v)$ be the integer defined as follows.

- If v is the root of T, then $p(v) = 1$.
- If v is the left child of node u, then $p(v) = 2p(u)$.
- If v is the right child of node u, then $p(v) = 2p(u) + 1$.

The numbering function p is known as a ***level numbering*** of the nodes in a binary tree T, for it numbers the nodes on each level of T in increasing order from left to right, although it may skip some numbers. (See Figure 7.15.)

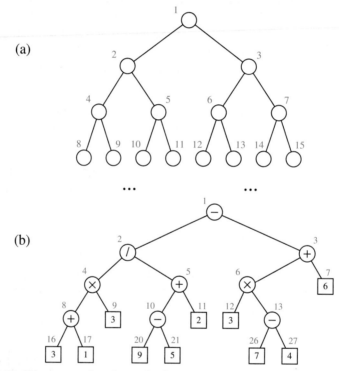

Figure 7.15: Binary tree level numbering: (a) general scheme; (b) an example.

The level numbering function p suggests a representation of a binary tree T by means of an array list S such that node v of T is the element of S at index $p(v)$. As mentioned in the previous chapter, we realize the array list S by means of an extendable array. (See Section 6.1.4.) Such an implementation is simple and efficient, for we can use it to easily perform the methods root, parent, left, right, hasLeft, hasRight, isInternal, isExternal, and isRoot by using simple arithmetic operations on the numbers $p(v)$ associated with each node v involved in the operation. We leave the details of this implementation as an exercise (R-7.27).

We show an example array-list representation of a binary tree in Figure 7.16.

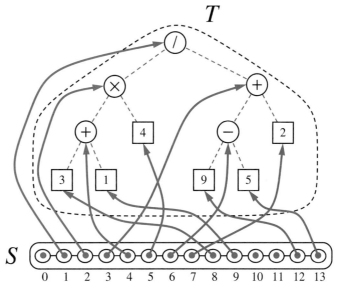

Figure 7.16: Representation of a binary tree T by means of an array list S.

Let n be the number of nodes of T, and let p_M be the maximum value of $p(v)$ over all the nodes of T. The array list S has size $N = p_M + 1$ since the element of S at index 0 is not associated with any node of T. Also, S will have, in general, a number of empty elements that do not refer to existing nodes of T. In fact, in the worst case, $N = 2^n$, the justification of which is left as an exercise (R-7.24). In Section 8.3, we will see a class of binary trees, called "heaps" for which $N = n + 1$. Thus, in spite of the worst-case space usage, there are applications for which the array-list representation of a binary tree is space efficient. Still, for general binary trees, the exponential worst-case space requirement of this representation is prohibitive.

Table 7.3 summarizes running times of the methods of a binary tree implemented with an array list. We do not include any tree update methods here.

Operation	Time
size, isEmpty	$O(1)$
iterator, positions	$O(n)$
replace	$O(1)$
root, parent, children, left, right	$O(1)$
hasLeft, hasRight, isInternal, isExternal, isRoot	$O(1)$

Table 7.3: Running times for a binary tree T implemented with an array list S. We denote the number of nodes of T with n, and N denotes the size of S. The space usage is $O(N)$, which is $O(2^n)$ in the worst case.

7.3.6   Traversals of Binary Trees

As with general trees, binary tree computations often involve traversals.

Building an Expression Tree

Consider the problem of constructing an expression tree from a fully parenthesized arithmetic expression of size n. (Recall Example 7.9 and see Code Fragment 7.24.) In Code Fragment 7.21, we give algorithm buildExpression for building such an expression tree, assuming all arithmetic operations are binary and variables are not parenthesized. Thus, every parenthesized subexpression contains an operator in the middle. The algorithm uses a stack S while scanning the input expression E looking for variables, operators, and right parentheses.

- When we see a variable or operator x, we create a single-node binary tree T, whose root stores x and we push T on the stack.
- When we see a right parenthesis, ")", we pop the top three trees from the stack S, which represent a subexpression $(E_1 \circ E_2)$. We then attach the trees for E_1 and E_2 to the one for $\circ$, and push the resulting tree back on S.

We repeat this until the expression E has been processed, at which time the top element on the stack is the expression tree for E. The total running time is $O(n)$.

Algorithm buildExpression(E):
   Input: A fully-parenthesized arithmetic expression $E = e_0, e_1, \ldots, e_{n-1}$, with
        each e_i being a variable, operator, or parenthetic symbol
   Output: A binary tree T representing arithmetic expression E
   $S \leftarrow$ a new initially-empty stack
   for $i \leftarrow 0$ to $n - 1$ **do**
      if e_i is a variable or an operator **then**
         $T \leftarrow$ a new empty binary tree
         T.addRoot(e_i)
         S.push(T)
      else if $e_i = '($' **then**
         Continue looping
      else $\{e_i = ')'\}$
         $T_2 \leftarrow S$.pop()   {the tree representing E_2}
         $T \leftarrow S$.pop()   {the tree representing $\circ$}
         $T_1 \leftarrow S$.pop()   {the tree representing E_1}
         T.attach(T.root(), T_1, T_2)
         S.push(T)
   return S.pop()

Code Fragment 7.21: Algorithm buildExpression.

Preorder Traversal of a Binary Tree

Since any binary tree can also be viewed as a general tree, the preorder traversal for general trees (Code Fragment 7.8) can be applied to any binary tree. We can simplify the algorithm in the case of a binary tree traversal, however, as we show in Code Fragment 7.22.

Algorithm binaryPreorder(T, v):
     perform the "visit" action for node v
     if v has a left child u in T **then**
        binaryPreorder(T, u)   {recursively traverse left subtree}
     if v has a right child w in T **then**
        binaryPreorder(T, w)   {recursively traverse right subtree}

Code Fragment 7.22: Algorithm binaryPreorder for performing the preorder traversal of the subtree of a binary tree T rooted at a node v.

As is the case for general trees, there are many applications of the preorder traversal for binary trees.

Postorder Traversal of a Binary Tree

Analogously, the postorder traversal for general trees (Code Fragment 7.11) can be specialized for binary trees, as shown in Code Fragment 7.23.

Algorithm binaryPostorder(T, v):
     if v has a left child u in T **then**
        binaryPostorder(T, u)   {recursively traverse left subtree}
     if v has a right child w in T **then**
        binaryPostorder(T, w)   {recursively traverse right subtree}
     perform the "visit" action for node v

Code Fragment 7.23: Algorithm binaryPostorder for performing the postorder traversal of the subtree of a binary tree T rooted at node v.

Expression Tree Evaluation

The postorder traversal of a binary tree can be used to solve the expression tree evaluation problem. In this problem, we are given an arithmetic expression tree, that is, a binary tree where each external node has a value associated with it and each internal node has an arithmetic operation associated with it (see Example 7.9), and we want to compute the value of the arithmetic expression represented by the tree.

Algorithm evaluateExpression, given in Code Fragment 7.24, evaluates the expression associated with the subtree rooted at a node v of an arithmetic expression tree T by performing a postorder traversal of T starting at v. In this case, the "visit" action consists of performing a single arithmetic operation. Note that we use the fact that an arithmetic expression tree is a proper binary tree.

Algorithm evaluateExpression(T, v):
    if v is an internal node in T **then**
        let $\circ$ be the operator stored at v
        $x \leftarrow$ evaluateExpression(T, T.left(v))
        $y \leftarrow$ evaluateExpression(T, T.right(v))
        return $x \circ y$
    else
        return the value stored at v

Code Fragment 7.24: Algorithm evaluateExpression for evaluating the expression represented by the subtree of an arithmetic expression tree T rooted at node v.

The expression-tree evaluation application of the postorder traversal provides an $O(n)$-time algorithm for evaluating an arithmetic expression represented by a binary tree with n nodes. Indeed, like the general postorder traversal, the postorder traversal for binary trees can be applied to other "bottom-up" evaluation problems (such as the size computation given in Example 7.7) as well.

Inorder Traversal of a Binary Tree

An additional traversal method for a binary tree is the *inorder* traversal. In this traversal, we visit a node between the recursive traversals of its left and right subtrees. The inorder traversal of the subtree rooted at a node v in a binary tree T is given in Code Fragment 7.25.

Algorithm inorder(T, v):
    if v has a left child u in T **then**
        inorder(T, u)   {recursively traverse left subtree}
    perform the "visit" action for node v
    if v has a right child w in T **then**
        inorder(T, w)   {recursively traverse right subtree}

Code Fragment 7.25: Algorithm inorder for performing the inorder traversal of the subtree of a binary tree T rooted at a node v.

The inorder traversal of a binary tree T can be informally viewed as visiting the nodes of T "from left to right." Indeed, for every node v, the inorder traversal visits v after all the nodes in the left subtree of v and before all the nodes in the right subtree of v. (See Figure 7.17.)

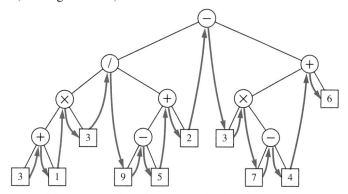

Figure 7.17: Inorder traversal of a binary tree.

Binary Search Trees

Let S be a set whose elements have an order relation. For example, S could be a set of integers. A ***binary search*** tree for S is a proper binary tree T such that

- Each internal node v of T stores an element of S, denoted with $x(v)$.
- For each internal node v of T, the elements stored in the left subtree of v are less than or equal to $x(v)$ and the elements stored in the right subtree of v are greater than or equal to $x(v)$.
- The external nodes of T do not store any element.

An inorder traversal of the internal nodes of a binary search tree T visits the elements in nondecreasing order. (See Figure 7.18.)

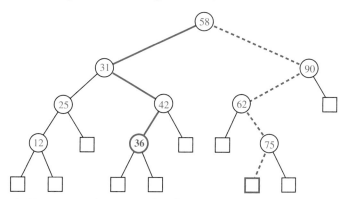

Figure 7.18: A binary search tree storing integers. The blue solid path is traversed when searching (successfully) for 36. The blue dashed path is traversed when searching (unsuccessfully) for 70.

We can use a binary search tree T for set S to find whether a given search value y is in S, by traversing a path down the tree T, starting at the root. (See Figure 7.18.) At each internal node v encountered, we compare our search value y with the element $x(v)$ stored at v. If $y \leq x(v)$, then the search continues in the left subtree of v. If $y = x(v)$, then the search terminates successfully. If $y \geq x(v)$, then the search continues in the right subtree of v. Finally, if we reach an external node, the search terminates unsuccessfully. In other words, a binary search tree can be viewed as a binary decision tree (recall Example 7.8), where the question asked at each internal node is whether the element at that node is less than, equal to, or larger than the element being searched for. Indeed, it is exactly this correspondence to a binary decision tree that motivates restricting binary search trees to be proper binary trees (with "place-holder" external nodes).

Note that the running time of searching in a binary search tree T is proportional to the height of T. Recall from Proposition 7.10 that the height of a proper binary tree with n nodes can be as small as $\log(n+1) - 1$ or as large as $(n-1)/2$. Thus, binary search trees are most efficient when they have small height. We illustrate an example search operation in a binary search tree in Figure 7.18, and we study binary search trees in more detail in Section 10.1.

Using Inorder Traversal for Tree Drawing

The inorder traversal can also be applied to the problem of computing a drawing of a binary tree. We can draw a binary tree T with an algorithm that assigns x- and y-coordinates to a node v of T using the following two rules (see Figure 7.19):

- $x(v)$ is the number of nodes visited before v in the inorder traversal of T
- $y(v)$ is the depth of v in T.

In this application, we take the convention common in computer graphics that x-coordinates increase left to right and y-coordinates increase top to bottom. So the origin is in the upper left corner of the computer screen.

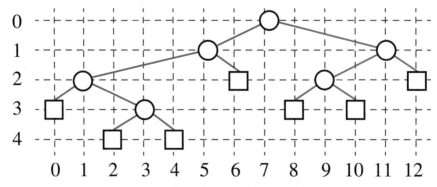

Figure 7.19: An inorder drawing of a binary tree.

The Euler Tour Traversal of a Binary Tree

The tree-traversal algorithms we have discussed so far are all forms of iterators. Each traversal visits the nodes of a tree in a certain order, and is guaranteed to visit each node exactly once. We can unify the tree-traversal algorithms given above into a single framework, however, by relaxing the requirement that each node be visited exactly once. The resulting traversal method is called the ***Euler tour traversal***, which we study next. The advantage of this traversal is that it allows for more general kinds of algorithms to be expressed easily.

The Euler tour traversal of a binary tree T can be informally defined as a "walk" around T, where we start by going from the root toward its left child, viewing the edges of T as being "walls" that we always keep to our left. (See Figure 7.20.) Each node v of T is encountered three times by the Euler tour:

- "On the left" (before the Euler tour of v's left subtree)
- "From below" (between the Euler tours of v's two subtrees)
- "On the right" (after the Euler tour of v's right subtree).

If v is external, then these three "visits" actually all happen at the same time. We describe the Euler tour of the subtree rooted at v in Code Fragment 7.26.

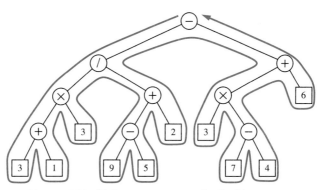

Figure 7.20: Euler tour traversal of a binary tree.

Algorithm eulerTour(T, v):

    perform the action for visiting node v on the left
    if v has a left child u in T **then**
        eulerTour(T, u)   { recursively tour the left subtree of v }
    perform the action for visiting node v from below
    if v has a right child w in T **then**
        eulerTour(T, w)   { recursively tour the right subtree of v }
    perform the action for visiting node v on the right

Code Fragment 7.26: The Euler tour of the subtree of a binary tree T rooted at v.

The running time of the Euler tour traversal of an n-node tree is easy to analyze, assuming each visit action takes $O(1)$ time. Since we spend a constant amount of time at each node of the tree during the traversal, the overall running time is $O(n)$.

The preorder traversal of a binary tree is equivalent to an Euler tour traversal such that each node has an associated "visit" action occur only when it is encountered on the left. Likewise, the inorder and postorder traversals of a binary tree are equivalent to an Euler tour such that each node has an associated "visit" action occur only when it is encountered from below or on the right, respectively. The Euler tour traversal extends the preorder, inorder, and postorder traversals, but it can also perform other kinds of traversals. For example, suppose we wish to compute the number of descendents of each node v in an n-node binary tree. We start an Euler tour by initializing a counter to 0, and then increment the counter each time we visit a node on the left. To determine the number of descendents of a node v, we compute the difference between the values of the counter when v is visited on the left and when it is visited on the right, and add 1. This simple rule gives us the number of descendents of v, because each node in the subtree rooted at v is counted between v's visit on the left and v's visit on the right. Therefore, we have an $O(n)$-time method for computing the number of descendents of each node.

Another application of the Euler tour traversal is to print a fully parenthesized arithmetic expression from its expression tree (Example 7.9). Algorithm printExpression, shown in Code Fragment 7.27, accomplishes this task by performing the following actions in an Euler tour:

- "On the left" action: if the node is internal, print "("
- "From below" action: print the value or operator stored at the node
- "On the right" action: if the node is internal, print ")".

Algorithm printExpression(T,v):

    if T.isInternal(v) **then**
        print "("
    if T.hasLeft(v) **then**
        printExpression$(T,T$.left$(v))$
    if T.isInternal(v) **then**
        print the operator stored at v
    else
        print the value stored at v
    if T.hasRight(v) **then**
        printExpression$(T,T$.right$(v))$
    if T.isInternal(v) **then**
        print ")"

Code Fragment 7.27: An algorithm for printing the arithmetic expression associated with the subtree of an arithmetic expression tree T rooted at v.

7.3.7 The Template Method Pattern

The tree traversal methods described above are actually examples of an interesting object-oriented software design pattern, the ***template method pattern***. The template method pattern describes a generic computation mechanism that can be specialized for a particular application by redefining certain steps. Following the template method pattern, we design an algorithm that implements a generic Euler tour traversal of a binary tree. This algorithm, called templateEulerTour, is shown in Code Fragment 7.28.

Algorithm templateEulerTour(T, v):
  $r \leftarrow$ new object of type TourResult
  visitLeft(T, v, r)
  if T.hasLeft(v) **then**
    r.left $\leftarrow$ templateEulerTour(T, T.left(v))
  visitBelow(T, v, r)
  if T.hasRight(v) **then**
    r.right $\leftarrow$ templateEulerTour(T, T.right(v))
  visitRight(T, v, r)
  return r.out

Code Fragment 7.28: An Euler tour traversal of the subtree of a binary tree T rooted at a node v, following the template method pattern.

When called on a node v, method templateEulerTour calls several other auxiliary methods at different phases of the traversal. Namely, it

- Creates a local variable r of type TourResult, which is used to store intermediate results of the computation and has fields left, right, and out
- Calls auxiliary method visitLeft(T, v, r), which performs the computations associated with encountering the node on the left
- If v has a left child, recursively calls itself on the left child of v and stores the returned value in r.left
- Calls auxiliary method visitBelow(T, v, r), which performs the computations associated with encountering the node from below
- If v has a right child, recursively calls itself on the right child and stores the returned value in r.right
- Calls auxiliary method visitRight(T, v, r), which performs the computations associated with encountering the node on the right
- Returns r.out.

Method templateEulerTour can be viewed as a ***template*** or "skeleton" of an Euler tour. (See Code Fragment 7.28.)

Java Implementation

Java class EulerTour, shown in Code Fragment 7.29, implements an Euler tour traversal using the template method pattern. The recursive traversal is performed by method eulerTour. The auxiliary methods called by eulerTour are empty place holders. That is, they have an empty body or they just return null. Class EulerTour is abstract and thus cannot be instantiated. It contains an abstract method, called execute, which needs to be specified in the concrete subclass of EulerTour. Class TourResult, with fields left, right, and out, is not shown.

```
/**
 * Template for algorithms traversing a binary tree using an Euler
 * tour. The subclasses of this class will redefine some of the
 * methods of this class to create a specific traversal.
 */
public abstract class EulerTour<E, R> {
  protected BinaryTree<E> tree;
  /** Execution of the traversal. This abstract method must be
   * specified in a concrete subclass. */
  public abstract R execute(BinaryTree<E> T);
  /** Initialization of the traversal */
  protected void init(BinaryTree<E> T) { tree = T; }
  /** Template method */
  protected R eulerTour(Position<E> v) {
    TourResult<R> r = new TourResult<R>();
    visitLeft(v, r);
    if (tree.hasLeft(v))
      r.left = eulerTour(tree.left(v));        // recursive traversal
    visitBelow(v, r);
    if (tree.hasRight(v))
      r.right = eulerTour(tree.right(v));      // recursive traversal
    visitRight(v, r);
    return r.out;
  }
  // Auxiliary methods that can be redefined by subclasses:
  /** Method called for the visit on the left */
  protected void visitLeft(Position<E> v, TourResult<R> r) {}
  /** Method called for the visit on from below */
  protected void visitBelow(Position<E> v, TourResult<R> r) {}
  /** Method called for the visit on the right */
  protected void visitRight(Position<E> v, TourResult<R> r) {}
}
```

Code Fragment 7.29: Java class EulerTour defining a generic Euler tour of a binary tree. This class realizes the template method pattern and must be specialized in order to get an interesting computation.

The class, EulerTour, itself does not perform any useful computation. Nevertheless, we can extend it and override the empty auxiliary methods to do useful tasks. We illustrate this concept using arithmetic expression trees (see Example 7.9). We assume that an arithmetic expression tree has objects of type ExpressionTerm at each node. Class ExpressionTerm has subclasses ExpressionVariable (for variables) and ExpressionOperator (for operators). In turn, class ExpressionOperator has subclasses for the arithmetic operators, such as AdditionOperator and MultiplicationOperator. Method value of ExpressionTerm is overridden by its subclasses. For a variable, it returns the value of the variable. For an operator, it returns the result of applying the operator to its operands. The operands of an operator are set by method setOperands of ExpressionOperator. In Code Fragment 7.30, we show the classes ExpressionTerm, ExpressionVariable, ExpressionOperator and AdditionOperator.

```java
/** Class for a term (operator or variable) of an arithmetic expression. */
public class ExpressionTerm {
  public Integer getValue() { return 0; }
  public String toString() { return new String(""); }
}
/** Class for a variable of an arithmetic expression. */
public class ExpressionVariable extends ExpressionTerm {
  protected Integer var;
  public ExpressionVariable(Integer x) { var = x; }
  public void setVariable(Integer x) { var = x; }
  public Integer getValue() { return var; }
  public String toString() { return var.toString(); }
}
/** Class for an operator of an arithmetic expression */
public class ExpressionOperator extends ExpressionTerm {
  protected Integer firstOperand, secondOperand;
  public void setOperands(Integer x, Integer y) {
    firstOperand = x;
    secondOperand = y;
  }
}
/** Class for the addition operator in an arithmetic expression. */
public class AdditionOperator extends ExpressionOperator {
  public Integer getValue() {
    return (firstOperand + secondOperand);   // unboxing and then autoboxing
  }
  public String toString() { return new String("+"); }
}
```

Code Fragment 7.30: Classes for a variable, generic operator, and addition operator of an arithmetic expression.

In Code Fragments 7.31 and 7.32, we show classes EvaluateExpressionTour and PrintExpressionTour, specializing EulerTour, that evaluate and print the arithmetic expression stored in a binary tree, respectively. Class EvaluateExpression-Tour overrides auxiliary method visitRight(T, v, r) with the following computation:

- If v is an external node, set r.out equal to the value of the variable stored at v
- Else (v is an internal node), combine r.left and r.right with the operator stored at v, and set r.out equal to the result of the operation.

Class PrintExpressionTour overrides methods visitLeft, visitBelow, and visitRight following the approach of pseudo-code version shown in Code Fragment 7.27.

```
/** Compute the value of an arithmetic expression tree. */
public class EvaluateExpressionTour extends EulerTour<ExpressionTerm, Integer> {
  public Integer execute(BinaryTree<ExpressionTerm> T) {
    init(T); // calls method of superclass
    return eulerTour(tree.root());  // returns the value of the expression
  }
  protected void visitRight(Position<ExpressionTerm> v, TourResult<Integer> r) {
    ExpressionTerm term = v.element();
    if (tree.isInternal(v)) {
      ExpressionOperator op = (ExpressionOperator) term;
      op.setOperands(r.left, r.right);
    }
    r.out = term.getValue();
  }
}
```

Code Fragment 7.31: Class EvaluateExpressionTour that specializes EulerTour to evaluate the expression associated with an arithmetic expression tree.

```
/** Print out the expression stored in an arithmetic expression tree. */
public class PrintExpressionTour extends EulerTour<ExpressionTerm, String> {
  public String execute(BinaryTree<ExpressionTerm> T) {
    init(T);
    System.out.print("Expression: ");
    eulerTour(T.root());
    System.out.println();
    return null;      // nothing to return
  }
  protected void visitLeft(Position<ExpressionTerm> v, TourResult<String> r) {
    if (tree.isInternal(v)) System.out.print("("); }
  protected void visitBelow(Position<ExpressionTerm> v, TourResult<String> r) {
    System.out.print(v.element()); }
  protected void visitRight(Position<ExpressionTerm> v, TourResult<String> r) {
    if (tree.isInternal(v)) System.out.print(")"); }
}
```

Code Fragment 7.32: Class PrintExpressionTour that specializes EulerTour to print the expression associated with an arithmetic expression tree.

7.4 Exercises

For help with exercises, please visit the web site, www.wiley.com/college/goodrich.

Reinforcement

R-7.1 Describe an algorithm for counting the number of left external nodes in a binary tree, using the Binary tree ADT.

R-7.2 The following questions refer to the tree of Figure 7.3.

   a. Which node is the root?
   b. What are the internal nodes?
   c. How many descendents does node cs016/ have?
   d. How many ancestors does node cs016/ have?
   e. What are the siblings of node homeworks/?
   f. Which nodes are in the subtree rooted at node projects/?
   g. What is the depth of node papers/?
   h. What is the height of the tree?

R-7.3 Find the value of the arithmetic expression associated with each subtree of the binary tree of Figure 7.11.

R-7.4 Let T be an n-node binary tree that may be improper. Describe how to represent T by means of a ***proper*** binary tree T' with $O(n)$ nodes.

R-7.5 What are the minimum and maximum number of internal and external nodes in an improper binary tree with n nodes?

R-7.6 Show a tree achieving the worst-case running time for algorithm depth.

R-7.7 Give a justification of Proposition 7.4.

R-7.8 What is the running time of algorithm height2(T, v) (Code Fragment 7.6) when called on a node v distinct from the root of T?

R-7.9 Let T be the tree of Figure 7.3, and refer to Code Fragments 7.9 and 7.10.

   a. Give the output of toStringPostorder$(T, T.$root$())$.
   b. Give the output of parentheticRepresentation$(T, T.$root$())$.

R-7.10 Describe a modification to parentheticRepresentation, from Code Fragment 7.10, so that it uses the length() method for String objects to output the parenthetic representation of a tree with line breaks and spaces added to display the tree in a text window that is 80 characters wide.

R-7.11 Draw an arithmetic expression tree that has four external nodes, storing the numbers 1, 5, 6, and 7 (with each number stored in a distinct external node, but not necessarily in this order), and has three internal nodes, each storing an operator from the set $\{+, -, \times, /\}$, so that the value of the root is 21. The operators may return and act on fractions, and an operator may be used more than once.

R-7.12 Let T be an ordered tree with more than one node. Is it possible that the preorder traversal of T visits the nodes in the same order as the postorder traversal of T? If so, give an example; otherwise, argue why this cannot occur. Likewise, is it possible that the preorder traversal of T visits the nodes in the reverse order of the postorder traversal of T? If so, give an example; otherwise, argue why this cannot occur.

R-7.13 Answer the previous question for the case when T is a proper binary tree with more than one node.

R-7.14 What is the running time of parentheticRepresentation(T, T.root()) (Code Fragment 7.10) for a tree T with n nodes?

R-7.15 Draw a (single) binary tree T such that

- Each internal node of T stores a single character
- A *preorder* traversal of T yields EXAMFUN
- An *inorder* traversal of T yields MAFXUEN.

R-7.16 Answer the following questions so as to justify Proposition 7.10.

a. What is the minimum number of external nodes for a proper binary tree with height h? Justify your answer.

b. What is the maximum number of external nodes for a proper binary tree with height h? Justify your answer.

c. Let T be a proper binary tree with height h and n nodes. Show that

$$\log(n+1) - 1 \leq h \leq (n-1)/2.$$

d. For which values of n and h can the above lower and upper bounds on h be attained with equality?

R-7.17 Describe a generalization of the Euler tour traversal to trees such that each internal node has three children. Describe how you could use this traversal to compute the height of each node in such a tree.

R-7.18 Compute the output of algorithm toStringPostorder(T, T.root()), from Code Fragment 7.12, on the tree T of Figure 7.3.

R-7.19 Illustrate the execution of algorithm diskSpace(T, T.root()) (Code Fragment 7.13) on the tree T of Figure 7.9.

R-7.20 Let T be the binary tree of Figure 7.11.

a. Give the output of toStringPostorder(T, T.root()) (Code Fragment 7.9).

b. Give the output of parentheticRepresentation(T, T.root()) (Code Fragment 7.10).

R-7.21 Let T be the binary tree of Figure 7.11.

a. Give the output of toStringPostorder(T, T.root()) (Code Fragment 7.12).

b. Give the output of printExpression(T, T.root()) (Code Fragment 7.27).

R-7.22 Describe, in pseudo-code, an algorithm for computing the number of descendents of each node of a binary tree. The algorithm should be based on the Euler tour traversal.

R-7.23 Let T be a (possibly improper) binary tree with n nodes, and let D be the sum of the depths of all the external nodes of T. Show that if T has the minimum number of external nodes possible, then D is $O(n)$ and if T has the maximum number of external nodes possible, then D is $O(n \log n)$.

R-7.24 Let T be a binary tree with n nodes, and let p be the level numbering of the nodes of T, as given in Section 7.3.5.
   a. Show that, for every node v of T, $p(v) \leq 2^n - 1$.
   b. Show an example of a binary tree with seven nodes that attains the above upper bound on $p(v)$ for some node v.

R-7.25 Show how to use the Euler tour traversal to compute the level number, defined in Section 7.3.5, of each node in a binary tree T.

R-7.26 Draw the binary tree representation of the following arithmetic expression: "$(((5+2)*(2-1))/((2+9)+((7-2)-1))*8)$".

R-7.27 Let T be a binary tree with n nodes that is realized with an array list, S, and let p be the level numbering of the nodes in T, as given in Section 7.3.5. Give pseudo-code descriptions of each of the methods root, parent, left, right, hasLeft, hasRight, isInternal, isExternal, and isRoot.

Creativity

C-7.1 Show that there are more than 2^n different potentially improper binary trees with n internal nodes, where two trees are considered different if they would be drawn as different looking trees.

C-7.2 Describe an efficient algorithm for converting a fully balanced string of parentheses into an equivalent tree. The tree associated with such a string is defined recursively. The outer-most pair of balanced parentheses is associated with the root and each substring inside this pair, defined by the substring between two balanced parentheses, is associated with a subtree of this root.

C-7.3 For each node v in a tree T, let pre(v) be the rank of v in a preorder traversal of T, let post(v) be the rank of v in a postorder traversal of T, let depth(v) be the depth of v, and let desc(v) be the number of descendents of v, not counting v itself. Derive a formula defining post(v) in terms of desc(v), depth(v), and pre(v), for each node v in T.

C-7.4 Let T be a tree whose nodes store strings. Give an efficient algorithm that computes and prints, for every node v of T, the string stored at v and the height of the subtree rooted at v.

C-7.5 Design algorithms for the following operations for a binary tree T:

- preorderNext(v): return the node visited after node v in a preorder traversal of T
- inorderNext(v): return the node visited after node v in an inorder traversal of T
- postorderNext(v): return the node visited after node v in a postorder traversal of T.

What are the worst-case running times of your algorithms?

C-7.6 Give an $O(n)$-time algorithm for computing the depth of all the nodes of a tree T, where n is the number of nodes of T.

C-7.7 The *indented parenthetic representation* of a tree T is a variation of the parenthetic representation of T (see Figure 7.7) that uses indentation and line breaks as illustrated in Figure 7.21. Give an algorithm that prints this representation of a tree.

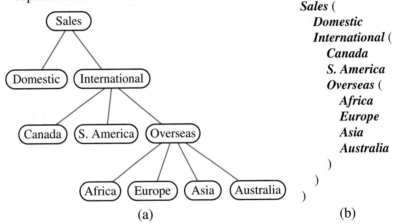

Figure 7.21: (a) Tree T; (b) indented parenthetic representation of T.

C-7.8 Let T be a (possibly improper) binary tree with n nodes, and let D be the sum of the depths of all the external nodes of T. Describe a configuration for T such that D is $\Omega(n^2)$. Such a tree would be the worst case for the asymptotic running time of Algorithm height1 (Code Fragment 7.5).

C-7.9 For a tree T, let n_I denote the number of its internal nodes, and let n_E denote the number of its external nodes. Show that if every internal node in T has exactly 3 children, then $n_E = 2n_I + 1$.

C-7.10 Describe how to clone a proper binary tree using the attach method instead of methods insertLeft and insertRight.

C-7.11 The **balance factor** of an internal node v of a proper binary tree is the difference between the heights of the right and left subtrees of v. Show how to specialize the Euler tour traversal of Section 7.3.7 to print the balance factors of all the internal nodes of a proper binary tree.

C-7.12 Two ordered trees T' and T'' are said to be ***isomorphic*** if one of the following holds:
  - Both T' and T'' are empty
  - Both T' and T'' consist of a single node
  - Both T' and T'' have the same number $k \geq 1$ of subtrees, and the ith subtree of T' is isomorphic to the ith subtree of T'', for $i = 1,\ldots,k$.

  Design an algorithm that tests whether two given ordered trees are isomorphic. What is the running time of your algorithm?

C-7.13 Extend the concept of an Euler tour to an ordered tree that is not necessarily a binary tree.

C-7.14 We can define a ***binary tree representation*** T' for an ordered general tree T as follows (see Figure 7.22):
  - For each node u of T, there is an internal node u' of T' associated with u.
  - If u is an external node of T and does not have a sibling immediately following it, then the children of u' in T' are external nodes.
  - If u is an internal node of T and v is the first child of u in T, then v' is the left child of u' in T.
  - If node v has a sibling w immediately following it, then w' is the right child of v' in T'.

  Given such a representation T' of a general ordered tree T, answer each of the following questions:
  a. Is a preorder traversal of T' equivalent to a preorder traversal of T?
  b. Is a postorder traversal of T' equivalent to a postorder traversal of T?
  c. Is an inorder traversal of T' equivalent to one of the standard traversals of T? If so, which one?

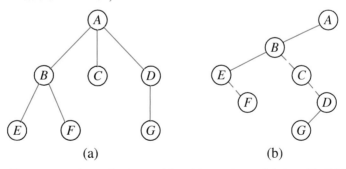

(a)   (b)

Figure 7.22: Representation of a tree with a binary tree: (a) tree T; (b) binary tree T' for T. The dashed edges connect nodes of T' that are siblings in T.

C-7.15 As mentioned in Exercise C-5.8, ***postfix notation*** is an unambiguous way of writing an arithmetic expression without parentheses. It is defined so that if "$(exp_1)\mathbf{op}(exp_2)$" is a normal (infix) fully parenthesized expression with operation **op**, then its postfix equivalent is "*pexp*$_1$ *pexp*$_2$ **op**", where *pexp*$_1$ is the postfix version of *exp*$_1$ and *pexp*$_2$ is the postfix version of *exp*$_2$. The postfix version of a single number of variables is just that number or variable. So, for example, the postfix version of the infix expression "$((5+2)*(8-3))/4$" is "$5\ 2 + 8\ 3 - *\ 4\ /$". Give an efficient algorithm for converting an infix arithmetic expression to its equivalent postfix notation. (Hint: First convert the infix expression into its equivalent binary tree representation, using the algorithm of Code Fragment 7.21.)

C-7.16 Given a proper binary tree T, define the **reflection** of T to be the binary tree T' such that each node v in T is also in T', but the left child of v in T is v's right child in T' and the right child of v in T is v's left child in T'. Show that a preorder traversal of a proper binary tree T is the same as the postorder traversal of T's reflection, but in reverse order.

C-7.17 Algorithm preorderDraw draws a binary tree T by assigning x- and y-coordinates to each node v such that $x(v)$ is the number of nodes preceding v in the preorder traversal of T and $y(v)$ is the depth of v in T. Algorithm postorderDraw is similar to preorderDraw but assigns x-coordinates using a postorder traversal.

   a. Show that the drawing of T produced by preorderDraw has no pairs of crossing edges.
   b. Redraw the binary tree of Figure 7.19 using preorderDraw.
   c. Show that the drawing of T produced by postorderDraw has no pairs of crossing edges.
   d. Redraw the binary tree of Figure 7.19 using postorderDraw.

C-7.18 Design an algorithm for drawing general trees that generalizes the inorder traversal approach for drawing binary trees.

C-7.19 Let a visit action in the Euler tour traversal be denoted by a pair (v,a), where v is the visited node and a is one of **left**, **below**, or **right**. Design and analyze an algorithm for performing operation tourNext(v,a), which returns the visit action (w,b) following (v,a).

C-7.20 Consider a variation of the linked data structure for binary trees where each node object has references to the node objects of the children but not to the node object of the parent. Describe an implementation of the methods of a binary tree with this data structure and analyze the time complexity for these methods.

C-7.21 Design an alternative implementation of the linked data structure for proper binary trees using a class for nodes that specializes into subclasses for an internal node, an external node, and the root node.

C-7.22 Within the linked data structure for binary trees, explore an alternative design for implementing the iterators returned by the methods iterator(), positions().iterator(), and children(v).iterator() such that each of these methods takes $O(1)$ time. Can you still achieve constant time implementations for the methods hasNext() and next() of the iterators returned?

C-7.23 Let T be a tree with n nodes. Define the *lowest common ancestor* (LCA) between two nodes v and w as the lowest node in T that has both v and w as descendents (where we allow a node to be a descendent of itself). Given two nodes v and w, describe an efficient algorithm for finding the LCA of v and w. What is the running time of your algorithm?

C-7.24 Let T be a binary tree with n nodes, and, for any node v in T, let d_v denote the depth of v in T. The *distance* between two nodes v and w in T is $d_v + d_w - 2d_u$, where u is the lowest common ancestor (LCA) u of v and w. The *diameter* of T is the maximum distance between two nodes in T. Describe an efficient algorithm for finding the diameter of T. What is the running time of your algorithm?

C-7.25 Suppose each node v of a binary tree T is labeled with its value $p(v)$ in a level numbering of T. Design a fast method for determining $p(u)$ for the lowest common ancestor (LCA), u, of two nodes v and w in T, given $p(v)$ and $p(w)$. You do not need to find node u, just compute its level-numbering label.

C-7.26 Justify the bounds in Table 7.3 by providing a detailed analysis of the running times of the methods of a binary tree T implemented with an array list, S, where S is realized by means of an array.

C-7.27 Justify Table 7.1, summarizing the running time of the methods of a tree represented with a linked structure, by providing, for each method, a description of its implementation, and an analysis of its running time.

C-7.28 Describe a nonrecursive method for evaluating a binary tree representing an arithmetic expression.

C-7.29 Let T be a binary tree with n nodes. Define a *Roman node* to be a node v in T, such that the number of descendents in v's left subtree differ from the number of descendents in v's right subtree by at most 5. Describe a linear-time method for finding each node v of T, such that v is not a Roman node, but all of v's descendents are Roman nodes.

C-7.30 Describe a nonrecursive method for performing an Euler tour traversal of a binary tree that runs in linear time and does not use a stack.

C-7.31 Describe, in pseudo-code, a nonrecursive method for performing an inorder traversal of a binary tree in linear time.

C-7.32 Let T be a binary tree with n nodes (T may be realized with an array list or a linked structure). Give a linear-time algorithm that uses the methods of the BinaryTree interface to traverse the nodes of T by increasing values of the level numbering function p given in Section 7.3.5. This traversal is known as the *level order traversal*.

C-7.33 The *path length* of a tree T is the sum of the depths of all the nodes in T. Describe a linear-time method for computing the path length of a tree T (which is not necessarily binary).

C-7.34 Define the *internal path length*, $I(T)$, of a tree T to be the sum of the depths of all the internal nodes in T. Likewise, define the *external path length*, $E(T)$, of a tree T to be the sum of the depths of all the external nodes in T. Show that if T is a proper binary tree with n nodes, then $E(T) = I(T) + n - 1$.

Projects

P-7.1 Write a program that takes as input a rooted tree T and a node v of T and converts T to another tree with the same set of node adjacencies but now rooted at v.

P-7.2 Implement the binary tree ADT using an array list.

P-7.3 Implement the tree ADT using a linked structure.

P-7.4 Write a program that draws a binary tree.

P-7.5 A *slicing floorplan* divides a rectangle with horizontal and vertical sides using horizontal and vertical *cuts*. (See Figure 7.23a.) A slicing floorplan can be represented by a proper binary tree, called a *slicing tree*, whose internal nodes represent the cuts, and whose external nodes represent the *basic rectangles* into which the floorplan is decomposed by the cuts. (See Figure 7.23b.) The *compaction problem* for a slicing floorplan is defined as follows. Assume that each basic rectangle of a slicing floorplan is assigned a minimum width w and a minimum height h. The compaction problem is to find the smallest possible height and width for each rectangle of the slicing floorplan that is compatible with the minimum dimensions of the basic rectangles. Namely, this problem requires the assignment of values $h(v)$ and $w(v)$ to each node v of the slicing tree such that:

$$
\mathsf{w}(v) = \begin{cases}
w & \text{if } v \text{ is an external node whose basic rectangle has minimum width } w \\[1em]
\max(\mathsf{w}(w), \mathsf{w}(z)) & \text{if } v \text{ is an internal node associated with a horizontal cut with left child } w \text{ and right child } z \\[1em]
\mathsf{w}(w) + \mathsf{w}(z) & \text{if } v \text{ is an internal node associated with a vertical cut with left child } w \text{ and right child } z
\end{cases}
$$

$$h(v) = \begin{cases} h & \text{if } v \text{ is an external node whose basic rect-angle has minimum height } h \\ \\ h(w) + h(z) & \text{if } v \text{ is an internal node associated with a horizontal cut with left child } w \text{ and right child } z \\ \\ \max(h(w), h(z)) & \text{if } v \text{ is an internal node associated with a vertical cut with left child } w \text{ and right child } z \end{cases}$$

Design a data structure for slicing floorplans that supports the operations:

- Create a floorplan consisting of a single basic rectangle.
- Decompose a basic rectangle by means of a horizontal cut.
- Decompose a basic rectangle by means of a vertical cut.
- Assign minimum height and width to a basic rectangle.
- Draw the slicing tree associated with the floorplan.
- Compact and draw the floorplan.

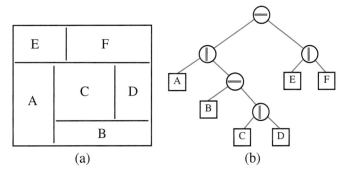

(a)   (b)

Figure 7.23: (a) Slicing floorplan; (b) slicing tree associated with the floorplan.

P-7.6 Write a program that takes as input a fully parenthesized, arithmetic expression and converts it to a binary expression tree. Your program should display the tree in some way and also print the value associated with the root. For an additional challenge, allow for the leaves to store variables of the form x_1, x_2, x_3, and so on, which are initially 0 and which can be updated interactively by your program, with the corresponding update in the printed value of the root of the expression tree.

P-7.7 Write a program that draws a general tree.

P-7.8 Write a program that can input and display a person's family tree.

P-7.9 Implement the tree ADT using the binary tree representation described in Exercise C-7.14. You may reuse the LinkedBinaryTree implementation of a binary tree.

P-7.10 Write a program that visualizes an Euler tour traversal of a proper binary tree, including the movements from node to node and the actions associated with visits on the left, from below, and on the right. Illustrate your program by having it compute and display preorder labels, inorder labels, postorder labels, ancestor counts, and descendent counts for each node in the tree (not necessarily all at the same time).

P-7.11 The arithmetic expression code in Code Fragments 7.29–7.32 only works for Integer expressions with the addition operator. Write a Java program that can evaluation arbitrary expressions of any Number type of object.

P-7.12 Write a program that can play Tic-Tac-Toe effectively. (See Section 3.1.5.) To do this, you will need to create a *game tree* T, which is a tree where each node corresponds to a *game configuration*, which, in this case, is a representation of the tic-tac-toe board. The root node corresponds to the initial configuration. For each internal node v in T, the children of v correspond to the game states we can reach from v's game state in a single legal move for the appropriate player, A (the first player) or B (the second player). Nodes at even depths correspond to moves for A and nodes at odd depths correspond to moves for B. External nodes are either final game states or are at a depth beyond which we don't want to explore. We score each external node with a value that indicates how good this state is for player A. In large games, like chess, we have to use a heuristic scoring function, but for small games, like tic-tac-toe, we can construct the entire game tree and score external nodes as $+1$, 0, -1, indicating whether player A has a win, draw, or lose in that configuration. A good algorithm for choosing moves is *minimax*. In this algorithm, we assign a score to each internal node v in T, such that if v represents A's turn, we compute v's score as the maximum of the scores of v's children (which corresponds to A's optimal play from v). If an internal node v represents B's turn, then we compute v's score as the minimum of the scores of v's children (which corresponds to B's optimal play from v).

Chapter Notes

Discussions of the classic preorder, inorder, and postorder tree traversal methods can be found in Knuth's *Fundamental Algorithms* book [62]. The Euler tour traversal technique comes from the parallel algorithms community, as it is introduced by Tarjan and Vishkin [89] and is discussed by JáJá [53] and by Karp and Ramachandran [57]. The algorithm for drawing a tree is generally considered to be a part of the "folklore" of graph drawing algorithms. The reader interested in graph drawing is referred to the book by Di Battista, Eades, Tamassia and Tollis [28] and the survey by Tamassia and Liotta [88]. The puzzler in Exercise R-7.11 was communicated by Micha Sharir.

Chapter

8

Heaps and Priority Queues

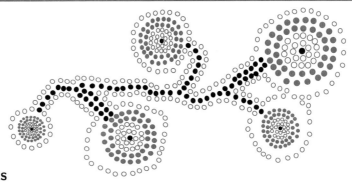

Contents

8.1 The Priority Queue Abstract Data Type

A *priority queue* is an abstract data type for storing a collection of prioritized elements that supports arbitrary element insertion but supports removal of elements in order of priority, that is, the element with first priority can be removed at any time. This ADT is fundamentally different from the position-based data structures we discussed in previous chapters, such as stacks, queues, deques, lists, and even trees. These other data structures store elements at specific positions, which are often positions in a linear arrangement of the elements determined by the insertion and deletion operations performed. The priority queue ADT stores elements according to their priorities, and exposes no notion of "position" to the user.

8.1.1 Keys, Priorities, and Total Order Relations

Applications commonly require that we compare objects according to parameters or properties, called "keys," that are assigned for each object in a collection. Formally, we define a *key* to be an object that is assigned to an element as a specific attribute for that element, which can be used to identify or weigh that element. Note that the key is assigned to an element, typically by a user or application; hence, a key might represent a property that an element did not originally possess.

The key an application assigns to an element is not necessarily unique, however, and an application may even change an element's key if it needs to. For example, we can compare companies by earnings or by number of employees; hence, either of these parameters can be used as a key for a company, depending on the information we wish to extract. Likewise, we can compare restaurants by a critic's food quality rating or by average entrée price. To achieve the most generality then, we allow a key to be of any type that is appropriate for a particular application.

As in the examples above from an airport, the key used for comparisons is often more than a single numerical value, such as price, length, weight, or speed. That is, a key can sometimes be a more complex property that cannot be quantified with a single number. For example, the priority of standby passengers is usually determined by taking into account a host of different factors, including frequent-flyer status, the fare paid, and check-in time. In some applications, the key for an object is part of the object itself (for example, it might be an instance variable storing the list price of a book, or the weight of a car). In other applications, the key is not part of the object but the object gets assigned its key by the application (for example, the quality rating given to a stock by a financial analyst, or the priority assigned to a standby passenger by a gate agent).

Comparing Keys with Total Orders

A priority queue needs a comparison rule that will never contradict itself. In order for a comparison rule, which we denote by $\leq$, to be robust in this way, it must define a ***total order*** relation, which is to say that the comparison rule is defined for every pair of keys and it must satisfy the following properties:

- **Reflexive property**: $k \leq k$.
- **Antisymmetric property**: if $k_1 \leq k_2$ and $k_2 \leq k_1$, then $k_1 = k_2$.
- **Transitive property**: if $k_1 \leq k_2$ and $k_2 \leq k_3$, then $k_1 \leq k_3$.

Any comparison rule, $\leq$, that satisfies these three properties will never lead to a comparison contradiction. In fact, such a rule defines a linear ordering relationship among a set of keys; hence, if a (finite) collection of elements has a total order defined for it, then the notion of a ***smallest*** key, k_{min}, is well defined, as a key in which $k_{min} \leq k$, for any other key k in our collection.

A ***priority queue*** is a collection of elements, called ***values***, each having an associated key that is provided at the time the element is inserted. A key-value pair inserted into a priority queue is called an ***entry*** of the priority queue. The name "priority queue" comes from the fact that keys determine the "priority" used to pick entries to be removed. The two fundamental methods of a priority queue P are as follows:

- insert(k,x): Insert a value x with key k into P.
- removeMin(): Return and remove from P an entry with the smallest key, that is, an entry whose key is less than or equal to that of every other entry in P.

By the way, some people refer to the removeMin method as the "extractMin" method, so as to stress that this method simultaneously removes and returns an entry P. There are many applications where the insert and removeMin operations play an important role. We consider such an application in the example that follows.

Example 8.1: *Suppose a certain flight is fully booked an hour prior to departure. Because of the possibility of cancellations, the airline maintains a priority queue of standby passengers hoping to get a seat. The priority of each standby passenger is determined by the airline taking into account the fare paid, the frequent-flyer status, and the time that the passenger is inserted into the priority queue. A standby passenger reference is inserted into the priority queue with an* insert *operation as soon as he or she requests to fly standby. Shortly before the flight departure, if seats become available (for example, due to no-shows or last-minute cancellations), the airline removes a standby passenger with first priority from the priority queue, using a* removeMin *operation and lets this person board. This process is then repeated until all available seats have been filled or the priority queue becomes empty.*

8.1.2   Entries and Comparators

There are still two important issues that we have left undetermined to this point:

- How do we keep track of the associations between keys and values?
- How do we compare keys so as to determine a smallest key?

Answering these questions involves the use of two interesting design patterns.

The definition of a priority queue implicitly makes use of two special kinds of objects that answer the above questions, the *entry* and *comparator*, which we discuss in this subsection.

Entries

An entry is an association between a key k and a value x, that is, an *entry* is simply a key-value pair. We use entries in a priority queue Q to keep track of the way Q is associating keys and their corresponding values.

An entry is actually an example of a more general object-oriented design pattern, the *composition pattern*, which defines a single object that is composed of other objects. We use this pattern in a priority queue when we define the entries being stored in the priority queue to be pairs consisting of a key k and a value x. A pair is the simplest composition, for it combines two objects into a single pair object. To implement this concept, we define a class that stores two objects in its first and second instance variables, respectively, and provides methods to access and update these variables.

In Code Fragment 8.1, we show an implementation of the composition pattern for entries storing key-value pairs in a priority queue. We realize this composition with an interface called Entry (the java.util package includes a similar Entry interface, by the way). Other kinds of compositions include triples, which store three objects, quadruples, which store four objects, and so on.

```
/** Interface for a key-value pair entry **/
public interface Entry<K,V> {
  /** Returns the key stored in this entry. */
  public K getKey();
  /** Returns the value stored in this entry. */
  public V getValue();
}
```

Code Fragment 8.1: Java interface for an entry storing key-value pairs in a priority queue.

Comparators

Another important issue in the priority queue ADT that we need to define is how to specify the total order relation for comparing keys. One possibility is to implement a different priority queue for each key type we want to use and each possible way of comparing keys of such types. The problem with this approach is that it is not very general and it requires that we create a lot of similar code.

An alternative strategy is to require that keys be able to compare themselves to one another. This solution allows us to write a general priority queue class that can store instances of a key class that has a well-established *natural ordering*, that is, a natural way of comparing such keys in a way that defines a total order. Such an ordering is defined in Java, for instance, by objects that implement the java.lang.Comparable interface. This solution is an improvement over the specialized approach, for it allows us to write a single priority queue class that can handle lots of different types of keys. But there are contexts in which this solution is asking too much of the keys, such as when there are at least two natural ways for comparing them, as in the following example.

Example 8.2: *There are at least two ways of comparing the strings, "4" and "12". In the **lexicographic ordering**, which is an extension of the alphabetic ordering to Unicode, we have "4" > "12". But if we interpret these strings as integers, then "4" < "12".*

Thus, for a general and reusable form of a priority queue, we should not rely on the keys to provide their comparison rules. Instead, we use special *comparator* objects that are external to the keys to supply the comparison rules. A comparator is an object that compares two keys. We assume that a priority queue P is given a comparator when P is constructed, and we might also imagine the ability of a priority queue to be given a new comparator if its old one ever becomes "out of date." When P needs to compare two keys, it uses the comparator it was given to perform the comparison. Thus, a programmer can write a general priority queue implementation that works correctly in a wide variety of contexts. Formally, the comparator ADT provides the following method:

> compare(a,b): Returns an integer i such that $i < 0$ if $a < b$, $i = 0$ if $a = b$, and $i > 0$ if $a > b$; an error occurs if a and b cannot be compared.

The standard Java interface java.util.Comparator corresponds to the comparator ADT above, which offers a general, dynamic, reusable way to compare objects. It also includes an equals() method for comparing a comparator to other comparators.

8.1.3   The Priority Queue ADT

Having described the composition and comparator patterns, let us now define the priority queue ADT, to support the following method for a priority queue P:

size(): Return the number of entries in P.

isEmpty(): Test whether P is empty.

min(): Return (but do not remove) an entry of P with smallest key; an error condition occurs if P is empty.

insert(k,x): Insert into P key k with value x and return the entry storing them; an error condition occurs if k is invalid (that is, k cannot be compared with other keys.

removeMin(): Remove from P and return an entry with smallest key; an error condition occurs if P is empty.

As mentioned above, the primary methods of the priority queue ADT are the insert and removeMin operations. The other methods are query operation min and the generic collection operations size and isEmpty. Note that we allow a priority queue to have multiple entries with the same key.

Example 8.3: *The following table shows a series of operations and their effects on an initially empty priority queue P. We denote with e_i an entry object returned by method* insert. *The "Priority Queue" column is somewhat deceiving since it shows the entries sorted by key. This is more than is required of a priority queue.*

Operation	*Output*	*Priority Queue*
insert$(5,A)$	$e_1[=(5,A)]$	$\{(5,A)\}$
insert$(9,C)$	$e_2[=(9,C)]$	$\{(5,A),(9,C)\}$
insert$(3,B)$	$e_3[=(3,B)]$	$\{(3,B),(5,A),(9,C)\}$
insert$(7,D)$	$e_4[=(7,D)]$	$\{(3,B),(5,A),(7,D),(9,C)\}$
min()	e_3	$\{(3,B),(5,A),(7,D),(9,C)\}$
removeMin()	e_3	$\{(5,A),(7,D),(9,C)\}$
size()	3	$\{(5,A),(7,D),(9,C)\}$
removeMin()	e_1	$\{(7,D),(9,C)\}$
removeMin()	e_4	$\{(9,C)\}$
removeMin()	e_2	$\{\}$

8.1.4   Sorting with a Priority Queue

Another important application of a priority queue is sorting, where we are given a collection S of n elements that can be compared according to a total order relation, and we want to rearrange them in increasing order (or at least in nondecreasing order if there are ties). The algorithm for sorting S with a priority queue Q, called PriorityQueueSort, is quite simple and consists of the following two phases:

1. In the first phase, we put the elements of S into an initially empty priority queue P by means of a series of n insert operations, one for each element.

2. In the second phase, we extract the elements from P in nondecreasing order by means of a series of n removeMin operations, putting them back into S in order.

We give pseudo-code for this algorithm in Code Fragment 8.2, assuming that S is a sequence (pseudo-code for a different type of collection, such as an array list or node list, would be similar). The algorithm works correctly for any priority queue P, no matter how P is implemented. However, the running time of the algorithm is determined by the running times of operations insert and removeMin, which do depend on how P is implemented. Indeed, PriorityQueueSort should be considered more a sorting "scheme" than a sorting "algorithm," because it does not specify how the priority queue P is implemented. The PriorityQueueSort scheme is the paradigm of several popular sorting algorithms, including selection-sort, insertion-sort, and heap-sort, which we discuss in this chapter.

Algorithm PriorityQueueSort(S, P):
  Input: A sequence S storing n elements, on which a total order relation is defined, and a priority queue, P, that compares keys using the same total order relation
  Output: The sequence S sorted by the total order relation
  while !S.isEmpty() **do**
    $e \leftarrow S$.removeFirst()
    P.insert($e, \emptyset$)   {a null value is used}
  while !P.isEmpty() **do**
    $e \leftarrow P$.removeMin().getKey()
    S.addLast(e)   {the smallest key in P is added to the end of S}

Code Fragment 8.2: Algorithm PriorityQueueSort. Note that the elements of the input sequence S serve as keys of the priority queue P.

8.2   Implementing a Priority Queue with a List

In this section, we show how to implement a priority queue by storing its entries in a list S. (See Chapter 6.2.) We provide two realizations, depending on whether or not we keep the entries in S sorted by key. When analyzing the running time of the methods of a priority queue implemented with a list, we will assume that a comparison of two keys takes $O(1)$ time.

Implementation with an Unsorted List

As our first implementation of a priority queue P, let us consider storing the entries of P in a list S, where S is implemented with a doubly linked list. Thus, the elements of S are entries (k,x), where k is the key and x is the value.

A simple way of performing operation insert(k,x) on P is to create a new entry object $e = (k,x)$ and add it at the end of list S, by executing method addLast(e) on S. This implementation of method insert takes $O(1)$ time.

The above insertion algorithm implies that S will be unsorted, for always inserting entries at the end of S does not take into account the ordering of the keys. As a consequence, to perform operation min or removeMin on P, we must inspect all the elements of list S to find an entry (k,x) of S with minimum k. Thus, methods min and removeMin take $O(n)$ time each, where n is the number of entries in P at the time the method is executed. Moreover, these methods run in time proportional to n even in the best case, since they each require searching the entire list to find a minimum-key entry. That is, using the notation of Section 4.2.3, we can say that these methods run in $\Theta(n)$ time. Finally, we implement methods size and isEmpty by simply returning the output of the corresponding methods executed on list S.

Thus, by using an unsorted list to implement a priority queue, we achieve constant-time insertion, but linear-time search and removal.

Implementation with a Sorted List

An alternative implementation of a priority queue P also uses a list S, except that this time let us store the entries sorted by key. Specifically, we represent the priority queue P by using a list S of entries sorted by nondecreasing keys, which means that the first element of S is an entry with the smallest key.

We can implement method min in this case simply by accessing the first element of the list with the first method of S. Likewise, we can implement the removeMin method of P as S.remove(S.first()). Assuming that S is implemented with a doubly linked list, operations min and removeMin in P take $O(1)$ time. Thus, using a sorted list allows for simple and fast implementations of priority queue access and removal methods.

This benefit comes at a cost, however, for now method insert of P requires that we scan through the list S to find the appropriate position to insert the new entry. Thus, implementing the insert method of P now takes $O(n)$ time, where n is the number of entries in P at the time the method is executed. In summary, when using a sorted list to implement a priority queue, insertion runs in linear time whereas finding and removing the minimum can be done in constant time.

Table 8.1 compares the running times of the methods of a priority queue realized by means of a sorted and unsorted list, respectively. We see an interesting trade-off when we use a list to implement the priority queue ADT. An unsorted list allows for fast insertions but slow queries and deletions, while a sorted list allows for fast queries and deletions, but slow insertions.

Method	Unsorted List	Sorted List
size, isEmpty	$O(1)$	$O(1)$
insert	$O(1)$	$O(n)$
min, removeMin	$O(n)$	$O(1)$

Table 8.1: Worst-case running times of the methods of a priority queue of size n, realized by means of an unsorted or sorted list, respectively. We assume that the list is implemented by a doubly linked list. The space requirement is $O(n)$.

8.2.1 A Java Priority Queue Implementation Using a List

Let us consider how we could implement a priority queue in Java using a sorted list. We begin with a Java interface, called PriorityQueue, for the priority queue ADT, which is shown in Code Fragment 8.3.

```
/** Interface for the priority queue ADT */
public interface PriorityQueue<K,V> {
    /** Returns the number of items in the priority queue. */
    public int size();
    /** Returns whether the priority queue is empty. */
    public boolean isEmpty();
    /** Returns but does not remove an entry with minimum key. */
    public Entry<K,V> min() throws EmptyPriorityQueueException;
    /** Inserts a key-value pair and return the entry created. */
    public Entry<K,V> insert(K key, V value) throws InvalidKeyException;
    /** Removes and returns an entry with minimum key. */
    public Entry<K,V> removeMin() throws EmptyPriorityQueueException;
}
```

Code Fragment 8.3: Java interface for the priority queue ADT.

A Java Implementation with a Sorted List

In Code Fragments 8.5 and 8.6, we give a Java implementation of the priority queue ADT that uses a sorted node list. This implementation uses a class, DefaultComparator, which realizes a comparator using the natural ordering, as shown in Code Fragment 8.4. This implementation also uses a nested class, called MyEntry, to implement the Entry interface (see Section 6.5.1). We do not show an auxiliary method, checkKey(k), which throws an InvalidKeyException if key k cannot be compared with the comparator of the priority queue.

```java
public class DefaultComparator<E> implements Comparator<E> {
  public int compare(E a, E b) throws ClassCastException {
    return ((Comparable<E>) a).compareTo(b);
  }
}
```

Code Fragment 8.4: Java class DefaultComparator that implements a comparator using the natural ordering.

```java
public class SortedListPriorityQueue<K,V> implements PriorityQueue<K,V> {
  protected PositionList<Entry<K,V>> entries;
  protected Comparator<K> c;
  protected Position<Entry<K,V>> actionPos; // variable used by subclasses
  /** Inner class for entries */
  protected static class MyEntry<K,V> implements Entry<K,V> {
    protected K k; // key
    protected V v; // value
    public MyEntry(K key, V value) {
      k = key;
      v = value;
    }
    // methods of the Entry interface
    public K getKey() { return k; }
    public V getValue() { return v; }
  }
  /** Creates the priority queue with the default comparator. */
  public SortedListPriorityQueue () {
    entries = new NodePositionList<Entry<K,V>>();
    c = new DefaultComparator<K>();
  }
  /** Creates the priority queue with the given comparator. */
  public SortedListPriorityQueue (Comparator<K> comp) {
    entries = new NodePositionList<Entry<K,V>>();
    c = comp;
  }
```

Code Fragment 8.5: Portions of the Java class SortedListPriorityQueue, which implements the PriorityQueue interface. (Continues in Code Fragment 8.6.)

```java
/** Returns but does not remove an entry with minimum key. */
public Entry<K,V> min () throws EmptyPriorityQueueException {
  if (entries.isEmpty())
    throw new EmptyPriorityQueueException("priority queue is empty");
  else
    return entries.first().element();
}
/** Inserts a key-value pair and return the entry created. */
public Entry<K,V> insert (K k, V v) throws InvalidKeyException {
  checkKey(k); // auxiliary key-checking method (could throw exception)
  Entry<K,V> entry = new MyEntry<K,V>(k, v);
  insertEntry(entry);          // auxiliary insertion method
  return entry;
}
/** Auxiliary method used for insertion. */
protected void insertEntry(Entry<K,V> e) {
  if (entries.isEmpty()) {
    entries.addFirst(e);          // insert into empty list
    actionPos = entries.first();  // insertion position
  }
  else if (c.compare(e.getKey(), entries.last().element().getKey()) > 0) {
    entries.addLast(e);           // insert at the end of the list
    actionPos = entries.last();   // insertion position
  }
  else {
    Position<Entry<K,V>> curr = entries.first();
    while (c.compare(e.getKey(), curr.element().getKey())> 0) {
      curr = entries.next(curr);   // advance toward insertion position
    }
    entries.addBefore(curr, e);
    actionPos = entries.prev(curr); // insertion position
  }
}
/** Removes and returns an entry with minimum key. */
public Entry<K,V> removeMin() throws EmptyPriorityQueueException {
  if (entries.isEmpty())
    throw new EmptyPriorityQueueException("priority queue is empty");
  else
    return entries.remove(entries.first());
}
```

Code Fragment 8.6: Portions of the Java class SortedListPriorityQueue, which implements the PriorityQueue interface. (Continued from Code Fragment 8.5.)

8.2.2   Selection-Sort and Insertion-Sort

Recall the PriorityQueueSort scheme introduced in Section 8.1.4. We are given an unsorted sequence S containing n elements, which we sort using a priority queue P in two phases. In Phase 1 we insert all the elements into P and in Phase 2 we repeatedly remove the elements from P using the removeMin() method.

Selection-Sort

If we implement P with an unsorted list, then Phase 1 of PriorityQueueSort takes $O(n)$ time, for we can insert each element in $O(1)$ time. In Phase 2, the running time of each removeMin operation is proportional to the size of P. Thus, the bottleneck computation is the repeated "selection" of the minimum element in Phase 2. For this reason, this algorithm is better known as **selection-sort**. (See Figure 8.1.)

As noted above, the bottleneck is in Phase 2 where we repeatedly remove an entry with smallest key from the priority queue P. The size of P starts at n and incrementally decreases with each removeMin until it becomes 0. Thus, the first removeMin operation takes time $O(n)$, the second one takes time $O(n-1)$, and so on, until the last (nth) operation takes time $O(1)$. Therefore, the total time needed for the second phase is

$$O\left(n+(n-1)+\cdots+2+1\right) = O\left(\sum_{i=1}^{n} i\right).$$

By Proposition 4.3, we have $\sum_{i=1}^{n} i = n(n+1)/2$. Thus, Phase 2 takes time $O(n^2)$, as does the entire selection-sort algorithm.

		Sequence S	*Priority Queue P*
Input		$(7,4,8,2,5,3,9)$	$()$
Phase 1	(a)	$(4,8,2,5,3,9)$	(7)
	(b)	$(8,2,5,3,9)$	$(7,4)$
	⋮	⋮	⋮
	(g)	$()$	$(7,4,8,2,5,3,9)$
Phase 2	(a)	(2)	$(7,4,8,5,3,9)$
	(b)	$(2,3)$	$(7,4,8,5,9)$
	(c)	$(2,3,4)$	$(7,8,5,9)$
	(d)	$(2,3,4,5)$	$(7,8,9)$
	(e)	$(2,3,4,5,7)$	$(8,9)$
	(f)	$(2,3,4,5,7,8)$	(9)
	(g)	$(2,3,4,5,7,8,9)$	$()$

Figure 8.1: Execution of selection-sort on sequence $S = (7,4,8,2,5,3,9)$.

Insertion-Sort

If we implement the priority queue P using a sorted list, then we improve the running time of Phase 2 to $O(n)$, for each operation removeMin on P now takes $O(1)$ time. Unfortunately, Phase 1 now becomes the bottleneck for the running time, since, in the worst case, each insert operation takes time proportional to the size of P. This sorting algorithm is therefore better known as ***insertion-sort*** (see Figure 8.2), for the bottleneck in this sorting algorithm involves the repeated "insertion" of a new element at the appropriate position in a sorted list.

		Sequence S	*Priority queue P*
Input		$(7,4,8,2,5,3,9)$	$()$
Phase 1	(a)	$(4,8,2,5,3,9)$	(7)
	(b)	$(8,2,5,3,9)$	$(4,7)$
	(c)	$(2,5,3,9)$	$(4,7,8)$
	(d)	$(5,3,9)$	$(2,4,7,8)$
	(e)	$(3,9)$	$(2,4,5,7,8)$
	(f)	(9)	$(2,3,4,5,7,8)$
	(g)	$()$	$(2,3,4,5,7,8,9)$
Phase 2	(a)	(2)	$(3,4,5,7,8,9)$
	(b)	$(2,3)$	$(4,5,7,8,9)$
	$\vdots$	$\vdots$	$\vdots$
	(g)	$(2,3,4,5,7,8,9)$	$()$

Figure 8.2: Execution of insertion-sort on sequence $S = (7,4,8,2,5,3,9)$. In Phase 1, we repeatedly remove the first element of S and insert it into P, by scanning the list implementing P, until we find the correct place for this element. In Phase 2, we repeatedly perform removeMin operations on P, each of which returns the first element of the list implementing P, and we add the element at the end of S.

Analyzing the running time of Phase 1 of insertion-sort, we note that it is

$$O(1+2+\ldots+(n-1)+n) = O\left(\sum_{i=1}^{n} i\right).$$

Again, by recalling Proposition 4.3, Phase 1 runs in $O(n^2)$ time, and hence, so does the entire insertion-sort algorithm.

Alternatively, we could change our definition of insertion-sort so that we insert elements starting from the end of the priority-queue list in Phase 1, in which case performing insertion-sort on a sequence that is already sorted would run in $O(n)$ time. Indeed, the running time of insertion-sort in this case is $O(n+I)$, where I is the number of ***inversions*** in the sequence, that is, the number of pairs of elements that start out in the input sequence in the wrong relative order.

8.3   Heaps

The two implementations of the PriorityQueueSort scheme presented in the previous section suggest a possible way of improving the running time for priority-queue sorting. For one algorithm (selection-sort) achieves a fast running time for Phase 1, but has a slow Phase 2, whereas the other algorithm (insertion-sort) has a slow Phase 1, but achieves a fast running time for Phase 2. If we can somehow balance the running times of the two phases, we might be able to significantly speed up the overall running time for sorting. This is, in fact, exactly what we can achieve using the priority-queue implementation discussed in this section.

An efficient realization of a priority queue uses a data structure called a ***heap***. This data structure allows us to perform both insertions and removals in logarithmic time, which is a significant improvement over the list-based implementations discussed in Section 8.2. The fundamental way the heap achieves this improvement is to abandon the idea of storing entries in a list and take the approach of storing entries in a binary tree instead.

8.3.1   The Heap Data Structure

A heap (see Figure 8.3) is a binary tree T that stores a collection of entries at its nodes and that satisfies two additional properties: a relational property defined in terms of the way keys are stored in T and a structural property defined in terms of the nodes of T itself. We assume that a total order relation on the keys is given, for example, by a comparator.

The relational property of T, defined in terms of the way keys are stored, is the following:

Heap-Order Property: In a heap T, for every node v other than the root, the key stored at v is greater than or equal to the key stored at v's parent.

As a consequence of the heap-order property, the keys encountered on a path from the root to an external node of T are in nondecreasing order. Also, a minimum key is always stored at the root of T. This is the most important key and is informally said to be "at the top of the heap"; hence, the name "heap" for the data structure. By the way, the heap data structure defined here has nothing to do with the memory heap (Section 14.1.2) used in the run-time environment supporting a programming language like Java.

If we define our comparator to indicate the opposite of the standard total order relation between keys (so that, for example, compare$(3,2) < 0$), then the root of the heap stores the largest key. This versatility comes essentially "for free" from our use of the comparator pattern. By defining the minimum key in terms of the comparator, the "minimum" key with a "reverse" comparator is in fact the largest.

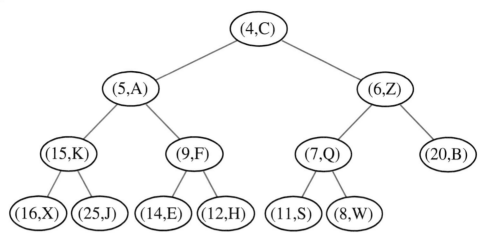

Figure 8.3: Example of a heap storing 13 entries with integer keys. The last node is the one storing entry $(8, W)$.

Thus, without loss of generality, we assume that we are always interested in the minimum key, which will always be at the root of the heap.

For the sake of efficiency, as will become clear later, we want the heap T to have as small a height as possible. We enforce this requirement by insisting that the heap T satisfy an additional structural property: it must be *complete*. Before we define this structural property, we need some definitions. We recall from Section 7.3.3 that level i of a binary tree T is the set of nodes of T that have depth i. Given nodes v and w on the same level of T, we say that v is *to the left of* w if v is encountered before w in an inorder traversal of T. That is, there is a node u of T such that v is in the left subtree of u and w is in the right subtree of u. For example, in the binary tree of Figure 8.3, the node storing entry $(15, K)$ is to the left of the node storing entry $(7, Q)$. In a standard drawing of a binary tree, the "to the left of" relation is visualized by the relative horizontal placement of the nodes.

Complete Binary Tree Property: A heap T with height h is a *complete* binary tree if levels $0, 1, 2, \ldots, h - 1$ of T have the maximum number of nodes possible (namely, level i has 2^i nodes, for $0 \le i \le h - 1$) and in level $h - 1$, all the internal nodes are to the left of the external nodes and there is at most one node with one child, which must be a left child.

By insisting that a heap T be complete, we identify another important node in a heap T, other than the root, namely, the *last node* of T, which we define to be the right-most, deepest external node of T (see Figure 8.3).

The Height of a Heap

Let h denote the height of T. Another way of defining the last node of T is that it is the node on level h such that all the other nodes of level h are to the left of it. Insisting that T be complete also has an important consequence, as shown in Proposition 8.4.

Proposition 8.4: *A heap T storing n entries has height*

$$h = \lfloor \log n \rfloor.$$

Justification: From the fact that T is complete, we know that the number of nodes of T is at least

$$
\begin{aligned}
1 + 2 + 4 + \cdots + 2^{h-1} + 1 &= 2^h - 1 + 1 \\
&= 2^h.
\end{aligned}
$$

This lower bound is achieved when there is only one node on level h. In addition, also following from T being complete, we have that the number of nodes of T is at most

$$1 + 2 + 4 + \cdots + 2^h = 2^{h+1} - 1.$$

This upper bound is achieved when level h has 2^h nodes. Since the number of nodes is equal to the number n of entries, we obtain

$$2^h \le n$$

and

$$n \le 2^{h+1} - 1.$$

Thus, by taking logarithms of both sides of these two inequalities, we see that

$$h \le \log n$$

and

$$\log(n+1) - 1 \le h.$$

Since h is an integer, the two inequalities above imply that

$$h = \lfloor \log n \rfloor.$$

$\blacksquare$

Proposition 8.4 has an important consequence, for it implies that if we can perform update operations on a heap in time proportional to its height, then those operations will run in logarithmic time. Let us therefore turn to the problem of how to efficiently perform various priority queue methods using a heap.

8.3.2 Complete Binary Trees and Their Representation

Let us discuss more about complete binary trees and how they are represented.

The Complete Binary Tree ADT

As an abstract data type, a complete binary T supports all the methods of binary tree ADT (Section 7.3.1), plus the following two methods:

> add(o): Add to T and return a new external node v storing element o such that the resulting tree is a complete binary tree with last node v.

> remove(): Remove the last node of T and return its element.

Using only these update operations guarantees that we will always have a complete binary tree. As shown in Figure 8.4, there are two cases for the effect of an add or remove. Specifically, for an add, we have the following (remove is similar).

- If the bottom level of T is not full, then add inserts a new node on the bottom level of T, immediately after the right-most node of this level (that is, the last node); hence, T's height remains the same.
- If the bottom level is full, then add inserts a new node as the left child of the left-most node of the bottom level of T; hence, T's height increases by one.

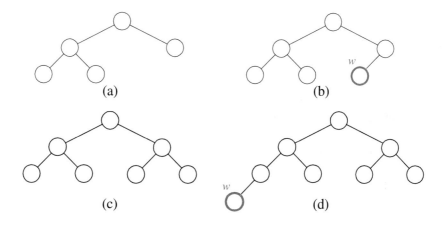

Figure 8.4: Examples of operations add and remove on a complete binary tree, where w denotes the node inserted by add or deleted by remove. The trees shown in (b) and (d) are the results of performing add operations on the trees in (a) and (c), respectively. Likewise, the trees shown in (a) and (c) are the results of performing remove operations on the trees in (b) and (d), respectively.

The Array List Representation of a Complete Binary Tree

The array-list binary tree representation (Section 7.3.5) is especially suitable for a complete binary tree T. We recall that in this implementation, the nodes of T are stored in an array list A such that node v in T is the element of A with index equal to the level number $p(v)$ of v, defined as follows:

- If v is the root of T, then $p(v) = 1$.
- If v is the left child of node u, then $p(v) = 2p(u)$.
- If v is the right child of node u, then $p(v) = 2p(u) + 1$.

With this implementation, the nodes of T have contiguous indices in the range $[1, n]$ and the last node of T is always at index n, where n is the number of nodes of T. Figure 8.5 shows two examples illustrating this property of the last node.

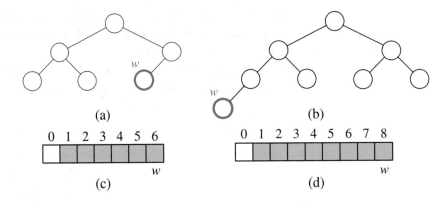

Figure 8.5: Two examples showing that the last node w of a heap with n nodes has level number n: (a) heap T_1 with more than one node on the bottom level; (b) heap T_2 with one node on the bottom level; (c) array-list representation of T_1; (d) array-list representation of T_2.

The simplifications that come from representing a complete binary tree T with an array list aid in the implementation of methods add and remove. Assuming that no array expansion is necessary, methods add and remove can be performed in $O(1)$ time, for they simply involve adding or removing the last element of the array list. Moreover, the array list associated with T has $n + 1$ elements (the element at index 0 is a place-holder). If we use an extendable array that grows and shrinks for the implementation of the array list (Section 6.1.4 and Exercise C-6.2), the space used by the array-list representation of a complete binary tree with n nodes is $O(n)$ and operations add and remove take $O(1)$ amortized time.

Java Implementation of a Complete Binary Tree

We represent the complete binary tree ADT in interface CompleteBinaryTree shown in Code Fragment 8.7. We provide a Java class ArrayListCompleteBinaryTree that implements the CompleteBinaryTree interface with an array list and supports methods add and remove in $O(1)$ time in Code Fragments 8.8–8.10.

```java
public interface CompleteBinaryTree<E> extends BinaryTree<E> {
  public Position<E> add(E elem);
  public E remove();
}
```

Code Fragment 8.7: Interface CompleteBinaryTree for a complete binary tree.

```java
public class ArrayListCompleteBinaryTree<E>
    implements CompleteBinaryTree<E> {
  protected ArrayList<BTPos<E>> T; // indexed list of tree positions
  /** Nested class for a index list-based complete binary tree node. */
  protected static class BTPos<E> implements Position<E> {
    E element; // element stored at this position
    int index;     // index of this position in the array list
    public BTPos(E elt, int i) {
      element = elt;
      index = i;
    }
    public E element() { return element; }
    public int index() { return index; }
    public E setElement(E elt) {
      E temp = element;
      element = elt;
      return temp;
    }
  }
  /** default constructor */
  public ArrayListCompleteBinaryTree() {
    T = new ArrayList<BTPos<E>>();
    T.add(0, null); // the location at rank 0 is deliberately empty
  }
  /** Returns the number of (internal and external) nodes. */
  public int size() { return T.size() − 1; }
  /** Returns whether the tree is empty. */
  public boolean isEmpty() { return (size() == 0); }
```

Code Fragment 8.8: Class ArrayListCompleteBinaryTree implementing interface CompleteBinaryTree using a java.util.ArrayList. (Continues in Code Fragment 8.9.)

```java
/** Returns whether v is an internal node. */
public boolean isInternal(Position<E> v) throws InvalidPositionException {
  return hasLeft(v); // if v has a right child it will have a left child
}
/** Returns whether v is an external node. */
public boolean isExternal(Position<E> v) throws InvalidPositionException {
  return !isInternal(v);
}
/** Returns whether v is the root node. */
public boolean isRoot(Position<E> v) throws InvalidPositionException {
  BTPos<E> vv = checkPosition(v);
  return vv.index() == 1;
}
/** Returns whether v has a left child. */
public boolean hasLeft(Position<E> v) throws InvalidPositionException {
  BTPos<E> vv = checkPosition(v);
  return 2*vv.index() <= size();
}
/** Returns whether v has a right child. */
public boolean hasRight(Position<E> v) throws InvalidPositionException {
  BTPos<E> vv = checkPosition(v);
  return 2*vv.index() + 1 <= size();
}
/** Returns the root of the tree. */
public Position<E> root() throws EmptyTreeException {
  if (isEmpty()) throw new EmptyTreeException("Tree is empty");
  return T.get(1);
}
/** Returns the left child of v. */
public Position<E> left(Position<E> v)
    throws InvalidPositionException, BoundaryViolationException {
  if (!hasLeft(v)) throw new BoundaryViolationException("No left child");
  BTPos<E> vv = checkPosition(v);
  return T.get(2*vv.index());
}
/** Returns the right child of v. */
public Position<E> right(Position<E> v)
    throws InvalidPositionException {
  if (!hasRight(v)) throw new BoundaryViolationException("No right child");
  BTPos<E> vv = checkPosition(v);
  return T.get(2*vv.index() + 1);
}
```

Code Fragment 8.9: Class ArrayListCompleteBinaryTree implementing the complete binary tree ADT. (Continues in Code Fragment 8.10.)

```java
/** Returns the parent of v. */
public Position<E> parent(Position<E> v)
  throws InvalidPositionException, BoundaryViolationException {
  if (isRoot(v)) throw new BoundaryViolationException("No parent");
  BTPos<E> vv = checkPosition(v);
  return T.get(vv.index()/2);
}
/** Replaces the element at v. */
public E replace(Position<E> v, E o) throws InvalidPositionException {
  BTPos<E> vv = checkPosition(v);
  return vv.setElement(o);
}
/** Adds an element just after the last node (in a level numbering). */
public Position<E> add(E e) {
  int i = size() + 1;
  BTPos<E> p = new BTPos<E>(e,i);
  T.add(i, p);
  return p;
}
/** Removes and returns the element at the last node. */
public E remove() throws EmptyTreeException {
  if(isEmpty()) throw new EmptyTreeException("Tree is empty");
  return T.remove(size()).element();
}
/** Determines whether the given position is a valid node. */
protected BTPos<E> checkPosition(Position<E> v)
  throws InvalidPositionException
{
  if (v == null || !(v instanceof BTPos))
    throw new InvalidPositionException("Position is invalid");
  return (BTPos<E>) v;
}
/** Returns an iterator of the elements stored at all nodes in the tree. */
public Iterator<E> iterator() {
  ArrayList<E> list = new ArrayList<E>();
  Iterator<BTPos<E>> iter = T.iterator();
  iter.next(); // skip the first element
  while (iter.hasNext())
    list.add(iter.next().element());
  return list.iterator();
  }
}
```

Code Fragment 8.10: Class ArrayListCompleteBinaryTree implementing the complete binary tree ADT. Methods children and positions are omitted. (Continued from Code Fragment 8.9.)

8.3.3 Implementing a Priority Queue with a Heap

We now discuss how to implement a priority queue using a heap. Our heap-based representation for a priority queue P consists of the following (see Figure 8.6):

- **heap**, a complete binary tree T whose internal nodes store entries so that the heap-order property is satisfied. We assume T is implemented using an array list, as described in Section 8.3.2. For each internal node v of T, we denote the key of the entry stored at v as $k(v)$.
- **comp**, a comparator that defines the total order relation among the keys.

With this data structure, methods size and isEmpty take $O(1)$ time, as usual. In addition, method min can also be easily performed in $O(1)$ time by accessing the entry stored at the root of the heap (which is at index 1 in the array list).

Insertion

Let us consider how to perform insert on a priority queue implemented with a heap T. To store a new entry (k,x) into T we add a new node z to T with operation add so that this new node becomes the last node of T and stores entry (k,x).

After this action, the tree T is complete, but it may violate the heap-order property. Hence, unless node z is the root of T (that is, the priority queue was empty before the insertion), we compare key $k(z)$ with the key $k(u)$ stored at the parent u of z. If $k(z) \geq k(u)$, the heap-order property is satisfied and the algorithm terminates. If instead $k(z) < k(u)$, then we need to restore the heap-order property, which can be locally achieved by swapping the entries stored at z and u. (See Figure 8.7c and d.) This swap causes the new entry (k,e) to move up one level. Again, the heap-order property may be violated, and we continue swapping, going up in T until no violation of the heap-order property occurs. (See Figure 8.7e and h.)

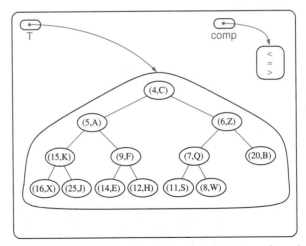

Figure 8.6: Illustration of the heap-based implementation of a priority queue.

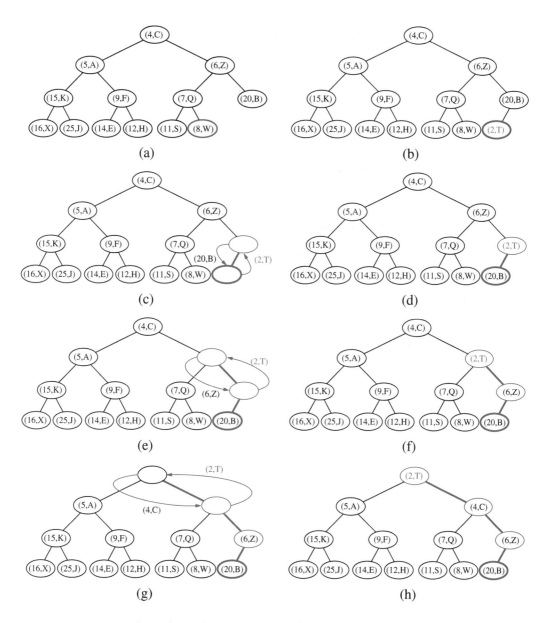

Figure 8.7: Insertion of a new entry with key 2 into the heap of Figure 8.6: (a) initial heap; (b) after performing operation add; (c and d) swap to locally restore the partial order property; (e and f) another swap; (g and h) final swap.

The upward movement of the newly inserted entry by means of swaps is conventionally called ***up-heap bubbling***. A swap either resolves the violation of the heap-order property or propagates it one level up in the heap. In the worst case, up-heap bubbling causes the new entry to move all the way up to the root of heap T. (See Figure 8.7.) Thus, in the worst case, the number of swaps performed in the execution of method insert is equal to the height of T, that is, it is $\lfloor \log n \rfloor$ by Proposition 8.4.

Removal

Let us now turn to method removeMin of the priority queue ADT. The algorithm for performing method removeMin using heap T is illustrated in Figure 8.8.

We know that an entry with the smallest key is stored at the root r of T (even if there is more than one entry with smallest key). However, unless r is the only internal node of T, we cannot simply delete node r, because this action would disrupt the binary tree structure. Instead, we access the last node w of T, copy its entry to the root r, and then delete the last node by performing operation remove of the complete binary tree ADT. (See Figure 8.8a and b.)

Down-Heap Bubbling after a Removal

We are not necessarily done, however, for, even though T is now complete, T may now violate the heap-order property. If T has only one node (the root), then the heap-order property is trivially satisfied and the algorithm terminates. Otherwise, we distinguish two cases, where r denotes the root of T:

- If r has no right child, let s be the left child of r.
- Otherwise (r has both children), let s be a child of r with the smallest key.

If $k(r) \leq k(s)$, the heap-order property is satisfied and the algorithm terminates. If instead $k(r) > k(s)$, then we need to restore the heap-order property, which can be locally achieved by swapping the entries stored at r and s. (See Figure 8.8c and d.) (Note that we shouldn't swap r with s's sibling.) The swap we perform restores the heap-order property for node r and its children, but it may violate this property at s; hence, we may have to continue swapping down T until no violation of the heap-order property occurs. (See Figure 8.8e and h.)

This downward swapping process is called ***down-heap bubbling***. A swap either resolves the violation of the heap-order property or propagates it one level down in the heap. In the worst case, an entry moves all the way down to the bottom level. (See Figure 8.8.) Thus, the number of swaps performed in the execution of method removeMin is, in the worst case, equal to the height of heap T, that is, it is $\lfloor \log n \rfloor$ by Proposition 8.4.

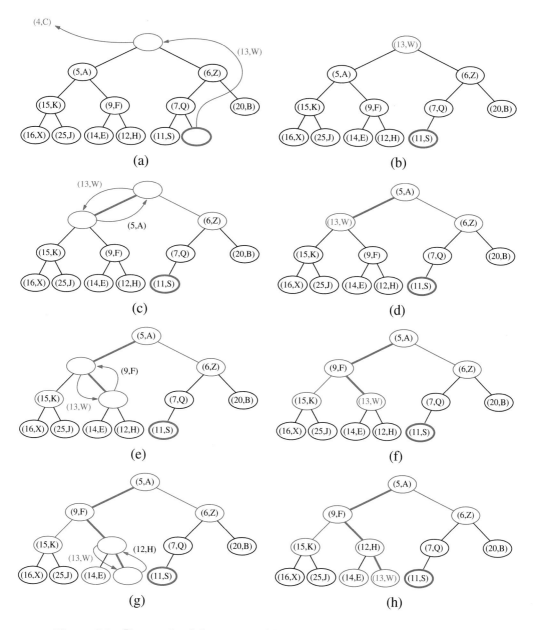

Figure 8.8: Removal of the entry with the smallest key from a heap: (a and b) deletion of the last node, whose entry gets stored into the root; (c and d) swap to locally restore the heap-order property; (e and f) another swap; (g and h) final swap.

Analysis

Table 8.2 shows the running time of the priority queue ADT methods for the heap implementation of a priority queue, assuming that two keys can be compared in $O(1)$ time and that the heap T is implemented with either an array list or linked structure.

Operation	Time
size, isEmpty	$O(1)$
min,	$O(1)$
insert	$O(\log n)$
removeMin	$O(\log n)$

Table 8.2: Performance of a priority queue realized by means of a heap, which is in turn implemented with an array list or linked structure. We denote with n the number of entries in the priority queue at the time a method is executed. The space requirement is $O(n)$. The running time of operations insert and removeMin is worst case for the array-list implementation of the heap and amortized for the linked representation.

In short, each of the priority queue ADT methods can be performed in $O(1)$ or in $O(\log n)$ time, where n is the number of entries at the time the method is executed. The analysis of the running time of the methods is based on the following:

- The heap T has n nodes, each storing a reference to an entry.

- Operations add and remove on T take either $O(1)$ amortized time (array-list representation) or $O(\log n)$ worst-case time.

- In the worst case, up-heap and down-heap bubbling perform a number of swaps equal to the height of T.

- The height of heap T is $O(\log n)$, since T is complete (Proposition 8.4).

We conclude that the heap data structure is a very efficient realization of the priority queue ADT, independent of whether the heap is implemented with a linked structure or an array list. The heap-based implementation achieves fast running times for both insertion and removal, unlike the list-based priority queue implementations. Indeed, an important consequence of the efficiency of the heap-based implementation is that it can speed up priority-queue sorting to be much faster than the list-based insertion-sort and selection-sort algorithms.

8.3.4 A Java Heap Implementation

A Java implementation of a heap-based priority queue is shown in Code Fragments 8.11–8.13. To aid in modularity, we delegate the maintenance of the structure of the heap itself to a complete binary tree.

```java
/**
 * Realization of a priority queue by means of a heap. A complete
 * binary tree realized by means of an array list is used to
 * represent the heap.
 */
public class HeapPriorityQueue<K,V> implements PriorityQueue<K,V> {
  protected CompleteBinaryTree<Entry<K,V>> heap; // underlying heap
  protected Comparator<K> comp; // comparator for the keys
  /** Inner class for heap entries. */
  protected static class MyEntry<K,V> implements Entry<K,V> {
    protected K key;
    protected V value;
    public MyEntry(K k, V v) { key = k; value = v; }
    public K getKey() { return key; }
    public V getValue() { return value; }
    public String toString() { return "(" + key + "," + value + ")"; }
  }
  /** Creates an empty heap with the default comparator */
  public HeapPriorityQueue() {
    heap = new ArrayListCompleteBinaryTree<Entry<K,V>>(); // use an array list
    comp = new DefaultComparator<K>(); // use the default comparator
  }
  /** Creates an empty heap with the given comparator */
  public HeapPriorityQueue(Comparator<K> c) {
    heap = new ArrayListCompleteBinaryTree<Entry<K,V>>();
    comp = c;
  }
  /** Returns the size of the heap */
  public int size() { return heap.size(); }
  /** Returns whether the heap is empty */
  public boolean isEmpty() { return heap.size() == 0; }
```

Code Fragment 8.11: Class HeapPriorityQueue, which implements a priority queue with a heap. A nested class MyEntry is used for the entries of the priority queue, which form the elements in the heap tree. (Continues in Code Fragment 8.12.)

```
/** Returns but does not remove an entry with minimum key */
public Entry<K,V> min() throws EmptyPriorityQueueException {
  if (isEmpty())
    throw new EmptyPriorityQueueException("Priority queue is empty");
  return heap.root().element();
}
/** Inserts a key-value pair and returns the entry created */
public Entry<K,V> insert(K k, V x) throws InvalidKeyException {
  checkKey(k); // may throw an InvalidKeyException
  Entry<K,V> entry = new MyEntry<K,V>(k,x);
  upHeap(heap.add(entry));
  return entry;
}
/** Removes and returns an entry with minimum key */
public Entry<K,V> removeMin() throws EmptyPriorityQueueException {
  if (isEmpty())
    throw new EmptyPriorityQueueException("Priority queue is empty");
  Entry<K,V> min = heap.root().element();
  if (size() == 1)
    heap.remove();
  else {
    heap.replace(heap.root(), heap.remove());
    downHeap(heap.root());
  }
  return min;
}
/** Determines whether a given key is valid */
protected void checkKey(K key) throws InvalidKeyException {
  try {
    comp.compare(key,key);
  }
  catch(Exception e) {
    throw new InvalidKeyException("Invalid key");
  }
}
```

Code Fragment 8.12: Methods min, insert and removeMin and some auxiliary methods of class HeapPriorityQueue. (Continues in Code Fragment 8.13.)

```
/** Performs up-heap bubbling */
protected void upHeap(Position<Entry<K,V>> v) {
  Position<Entry<K,V>> u;
  while (!heap.isRoot(v)) {
    u = heap.parent(v);
    if (comp.compare(u.element().getKey(), v.element().getKey()) <= 0) break;
    swap(u, v);
    v = u;
  }
}
/** Performs down-heap bubbling */
protected void downHeap(Position<Entry<K,V>> r) {
  while (heap.isInternal(r)) {
    Position<Entry<K,V>> s;          // the position of the smaller child
    if (!heap.hasRight(r))
      s = heap.left(r);
    else if (comp.compare(heap.left(r).element().getKey(),
                          heap.right(r).element().getKey()) <=0)
      s = heap.left(r);
    else
      s = heap.right(r);
    if (comp.compare(s.element().getKey(), r.element().getKey()) < 0) {
      swap(r, s);
      r = s;
    }
    else
      break;
  }
}
/** Swaps the entries of the two given positions */
protected void swap(Position<Entry<K,V>> x, Position<Entry<K,V>> y) {
  Entry<K,V> temp = x.element();
  heap.replace(x, y.element());
  heap.replace(y, temp);
}
/** Text visualization for debugging purposes */
public String toString() {
  return heap.toString();
}
```

Code Fragment 8.13: Remaining auxiliary methods of class HeapPriorityQueue. (Continued from Code Fragment 8.12.)

8.3.5 Heap-Sort

As we have previously observed, realizing a priority queue with a heap has the advantage that all the methods in the priority queue ADT run in logarithmic time or better. Hence, this realization is suitable for applications where fast running times are sought for all the priority queue methods. Therefore, let us again consider the PriorityQueueSort sorting scheme from Section 8.1.4, which uses a priority queue P to sort a sequence S with n elements.

During Phase 1, the i-th insert operation ($1 \leq i \leq n$) takes $O(1 + \log i)$ time, since the heap has i entries after the operation is performed. Likewise, during Phase 2, the j-th removeMin operation ($1 \leq j \leq n$) runs in time $O(1 + \log(n - j + 1))$, since the heap has $n - j + 1$ entries at the time the operation is performed. Thus, each phase takes $O(n \log n)$ time, so the entire priority-queue sorting algorithm runs in $O(n \log n)$ time when we use a heap to implement the priority queue. This sorting algorithm is better known as ***heap-sort***, and its performance is summarized in the following proposition.

Proposition 8.5: *The heap-sort algorithm sorts a sequence S of n elements in $O(n \log n)$ time, assuming two elements of S can be compared in $O(1)$ time.*

Let us stress that the $O(n \log n)$ running time of heap-sort is considerably better than the $O(n^2)$ running time of selection-sort and insertion-sort (Section 8.2.2).

Implementing Heap-Sort In-Place

If the sequence S to be sorted is implemented by means of an array, we can speed up heap-sort and reduce its space requirement by a constant factor using a portion of the sequence S itself to store the heap, thus avoiding the use of an external heap data structure. This is accomplished by modifying the algorithm as follows:

1. We use a reverse comparator, which corresponds to a heap where an entry with the largest key is at the top. At any time during the execution of the algorithm, we use the left portion of S, up to a certain index $i - 1$, to store the entries of the heap, and the right portion of S, from index i to $n - 1$, to store the elements of the sequence. Thus, the first i elements of S (at indices $0, \ldots, i - 1$) provide the array-list representation of the heap (with modified level numbers starting at 0 instead of 1), that is, the element at index k is greater than or equal to its "children" at indices $2k + 1$ and $2k + 2$.

2. In the first phase of the algorithm, we start with an empty heap and move the boundary between the heap and the sequence from left to right, one step at a time. In step i ($i = 1, \ldots, n$), we expand the heap by adding the element at index $i - 1$.

3. In the second phase of the algorithm, we start with an empty sequence and move the boundary between the heap and the sequence from right to left, one step at a time. At step i ($i = 1, \ldots, n$), we remove a maximum element from the heap and store it at index $n - i$.

The variation of heap-sort above is said to be ***in-place*** because we use only a small amount of space in addition to the sequence itself. Instead of transferring elements out of the sequence and then back in, we simply rearrange them. We illustrate in-place heap-sort in Figure 8.9. In general, we say that a sorting algorithm is in-place if it uses only a small amount of memory in addition to the sequence storing the objects to be sorted.

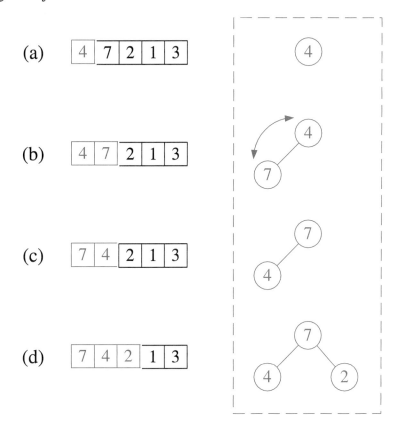

Figure 8.9: First three steps of Phase 1 of in-place heap-sort. The heap portion of the sequence is highlighted in blue. We draw next to the sequence a binary tree view of the heap, even though this tree is not actually constructed by the in-place algorithm.

8.3.6   Bottom-Up Heap Construction ⋆

The analysis of the heap-sort algorithm shows that we can construct a heap storing n entries in $O(n\log n)$ time, by means of n successive insert operations, and then use that heap to extract the entries in order by nondecreasing key. However, if all the n key-value pairs to be stored in the heap are given in advance, there is an alternative ***bottom-up*** construction method that runs in $O(n)$ time. We describe this method in this section, observing that it could be included as one of the constructors of a class implementing a heap-based priority queue. For simplicity of exposition, we describe this bottom-up heap construction assuming the number n of keys is an integer of the type $n = 2^{h+1} - 1$. That is, the heap is a complete binary tree with every level being full, so the heap has height $h = \log(n+1) - 1$. Viewed nonrecursively, bottom-up heap construction consists of the following $h + 1 = \log(n+1)$ steps:

1. In the first step (see Figure 8.10a), we construct $(n+1)/2$ elementary heaps storing one entry each.

2. In the second step (see Figure 8.10b–c), we form $(n+1)/4$ heaps, each storing three entries, by joining pairs of elementary heaps and adding a new entry. The new entry is placed at the root and may have to be swapped with the entry stored at a child to preserve the heap-order property.

3. In the third step (see Figure 8.10d–e), we form $(n+1)/8$ heaps, each storing 7 entries, by joining pairs of 3-entry heaps (constructed in the previous step) and adding a new entry. The new entry is placed initially at the root, but may have to move down with a down-heap bubbling to preserve the heap-order property.

                      ⋮

i. In the generic ith step, $2 \le i \le h$, we form $(n+1)/2^i$ heaps, each storing $2^i - 1$ entries, by joining pairs of heaps storing $(2^{i-1} - 1)$ entries (constructed in the previous step) and adding a new entry. The new entry is placed initially at the root, but may have to move down with a down-heap bubbling to preserve the heap-order property.

                      ⋮

$h+1$. In the last step (see Figure 8.10f–g), we form the final heap, storing all the n entries, by joining two heaps storing $(n-1)/2$ entries (constructed in the previous step) and adding a new entry. The new entry is placed initially at the root, but may have to move down with a down-heap bubbling to preserve the heap-order property.

We illustrate bottom-up heap construction in Figure 8.10 for $h = 3$.

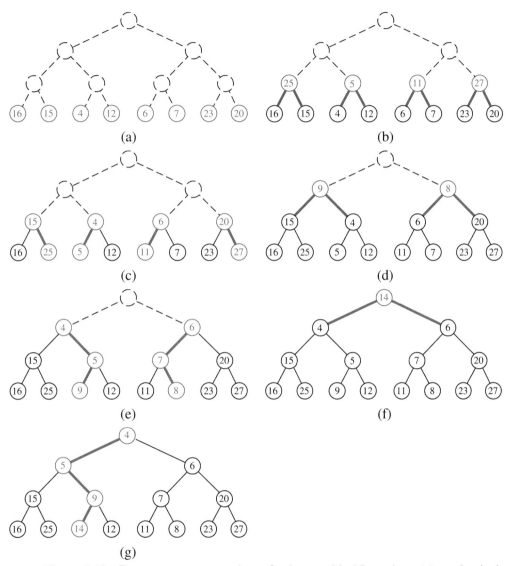

Figure 8.10: Bottom-up construction of a heap with 15 entries: (a) we begin by constructing 1-entry heaps on the bottom level; (b and c) we combine these heaps into 3-entry heaps and then (d and e) 7-entry heaps, until (f and g) we create the final heap. The paths of the down-heap bubblings are highlighted in blue. For simplicity, we only show the key within each node instead of the entire entry.

Recursive Bottom-Up Heap Construction

We can also describe bottom-up heap construction as a recursive algorithm, as shown in Code Fragment 8.14, which we call by passing a list storing the key-value pairs for which we wish to build a heap.

Algorithm BottomUpHeap(S):

    Input: A list L storing $n = 2^{h+1} - 1$ entries

    Output: A heap T storing the entries in L.

    if S.isEmpty() **then**

        return an empty heap

    $e \leftarrow L$.remove(L.first())

    Split L into two lists, L_1 and L_2, each of size $(n-1)/2$

    $T_1 \leftarrow$ BottomUpHeap(L_1)

    $T_2 \leftarrow$ BottomUpHeap(L_2)

    Create binary tree T with root r storing e, left subtree T_1, and right subtree T_2

    Perform a down-heap bubbling from the root r of T, if necessary

    return T

Code Fragment 8.14: Recursive bottom-up heap construction.

Bottom-up heap construction is asymptotically faster than incrementally inserting n keys into an initially empty heap, as the following proposition shows.

Proposition 8.6: *Bottom-up construction of a heap with n entries takes $O(n)$ time, assuming two keys can be compared in $O(1)$ time.*

Justification: We analyze bottom-up heap construction using a "visual" approach, which is illustrated in Figure 8.11.

Let T be the final heap, let v be a node of T, and let $T(v)$ denote the subtree of T rooted at v. In the worst case, the time for forming $T(v)$ from the two recursively formed subtrees rooted at v's children is proportional to the height of $T(v)$. The worst case occurs when down-heap bubbling from v traverses a path from v all the way to a bottom-most node of $T(v)$.

Now consider the path $p(v)$ of T from node v to its inorder successor external node, that is, the path that starts at v, goes to the right child of v, and then goes down leftward until it reaches an external node. We say that path $p(v)$ is ***associated***

with node v. Note that $p(v)$ is not necessarily the path followed by down-heap bubbling when forming $T(v)$. Clearly, the size (number of nodes) of $p(v)$ is equal to the height of $T(v)$ plus one. Hence, forming $T(v)$ takes time proportional to the size of of $p(v)$, in the worst case. Thus, the total running time of bottom-up heap construction is proportional to the sum of the sizes of the paths associated with the nodes of T.

Observe that each node v of T belongs to at most two such paths: the path $p(v)$ associated with v itself and possibly also the path $p(u)$ associated with the closest ancestor u of v preceding v in an inorder traversal. (See Figure 8.11.) In particular, the root r of T and the nodes on the leftmost root-to-leaf path each belong only to one path, the one associated with the node itself. Therefore, the sum of the sizes of the paths associated with the internal nodes of T is at most $2n-1$. We conclude that the bottom-up construction of heap T takes $O(n)$ time.   ■

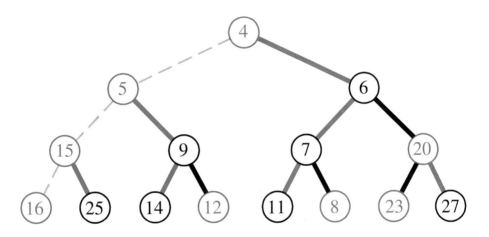

Figure 8.11: Visual justification of the linear running time of bottom-up heap construction, where the paths associated with the internal nodes have been highlighted with alternating colors. For example, the path associated with the root consists of the nodes storing keys 4, 6, 7, and 11. Also, the path associated with the right child of the root consists of the internal nodes storing keys 6, 20, and 23.

To summarize, Proposition 8.6 states that the running time for the first phase of heap-sort can be reduced to be $O(n)$. Unfortunately, the running time of the second phase of heap-sort cannot be made asymptotically better than $O(n \log n)$ (that is, it will always be $\Omega(n \log n)$ in the worst case). We will not justify this lower bound until Chapter 11, however. Instead, we conclude this chapter by discussing a design pattern that allows us to extend the priority queue ADT to have additional functionality.

8.4   Adaptable Priority Queues

The methods of the priority queue ADT given in Section 8.1.3 are sufficient for most basic applications of priority queues, such as sorting. However, there are situations where additional methods would be useful, as shown in the scenarios below, which refer to the standby airline passenger application.

- A standby passenger with a pessimistic attitude may become tired of waiting and decide to leave ahead of the boarding time, requesting to be removed from the waiting list. Thus, we would like to remove from the priority queue the entry associated with this passenger. Operation removeMin is not suitable for this purpose since the passenger leaving is unlikely to have first priority. Instead, we would like to have a new operation remove(e) that removes an arbitrary entry e.

- Another standby passenger finds her gold frequent-flyer card and shows it to the agent. Thus, her priority has to be modified accordingly. To achieve this change of priority, we would like to have a new operation replaceKey(e, k) that replaces with k the key of entry e in the priority queue.

- Finally, a third standby passenger notices her name is misspelled on the ticket and asks it to be corrected. To perform the change, we need to update the passenger's record. Hence, we would like to have a new operation replaceValue(e, x) that replaces with x the value of entry e in the priority queue.

Methods of the Adaptable Priority Queue ADT

The above scenarios motivate the definition of a new ADT that extends the priority queue ADT with methods remove, replaceKey, and replaceValue. Namely, an **adaptable priority queue** P supports the following methods in addition to those of the priority queue ADT:

remove(e): Remove from P and return entry e.

replaceKey(e, k): Replace with k and return the key of entry e of P; an error condition occurs if k is invalid (that is, k cannot be compared with other keys).

replaceValue(e, x): Replace with x and return the value of entry e of P.

8.4.1 Using the java.util.PriorityQueue Class

There is no priority queue interface built into Java, but Java does include a class, java.util.PriorityQueue, which implements the java.util.Queue interface. Instead of adding and removing elements according to the FIFO policy, however, which is the standard queue policy, the java.util.PriorityQueue class processes its entries according to a priority. This priority is defined by a given comparator object, which is passed to the queue in a constructor, or it is defined by the natural ordering of the elements being stored in the queue. Thus, the java.util.PriorityQueue class is a type of priority queue, which is based on inserting and removing general elements rather than key-value pair entries.

The java.util.PriorityQueue class is implemented with a heap, so it guarantees $O(\log n)$ time performance for inserting an element and removing the minimum element. In addition, it provides a method, remove(e), for removing an element, e. It doesn't have methods for replacing keys or values, though, since it operates on general objects, not entries. Still, we can define it to use entry objects as its elements, and we can perform key and value replacement by the appropriate element removal and insertion. Indeed, the Java Collections Framework includes an entry object, called java.util.AbstractMap.SimpleEntry, which implements an interface, java.util.Map.Entry, that includes the entry ADT discussed above in Section 8.1.2. Thus, we can use built-in Java classes to construct a simple adapter pattern implementation of the adaptable priority queue ADT, as shown in Table 8.3.

The only drawback with this implementation of the adaptable priority queue ADT is that, even though the priority queue methods min() and removeMin() run in $O(\log n)$ time using this implementation, the methods remove(e), replaceKey(e,k), and replaceValue(e,x) run in $O(n)$ time. The main problem is that this adaptation has no fast way of locating element e in the heap; so we have to search through the entire heap to find e and remove it.

Method	java.util.PriorityQueue **Adaptation**
size()	size()
isEmpty()	isEmpty()
insert(k,v)	add(**new** SimpleEntry(k,v))
min()	peek()
removeMin()	remove()
remove(e)	remove(e)
replaceKey(e,k)	remove(e); add(**new** SimpleEntry(k,e.getValue()))
replaceValue(e,x)	remove(e); add(**new** SimpleEntry(e.getKey(),x))

Table 8.3: Methods of the adaptable priority queue ADT and corresponding adapter pattern implementations using the java.util.PriorityQueue class.

8.4.2   Location-Aware Entries

In order to implement methods remove, replaceKey, and replaceValue of an adaptable priority queue P efficiently, we need a mechanism for finding the position of an entry of P. Namely, given the entry e of P passed as an argument to one of the above methods, we need to find the position storing e in the the data structure implementing P (for example, a doubly linked list or a heap). This position is called the *location* of the entry.

Instead of searching for the location of a given entry e, we augment the entry object with an instance variable of type Position storing the location. This implementation of an entry that keeps track of its position is called a *location-aware entry*. A summary description of the the use of location-aware entries for the sorted list and heap implementations of an adaptable priority queue is provided below. We denote the number of entries in the priority queue at the time an operation is performed, with n.

- **Sorted list implementation.** In this implementation, after an entry is inserted, we set the location of the entry to refer to the position of the list containing the entry. Also, we update the location of the entry whenever it changes position in the list. Operations remove(e) and replaceValue(e,x) take $O(1)$ time, since we can obtain the position p of entry e in $O(1)$ time following the location reference stored with the entry. Instead, operation replaceKey(e,k) runs in $O(n)$ time, because the modification of the key of entry e may require moving the entry to a different position in the list to preserve the ordering of the keys. The use of location-aware entries increases the running time of the standard priority queue operations by a constant factor.

- **Heap implementation.** In this implementation, after an entry is inserted, we set the location of the entry to refer to the node of the heap containing the entry. Also, we update the location of the entry whenever it changes node in the heap (for example, because of the swaps in a down-heap or up-heap bubbling). Operation replaceValue(e,x) takes $O(1)$ time since we can obtain the position p of entry e in $O(1)$ time following the location reference stored with the entry. Operations remove(e) and replaceKey(e,k) run instead in $O(\log n)$ (details are explored in Exercise C-8.23). The use of location-aware entries increases the running time of operations insert and removeMin by a constant factor overhead.

The use of location-aware entries for the unsorted list implementation is explored in Exercise C-8.22.

Performance of Adaptable Priority Queue Implementations

The performance of an adaptable priority queue implemented by means of various data structures with location-aware entries is summarized in Table 8.4.

Method	Unsorted List	Sorted List	Heap
size, isEmpty	$O(1)$	$O(1)$	$O(1)$
insert	$O(1)$	$O(n)$	$O(\log n)$
min	$O(n)$	$O(1)$	$O(1)$
removeMin	$O(n)$	$O(1)$	$O(\log n)$
remove	$O(1)$	$O(1)$	$O(\log n)$
replaceKey	$O(1)$	$O(n)$	$O(\log n)$
replaceValue	$O(1)$	$O(1)$	$O(1)$

Table 8.4: Running times of the methods of an adaptable priority queue of size n, realized by means of an unsorted list, sorted list, and heap, respectively. The space requirement is $O(n)$.

8.4.3 Implementing an Adaptable Priority Queue

In Code Fragment 8.15 and 8.16, we show the Java implementation of an adaptable priority queue based on a sorted list. This implementation is obtained by extending class SortedListPriorityQueue shown in Code Fragment 8.5. In particular, Code Fragment 8.16 shows how to realize a location-aware entry in Java by extending a regular entry.

The main idea behind this implementation is that the LocationAwareEntry class, which implements the Entry interface, now contains a field, loc, that stores the location of each entry. That is, loc is a pointer to the position of this entry in the list representing the priority queue. In addition, location-aware entry objects support a method, setLocation, and each time the list-based priority queue moves an entry, it notifies the entry of this change using its setLocation method. This allows for each update operation to have the same asymptotic time performance as in a nonadaptive priority queue while also allowing for constant-time location of any location-aware entry.

```java
/** Implementation of an adaptable priority queue by means of a sorted list. */
public class SortedListAdaptablePriorityQueue<K,V>
    extends SortedListPriorityQueue<K,V>
    implements AdaptablePriorityQueue<K,V> {
  /** Creates the priority queue with the default comparator */
  public SortedListAdaptablePriorityQueue() {
    super();
  }
  /** Creates the priority queue with the given comparator */
  public SortedListAdaptablePriorityQueue(Comparator<K> comp) {
    super(comp);
  }
  /** Inserts a key-value pair and returns the entry created */
  public Entry<K,V> insert (K k, V v) throws InvalidKeyException {
    checkKey(k);
    LocationAwareEntry<K,V> entry = new LocationAwareEntry<K,V>(k,v);
    insertEntry(entry);
    entry.setLocation(actionPos);        // position of the new entry
    return entry;
  }
  /** Removes and returns the given entry */
  public Entry<K,V> remove(Entry<K,V> entry) {
    checkEntry(entry);
    LocationAwareEntry<K,V> e = (LocationAwareEntry<K,V>) entry;
    Position<Entry<K,V>> p = e.location();
    entries.remove(p);
    e.setLocation(null);
    return e;
  }
  /** Replaces the key of the given entry */
  public K replaceKey(Entry<K,V> entry, K k) {
    checkKey(k);
    checkEntry(entry);
    LocationAwareEntry<K,V> e = (LocationAwareEntry<K,V>) remove(entry);
    K oldKey = e.setKey(k);
    insertEntry(e);
    e.setLocation(actionPos); // position of new entry
    return oldKey;
  }
}
```

Code Fragment 8.15: Java implementation of an adaptable priority queue by means of a sorted list storing location-aware entries. Class SortedListAdaptablePriorityQueue extends class SortedListPriorityQueue (Code Fragment 8.5) and implements interface AdaptablePriorityQueue. (Continues in Code Fragment 8.16.)

```java
/** Replaces the value of the given entry */
public V replaceValue(Entry<K,V> e, V value) {
  checkEntry(e);
  V oldValue = ((LocationAwareEntry<K,V>) e).setValue(value);
  return oldValue;
}
/** Determines whether a given entry is valid */
protected void checkEntry(Entry ent) throws InvalidEntryException {
  if(ent == null || !(ent instanceof LocationAwareEntry))
    throw new InvalidEntryException("invalid entry");
}
/** Inner class for a location-aware entry */
protected static class LocationAwareEntry<K,V>
  extends MyEntry<K,V> implements Entry<K,V> {
  /** Position where the entry is stored. */
  private Position<Entry<K,V>> loc;
  public LocationAwareEntry(K key, V value) {
    super(key, value);
  }
  public LocationAwareEntry(K key, V value, Position<Entry<K,V>> pos) {
    super(key, value);
    loc = pos;
  }
  protected Position<Entry<K,V>> location() {
    return loc;
  }
  protected Position<Entry<K,V>> setLocation(Position<Entry<K,V>> pos) {
    Position<Entry<K,V>> oldPosition = location();
    loc = pos;
    return oldPosition;
  }
  protected K setKey(K key) {
    K oldKey = getKey();
    k = key;
    return oldKey;
  }
  protected V setValue(V value) {
    V oldValue = getValue();
    v = value;
    return oldValue;
  }
}
}
```

Code Fragment 8.16: An adaptable priority queue implemented with a sorted list storing location-aware entries. (Continued from Code Fragment 8.15.) The nested class LocationAwareEntry realizes a location-aware entry and extends nested class MyEntry of SortedListPriorityQueue shown in Code Fragment 8.5.

8.5   Exercises

For help with exercises, please visit the web site, www.wiley.com/college/goodrich.

Reinforcement

R-8.1 What are the running times of each of the methods of the (standard) priority queue ADT if we implement it using the java.util.PriorityQueue adaptation given in Table 8.3?

R-8.2 How long would it take to remove the $\lceil \log n \rceil$ smallest elements from a heap that contains n entries, using the removeMin() operation?

R-8.3 Suppose you label each node v of a binary tree T with a key equal to the preorder rank of v. Under what circumstances is T a heap?

R-8.4 What is the output from the following sequence of priority queue ADT methods: insert(5, A), insert(4, B), insert(7, I), insert(1, D), removeMin(), insert(3, J), insert(6, L), removeMin(), removeMin(), insert(8, G), removeMin(), insert(2, H), removeMin(), removeMin() ?

R-8.5 An airport is developing a computer simulation of air-traffic control that handles events such as landings and takeoffs. Each event has a *time-stamp* that denotes the time when the event occurs. The simulation program needs to efficiently perform the following two fundamental operations:

   • Insert an event with a given time-stamp (that is, add a future event).
   • Extract the event with smallest time-stamp (that is, determine the next event to process).

Which data structure should be used for the above operations? Why?

R-8.6 Although it is correct to use a "reverse" comparator with the priority queue ADT so that we retrieve and remove an entry with the maximum key each time, it is confusing to have an entry with maximum key returned by a method named "removeMin." Write a short adapter class that can take any priority queue P and an associated comparator C and implement a priority queue that concentrates on the element with maximum key, using methods with names like removeMax.

R-8.7 Illustrate the execution of the selection-sort algorithm on the following input sequence: $(22, 15, 36, 44, 10, 3, 9, 13, 29, 25)$.

R-8.8 Illustrate the execution of the insertion-sort algorithm on the input sequence of the previous problem.

R-8.9 Give an example of a worst-case sequence with n elements for insertion-sort, and show that insertion-sort runs in $\Omega(n^2)$ time on such a sequence.

R-8.10 At which nodes of a heap can an entry with the largest key be stored?

R-8.11 In defining the relation "to the left of" for two nodes of a binary tree (Section 8.3.1), can we use a preorder traversal instead of an inorder traversal? How about a postorder traversal?

R-8.12 Illustrate the execution of the heap-sort algorithm on the following input sequence: $(2, 5, 16, 4, 10, 23, 39, 18, 26, 15)$.

R-8.13 Let T be a complete binary tree such that node v stores the entry $(p(v), 0)$, where $p(v)$ is the level number of v. Is tree T a heap? Why or why not?

R-8.14 Explain why the case where node r has a right child but not a left child was not considered in the description of down-heap bubbling.

R-8.15 Is there a heap T storing seven entries with distinct keys such that a preorder traversal of T yields the entries of T in increasing or decreasing order by key? How about an inorder traversal? How about a postorder traversal? If so, give an example; if not, say why.

R-8.16 Let H be a heap storing 15 entries using the array-list representation of a complete binary tree. What is the sequence of indices of the array list that are visited in a preorder traversal of H? What about an inorder traversal of H? What about a postorder traversal of H?

R-8.17 Show that the sum

$$\sum_{i=1}^{n} \log i,$$

which appears in the analysis of heap-sort, is $\Omega(n \log n)$.

R-8.18 Bill claims that a preorder traversal of a heap will list its keys in nondecreasing order. Draw an example of a heap that proves him wrong.

R-8.19 Hillary claims that a postorder traversal of a heap will list its keys in nonincreasing order. Draw an example of a heap that proves her wrong.

R-8.20 Show all the steps of the algorithm for removing key 16 from the heap of Figure 8.3.

R-8.21 Show all the steps of the algorithm for replacing key 5 with 18 in the heap of Figure 8.3.

R-8.22 Draw an example of a heap whose keys are all the odd numbers from 1 to 59 (with no repeats), such that the insertion of an entry with key 32 would cause up-heap bubbling to proceed all the way up to a child of the root (replacing that child's key with 32).

R-8.23 Complete Figure 8.9 by showing all the steps of the in-place heap-sort algorithm. Show both the array and the associated heap at the end of each step.

R-8.24 Give a pseudo-code description of a nonrecursive in-place heap-sort algorithm.

R-8.25 A group of children want to play a game, called *Unmonopoly*, where in each turn the player with the most money must give half of his/her money to the player with the least amount of money. What data structure(s) should be used to play this game efficiently? Why?

Creativity

C-8.1 Suppose you have a heap H that stores n entries with keys consisting of strings of digits, ordered according to the lexicographic ordering. Describe a linear-time method for converting H into a heap that is ordered according to the numeric values of the integers represented by the keys of the entries of H.

C-8.2 An online computer system for trading stock needs to process orders of the form "buy 100 shares at $\$x$ each" or "sell 100 shares at $\$y$ each." A buy order for $\$x$ can only be processed if there is an existing sell order with price $\$y$ such that $y \leq x$. Likewise, a sell order for $\$y$ can only be processed if there is an existing buy order with price $\$x$ such that $y \leq x$. If a buy or sell order is entered but cannot be processed, it must wait for a future order that allows it to be processed. Describe a scheme that allows for buy and sell orders to be entered in $O(\log n)$ time, independent of whether or not they can be immediately processed.

C-8.3 Extend a solution to the previous problem so that users are allowed to update the prices for their buy or sell orders that have yet to be processed.

C-8.4 Write a comparator for nonnegative integers that determines order based on the number of 1's in each integer's binary expansion, so that $i < j$ if the number of 1's in the binary representation of i is less than the number of 1's in the binary representation of j.

C-8.5 Show how to implement the stack ADT using only a priority queue and one additional integer instance variable.

C-8.6 Show how to implement the (standard) queue ADT using only a priority queue and one additional integer instance variable.

C-8.7 Describe in detail an implementation of a priority queue based on a sorted array. Show that this implementation achieves $O(1)$ time for operations min and removeMin and $O(n)$ time for operation insert.

C-8.8 Describe an in-place version of the selection-sort algorithm that uses only $O(1)$ space for instance variables in addition to an input array itself.

C-8.9 Assuming the input to the sorting problem is given in an array A, describe how to implement the insertion-sort algorithm using only the array A and, at most, six additional (base-type) variables.

C-8.10 Describe how to implement the heap-sort algorithm using, at most, six integer variables in addition to an input array itself.

C-8.11 Describe a sequence of n insertions in a heap that requires $\Omega(n\log n)$ time to process.

C-8.12 An alternative method for finding the last node during an insertion in a heap T is to store, in the last node and each external node of T, a reference to the external node immediately to its right (wrapping to the first node in the next lower level for the right-most external node). Show how to maintain such references in $O(1)$ time per operation of the priority queue ADT assuming T is implemented as a linked structure.

C-8.13 Describe an implementation of complete binary tree T by means of a linked structure and a reference to the last node. In particular, show how to update the reference to the last node after operations add and remove in $O(\log n)$ time, where n is the current number of nodes of T. Be sure and handle all possible cases, as illustrated in Figure 8.12.

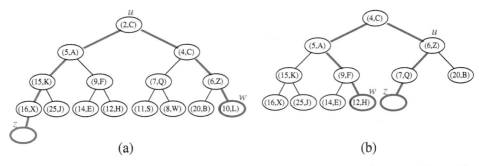

(a)   (b)

Figure 8.12: Updating the last node in a complete binary tree after operation add or remove. Node w is the last node before operation add or after operation remove. Node z is the last node after operation add or before operation remove.

C-8.14 We can represent a path from the root to a given node of a binary tree by means of a binary string, where 0 means "go to the left child" and 1 means "go to the right child." For example, the path from the root to the node storing $(8,W)$ in the heap of Figure 8.12a is represented by "101." Design an $O(\log n)$-time algorithm for finding the last node of a complete binary tree with n nodes, based on the above representation. Show how this algorithm can be used in the implementation of a complete binary tree by means of a linked structure that does not keep a reference to the last node.

C-8.15 Given a heap T and a key k, give an algorithm to compute all the entries in T with key less than or equal to k. For example, given the heap of Figure 8.12a and query $k = 7$, the algorithm should report the entries with keys 2, 4, 5, 6, and 7 (but not necessarily in this order). Your algorithm should run in time proportional to the number of entries returned.

C-8.16 Provide a justification of the time bounds in Table 8.4.

C-8.17 Tamarindo Airlines wants to give a first-class upgrade coupon to their top $\log n$ frequent flyers, based on the number of miles accumulated, where n is the total number of the airlines' frequent flyers. The algorithm they currently use, which runs in $O(n \log n)$ time, sorts the flyers by the number of miles flown and then scans the sorted list to pick the top $\log n$ flyers. Describe an algorithm that identifies the top $\log n$ flyers in $O(n)$ time.

C-8.18 Develop an algorithm that computes the kth smallest element of a set of n distinct integers in $O(n + k \log n)$ time.

C-8.19 Suppose two binary trees, T_1 and T_2, hold entries satisfying the heap-order property. Describe a method for combining T_1 and T_2 into a tree T whose internal nodes hold the union of the entries in T_1 and T_2 and also satisfy the heap-order property. Your algorithm should run in time $O(h_1 + h_2)$ where h_1 and h_2 are the respective heights of T_1 and T_2.

C-8.20 Give an alternative analysis of bottom-up heap construction by showing the following summation is $O(1)$, for any positive integer h:

$$\sum_{i=1}^{h} \left(i/2^i \right).$$

C-8.21 Give an alternate description of the in-place heap-sort algorithm that uses a standard comparator instead of a reverse one.

C-8.22 Describe efficient algorithms for performing operations remove(e) and replaceKey(e,k) on an adaptable priority queue realized by means of an unsorted list with location-aware entries.

C-8.23 Describe efficient algorithms for performing operations remove(e) and replaceKey(e,k) on an adaptable priority queue realized by means of a heap with location-aware entries.

C-8.24 Let S be a set of n points in the plane with distinct integer x- and y-coordinates. Let T be a complete binary tree storing the points from S at its external nodes, such that the points are ordered left-to-right by increasing x-coordinates. For each node v in T, let $S(v)$ denote the subset of S consisting of points stored in the subtree rooted at v. For the root r of T, define $top(r)$ to be the point in $S = S(r)$ with maximum y-coordinate. For every other node v, define $top(r)$ to be the point in S with highest y-coordinate in $S(v)$ that is not also the highest y-coordinate in $S(u)$, where u is the parent of v in T (if such a point exists). Such labeling turns T into a ***priority search tree***. Describe a linear-time algorithm for turning T into a priority search tree.

Projects

P-8.1 Implement a complete adapter class for using the java.util.PriorityQueue class to implement the adaptable priority queue ADT. Your class should fix an omission in the adapter from the book that the version of the adabtable priority queue methods given there do not have the right return values. Test the performance of your adapter class on a representative sequence of adapter priority queue methods. Test the hypothesis that standard priority queue methods run in $O(\log n)$ time whereas the additional methods of the adaptable priority queue run in $O(n)$ time.

P-8.2 Give a Java implementation of a priority queue based on an unsorted list.

P-8.3 Write an applet or stand-alone graphical program that animates both the insertion-sort and selection-sort algorithms. Your animation should visualize the movement of elements to their correct locations.

P-8.4 Write an applet or stand-alone graphical program that animates a heap. Your program should support all the priority queue operations and should visualize the swaps in the up-heap and down-heap bubblings. (Extra: Visualize bottom-up heap construction as well.)

P-8.5 Implement the heap-sort algorithm using bottom-up heap construction.

P-8.6 Implement the in-place heap-sort algorithm. Experimentally compare its running time with that of the standard heap-sort that is not in-place.

P-8.7 Implement a heap-based priority queue that supports the following additional operation in linear time:

replaceComparator(c): Replace the current comparator with c.

(Hint: Utilize the bottom-up heap construction algorithm.)

P-8.8 Write a program that can process a sequence of stock buy and sell orders as described in Exercise C-8.2.

P-8.9 One of the main applications of priority queues is in operating systems— for *scheduling jobs* on a CPU. In this project you are to build a program that schedules simulated CPU jobs. Your program should run in a loop, each iteration of which corresponds to a *time slice* for the CPU. Each job is assigned a priority, which is an integer between -20 (highest priority) and 19 (lowest priority), inclusive. From among all jobs waiting to be processed in a time slice, the CPU must work on a job with highest priority. In this simulation, each job will also come with a *length* value, which is an integer between 1 and 100, inclusive, indicating the number of time slices that are needed to process this job. For simplicity, you may assume jobs cannot be interrupted—once it is scheduled on the CPU, a job runs for a number of time slices equal to its length. Your simulator must output the name of the job running on the CPU in each time slice and must process a sequence of commands, one per time slice, each of which is of the form "add job *name* with length n and priority p" or "no new job this slice".

P-8.10 Develop a Java implementation of an adaptable priority queue that is based on an unsorted list and supports location-aware entries.

P-8.11 Develop a Java implementation of an adaptable priority queue that is based on a heap and supports location-aware entries.

Chapter Notes

Knuth's book on sorting and searching [63] describes the motivation and history for the selection-sort, insertion-sort, and heap-sort algorithms. The heap-sort algorithm is due to Williams [99], and the linear-time heap construction algorithm is due to Floyd [34]. Additional algorithms and analyses for heaps and heap-sort variations can be found in papers by Bentley [13], Carlsson [21], Gonnet and Munro [40], McDiarmid and Reed [71], and Schaffer and Sedgewick [85]. The design pattern of using location-aware entries (also described in [41]) appears to be new.

Chapter

9

Hash Tables, Maps, and Skip Lists

Contents

9.1   Maps

Figure 9.1: A conceptual illustration of the map ADT. Keys (labels) are assigned to values (folders) by a user. The resulting entries (labeled folders) are inserted into the map (file cabinet). The keys can be used later to retrieve or remove values.

A *map* allows us to store elements so they can be located quickly using keys. The motivation for such searches is that each element typically stores additional useful information besides its search key, but the only way to get at that information is to use the search key. Specifically, a map stores key-value pairs (k, v), which we call *entries*, where k is the key and v is its corresponding value. In addition, the map ADT requires that each key be unique, so the association of keys to values defines a mapping. In order to achieve the highest level of generality, we allow both the keys and the values stored in a map to be of any object type. (See Figure 9.1.) In a map storing student records (such as the student's name, address, and course grades), the key might be the student's ID number. In some applications, the key and the value may be the same. For example, if we had a map storing prime numbers, we could use each number itself as both a key and its value.

In either case, we use a *key* as a unique identifier that is assigned by an application or user to an associated value object. Thus, a map is most appropriate in situations where each key is to be viewed as a kind of unique *index* address for its value, that is, an object that serves as a kind of location for that value. For example, if we wish to store student records, we would probably want to use student ID objects as keys (and disallow two students having the same student ID). In other words, the key associated with an object can be viewed as an "address" for that object. Indeed, maps are sometimes referred to as *associative stores*, because the key associated with an object determines its "location" in the data structure.

9.1.1 The Map ADT

Since a map stores a collection of objects, it should be viewed as a collection of key-value pairs. As an ADT, a ***map*** *M* supports the following methods:

size(): Return the number of entries in *M*.

isEmpty(): Test whether *M* is empty.

get(k): If *M* contains an entry $e = (k, v)$, with key equal to k, then return the value, v, for e, else return **null**.

put(k, v): If *M* does not have an entry with key equal to k, then add entry (k, v) to *M* and return **null**; else, replace with v the existing value of the entry with key equal to k and return the old value.

remove(k): Remove from *M* the entry with key equal to k, and return its value; if *M* has no such entry, then return **null**.

keySet(): Return an iterable collection containing all the keys stored in *M* (so keySet().iterator() returns an iterator of keys).

values(): Return an iterable collection containing all the values associated with keys stored in *M* (so values().iterator() returns an iterator of values).

entrySet(): Return an iterable collection containing all the key-value entries in *M* (so entrySet().iterator() returns an iterator of entries).

When operations get(k), put(k, v) and remove(k) are performed on a map *M* that has no entry with key equal to k, we use the convention of returning **null**. A special value such as this is known as a ***sentinel***. (See also Section 3.3.) The disadvantage with using **null** as such a sentinel is that this choice can create ambiguity should we ever want to have an entry $(k, \textbf{null})$ with value **null** in the map. Another choice, of course, would be to throw an exception when someone requests a key that is not in our map. This would probably not be an appropriate use of an exception, however, since it is normal to ask for something that might not be in our map. Moreover, throwing and catching an exception is typically slower than a test against a sentinel; hence, using a sentinel is more efficient (and, in this case, conceptually more appropriate). So we use **null** as a sentinel for a value associated with a missing key.

Example 9.1: *In the following, we show the effect of a series of operations on an initially empty map storing entries with integer keys and single-character values.*

Operation	Output	Map
isEmpty()	true	$\emptyset$
put(5,A)	null	$\{(5,A)\}$
put(7,B)	null	$\{(5,A),(7,B)\}$
put(2,C)	null	$\{(5,A),(7,B),(2,C)\}$
put(8,D)	null	$\{(5,A),(7,B),(2,C),(8,D)\}$
put(2,E)	C	$\{(5,A),(7,B),(2,E),(8,D)\}$
get(7)	B	$\{(5,A),(7,B),(2,E),(8,D)\}$
get(4)	null	$\{(5,A),(7,B),(2,E),(8,D)\}$
get(2)	E	$\{(5,A),(7,B),(2,E),(8,D)\}$
size()	4	$\{(5,A),(7,B),(2,E),(8,D)\}$
remove(5)	A	$\{(7,B),(2,E),(8,D)\}$
remove(2)	E	$\{(7,B),(8,D)\}$
get(2)	null	$\{(7,B),(8,D)\}$
isEmpty()	false	$\{(7,B),(8,D)\}$
entrySet()	$\{(7,B),(8,D)\}$	$\{(7,B),(8,D)\}$
keySet()	$\{7,8\}$	$\{(7,B),(8,D)\}$
values()	$\{B,D\}$	$\{(7,B),(8,D)\}$

Maps in the java.util Package

The Java package java.util includes an interface for the map ADT, which is called java.util.Map. This interface is defined so that an implementing class enforces unique keys, and it includes all of the methods of the map ADT given above. It also includes some additional methods, as well, for adding and removing large collections of entries at once.

In addition, the java.util.Map interface assumes that all the associated entries, which would be returned in the collection provided by entrySet(), are of type java.util.Map.Entry. As we have noted above, the java.util.Map.Entry interface includes all the methods of the entry ADT given in Section 8.1.2, including the methods getKey() and getValue().

Having defined the map abstract data type, and its Java counterpart, let us now discuss some ways of implementing this ADT.

9.1.2 A Simple List-Based Map Implementation

A simple way of implementing a map is to store its n entries in a list S, implemented as a doubly linked list. Performing the fundamental methods, get(k), put(k,v), and remove(k), involves simple scans down S looking for an entry with key k. We give pseudo-code for performing these methods on a map M in Code Fragment 9.1.

This list-based map implementation is simple, but it is only efficient for very small maps. Every one of the fundamental methods takes $O(n)$ time on a map with n entries, because each method involves searching through the entire list in the worst case. Thus, we would like something faster.

Algorithm get(k):
  Input: A key k
  Output: The value for key k in M, or **null** if there is no key k in M

  for each position p in S.positions() **do**
    if p.element().getKey() $= k$ **then**
      return p.element().getValue()
  return null   {there is no entry with key equal to k}

Algorithm put(k,v):
  Input: A key-value pair (k,v)
  Output: The old value associated with key k in M, or **null** if k is new

  for each position p in S.positions() **do**
    if p.element().getKey() $= k$ **then**
      $t \leftarrow p$.element().getValue()
      B.set$(p,(k,v))$
      return t {return the old value}
  S.addLast$((k,v))$
  $n \leftarrow n+1$ {increment variable storing number of entries}
  return null   {there was no previous entry with key equal to k}

Algorithm remove(k):
  Input: A key k
  Output: The (removed) value for key k in M, or **null** if k is not in M

  for each position p in S.positions() **do**
    if p.element().getKey() $= k$ **then**
      $t \leftarrow p$.element().getValue()
      S.remove(p)
      $n \leftarrow n-1$ {decrement variable storing number of entries}
      return t {return the removed value}
  return null   {there is no entry with key equal to k}

Code Fragment 9.1: Algorithms for the fundamental map methods with a list S.

9.2   Hash Tables

The keys associated with values in a map are typically thought of as "addresses" for those values. Examples of such applications include a compiler's symbol table and a registry of environment variables. Both of these structures consist of a collection of symbolic names where each name serves as the "address" for properties about a variable's type and value. One of the most efficient ways to implement a map in such circumstances is to use a ***hash table***. Although, as we will see, the worst-case running time of map operations in an n-entry hash table is $O(n)$, a hash table can usually perform these operations in $O(1)$ expected time. In general, a hash table consists of two major components, a ***bucket array*** and a ***hash function***.

9.2.1   Bucket Arrays

A ***bucket array*** for a hash table is an array A of size N, where each cell of A is thought of as a "bucket" (that is, a collection of key-value pairs) and the integer N defines the ***capacity*** of the array. If the keys are integers well distributed in the range $[0, N-1]$, this bucket array is all that is needed. An entry e with key k is simply inserted into the bucket $A[k]$. (See Figure 9.2.) To save space, an empty bucket may be replaced by a **null** object.

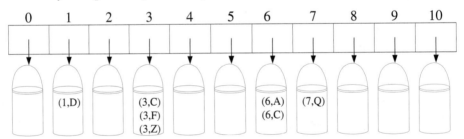

Figure 9.2: A bucket array of size 11 for the entries (1,D), (3,C), (3,F), (3,Z), (6,A), (6,C) and (7,Q),

If our keys are unique integers in the range $[0, N-1]$, then each bucket holds at most one entry. Thus, searches, insertions, and removals in the bucket array take $O(1)$ time. This sounds like a great achievement, but it has two drawbacks. First, the space used is proportional to N. Thus, if N is much larger than the number of entries n actually present in the map, we have a waste of space. The second drawback is that keys are required to be integers in the range $[0, N-1]$, which is often not the case. Because of these two drawbacks, we use the bucket array in conjunction with a "good" mapping from the keys to the integers in the range $[0, N-1]$.

9.2.2 Hash Functions

The second part of a hash table structure is a function, h, called a ***hash function***, that maps each key k in our map to an integer in the range $[0, N-1]$, where N is the capacity of the bucket array for this table. Equipped with such a hash function, h, we can apply the bucket array method to arbitrary keys. The main idea of this approach is to use the hash function value, $h(k)$, as an index into our bucket array, A, instead of the key k (which is most likely inappropriate for use as a bucket array index). That is, we store the entry (k, v) in the bucket $A[h(k)]$.

Of course, if there are two or more keys with the same hash value, then two different entries will be mapped to the same bucket in A. In this case, we say that a ***collision*** has occurred. Clearly, if each bucket of A can store only a single entry, then we cannot associate more than one entry with a single bucket, which is a problem in the case of collisions. To be sure, there are ways of dealing with collisions, which we will discuss later, but the best strategy is to try to avoid them in the first place. We say that a hash function is "good" if it maps the keys in our map so as to minimize collisions as much as possible. For practical reasons, we also would like a hash function to be fast and easy to compute.

Following the convention in Java, we view the evaluation of a hash function, $h(k)$, as consisting of two actions—mapping the key k to an integer, called the ***hash code***, and mapping the hash code to an integer within the range of indices ($[0, N-1]$) of a bucket array, called the ***compression function***. (See Figure 9.3.)

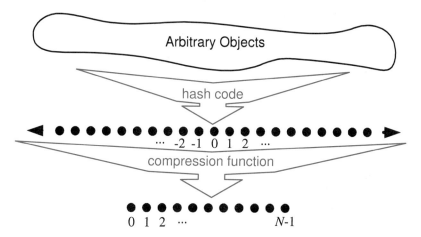

Figure 9.3: The two parts of a hash function: a hash code and a compression function.

9.2.3 Hash Codes

The first action that a hash function performs is to take an arbitrary key k in our map and assign it an integer value. The integer assigned to a key k is called the **hash code** for k. This integer value need not be in the range $[0, N-1]$, and may even be negative, but we desire that the set of hash codes assigned to our keys should avoid collisions as much as possible. For if the hash codes of our keys cause collisions, then there is no hope for our compression function to avoid them. In addition, to be consistent with all of our keys, the hash code we use for a key k should be the same as the hash code for any key that is equal to k.

Hash Codes in Java

The generic Object class defined in a Java comes with a default hashCode() method for mapping each object instance to an integer that is a "representation" of that object. Specifically, the hashCode() method returns a 32-bit integer of type **int**. Unless specifically overridden, this method is inherited by every object used in a Java program. We should be careful in using the default Object version of hashCode(), however, as this could just be an integer interpretation of the object's location in memory (as is the case in many Java implementations). This type of hash code works poorly with character strings, for example, because two different string objects in memory might actually be equal, in which case we would like them to have the same hash code. Indeed, the Java String class overrides the hashCode method of the Object class to be something more appropriate for character strings. Likewise, if we intend to use certain objects as keys in a map, then we should override the built-in hashCode() method for these objects, replacing it with a mapping that assigns well-spread, consistent integers to these types of objects.

Let us consider, then, several common data types and some example methods for assigning hash codes to objects of these types.

Casting to an Integer

To begin, we note that, for any data type X that is represented using at most as many bits as our integer hash codes, we can simply take as a hash code for X an integer interpretation of its bits. Thus, for Java base types **byte**, **short**, **int**, and **char**, we can achieve a good hash code simply by casting this type to **int**. Likewise, for a variable x of base type **float**, we can convert x to an integer using a call to Float.floatToIntBits(x), and then use this integer as x's hash code.

Summing Components

For base types, such as **long** and **double**, whose bit representation is double that of a hash code, the above scheme is not immediately applicable. Still, one possible hash code, and indeed one that is used by many Java implementations, is to simply cast a (long) integer representation of the type down to an integer the size of a hash code. This hash code, of course, ignores half of the information present in the original value, and if many of the keys in our map only differ in these bits, then they will collide using this simple hash code. An alternative hash code, then, which takes all the original bits into consideration, is to sum an integer representation of the high-order bits with an integer representation of the low-order bits. Such a hash code can be written in Java as follows:

```
static int hashCode(long i) {return (int)((i >> 32) + (int) i);}
```

Indeed, the approach of summing components can be extended to any object x whose binary representation can be viewed as a k-tuple $(x_0, x_1, \ldots, x_{k-1})$ of integers, for we can then form a hash code for x as $\sum_{i=0}^{k-1} x_i$. For example, given any floating-point number, we can sum its mantissa and exponent as long integers, and then apply a hash code for long integers to the result.

Polynomial Hash Codes

The summation hash code, described above, is not a good choice for character strings or other variable-length objects that can be viewed as tuples of the form $(x_0, x_1, \ldots, x_{k-1})$, where the order of the x_i's is significant. For example, consider a hash code for a character string s that sums the ASCII (or Unicode) values of the characters in s. This hash code unfortunately produces lots of unwanted collisions for common groups of strings. In particular, "temp01" and "temp10" collide using this function, as do "stop", "tops", "pots", and "spot". A better hash code should somehow take into consideration the positions of the x_i's. An alternative hash code, which does exactly this, is to choose a nonzero constant, $a \neq 1$, and use as a hash code the value

$$x_0 a^{k-1} + x_1 a^{k-2} + \cdots + x_{k-2} a + x_{k-1}.$$

Mathematically speaking, this is simply a polynomial in a that takes the components $(x_0, x_1, \ldots, x_{k-1})$ of an object x as its coefficients. This hash code is therefore called a ***polynomial hash code***. By Horner's rule (see Exercise C-4.16), this polynomial can be written as

$$x_{k-1} + a(x_{k-2} + a(x_{k-3} + \cdots + a(x_2 + a(x_1 + ax_0)) \cdots)).$$

Intuitively, a polynomial hash code uses multiplication by the constant a as a way of "making room" for each component in a tuple of values while also preserving a characterization of the previous components.

Of course, on a typical computer, evaluating a polynomial will be done using the finite bit representation for a hash code; hence, the value will periodically overflow the bits used for an integer. Since we are more interested in a good spread of the object x with respect to other keys, we simply ignore such overflows. Still, we should be mindful that such overflows are occurring and choose the constant a so that it has some nonzero, low-order bits, which will serve to preserve some of the information content even as we are in an overflow situation.

We have done some experimental studies that suggest that 33, 37, 39, and 41 are particularly good choices for a when working with character strings that are English words. In fact, in a list of over 50,000 English words formed as the union of the word lists provided in two variants of Unix, we found that taking a to be 33, 37, 39, or 41 produced less than 7 collisions in each case! It should come as no surprise, then, to learn that many Java implementations choose the polynomial hash function, using one of these constants for a, as a default hash code for strings. For the sake of speed, however, some Java implementations only apply the polynomial hash function to a fraction of the characters in long strings.

Cyclic Shift Hash Codes

A variant of the polynomial hash code replaces multiplication by a with a cyclic shift of a partial sum by a certain number of bits. Such a function, applied to character strings in Java could, for example, look like the following:

```java
static int hashCode(String s) {
    int h=0;
    for (int i=0; i<s.length(); i++) {
        h = (h << 5) | (h >>> 27);  // 5-bit cyclic shift of the running sum
        h += (int) s.charAt(i);     // add in next character
    }
    return h;
}
```

As with the traditional polynomial hash code, using the cyclic-shift hash code requires some fine-tuning. In this case, we must wisely choose the amount to shift by for each new character. We show in Table 9.1 the results of some experiments run on a list of just over 25,000 English words, which compare the number of collisions for various shift amounts. These and our previous experiments show that if we choose our constant a or our shift value wisely, then either the polynomial hash code or its cyclic-shift variant are suitable for any object that can be written as a tuple $(x_0, x_1, \ldots, x_{k-1})$, where the order in tuples matters.

Shift	Collisions	
	Total	**Max**
0	23739	86
1	10517	21
2	2254	6
3	448	3
4	89	2
5	4	2
6	6	2
7	14	2
8	105	2
9	18	2
10	277	3
11	453	4
12	43	2
13	13	2
14	135	3
15	1082	6
16	8760	9

Table 9.1: Comparison of collision behavior for the cyclic shift variant of the polynomial hash code as applied to a list of just over 25,000 English words. The "Total" column records the total number of collisions and the "Max" column records the maximum number of collisions for any one hash code. Note that with a cyclic shift of 0, this hash code reverts to the one that simply sums all the characters.

9.2.4 Compression Functions

The hash code for a key k will typically not be suitable for immediate use with a bucket array, because the range of possible hash codes for our keys will typically exceed the range of legal indices of our bucket array A. That is, incorrectly using a hash code as an index into our bucket array may result in an array out-of-bounds exception being thrown, either because the index is negative or it exceeds the capacity of A. Thus, once we have determined an integer hash code for a key object k, there is still the issue of mapping that integer into the range $[0, N-1]$. This mapping is the second action that a hash function performs, and a good compression function is one that minimizes the possible number of collisions in a given set of hash codes.

The Division Method

One simple *compression function* is the *division method*, which maps an integer i to

$$i \bmod N,$$

where N, the size of the bucket array, is a fixed positive integer. Additionally, if we take N to be a prime number, then this compression function helps "spread out" the distribution of hashed values. Indeed, if N is not prime, then there is a higher likelihood that patterns in the distribution of hash codes will be repeated in the distribution of hash values, thereby causing collisions. For example, if we insert keys with hash codes $\{200, 205, 210, 215, 220, \ldots, 600\}$ into a bucket array of size 100, then each hash code will collide with three others. But if we use a bucket array of size 101, then there will be no collisions. If a hash function is chosen well, it should ensure that the probability of two different keys getting hashed to the same bucket is $1/N$. Choosing N to be a prime number is not always enough, however, for if there is a repeated pattern of hash codes of the form $pN + q$ for several different p's, then there will still be collisions.

The MAD Method

A more sophisticated compression function, which helps eliminate repeated patterns in a set of integer keys is the *multiply-add-and-divide* (or "MAD") method. This method maps an integer i to

$$[(ai + b) \bmod p] \bmod N,$$

where N is the size of the bucket array, p is a prime number larger than N, and a and b are integers chosen at random from the interval $[0, p-1]$, with $a > 0$. This compression function is chosen in order to eliminate repeated patterns in the set of hash codes and get us closer to having a "good" hash function, that is, one such that the probability any two different keys collide is $1/N$. This good behavior would be the same as we would have if these keys were "thrown" into A uniformly at random.

With a compression function such as this, which spreads integers fairly evenly in the range $[0, N-1]$, and a hash code that transforms the keys in our map into integers, we have an effective hash function. Together, such a hash function and a bucket array define the main ingredients of the hash table implementation of the map ADT.

But before we can give the details of how to perform such operations as put, get, and remove, we must first resolve the issue of how we will be handling collisions.

9.2.5 Collision-Handling Schemes

The main idea of a hash table is to take a bucket array, A, and a hash function, h, and use them to implement a map by storing each entry (k, v) in the "bucket" $A[h(k)]$. This simple idea is challenged, however, when we have two distinct keys, k_1 and k_2, such that $h(k_1) = h(k_2)$. The existence of such **collisions** prevents us from simply inserting a new entry (k, v) directly in the bucket $A[h(k)]$. They also complicate our procedure for performing the get(k), put(k, v), and remove(k) operations.

Separate Chaining

A simple and efficient way for dealing with collisions is to have each bucket $A[i]$ store a small map, M_i, implemented using a list, as described in Section 9.1.2, holding entries (k, v) such that $h(k) = i$. That is, each separate M_i chains together the entries that hash to index i in a linked list. This **collision resolution** rule is known as **separate chaining**. Assuming that we initialize each bucket $A[i]$ to be an empty list-based map, we can easily use the separate chaining rule to perform the fundamental map operations, as shown in Code Fragment 9.2.

Algorithm get(k):
    Output: The value associated with the key k in the map, or **null** if there is no entry with key equal to k in the map
    return $A[h(k)]$.get(k) {delegate the get to the list-based map at $A[h(k)]$}

Algorithm put(k, v):
    Output: If there is an existing entry in our map with key equal to k, then we return its value (replacing it with v); otherwise, we return **null**
    $t \leftarrow A[h(k)]$.put(k, v) {delegate the put to the list-based map at $A[h(k)]$}
    if $t = $ **null then** {k is a new key}
        $n \leftarrow n + 1$
    return t

Algorithm remove(k):
    Output: The (removed) value associated with key k in the map, or **null** if there is no entry with key equal to k in the map
    $t \leftarrow A[h(k)]$.remove(k) {delegate the remove to the list-based map at $A[h(k)]$}
    if $t \neq $ **null then** {k was found}
        $n \leftarrow n - 1$
    return t

Code Fragment 9.2: The fundamental methods of the map ADT, implemented with a hash table that uses separate chaining to resolve collisions among its n entries.

For each fundamental map operation, involving a key k, the separate-chaining approach delegates the handling of this operation to the miniature list-based map stored at $A[h(k)]$. So, $\text{put}(k,v)$ will scan this list looking for an entry with key equal to k; if it finds one, it replaces its value with v, otherwise, it puts (k,v) at the end of this list. Likewise, $\text{get}(k)$ will search through this list until it reaches the end or finds an entry with key equal to k. And $\text{remove}(k)$ will perform a similar search but additionally remove an entry after it is found. We can "get away" with this simple list-based approach, because the spreading properties of the hash function help keep each bucket's list small. Indeed, a good hash function will try to minimize collisions as much as possible, which will imply that most of our buckets are either empty or store just a single entry. This observation allows us to make a slight change to our implementation so that, if a bucket $A[i]$ is empty, it stores **null**, and if $A[i]$ stores just a single entry (k,v), we can simply have $A[i]$ point directly to the entry (k,v) rather than to a list-based map holding only the one entry. We leave the details of this final space optimization to an exercise (C-9.6). In Figure 9.4, we give an illustration of a hash table with separate chaining.

Assuming we use a good hash function to index the n entries of our map in a bucket array of capacity N, we expect each bucket to be of size n/N. This value, called the *load factor* of the hash table (and denoted with λ), should be bounded by a small constant, preferably below 1. For, given a good hash function, the expected running time of operations get, put, and remove in a map implemented with a hash table that uses this function is $O(\lceil n/N \rceil)$. Thus, we can implement these operations to run in $O(1)$ expected time, provided n is $O(N)$.

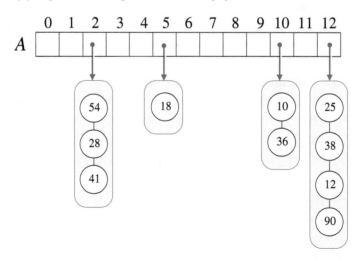

Figure 9.4: A hash table of size 13, storing 10 entries with integer keys, with collisions resolved by separate chaining. The compression function is $h(k) = k \bmod 13$. For simplicity, we do not show the values associated with the keys.

Open Addressing

The separate chaining rule has many nice properties, such as allowing for simple implementations of map operations, but it nevertheless has one slight disadvantage: it requires the use of an auxiliary data structure—a list—to hold entries with colliding keys. We can handle collisions in other ways besides using the separate chaining rule, however. In particular, if space is at a premium (for example, if we are writing a program for a small handheld device), then we can use the alternative approach of always storing each entry directly in a bucket, at most one entry per bucket. This approach saves space because no auxiliary structures are employed, but it requires a bit more complexity to deal with collisions. There are several variants of this approach, collectively referred to as **open addressing** schemes, which we discuss next. Open addressing requires that the load factor is always at most 1 and that entries are stored directly in the cells of the bucket array itself.

Linear Probing and its Variants

A simple open addressing method for collision handling is **linear probing**. In this method, if we try to insert an entry (k, v) into a bucket $A[i]$ that is already occupied, where $i = h(k)$, then we try next at $A[(i+1) \bmod N]$. If $A[(i+1) \bmod N]$ is also occupied, then we try $A[(i+2) \bmod N]$, and so on, until we find an empty bucket that can accept the new entry. Once this bucket is located, we simply insert the entry there. Of course, this collision resolution strategy requires that we change the implementation of the get(k, v) operation. In particular, to perform such a search, followed by either a replacement or insertion, we must examine consecutive buckets, starting from $A[h(k)]$, until we either find an entry with key equal to k or we find an empty bucket. (See Figure 9.5.) The name "linear probing" comes from the fact that accessing a cell of the bucket array can be viewed as a "probe."

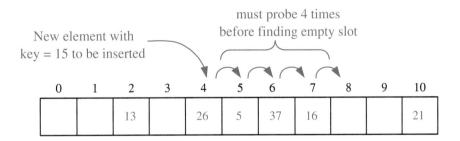

Figure 9.5: Insertion into a hash table with integer keys using linear probing. The hash function is $h(k) = k \bmod 11$. Values associated with keys are not shown.

To implement remove(k), we might, at first, think we need to do a considerable amount of shifting of entries to make it look as though the entry with key k was never inserted, which would be very complicated. A typical way to get around this difficulty is to replace a deleted entry with a special "available" marker object. With this special marker possibly occupying buckets in our hash table, we modify our search algorithm for remove(k) or get(k) so that the search for a key k will skip over cells containing the available marker and continue probing until reaching the desired entry or an empty bucket (or returning back to where we started from). Additionally, our algorithm for put(k,v) should remember an available cell encountered during the search for k, since this is a valid place to put a new entry (k,v). Thus, linear probing saves space, but it complicates removals.

Even with the use of the available marker object, linear probing suffers from an additional disadvantage. It tends to cluster the entries of the map into contiguous runs, which may even overlap (particularly if more than half of the cells in the hash table are occupied). Such contiguous runs of occupied hash cells causes searches to slow down considerably.

Another open addressing strategy, known as **quadratic probing**, involves iteratively trying the buckets $A[(i + f(j)) \bmod N]$, for $j = 0, 1, 2, \ldots$, where $f(j) = j^2$, until finding an empty bucket. As with linear probing, the quadratic probing strategy complicates the removal operation, but it does avoid the kinds of clustering patterns that occur with linear probing. Nevertheless, it creates its own kind of clustering, called **secondary clustering**, where the set of filled array cells "bounces" around the array in a fixed pattern. If N is not chosen as a prime, then the quadratic probing strategy may not find an empty bucket in A even if one exists. In fact, even if N is prime, this strategy may not find an empty slot, if the bucket array is at least half full; we explore the cause of this type of clustering in an exercise (C-9.10).

Another open addressing strategy that does not cause clustering of the kind produced by linear probing or the kind produced by quadratic probing is the **double hashing** strategy. In this approach, we choose a secondary hash function, h', and if h maps some key k to a bucket $A[i]$, with $i = h(k)$, that is already occupied, then we iteratively try the buckets $A[(i + f(j)) \bmod N]$ next, for $j = 1, 2, 3, \ldots$, where $f(j) = j \cdot h'(k)$. In this scheme, the secondary hash function is not allowed to evaluate to zero; a common choice is $h'(k) = q - (k \bmod q)$, for some prime number $q < N$. Also, N should be a prime. Moreover, we should choose a secondary hash function that will attempt to minimize clustering as much as possible.

These **open addressing** schemes save some space over the separate chaining method, but they are not necessarily faster. In experimental and theoretical analyses, the chaining method is either competitive or faster than the other methods, depending on the load factor of the bucket array. So, if memory space is not a major issue, the collision-handling method of choice seems to be separate chaining.

9.2.6 A Java Hash Table Implementation

The Java Collections Framework provides a hash table implementation in the class java.util.HashMap. This class implements the java.util.Map interface; hence, it performs all the methods of the map ADT, as well as several others, such as a clear() method, which removes all the entries from the map. It implements collision resolution using the separate chaining scheme described above, and it even allows users to specify the initial capacity of the hash table and the load factor that the table should not exceed. Standard instances of this class start with a default capacity of 11 and default load factor of 0.75. Thus, if we want to have a hash table that uses some form of linear probing to resolve collisions, we will have to implement it "from scratch."

In Code Fragments 9.3–9.5, we show a class, HashTableMap, which implements the map ADT using a hash table with linear probing to resolve collisions. These code fragments include the entire implementation of the map ADT, except for the methods values() and entrySet(), which we leave as an Exercise (R-9.12).

The main design elements of the Java class HashTableMap are as follows:

- We maintain, in instance variables, the size, n, of the map, the bucket array, A, and the capacity, N, of A.
- We use method hashValue to compute the hash function of a key by means of the built-in hashCode method and the multiply-add-and-divide (MAD) compression function.
- We define a sentinel, AVAILABLE, as a marker for deactivated entries.
- We provide an optional constructor that allows us to specify the initial capacity of the bucket array.
- If the current bucket array is full and one tries to insert a new entry, we rehash the entire contents into a new array that is twice the size as the old version.
- The following (protected) auxiliary methods are used:
  - checkKey(k), which checks if the key k is valid. This method currently just checks that k is not **null**, but a class that extends HashTableMap can override this method with a more elaborate test.
  - rehash(), which computes a new MAD hash function with random parameters and rehashes the entries into a new array with double capacity.
  - findEntry(k), which looks for an entry with key equal to k, starting at the index $A[h(k)]$ and going through the array in a circular fashion. If the method finds a cell with such an entry, then it returns the index i of this cell. Otherwise, it returns $-i-1$, where i is the index of the last empty or available cell encountered.

```java
/** A hash table with linear probing and the MAD hash function */
public class HashTableMap<K,V> implements Map<K,V> {
  public static class HashEntry<K,V> implements Entry<K,V> {
    protected K key;
    protected V value;
    public HashEntry(K k, V v) { key = k; value = v; }
    public V getValue() { return value; }
    public K getKey() { return key; }
    public V setValue(V val) {
      V oldValue = value;
      value = val;
      return oldValue;
    }
    public boolean equals(Object o) {
      HashEntry<K,V> ent;
      try { ent = (HashEntry<K,V>) o; }
      catch (ClassCastException ex) { return false; }
      return (ent.getKey() == key) && (ent.getValue() == value);
    }
  }
  protected Entry<K,V> AVAILABLE = new HashEntry<K,V>(null, null);
  protected int n = 0;          // number of entries in the dictionary
  protected int prime, capacity; // prime factor and capacity of bucket array
  protected Entry<K,V>[] bucket;// bucket array
  protected long scale, shift;   // the shift and scaling factors
  /** Creates a hash table with prime factor 109345121 and given capacity. */
  public HashTableMap(int cap) { this(109345121, cap); }
  /** Creates a hash table with the given prime factor and capacity. */
  public HashTableMap(int p, int cap) {
    prime = p;
    capacity = cap;
    bucket = (Entry<K,V>[]) new Entry[capacity]; // safe cast
    java.util.Random rand = new java.util.Random();
    scale = rand.nextInt(prime−1) + 1;
    shift = rand.nextInt(prime);
  }
  /** Determines whether a key is valid. */
  protected void checkKey(K k) {
    if (k == null) throw new InvalidKeyException("Invalid key: null.");
  }
  /** Hash function applying MAD method to default hash code. */
  public int hashValue(K key) {
    return (int) ((Math.abs(key.hashCode()*scale + shift) % prime) % capacity);
  }
```

Code Fragment 9.3: Class HashTableMap implementing the map ADT using a hash table with linear probing. (Continues in Code Fragment 9.4.)

```
/** Returns the number of entries in the hash table. */
public int size() { return n; }
/** Returns whether or not the table is empty. */
public boolean isEmpty() { return (n == 0); }
/** Returns an iterable object containing all of the keys. */
public Iterable<K> keySet() {
  PositionList<K> keys = new NodePositionList<K>();
  for (int i=0; i<capacity; i++)
    if ((bucket[i] != null) && (bucket[i] != AVAILABLE))
      keys.addLast(bucket[i].getKey());
  return keys;
}
/** Helper search method - returns index of found key or -(a + 1),
 * where a is the index of the first empty or available slot found. */
protected int findEntry(K key) throws InvalidKeyException {
  int avail = −1;
  checkKey(key);
  int i = hashValue(key);
  int j = i;
  do {
    Entry<K,V> e = bucket[i];
    if ( e == null) {
      if (avail < 0)
        avail = i;     // key is not in table
      break;
    }
    if (key.equals(e.getKey())) // we have found our key
      return i;        // key found
    if (e == AVAILABLE) { // bucket is deactivated
      if (avail < 0)
        avail = i;     // remember that this slot is available
    }
    i = (i + 1) % capacity; // keep looking
  } while (i != j);
  return −(avail + 1); // first empty or available slot
}
/** Returns the value associated with a key. */
public V get (K key) throws InvalidKeyException {
  int i = findEntry(key);  // helper method for finding a key
  if (i < 0) return null;  // there is no value for this key, so reutrn null
  return bucket[i].getValue();     // return the found value in this case
}
```

Code Fragment 9.4: Class HashTableMap implementing the map ADT using a hash table with linear probing. (Continues in Code Fragment 9.5.)

```
/** Put a key-value pair in the map, replacing previous one if it exists. */
public V put (K key, V value) throws InvalidKeyException {
  int i = findEntry(key); //find the appropriate spot for this entry
  if (i >= 0) // this key has a previous value
    return ((HashEntry<K,V>) bucket[i]).setValue(value); // set new value
  if (n >= capacity/2) {
    rehash(); // rehash to keep the load factor <= 0.5
    i = findEntry(key); //find again the appropriate spot for this entry
  }
  bucket[-i-1] = new HashEntry<K,V>(key, value); // convert to proper index
  n++;
  return null;        // there was no previous value
}
/** Doubles the size of the hash table and rehashes all the entries. */
protected void rehash() {
  capacity = 2*capacity;
  Entry<K,V>[] old = bucket;
  bucket = (Entry<K,V>[]) new Entry[capacity]; // new bucket is twice as big
  java.util.Random rand = new java.util.Random();
  scale = rand.nextInt(prime-1) + 1;      // new hash scaling factor
  shift = rand.nextInt(prime);            // new hash shifting factor
  for (int i=0; i<old.length; i++) {
    Entry<K,V> e = old[i];
    if ((e != null) && (e != AVAILABLE)) { // a valid entry
      int j = - 1 - findEntry(e.getKey());
      bucket[j] = e;
    }
  }
}
/** Removes the key-value pair with a specified key. */
public V remove (K key) throws InvalidKeyException {
  int i = findEntry(key);     // find this key first
  if (i < 0) return null;     // nothing to remove
  V toReturn = bucket[i].getValue();
  bucket[i] = AVAILABLE;            // mark this slot as deactivated
  n--;
  return toReturn;
}
}
```

Code Fragment 9.5: Class HashTableMap implementing the map ADT using a hash table with linear probing. (Continued from Code Fragment 9.4.) We have omitted the values() and entrySet() methods in the listing above, as they are similar to keySet().

9.2.7 Load Factors and Rehashing

In the hash table schemes described above, we should desire that the load factor, $\lambda = n/N$, be kept below 1. Experiments and average-case analyses suggest that we should maintain $\lambda < 0.5$ for the open addressing schemes and we should maintain $\lambda < 0.9$ for separate chaining. As we mention above, the Java Collections Framework class java.util.HashMap, which implements the map ADT, uses the threshold 0.75 as a default maximum load factor and rehashes any time the load factor exceeds this (or an optional user-set load factor). The choice of 0.75 is fine for separate chaining (which is the implementation in java.util.HashMap), but, as we explore in Exercise C-9.10, the performance of some open addressing schemes can start to degrade when $\lambda \geq 0.5$. Although the details of the average-case analysis of hashing are beyond the scope of this book, its probabilistic basis is quite intuitive. If our hash function is good, then we expect the entries to be uniformly distributed in the N cells of the bucket array. Thus, to store n entries, the expected number of keys in a bucket would be $\lceil n/N \rceil$, which is $O(1)$ if n is $O(N)$.

With separate chaining, as λ gets very close to 1, the probability of a collision also approaches 1, which adds overhead to our operations, since we must revert to linear-time list-based methods in buckets that have collisions. Of course, in the worst case, a poor hash function could map every entry to the same bucket, which would result in linear-time performance for all map operations, but this is unlikely.

With open addressing, on the other hand, as the load factor λ grows beyond 0.5 and starts approaching 1, clusters of entries in the bucket array start to grow as well. These clusters cause the probing strategies to "bounce around" the bucket array for a considerable amount of time before they can finish.

Thus, keeping the load factor below a certain threshold is vital for open addressing schemes and is also of concern with the separate chaining method. If the load factor of a hash table goes significantly above the specified threshold, then it is common to require that the table be resized (to regain the specified load factor) and all the objects inserted into this new table. When *rehashing* to a new table, it is a good requirement for the new array's size to be at least double the previous size. Once we have allocated this new bucket array, we must define a new hash function to go with it, possibly computing new parameters. We then reinsert every entry from the old array into the new array using this new hash function. In our implementation of a hash table with linear probing given in Code Fragments 9.3–9.5, rehashing is used to keep the load factor less than or equal to 0.5.

Even with periodic rehashing, a hash table is an efficient means of implementing a map. Indeed, if we always double the size of the table with each rehashing operation, then we can amortize the cost of rehashing all the entries in the table against the time used to insert them in the first place. (See Section 6.1.4.) Each rehashing will generally scatter the entries throughout the new bucket array.

9.2.8   Application: Counting Word Frequencies

As a miniature case study of using a hash table, consider the problem of counting the number of occurrences of different words in a document, which arises, for example, when pundits study political speeches looking for themes. A hash table is an ideal data structure to use here, for we can use words as keys and word counts as values. We show such an application in Code Fragment 9.6.

```java
import java.io.*;
import java.util.Scanner;
import net.datastructures.*;
/** A program that counts words in a document, printing the most frequent. */
public class WordCount {
  public static void main(String[] args) throws IOException {
    Scanner doc = new Scanner(System.in);
    doc.useDelimiter("[^a-zA-Z]"); // ignore non-letters
    HashTableMap<String,Integer> h = new HashTableMap<String,Integer>();
    String word;
    Integer count;
    while (doc.hasNext()) {
      word = doc.next();
      if (word.equals("")) continue; // ignore null strings between delimiters
      word = word.toLowerCase();   // ignore case
      count = h.get(word); // get the previous count for this word
      if (count == null)
        h.put(word, 1);        // autoboxing allows this
      else
        h.put(word, ++count); // autoboxing/unboxing allows this
    }
    int maxCount = 0;
    String maxWord = "no word";
    for (Entry<String,Integer> ent : h.entries()) { // find max-count word
      if (ent.getValue() > maxCount) {
        maxWord = ent.getKey();
        maxCount = ent.getValue();
      }
    }
    System.out.print("The most frequent word is \"" + maxWord);
    System.out.println(",\" with word-count = " + maxCount + ".");
  }
}
```

Code Fragment 9.6: A program for counting word frequencies in a document, printing the most frequent word. The document is parsed using the Scanner class, for which we change the delimiter for separating tokens from whitespace to any non-letter. We also convert words to lowercase.

9.3 Ordered Maps

In some applications, simply looking up values based on associated keys is not enough. We often also want to keep the entries in a map sorted according to some total order and be able to look up keys and values based on this ordering. That is, in an *ordered map*, we want to perform the usual map operations, but also maintain an order relation for the keys in our map and use this order in some of the map methods. We can use a comparator to provide the order relation among keys, allowing us to define an ordered map relative to this comparator, which can be provided to the ordered map as an argument to its constructor.

When the entries of a map are stored in order, we can provide efficient implementations for additional methods in the map ADT. In particular, as an ADT, the ordered map includes all the methods of the standard map ADT plus the following:

firstEntry(k): Returns the entry with smallest key value; if the map is empty, then it returns **null**.

lastEntry(k): Returns the entry with largest key value; if the map is empty, then it returns **null**.

ceilingEntry(k): Returns the entry with the least key value greater than or equal to k; if there is no such entry, then it returns **null**.

floorEntry(k): Returns the entry with the greatest key value less than or equal to k; if there is no such entry, then it returns **null**.

lowerEntry(k): Returns the entry with the greatest key value strictly less than k; if there is no such entry, then it returns **null**.

higherEntry(k): Returns the entry with the least key value strictly greater than k; if there is no such entry, then it returns **null**.

Incidentally, each of these methods is included in the java.util.NavigableMap interface; hence, Java provides a superset of the ordered map ADT.

Implementing an Ordered Map

The ordered nature of the operations given above for the ordered map ADT makes the use of an unordered list or a hash table inappropriate, because neither of these data structures maintains any ordering information for the keys in the map. Indeed, hash tables achieve their best search speeds when their keys are distributed almost at random. Thus, we should consider an alternative implementation when dealing with ordered maps. We discuss one such implementation next, and we discuss other implementations in Section 9.4 and Chapter 10.

9.3.1   Ordered Search Tables and Binary Search

If the keys in a map come from a total order, we can store the map's entries in an array list S in increasing order of the keys. (See Figure 9.6.) We specify that S is an array list, rather than a node list, because the ordering of the keys in the array list S allows for faster searching than would be possible had S been, say, implemented with a linked list. Admittedly, a hash table has good expected running time for searching. But its worst-case time for searching is no better than a linked list, and in some applications, such as in real-time processing, we need to guarantee a worst-case searching bound. The fast algorithm for searching in an ordered array list, which we discuss in this subsection, has a good worst-case guarantee on its running time. So it might be preferred over a hash table in certain applications. We refer to this ordered array list implementation of a map as an ***ordered search table***.

0	1	2	3	4	5	6	7	8	9	10
4	6	9	12	15	16	18	28	34		

Figure 9.6: Realization of a map by means of an ordered search table. We show only the keys for this map, so as to highlight their ordering.

The space requirement of an ordered search table is $O(n)$, which is similar to the list-based map implementation (Section 9.1.2), assuming we grow and shrink the array supporting the array list S to keep the size of this array proportional to the number of entries in S. Unlike an unordered list, however, performing updates in a search table takes a considerable amount of time. In particular, performing the $put(k, v)$ operation in a search table requires $O(n)$ time in the worst case, since we need to shift up all the entries in the array list with key greater than k to make room for the new entry (k, v). A similar observation applies to the operation $remove(k)$, since it takes $O(n)$ time in the worst case to shift all the entries in the array list with key greater than k to close the "hole" left by the removed entry (or entries). The search table implementation is therefore inferior to the linked list implementation in terms of the worst-case running times of the map update operations. Nevertheless, we can perform the get method much faster in a search table.

Binary Search

A significant advantage of using an ordered array list S to implement a map with n entries is that accessing an element of S by its ***index*** takes $O(1)$ time. We recall, from Section 6.1, that the index of an element in an array list is the number of elements preceding it. Thus, the first element in S has index 0, and the last element has index $n - 1$. In this subsection, we give a classic algorithm, ***binary search***, to locate an entry in an ordered search table. We show how this method can be used to quickly perform the get() method of the map ADT, but a similar method can be used for each of the ordered map methods, ceilingEntry(), floorEntry(), lowerEntry(), and higherEntry().

The elements stored in S are the entries of a map, and since S is ordered, the entry at index i has a key no smaller than the keys of the entries at indices $0, \ldots, i-1$, and no larger than the keys of the entries at indices $i+1, \ldots, n-1$. This observation allows us to quickly "home in" on a search key k using a variant of the children's game "high-low." We call an entry of our map a **candidate** if, at the current stage of the search, we cannot rule out that this entry has key equal to k. The algorithm maintains two parameters, low and high, such that all the candidate entries have index at least low and at most high in S. Initially, low $= 0$ and high $= n-1$. We then compare k to the key of the median candidate e, that is, the entry e with index

$$\text{mid} = \lfloor (\text{low} + \text{high})/2 \rfloor.$$

We consider three cases:

- If $k = e.\text{getKey}()$, then we have found the entry we were looking for, and the search terminates successfully returning e.
- If $k < e.\text{getKey}()$, then we recur on the first half of the array list, that is, on the range of indices from low to mid $- 1$.
- If $k > e.\text{getKey}()$, we recur on the range of indices from mid $+ 1$ to high.

This search method is called **binary search**, and is given in pseudo-code in Code Fragment 9.7. Operation get(k) on an n-entry map implemented with an ordered array list S consists of calling BinarySearch$(S, k, 0, n-1)$.

Algorithm BinarySearch$(S, k, \text{low}, \text{high})$:

　Input: An ordered array list S storing n entries and integers low and high
　Output: An entry of S with key equal to k and index between low and high, if such an entry exists, and otherwise **null**

　if low $>$ high **then**
　　return null
　else
　　mid $\leftarrow \lfloor (\text{low} + \text{high})/2 \rfloor$
　　$e \leftarrow S.\text{get}(\text{mid})$
　　if $k = e.\text{getKey}()$ **then**
　　　return e
　　else if $k < e.\text{getKey}()$ **then**
　　　return BinarySearch$(S, k, \text{low}, \text{mid} - 1)$
　　else
　　　return BinarySearch$(S, k, \text{mid} + 1, \text{high})$

Code Fragment 9.7: Binary search in an ordered array list.

We illustrate the binary search algorithm in Figure 9.7.

2	4	5	7	8	9	12	14	17	19	22	25	27	28	33	37

  ↑ low   ↑ mid   ↑ high

2	4	5	7	8	9	12	14	17	19	22	25	27	28	33	37

      ↑ low   ↑ mid   ↑ high

2	4	5	7	8	9	12	14	17	19	22	25	27	28	33	37

      ↑ low mid high

2	4	5	7	8	9	12	14	17	19	22	25	27	28	33	37

      ↑ low=mid=high

Figure 9.7: Example of a binary search to perform operation get(22), in a map with integer keys, implemented with an ordered array list. For simplicity, we show the keys, not the whole entries.

Considering the running time of binary search, we observe that a constant number of primitive operations are executed at each recursive call of method Binary-Search. Hence, the running time is proportional to the number of recursive calls performed. A crucial fact is that with each recursive call the number of candidate entries still to be searched in the array list S is given by the value

$$\text{high} - \text{low} + 1.$$

Moreover, the number of remaining candidates is reduced by at least one half with each recursive call. Specifically, from the definition of mid, the number of remaining candidates is either

$$(\text{mid} - 1) - \text{low} + 1 = \left\lfloor \frac{\text{low} + \text{high}}{2} \right\rfloor - \text{low} \leq \frac{\text{high} - \text{low} + 1}{2}$$

or

$$\text{high} - (\text{mid} + 1) + 1 = \text{high} - \left\lfloor \frac{\text{low} + \text{high}}{2} \right\rfloor \leq \frac{\text{high} - \text{low} + 1}{2}.$$

Initially, the number of candidate entries is n; after the first call to BinarySearch, it is at most $n/2$; after the second call, it is at most $n/4$; and so on. In general, after the ith call to BinarySearch, the number of candidate entries remaining is at most $n/2^i$. In the worst case (unsuccessful search), the recursive calls stop when there are no more candidate entries. Hence, the maximum number of recursive calls performed, is the smallest integer m such that

$$n/2^m < 1.$$

In other words (recalling that we omit a logarithm's base when it is 2), $m > \log n$. Thus, we have

$$m = \lfloor \log n \rfloor + 1,$$

which implies that binary search runs in $O(\log n)$ time.

Thus, we can use an ordered search table to perform fast searches in an ordered map, but using such a table for lots of map updates would take a considerable amount of time. For this reason, the primary applications for search tables are in situations where we expect few updates but many searches. Such a situation could arise, for example, in an ordered list of English words we use to order entries in an encyclopedia or help file.

Comparing Map Implementations

Note that we can use an ordered search table to implement the map ADT even if we don't want to use the additional methods of the ordered map ADT. Table 9.2 compares the running times of the methods of a (standard) map realized by either an unordered list, a hash table, or an ordered search table. Note that an unordered list allows for fast insertions but slow searches and removals, whereas a search table allows for fast searches but slow insertions and removals. Incidentally, although we don't explicitly discuss it, we note that a sorted list implemented with a doubly linked list would be slow in performing almost all the map operations. (See Exercise R-9.5.) Nevertheless, the list-like data structure we discuss in the next section can perform the methods of the ordered map ADT quite efficiently.

Method	List	Hash Table	Search Table
size, isEmpty	$O(1)$	$O(1)$	$O(1)$
entrySet	$O(n)$	$O(n)$	$O(n)$
get	$O(n)$	$O(1)$ exp., $O(n)$ worst-case	$O(\log n)$
put	$O(1)$	$O(1)$	$O(n)$
remove	$O(n)$	$O(1)$ exp., $O(n)$ worst-case	$O(n)$

Table 9.2: Comparison of the running times of the methods of a map realized by means of an unordered list, a hash table, or an ordered search table. We let n denote the number of entries in the map and we let N denote the capacity of the bucket array in the hash table implementation. The space requirement of all the implementations is $O(n)$, assuming that the arrays supporting the hash table and search table implementations are maintained such that their capacity is proportional to the number of entries in the map.

9.3.2   Two Applications of Ordered Maps

As we have mentioned in the preceding sections, unordered and ordered maps have many applications.

In this section, we explore some specific applications of ordered maps.

Flight Databases

There are several web sites on the Internet that allow users to perform queries on flight databases to find flights between various cities, typically with the intent to buy a ticket. To make a query, a user specifies origin and destination cities, a departure date, and a departure time. To support such queries, we can model the flight database as a map, where keys are Flight objects that contain fields corresponding to these four parameters. That is, a key is a *tuple*

$$k = (\text{origin}, \text{destination}, \text{date}, \text{time}).$$

Additional information about a flight, such as the flight number, the number of seats still available in first (F) and coach (Y) class, the flight duration, and the fare, can be stored in the value object.

Finding a requested flight is not simply a matter of finding a key in the map matching the requested query, however. The main difficulty is that, although a user typically wants to exactly match the origin and destination cities, as well as the departure date, he or she will probably be content with any departure time that is close to his or her requested departure time. We can handle such a query, of course, by ordering our keys lexicographically. Thus, given a user query key k, we could, for instance, call ceilingEntry(k) to return the flight between the desired cities on the desired date, with departure time at the desired time or after. A similar use of floorEntry(k) would give us the flight with departure time at the desired time or before. Given these entries, we could then use the higherEntry() or lowerEntry() methods to find flights with the next close-by departure times that are respectively higher or lower than the desired time, k. Therefore, an efficient implementation for an ordered map would be a good way to satisfy such queries. For example, calling ceilingEntry(k) on a query key $k = $ (ORD, PVD, 05May, 09:30), followed by the respective calls to higherEntry(), might result in the following sequence of entries:

```
( (ORD, PVD, 05May, 09:53),   (AA 1840, F5, Y15, 02:05, $251) )
( (ORD, PVD, 05May, 13:29),   (AA 600, F2, Y0, 02:16, $713) )
( (ORD, PVD, 05May, 17:39),   (AA 416, F3, Y9, 02:09, $365) )
( (ORD, PVD, 05May, 19:50),   (AA 1828, F9, Y25, 02:13, $186) )
```

Maxima Sets

Life is full of trade-offs. We often have to trade off a desired performance measure against a corresponding cost. Suppose, for the sake of an example, we are interested in maintaining a database rating automobiles by their maximum speeds and their cost. We would like to allow someone with a certain amount to spend to query our database to find the fastest car they can possibly afford.

We can model such a trade-off problem as this by using a key-value pair to model the two parameters that we are trading off, which in this case would be the pair (cost, speed) for each car. Notice that some cars are strictly better than other cars using this measure. For example, a car with cost-speed pair $(20,000, 100)$ is strictly better than a car with cost-speed pair $(30,000, 90)$. At the same time, there are some cars that are not strictly dominated by another car. For example, a car with cost-speed pair $(20000, 100)$ may be better or worse than a car with cost-speed pair $(30000, 120)$, depending on how much money we have to spend. (See Figure 9.8.)

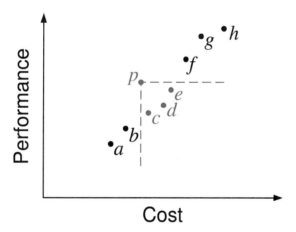

Figure 9.8: Illustrating the cost-performance trade-off with key-value pairs represented by points in the plane. Notice that point p is strictly better than points c, d, and e, but may be better or worse than points a, b, f, g, and h, depending on the price we are willing to pay. Thus, if we were to add p to our set, we could remove the points c, d, and e, but not the others.

Formally, we say a price-performance pair (a, b) **dominates** a pair (c, d) if $a < c$ and $b > d$. A pair (a, b) is called a **maximum** pair if it is not dominated by any other pairs. We are interested in maintaining the set of maxima of a collection C of price-performance pairs. That is, we would like to add new pairs to this collection (for example, when a new car is introduced), and we would like to query this collection for a given dollar amount, d, to find the fastest car that costs no more than d dollars.

Maintaining a Maxima Set with an Ordered Map

We can store the set of maxima pairs in an ordered map, M, ordered by cost, so that the cost is the key field and performance (speed) is the value field. We can then implement operations add(c, p), which adds a new cost-performance pair (c, p), and best(c), which returns the best pair with cost at most c, as shown in Code Fragments 9.8. and 9.9.

Algorithm best(c):
    Input: A cost c
    Output: The cost-performance pair in M with largest cost less than or equal to
        c or or **null** if there is no such pair
    return M.floorEntry(c)

Code Fragment 9.8: The best() method, used in a class maintaining a set of maxima implemented with an ordered map M.

Algorithm add(c, p):
    Input: A cost-performance pair (c, p)
    Output: None (but M will have (c, p) added to the set of cost-performance
        pairs)
    $e \leftarrow M$.floorEntry(c) {the greatest pair with cost at most c}
    if $e \neq$ **null then**
        if e.getValue$() > p$ **then**
            return   {(c, p) is dominated, so don't insert it in M}
    $e \leftarrow M$.ceilingEntry(c) {next pair with cost at least c}
    {Remove all the pairs that are dominated by (c, p)}
    while $e \neq$ **null and** e.getValue$() < p$ **do** {assume conditional **and** as in Java}
        M.remove$(e$.getKey$())$ {this pair is dominated by (c, p)}
        $e \leftarrow M$.higherEntry$(e$.getKey$())$ {the next pair after e}
    M.put(c, p) {Add the pair (c, p), which is not dominated}

Code Fragment 9.9: The add(c, p) method used in a class for maintaining a set of maxima implemented with an ordered map M.

Unfortunately, if we implement M using any of the data structures described above, it will result in a poor running time for the above algorithm. If, on the other hand, we implement M using a skip list, which we describe next, then we can perform best(c) queries in $O(\log n)$ expected time and add(c, p) updates in $O((1+r)\log n)$ expected time, where r is the number of points removed.

9.4 Skip Lists

An interesting data structure for efficiently realizing the ordered map ADT is the *skip list*. This data structure makes random choices in arranging the entries in such a way that search and update times are $O(\log n)$ *on average*, where n is the number of entries in the dictionary. Interestingly, the notion of average time complexity used here does not depend on the probability distribution of the keys in the input. Instead, it depends on the use of a random-number generator in the implementation of the insertions to help decide where to place the new entry. The running time is averaged over all possible outcomes of the random numbers used when inserting entries. Interestingly, Java includes an implementation of the ordered map ADT using a skip list, in the ConcurrentSkipListMap class, which guarantees $O(\log n)$ expected time performance for the get, put, and remove methods and their variants.

Because they are used extensively in computer games, cryptography, and computer simulations, methods that generate numbers that can be viewed as random numbers are built into most modern computers. Some methods, called *pseudo-random number generators* (Section 3.1.3), generate random-like numbers, starting with an initial *seed*. Other methods use hardware devices to extract "true" random numbers from nature. In any case, we will assume that our computer has access to numbers that are sufficiently random for our analysis.

The main advantage of using *randomization* in data structure and algorithm design is that the structures and methods that result are usually simple and efficient. We can devise a simple randomized data structure, called the skip list, which has the same logarithmic time bounds for searching as is achieved by the binary searching algorithm. Nevertheless, the bounds are *expected* for the skip list, while they are *worst-case* bounds for binary searching in a look-up table. On the other hand, skip lists are much faster than look-up tables for map updates.

A *skip list* S for a map M consists of a series of lists $\{S_0, S_1, \ldots, S_h\}$. Each list S_i stores a subset of the entries of M sorted by increasing keys plus entries with two special keys, denoted $-\infty$ and $+\infty$, where $-\infty$ is smaller than every possible key that can be inserted in M and $+\infty$ is larger than every possible key that can be inserted in M. In addition, the lists in S satisfy the following:

- List S_0 contains every entry of the map M (plus the special entries with keys $-\infty$ and $+\infty$).
- For $i = 1, \ldots, h-1$, list S_i contains (in addition to $-\infty$ and $+\infty$) a randomly generated subset of the entries in list S_{i-1}.
- List S_h contains only $-\infty$ and $+\infty$.

An example of a skip list is shown in Figure 9.9. It is customary to visualize a skip list S with list S_0 at the bottom and lists $S_1, \ldots, S_h$ above it. Also, we refer to h as the *height* of skip list S.

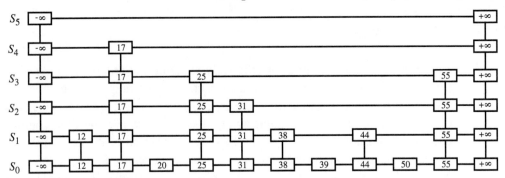

Figure 9.9: Example of a skip list storing 10 entries. For simplicity, we show only the keys of the entries.

Intuitively, the lists are set up so that S_{i+1} contains more or less every other entry in S_i. As we shall see in the details of the insertion method, the entries in S_{i+1} are chosen at random from the entries in S_i by picking each entry from S_i to also be in S_{i+1} with probability $1/2$. That is, in essence, we "flip a coin" for each entry in S_i and place that entry in S_{i+1} if the coin comes up "heads." Thus, we expect S_1 to have about $n/2$ entries, S_2 to have about $n/4$ entries, and, in general, S_i to have about $n/2^i$ entries. In other words, we expect the height h of S to be about $\log n$. The halving of the number of entries from one list to the next is not enforced as an explicit property of skip lists, however. Instead, randomization is used.

Using the position abstraction used for lists and trees, we view a skip list as a two-dimensional collection of positions arranged horizontally into **levels** and vertically into **towers**. Each level is a list S_i and each tower contains positions storing the same entry across consecutive lists. The positions in a skip list can be traversed using the following operations:

next(p): Return the position following p on the same level.

prev(p): Return the position preceding p on the same level.

below(p): Return the position below p in the same tower.

above(p): Return the position above p in the same tower.

We conventionally assume that the above operations return a **null** position if the position requested does not exist. Without going into the details, we note that we can easily implement a skip list by means of a linked structure such that the above traversal methods each take $O(1)$ time, given a skip-list position p. Such a linked structure is essentially a collection of h doubly linked lists aligned at towers, which are also doubly linked lists.

9.4.1 Search and Update Operations in a Skip List

The skip list structure allows for simple map search and update algorithms. In fact, all of the skip list search and update algorithms are based on an elegant SkipSearch method that takes a key k and finds the position p of the entry e in list S_0 such that e has the largest key (which is possibly $-\infty$) less than or equal to k.

Searching in a Skip List

Suppose we are given a search key k. We begin the SkipSearch method by setting a position variable p to the top-most, left position in the skip list S, called the ***start position*** of S. That is, the start position is the position of S_h storing the special entry with key $-\infty$. We then perform the following steps (see Figure 9.10), where $\text{key}(p)$ denotes the key of the entry at position p:

1. If $S.\text{below}(p)$ is null, then the search terminates—we are ***at the bottom*** and have located the largest entry in S with key less than or equal to the search key k. Otherwise, we ***drop down*** to the next lower level in the present tower by setting $p \leftarrow S.\text{below}(p)$.

2. Starting at position p, we move p forward until it is at the right-most position on the present level such that $\text{key}(p) \leq k$. We call this the ***scan forward*** step. Note that such a position always exists, since each level contains the keys $+\infty$ and $-\infty$. In fact, after we perform the scan forward for this level, p may remain where it started. In any case, we then repeat the previous step.

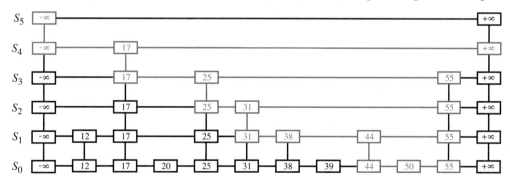

Figure 9.10: Example of a search in a skip list. The positions visited when searching for key 50 are highlighted in blue.

We give a pseudo-code description of the skip-list search algorithm, SkipSearch, in Code Fragment 9.10. Given this method, it is now easy to implement the operation $\text{get}(k)$—we simply perform $p \leftarrow \text{SkipSearch}(k)$ and test whether or not $\text{key}(p) = k$. If these two keys are equal, we return p; otherwise, we return **null**.

Algorithm SkipSearch(k):

    Input: A search key k

    Output: Position p in the bottom list S_0 such that the entry at p has the largest key less than or equal to k

    $p \leftarrow s$

    while below$(p) \neq$ **null do**

        $p \leftarrow$ below(p) {drop down}

        while $k \geq$ key(next(p)) **do**

            $p \leftarrow$ next(p) {scan forward}

    return p.

Code Fragment 9.10: Search in a skip list S. Variable s holds the start position of S.

As it turns out, the expected running time of algorithm SkipSearch on a skip list with n entries is $O(\log n)$. We postpone the justification of this fact, however, until after we discuss the implementation of the update methods for skip lists.

Insertion in a Skip List

The insertion algorithm for skip lists uses randomization to decide the height of the tower for the new entry. We begin the insertion of a new entry (k, v) by performing a SkipSearch(k) operation. This gives us the position p of the bottom-level entry with the largest key less than or equal to k (note that p may hold the special entry with key $-\infty$). We then insert (k, v) immediately after position p. After inserting the new entry at the bottom level, we "flip" a coin. If the flip comes up tails, then we stop here. Else (the flip comes up heads), we backtrack to the previous (next higher) level and insert (k, v) in this level at the appropriate position. We again flip a coin; if it comes up heads, we go to the next higher level and repeat. Thus, we continue to insert the new entry (k, v) in lists until we finally get a flip that comes up tails. We link together all the references to the new entry (k, v) created in this process to create the tower for the new entry. A coin flip can be simulated with Java's built-in pseudo-random number generator java.util.Random by calling nextInt(2), which returns 0 of 1, each with probability $1/2$.

We give the insertion algorithm for a skip list S in Code Fragment 9.11 and we illustrate it in Figure 9.11. The algorithm uses method insertAfterAbove$(p, q, (k, v))$ that inserts a position storing the entry (k, v) after position p (on the same level as p) and above position q, returning the position r of the new entry (and setting internal references so that next, prev, above, and below methods will work correctly for p, q, and r). The expected running time of the insertion algorithm on a skip list with n entries is $O(\log n)$, which we show in Section 9.4.2.

Algorithm SkipInsert(k, v):

   Input: Key k and value v

   Output: Topmost position of the entry inserted in the skip list

   $p \leftarrow$ SkipSearch(k)

   $q \leftarrow$ **null**

   $e \leftarrow (k, v)$

   $i \leftarrow -1$

   repeat

      $i \leftarrow i + 1$

      if $i \geq h$ **then**

         $h \leftarrow h + 1$ {add a new level to the skip list}

         $t \leftarrow$ next(s)

         $s \leftarrow$ insertAfterAbove(**null**, $s, (-\infty, \textbf{null})$)

         insertAfterAbove($s, t, (+\infty, \textbf{null})$)

      while above(p) = **null do**

         $p \leftarrow$ prev(p)   {scan backward}

      $p \leftarrow$ above(p)   {jump up to higher level}

      $q \leftarrow$ insertAfterAbove(p, q, e) {add a position to the tower of the new entry}

   until coinFlip() = tails

   $n \leftarrow n + 1$

   return q

Code Fragment 9.11: Insertion in a skip list. Method coinFlip() returns "heads" or "tails", each with probability $1/2$. Variables n, h, and s hold the number of entries, the height, and the start node of the skip list.

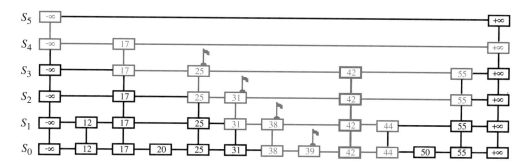

Figure 9.11: Insertion of an entry with key 42 into the skip list of Figure 9.9. We assume that the random "coin flips" for the new entry came up heads three times in a row, followed by tails. The positions visited are highlighted in blue. The positions inserted to hold the new entry are drawn with thick lines, and the positions preceding them are flagged.

Removal in a Skip List

Like the search and insertion algorithms, the removal algorithm for a skip list is quite simple. In fact, it is even easier than the insertion algorithm. That is, to perform a remove(k) operation, we begin by executing method SkipSearch(k). If the position p stores an entry with key different from k, we return **null**. Otherwise, we remove p and all the positions above p, which are easily accessed by using above operations to climb up the tower of this entry in S starting at position p. The removal algorithm is illustrated in Figure 9.12 and a detailed description of it is left as an exercise (R-9.19). As we show in the next subsection, operation remove in a skip list with n entries has $O(\log n)$ expected running time.

Before we give this analysis, however, there are some minor improvements to the skip list data structure we would like to discuss. First, we don't actually need to store references to entries at the levels of the skip list above the bottom level, because all that is needed at these levels are references to keys. Second, we don't actually need the above method. In fact, we don't need the prev method either. We can perform entry insertion and removal in strictly a top-down, scan-forward fashion, thus saving space for "up" and "prev" references. We explore the details of this optimization in Exercise C-9.11. Neither of these optimizations improve the asymptotic performance of skip lists by more than a constant factor, but these improvements can, nevertheless, be meaningful in practice. In fact, experimental evidence suggests that optimized skip lists are faster in practice than AVL trees and other balanced search trees, which are discussed in Chapter 10.

The expected running time of the removal algorithm is $O(\log n)$, which we show in Section 9.4.2.

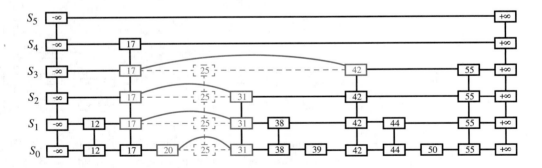

Figure 9.12: Removal of the entry with key 25 from the skip list of Figure 9.11. The positions visited after the search for the position of S_0 holding the entry are highlighted in blue. The positions removed are drawn with dashed lines.

Maintaining the Top-most Level

A skip-list S must maintain a reference to the start position (the top-most, left position in S) as an instance variable, and must have a policy for any insertion that wishes to continue inserting a new entry past the top level of S. There are two possible courses of action we can take, both of which have their merits.

One possibility is to restrict the top level, h, to be kept at some fixed value that is a function of n, the number of entries currently in the map (from the analysis we will see that $h = \max\{10, 2\lceil \log n \rceil\}$ is a reasonable choice, and picking $h = 3\lceil \log n \rceil$ is even safer). Implementing this choice means that we must modify the insertion algorithm to stop inserting a new position once we reach the top-most level (unless $\lceil \log n \rceil < \lceil \log(n+1) \rceil$, in which case we can now go at least one more level, since the bound on the height is increasing).

The other possibility is to let an insertion continue inserting a new position as long as heads keeps getting returned from the random number generator. This is the approach taken in Algorithm SkipInsert of Code Fragment 9.11. As we show in the analysis of skip lists, the probability that an insertion will go to a level that is more than $O(\log n)$ is very low, so this design choice should also work.

Either choice will still result in the expected $O(\log n)$ time to perform search, insertion, and removal, however, which we show in the next section.

9.4.2 A Probabilistic Analysis of Skip Lists $\star$

As we have shown above, skip lists provide a simple implementation of an ordered map. In terms of worst-case performance, however, skip lists are not a superior data structure. In fact, if we don't officially prevent an insertion from continuing significantly past the current highest level, then the insertion algorithm can go into what is almost an infinite loop (it is not actually an infinite loop, however, since the probability of having a fair coin repeatedly come up heads forever is 0). Moreover, we cannot infinitely add positions to a list without eventually running out of memory. In any case, if we terminate position insertion at the highest level h, then the **worst-case** running time for performing the get, put, and remove operations in a skip list S with n entries and height h is $O(n+h)$. This worst-case performance occurs when the tower of every entry reaches level $h - 1$, where h is the height of S. However, this event has very low probability. Judging from this worst case, we might conclude that the skip list structure is strictly inferior to the other map implementations discussed earlier in this chapter. But this would not be a fair analysis, for this worst-case behavior is a gross overestimate.

---

*We use a star ($\star$) to indicate sections containing material more advanced than the material in the rest of the chapter; this material can be considered optional in a first reading.

Bounding the Height of a Skip List

Because the insertion step involves randomization, a more accurate analysis of skip lists involves a bit of probability. At first, this might seem like a major undertaking, for a complete and thorough probabilistic analysis could require deep mathematics (and, indeed, there are several such deep analyses that have appeared in data structures research literature). Fortunately, such an analysis is not necessary to understand the expected asymptotic behavior of skip lists. The informal and intuitive probabilistic analysis we give below uses only basic concepts of probability theory.

Let us begin by determining the expected value of the height h of a skip list S with n entries (assuming that we do not terminate insertions early). The probability that a given entry has a tower of height $i \geq 1$ is equal to the probability of getting i consecutive heads when flipping a coin, that is, this probability is $1/2^i$. Hence, the probability P_i that level i has at least one position is at most

$$P_i \leq \frac{n}{2^i},$$

for the probability that any one of n different events occurs is at most the sum of the probabilities that each occurs.

The probability that the height h of S is larger than i is equal to the probability that level i has at least one position, that is, it is no more than P_i. This means that h is larger than, say, $3\log n$ with probability at most

$$P_{3\log n} \leq \frac{n}{2^{3\log n}}$$
$$= \frac{n}{n^3} = \frac{1}{n^2}.$$

For example, if $n = 1000$, this probability is a one-in-a-million long shot. More generally, given a constant $c > 1$, h is larger than $c\log n$ with probability at most $1/n^{c-1}$. That is, the probability that h is smaller than $c\log n$ is at least $1 - 1/n^{c-1}$. Thus, with high probability, the height h of S is $O(\log n)$.

Analyzing Search Time in a Skip List

Next, consider the running time of a search in skip list S, and recall that such a search involves two nested **while** loops. The inner loop performs a scan forward on a level of S as long as the next key is no greater than the search key k, and the outer loop drops down to the next level and repeats the scan forward iteration. Since the height h of S is $O(\log n)$ with high probability, the number of drop-down steps is $O(\log n)$ with high probability.

So we have yet to bound the number of scan-forward steps we make. Let n_i be the number of keys examined while scanning forward at level i. Observe that, after the key at the starting position, each additional key examined in a scan-forward at level i cannot also belong to level $i+1$. If any of these keys were on the previous level, we would have encountered them in the previous scan-forward step. Thus, the probability that any key is counted in n_i is $1/2$. Therefore, the expected value of n_i is exactly equal to the expected number of times we must flip a fair coin before it comes up heads. This expected value is 2. Hence, the expected amount of time spent scanning forward at any level i is $O(1)$. Since S has $O(\log n)$ levels with high probability, a search in S takes expected time $O(\log n)$. By a similar analysis, we can show that the expected running time of an insertion or a removal is $O(\log n)$.

Space Usage in a Skip List

Finally, let us turn to the space requirement of a skip list S with n entries. As we observed above, the expected number of positions at level i is $n/2^i$, which means that the expected total number of positions in S is

$$\sum_{i=0}^{h} \frac{n}{2^i} = n \sum_{i=0}^{h} \frac{1}{2^i}.$$

Using Proposition 4.5 on geometric summations, we have

$$\sum_{i=0}^{h} \frac{1}{2^i} = \frac{\left(\frac{1}{2}\right)^{h+1} - 1}{\frac{1}{2} - 1} = 2 \cdot \left(1 - \frac{1}{2^{h+1}}\right) < 2 \quad \text{for all } h \geq 0.$$

Hence, the expected space requirement of S is $O(n)$.

Table 9.3 summarizes the performance of an ordered map realized by a skip list.

Operation	Time
size, isEmpty	$O(1)$
firstEntry, lastEntry	$O(1)$
keySet, values, entrySet	$O(n)$
get, put, remove	$O(\log n)$ (expected)
ceilingEntry, floorEntry, lowerEntry, higherEntry	$O(\log n)$ (expected)

Table 9.3: Performance of an ordered map implemented with a skip list, as in the class, java.util.concurrent.ConcurrentSkipListMap. We use n to denote the number of entries in the dictionary at the time the operation is performed. The expected space requirement is $O(n)$.

9.5   Dictionaries

Like a map, a dictionary stores key-value pairs (k, v), which we call **entries**, where k is the key and v is the value. Similarly, a dictionary allows for keys and values to be of any object type. But, whereas a map insists that entries have unique keys, a dictionary allows for multiple entries to have the same key, much like an English dictionary, which allows for multiple definitions for the same word.

The ability to store multiple entries with the same key has several applications. For example, we might want to store records for computer science authors indexed by their first and last names. Since there are a few cases of different authors with the same first and last name, there will naturally be some instances where we have to deal with different entries having equal keys. Likewise, a multi-user computer game involving players visiting various rooms in a large castle might need a mapping from rooms to players. It is natural in this application to allow users to be in the same room simultaneously, however, to engage in battles. Thus, this game would naturally be another application where it would be useful to allow for multiple entries with equal keys.

9.5.1   The Dictionary ADT

As an ADT, an (unordered) **dictionary** D supports the following methods:

size(): Return the number of entries in D.

isEmpty(): Test whether D is empty.

get(k): If D contains an entry with key equal to k, then return such an entry, else return **null**.

getAll(k): Return an iterable collection containing all entries with key equal to k.

put(k, v): Insert an entry with key k and value v into D, returning the entry created.

remove(e): Remove from D an entry e, returning the removed entry; an error occurs if e is not in D.

entrySet(): Return an iterable collection of the key-value entries in D.

Notice that our dictionary operations use entries, as in the map ADT, which are the key-value pairs stored in the dictionary. As mentioned above, we allow for multiple entries with equal keys. For this reason, we define the put method to return a reference to the newly created entry, as this gives us a way to directly reference entries in addition to the entrySet() method. Such references are required, for example, by the dictionary method, remove(e).

Additional Details

When the method get(k) is unsuccessful (that is, there is no entry with key equal to k), we use the convention of returning a sentinel **null**. Another choice, of course, would be to throw an exception for an unsuccessful get(k), but that would not be a good use of an exception, since it is normal to ask for a key that might not be in our dictionary, and throwing and catching an exception is slower than testing against a sentinel.

Note that, as we have defined it, a dictionary D can contain different entries with equal keys. In this case, operation get(k) returns an ***arbitrary*** entry (k,v), whose key is equal to k. We also mention, in passing, that this dictionary ADT should not be confused with the abstract class java.util.Dictionary, which actually corresponds to the map ADT given above and is now considered obsolete. Indeed, as of this writing, there is no data structure in the Java Collections Framework that allows for multiple entries with equal keys, as in the dictionary ADT.

As with the entries used with the map ADT, we assume each entry in a dictionary comes equipped with getKey() and getValue() methods to access its key and value components respectively. Incidentally, if we wish to store an element e in a dictionary so that the element is itself its own key, then we would insert e with the method call put(e,e). In this case, the getKey() and getValue() methods would return the same thing.

Example 9.2: *In the following, we show a series of operations on an initially empty dictionary storing entries with integer keys and character values.*

Operation	Output	Dictionary
put($5,A$)	$(5,A)$	$\{(5,A)\}$
put($7,B$)	$(7,B)$	$\{(5,A),(7,B)\}$
put($2,C$)	$(2,C)$	$\{(5,A),(7,B),(2,C)\}$
put($8,D$)	$(8,D)$	$\{(5,A),(7,B),(2,C),(8,D)\}$
put($2,E$)	$(2,E)$	$\{(5,A),(7,B),(2,C),(8,D),(2,E)\}$
get(7)	$(7,B)$	$\{(5,A),(7,B),(2,C),(8,D),(2,E)\}$
get(4)	**null**	$\{(5,A),(7,B),(2,C),(8,D),(2,E)\}$
get(2)	$(2,C)$	$\{(5,A),(7,B),(2,C),(8,D),(2,E)\}$
getAll(2)	$\{(2,C),(2,E)\}$	$\{(5,A),(7,B),(2,C),(8,D),(2,E)\}$
size()	5	$\{(5,A),(7,B),(2,C),(8,D),(2,E)\}$
remove(get(5))	$(5,A)$	$\{(7,B),(2,C),(8,D),(2,E)\}$
get(5)	**null**	$\{(7,B),(2,C),(8,D),(2,E)\}$

9.5.2   Implementations with Location-Aware Entries

As with the map ADT, there are several possible ways we can implement the dictionary ADT, including with an unordered list, a hash table, an ordered search table, or a skip list. As we did for adaptable priority queues (Section 8.4.2), we can also use location-aware entries to speed up the running time for some operations in a dictionary. In removing a location-aware entry e, for instance, we could simply go directly to the place in our data structure where we are storing e and remove it. We could implement a location-aware entry, for example, by augmenting our entry class with a private location variable and protected methods, location() and setLocation(p), which return and set this variable respectively. We would then require that the location variable for an entry e would always refer to e's position or index in the data structure. We would, of course, have to update this variable any time we moved an entry, as follows.

- **Unordered list**: In an unordered list, L, implementing a dictionary, we can maintain the location variable of each entry e to point to e's position in the underlying linked list for L. This choice allows us to perform remove(e) as L.remove(e.location()), which would run in $O(1)$ time.
- **Hash table with separate chaining**: Consider a hash table, with bucket array A and hash function h, that uses separate chaining for handling collisions. We use the location variable of each entry e to point to e's position in the list L implementing the list $A[h(k)]$. This choice allows us to perform a remove(e) as L.remove(e.location()), which would run in constant expected time.
- **Ordered search table**: In an ordered table, T, implementing a dictionary, we should maintain the location variable of each entry e to be e's index in T. This choice would allow us to perform remove(e) as T.remove(e.location()). (Recall that location() now returns an integer.) This approach would run fast if entry e was stored near the end of T.
- **Skip list**: In a skip list, S, implementing a dictionary, we should maintain the location variable of each entry e to point to e's position in the bottom level of S. This choice would allow us to skip the search step in our algorithm for performing remove(e) in a skip list.

We summarize the performance of entry removal in a dictionary with location-aware entries in Table 9.4.

List	Hash Table	Search Table	Skip List
$O(1)$	$O(1)$ (expected)	$O(n)$	$O(\log n)$ (expected)

Table 9.4: Performance of the remove method in dictionaries implemented with location-aware entries. We use n to denote the number of entries in the dictionary.

9.5.3 An Implementation Using the java.util Package

Since, as of this writing, Java provides no equivalent to the dictionary ADT in the Java Collections Framework, we provide, in this section, a complete Java implementation of the dictionary ADT using only classes and interfaces from the java.util package. Key features of this implementation include the following:

- The dictionary ADT is specified in an interface, MultiMap, given in Code Fragment 9.12. This interface defines the dictionary entries to be instances of classes that implement the interface, java.util.Map.Entry<K,V>. In addition, it specifies that the getAll and entrySet methods return objects that implement the java.util.Iterable interface over these types of entries. Finally, it specifies that the methods that take arguments may throw an exception in java.lang, namely, IllegalArgumentException.

- The class, HashTableMultiMap, which implements the MultiMap interface, is specified in Code Fragments 9.13 and 9.14. It implements the dictionary ADT using a java.util.HashMap object, m. Rather than store each key-value pair entry directly in this hash table, it stores a java.util.LinkedList object for each key in m. Each such linked list stores all the key-value pair entries having the same key. This design choice is, in fact, the main idea that allows us to store multiple entries with equal keys.

- Since the size of the underlying hash table is the number of linked lists that it stores, the HashTableMultiMap class explicitly keeps track of its own size, rather than using the value, m.size(). Specifically, the HashTableMultiMap class uses its own size instance variable, nSize, to implement its size() and isEmpty() methods.

- When adding a new key-value pair entry, with the put(k, v) method, we first check if there is already a linked list existing for this key, and, if not, then we create one. Once we have a linked list established for this key, k, we add a new entry for this pair, (k, v), to the list, using an object of type java.util.AbstractMap.SimpleEntry.

- When performing a get(k) or getAll(k), we consult the linked list for the key k. In the former case, we simply return the first entry in this list and, in the latter case, we return the entire list.

- To perform a remove(e) operation, we delegate the removal action to the linked list for the key e.getKey().

- Performing the entrySet() method is more interesting. In this case, we ask for each of the values in the underlying HashMap, m, storing our entries. Since each value in this map is a linked list of entries, we perform an addAll call to add all the entries from each such list to our output list, which we return after we have added all the lists from m into this list.

```java
import java.util.*;
public interface MultiMap<K,V> {
  public int size();
  public boolean isEmpty();
  public Map.Entry<K,V> get(K k) throws IllegalArgumentException;
  public Iterable<Map.Entry<K,V>> getAll(K k) throws IllegalArgumentException;
  public Map.Entry<K,V> put(K k, V v) throws IllegalArgumentException;
  public Map.Entry<K,V> remove(Map.Entry<K,V> e)
                      throws IllegalArgumentException;
  public Iterable<Map.Entry<K,V>> entrySet();
}
```

Code Fragment 9.12: The MultiMap interface, which is defined to use only classes and interfaces in java.util.

```java
import java.util.*;
public class HashTableMultiMap<K,V> implements MultiMap<K,V> {
  Map<K,LinkedList<Map.Entry<K,V>>> m; // a map of keys to lists of entries
  int nSize; // the size of this MapDictionary
  /** Default constructor, which uses a HashMap. */
  public HashTableMultiMap() {
    m = new HashMap<K,LinkedList<Map.Entry<K,V>>>(); // default map
    nSize = 0;
  }
  /** Returns the number of entries in the dictionary. */
  public int size() { return nSize; }
  /** Returns whether the dictionary is empty. */
  public boolean isEmpty() { return nSize == 0; }
  /** Inserts an item into the dictionary.  Returns the newly created
   * entry. */
  public Map.Entry<K,V> put(K key, V value)
                      throws IllegalArgumentException {
    LinkedList<Map.Entry<K,V>> ll;
    if (key == null) throw new IllegalArgumentException();
    if ((ll = m.get(key)) == null) { // nothing there yet
      ll = new LinkedList<Map.Entry<K,V>>();
      m.put(key,ll);
    }
    Map.Entry<K,V> e = new AbstractMap.SimpleEntry<K,V>(key,value);
    ll.add(e); // add the new entry to the list for this key
    nSize++;
    return e;
  }
}
```

Code Fragment 9.13: The HashTableMultiMap class, which is defined to use only classes and interfaces in java.util. (Continues in Code Fragment 9.14.)

```java
/** Returns an entry containing the given key, or <tt>null</tt> if
 * no such entry exists. */
public Map.Entry<K,V> get(K key)
                        throws IllegalArgumentException {
  LinkedList<Map.Entry<K,V>> ll;
  if (key == null) throw new IllegalArgumentException();
  if ((ll = m.get(key)) == null) return null; // nothing there yet
  return ll.peekFirst();   // the first element is as good as any
}

/** Returns an iterator containing all the entries containing the
 * given key, or an empty iterator if no such entries exist. */
public Iterable<Map.Entry<K,V>> getAll(K key)
                              throws IllegalArgumentException {
  LinkedList<Map.Entry<K,V>> ll;
  if (key == null) throw new IllegalArgumentException();
  if ((ll = m.get(key)) == null) return null; // nothing there yet
  return ll;
}

/** Removes and returns the given entry from the dictionary. */
public Map.Entry<K,V> remove(Map.Entry<K,V> e)
                        throws IllegalArgumentException {
  LinkedList<Map.Entry<K,V>> ll;
  if (e == null) throw new IllegalArgumentException();
  K key = e.getKey();
  ll = m.get(key);
  if (ll == null) throw new IllegalArgumentException(); // no such key in m
  if (ll.remove(e)) {
    nSize--;
    if (ll.isEmpty()) m.remove(key); // remove the empty list in this case
    return e; // e was in ll, so return the removed entry
  }
  else
    throw new IllegalArgumentException(); // e was not in ll
}

/** Returns an iterator containing all the entries in the dictionary. */
public Iterable<Map.Entry<K,V>> entrySet() {
  LinkedList<Map.Entry<K,V>> ll = new LinkedList<Map.Entry<K,V>>();
  for (LinkedList<Map.Entry<K,V>> sub : m.values())
    ll.addAll(sub);   // add all the entries in this list to ll
  return ll;
}
}
```

Code Fragment 9.14: The HashTableMultiMap class, which is defined to use only classes and interfaces in java.util. (Continued from Code Fragment 9.13.)

9.6   Exercises

For help with exercises, please visit the web site, www.wiley.com/college/goodrich.

Reinforcement

R-9.1 Which of the hash table collision-handling schemes could tolerate a load factor above 1 and which could not?

R-9.2 What is the worst-case running time for inserting n key-value entries into an initially empty map M that is implemented with a list?

R-9.3 What is the worst-case asymptotic running time for performing n (correct) remove() operations on a map, implemented with an ordered search table, that initially contains $2n$ entries?

R-9.4 Describe how to use a skip-list map to implement the dictionary ADT, allowing for the user to insert different entries with equal keys.

R-9.5 Describe how an ordered list implemented as a doubly linked list could be used to implement the map ADT.

R-9.6 What would be a good hash code for a vehicle identification number, that is a string of numbers and letters of the form "9X9XX99X9XX999999," where a "9" represents a digit and an "X" represents a letter?

R-9.7 Draw the 11-entry hash table that results from using the hash function, $h(i) = (3i + 5) \bmod 11$, to hash the keys 12, 44, 13, 88, 23, 94, 11, 39, 20, 16, and 5, assuming collisions are handled by chaining.

R-9.8 What is the result of the previous exercise, assuming collisions are handled by linear probing?

R-9.9 Show the result of Exercise R-9.7, assuming collisions are handled by quadratic probing, up to the point where the method fails.

R-9.10 What is the result of Exercise R-9.7 when collisions are handled by double hashing using the secondary hash function $h'(k) = 7 - (k \bmod 7)$?

R-9.11 Give a pseudo-code description of an insertion into a hash table that uses quadratic probing to resolve collisions, assuming we also use the trick of replacing deleted entries with a special "deactivated entry" object.

R-9.12 Give a Java description of the values() and entrySet() methods that could be included in the hash table implementation of Code Fragments 9.3–9.5.

R-9.13 Describe a set of operations for an ordered dictionary ADT that would correspond to the methods of the ordered map ADT. Be sure to define the meaning of the methods so that they can deal with the possibility of different entries with equal keys.

R-9.14 Explain how to modify class HashTableMap given in Code Fragments 9.3–9.5, so that it implements the dictionary ADT instead of the map ADT.

R-9.15 Show the result of rehashing the hash table shown in Figure 9.4 into a table of size 19 using the new hash function $h(k) = 3k \bmod 17$.

R-9.16 Argue why a hash table is not suited to implement an ordered dictionary.

R-9.17 What is the worst-case time for putting n entries in an initially empty hash table, with collisions resolved by chaining? What is the best case?

R-9.18 Draw an example skip list that results from performing the following series of operations on the skip list shown in Figure 9.12: remove(38), put(48,x), put(24,y), remove(55). Record your coin flips, as well.

R-9.19 Give a pseudo-code description of the remove operation in a skip list.

R-9.20 What is the expected running time of the methods for maintaining a maxima set if we insert n pairs such that each pair has lower cost and performance than one before it? What is contained in the ordered dictionary at the end of this series of operations? What if each pair had a lower cost and higher performance than the one before it?

R-9.21 Argue why location-aware entries are not really needed for a dictionary implemented with a good hash table.

Creativity

C-9.1 Describe how you could perform each of the additional methods of the ordered map ADT using a skip list.

C-9.2 Describe how to use a skip list to implement the array list ADT, so that index-based insertions and removals both run in $O(\log n)$ expected time.

C-9.3 Suppose we are given two ordered search tables S and T, each with n entries (with S and T being implemented with arrays). Describe an $O(\log^2 n)$-time algorithm for finding the kth smallest key in the union of the keys from S and T (assuming no duplicates).

C-9.4 Give an $O(\log n)$-time solution for the previous problem.

C-9.5 Design a variation of binary search for performing operation getAll(k) in a dictionary implemented with an ordered search table, and show that it runs in time $O(\log n + s)$, where n is the number of elements in the dictionary and s is the size of the iterator returned.

C-9.6 Describe the changes that must be made in the pseudo-code descriptions of the (unordered) map methods when we implement the map with a hash table such that collisions are handled via separate chaining, but we add the space optimization that if a bucket stores just a single entry, then we simply have the bucket reference that entry directly.

C-9.7 The hash table dictionary implementation requires that we find a prime number between a number M and a number $2M$. Implement a method for finding such a prime by using the *sieve algorithm*. In this algorithm, we allocate a $2M$ cell Boolean array A, such that cell i is associated with the integer i. We then initialize the array cells to all be "true" and we "mark off" all the cells that are multiples of 2, 3, 5, 7, and so on. This process can stop after it reaches a number larger than $\sqrt{2M}$.   (Hint: Consider a bootstrapping method for finding the primes up to $\sqrt{2M}$.)

C-9.8 Describe how to perform a removal from a hash table that uses linear probing to resolve collisions where we do not use a special marker to represent deleted elements. That is, we must rearrange the contents so that it appears that the removed entry was never inserted in the first place.

C-9.9 Given a collection C of n cost-performance pairs (c, p), describe an algorithm for finding the maxima pairs of C in $O(n \log n)$ time.

C-9.10 The quadratic probing strategy has a clustering problem related to the way it looks for open slots. Namely, when a collision occurs at bucket $h(k)$, it checks buckets $A[(h(k) + j^2) \bmod N]$, for $j = 1, 2, \ldots, N-1$.

a. Show that $j^2 \bmod N$ will assume at most $(N+1)/2$ distinct values, for N prime, as j ranges from 1 to $N-1$. As a part of this justification, note that $j^2 \bmod N = (N-j)^2 \bmod N$ for all j.

b. A better strategy is to choose a prime N such that $N \bmod 4 = 3$ and then to check the buckets $A[(h(k) \pm j^2) \bmod N]$ as j ranges from 1 to $(N-1)/2$, alternating between plus and minus. Show that this alternate version is guaranteed to check every bucket in A.

C-9.11 Show that the methods above(p) and prev(p) are not actually needed to efficiently implement a dictionary using a skip list. That is, we can implement entry insertion and removal in a skip list using a strictly top-down, scan-forward approach, without ever using the above or prev methods. (Hint: In the insertion algorithm, first repeatedly flip the coin to determine the level where you should start inserting the new entry.)

C-9.12 Describe how to implement method successors(k) in an ordered map realized using an ordered search table. This method returns an iterable collection of all the entries in the map that have keys greater than or equal to k. What is the running time of your scheme?

C-9.13 Repeat the previous exercise using a skip list. What is the expected running time in this case?

C-9.14 Suppose that each row of an $n \times n$ array A consists of 1's and 0's such that, in any row of A, all the 1's come before any 0's in that row. Assuming A is already in memory, describe a method running in $O(n \log n)$ time (not $O(n^2)$ time!) for counting the number of 1's in A.

C-9.15 Describe an efficient dictionary structure for storing n entries that have an associated set of $r < n$ keys that come from a total order. That is, the set of keys is smaller than the number of entries. Your structure should perform operation getAll in $O(\log r + s)$ expected time, where s is the number of entries returned, operation entrySet() in $O(n)$ time, and the remaining operations of the dictionary ADT in $O(\log r)$ expected time.

C-9.16 Describe an efficient dictionary structure for storing n entries whose $r < n$ keys have distinct hash codes. Your structure should perform operation getAll in $O(1 + s)$ expected time, where s is the number of entries returned, operation entrySet() in $O(n)$ time, and the remaining operations of the dictionary ADT in $O(1)$ expected time.

C-9.17 Describe an efficient data structure for implementing the **bag** ADT, which supports a method add(e), for adding an element e to the bag, and a method remove(), which removes an arbitrary element in the bag, allowing for multiple copies of duplicate elements, if they were added separately. Show that both of these methods can be done in $O(1)$ time.

C-9.18 Describe how to modify the skip list data structure to support the method median(), which returns the position of the element in the "bottom" list S_0 at index $\lfloor n/2 \rfloor$. Show that your implementation of this method runs in $O(\log n)$ expected time.

Projects

P-9.1 Write a spell-checker class that stores a set of words, W, in a hash table and implements a method, spellCheck(s), which performs a **spell check** on the string s with respect to the set of words, W. If s is in W, then the call to spellCheck(s) returns an iterable collection that contains only s, as it is assumed to be spelled correctly in this case. Otherwise, if s is not in W, then the call to spellCheck(s) returns an iterable collection of every word in W that could be a correct spelling of s. Your program should be able to handle all the common ways that s might be a misspelling of a word in W, including swapping adjacent characters in a word, inserting a single character inbetween two adjacent characters in a word, deleting a single character from a word, and replacing a character in a word with another character. For an extra challenge, consider phonetic substitutions as well.

P-9.2 Write an implementation of the dictionary ADT using a linked list.

P-9.3 Write an implementation of the map ADT using an array list.

P-9.4 Implement a class that implements a version of an ordered dictionary ADT using a skip list. Be sure to carefully define and implement dictionary versions of corresponding methods of the ordered map ADT.

P-9.5 Implement the map ADT with a hash table with separate chaining collision handling (do not adapt any java.util classes).

P-9.6 Implement the ordered map ADT using a skip list.

P-9.7 Extend the previous project by providing a graphical animation of the skip list operations. Visualize how entries move up the skip list during insertions and are linked out of the skip list during removals. Also, in a search operation, visualize the scan-forward and drop-down actions.

P-9.8 Implement a dictionary that supports location-aware entries by means of an ordered list.

P-9.9 Perform a comparative analysis that studies the collision rates for various hash codes for character strings, such as various polynomial hash codes for different values of the parameter a. Use a hash table to determine collisions, but only count collisions where different strings map to the same hash code (not if they map to the same location in this hash table). Test these hash codes on text files found on the Internet.

P-9.10 Perform a comparative analysis as in the previous exercise but for 10-digit telephone numbers instead of character strings.

P-9.11 Design a Java class that implements the skip list data structure. Use this class to create implementations of both the map and dictionary ADTs, including location-aware methods for the dictionary.

Chapter Notes

Hashing is a well-studied technique. The reader interested in further study is encouraged to explore the book by Knuth [63], as well as the book by Vitter and Chen [96]. Interestingly, binary search was first published in 1946, but was not published in a fully correct form until 1962. For further discussions on lessons learned, please see papers by Bentley [12] and Levisse [67]. Skip lists were introduced by Pugh [83]. Our analysis of skip lists is a simplification of a presentation given by Motwani and Raghavan [79]. For a more in-depth analysis of skip lists, please see the various research papers on skip lists that have appeared in the data structures literature [58, 80, 81]. Exercise C-9.10 was contributed by James Lee.

Chapter

10

Search Trees

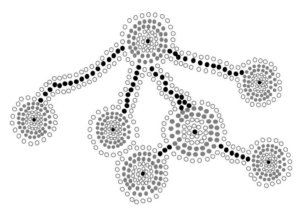

Contents

10.1 Binary Search Trees

All of the structures we discuss in this chapter are *search trees*, that is, tree data structures that can be used to implement a map. Let us, therefore, begin by briefly reviewing the fundamental methods of the map ADT (Section 9.1):

get(k): Return the value v for the entry, (k,v), with key equal to k, if it exists.

put(k,v): Enter the entry (k,v) as the mapping of k to v.

remove(k): Remove the entry with key equal to k, and return its value.

The ordered map ADT also includes some additional methods for finding predecessor and successor entries with respect to a given key or entry, but their performance is similar to that of get(). So we will be focusing on get() as the primary search operation in this chapter.

Binary trees are an excellent data structure for storing the entries of a map, assuming we have an order relation defined on the keys. As mentioned previously (Section 7.3.6), a *binary search tree* is a binary tree T such that each internal node v of T stores an entry (k,x) such that:

- Keys stored at nodes in the left subtree of v are less than or equal to k.
- Keys stored at nodes in the right subtree of v are greater than or equal to k.

As we show below, the keys stored at the nodes of T provide a way of performing a search by making comparisons at a series of internal nodes. The search can stop at the current node v or continue at v's left or right child. Thus, we take the view here that binary search trees are nonempty proper binary trees. That is, we store entries only at the internal nodes of a binary search tree, and the external nodes serve as "placeholders." This approach simplifies several of our search and update algorithms. Incidentally, we could have allowed for improper binary search trees, which have better space usage, but at the expense of more complicated search and update methods.

Independent of whether we view binary search trees as proper or not, the important property of a binary search tree is the realization of an ordered map (or dictionary). That is, a binary search tree should hierarchically represent an ordering of its keys, using relationships between parent and children. Specifically, an inorder traversal (Section 7.3.6) of the nodes of a binary search tree T should visit the keys in nondecreasing order.

10.1.1 Searching

To perform operation get(k) in a map M that is represented with a binary search tree T, we view the tree T as a decision tree (recall Figure 7.10). In this case, the question asked at each internal node v of T is whether the search key k is less than, equal to, or greater than the key stored at node v, denoted with key(v). If the answer is "smaller," then the search continues in the left subtree. If the answer is "equal," then the search terminates successfully. If the answer is "greater," then the search continues in the right subtree. Finally, if we reach an external node, then the search terminates unsuccessfully. (See Figure 10.1.)

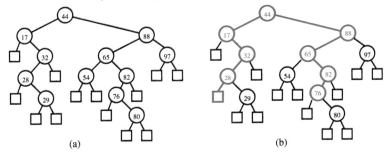

Figure 10.1: (a) A binary search tree T representing a map with integer keys; (b) nodes of T visited when executing operations get(76) (successful) and get(25) (unsuccessful) on M. For simplicity, we show only the keys of the entries.

We describe this approach in detail in Code Fragment 10.1. Given a search key k and a node v of T, this method, TreeSearch, returns a node (position) w of the subtree $T(v)$ of T rooted at v, such that one of the following occurs:

- w is an internal node and w's entry has key equal to k.
- w is an external node representing k's proper place in an inorder traversal of $T(v)$, but k is not a key contained in $T(v)$.

Thus, method get(k) can be performed by calling TreeSearch(k, T.root()). Let w be the node of T returned by this call. If w is an internal node, then we return w's entry; otherwise, we return **null**.

Algorithm TreeSearch(k, v):
    if T.isExternal(v) **then**
        return v
    if $k <$ key(v) **then**
        return TreeSearch(k, T.left(v))
    else if $k >$ key(v) **then**
        return TreeSearch(k, T.right(v))
    return v {we know $k =$ key(v)}

    Code Fragment 10.1: Recursive search in a binary search tree.

Analysis of Binary Tree Searching

The analysis of the worst-case running time of searching in a binary search tree T is simple. Algorithm TreeSearch is recursive and executes a constant number of primitive operations for each recursive call. Each recursive call of TreeSearch is made on a child of the previous node. That is, TreeSearch is called on the nodes of a path of T that starts at the root and goes down one level at a time. Thus, the number of such nodes is bounded by $h+1$, where h is the height of T. In other words, since we spend $O(1)$ time per node encountered in the search, method get on map M runs in $O(h)$ time, where h is the height of the binary search tree T used to implement M. (See Figure 10.2.)

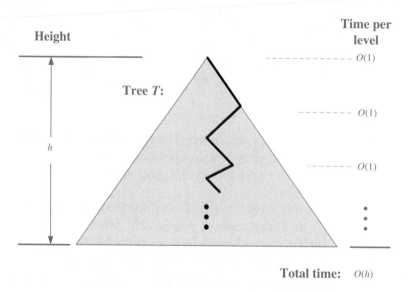

Figure 10.2: Illustrating the running time of searching in a binary search tree. The figure uses standard visualization shortcuts of viewing a binary search tree as a big triangle and a path from the root as a zig-zag line.

We can also show that a variation of the above algorithm performs operation getAll(k) of the dictionary ADT in time $O(h+s)$, where s is the number of entries returned. However, this method is slightly more complicated, and the details are left as an exercise (C-10.2).

Admittedly, the height h of T can be as large as the number of entries, n, but we expect that it is usually much smaller. Indeed, we will show how to maintain an upper bound of $O(\log n)$ on the height of a search tree T in Section 10.2. Before we describe such a scheme, however, let us describe implementations for map update methods.

10.1.2 Update Operations

Binary search trees allow implementations of the put and remove operations using algorithms that are fairly straightforward, but not trivial.

Insertion

Let us assume a proper binary tree T supports the following update operation:

insertAtExternal(v,e): Insert the element e at the external node v, and expand v to be internal, having new (empty) external node children; an error occurs if v is an internal node.

Given this method, we perform put(k,x) for a map implemented with a binary search tree T by calling TreeInsert$(k,x,T.\text{root}())$, which is given in Code Fragment 10.2.

Algorithm TreeInsert(k,x,v):

    Input: A search key k, an associated value, x, and a node v of T

    Output: A new node w in the subtree $T(v)$ that stores the entry (k,x)

    $w \leftarrow$ TreeSearch(k,v)

    if $T.\text{isInternal}(w)$ **then**

        return TreeInsert$(k,x,T.\text{left}(w))$ {going to the right would be correct too}

    $T.\text{insertAtExternal}(w,(k,x))$ {this is an appropriate place to put (k,x)}

    return w

Code Fragment 10.2: Recursive algorithm for insertion in a binary search tree.

This algorithm traces a path from T's root to an external node, which is expanded into a new internal node accommodating the new entry. An example of insertion into a binary search tree is shown in Figure 10.3.

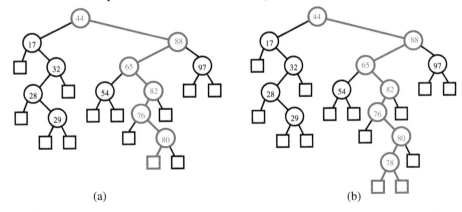

(a)   (b)

Figure 10.3: Insertion of an entry with key 78 into the search tree of Figure 10.1. Finding the position to insert is shown in (a), and the resulting tree is shown in (b).

Removal

The implementation of the remove(k) operation on a map M implemented with a binary search tree T is a bit more complex, since we do not wish to create any "holes" in the tree T. We assume, in this case, that a proper binary tree supports the following additional update operation:

> removeExternal(v): Remove an external node v and its parent, replacing v's parent with v's sibling; an error occurs if v is not external.

Given this operation, we begin our implementation of operation remove(k) of the map ADT by calling TreeSearch(k, T.root()) on T to find a node of T storing an entry with key equal to k. If TreeSearch returns an external node, then there is no entry with key k in map M, and we return **null** (and we are done). If TreeSearch returns an internal node w instead, then w stores an entry we wish to remove, and we distinguish two cases (of increasing difficulty):

- If one of the children of node w is an external node, say node z, we simply remove w and z from T by means of operation removeExternal(z) on T. This operation restructures T by replacing w with the sibling of z, removing both w and z from T. (See Figure 10.4.)

- If both children of node w are internal nodes, we cannot simply remove the node w from T, since this would create a "hole" in T. Instead, we proceed as follows (see Figure 10.5):

  - We find the first internal node y that follows w in an inorder traversal of T. Node y is the left-most internal node in the right subtree of w, and is found by going first to the right child of w and then down T from there, following left children. Also, the left child x of y is the external node that immediately follows node w in the inorder traversal of T.

  - We save the entry stored at w in a temporary variable t, and move the entry of y into w. This action has the effect of removing the former entry stored at w.

  - We remove nodes x and y from T by calling removeExternal(x) on T. This action replaces y with x's sibling, and removes both x and y from T.

  - We return the entry previously stored at w, which we had saved in the temporary variable t.

As with searching and insertion, this removal algorithm traverses a path from the root to an external node, possibly moving an entry between two nodes of this path, and then performs a removeExternal operation at that external node.

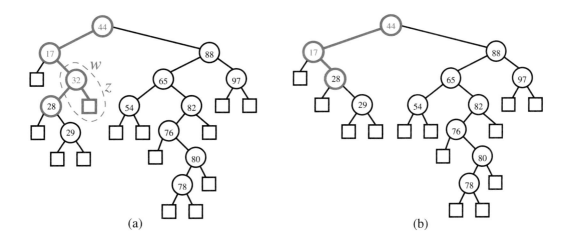

Figure 10.4: Removal from the binary search tree of Figure 10.3b, where the entry to remove (with key 32) is stored at a node (w) with an external child: (a) before the removal; (b) after the removal.

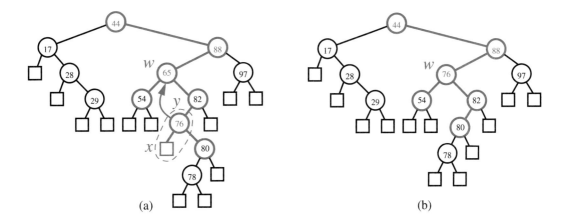

Figure 10.5: Removal from the binary search tree of Figure 10.3b, where the entry to remove (with key 65) is stored at a node (w) whose children are both internal: (a) before the removal; (b) after the removal.

Performance of a Binary Search Tree

The analysis of the search, insertion, and removal algorithms are similar. We spend $O(1)$ time at each node visited, and, in the worst case, the number of nodes visited is proportional to the height h of T. Thus, in a map M implemented with a binary search tree T, the get, put, and remove methods run in $O(h)$ time, where h is the height of T. Thus, a binary search tree T is an efficient implementation of a map with n entries only if the height of T is small. In the best case, T has height $h = \lceil \log(n+1) \rceil$, which yields logarithmic-time performance for all the map operations. In the worst case, however, T has height n, in which case it would look and feel like an ordered list implementation of a map. Such a worst-case configuration arises, for example, if we insert a series of entries with keys in increasing or decreasing order. (See Figure 10.6.)

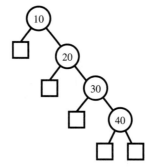

Figure 10.6: Example of a binary search tree with linear height, obtained by inserting entries with keys in increasing order.

The performance of a map implemented with a binary search tree is summarized in the following proposition and in Table 10.1.

Proposition 10.1: *A binary search tree T with height h for n key-value entries uses $O(n)$ space and executes the map ADT operations with the following running times. Operations* size *and* isEmpty *each take $O(1)$ time. Operations* get, put, *and* remove *each take $O(h)$ time.*

Method	Time
size, isEmpty	$O(1)$
get, put, remove	$O(h)$

Table 10.1: Running times of the main methods of a map realized by a binary search tree. We denote the current height of the tree with h. The space usage is $O(n)$, where n is the number of entries stored in the map.

Note that the running time of search and update operations in a binary search tree varies dramatically depending on the tree's height. We can nevertheless take comfort that, on average, a binary search tree with n keys generated from a random series of insertions and removals of keys has expected height $O(\log n)$. Such a statement requires careful mathematical language to precisely define what we mean by a random series of insertions and removals, and sophisticated probability theory to prove; hence, its justification is beyond the scope of this book. Nevertheless, keep in mind the poor worst-case performance and take care in using standard binary search trees in applications where updates are not random. There are, after all, applications where it is essential to have a map with fast worst-case search and update times. The data structures presented in the next sections address this need.

10.1.3 Java Implementation

In Code Fragments 10.3 through 10.5, we describe a binary search tree class, BinarySearchTree, which stores objects of class BSTEntry (implementing the Entry interface) at its nodes. Class BinarySearchTree extends class LinkedBinaryTree from Code Fragments 7.16 through 7.18, thus taking advantage of code reuse. For space reasons, however, we omit showing the keySet, values, and entrySet methods.

This class makes use of several auxiliary methods to do much of the heavy lifting. The auxiliary method treeSearch, based on the TreeSearch algorithm (Code Fragment 10.1), is invoked by the get and put methods. We use two additional update methods, insertAtExternal, which inserts a new entry at an external node, and removeExternal, which removes an external node and its parent.

Class BinarySearchTree uses location-aware entries (see Section 8.4.2). Thus, its update methods inform any moved BSTEntry objects of their new positions. We also use several simple auxiliary methods for accessing and testing data, such as checkKey, which checks if a key is valid (albeit using a fairly simple rule in this case). We also use an instance variable, actionPos, which stores the position where the most recent search, insertion, or removal ended. This instance variable is not necessary to the implementation of a binary search tree, but is useful to classes that will extend BinarySearchTree (see Code Fragments 10.7, 10.8, 10.10, and 10.11) to identify the position where the previous search, insertion, or removal has taken place. Position actionPos has the intended meaning provided it is used right after executing the method get, put, or remove.

```java
// Realization of a map by means of a binary search tree
public class BinarySearchTreeMap<K,V>
  extends LinkedBinaryTree<Entry<K,V>> implements Map<K,V> {
  protected Comparator<K> C; // comparator
  protected Position<Entry<K,V>>
            actionPos; // insert node or removed node's parent
  protected int numEntries = 0; // number of entries
  /** Creates a BinarySearchTree with a default comparator. */
  public BinarySearchTreeMap() {
    C = new DefaultComparator<K>();
    addRoot(null);
  }
  public BinarySearchTreeMap(Comparator<K> c) {
    C = c;
    addRoot(null);
  }
  /** Nested class for location-aware binary search tree entries */
  protected static class BSTEntry<K,V> implements Entry<K,V> {
    protected K key;
    protected V value;
    protected Position<Entry<K,V>> pos;
    BSTEntry() { /* default constructor */ }
    BSTEntry(K k, V v, Position<Entry<K,V>> p) {
      key = k; value = v; pos = p;
    }
    public K getKey() { return key; }
    public V getValue() { return value; }
    public Position<Entry<K,V>> position() { return pos; }
  }
  /** Extracts the key of the entry at a given node of the tree. */
  protected K key(Position<Entry<K,V>> position) {
    return position.element().getKey();
  }
  /** Extracts the value of the entry at a given node of the tree. */
  protected V value(Position<Entry<K,V>> position) {
    return position.element().getValue();
  }
  /** Extracts the entry at a given node of the tree. */
  protected Entry<K,V> entry(Position<Entry<K,V>> position) {
    return position.element();
  }
```

Code Fragment 10.3: Class BinarySearchTree. (Continues in Code Fragment 10.4.)

```
/** Replaces an entry with a new entry (and reset the entry's location) */
protected V replaceEntry(Position <Entry<K,V>> pos, Entry<K,V> ent) {
  ((BSTEntry<K,V>) ent).pos = pos;
  return replace(pos, ent).getValue();
}
/** Checks whether a given key is valid. */
protected void checkKey(K key) throws InvalidKeyException {
  if(key == null) // just a simple test for now
    throw new InvalidKeyException("null key");
}
/** Checks whether a given entry is valid. */
protected void checkEntry(Entry<K,V> ent) throws InvalidEntryException {
  if(ent == null || !(ent instanceof BSTEntry))
    throw new InvalidEntryException("invalid entry");
}
/** Auxiliary method for inserting an entry at an external node */
protected Entry<K,V> insertAtExternal(Position<Entry<K,V>> v, Entry<K,V> e) {
  expandExternal(v,null,null);
  replace(v, e);
  numEntries++;
  return e;
}
/** Auxiliary method for removing an external node and its parent */
protected void removeExternal(Position<Entry<K,V>> v) {
  removeAboveExternal(v);
  numEntries--;
}
/** Auxiliary method used by find, insert, and remove. */
protected Position<Entry<K,V>> treeSearch(K key, Position<Entry<K,V>> pos) {
  if (isExternal(pos)) return pos; // key not found; return external node
  else {
    K curKey = key(pos);
    int comp = C.compare(key, curKey);
    if (comp < 0)
      return treeSearch(key, left(pos));        // search left subtree
    else if (comp > 0)
      return treeSearch(key, right(pos));       // search right subtree
    return pos;          // return internal node where key is found
  }
}
```

Code Fragment 10.4: Class BinarySearchTree. (Continues in Code Fragment 10.5.)

```
// methods of the map ADT
public int size() { return numEntries; }
public boolean isEmpty() { return size() == 0; }
public V get(K key) throws InvalidKeyException {
  checkKey(key);                    // may throw an InvalidKeyException
  Position<Entry<K,V>> curPos = treeSearch(key, root());
  actionPos = curPos;          // node where the search ended
  if (isInternal(curPos)) return value(curPos);
  return null;
}
public V put(K k, V x) throws InvalidKeyException {
  checkKey(k);          // may throw an InvalidKeyException
  Position<Entry<K,V>> insPos = treeSearch(k, root());
  BSTEntry<K,V> e = new BSTEntry<K,V>(k, x, insPos);
  actionPos = insPos; // node where the entry is being inserted
  if (isExternal(insPos)) { // we need a new node, key is new
    return insertAtExternal(insPos, e).getValue();
  }
  return replaceEntry(insPos, e); // key already exists
}
public V remove(K k) throws InvalidKeyException {
  checkKey(k);                       // may throw an InvalidKeyException
  Position<Entry<K,V>> remPos = treeSearch(k, root());
  if (isExternal(remPos)) return null; // key not found
  Entry<K,V> toReturn = entry(remPos);   // old entry
  if (isExternal(left(remPos))) remPos = left(remPos); // left easy case
  else if (isExternal(right(remPos))) remPos = right(remPos); // right easy case
  else {                            // entry is at a node with internal children
    Position<Entry<K,V>> swapPos = remPos; // find node for moving entry
    remPos = right(swapPos);
    do
      remPos = left(remPos);
    while (isInternal(remPos));
    replaceEntry(swapPos, (Entry<K,V>) parent(remPos).element());
  }
  actionPos = sibling(remPos);         // sibling of the leaf to be removed
  removeExternal(remPos);
  return toReturn.getValue();
}
}
```

Code Fragment 10.5: Class BinarySearchTree. (Continued from Code Fragment 10.4.)

10.2 AVL Trees

In the previous section, we discussed what should be an efficient map data structure, but the worst-case performance it achieves for the various operations is linear time, which is no better than the performance of list- and array-based map implementations (such as unordered lists and search tables discussed in Chapter 9). In this section, we describe a simple way of correcting this problem so as to achieve logarithmic time for all the fundamental map operations.

Definition of an AVL Tree

The simple correction is to add a rule to the binary search tree definition that will maintain a logarithmic height for the tree. The rule we consider in this section is the following **height-balance property**, which characterizes the structure of a binary search tree T in terms of the heights of its internal nodes (recall from Section 7.2.1 that the height of a node v in a tree is the length of a longest path from v to an external node):

Height-Balance Property: For every internal node v of T, the heights of the children of v differ by at most 1.

Any binary search tree T that satisfies the height-balance property is said to be an **AVL tree**, named after the initials of its inventors: Adel'son-Vel'skii and Landis. An example of an AVL tree is shown in Figure 10.7.

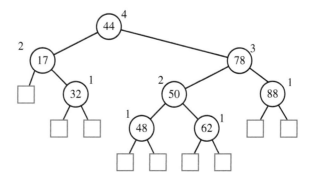

Figure 10.7: An example of an AVL tree. The keys of the entries are shown inside the nodes, and the heights of the nodes are shown next to the nodes.

An immediate consequence of the height-balance property is that a subtree of an AVL tree is itself an AVL tree. The height-balance property has also the important consequence of keeping the height small, as shown in the following proposition.

Proposition 10.2: *The height of an AVL tree storing n entries is $O(\log n)$.*

Justification: Instead of trying to find an upper bound on the height of an AVL tree directly, it turns out to be easier to work on the "inverse problem" of finding a lower bound on the minimum number of internal nodes $n(h)$ of an AVL tree with height h. We will show that $n(h)$ grows at least exponentially. From this, it will be an easy step to derive that the height of an AVL tree storing n entries is $O(\log n)$.

To start with, notice that $n(1) = 1$ and $n(2) = 2$, because an AVL tree of height 1 must have at least one internal node and an AVL tree of height 2 must have at least two internal nodes. Now, for $h \geq 3$, an AVL tree with height h and the minimum number of nodes is such that both its subtrees are AVL trees with the minimum number of nodes: one with height $h-1$ and the other with height $h-2$. Taking the root into account, we obtain the following formula that relates $n(h)$ to $n(h-1)$ and $n(h-2)$, for $h \geq 3$:

$$n(h) = 1 + n(h-1) + n(h-2). \tag{10.1}$$

At this point, the reader familiar with the properties of Fibonacci progressions (Section 2.2.3 and Exercise C-4.17) will already see that $n(h)$ is a function exponential in h. For the rest of the readers, we will proceed with our reasoning.

Formula 10.1 implies that $n(h)$ is a strictly increasing function of h. Thus, we know that $n(h-1) > n(h-2)$. Replacing $n(h-1)$ with $n(h-2)$ in Formula 10.1 and dropping the 1, we get, for $h \geq 3$,

$$n(h) > 2 \cdot n(h-2). \tag{10.2}$$

Formula 10.2 indicates that $n(h)$ at least doubles each time h increases by 2, which intuitively means that $n(h)$ grows exponentially. To show this fact in a formal way, we apply Formula 10.2 repeatedly, yielding the following series of inequalities:

$$
\begin{aligned}
n(h) &> 2 \cdot n(h-2) \\
&> 4 \cdot n(h-4) \\
&> 8 \cdot n(h-6) \\
&\ \ \vdots \\
&> 2^i \cdot n(h-2i).
\end{aligned}
\tag{10.3}
$$

That is, $n(h) > 2^i \cdot n(h-2i)$, for any integer i, such that $h - 2i \geq 1$. Since we already know the values of $n(1)$ and $n(2)$, we pick i so that $h - 2i$ is equal to either 1 or 2. That is, we pick

$$i = \left\lceil \frac{h}{2} \right\rceil - 1.$$

By substituting the above value of i in formula 10.3, we obtain, for $h \geq 3$,

$$
\begin{aligned}
n(h) \; &> \; 2^{\lceil \frac{h}{2} \rceil - 1} \cdot n\left(h - 2\left\lceil \frac{h}{2} \right\rceil + 2 \right) \\
&\geq \; 2^{\lceil \frac{h}{2} \rceil - 1} n(1) \\
&\geq \; 2^{\frac{h}{2} - 1}.
\end{aligned}
\tag{10.4}
$$

By taking logarithms of both sides of formula 10.4, we obtain

$$
\log n(h) \; > \; \frac{h}{2} - 1,
$$

from which we get

$$
h \; < \; 2\log n(h) + 2,
\tag{10.5}
$$

which implies that an AVL tree storing n entries has height at most $2\log n + 2$. ∎

By Proposition 10.2 and the analysis of binary search trees given in Section 10.1, the operation get, in a map implemented with an AVL tree, runs in time $O(\log n)$, where n is the number of entries in the map. Of course, we still have to show how to maintain the height-balance property after an insertion or removal.

10.2.1 Update Operations

The insertion and removal operations for AVL trees are similar to those for binary search trees, but with AVL trees we must perform additional computations.

Insertion

An insertion in an AVL tree T begins as in a put operation described in Section 10.1.2 for a (simple) binary search tree. Recall that this operation always inserts the new entry at a node w in T that was previously an external node, and it makes w become an internal node with operation insertAtExternal. That is, it adds two external node children to w. This action may violate the height-balance property, however, for some nodes increase their heights by one. In particular, node w, and possibly some of its ancestors, increase their heights by one. Therefore, let us describe how to restructure T to restore its height balance.

Given a binary search tree T, we say that an internal node v of T is **balanced** if the absolute value of the difference between the heights of the children of v is at most 1, and we say that it is **unbalanced** otherwise. Thus, the height-balance property characterizing AVL trees is equivalent to saying that every internal node is balanced.

Suppose that T satisfies the height-balance property, and hence is an AVL tree, prior to our inserting the new entry. As we have mentioned, after performing the operation insertAtExternal on T, the heights of some nodes of T, including w, increase. All such nodes are on the path of T from w to the root of T, and these are the only nodes of T that may have just become unbalanced. (See Figure 10.8a.) Of course, if this happens, then T is no longer an AVL tree; hence, we need a mechanism to fix the "unbalance" that we have just caused.

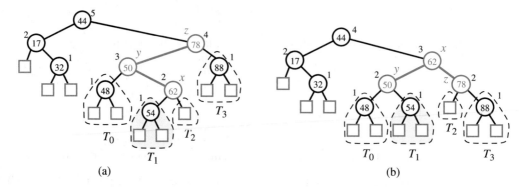

(a)   (b)

Figure 10.8: An example insertion of an entry with key 54 in the AVL tree of Figure 10.7: (a) after adding a new node for key 54, the nodes storing keys 78 and 44 become unbalanced; (b) a trinode restructuring restores the height-balance property. We show the heights of nodes next to them, and we identify the nodes x, y, and z participating in the trinode restructuring.

We restore the balance of the nodes in the binary search tree T by a simple "search-and-repair" strategy. In particular, let z be the first node we encounter in going up from w toward the root of T such that z is unbalanced. (See Figure 10.8a.) Also, let y denote the child of z with higher height (and note that node y must be an ancestor of w). Finally, let x be the child of y with higher height (there cannot be a tie and node x must be an ancestor of w). Also, node x is a grandchild of z and could be equal to w. Since z became unbalanced because of an insertion in the subtree rooted at its child y, the height of y is 2 greater than its sibling.

We now rebalance the subtree rooted at z by calling the ***trinode restructuring*** method, restructure(x), given in Code Fragment 10.6 and illustrated in Figures 10.8 and 10.9. A trinode restructuring temporarily renames the nodes x, y, and z as a, b, and c, so that a precedes b and b precedes c in an inorder traversal of T. There are four possible ways of mapping x, y, and z to a, b, and c, as shown in Figure 10.9, which are unified into one case by our relabeling. The trinode restructuring then replaces z with the node called b, makes the children of this node be a and c, and makes the children of a and c be the four previous children of x, y, and z (other than x and y) while maintaining the inorder relationships of all the nodes in T.

Algorithm restructure(*x*):

> *Input:* A node *x* of a binary search tree *T* that has both a parent *y* and a grand-parent *z*
>
> *Output:* Tree *T* after a trinode restructuring (which corresponds to a single or double rotation) involving nodes *x*, *y*, and *z*

1: Let (a, b, c) be a left-to-right (inorder) listing of the nodes *x*, *y*, and *z*, and let (T_0, T_1, T_2, T_3) be a left-to-right (inorder) listing of the four subtrees of *x*, *y*, and *z* not rooted at *x*, *y*, or *z*.
2: Replace the subtree rooted at *z* with a new subtree rooted at *b*.
3: Let *a* be the left child of *b* and let T_0 and T_1 be the left and right subtrees of *a*, respectively.
4: Let *c* be the right child of *b* and let T_2 and T_3 be the left and right subtrees of *c*, respectively.

Code Fragment 10.6: The trinode restructuring operation in a binary search tree.

The modification of a tree *T* caused by a trinode restructuring operation is often called a ***rotation***, because of the geometric way we can visualize the way it changes *T*. If $b = y$, the trinode restructuring method is called a ***single rotation***, for it can be visualized as "rotating" *y* over *z*. (See Figure 10.9a and b.) Otherwise, if $b = x$, the trinode restructuring operation is called a ***double rotation***, for it can be visualized as first "rotating" *x* over *y* and then over *z*. (See Figure 10.9c and d, and Figure 10.8.) Some computer researchers treat these two kinds of rotations as separate methods, each with two symmetric types. We have chosen, however, to unify these four types of rotations into a single trinode restructuring operation. No matter how we view it, though, the trinode restructuring method modifies parent-child relationships of $O(1)$ nodes in *T*, while preserving the inorder traversal ordering of all the nodes in *T*.

In addition to its order-preserving property, a trinode restructuring changes the heights of several nodes in *T*, so as to restore balance. Recall that we execute the method restructure(*x*) because *z*, the grandparent of *x*, is unbalanced. Moreover, this unbalance is due to one of the children of *x* now having too large a height relative to the height of *z*'s other child. As a result of a rotation, we move up the "tall" child of *x* while pushing down the "short" child of *z*. Thus, after performing restructure(*x*), all the nodes in the subtree now rooted at the node we called *b* are balanced. (See Figure 10.9.) Thus, we restore the height-balance property ***locally*** at the nodes *x*, *y*, and *z*. In addition, since after performing the new entry insertion the subtree rooted at *b* replaces the one formerly rooted at *z*, which was taller by one unit, all the ancestors of *z* that were formerly unbalanced become balanced. (See Figure 10.8.) (The justification of this fact is left as Exercise C-10.14.) Therefore, this one restructuring also restores the height-balance property ***globally***.

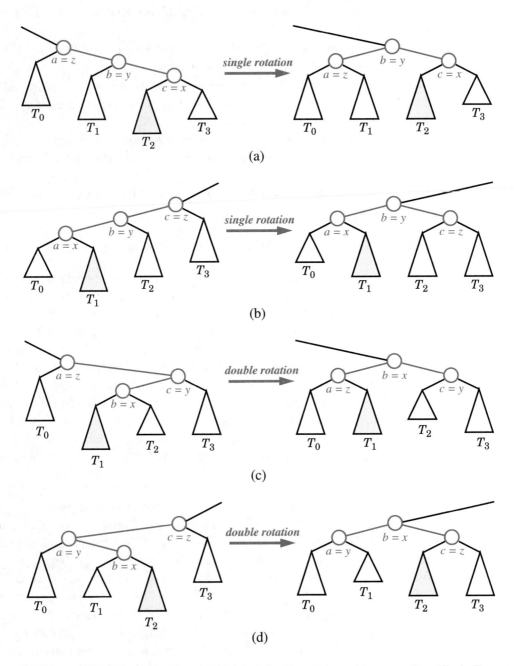

Figure 10.9: Schematic illustration of a trinode restructuring operation (Code Fragment 10.6): (a) and (b) a single rotation; (c) and (d) a double rotation.

Removal

As was the case for the put map operation, we begin the implementation of the remove map operation on an AVL tree T by using the algorithm for performing this operation on a regular binary search tree. The added difficulty in using this approach with an AVL tree is that it may violate the height-balance property. In particular, after removing an internal node with operation removeExternal and elevating one of its children into its place, there may be an unbalanced node in T on the path from the parent w of the previously removed node to the root of T. (See Figure 10.10a.) In fact, there can be one such unbalanced node at most. (The justification of this fact is left as Exercise C-10.13.)

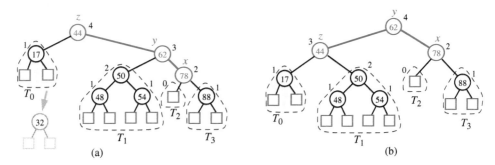

Figure 10.10: Removal of the entry with key 32 from the AVL tree of Figure 10.7: (a) after removing the node storing key 32, the root becomes unbalanced; (b) a (single) rotation restores the height-balance property.

As with insertion, we use trinode restructuring to restore balance in the tree T. In particular, let z be the first unbalanced node encountered going up from w toward the root of T. Also, let y be the child of z with larger height (note that node y is the child of z that is not an ancestor of w), and let x be the child of y defined as follows: if one of the children of y is taller than the other, let x be the taller child of y; else (both children of y have the same height), let x be the child of y on the same side as y (that is, if y is a left child, let x be the left child of y, else let x be the right child of y). In any case, we then perform a restructure(x) operation, which restores the height-balance property *locally*, at the subtree that was formerly rooted at z and is now rooted at the node we temporarily called b. (See Figure 10.10b.)

Unfortunately, this trinode restructuring may reduce the height of the subtree rooted at b by 1, which may cause an ancestor of b to become unbalanced. So, after rebalancing z, we continue walking up T looking for unbalanced nodes. If we find another, we perform a restructure operation to restore its balance, and continue marching up T looking for more, all the way to the root. Still, since the height of T is $O(\log n)$, where n is the number of entries, by Proposition 10.2, $O(\log n)$ trinode restructurings are sufficient to restore the height-balance property.

Performance of AVL Trees

We summarize the analysis of the performance of an AVL tree T as follows. Operations get, put, and remove visit the nodes along a root-to-leaf path of T, plus, possibly, their siblings, and spend $O(1)$ time per node. Thus, since the height of T is $O(\log n)$ by Proposition 10.2, each of the above operations takes $O(\log n)$ time. In Table 10.2, we summarize the performance of a map implemented with an AVL tree. We illustrate this performance in Figure 10.11.

Operation	Time
size, isEmpty	$O(1)$
get, put, remove	$O(\log n)$

Table 10.2: Performance of an n-entry map realized by an AVL tree. The space usage is $O(n)$.

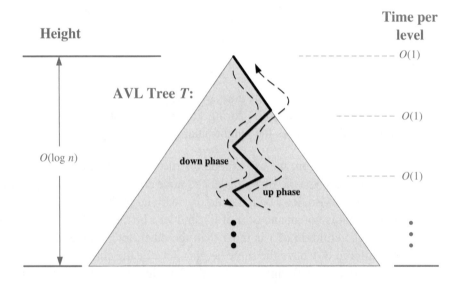

Figure 10.11: Illustrating the running time of searches and updates in an AVL tree. The time performance is $O(1)$ per level, broken into a down phase, which typically involves searching, and an up phase, which typically involves updating height values and performing local trinode restructurings (rotations).

10.2.2 Java Implementation

Let us now turn to the implementation details and analysis of using an AVL tree T with n internal nodes to implement an ordered map of n entries. The insertion and removal algorithms for T require that we are able to perform trinode restructurings and determine the difference between the heights of two sibling nodes. Regarding restructurings, we now need to make sure our underlying implementation of a binary search tree includes the method restructure(x), which performs a trinode restructuring operation (Code Fragment 10.6). It is easy to see that a restructure operation can be performed in $O(1)$ time if T is implemented with a linked structure (Section 7.3.4). In our case, we assume that the BinarySearchTree class includes this method.

Regarding height information, we can explicitly store the height of each internal node, v, in the node itself. Alternatively, we can store the **balance factor** of v at v, which is defined as the height of the left child of v minus the height of the right child of v. Thus, the balance factor of v is always equal to -1, 0, or 1, except during an insertion or removal, when it may become **temporarily** equal to -2 or $+2$. During the execution of an insertion or removal, the heights and balance factors of $O(\log n)$ nodes are affected and can be maintained in $O(\log n)$ time.

In Code Fragments 10.7 and 10.8, we show a complete Java class, AVLTree, implementing a map using an AVL tree (assuming the parent class includes an implementation of the restructure method). This class extends BinarySearchTree (Code Fragments 10.3–10.5) and includes a nested class, AVLNode, which extends the BTNode class used to represent the nodes of a binary tree. The AVLNode class defines an additional instance variable height, representing the height of the node. We get our binary tree to use this node class instead of the BTNode class simply by overriding the createNode method, which is used exclusively to create new binary tree nodes. Class AVLTree inherits methods size, isEmpty, and get from its superclass, BinarySearchTree, but overrides methods put and remove to keep the search tree balanced.

Method put (Code Fragment 10.8) starts by calling the superclass's put method, which inserts the new entry and assigns the insertion position (for example, the node storing key 54 in Figure 10.8) to the instance variable actionPos. The auxiliary method rebalance is then used to traverse the path from the insertion position to the root. This traversal updates the heights of all the nodes visited, and performs a trinode restructuring if necessary. Similarly, method remove (Code Fragment 10.8) begins by calling the superclass's remove method, which performs the removal of the entry and assigns the position replacing the deleted one to instance variable actionPos. The auxiliary method rebalance is then used to traverse the path from the removed position to the root, performing any needed restructurings.

```
/** Implementation of an AVL tree. */
public class AVLTreeMap<K,V>
  extends BinarySearchTreeMap<K,V> implements Map<K,V> {
  public AVLTreeMap(Comparator<K> c) { super(c); }
  public AVLTreeMap() { super(); }
  /** Nested class for the nodes of an AVL tree. */
  protected static class AVLNode<K,V> extends BTNode<Entry<K,V>> {
    protected int height; // we add a height field to a BTNode
    AVLNode() {/* default constructor */}
    /** Preferred constructor */
    AVLNode(Entry<K,V> element, BTPosition<Entry<K,V>> parent,
            BTPosition<Entry<K,V>> left, BTPosition<Entry<K,V>> right) {
      super(element, parent, left, right);
      height = 0;
      if (left != null)
        height = Math.max(height, 1 + ((AVLNode<K,V>) left).getHeight());
      if (right != null)
        height = Math.max(height, 1 + ((AVLNode<K,V>) right).getHeight());
    } // we assume that the parent will revise its height if needed
    public void setHeight(int h) { height = h; }
    public int getHeight() { return height; }
  }
  /** Creates a new binary search tree node (overrides super's version). */
  protected BTPosition<Entry<K,V>> createNode(Entry<K,V> element,
      BTPosition<Entry<K,V>> parent, BTPosition<Entry<K,V>> left,
      BTPosition<Entry<K,V>> right) {
    return new AVLNode<K,V>(element,parent,left,right); // now use AVL nodes
  }
  /** Returns the height of a node (call back to an AVLNode). */
  protected int height(Position<Entry<K,V>> p) {
    return ((AVLNode<K,V>) p).getHeight();
  }
  /** Sets the height of an internal node (call back to an AVLNode). */
  protected void setHeight(Position<Entry<K,V>> p) {
    ((AVLNode<K,V>) p).setHeight(1+Math.max(height(left(p)), height(right(p))));
  }
  /** Returns whether a node has balance factor between -1 and 1. */
  protected boolean isBalanced(Position<Entry<K,V>> p) {
    int bf = height(left(p)) − height(right(p));
    return ((−1 <= bf) && (bf <= 1));
  }
```

Code Fragment 10.7: Constructor and auxiliary methods of class AVLTree.

```
/** Returns a child of p with height no smaller than that of the other child */
protected Position<Entry<K,V>> tallerChild(Position<Entry<K,V>> p) {
  if (height(left(p)) > height(right(p))) return left(p);
  else if (height(left(p)) < height(right(p))) return right(p);
  // equal height children - break tie using parent's type
  if (isRoot(p)) return left(p);
  if (p == left(parent(p))) return left(p);
  else return right(p);
}
/**
 * Rebalance method called by insert and remove. Traverses the path from
 * zPos to the root. For each node encountered, we recompute its height
 * and perform a trinode restructuring if it's unbalanced.
 */
protected void rebalance(Position<Entry<K,V>> zPos) {
  if(isInternal(zPos))
     setHeight(zPos);
  while (!isRoot(zPos)) { // traverse up the tree towards the root
    zPos = parent(zPos);
    setHeight(zPos);
    if (!isBalanced(zPos)) {
      // perform a trinode restructuring at zPos's tallest grandchild
      Position<Entry<K,V>> xPos = tallerChild(tallerChild(zPos));
      zPos = restructure(xPos); // tri-node restructure (from parent class)
      setHeight(left(zPos));   // recompute heights
      setHeight(right(zPos));
      setHeight(zPos);
    }
  }
}
// overridden methods of the dictionary ADT
public V put(K k, V v) throws InvalidKeyException {
  V toReturn = super.put(k, v); // calls our createNode method if k is new
  rebalance(actionPos); // rebalance up from the insertion position
  return toReturn;
}
public V remove(K k) throws InvalidKeyException {
  V toReturn = super.remove(k);
  if (toReturn != null)   // we actually removed something
    rebalance(actionPos); // rebalance up the tree
  return toReturn;
}
} // end of AVLTree class
```

Code Fragment 10.8: Auxiliary methods tallerChild and rebalance and map methods put and remove of class AVLTree.

10.3   Splay Trees

Another way we can implement the fundamental map operations is to use a balanced search tree data structure known as a *splay tree*. This structure is conceptually quite different from the other balanced search trees we discuss in this chapter, for a splay tree does not use any explicit rules to enforce its balance. Instead, it applies a certain move-to-root operation, called *splaying*, after every access, in order to keep the search tree balanced in an amortized sense. The splaying operation is performed at the bottom-most node *x* reached during an insertion, deletion, or even a search. The surprising thing about splaying is that it allows us to guarantee an amortized running time, for insertions, deletions, and searches, that is logarithmic. The structure of a *splay tree* is simply a binary search tree *T*. In fact, there are no additional height, balance, or color labels that we associate with the nodes of this tree.

10.3.1   Splaying

Given an internal node *x* of a binary search tree *T*, we *splay* *x* by moving *x* to the root of *T* through a sequence of restructurings. The particular restructurings we perform are important, for it is not sufficient to move *x* to the root of *T* by just any sequence of restructurings. The specific operation we perform to move *x* up depends upon the relative positions of *x*, its parent *y*, and (if it exists) *x*'s grandparent *z*. There are three cases that we consider.

zig-zig: The node *x* and its parent *y* are both left children or both right children. (See Figure 10.12.) We replace *z* by *x*, making *y* a child of *x* and *z* a child of *y*, while maintaining the inorder relationships of the nodes in *T*.

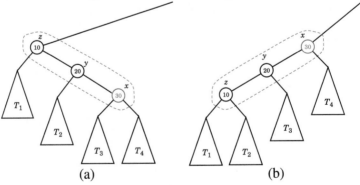

Figure 10.12: Zig-zig: (a) before; (b) after. There is another symmetric configuration where *x* and *y* are left children.

zig-zag: One of x and y is a left child and the other is a right child. (See Figure 10.13.) In this case, we replace z by x and make x have y and z as its children, while maintaining the inorder relationships of the nodes in T.

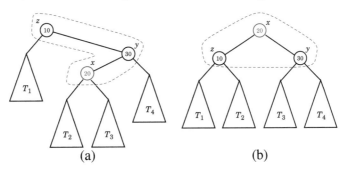

Figure 10.13: Zig-zag: (a) before; (b) after. There is another symmetric configuration where x is a right child and y is a left child.

zig: x does not have a grandparent (or we are not considering x's grandparent for some reason). (See Figure 10.14.) In this case, we rotate x over y, making x's children be the node y and one of x's former children w, so as to maintain the relative inorder relationships of the nodes in T.

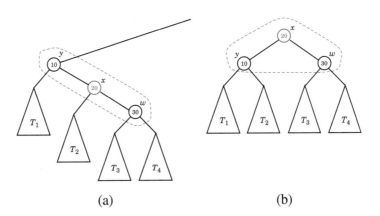

Figure 10.14: Zig: (a) before; (b) after. There is another symmetric configuration where x and w are left children.

We perform a zig-zig or a zig-zag when x has a grandparent, and we perform a zig when x has a parent but not a grandparent. A **splaying** step consists of repeating these restructurings at x until x becomes the root of T. Note that this is not the same as a sequence of simple rotations that brings x to the root. An example of the splaying of a node is shown in Figures 10.15 and 10.16.

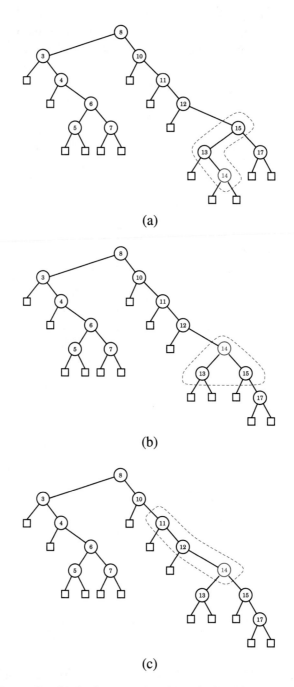

Figure 10.15: Example of splaying a node: (a) splaying the node storing 14 starts with a zig-zag; (b) after the zig-zag; (c) the next step is a zig-zig. (Continues in Figure 10.16.)

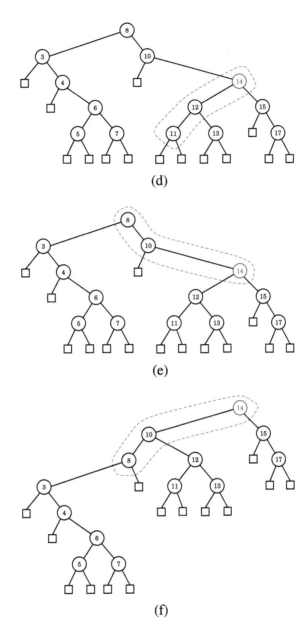

Figure 10.16: Example of splaying a node:(d) after the zig-zig; (e) the next step is again a zig-zig; (f) after the zig-zig (Continued from Figure 10.16.)

10.3.2 When to Splay

The rules that dictate when splaying is performed are as follows:

- When searching for key k, if k is found at a node x, we splay x, else we splay the parent of the external node at which the search terminates unsuccessfully. For example, the splaying in Figures 10.15 and 10.16 would be performed after searching successfully for key 14 or unsuccessfully for key 14.5.

- When inserting key k, we splay the newly created internal node where k gets inserted. For example, the splaying in Figures 10.15 and 10.16 would be performed if 14 were the newly inserted key. We show a sequence of insertions in a splay tree in Figure 10.17.

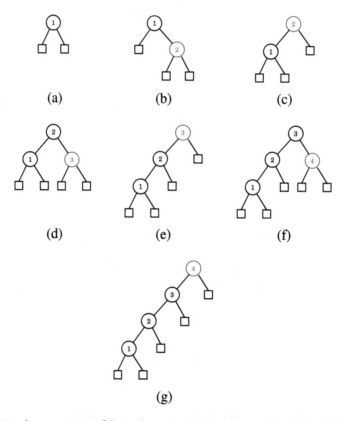

Figure 10.17: A sequence of insertions in a splay tree: (a) initial tree; (b) after inserting 2; (c) after splaying; (d) after inserting 3; (e) after splaying; (f) after inserting 4; (g) after splaying.

- When deleting a key k, we splay the parent of the node w that gets removed, that is, w is either the node storing k or one of its descendents. (Recall the removal algorithm for binary search trees.) An example of splaying following a deletion is shown in Figure 10.18.

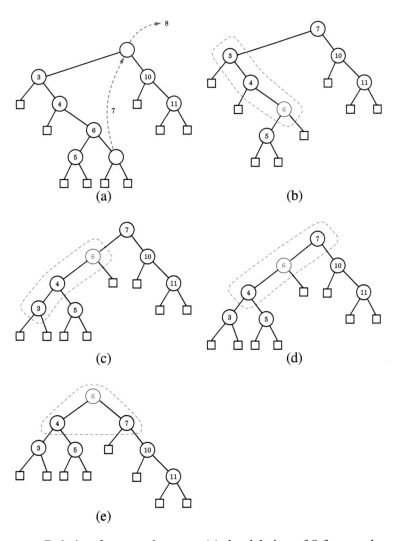

Figure 10.18: Deletion from a splay tree: (a) the deletion of 8 from node r is performed by moving to r the key of the right-most internal node v, in the left subtree of r, deleting v, and splaying the parent u of v; (b) splaying u starts with a zig-zig; (c) after the zig-zig; (d) the next step is a zig; (e) after the zig.

10.3.3   Amortized Analysis of Splaying ⋆

After a zig-zig or zig-zag, the depth of x decreases by two, and after a zig the depth of x decreases by one. Thus, if x has depth d, splaying x consists of a sequence of $\lfloor d/2 \rfloor$ zig-zigs and/or zig-zags, plus one final zig if d is odd. Since a single zig-zig, zig-zag, or zig affects a constant number of nodes, it can be done in $O(1)$ time. Thus, splaying a node x in a binary search tree T takes time $O(d)$, where d is the depth of x in T. In other words, the time for performing a splaying step for a node x is asymptotically the same as the time needed just to reach that node in a top-down search from the root of T.

Worst Case Time

In the worst case, the overall running time of a search, insertion, or deletion in a splay tree of height h is $O(h)$, since the node we splay might be the deepest node in the tree. Moreover, it is possible for h to be as large as n, as shown in Figure 10.17. Thus, from a worst-case point of view, a splay tree is not an attractive data structure.

In spite of its poor worst-case performance, a splay tree performs well in an amortized sense. That is, in a sequence of intermixed searches, insertions, and deletions, each operation takes on average logarithmic time. We perform the amortized analysis of splay trees using the accounting method.

Amortized Performance of Splay Trees

For our analysis, we note that the time for performing a search, insertion, or deletion is proportional to the time for the associated splaying. So let us consider only splaying time.

Let T be a splay tree with n keys, and let v be a node of T. We define the *size* $n(v)$ of v as the number of nodes in the subtree rooted at v. Note that this definition implies that the size of an internal node is one more than the sum of the sizes of its two children. We define the *rank* $r(v)$ of a node v as the logarithm in base 2 of the size of v, that is, $r(v) = \log(n(v))$. Clearly, the root of T has the maximum size $(2n + 1)$ and the maximum rank, $\log(2n + 1)$, while each external node has size 1 and rank 0.

We use cyber-dollars to pay for the work we perform in splaying a node x in T, and we assume that one cyber-dollar pays for a zig, while two cyber-dollars pay for a zig-zig or a zig-zag. Hence, the cost of splaying a node at depth d is d cyber-dollars. We keep a virtual account storing cyber-dollars at each internal node of T. Note that this account exists only for the purpose of our amortized analysis, and does not need to be included in a data structure implementing the splay tree T.

An Accounting Analysis of Splaying

When we perform a splaying, we pay a certain number of cyber-dollars (the exact value of the payment will be determined at the end of our analysis). We distinguish three cases:

- If the payment is equal to the splaying work, then we use it all to pay for the splaying.

- If the payment is greater than the splaying work, we deposit the excess in the accounts of several nodes.

- If the payment is less than the splaying work, we make withdrawals from the accounts of several nodes to cover the deficiency.

We show below that a payment of $O(\log n)$ cyber-dollars per operation is sufficient to keep the system working, that is, to ensure that each node keeps a nonnegative account balance.

An Accounting Invariant for Splaying

We use a scheme in which transfers are made between the accounts of the nodes to ensure that there will always be enough cyber-dollars to withdraw for paying for splaying work when needed.

In order to use the accounting method to perform our analysis of splaying, we maintain the following invariant:

> *Before and after a splaying, each node v of T has r(v) cyber-dollars in its account.*

Note that the invariant is "financially sound," since it does not require us to make a preliminary deposit to endow a tree with zero keys.

Let $r(T)$ be the sum of the ranks of all the nodes of T. To preserve the invariant after a splaying, we must make a payment equal to the splaying work plus the total change in $r(T)$. We refer to a single zig, zig-zig, or zig-zag operation in a splaying as a splaying *substep*. Also, we denote the rank of a node v of T before and after a splaying substep with $r(v)$ and $r'(v)$, respectively. The following proposition gives an upper bound on the change of $r(T)$ caused by a single splaying substep. We will repeatedly use this lemma in our analysis of a full splaying of a node to the root.

Proposition 10.3: *Let* δ *be the variation of* $r(T)$ *caused by a single splaying sub-step (a zig, zig-zig, or zig-zag) for a node* x *in* T. *We have the following:*

- $\delta \leq 3(r'(x) - r(x)) - 2$ *if the substep is a zig-zig or zig-zag.*
- $\delta \leq 3(r'(x) - r(x))$ *if the substep is a zig.*

Justification: We use the fact (see Proposition A.1, Appendix A) that, if $a > 0$, $b > 0$, and $c > a + b$,

$$\log a + \log b \leq 2\log c - 2. \tag{10.6}$$

Let us consider the change in $r(T)$ caused by each type of splaying substep.

zig-zig: (Recall Figure 10.12.) Since the size of each node is one more than the size of its two children, note that only the ranks of x, y, and z change in a zig-zig operation, where y is the parent of x and z is the parent of y. Also, $r'(x) = r(z)$, $r'(y) \leq r'(x)$, and $r(y) \geq r(x)$. Thus

$$
\begin{aligned}
\delta & = r'(x) + r'(y) + r'(z) - r(x) - r(y) - r(z) \\
& \leq r'(y) + r'(z) - r(x) - r(y) \\
& \leq r'(x) + r'(z) - 2r(x).
\end{aligned} \tag{10.7}
$$

Note that $n(x) + n'(z) \leq n'(x)$. Thus, by 10.6, $r(x) + r'(z) \leq 2r'(x) - 2$, that is,

$$r'(z) \leq 2r'(x) - r(x) - 2.$$

This inequality and 10.7 imply

$$
\begin{aligned}
\delta & \leq r'(x) + (2r'(x) - r(x) - 2) - 2r(x) \\
& \leq 3(r'(x) - r(x)) - 2.
\end{aligned}
$$

zig-zag: (Recall Figure 10.13.) Again, by the definition of size and rank, only the ranks of x, y, and z change, where y denotes the parent of x and z denotes the parent of y. Also, $r'(x) = r(z)$ and $r(x) \leq r(y)$. Thus

$$
\begin{aligned}
\delta & = r'(x) + r'(y) + r'(z) - r(x) - r(y) - r(z) \\
& \leq r'(y) + r'(z) - r(x) - r(y) \\
& \leq r'(y) + r'(z) - 2r(x).
\end{aligned} \tag{10.8}
$$

Note that $n'(y) + n'(z) \leq n'(x)$; hence, by 10.6, $r'(y) + r'(z) \leq 2r'(x) - 2$. Thus,

$$
\begin{aligned}
\delta & \leq 2r'(x) - 2 - 2r(x) \\
& \leq 3(r'(x) - r(x)) - 2.
\end{aligned}
$$

zig: (Recall Figure 10.14.) In this case, only the ranks of x and y change, where y denotes the parent of x. Also, $r'(y) \leq r(y)$ and $r'(x) \geq r(x)$. Thus

$$
\begin{aligned}
\delta & = r'(y) + r'(x) - r(y) - r(x) \\
& \leq r'(x) - r(x) \\
& \leq 3(r'(x) - r(x)).
\end{aligned}
$$

∎

Proposition 10.4: *Let T be a splay tree with root t, and let Δ be the total variation of $r(T)$ caused by splaying a node x at depth d. We have*

$$\Delta \le 3(r(t) - r(x)) - d + 2.$$

Justification: Splaying node x consists of $p = \lceil d/2 \rceil$ splaying substeps, each of which is a zig-zig or a zig-zag, except possibly the last one, which is a zig if d is odd. Let $r_0(x) = r(x)$ be the initial rank of x, and for $i = 1, \ldots, p$, let $r_i(x)$ be the rank of x after the ith substep and δ_i be the variation of $r(T)$ caused by the ith substep. By Lemma 10.3, the total variation Δ of $r(T)$ caused by splaying x is

$$
\begin{aligned}
\Delta &= \sum_{i=1}^{p} \delta_i \\
&\le \sum_{i=1}^{p} (3(r_i(x) - r_{i-1}(x)) - 2) + 2 \\
&= 3(r_p(x) - r_0(x)) - 2p + 2 \\
&\le 3(r(t) - r(x)) - d + 2.
\end{aligned}
$$
■

By Proposition 10.4, if we make a payment of $3(r(t) - r(x)) + 2$ cyber-dollars towards the splaying of node x, we have enough cyber-dollars to maintain the invariant, keeping $r(v)$ cyber-dollars at each node v in T, and pay for the entire splaying work, which costs d dollars. Since the size of the root t is $2n + 1$, its rank $r(t) = \log(2n + 1)$. In addition, we have $r(x) < r(t)$. Thus, the payment to be made for splaying is $O(\log n)$ cyber-dollars. To complete our analysis, we have to compute the cost for maintaining the invariant when a node is inserted or deleted.

When inserting a new node v into a splay tree with n keys, the ranks of all the ancestors of v are increased. Namely, let $v_0, v_1, \ldots, v_d$ be the ancestors of v, where $v_0 = v$, v_i is the parent of v_{i-1}, and v_d is the root. For $i = 1, \ldots, d$, let $n'(v_i)$ and $n(v_i)$ be the size of v_i before and after the insertion, respectively, and let $r'(v_i)$ and $r(v_i)$ be the rank of v_i before and after the insertion, respectively. We have

$$n'(v_i) = n(v_i) + 1.$$

Also, since $n(v_i) + 1 \le n(v_{i+1})$, for $i = 0, 1, \ldots, d - 1$, we have the following for each i in this range:

$$r'(v_i) = \log(n'(v_i)) = \log(n(v_i) + 1) \le \log(n(v_{i+1})) = r(v_{i+1}).$$

Thus, the total variation of $r(T)$ caused by the insertion is

$$
\begin{aligned}
\sum_{i=1}^{d} (r'(v_i) - r(v_i)) &\le r'(v_d) + \sum_{i=1}^{d-1} (r(v_{i+1}) - r(v_i)) \\
&= r'(v_d) - r(v_0) \\
&\le \log(2n + 1).
\end{aligned}
$$

Therefore, a payment of $O(\log n)$ cyber-dollars is sufficient to maintain the invariant when a new node is inserted.

When deleting a node v from a splay tree with n keys, the ranks of all the ancestors of v are decreased. Thus, the total variation of $r(T)$ caused by the deletion is negative, and we do not need to make any payment to maintain the invariant when a node is deleted. Therefore, we may summarize our amortized analysis in the following proposition (which is sometimes called the "balance proposition" for splay trees):

Proposition 10.5: *Consider a sequence of m operations on a splay tree, each one a search, insertion, or deletion, starting from a splay tree with zero keys. Also, let n_i be the number of keys in the tree after operation i, and n be the total number of insertions. The total running time for performing the sequence of operations is*

$$ O\left(m + \sum_{i=1}^{m} \log n_i \right), $$

which is $O(m \log n)$.

In other words, the amortized running time of performing a search, insertion, or deletion in a splay tree is $O(\log n)$, where n is the size of the splay tree at the time. Thus, a splay tree can achieve logarithmic-time amortized performance for implementing an ordered map ADT. This amortized performance matches the worst-case performance of AVL trees, $(2,4)$ trees, and red-black trees, but it does so using a simple binary tree that does not need any extra balance information stored at each of its nodes. In addition, splay trees have a number of other interesting properties that are not shared by these other balanced search trees. We explore one such additional property in the following proposition (which is sometimes called the "Static Optimality" proposition for splay trees):

Proposition 10.6: *Consider a sequence of m operations on a splay tree, each one a search, insertion, or deletion, starting from a splay tree T with zero keys. Also, let $f(i)$ denote the number of times the entry i is accessed in the splay tree, that is, its frequency, and let n denote the total number of entries. Assuming that each entry is accessed at least once, then the total running time for performing the sequence of operations is*

$$ O\left(m + \sum_{i=1}^{n} f(i) \log(m/f(i)) \right). $$

We omit the proof of this proposition, but it is not as hard to justify as one might imagine. The remarkable thing is that this proposition states that the amortized running time of accessing an entry i is $O(\log(m/f(i)))$.

10.4   (2,4) Trees

Some data structures we discuss in this chapter, including $(2,4)$ trees, are multi-way search trees, that is, trees with internal nodes that have two or more children. Thus, before we define $(2,4)$ trees, let us discuss multi-way search trees.

10.4.1   Multi-Way Search Trees

Recall that multi-way trees are defined so that each internal node can have many children. In this section, we discuss how multi-way trees can be used as search trees. Recall that the ***entries*** that we store in a search tree are pairs of the form (k, x), where k is the ***key*** and x is the value associated with the key. However, we do not discuss how to perform updates in multi-way search trees now, since the details for update methods depend on additional properties we wish to maintain for multi-way trees, which we discuss in Section 14.3.1.

Definition of a Multi-way Search Tree

Let v be a node of an ordered tree. We say that v is a ***d-node*** if v has d children. We define a ***multi-way search tree*** to be an ordered tree T that has the following properties, which are illustrated in Figure 10.19a:

- Each internal node of T has at least two children. That is, each internal node is a d-node such that $d \geq 2$.
- Each internal d-node v of T with children $v_1, \ldots, v_d$ stores an ordered set of $d-1$ key-value entries $(k_1, x_1), \ldots, (k_{d-1}, x_{d-1})$, where $k_1 \leq \cdots \leq k_{d-1}$.
- Let us conventionally define $k_0 = -\infty$ and $k_d = +\infty$. For each entry (k, x) stored at a node in the subtree of v rooted at v_i, $i = 1, \ldots, d$, we have that $k_{i-1} \leq k \leq k_i$.

That is, if we think of the set of keys stored at v as including the special fictitious keys $k_0 = -\infty$ and $k_d = +\infty$, then a key k stored in the subtree of T rooted at a child node v_i must be "in between" two keys stored at v. This simple viewpoint gives rise to the rule that a d-node stores $d-1$ regular keys, and it also forms the basis of the algorithm for searching in a multi-way search tree.

By the above definition, the external nodes of a multi-way search do not store any entries and serve only as "placeholders," as has been our convention with binary search trees (Section 10.1); hence, a binary search tree can be viewed as a special case of a multi-way search tree, where each internal node stores one entry and has two children. In addition, while the external nodes could be **null**, we make the simplifying assumption here that they are actual nodes that don't store anything.

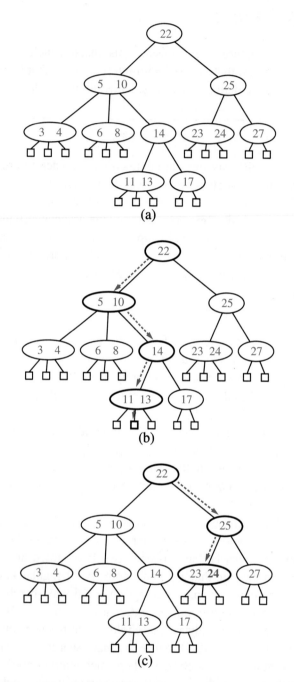

Figure 10.19: (a) A multi-way search tree T; (b) search path in T for key 12 (unsuccessful search); (c) search path in T for key 24 (successful search).

Whether internal nodes of a multi-way tree have two children or many, however, there is an interesting relationship between the number of entries and the number of external nodes.

Proposition 10.7: *An n-entry multi-way search tree has $n + 1$ external nodes.*

We leave the justification of this proposition as an exercise (C-10.17).

Searching in a Multi-Way Tree

Given a multi-way search tree T, we note that searching for an entry with key k is simple. We perform such a search by tracing a path in T starting at the root. (See Figure 10.19b and c.) When we are at a d-node v during this search, we compare the key k with the keys $k_1, \ldots, k_{d-1}$ stored at v. If $k = k_i$ for some i, the search is successfully completed. Otherwise, we continue the search in the child v_i of v such that $k_{i-1} < k < k_i$. (Recall that we conventionally define $k_0 = -\infty$ and $k_d = +\infty$.) If we reach an external node, then we know that there is no entry with key k in T, and the search terminates unsuccessfully.

Data Structures for Representing Multi-way Search Trees

In Section 7.1.3, we discuss a linked data structure for representing a general tree. This representation can also be used for a multi-way search tree. In fact, in using a general tree to implement a multi-way search tree, the only additional information that we need to store at each node is the set of entries (including keys) associated with that node. That is, we need to store with v a reference to some collection that stores the entries for v.

Recall that when we use a binary search tree to represent an ordered map M, we simply store a reference to a single entry at each internal node. In using a multi-way search tree T to represent M, we must store a reference to the ordered set of entries associated with v at each internal node v of T. This reasoning may at first seem like a circular argument, since we need a representation of an ordered map to represent an ordered map. We can avoid any circular arguments, however, by using the ***bootstrapping*** technique, where we use a previous (less advanced) solution to a problem to create a new (more advanced) solution. In this case, bootstrapping consists of representing the ordered set associated with each internal node using a map data structure that we have previously constructed (for example, a search table based on a sorted array, as shown in Section 9.3.1). In particular, assuming we already have a way of implementing ordered maps, we can realize a multi-way search tree by taking a tree T and storing such a map at each node of T.

The map we store at each node v is known as a **secondary** data structure, for we are using it to support the bigger, **primary** data structure. We denote the map stored at a node v of T as $M(v)$. The entries we store in $M(v)$ will allow us to find which child node to move to next during a search operation. Specifically, for each node v of T, with children $v_1, \ldots, v_d$ and entries $(k_1, x_1), \ldots, (k_{d-1}, x_{d-1})$, we store in the map $M(v)$ the entries

$$(k_1, (x_1, v_1)), (k_2, (x_2, v_2)), \ldots, (k_{d-1}, (x_{d-1}, v_{d-1})), (+\infty, (\emptyset, v_d)).$$

That is, an entry $(k_i, (x_i, v_i))$ of map $M(v)$ has key k_i and value (x_i, v_i). Note that the last entry stores the special key $+\infty$.

With the realization of the multi-way search tree T above, processing a d-node v while searching for an entry of T with key k can be done by performing a search operation to find the entry $(k_i, (x_i, v_i))$ in $M(v)$ with smallest key greater than or equal to k. We distinguish two cases:

- If $k < k_i$, then we continue the search by processing child v_i. (Note that if the special key $k_d = +\infty$ is returned, then k is greater than all the keys stored at node v, and we continue the search processing child v_d.)

- Otherwise ($k = k_i$), then the search terminates successfully.

Consider the space requirement for the above realization of a multi-way search tree T storing n entries. By Proposition 10.7, using any of the common realizations of ordered map (Chapter 9) for the secondary structures of the nodes of T, the overall space requirement for T is $O(n)$.

Consider next the time spent answering a search in T. The time spent at a d-node v of T during a search depends on how we realize the secondary data structure $M(v)$. If $M(v)$ is realized with a sorted array (that is, an ordered search table), then we can process v in $O(\log d)$ time. If instead $M(v)$ is realized using an unsorted list instead, then processing v takes $O(d)$ time. Let $d_{\max}$ denote the maximum number of children of any node of T, and let h denote the height of T. The search time in a multi-way search tree is either $O(h d_{\max})$ or $O(h \log d_{\max})$, depending on the specific implementation of the secondary structures at the nodes of T (the map $M(v)$). If $d_{\max}$ is a constant, the running time for performing a search is $O(h)$, irrespective of the implementation of the secondary structures.

Thus, the primary efficiency goal for a multi-way search tree is to keep the height as small as possible, that is, we want h to be a logarithmic function of n, the total number of entries stored in the map. A search tree with logarithmic height, such as this, is called a **balanced search tree**. We discuss a balanced search tree that caps $d_{\max}$ at 4 next.

Definition of a (2,4) Tree

A multi-way search tree that keeps the secondary data structures stored at each node small and also keeps the primary multi-way tree balanced is the **(2,4)** *tree*, which is sometimes called 2-4 tree or 2-3-4 tree. This data structure achieves these goals by maintaining two simple properties (see Figure 10.20):

Size Property: Every internal node has at most four children.

Depth Property: All the external nodes have the same depth.

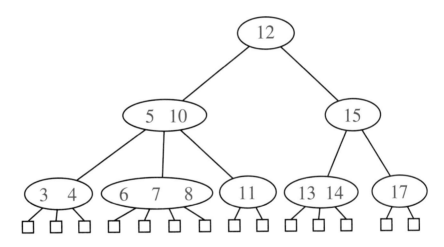

Figure 10.20: A (2,4) tree.

Again, we assume that external nodes are empty and, for the sake of simplicity, we describe our search and update methods assuming that external nodes are real nodes, although this latter requirement is not strictly needed.

Enforcing the size property for (2,4) trees keeps the nodes in the multi-way search tree simple. It also gives rise to the alternative name "2-3-4 tree," since it implies that each internal node in the tree has 2, 3, or 4 children. Another implication of this rule is that we can represent the map $M(v)$ stored at each internal node v using an unordered list or an ordered array, and still achieve $O(1)$-time performance for all operations (since $d_{max} = 4$). The depth property, on the other hand, enforces an important bound on the height of a (2,4) tree.

Proposition 10.8: *The height of a* $(2,4)$ *tree storing* n *entries is* $O(\log n)$.

Justification: Let h be the height of a $(2,4)$ tree T storing n entries. We justify the proposition by showing that the claims

$$\frac{1}{2}\log(n+1) \leq h \qquad\qquad (10.9)$$

and

$$h \leq \log(n+1) \qquad\qquad (10.10)$$

are true.

To justify these claims note first that, by the size property, we can have at most 4 nodes at depth 1, at most 4^2 nodes at depth 2, and so on. Thus, the number of external nodes in T is at most 4^h. Likewise, by the depth property and the definition of a $(2,4)$ tree, we must have at least 2 nodes at depth 1, at least 2^2 nodes at depth 2, and so on. Thus, the number of external nodes in T is at least 2^h. In addition, by Proposition 10.7, the number of external nodes in T is $n+1$. Therefore, we obtain

$$2^h \leq n+1$$

and

$$n+1 \leq 4^h.$$

Taking the logarithm in base 2 of each of the above terms, we get that

$$h \leq \log(n+1)$$

and

$$\log(n+1) \leq 2h,$$

which justifies our claims (10.9 and 10.10).   ∎

Proposition 10.8 states that the size and depth properties are sufficient for keeping a multi-way tree balanced (Section 10.4.1). Moreover, this proposition implies that performing a search in a $(2,4)$ tree takes $O(\log n)$ time and that the specific realization of the secondary structures at the nodes is not a crucial design choice, since the maximum number of children d_{max} is a constant (4). We can, for example, use a simple ordered map implementation, such as an array-list search table, for each secondary structure.

10.4.2 Update Operations for (2,4) Trees

Maintaining the size and depth properties requires some effort after performing insertions and removals in a $(2,4)$ tree, however. We discuss these operations next.

Insertion

To insert a new entry (k,x), with key k, into a $(2,4)$ tree T, we first perform a search for k. Assuming that T has no entry with key k, this search terminates unsuccessfully at an external node z. Let v be the parent of z. We insert the new entry into node v and add a new child w (an external node) to v on the left of z. That is, we add entry (k,x,w) to the map $M(v)$.

Our insertion method preserves the depth property, since we add a new external node at the same level as existing external nodes. Nevertheless, it may violate the size property. Indeed, if a node v was previously a 4-node, then it may become a 5-node after the insertion, which causes the tree T to no longer be a $(2,4)$ tree. This type of violation of the size property is called an ***overflow*** at node v, and it must be resolved in order to restore the properties of a $(2,4)$ tree. Let $v_1,\dots,v_5$ be the children of v, and let $k_1,\dots,k_4$ be the keys stored at v. To remedy the overflow at node v, we perform a ***split*** operation on v as follows (see Figure 10.21):

- Replace v with two nodes v' and v'', where
  - v' is a 3-node with children v_1,v_2,v_3 storing keys k_1 and k_2
  - v'' is a 2-node with children v_4,v_5 storing key k_4.

- If v was the root of T, create a new root node u; else, let u be the parent of v.
- Insert key k_3 into u and make v' and v'' children of u, so that if v was child i of u, then v' and v'' become children i and $i+1$ of u, respectively.

We show a sequence of insertions in a $(2,4)$ tree in Figure 10.22.

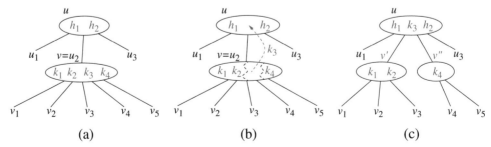

Figure 10.21: A node split: (a) overflow at a 5-node v; (b) the third key of v inserted into the parent u of v; (c) node v replaced with a 3-node v' and a 2-node v''.

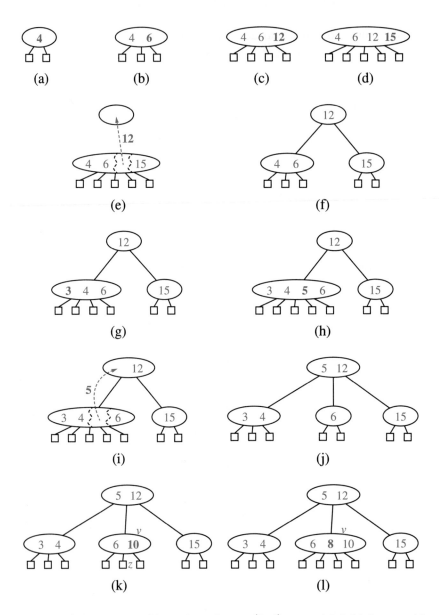

Figure 10.22: A sequence of insertions into a $(2,4)$ tree: (a) initial tree with one entry; (b) insertion of 6; (c) insertion of 12; (d) insertion of 15, which causes an overflow; (e) split, which causes the creation of a new root node; (f) after the split; (g) insertion of 3; (h) insertion of 5, which causes an overflow; (i) split; (j) after the split; (k) insertion of 10; (l) insertion of 8.

Analysis of Insertion in a $(2,4)$ Tree

A split operation affects a constant number of nodes of the tree and $O(1)$ entries stored at such nodes. Thus, it can be implemented to run in $O(1)$ time.

As a consequence of a split operation on node v, a new overflow may occur at the parent u of v. If such an overflow occurs, it triggers in turn a split at node u. (See Figure 10.23.) A split operation either eliminates the overflow or propagates it into the parent of the current node. Hence, the number of split operations is bounded by the height of the tree, which is $O(\log n)$ by Proposition 10.8. Therefore, the total time to perform an insertion in a $(2,4)$ tree is $O(\log n)$.

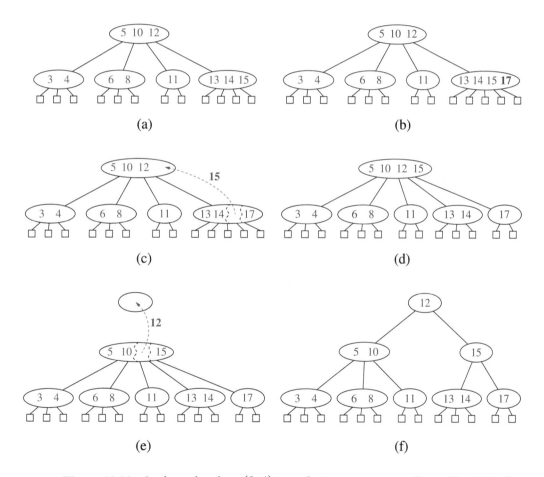

Figure 10.23: An insertion in a $(2,4)$ tree that causes a cascading split: (a) before the insertion; (b) insertion of 17, causing an overflow; (c) a split; (d) after the split a new overflow occurs; (e) another split, creating a new root node; (f) final tree.

Removal

Let us now consider the removal of an entry with key k from a $(2,4)$ tree T. We begin such an operation by performing a search in T for an entry with key k. Removing such an entry from a $(2,4)$ tree can always be reduced to the case where the entry to be removed is stored at a node v whose children are external nodes. Suppose, for instance, that the entry with key k that we wish to remove is stored in the ith entry (k_i, x_i) at a node z that has only internal-node children. In this case, we swap the entry (k_i, x_i) with an appropriate entry that is stored at a node v with external-node children as follows (see Figure 10.24d):

1. We find the right-most internal node v in the subtree rooted at the ith child of z, noting that the children of node v are all external nodes.

2. We swap the entry (k_i, x_i) at z with the last entry of v.

Once we ensure that the entry to remove is stored at a node v with only external-node children (because either it was already at v or we swapped it into v), we simply remove the entry from v (that is, from the map $M(v)$) and remove the ith external node of v.

Removing an entry (and a child) from a node v as described above preserves the depth property, for we always remove an external node child from a node v with only external-node children. However, in removing such an external node we may violate the size property at v. Indeed, if v was previously a 2-node, then it becomes a 1-node with no entries after the removal (Figure 10.24d and e), which is not allowed in a $(2,4)$ tree. This type of violation of the size property is called an **underflow** at node v. To remedy an underflow, we check whether an immediate sibling of v is a 3-node or a 4-node. If we find such a sibling w, then we perform a **transfer** operation, in which we move a child of w to v, a key of w to the parent u of v and w, and a key of u to v. (See Figure 10.24b and c.) If v has only one sibling, or if both immediate siblings of v are 2-nodes, then we perform a **fusion** operation, in which we merge v with a sibling, creating a new node v', and move a key from the parent u of v to v'. (See Figure 10.25e and f.)

A fusion operation at node v may cause a new underflow to occur at the parent u of v, which in turn triggers a transfer or fusion at u. (See Figure 10.25.) Hence, the number of fusion operations is bounded by the height of the tree, which is $O(\log n)$ by Proposition 10.8. If an underflow propagates all the way up to the root, then the root is simply deleted. (See Figure 10.25c and d.) We show a sequence of removals from a $(2,4)$ tree in Figures 10.24 and 10.25.

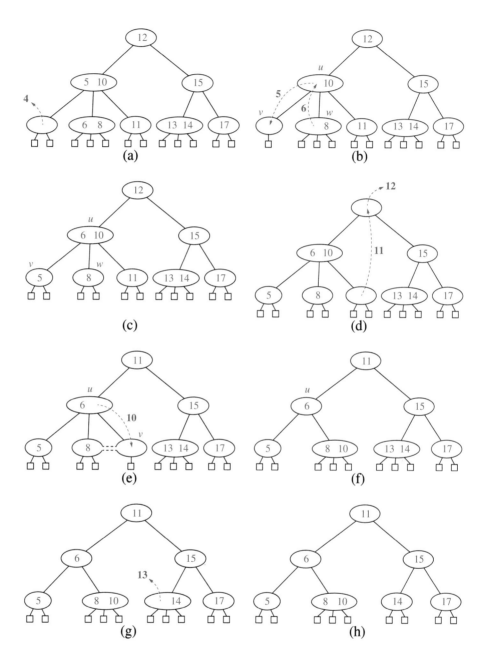

Figure 10.24: A sequence of removals from a $(2,4)$ tree: (a) removal of 4, causing an underflow; (b) a transfer operation; (c) after the transfer operation; (d) removal of 12, causing an underflow; (e) a fusion operation; (f) after the fusion operation; (g) removal of 13; (h) after removing 13.

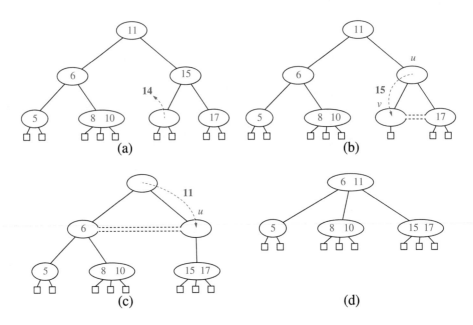

Figure 10.25: A propagating sequence of fusions in a $(2,4)$ tree: (a) removal of 14, which causes an underflow; (b) fusion, which causes another underflow; (c) second fusion operation, which causes the root to be removed; (d) final tree.

Performance of $(2,4)$ Trees

Table 10.3 summarizes the running times of the main operations of a map realized with a $(2,4)$ tree. The time complexity analysis is based on the following:

- The height of a $(2,4)$ tree storing n entries is $O(\log n)$, by Proposition 10.8.
- A split, transfer, or fusion operation takes $O(1)$ time.
- A search, insertion, or removal of an entry visits $O(\log n)$ nodes.

Operation	Time
size, isEmpty	$O(1)$
get, put, remove	$O(\log n)$

Table 10.3: Performance of an *n*-entry map realized by a $(2,4)$ tree. The space usage is $O(n)$.

Thus, $(2,4)$ trees provide for fast map search and update operations. $(2,4)$ trees also have an interesting relationship to the data structure we discuss next.

10.5   Red-Black Trees

Although AVL trees and $(2,4)$ trees have a number of nice properties, there are some map applications for which they are not well suited. For instance, AVL trees may require many restructure operations (rotations) to be performed after a removal, and $(2,4)$ trees may require many fusing or split operations to be performed after either an insertion or removal. The data structure we discuss in this section, the red-black tree, does not have these drawbacks, however, as it requires that only $O(1)$ structural changes be made after an update in order to stay balanced.

A ***red-black tree*** is a binary search tree (see Section 10.1) with nodes colored red and black in a way that satisfies the following properties:

Root Property: The root is black.

External Property: Every external node is black.

Internal Property: The children of a red node are black.

Depth Property: All the external nodes have the same ***black depth***, defined as the number of black ancestors minus one. (Recall that a node is an ancestor of itself.)

An example of a red-black tree is shown in Figure 10.26.

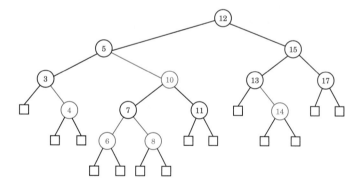

Figure 10.26: Red-black tree associated with the $(2,4)$ tree of Figure 10.20. Each external node of this red-black tree has 4 black ancestors (including itself); hence, it has black depth 3. We use the color blue instead of red. Also, we use the convention of giving an edge of the tree the same color as the child node.

As for previous types of search trees, we assume that entries are stored at the internal nodes of a red-black tree, with the external nodes being empty placeholders. Also, we assume that the external nodes are actual nodes, but we note that, at the expense of slightly more complicated methods, external nodes could be **null**.

We can make the red-black tree definition more intuitive by noting an interesting correspondence between red-black trees and $(2,4)$ trees, as illustrated in Figure 10.27. Namely, given a red-black tree, we can construct a corresponding $(2,4)$ tree by merging every red node v into its parent and storing the entry from v at its parent. Conversely, we can transform any $(2,4)$ tree into a corresponding red-black tree by coloring each node black and performing the following transformation for each internal node v:

- If v is a 2-node, then keep the (black) children of v as is.

- If v is a 3-node, then create a new red node w, give v's first two (black) children to w, and make w and v's third child be the two children of v.

- If v is a 4-node, then create two new red nodes w and z, give v's first two (black) children to w, give v's last two (black) children to z, and make w and z be the two children of v.

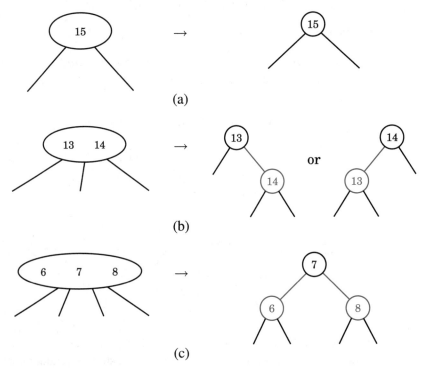

Figure 10.27: Correspondence between a $(2,4)$ tree and a red-black tree: (a) 2-node; (b) 3-node; (c) 4-node.

The correspondence between $(2,4)$ trees and red-black trees provides important intuition that we will use in our discussion of how to perform updates in red-black trees. In fact, the update algorithms for red-black trees are mysteriously complex without this intuition.

Proposition 10.9: *The height of a red-black tree storing n entries is $O(\log n)$.*

Justification: Let T be a red-black tree storing n entries, and let h be the height of T. We justify this proposition by establishing the following fact:

$$\log(n+1) \leq h \leq 2\log(n+1).$$

Let d be the common black depth of all the external nodes of T. Let T' be the $(2,4)$ tree associated with T, and let h' be the height of T'. Because of the correspondence between red-black trees and $(2,4)$ trees, we know that $h' = d$. Hence, by Proposition 10.8, $d = h' \leq \log(n+1)$. By the internal node property, $h \leq 2d$. Thus, we obtain $h \leq 2\log(n+1)$. The other inequality, $\log(n+1) \leq h$, follows from Proposition 7.10 and the fact that T has n internal nodes. ∎

We assume that a red-black tree is realized with a linked structure for binary trees (Section 7.3.4), in which we store a map entry and a color indicator at each node. Thus the space requirement for storing n keys is $O(n)$. The algorithm for searching in a red-black tree T is the same as that for a standard binary search tree (Section 10.1). Thus, searching in a red-black tree takes $O(\log n)$ time.

10.5.1 Update Operations

Performing the update operations in a red-black tree is similar to that of a binary search tree, except that we must additionally restore the color properties.

Insertion

Now consider the insertion of an entry with key k into a red-black tree T, keeping in mind the correspondence between T and its associated $(2,4)$ tree T' and the insertion algorithm for T'. The algorithm initially proceeds as in a binary search tree (Section 10.1.2). Namely, we search for k in T until we reach an external node of T, and we replace this node with an internal node z, storing (k,x) and having two external-node children. If z is the root of T, we color z black, else we color z red. We also color the children of z black. This action corresponds to inserting (k,x) into a node of the $(2,4)$ tree T' with external children. In addition, this action preserves the root, external, and depth properties of T, but it may violate the internal property. Indeed, if z is not the root of T and the parent v of z is red, then we have a parent and a child (namely, v and z) that are both red. Note that by the root property, v cannot be the root of T, and by the internal property (which was previously satisfied), the parent u of v must be black. Since z and its parent are red, but z's grandparent u is black, we call this violation of the internal property a ***double red*** at node z.

To remedy a double red, we consider two cases.

Case 1: *The Sibling* **w** *of* **v** *is Black.* (See Figure 10.28.) In this case, the double red denotes the fact that we have created in our red-black tree T a malformed replacement for a corresponding 4-node of the $(2,4)$ tree T', which has as its children the four black children of u, v, and z. Our malformed replacement has one red node (v) that is the parent of another red node (z), while we want it to have the two red nodes as siblings instead. To fix this problem, we perform a ***trinode restructuring*** of T. The trinode restructuring is done by the operation restructure(z), which consists of the following steps (see again Figure 10.28; this operation is also discussed in Section 10.2):

- Take node z, its parent v, and grandparent u, and temporarily relabel them as a, b, and c, in left-to-right order, so that a, b, and c will be visited in this order by an inorder tree traversal.
- Replace the grandparent u with the node labeled b, and make nodes a and c the children of b, keeping inorder relationships unchanged.

After performing the restructure(z) operation, we color b black and we color a and c red. Thus, the restructuring eliminates the double red problem.

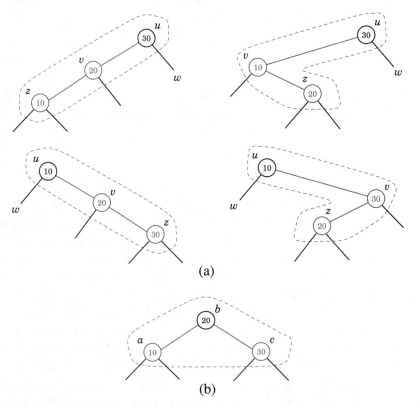

(a)

(b)

Figure 10.28: Restructuring a red-black tree to remedy a double red: (a) the four configurations for u, v, and z before restructuring; (b) after restructuring.

Case 2: *The Sibling* w *of* v *is Red.* (See Figure 10.29.) In this case, the double red denotes an overflow in the corresponding $(2,4)$ tree T. To fix the problem, we perform the equivalent of a split operation. Namely, we do a ***recoloring***: we color v and w black and their parent u red (unless u is the root, in which case, it is colored black). It is possible that, after such a recoloring, the double red problem reappears, albeit higher up in the tree T, since u may have a red parent. If the double red problem reappears at u, then we repeat the consideration of the two cases at u. Thus, a recoloring either eliminates the double red problem at node z, or propagates it to the grandparent u of z. We continue going up T performing recolorings until we finally resolve the double red problem (with either a final recoloring or a trinode restructuring). Thus, the number of recolorings caused by an insertion is no more than half the height of tree T, that is, no more than $\log(n+1)$ by Proposition 10.9.

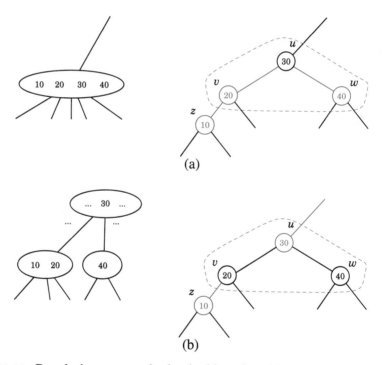

(a)

(b)

Figure 10.29: Recoloring to remedy the double red problem: (a) before recoloring and the corresponding 5-node in the associated $(2,4)$ tree before the split; (b) after the recoloring (and corresponding nodes in the associated $(2,4)$ tree after the split).

Figures 10.30 and 10.31 show a sequence of insertion operations in a red-black tree.

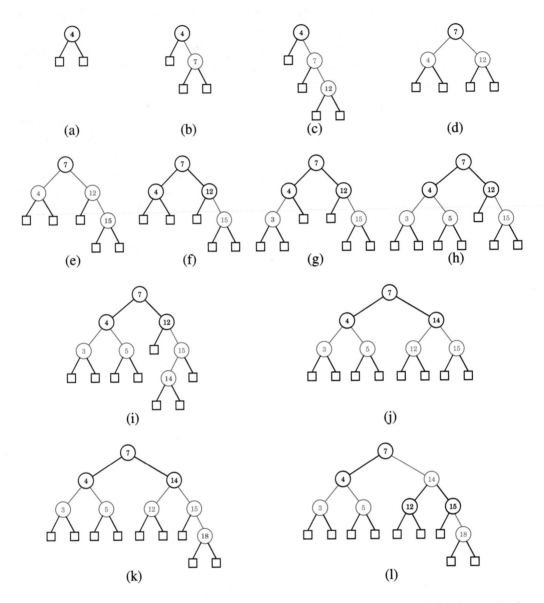

Figure 10.30: A sequence of insertions in a red-black tree: (a) initial tree; (b) insertion of 7; (c) insertion of 12, which causes a double red; (d) after restructuring; (e) insertion of 15, which causes a double red; (f) after recoloring (the root remains black); (g) insertion of 3; (h) insertion of 5; (i) insertion of 14, which causes a double red; (j) after restructuring; (k) insertion of 18, which causes a double red; (l) after recoloring. (Continues in Figure 10.31.)

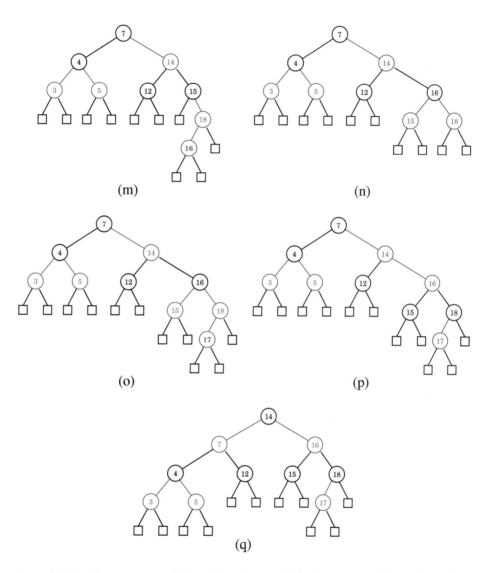

Figure 10.31: A sequence of insertions in a red-black tree: (m) insertion of 16, which causes a double red; (n) after restructuring; (o) insertion of 17, which causes a double red; (p) after recoloring there is again a double red, to be handled by a restructuring; (q) after restructuring. (Continued from Figure 10.30.)

The cases for insertion imply an interesting property for red-black trees. Namely, since the Case 1 action eliminates the double-red problem with a single trinode restructuring and the Case 2 action performs no restructuring operations, at most one restructuring is needed in a red-black tree insertion. By the above analysis and the fact that a restructuring or recoloring takes $O(1)$ time, we have the following:

Proposition 10.10: *The insertion of a key-value entry in a red-black tree storing* n *entries can be done in* $O(\log n)$ *time and requires* $O(\log n)$ *recolorings and one trinode restructuring (a* restructure *operation).*

Removal

Suppose now that we are asked to remove an entry with key k from a red-black tree T. Removing such an entry initially proceeds as for a binary search tree (Section 10.1.2). First, we search for a node u storing such an entry. If node u does not have an external child, we find the internal node v following u in the inorder traversal of T, move the entry at v to u, and perform the removal at v. Thus, we may consider only the removal of an entry with key k stored at a node v with an external child w. Also, as we did for insertions, we keep in mind the correspondence between red-black tree T and its associated $(2,4)$ tree T' (and the removal algorithm for T').

To remove the entry with key k from a node v of T with an external child w we proceed as follows. Let r be the sibling of w and x be the parent of v. We remove nodes v and w, and make r a child of x. If v was red (hence r is black) or r is red (hence v was black), we color r black and we are done. If, instead, r is black and v was black, then, to preserve the depth property, we give r a fictitious ***double black*** color. We now have a color violation, called the double black problem. A double black in T denotes an underflow in the corresponding $(2,4)$ tree T'. Recall that x is the parent of the double black node r. To remedy the double-black problem at r, we consider three cases.

Case 1: *The Sibling* **y** *of* r *is Black and has a Red Child* **z**. (See Figure 10.32.) Resolving this case corresponds to a transfer operation in the $(2,4)$ tree T'. We perform a ***trinode restructuring*** by means of operation restructure(z). Recall that the operation restructure(z) takes the node z, its parent y, and grandparent x, labels them temporarily left to right as a, b, and c, and replaces x with the node labeled b, making it the parent of the other two. (See also the description of restructure in Section 10.2.) We color a and c black, give b the former color of x, and color r black. This trinode restructuring eliminates the double black problem. Hence, at most one restructuring is performed in a removal operation in this case.

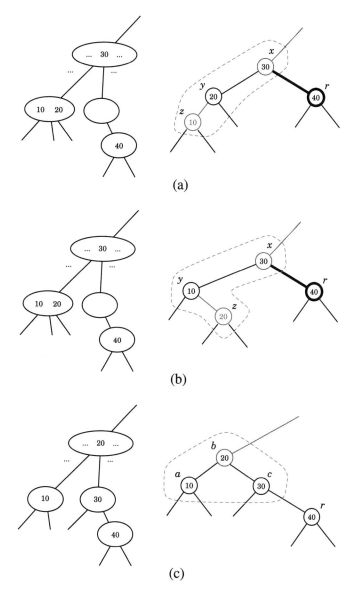

Figure 10.32: Restructuring of a red-black tree to remedy the double black problem: (a) and (b) configurations before the restructuring, where r is a right child and the associated nodes in the corresponding $(2,4)$ tree before the transfer (two other symmetric configurations where r is a left child are possible); (c) configuration after the restructuring and the associated nodes in the corresponding $(2,4)$ tree after the transfer. The grey color for node x in parts (a) and (b) and for node b in part (c) denotes the fact that this node may be colored either red or black.

Case 2: ***The Sibling y of r is Black and Both Children of y are Black.*** (See Figures 10.33 and 10.34.) Resolving this case corresponds to a fusion operation in the corresponding $(2,4)$ tree T'. We do a ***recoloring***; we color r black, we color y red, and, if x is red, we color it black (Figure 10.33); otherwise, we color x ***double black*** (Figure 10.34). Hence, after this recoloring, the double black problem may reappear at the parent x of r. (See Figure 10.34.) That is, this recoloring either eliminates the double black problem or propagates it into the parent of the current node. We then repeat a consideration of these three cases at the parent. Thus, since Case 1 performs a trinode restructuring operation and stops (and, as we will soon see, Case 3 is similar), the number of recolorings caused by a removal is no more than $\log(n+1)$.

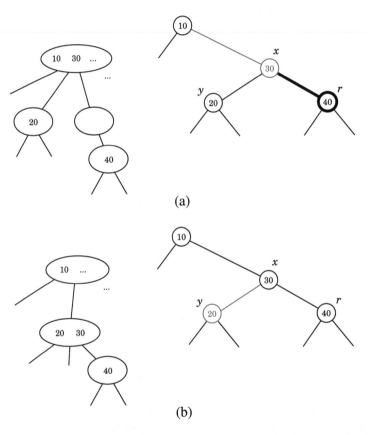

Figure 10.33: Recoloring of a red-black tree that fixes the double black problem: (a) before the recoloring and corresponding nodes in the associated $(2,4)$ tree before the fusion (other similar configurations are possible); (b) after the recoloring and corresponding nodes in the associated $(2,4)$ tree after the fusion.

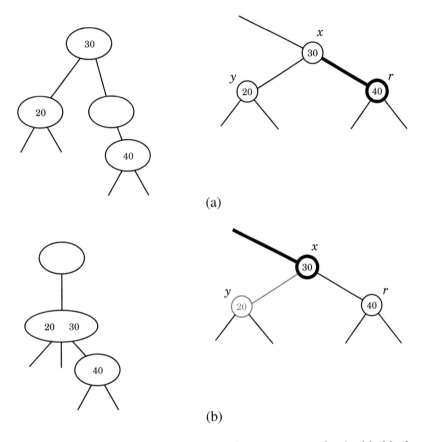

(a)

(b)

Figure 10.34: Recoloring of a red-black tree that propagates the double black problem: (a) configuration before the recoloring and corresponding nodes in the associated $(2,4)$ tree before the fusion (other similar configurations are possible); (b) configuration after the recoloring and corresponding nodes in the associated $(2,4)$ tree after the fusion.

Case 3: *The Sibling* y *of* r *is Red.* (See Figure 10.35.) In this case, we perform an ***adjustment*** operation, as follows. If y is the right child of x, let z be the right child of y; otherwise, let z be the left child of y. Execute the trinode restructuring operation restructure(z), which makes y the parent of x. Color y black and x red. An adjustment corresponds to choosing a different representation of a 3-node in the $(2,4)$ tree T'. After the adjustment operation, the sibling of r is black, and either Case 1 or Case 2 applies, with a different meaning of x and y. Note that if Case 2 applies, the double-black problem cannot reappear. Thus, to complete Case 3 we make one more application of either Case 1 or Case 2 above and we are done. Therefore, at most one adjustment is performed in a removal operation.

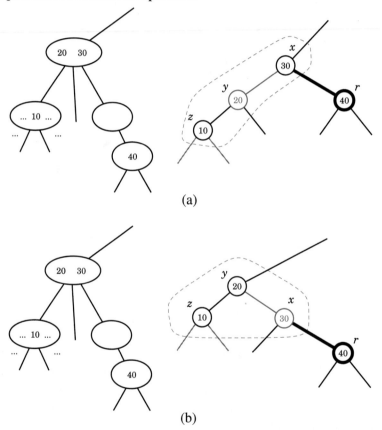

Figure 10.35: Adjustment of a red-black tree in the presence of a double black problem: (a) configuration before the adjustment and corresponding nodes in the associated $(2,4)$ tree (a symmetric configuration is possible); (b) configuration after the adjustment with the same corresponding nodes in the associated $(2,4)$ tree.

From the above algorithm description, we see that the tree updating needed after a removal involves an upward march in the tree T, while performing at most a constant amount of work (in a restructuring, recoloring, or adjustment) per node. Thus, since any changes we make at a node in T during this upward march takes $O(1)$ time (because it affects a constant number of nodes), we have the following:

Proposition 10.11: *The algorithm for removing an entry from a red-black tree with n entries takes $O(\log n)$ time and performs $O(\log n)$ recolorings and at most one adjustment plus one additional trinode restructuring. Thus, it performs at most* two *restructure operations.*

In Figures 10.36 and 10.37, we show a sequence of removal operations on a red-black tree. We illustrate Case 1 restructurings in Figure 10.36c and d. We illustrate Case 2 recolorings at several places in Figures 10.36 and 10.37. Finally, in Figure 10.37i and j, we show an example of a Case 3 adjustment.

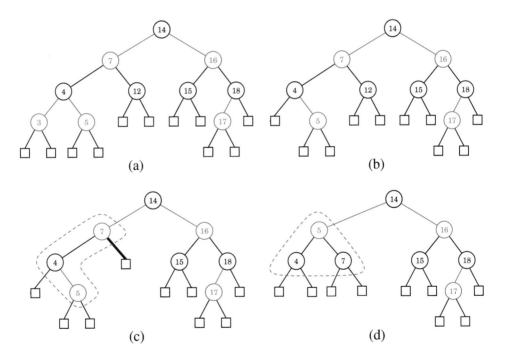

Figure 10.36: Sequence of removals from a red-black tree: (a) initial tree; (b) removal of 3; (c) removal of 12, causing a double black (handled by restructuring); (d) after restructuring. (Continues in Figure 10.37.)

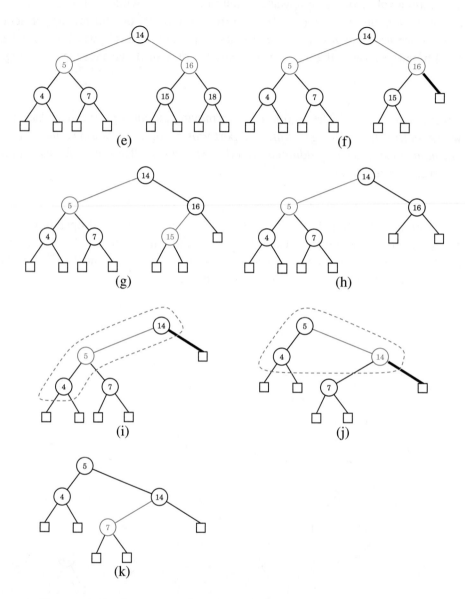

Figure 10.37: Sequence of removals in a red-black tree (continued): (e) removal of 17; (f) removal of 18, causing a double black (handled by recoloring); (g) after recoloring; (h) removal of 15; (i) removal of 16, causing a double black (handled by an adjustment); (j) after the adjustment the double black needs to be handled by a recoloring; (k) after the recoloring. (Continued from Figure 10.36.)

Performance of Red-Black Trees

Table 10.4 summarizes the running times of the main operations of a map realized by means of a red-black tree. We illustrate the justification for these bounds in Figure 10.38.

Operation	Time
size, isEmpty	$O(1)$
get, put, remove	$O(\log n)$

Table 10.4: Performance of an n-entry map realized by a red-black tree. The space usage is $O(n)$.

Figure 10.38: Illustrating the running time of searches and updates in a red-black tree. The time performance is $O(1)$ per level, broken into a down phase, which typically involves searching, and an up phase, which typically involves recolorings and performing local trinode restructurings (rotations).

Thus, a red-black tree achieves logarithmic worst-case running times for both searching and updating in a map. The red-black tree data structure is slightly more complicated than its corresponding $(2,4)$ tree. Even so, a red-black tree has a conceptual advantage that only a constant number of trinode restructurings are ever needed to restore the balance in a red-black tree after an update.

10.5.2   Java Implementation

Java provides an implementation of the java.util.Map and java.util.NavigableMap
interfaces using a red-black tree, in a class, java.util.TreeMap. It guarantees $O(\log n)$
time worst-case performance for the get, put, and remove methods and related operations.

In Code Fragments 10.9 through 10.11, we show the major portions of a Java
implementation of a map realized by means of a red-black tree. The main class
includes a nested class, RBNode, shown in Code Fragment 10.9, which extends
the BTNode class used to represent a key-value entry of a binary search tree. It
defines an additional instance variable isRed, representing the color of the node,
and methods to set and return it.

```
/** Realization of a dictionary by means of a red-black tree. */
public class RBTreeMap<K,V>
   extends BinarySearchTreeMap<K,V> implements Map<K,V> {
   public RBTreeMap() { super(); }
   public RBTreeMap(Comparator<K> C) { super(C); }
   /** Nested class for the nodes of a red-black tree */
   protected static class RBNode<K,V> extends BTNode<Entry<K,V>> {
      protected boolean isRed; // we add a color field to a BTNode
      RBNode() {/* default constructor */}
      /** Preferred constructor */
      RBNode(Entry<K,V> element, BTPosition<Entry<K,V>> parent,
            BTPosition<Entry<K,V>> left, BTPosition<Entry<K,V>> right) {
         super(element, parent, left, right);
         isRed = false;
      }
      public boolean isRed() {return isRed;}
      public void makeRed() {isRed = true;}
      public void makeBlack() {isRed = false;}
      public void setColor(boolean color) {isRed = color;}
   }
```

Code Fragment 10.9: Instance variables, nested class, and constructor for RBTree.

Class RBTree (Code Fragments 10.9 through 10.11) extends BinarySearchTree
(Code Fragments 10.3 through 10.5). We assume the parent class supports the
method restructure for performing trinode restructurings (rotations); its implementation is left as an exercise (P-10.4). Class RBTree inherits methods size, isEmpty,
and get from BinarySearchTree but overrides methods put and remove. It implements these two operations by first calling the corresponding method of the parent
class and then remedying any color violations that this update may have caused.
Several auxiliary methods of class RBTree are not shown, but their names suggest
their meanings and their implementations are straightforward.

```
/** Creates a new tree node. */
protected BTPosition<Entry<K,V>> createNode(Entry<K,V> element,
    BTPosition<Entry<K,V>> parent, BTPosition<Entry<K,V>> left,
    BTPosition<Entry<K,V>> right) {
  return new RBNode<K,V>(element,parent,left,right); // a red-black node
}
public V put(K k, V x) throws InvalidKeyException {
  V toReturn = super.put(k, x);
  Position<Entry<K,V>> posZ = actionPos; // start at the insertion position
  setRed(posZ);
  if (isRoot(posZ))
    setBlack(posZ);
  else
    remedyDoubleRed(posZ); // fix a double-red color violation
  return toReturn;
}
protected void remedyDoubleRed(Position<Entry<K,V>> posZ) {
  Position<Entry<K,V>> posV = parent(posZ);
  if (isRoot(posV))
    return;
  if (!isPosRed(posV))
    return;
  // we have a double red: posZ and posV
  if (!isPosRed(sibling(posV)))  { // Case 1: trinode restructuring
    posV = restructure(posZ);
    setBlack(posV);
    setRed(left(posV));
    setRed(right(posV));
  }
  else  { // Case 2: recoloring
    setBlack(posV);
    setBlack(sibling(posV));
    Position<Entry<K,V>> posU = parent(posV);
    if (isRoot(posU))
      return;
    setRed(posU);
    remedyDoubleRed(posU);
  }
}
```

Code Fragment 10.10: The map ADT method put and auxiliary methods createN-ode and remedyDoubleRed of class RBTree.

Methods put (Code Fragment 10.10) and remove (Code Fragment 10.11) call the corresponding methods of the superclass first and then rebalance the tree by calling auxiliary methods to perform rotations along the path from the update position (given by the actionPos variable inherited from the superclass) to the root.

```
        public V remove(K k) throws InvalidKeyException {
          V toReturn = super.remove(k);
          Position<Entry<K,V>> posR = actionPos;
          if (toReturn != null) {
            if (wasParentRed(posR) || isRoot(posR) || isPosRed(posR))
              setBlack(posR);
            else
              remedyDoubleBlack(posR);
          }
          return toReturn;
        }
        protected void remedyDoubleBlack(Position<Entry<K,V>> posR) {
          Position<Entry<K,V>> posX, posY, posZ;
          boolean oldColor;
          posX = parent(posR);
          posY = sibling(posR);
          if (!isPosRed(posY)) {
            posZ = redChild(posY);
            if (hasRedChild(posY)) { // Case 1: trinode restructuring
              oldColor = isPosRed(posX);
              posZ = restructure(posZ);
              setColor(posZ, oldColor);
              setBlack(posR);
              setBlack(left(posZ));
              setBlack(right(posZ));
              return;
            }
            setBlack(posR);
            setRed(posY);
            if (!isPosRed(posX)) { // Case 2: recoloring
              if (!isRoot(posX))
                remedyDoubleBlack(posX);
              return;
            }
            setBlack(posX);
            return;
          } // Case 3: adjustment
          if (posY == right(posX)) posZ = right(posY);
          else posZ = left(posY);
          restructure(posZ);
          setBlack(posY);
          setRed(posX);
          remedyDoubleBlack(posR);
        }
```

Code Fragment 10.11: Method remove and auxiliary method remedyDoubleBlack of class RBTree.

10.6 Exercises

For help with exercises, please visit the web site, www.wiley.com/college/goodrich.

Reinforcement

R-10.1 If we insert the entries $(1,A)$, $(2,B)$, $(3,C)$, $(4,D)$, and $(5,E)$, in this order, into an initially empty binary search tree, what will it look like?

R-10.2 We defined a binary search tree so that keys equal to a node's key can be in either the left or right subtree of that node. Suppose we change the definition so that we restrict equal keys to the right subtree. What must a subtree of a binary search tree containing only equal keys look like in this case?

R-10.3 Insert, into an empty binary search tree, entries with keys 30, 40, 24, 58, 48, 26, 11, 13 (in this order). Draw the tree after each insertion.

R-10.4 How many different binary search trees can store the keys $\{1,2,3\}$?

R-10.5 Suppose that the methods of BinarySearchTree (Code Fragments 10.3–10.5) are used to perform the updates shown in Figures 10.3, 10.4, and 10.5. What is the node referenced by actionPos after each update?

R-10.6 Dr. Amongus claims that the order in which a fixed set of entries is inserted into a binary search tree does not matter—the same tree results every time. Give a small example that proves he is wrong.

R-10.7 Dr. Amongus claims that the order in which a fixed set of entries is inserted into an AVL tree does not matter—the same AVL tree results every time. Give a small example that proves he is wrong.

R-10.8 Are the rotations in Figures 10.8 and 10.10 single or double rotations?

R-10.9 Draw the AVL tree resulting from the insertion of an entry with key 52 into the AVL tree of Figure 10.10b.

R-10.10 Draw the AVL tree resulting from the removal of the entry with key 62 from the AVL tree of Figure 10.10b.

R-10.11 Explain why performing a rotation in an n-node binary tree represented using an array list takes $\Omega(n)$ time.

R-10.12 Is the search tree of Figure 10.19a a $(2,4)$ tree? Why or why not?

R-10.13 An alternative way of performing a split at a node v in a $(2,4)$ tree is to partition v into v' and v'', with v' being a 2-node and v'' a 3-node. Which of the keys k_1, k_2, k_3, or k_4 do we store at v's parent in this case? Why?

R-10.14 Dr. Amongus claims that a $(2,4)$ tree storing a set of entries will always have the same structure, regardless of the order in which the entries are inserted. Show that he is wrong.

R-10.15 Draw four different red-black trees that correspond to the same $(2,4)$ tree.

R-10.16 Consider the set of keys $K = \{1,2,3,4,5,6,7,8,9,10,11,12,13,14,15\}$.

    a. Draw a $(2,4)$ tree storing K as its keys using the fewest number of nodes.

    b. Draw a $(2,4)$ tree storing K as its keys using the maximum number of nodes.

R-10.17 Consider the sequence of keys $(5,16,22,45,2,10,18,30,50,12,1)$. Draw the result of inserting entries with these keys (in the given order) into

    a. An initially empty $(2,4)$ tree.

    b. An initially empty red-black tree.

R-10.18 For the following statements about red-black trees, provide a justification for each true statement and a counterexample for each false one.

    a. A subtree of a red-black tree is itself a red-black tree.

    b. The sibling of an external node is either external or it is red.

    c. There is a unique $(2,4)$ tree associated with a given red-black tree.

    d. There is a unique red-black tree associated with a given $(2,4)$ tree.

R-10.19 Draw an example red-black tree that is not an AVL tree.

R-10.20 Consider a tree T storing 100,000 entries. What is the worst-case height of T in the following cases?

    a. T is an AVL tree.

    b. T is a $(2,4)$ tree.

    c. T is a red-black tree.

    d. T is a splay tree.

    e. T is a binary search tree.

R-10.21 Perform the following sequence of operations in an initially empty splay tree and draw the tree after each set of operations.

    a. Insert keys 0, 2, 4, 6, 8, 10, 12, 14, 16, 18, in this order.

    b. Search for keys 1, 3, 5, 7, 9, 11, 13, 15, 17, 19, in this order.

    c. Delete keys 0, 2, 4, 6, 8, 10, 12, 14, 16, 18, in this order.

R-10.22 What does a splay tree look like if its entries are accessed in increasing order by their keys?

R-10.23 Explain how to use an AVL tree or a red-black tree to sort n comparable elements in $O(n\log n)$ time in the worst case.

R-10.24 Can we use a splay tree to sort n comparable elements in $O(n\log n)$ time in the **worst case**? Why or why not?

R-10.25 Explain why you would get the same output in an inorder listing of the entries in a binary search tree, T, independent of whether T is maintained to be an AVL tree, splay tree, or red-black tree.

Creativity

C-10.1 Describe a modification to the binary search tree data structure that would allow you to find the median entry, that is the entry with rank $\lfloor n/2 \rfloor$, in a binary search tree. Describe both the modification and the algorithm for finding the median, assuming all keys are distinct.

C-10.2 Design a variation of algorithm TreeSearch for performing the operation getAll(k) in an ordered dictionary implemented with a binary search tree T, and show that it runs in time $O(h+s)$, where h is the height of T and s is the size of the collection returned.

C-10.3 Describe how to perform an operation removeAll(k), which removes all the entries whose keys equal k in an ordered dictionary implemented with a binary search tree T, and show that this method runs in time $O(h+s)$, where h is the height of T and s is the size of the iterator returned.

C-10.4 Draw a schematic of an AVL tree such that a single remove operation could require $\Omega(\log n)$ trinode restructurings (or rotations) from a leaf to the root in order to restore the height-balance property.

C-10.5 Show how to perform an operation, removeAll(k), which removes all entries with keys equal to K, in an ordered dictionary implemented with an AVL tree in time $O(s\log n)$, where n is the number of entries in the map and s is the size of the iterator returned.

C-10.6 Describe the changes that would need to be made to the binary search tree implementation given in the book to allow it to be used to support an ordered dictionary, where we allow for different entries with equal keys.

C-10.7 If we maintain a reference to the position of the left-most internal node of an AVL tree, then operation firstEntry (Section 9.3) can be performed in $O(1)$ time. Describe how the implementation of the other map methods needs to be modified to maintain a reference to the left-most position.

C-10.8 Show that any n-node binary tree can be converted to any other n-node binary tree using $O(n)$ rotations.

C-10.9 Let M be an ordered map with n entries implemented by means of an AVL tree. Show how to implement the following operation on M in time $O(\log n + s)$, where s is the size of the iterator returned:

    findAllInRange(k_1, k_2): Return an iterator of all the entries in M with key k such that $k_1 \leq k \leq k_2$.

C-10.10 Let M be an ordered map with n entries. Show how to modify the AVL tree to implement the following method for M in time $O(\log n)$:

    countAllInRange(k_1, k_2): Compute and return the number of entries in M with key k such that $k_1 \leq k \leq k_2$.

C-10.11 Draw a splay tree, T_1, together with the sequence of updates that produced it, and a red-black tree, T_2, on the same set of ten entries, such that a preorder traversal of T_1 would be the same as a preorder traversal of T_2.

C-10.12 Show that the nodes that become unbalanced in an AVL tree during a put operation may be nonconsecutive on the path from the newly inserted node to the root.

C-10.13 Show that at most one node in an AVL tree becomes unbalanced after operation removeExternal is performed within the execution of a remove map operation.

C-10.14 Show that at most one trinode restructuring operation is needed to restore balance after any insertion in an AVL tree.

C-10.15 Let T and U be $(2,4)$ trees storing n and m entries, respectively, such that all the entries in T have keys less than the keys of all the entries in U. Describe an $O(\log n + \log m)$ time method for *joining* T and U into a single tree that stores all the entries in T and U.

C-10.16 Repeat the previous problem for red-black trees T and U.

C-10.17 Justify Proposition 10.7.

C-10.18 The Boolean indicator used to mark nodes in a red-black tree as being "red" or "black" is not strictly needed when we have distinct keys. Describe a scheme for implementing a red-black tree without adding any extra space to standard binary search tree nodes.

C-10.19 Let T be a red-black tree storing n entries, and let k be the key of an entry in T. Show how to construct from T, in $O(\log n)$ time, two red-black trees T' and T'', such that T' contains all the keys of T less than k, and T'' contains all the keys of T greater than k. This operation destroys T.

C-10.20 Show that the nodes of any AVL tree T can be colored "red" and "black" so that T becomes a red-black tree.

C-10.21 The *mergeable heap* ADT consists of operations insert(k,x), removeMin(), unionWith(h), and min(), where the unionWith(h) operation performs a union of the mergeable heap h with the present one, destroying the old versions of both. Describe a concrete implementation of the mergeable heap ADT that achieves $O(\log n)$ performance for all its operations.

C-10.22 Consider a variation of splay trees, called *half-splay trees*, where splaying a node at depth d stops as soon as the node reaches depth $\lfloor d/2 \rfloor$. Perform an amortized analysis of half-splay trees.

C-10.23 The standard splaying step requires two passes, one downward pass to find the node x to splay, followed by an upward pass to splay the node x. Describe a method for splaying and searching for x in one downward pass. Each substep now requires that you consider the next two nodes in the path down to x, with a possible zig substep performed at the end. Describe how to perform the zig-zig, zig-zag, and zig steps.

C-10.24 Describe a sequence of accesses to an n-node splay tree T, where n is odd, that results in T consisting of a single chain of internal nodes with external node children, such that the internal-node path down T alternates between left children and right children.

C-10.25 Explain how to implement an array list of n elements so that the methods add and get take $O(\log n)$ time in the worst case.

Projects

P-10.1 Perform an experimental comparison of the performance of the class, java.util.TreeMap, which implements a map with a red-black tree, and java.util.concurrent.ConcurrentSkipListMap, which uses a skip list.

P-10.2 Write a program that performs a simple n-body simulation, called "Jumping Leprechauns." This simulation involves n leprechauns, numbered 1 to n. It maintains a gold value g_i for each leprechaun i, which begins with each leprechaun starting out with a million dollars worth of gold, that is, $g_i = 1\,000\,000$ for each $i = 1, 2, \ldots, n$. In addition, the simulation also maintains, for each leprechaun, i, a place on the horizon, which is represented as a double-precision floating point number, x_i. In each iteration of the simulation, the simulation processes the leprechauns in order. Processing a leprechaun i during this iteration begins by computing a new place on the horizon for i, which is determined by the assignment

$$x_i \leftarrow x_i + rg_i,$$

where r is a random floating-point number between -1 and 1. The leprechaun i then steals half the gold from the nearest leprechauns on either side of him and adds this gold to his gold value, g_i. Write a program that can perform a series of iterations in this simulation for a given number, n, of leprechauns. You must maintain the set of horizon positions using an ordered map data structure described in this chapter.

P-10.3 Extend class BinarySearchTree (Code Fragments 10.3–10.5) to support the methods of the ordered map ADT (see Section 9.3).

P-10.4 Implement a class RestructurableNodeBinaryTree that supports the methods of the binary tree ADT, plus a method restructure for performing a rotation operation. This class is a component of the implementation of an AVL tree given in Section 10.2.2.

P-10.5 Write a Java class that implements all the methods of the ordered map ADT (see Section 9.3) using an AVL tree.

P-10.6 Write a Java class that implements all the methods of the ordered map ADT (see Section 9.3) using a $(2,4)$ tree.

P-10.7 Write a Java class that implements all the methods of the ordered map ADT (see Section 9.3) using a red-black tree.

P-10.8 Form a three-programmer team and have each member implement a map using a different search tree data structure. Perform a cooperative experimental study to compare the speed of these three implementations.

P-10.9 Write a Java class that can take any red-black tree and convert it into its corresponding $(2,4)$ tree and can take any $(2,4)$ tree and convert it into its corresponding red-black tree.

P-10.10 Implement the java.util.Map interface using a splay tree, and compare its performance experimentally with the class, java.util.TreeMap, which uses a red-black tree, and java.util.concurrent.ConcurrentSkipListMap, which uses a skip list.

P-10.11 Prepare an implementation of splay trees that uses bottom-up splaying as described in this chapter and another that uses top-down splaying as described in Exercise C-10.23. Perform extensive experimental studies to see which implementation is better in practice, if any.

P-10.12 Implement a binary search tree data structure so that it can support the dictionary ADT, where different entries can have equal keys. In addition, support methods entrySetPreorder(), entrySetInorder(), and entrySetPostorder(), which produce an iterable collection of the entries in the binary search tree in the same order they would respectively be visited in a preorder, inorder, and postorder traversal of the tree.

Chapter Notes

Some of the data structures discussed in this chapter are extensively covered by Knuth in his *Sorting and Searching* book [63], and by Mehlhorn in [74]. AVL trees are due to Adel'son-Vel'skii and Landis [1], who invented this class of balanced search trees in 1962. Binary search trees, AVL trees, and hashing are described in Knuth's *Sorting and Searching* [63] book. Average-height analyses for binary search trees can be found in the books by Aho, Hopcroft, and Ullman [5] and Cormen, Leiserson, and Rivest [25]. The handbook by Gonnet and Baeza-Yates [39] contains a number of theoretical and experimental comparisons among map implementations. Aho, Hopcroft, and Ullman [4] discuss $(2,3)$ trees, which are similar to $(2,4)$ trees. Red-black trees were defined by Bayer [10]. Variations and interesting properties of red-black trees are presented in a paper by Guibas and Sedgewick [44]. The reader interested in learning more about different balanced tree data structures is referred to the books by Mehlhorn [74] and Tarjan [91], and the book chapter by Mehlhorn and Tsakalidis [76]. Knuth [63] is excellent additional reading that includes early approaches to balancing trees. Splay trees were invented by Sleator and Tarjan [86] (see also [91]).

Contents

11.1   Merge-Sort

In this section, we present a sorting technique, called ***merge-sort***, which can be
described in a simple and compact way using recursion.

11.1.1   Divide-and-Conquer

Merge-sort is based on an algorithmic design pattern called ***divide-and-conquer***.
The divide-and-conquer pattern consists of the following three steps:

1. ***Divide:*** If the input size is smaller than a certain threshold (say, one or two
   elements), solve the problem directly using a straightforward method and
   return the solution so obtained. Otherwise, divide the input data into two or
   more disjoint subsets.
2. ***Recur:*** Recursively solve the subproblems associated with the subsets.
3. ***Conquer:*** Take the solutions to the subproblems and "merge" them into a
   solution to the original problem.

Using Divide-and-Conquer for Sorting

Recall that in a sorting problem we are given a sequence of n objects, stored in a
linked list or an array, together with some comparator defining a total order on these
objects, and we are asked to produce an ordered representation of these objects. To
allow for sorting of either representation, we will describe our sorting algorithm at
a high level for sequences and explain the details needed to implement it for linked
lists and arrays. To sort a sequence S with n elements using the three divide-and-
conquer steps, the merge-sort algorithm proceeds as follows:

1. ***Divide:*** If S has zero or one element, return S immediately; it is already
   sorted. Otherwise (S has at least two elements), remove all the elements
   from S and put them into two sequences, S_1 and S_2, each containing about
   half of the elements of S; that is, S_1 contains the first $\lceil n/2 \rceil$ elements of S,
   and S_2 contains the remaining $\lfloor n/2 \rfloor$ elements.
2. ***Recur:*** Recursively sort sequences S_1 and S_2.
3. ***Conquer:*** Put back the elements into S by merging the sorted sequences S_1
   and S_2 into a sorted sequence.

In reference to the divide step, we recall that the notation $\lceil x \rceil$ indicates the ***ceiling***
of x, that is, the smallest integer m, such that $x \le m$. Similarly, the notation $\lfloor x \rfloor$
indicates the ***floor*** of x, that is, the largest integer k, such that $k \le x$.

We can visualize an execution of the merge-sort algorithm by means of a binary tree T, called the ***merge-sort tree***. Each node of T represents a recursive invocation (or call) of the merge-sort algorithm. We associate with each node v of T the sequence S that is processed by the invocation associated with v. The children of node v are associated with the recursive calls that process the subsequences S_1 and S_2 of S. The external nodes of T are associated with individual elements of S, corresponding to instances of the algorithm that make no recursive calls.

Figure 11.1 summarizes an execution of the merge-sort algorithm by showing the input and output sequences processed at each node of the merge-sort tree. The step-by-step evolution of the merge-sort tree is shown in Figures 11.2 through 11.4.

This algorithm visualization in terms of the merge-sort tree helps us analyze the running time of the merge-sort algorithm. In particular, since the size of the input sequence roughly halves at each recursive call of merge-sort, the height of the merge-sort tree is about $\log n$ (recall that the base of log is 2 if omitted).

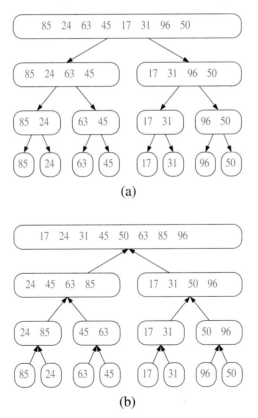

Figure 11.1: Merge-sort tree T for an execution of the merge-sort algorithm on a sequence with 8 elements: (a) input sequences processed at each node of T; (b) output sequences generated at each node of T.

Figure 11.2: Visualization of an execution of merge-sort. Each node of the tree represents a recursive call of merge-sort. The nodes drawn with dashed lines represent calls that have not been made yet. The node drawn with thick lines represents the current call. The empty nodes drawn with thin lines represent completed calls. The remaining nodes (drawn with thin lines and not empty) represent calls that are waiting for a child invocation to return. (Continues in Figure 11.3.)

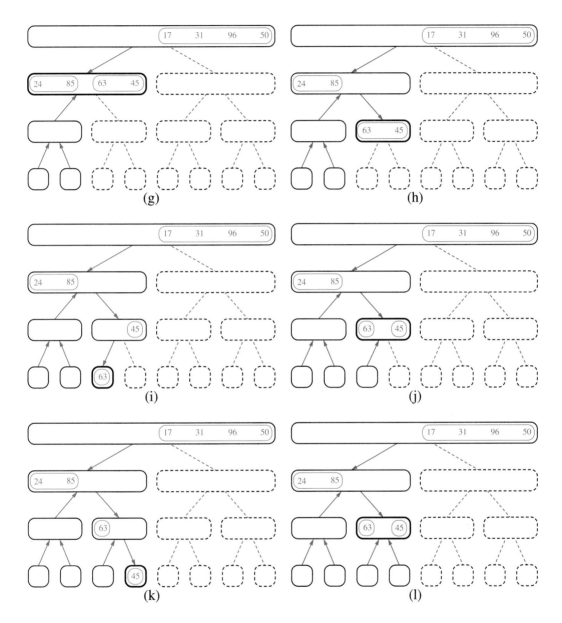

Figure 11.3: Visualization of an execution of merge-sort. (Continues in Figure 11.4.)

Figure 11.4: Visualization of an execution of merge-sort. Several invocations are omitted between (l) and (m) and between (m) and (n). Note the conquer step performed in step (p). (Continued from Figure 11.3.)

Proposition 11.1: *The merge-sort tree associated with an execution of merge-sort on a sequence of size n has height* $\lceil \log n \rceil$.

We leave the justification of Proposition 11.1 as a simple exercise (R-11.4). We will use this proposition to analyze the running time of the merge-sort algorithm.

Having given an overview of merge-sort and an illustration of how it works, let us consider each of the steps of this divide-and-conquer algorithm in more detail. The divide and recur steps of the merge-sort algorithm are simple; dividing a sequence of size n involves separating it at the element with index $\lceil n/2 \rceil$, and the recursive calls simply involve passing these smaller sequences as parameters. The difficult step is the conquer step, which merges two sorted sequences into a single sorted sequence. Thus, before we present our analysis of merge-sort, we need to say more about how this is done.

11.1.2 Merging Arrays and Lists

To merge two sorted sequences, it is helpful to know if they are implemented as arrays or lists. We begin with the array implementation, which we show in Code Fragment 11.1. We illustrate a step in the merge of two sorted arrays in Figure 11.5.

Algorithm merge(S_1, S_2, S):

    Input: Sorted sequences S_1 and S_2 and an empty sequence S, all of which are implemented as arrays

    Output: Sorted sequence S containing the elements from S_1 and S_2

    $i \leftarrow j \leftarrow 0$

    while $i < S_1.\text{size}()$ **and** $j < S_2.\text{size}()$ **do**

        if $S_1.\text{get}(i) \le S_2.\text{get}(j)$ **then**

            $S.\text{addLast}(S_1.\text{get}(i))$ { copy ith element of S_1 to end of S }

            $i \leftarrow i + 1$

        else

            $S.\text{addLast}(S_2.\text{get}(j))$ { copy jth element of S_2 to end of S }

            $j \leftarrow j + 1$

    while $i < S_1.\text{size}()$ **do** {copy the remaining elements of S_1 to S}

        $S.\text{addLast}(S_1.\text{get}(i))$

        $i \leftarrow i + 1$

    while $j < S_2.\text{size}()$ **do** {copy the remaining elements of S_2 to S}

        $S.\text{addLast}(S_2.\text{get}(j))$

        $j \leftarrow j + 1$

Code Fragment 11.1: Algorithm for merging two sorted array-based sequences.

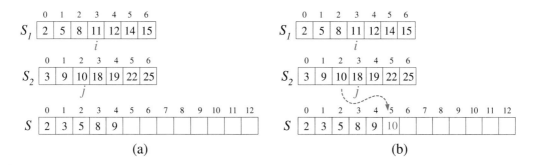

Figure 11.5: A step in the merge of two sorted arrays. We show the arrays before the copy step in (a) and after it in (b).

Merging Two Sorted Lists

In Code Fragment 11.2, we give a list-based version of algorithm merge, for merging two sorted sequences, S_1 and S_2, implemented as linked lists. The main idea is to iteratively remove the smallest element from the front of one of the two lists and add it to the end of the output sequence, S, until one of the two input lists is empty, at which point we copy the remainder of the other list to S. We show an example execution of this version of algorithm merge in Figure 11.6.

Algorithm merge(S_1, S_2, S):

    Input: Sorted sequences S_1 and S_2 and an empty sequence S, implemented as
       linked lists

    Output: Sorted sequence S containing the elements from S_1 and S_2

    while S_1 is not empty **and** S_2 is not empty **do**

       if S_1.first().element() $\leq$ S_2.first().element() **then**

          { move the first element of S_1 at the end of S }

          S.addLast(S_1.remove(S_1.first()))

       else

          { move the first element of S_2 at the end of S }

          S.addLast(S_2.remove(S_2.first()))

    { move the remaining elements of S_1 to S }

    while S_1 is not empty **do**

       S.addLast(S_1.remove(S_1.first()))

    { move the remaining elements of S_2 to S }

    while S_2 is not empty **do**

       S.addLast(S_2.remove(S_2.first()))

Code Fragment 11.2: Algorithm merge for merging two sorted sequences implemented as linked lists.

The Running Time for Merging

We analyze the running time of the merge algorithm by making some simple observations. Let n_1 and n_2 be the number of elements of S_1 and S_2, respectively. Algorithm merge has three **while** loops. Independent of whether we are analyzing the array-based version or the list-based version, the operations performed inside each loop take $O(1)$ time each. The key observation is that during each iteration of one of the loops, one element is copied or moved from either S_1 or S_2 into S (and that element is considered no further). Since no insertions are performed into S_1 or S_2, this observation implies that the overall number of iterations of the three loops is $n_1 + n_2$. Thus, the running time of algorithm merge is $O(n_1 + n_2)$.

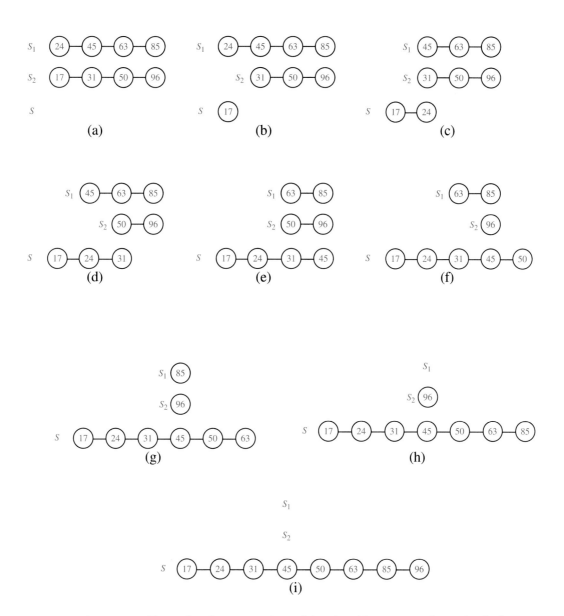

Figure 11.6: Example of an execution of the algorithm merge shown in Code Fragment 11.2.

11.1.3   The Running Time of Merge-Sort

Now that we have given the details of the merge-sort algorithm, in both its array-based and list-based versions, and we have analyzed the running time of the crucial merge algorithm used in the conquer step, let us analyze the running time of the entire merge-sort algorithm, assuming it is given an input sequence of n elements. For simplicity, we restrict our attention to the case where n is a power of 2. We leave it to an exercise (R-11.7) to show that the result of our analysis also holds when n is not a power of 2.

As we did in the analysis of the merge algorithm, we assume that the input sequence S and the auxiliary sequences S_1 and S_2, created by each recursive call of merge-sort, are implemented by either arrays or linked lists (the same as S), so that merging two sorted sequences can be done in linear time.

As we mentioned earlier, we analyze the merge-sort algorithm by referring to the merge-sort tree T. (Recall Figures 11.2 through 11.4.) We call the **time spent at a node** v of T the running time of the recursive call associated with v, excluding the time taken waiting for the recursive calls associated with the children of v to terminate. In other words, the time spent at node v includes the running times of the divide and conquer steps, but excludes the running time of the recur step. We have already observed that the details of the divide step are straightforward; this step runs in time proportional to the size of the sequence for v. In addition, as discussed above, the conquer step, which consists of merging two sorted subsequences, also takes linear time, independent of whether we are dealing with arrays or linked lists. That is, letting i denote the depth of node v, the time spent at node v is $O(n/2^i)$, since the size of the sequence handled by the recursive call associated with v is equal to $n/2^i$.

Looking at the tree T more globally, as shown in Figure 11.7, we see that, given our definition of "time spent at a node," the running time of merge-sort is equal to the sum of the times spent at the nodes of T. Observe that T has exactly 2^i nodes at depth i. This simple observation has an important consequence, for it implies that the overall time spent at all the nodes of T at depth i is $O(2^i \cdot n/2^i)$, which is $O(n)$. By Proposition 11.1, the height of T is $\lceil \log n \rceil$. Thus, since the time spent at each of the $\lceil \log n \rceil + 1$ levels of T is $O(n)$, we have the following result:

Proposition 11.2: *Algorithm merge-sort sorts a sequence S of size n in $O(n \log n)$ time, assuming two elements of S can be compared in $O(1)$ time.*

In other words, the merge-sort algorithm asymptotically matches the fast running time of the heap-sort algorithm.

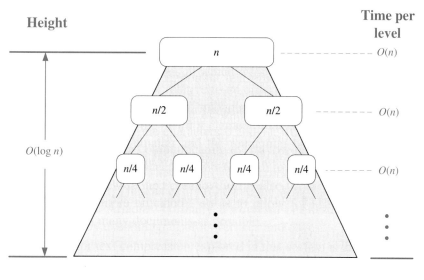

Figure 11.7: A visual time analysis of the merge-sort tree T. Each node is shown labeled with the size of its subproblem.

11.1.4 Java Implementations of Merge-Sort

The merge-sort algorithm is, in fact, the algorithm that is used in the method, java.util.Collections.sort(L), for sorting a list L that implements the java.util.List interface. Thus, this method guarantees $O(n \log n)$ worst-case performance and it applies equally well whether L is, for instance, of type java.util.ArrayList or java.util.LinkedList. The merge-sort algorithm is also the algorithm used in the method, java.util.Arrays.sort(A), for sorting an array, A, in the case when A is not an array of base types. In this subsection, we present two Java implementations of the merge-sort algorithm, one for lists and one for arrays.

In Code Fragment 11.3, we show a complete Java implementation of the list-based merge-sort algorithm as a static recursive method, mergeSort. A comparator (see Section 8.1.2) is used to decide the relative order of two elements.

In this implementation, the input is a list, L, and auxiliary lists, L1 and L2, are processed by the recursive calls. Each list is modified by insertions and deletions only at the head and tail; hence, each list update takes $O(1)$ time, assuming the lists are implemented with doubly linked lists (see Table 6.4). In our code, we use class NodeList (Code Fragments 6.9–6.11) for the auxiliary lists. Thus, for a list L of size n, method mergeSort(L,c) runs in time $O(n \log n)$ provided the list L is implemented with a doubly linked list and the comparator c can compare two elements of L in $O(1)$ time.

```java
/**
 * Sorts the elements of list in in nondecreasing order according
 * to comparator c, using the merge-sort algorithm.
 **/
public static <E> void mergeSort (PositionList<E> in, Comparator<E> c) {
  int n = in.size();
  if (n < 2)
    return;  // the in list is already sorted in this case
  // divide
  PositionList<E> in1 = new NodePositionList<E>();
  PositionList<E> in2 = new NodePositionList<E>();
  int i = 0;
  while (i < n/2) {
    in1.addLast(in.remove(in.first()));  // move the first n/2 elements to in1
    i++;
  }
  while (!in.isEmpty())
    in2.addLast(in.remove(in.first()));  // move the rest to in2
  // recur
  mergeSort(in1,c);
  mergeSort(in2,c);
  //conquer
  merge(in1,in2,c,in);
}


/**
 * Merges two sorted lists, in1 and in2, into a sorted list in.
 **/
public static <E> void merge(PositionList<E> in1, PositionList<E> in2,
        Comparator<E> c, PositionList<E> in) {
  while (!in1.isEmpty() && !in2.isEmpty())
    if (c.compare(in1.first().element(), in2.first().element()) <= 0)
      in.addLast(in1.remove(in1.first()));
    else
      in.addLast(in2.remove(in2.first()));
  while(!in1.isEmpty())  // move the remaining elements of in1
    in.addLast(in1.remove(in1.first()));
  while(!in2.isEmpty())  // move the remaining elements of in2
    in.addLast(in2.remove(in2.first()));
}
```

Code Fragment 11.3: Methods mergeSort and merge implementing the recursive merge-sort algorithm.

A Nonrecursive Array-Based Implementation of Merge-Sort

There is a nonrecursive version of array-based merge-sort, which runs in $O(n \log n)$ time. It is a bit faster than recursive list-based merge-sort in practice, as it avoids the extra overheads of recursive calls and node creation. The main idea is to perform merge-sort bottom-up, performing the merges level-by-level going up the merge-sort tree. Given an input array of elements, we begin by merging every odd-even pair of elements into sorted runs of length two. We merge these runs into runs of length four, merge these new runs into runs of length eight, and so on, until the array is sorted. To keep the space usage reasonable, we deploy an output array that stores the merged runs (swapping input and output arrays after each iteration). We give a Java implementation in Code Fragment 11.4, where we use the built-in method System.arraycopy to copy a range of cells between two arrays.

```java
/** Sorts an array with a comparator using nonrecursive merge sort. */
public static <E> void mergeSort(E[] orig, Comparator<E> c) {
  E[] in = (E[]) new Object[orig.length];  // make a new temporary array
  System.arraycopy(orig,0,in,0,in.length);  // copy the input
  E[] out = (E[]) new Object[in.length];  // output array
  E[] temp;  // temp array reference used for swapping
  int n = in.length;
  for (int i=1; i < n; i*=2) {  // each iteration sorts all length-2*i runs
    for (int j=0; j < n; j+=2*i)  // each iteration merges two length-i pairs
      merge(in,out,c,j,i);  // merge from in to out two length-i runs at j
    temp = in; in = out; out = temp;  // swap arrays for next iteration
  }
  // the "in" array contains the sorted array, so re-copy it
  System.arraycopy(in,0,orig,0,in.length);
}
/** Merges two subarrays, specified by a start and increment. */
protected static <E> void merge(E[] in, E[] out, Comparator<E> c, int start,
      int inc) {  // merge in[start..start+inc-1] and in[start+inc..start+2*inc-1]
  int x = start;  // index into run #1
  int end1 = Math.min(start+inc, in.length);  // boundary for run #1
  int end2 = Math.min(start+2*inc, in.length);  // boundary for run #2
  int y = start+inc;  // index into run #2 (could be beyond array boundary)
  int z = start;  // index into the out array
  while ((x < end1) && (y < end2))
    if (c.compare(in[x],in[y]) <= 0) out[z++] = in[x++];
    else out[z++] = in[y++];
  if (x < end1)  // first run didn't finish
    System.arraycopy(in, x, out, z, end1 - x);
  else if (y < end2)  // second run didn't finish
    System.arraycopy(in, y, out, z, end2 - y);
}
```

Code Fragment 11.4: An implementation of the nonrecursive merge-sort algorithm.

11.1.5   Merge-Sort and Recurrence Equations ⋆

There is another way to justify that the running time of the merge-sort algorithm is $O(n \log n)$ (Proposition 11.2). Namely, we can deal more directly with the recursive nature of the merge-sort algorithm. In this section, we present such an analysis of the running time of merge-sort, and in so doing introduce the mathematical concept of a ***recurrence equation*** (also known as ***recurrence relation***).

Let the function $t(n)$ denote the worst-case running time of merge-sort on an input sequence of size n. Since merge-sort is recursive, we can characterize function $t(n)$ by means of an equation where the function $t(n)$ is recursively expressed in terms of itself. In order to simplify our characterization of $t(n)$, let us restrict our attention to the case when n is a power of 2. (We leave the problem of showing that our asymptotic characterization still holds in the general case as an exercise.) In this case, we can specify the definition of $t(n)$ as

$$t(n) = \begin{cases} b & \text{if } n \le 1 \\ 2t(n/2) + cn & \text{otherwise.} \end{cases}$$

An expression such as the one above is called a ***recurrence equation***, since the function appears on both the left- and right-hand sides of the equal sign. Although such a characterization is correct and accurate, what we really desire is a big-Oh type of characterization of $t(n)$ that does not involve the function $t(n)$ itself. That is, we want a ***closed-form*** characterization of $t(n)$.

We can obtain a closed-form solution by applying the definition of a recurrence equation, assuming n is relatively large. For example, after one more application of the equation above, we can write a new recurrence for $t(n)$ as

$$\begin{aligned} t(n) &= 2(2t(n/2^2) + (cn/2)) + cn \\ &= 2^2 t(n/2^2) + 2(cn/2) + cn = 2^2 t(n/2^2) + 2cn. \end{aligned}$$

If we apply the equation again, we get $t(n) = 2^3 t(n/2^3) + 3cn$. At this point, we should see a pattern emerging, so that after applying this equation i times we get

$$t(n) = 2^i t(n/2^i) + icn.$$

The issue that remains, then, is to determine when to stop this process. To see when to stop, recall that we switch to the closed form $t(n) = b$ when $n \le 1$, which will occur when $2^i = n$. In other words, this will occur when $i = \log n$. Making this substitution, then, yields

$$\begin{aligned} t(n) &= 2^{\log n} t(n/2^{\log n}) + (\log n)cn \\ &= nt(1) + cn \log n \\ &= nb + cn \log n. \end{aligned}$$

That is, we get an alternative justification of the fact that $t(n)$ is $O(n \log n)$.

11.2 Quick-Sort

The next sorting algorithm we discuss is called *quick-sort*. Like merge-sort, this algorithm is also based on the *divide-and-conquer* paradigm, but it uses this technique in a somewhat opposite manner, as all the hard work is done *before* the recursive calls.

High-Level Description of Quick-Sort

The quick-sort algorithm sorts a sequence S using a simple recursive approach. The main idea is to apply the divide-and-conquer technique, whereby we divide S into subsequences, recur to sort each subsequence, and then combine the sorted subsequences by a simple concatenation. In particular, the quick-sort algorithm consists of the following three steps (see Figure 11.8):

1. *Divide:* If S has at least two elements (nothing needs to be done if S has zero or one element), select a specific element x from S, which is called the *pivot*. As is common practice, choose the pivot x to be the last element in S. Remove all the elements from S and put them into three sequences:

   - L, storing the elements in S less than x
   - E, storing the elements in S equal to x
   - G, storing the elements in S greater than x.

   Of course, if the elements of S are all distinct, then E holds just one element—the pivot itself.

2. *Recur:* Recursively sort sequences L and G.

3. *Conquer:* Put back the elements into S in order by first inserting the elements of L, then those of E, and finally those of G.

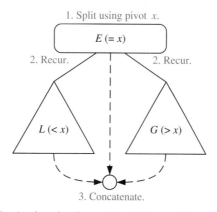

Figure 11.8: A visual schematic of the quick-sort algorithm.

Like merge-sort, the execution of quick-sort can be visualized by means of a binary recursion tree, called the ***quick-sort tree***. Figure 11.9 summarizes an execution of the quick-sort algorithm by showing the input and output sequences processed at each node of the quick-sort tree. The step-by-step evolution of the quick-sort tree is shown in Figures 11.10, 11.11, and 11.12.

Unlike merge-sort, however, the height of the quick-sort tree associated with an execution of quick-sort is linear in the worst case. This happens, for example, if the sequence consists of n distinct elements and is already sorted. Indeed, in this case, the standard choice of the pivot as the largest element yields a subsequence L of size $n-1$, while subsequence E has size 1 and subsequence G has size 0. At each invocation of quick-sort on subsequence L, the size decreases by 1. Hence, the height of the quick-sort tree is $n-1$.

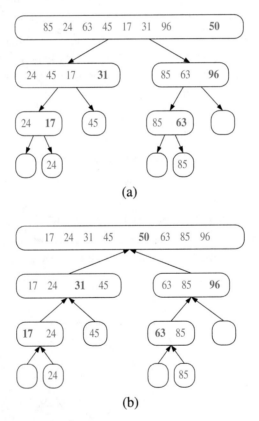

Figure 11.9: Quick-sort tree T for an execution of the quick-sort algorithm on a sequence with 8 elements: (a) input sequences processed at each node of T; (b) output sequences generated at each node of T. The pivot used at each level of the recursion is shown in bold.

Figure 11.10: Visualization of quick-sort. Each node of the tree represents a recursive call. The nodes drawn with dashed lines represent calls that have not been made yet. The node drawn with thick lines represents the running invocation. The empty nodes drawn with thin lines represent terminated calls. The remaining nodes represent suspended calls (that is, active invocations that are waiting for a child invocation to return). Note the divide steps performed in (b), (d), and (f). (Continues in Figure 11.11.)

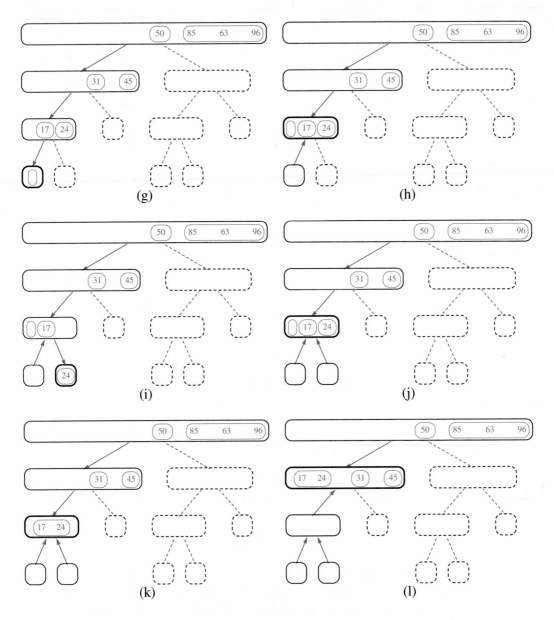

Figure 11.11: Visualization of an execution of quick-sort. Note the conquer step performed in (k). (Continues in Figure 11.12.)

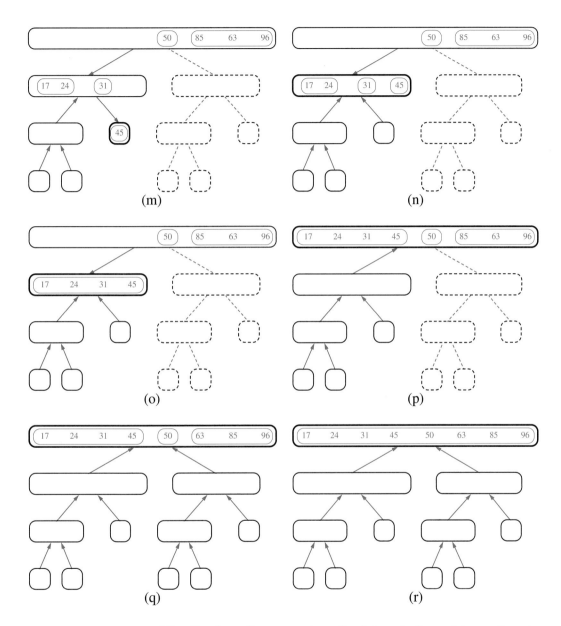

Figure 11.12: Visualization of an execution of quick-sort. Several invocations between (p) and (q) have been omitted. Note the conquer steps performed in (o) and (r). (Continued from Figure 11.11.)

Performing Quick-Sort on Arrays and Lists

In Code Fragment 11.5, we give a pseudo-code description of the quick-sort algorithm that is efficient for sequences implemented as arrays or linked lists. The algorithm follows the template for quick-sort given above, adding the detail of scanning the input sequence S backwards to divide it into the lists L, E, and G of elements that are respectively less than, equal to, and greater than the pivot. We perform this scan backwards, since removing the last element in a sequence is a constant-time operation independent of whether the sequence is implemented as an array or a linked list. We then recur on the L and G lists, and copy the sorted lists L, E, and G back to S. We perform this latter set of copies in the forward direction, since inserting elements at the end of a sequence is a constant-time operation independent of whether the sequence is implemented as an array or a linked list.

Algorithm QuickSort(S):

    Input: A sequence S implemented as an array or linked list

    Output: The sequence S in sorted order

    if S.size() ≤ 1 **then**

        return   {S is already sorted in this case}

    $p \leftarrow S$.last().element()   {the pivot}

    Let L, E, and G be empty list-based sequences

    while !S.isEmpty() **do** {scan S backwards, dividing it into L, E, and G}

        if S.last().element() $< p$ **then**

          L.addLast(S.remove(S.getLast()))

        else if S.last().element() $= p$ **then**

          E.addLast(S.remove(S.getLast()))

        else {the last element in S is greater than p}

          G.addLast(S.remove(S.getLast())))

    QuickSort(L)   {Recur on the elements less than p}

    QuickSort(G)   {Recur on the elements greater than p}

    while !L.isEmpty() **do** {copy back to S the sorted elements less than p}

        S.addLast(L.remove(L.getFirst()))

    while !E.isEmpty() **do** {copy back to S the elements equal to p}

        S.addLast(E.remove(E.getFirst()))

    while !G.isEmpty() **do** {copy back to S the sorted elements greater than p}

        S.addLast(G.remove(G.getFirst()))

    return   {S is now in sorted order}

Code Fragment 11.5: Quick-sort for an input sequence S implemented with a linked list or an array.

Running Time of Quick-Sort

We can analyze the running time of quick-sort with the same technique used for merge-sort in Section 11.1.3. Namely, we can identify the time spent at each node of the quick-sort tree T and sum up the running times for all the nodes.

Examining Code Fragment 11.5, we see that the divide step and the conquer step of quick-sort can be implemented in linear time. Thus, the time spent at a node v of T is proportional to the **input size** $s(v)$ of v, defined as the size of the sequence handled by the invocation of quick-sort associated with node v. Since subsequence E has at least one element (the pivot), the sum of the input sizes of the children of v is at most $s(v) - 1$.

Given a quick-sort tree T, let s_i denote the sum of the input sizes of the nodes at depth i in T. Clearly, $s_0 = n$, since the root r of T is associated with the entire sequence. Also, $s_1 \leq n - 1$, since the pivot is not propagated to the children of r. Consider next s_2. If both children of r have nonzero input size, then $s_2 = n - 3$. Otherwise (one child of the root has zero size, the other has size $n - 1$), $s_2 = n - 2$. Thus, $s_2 \leq n - 2$. Continuing this line of reasoning, we obtain that $s_i \leq n - i$. As observed in Section 11.2, the height of T is $n - 1$ in the worst case. Thus, the worst-case running time of quick-sort is $O\left(\sum_{i=0}^{n-1} s_i\right)$, which is $O\left(\sum_{i=0}^{n-1} (n - i)\right)$, that is, $O\left(\sum_{i=1}^{n} i\right)$. By Proposition 4.3, $\sum_{i=1}^{n} i$ is $O(n^2)$. Thus, quick-sort runs in $O(n^2)$ worst-case time.

Given its name, we would expect quick-sort to run quickly. However, the quadratic bound above indicates that quick-sort is slow in the worst case. Paradoxically, this worst-case behavior occurs for problem instances when sorting should be easy—if the sequence is already sorted.

Going back to our analysis, note that the best case for quick-sort on a sequence of distinct elements occurs when subsequences L and G happen to have roughly the same size. That is, in the best case, we have

$$
\begin{aligned}
s_0 &= n \\
s_1 &= n - 1 \\
s_2 &= n - (1 + 2) = n - 3 \\
&\;\;\vdots \\
s_i &= n - (1 + 2 + 2^2 + \cdots + 2^{i-1}) = n - (2^i - 1).
\end{aligned}
$$

Thus, in the best case, T has height $O(\log n)$ and quick-sort runs in $O(n \log n)$ time; we leave the justification of this fact as an exercise (R-11.12).

The informal intuition behind the expected behavior of quick-sort is that at each invocation the pivot will probably divide the input sequence about equally. Thus, we expect the average running time quick-sort to be similar to the best-case running time, that is, $O(n \log n)$. We will see in the next section that introducing randomization makes quick-sort behave exactly in this way.

11.2.1   Randomized Quick-Sort

One common method for analyzing quick-sort is to assume that the pivot will always divide the sequence almost equally. We feel such an assumption would presuppose knowledge about the input distribution that is typically not available, however. For example, we would have to assume that we will rarely be given "almost" sorted sequences to sort, which are actually common in many applications. Fortunately, this assumption is not needed in order for us to match our intuition to quick-sort's behavior.

In general, we desire some way of getting close to the best-case running time for quick-sort. The way to get close to the best-case running time, of course, is for the pivot to divide the input sequence S almost equally. If this outcome were to occur, then it would result in a running time that is asymptotically the same as the best-case running time. That is, having pivots close to the "middle" of the set of elements leads to an $O(n \log n)$ running time for quick-sort.

Picking Pivots at Random

Since the goal of the partition step of the quick-sort method is to divide the sequence S almost equally, let us introduce randomization into the algorithm and pick as the pivot a ***random element*** of the input sequence. That is, instead of picking the pivot as the last element of S, we pick an element of S at random as the pivot, keeping the rest of the algorithm unchanged. This variation of quick-sort is called ***randomized quick-sort***. The following proposition shows that the expected running time of randomized quick-sort on a sequence with n elements is $O(n \log n)$. This expectation is taken over all the possible random choices the algorithm makes, and is independent of any assumptions about the distribution of the possible input sequences the algorithm is likely to be given.

Proposition 11.3: *The expected running time of randomized quick-sort on a sequence S of size n is $O(n \log n)$.*

Justification: We assume two elements of S can be compared in $O(1)$ time. Consider a single recursive call of randomized quick-sort, and let n denote the size of the input for this call. Say that this call is "good" if the pivot chosen is such that subsequences L and G have size at least $n/4$ and at most $3n/4$ each; otherwise, a call is "bad."

Now, consider the implications of our choosing a pivot uniformly at random. Note that there are $n/2$ possible good choices for the pivot for any given call of size n of the randomized quick-sort algorithm. Thus, the probability that any call is good is $1/2$. Note further that a good call will at least partition a list of size n into two lists of size $3n/4$ and $n/4$, and a bad call could be as bad as producing a single call of size $n - 1$.

Now consider a recursion trace for randomized quick-sort. This trace defines a binary tree, T, such that each node in T corresponds to a different recursive call on a subproblem of sorting a portion of the original list.

Say that a node v in T is in *size group* i if the size of v's subproblem is greater than $(3/4)^{i+1}n$ and at most $(3/4)^i n$. Let us analyze the expected time spent working on all the subproblems for nodes in size group i. By the linearity of expectation (Proposition A.19), the expected time for working on all these subproblems is the sum of the expected times for each one. Some of these nodes correspond to good calls and some correspond to bad calls. But note that, since a good call occurs with probability $1/2$, the expected number of consecutive calls we have to make before getting a good call is 2. Moreover, notice that as soon as we have a good call for a node in size group i, its children will be in size groups higher than i. Thus, for any element x from in the input list, the expected number of nodes in size group i containing x in their subproblems is 2. In other words, the expected total size of all the subproblems in size group i is $2n$. Since the nonrecursive work we perform for any subproblem is proportional to its size, this implies that the total expected time spent processing subproblems for nodes in size group i is $O(n)$.

The number of size groups is $\log_{4/3} n$, since repeatedly multiplying by $3/4$ is the same as repeatedly dividing by $4/3$. That is, the number of size groups is $O(\log n)$. Therefore, the total expected running time of randomized quick-sort is $O(n \log n)$. (See Figure 11.13.) ∎

Figure 11.13: A visual time analysis of the quick-sort tree T. Each node is shown labeled with the size of its subproblem.

Actually, we can show that the running time of randomized quick-sort is $O(n \log n)$ with high probability.

11.2.2   Java Implementations and Optimizations

Recall from Section 8.3.5 that a sorting algorithm is *in-place* if it uses only a small amount of memory in addition to that needed for the objects being sorted themselves. The merge-sort algorithm, as described above, does not use this optimization technique, and making it be in-place seems to be quite difficult. In-place sorting is not inherently difficult, however. For, as with heap-sort, quick-sort can be adapted to be in-place, and this is the version of quick-sort that is used in most deployed implementations.

Performing the quick-sort algorithm in-place requires a bit of ingenuity, however, for we must use the input sequence itself to store the subsequences for all the recursive calls. We show algorithm inPlaceQuickSort, which performs in-place quick-sort, in Code Fragment 11.6. Algorithm inPlaceQuickSort assumes that the input sequence, S, is given as an array of *distinct* elements. The reason for this restriction is explored in Exercise R-11.15. The extension to the general case is discussed in Exercise C-11.9.

Algorithm inPlaceQuickSort(S, a, b):

    Input: An array S of distinct elements; integers a and b
    Output: Array S with elements originally from indices from a to b, inclusive,
        sorted in nondecreasing order from indices a to b

    if $a \geq b$ **then return**   {at most one element in subrange}
    $p \leftarrow S[b]$ {the pivot}
    $l \leftarrow a$ {will scan rightward}
    $r \leftarrow b - 1$ {will scan leftward}
    while $l \leq r$ **do**
        {find an element larger than the pivot}
        while $l \leq r$ **and** $S[l] \leq p$ **do**
            $l \leftarrow l + 1$
        {find an element smaller than the pivot}
        while $r \geq l$ **and** $S[r] \geq p$ **do**
            $r \leftarrow r - 1$
        if $l < r$ **then**
            swap the elements at $S[l]$ and $S[r]$
    {put the pivot into its final place}
    swap the elements at $S[l]$ and $S[b]$
    {recursive calls}
    inPlaceQuickSort($S, a, l - 1$)
    inPlaceQuickSort($S, l + 1, b$)
    {we are done at this point, since the sorted subarrays are already consecutive}

        Code Fragment 11.6: In-place quick-sort for an input array S.

In-place quick-sort modifies the input sequence using element swapping and does not explicitly create subsequences. Indeed, a subsequence of the input sequence is implicitly represented by a range of positions specified by a left-most index l and a right-most index r. The divide step is performed by scanning the array simultaneously from l forward and from r backward, swapping pairs of elements that are in reverse order, as shown in Figure 11.14. When these two indices "meet," subarrays L and G are on opposite sides of the meeting point. The algorithm completes by recurring on these two subarrays.

In-place quick-sort reduces the running time caused by the creation of new sequences and the movement of elements between them by a constant factor. We show a Java version of in-place quick-sort in Code Fragment 11.7.

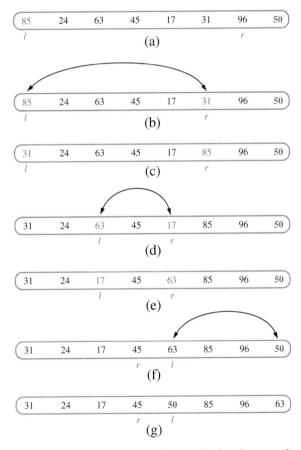

Figure 11.14: Divide step of in-place quick-sort. Index l scans the sequence from left to right, and index r scans the sequence from right to left. A swap is performed when l is at an element larger than the pivot and r is at an element smaller than the pivot. A final swap with the pivot completes the divide step.

```
public static <E> void quickSort (E[] s, Comparator<E> c) {
  if (s.length < 2) return; // the array is already sorted in this case
  quickSortStep(s, c, 0, s.length−1); // recursive sort method
}
private static <E> void quickSortStep (E[] s, Comparator<E> c,
                            int leftBound, int rightBound ) {
  if (leftBound >= rightBound) return; // the indices have crossed
  E temp; // temp object used for swapping
  E pivot = s[rightBound];
  int leftInd = leftBound;      // will scan rightward
  int rightInd = rightBound−1; // will scan leftward
  while (leftInd <= rightInd) { // scan right until larger than the pivot
    while ( (leftInd <= rightInd) && (c.compare(s[leftInd], pivot)<=0) )
      leftInd++;
    while ( (rightInd >= leftInd) && (c.compare(s[rightInd], pivot)>=0))
      rightInd−−;
    if (leftInd < rightInd) { // both elements were found, so swap
      temp = s[rightInd]; s[rightInd] = s[leftInd]; s[leftInd] = temp;
    }
  } // the loop continues until the indices cross
  temp = s[rightBound]; // swap pivot with element at leftInd
  s[rightBound] = s[leftInd];
  s[leftInd] = temp; // the pivot is now at leftInd
  quickSortStep(s, c, leftBound, leftInd−1); // left recursive call
  quickSortStep(s, c, leftInd+1, rightBound); // right recursive call
}
```

Code Fragment 11.7: A coding of in-place quick-sort, assuming distinct elements.

Interestingly, a version of quick-sort is used in the Java Collections Framework, in the method, java.util.Arrays.sort(A), for sorting an array, A, in the case when A is an array of base types. It is a recursive, in-place implementation of quick-sort, which includes several additional optimizations.

One optimization limits recursive steps to subarrays of A that are reasonably large, say, having at least eight elements. When the subarray to sort is below this threshold, the algorithm simply uses the insertion-sort algorithm (Section 8.2.2) to sort the subarray. This optimization is based on the fact that the insertion-sort algorithm has a low overhead and is relatively fast for sorting small arrays.

Another optimization is in how pivots are chosen. If the subarray is moderately sized, then the pivot is chosen as the median of three values, taken respectively from the front, middle, and tail of the array. This ***median-of-three*** heuristic performs like a random pivot on subarrays of moderate size. When the subarray is relatively large, the algorithm applies the median-of-three heuristic separately to the front, middle, and tail of the subarray, to select three candidate pivots, and then it selects the median of these three. This approach still has lower overhead than selecting a random pivot and it performs well in practice.

11.3 Studying Sorting through an Algorithmic Lens

Recapping our discussions on sorting to this point, we have described several methods with either a worst-case or expected running time of $O(n\log n)$ on an input sequence of size n. These methods include merge-sort and quick-sort, described in this chapter, as well as heap-sort (Section 8.3.5). In this section, we study sorting as an algorithmic problem, addressing general issues about sorting algorithms.

11.3.1 A Lower Bound for Sorting

A natural first question to ask is whether we can sort any faster than $O(n\log n)$ time. Interestingly, if the computational primitive used by a sorting algorithm is the comparison of two elements, then this is in fact the best we can do—comparison-based sorting has an $\Omega(n\log n)$ worst-case lower bound on its running time. (Recall the notation $\Omega(\cdot)$ from Section 4.2.3.) To focus on the main cost of comparison-based sorting, let us only count comparisons, for the sake of a lower bound.

Suppose we are given a sequence $S = (x_0, x_1, \ldots, x_{n-1})$ that we wish to sort, and assume that all the elements of S are distinct (this is not really a restriction since we are deriving a lower bound). We do not care if S is implemented as an array or a linked list, for the sake of our lower bound, since we are only counting comparisons. Each time a sorting algorithm compares two elements x_i and x_j (that is, it asks, "is $x_i < x_j$?"), there are two outcomes: "yes" or "no." Based on the result of this comparison, the sorting algorithm may perform some internal calculations (which we are not counting here) and will eventually perform another comparison between two other elements of S, which again will have two outcomes. Therefore, we can represent a comparison-based sorting algorithm with a decision tree T (recall Example 7.8). That is, each internal node v in T corresponds to a comparison and the edges from node v' to its children correspond to the computations resulting from either a "yes" or "no" answer. It is important to note that the hypothetical sorting algorithm in question probably has no explicit knowledge of the tree T. T simply represents all the possible sequences of comparisons that a sorting algorithm might make, starting from the first comparison (associated with the root) and ending with the last comparison (associated with the parent of an external node).

Each possible initial ordering, or *permutation*, of the elements in S will cause our hypothetical sorting algorithm to execute a series of comparisons, traversing a path in T from the root to some external node. Let us associate with each external node v in T, then, the set of permutations of S that cause our sorting algorithm to end up in v. The most important observation in our lower-bound argument is that each external node v in T can represent the sequence of comparisons for at most one permutation of S. The justification for this claim is simple: if two different permutations P_1 and P_2 of S are associated with the same external node, then there are at least two objects x_i and x_j, such that x_i is before x_j in P_1 but x_i is after x_j in P_2. At the same time, the output associated with v must be a specific reordering of S, with either x_i or x_j appearing before the other. But if P_1 and P_2 both cause the sorting algorithm to output the elements of S in this order, then that implies there is a way to trick the algorithm into outputting x_i and x_j in the wrong order. Since this cannot be allowed by a correct sorting algorithm, each external node of T must be associated with exactly one permutation of S. We use this property of the decision tree associated with a sorting algorithm to prove the following result:

Proposition 11.4: *The running time of any comparison-based algorithm for sorting an n-element sequence is $\Omega(n \log n)$ in the worst case.*

Justification: The running time of a comparison-based sorting algorithm must be greater than or equal to the height of the decision tree T associated with this algorithm, as described above. (See Figure 11.15.) By the argument above, each external node in T must be associated with one permutation of S. Moreover, each permutation of S must result in a different external node of T. The number of permutations of n objects is $n! = n(n-1)(n-2) \cdots 2 \cdot 1$. Thus, T must have at least $n!$ external nodes. By Proposition 7.10, the height of T is at least $\log(n!)$. This immediately justifies the proposition, because there are at least $n/2$ terms that are greater than or equal to $n/2$ in the product $n!$; hence

$$\log(n!) \geq \log\left(\frac{n}{2}\right)^{\frac{n}{2}} = \frac{n}{2} \log \frac{n}{2},$$

which is $\Omega(n \log n)$.   ∎

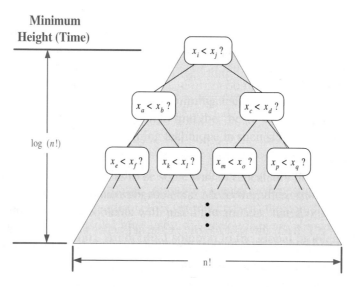

Figure 11.15: Visualizing the lower bound for comparison-based sorting.

11.3.2 Linear-Time Sorting: Bucket-Sort and Radix-Sort

In the previous section, we showed that $\Omega(n\log n)$ time is necessary, in the worst case, to sort an n-element sequence with a comparison-based sorting algorithm. A natural question to ask, then, is whether there are other kinds of sorting algorithms that can be designed to run asymptotically faster than $O(n\log n)$ time. Interestingly, such algorithms exist, but they require special assumptions about the input sequence to be sorted. Even so, such scenarios often arise in practice, so discussing them is worthwhile. In this section, we consider the problem of sorting a sequence of entries, each a key-value pair, where the keys have a restricted type.

Bucket-Sort

Consider a sequence S of n entries whose keys are integers in the range $[0, N-1]$, for some integer $N \geq 2$, and suppose that S should be sorted according to the keys of the entries. In this case, it is possible to sort S in $O(n+N)$ time. It might seem surprising, but this implies, for example, that if N is $O(n)$, then we can sort S in $O(n)$ time. Of course, the crucial point is that, because of the restrictive assumption about the format of the elements, we can avoid using comparisons.

The main idea is to use an algorithm called ***bucket-sort***, which is not based on comparisons, but on using keys as indices into a bucket array B that has cells indexed from 0 to $N-1$. An entry with key k is placed in the "bucket" $B[k]$, which itself is a sequence (of entries with key k). After inserting each entry of the input sequence S into its bucket, we can put the entries back into S in sorted order by enumerating the contents of the buckets $B[0], B[1], \ldots, B[N-1]$ in order. We describe the bucket-sort algorithm in Code Fragment 11.8.

Algorithm bucketSort(S):
    Input: Sequence S of entries with integer keys in the range $[0, N-1]$
    Output: Sequence S sorted in nondecreasing order of the keys
    let B be an array of N sequences, each of which is initially empty
    for each entry e in S **do**
        $k \leftarrow e.\text{getKey}()$
        remove e from S and insert it at the end bucket (sequence) $B[k]$
    for $i \leftarrow 0$ to $N-1$ **do**
        for each entry e in sequence $B[i]$ **do**
            remove e from $B[i]$ and insert it at the end of S

Code Fragment 11.8: Bucket-sort.

It is easy to see that bucket-sort runs in $O(n+N)$ time and uses $O(n+N)$ space. Hence, bucket-sort is efficient when the range N of values for the keys is small compared to the sequence size n, say $N = O(n)$ or $N = O(n\log n)$. Still, its performance deteriorates as N grows compared to n.

An important property of the bucket-sort algorithm is that it works correctly even if there are many different elements with the same key. Indeed, we described it in a way that anticipates such occurrences.

Stable Sorting

When sorting key-value pairs, an important issue is how equal keys are handled. Let $S = ((k_0,x_0),\dots,(k_{n-1},x_{n-1}))$ be a sequence of such entries. We say that a sorting algorithm is *stable* if, for any two entries (k_i,x_i) and (k_j,x_j) of S, such that $k_i = k_j$ and (k_i,x_i) precedes (k_j,x_j) in S before sorting (that is, $i < j$), entry (k_i,x_i) also precedes entry (k_j,x_j) after sorting. Stability is important for a sorting algorithm because applications may want to preserve the initial ordering of elements with the same key.

Our informal description of bucket-sort in Code Fragment 11.8 does not guarantee stability. This is not inherent in the bucket-sort method itself, however, for we can easily modify our description to make bucket-sort stable, while still preserving its $O(n+N)$ running time. Indeed, we can obtain a stable bucket-sort algorithm by always removing the *first* element from sequence S and from the sequences $B[i]$ during the execution of the algorithm.

Radix-Sort

One of the reasons that stable sorting is so important is that it allows the bucket-sort approach to be applied to more general contexts than to sort integers. Suppose, for example, that we want to sort entries with keys that are pairs (k,l), where k and l are integers in the range $[0,N-1]$, for some integer $N \geq 2$. In a context such as this, it is natural to define an ordering on these keys using the *lexicographical* (dictionary) convention, where $(k_1,l_1) < (k_2,l_2)$ if $k_1 < k_2$ or if $k_1 = k_2$ and $l_1 < l_2$ (Section 8.1.2). This is a pair-wise version of the lexicographic comparison function, usually applied to equal-length character strings (and it easily generalizes to tuples of d numbers for $d > 2$).

The *radix-sort* algorithm sorts a sequence S of entries with keys that are pairs, by applying a stable bucket-sort on the sequence twice; first using one component of the pair as the ordering key and then using the second component. But which order is correct? Should we first sort on the k's (the first component) and then on the l's (the second component), or should it be the other way around?

Before we answer this question, we consider the following example.

Example 11.5: *Consider the following sequence S (we show only the keys):*

$$S = ((3,3),(1,5),(2,5),(1,2),(2,3),(1,7),(3,2),(2,2)).$$

If we sort S stably on the first component, then we get the sequence

$$S_1 = ((1,5),(1,2),(1,7),(2,5),(2,3),(2,2),(3,3),(3,2)).$$

If we then stably sort this sequence S_1 using the second component, then we get the sequence

$$S_{1,2} = ((1,2),(2,2),(3,2),(2,3),(3,3),(1,5),(2,5),(1,7)),$$

which is not exactly a sorted sequence. On the other hand, if we first stably sort S using the second component, then we get the sequence

$$S_2 = ((1,2),(3,2),(2,2),(3,3),(2,3),(1,5),(2,5),(1,7)).$$

If we then stably sort sequence S_2 using the first component, then we get the sequence

$$S_{2,1} = ((1,2),(1,5),(1,7),(2,2),(2,3),(2,5),(3,2),(3,3)),$$

which is indeed sequence S lexicographically ordered.

So, from this example, we are led to believe that we should first sort using the second component and then again using the first component. This intuition is exactly right. By first stably sorting by the second component and then again by the first component, we guarantee that if two entries are equal in the second sort (by the first component), then their relative order in the starting sequence (which is sorted by the second component) is preserved. Thus, the resulting sequence is guaranteed to be sorted lexicographically every time. We leave to a simple exercise (R-11.20) the determination of how this approach can be extended to triples and other *d*-tuples of numbers. We can summarize this section as follows:

Proposition 11.6: *Let S be a sequence of n key-value pairs, each of which has a key $(k_1, k_2, \ldots, k_d)$, where k_i is an integer in the range $[0, N-1]$ for some integer $N \geq 2$. We can sort S lexicographically in time $O(d(n+N))$ using radix-sort.*

As important as it is, sorting is not the only interesting problem dealing with a total order relation on a set of elements. There are some applications, for example, that do not require an ordered listing of an entire set, but nevertheless call for some amount of ordering information about the set. Before we study such a problem (called "selection"), let us step back and briefly compare all of the sorting algorithms we have studied so far.

11.3.3   Comparing Sorting Algorithms

At this point, it might be useful for us to take a breath and consider all the algorithms we have studied in this book to sort an n-element array list, node list, or general sequence.

Considering Running Time and Other Factors

We have studied several methods, such as insertion-sort, and selection-sort, that have $O(n^2)$-time behavior in the average and worst case. We have also studied several methods with $O(n \log n)$-time behavior, including heap-sort, merge-sort, and quick-sort. Finally, we have studied a special class of sorting algorithms, namely, the bucket-sort and radix-sort methods, that run in linear time for certain types of keys. Certainly, the selection-sort algorithm is a poor choice in any application, since it runs in $O(n^2)$ time even in the best case. But, of the remaining sorting algorithms, which is the best?

As with many things in life, there is no clear "best" sorting algorithm from the remaining candidates. The sorting algorithm best suited for a particular application depends on several properties of that application. We can offer some guidance and observations, therefore, based on the known properties of the "good" sorting algorithms.

Insertion-Sort

If implemented well, the running time of **insertion-sort** is $O(n+m)$, where m is the number of **inversions** (that is, the number of pairs of elements out of order). Thus, insertion-sort is an excellent algorithm for sorting small sequences (say, less than 50 elements), because insertion-sort is simple to program, and small sequences necessarily have few inversions. Also, insertion-sort is quite effective for sorting sequences that are already "almost" sorted. By "almost," we mean that the number of inversions is small. But the $O(n^2)$-time performance of insertion-sort makes it a poor choice outside of these special contexts.

Merge-Sort

Merge-sort, on the other hand, runs in $O(n \log n)$ time in the worst case, which is optimal for comparison-based sorting methods. Still, experimental studies have shown that, since it is difficult to make merge-sort run in-place, the overheads needed to implement merge-sort make it less attractive than the in-place implementations of heap-sort and quick-sort for sequences that can fit entirely in a computer's main memory area. Even so, merge-sort is an excellent algorithm for situations where the input cannot all fit into main memory, but must be stored in blocks on an external memory device, such as a disk. In these contexts, the way that merge-sort processes runs of data in long merge streams makes the best use of all the data brought into main memory in a block from disk. Thus, for external memory sorting, the merge-sort algorithm tends to minimize the total number of disk reads and writes needed, which makes the merge-sort algorithm superior in such contexts.

Quick-Sort

Experimental studies have shown that if an input sequence can fit entirely in main memory, then the in-place versions of quick-sort and heap-sort run faster than merge-sort. The extra overhead needed for copying nodes or entries puts merge-sort at a disadvantage to quick-sort and heap-sort in these applications. In fact, quick-sort tends, on average, to beat heap-sort in these tests.

So, *quick-sort* is an excellent choice as a general-purpose, in-memory sorting algorithm. Indeed, it is included in the qsort sorting utility provided in C language libraries. Still, its $O(n^2)$ time worst-case performance makes quick-sort a poor choice in real-time applications where we must make guarantees on the time needed to complete a sorting operation.

Heap-Sort

In real-time scenarios where we have a fixed amount of time to perform a sorting operation and the input data can fit into main memory, the *heap-sort* algorithm is probably the best choice. It runs in $O(n \log n)$ worst-case time and can easily be made to execute in-place.

Bucket-Sort and Radix-Sort

Finally, if our application involves sorting entries with small integer keys or d-tuples of small integer keys, then *bucket-sort* or *radix-sort* is an excellent choice, for it runs in $O(d(n+N))$ time, where $[0, N-1]$ is the range of integer keys (and $d = 1$ for bucket sort). Thus, if $d(n+N)$ is significantly "below" the $n \log n$ function, then this sorting method should run faster than even quick-sort or heap-sort.

Thus, our study of all these different sorting algorithms provides us with a versatile collection of sorting methods in our algorithm engineering "toolbox."

11.4   Sets and Union/Find Structures

In this section, we study sets, including operations that define them and operations that can be applied to entire sets.

11.4.1   The Set ADT

A *set* is a collection of distinct objects. That is, there are no duplicate elements in a set, and there is no explicit notion of keys or even an order. Even so, if the elements in a set are comparable, then we can maintain sets to be ordered. The fundamental methods of the set ADT for a set S are the following:

> add(e): Adds the element e to S.
>
> remove(e): Removes the element e from S.
>
> contains(e): Returns whether e is in S.
>
> iterator(): Returns an iterator of the elements in S.

The Java Collections Framework includes all of these methods as a part of the java.util.Set interface, and this interface has the following implementation:

- java.util.HashSet: an implementation of the set ADT with a hash table.

If we wish to extend the set ADT to an ordered set ADT, then we could also include the following methods:

> pollFirst(): Returns and removes the smallest element in S.
>
> pollLast(): Returns and removes the largest element in S.
>
> ceiling(e): Returns the element that is the smallest element greater than or equal to e.
>
> floor(e): Returns the element that is the largest element less than or equal to e.
>
> lower(e): Returns the element that is the greatest element strictly less than e.
>
> higher(e): Returns the element that is the smallest element strictly greater than k.

Incidentally, each of these methods is included in the java.util.NavigableSet interface; hence, Java provides a superset of the ordered set ADT. This interface is implemented in the following classes in the Java Collections Framework:

- java.util.concurrent.ConcurrentSkipListSet: a skip-list implementation of the ordered set ADT
- java.util.TreeSet: a red-black tree implementation of the ordered set ADT.

11.4.2 Mergable Sets and the Template Method Pattern

Let us explore a further extension of the ordered set ADT that allows for operations between pairs of sets. This will also serve to motivate a software engineering design pattern known as the ***template method***.

First, we recall the mathematical definitions of the ***union***, ***intersection***, and ***subtraction*** of two sets A and B:

$$
\begin{aligned}
A \cup B &= \{x: x \text{ is in } A \text{ or } x \text{ is in } B\}, \\
A \cap B &= \{x: x \text{ is in } A \text{ and } x \text{ is in } B\}, \\
A - B &= \{x: x \text{ is in } A \text{ and } x \text{ is not in } B\}.
\end{aligned}
$$

Example 11.7: *Most Internet search engines store, for each word x in their dictionary database, a set, $W(x)$, of Web pages that contain x, where each Web page is identified by a unique Internet address. When presented with a query for a word x, such a search engine need only return the Web pages in the set $W(x)$, sorted according to some proprietary priority ranking of page "importance." But when presented with a two-word query for words x and y, such a search engine must first compute the intersection $W(x) \cap W(y)$, and then return the Web pages in the resulting set sorted by priority. Several search engines use the set intersection algorithm described in this section for this computation.*

Fundamental Methods of the Mergable Set ADT

The fundamental methods of the mergable set ADT, acting on a set A, are as follows:

union(B): Replace A with the union of A and B, that is, execute $A \leftarrow A \cup B$.

intersect(B): Replace A with the intersection of A and B, that is, execute $A \leftarrow A \cap B$.

subtract(B): Replace A with the difference of A and B, that is, execute $A \leftarrow A - B$.

A Simple Mergable Set Implementation

One of the simplest ways of implementing a set is to store its elements in an ordered sequence. This implementation is included in several software libraries for generic data structures, for example. Therefore, let us consider implementing the set ADT with an ordered sequence (we consider other implementations in several exercises). Any consistent total order relation among the elements of the set can be used, provided the same order is used for all the sets.

We implement each of the three fundamental set operations using a generic version of the merge algorithm that takes, as input, two sorted sequences representing the input sets, and constructs a sequence representing the output set, be it the union, intersection, or subtraction of the input sets. Incidentally, we have defined these operations so that they modify the contents of the set A involved. Alternatively, we could have defined these methods so that they do not modify A but return a new set instead.

The generic merge algorithm iteratively examines and compares the current elements a and b of the input sequence A and B, respectively, and finds out whether $a < b$, $a = b$, or $a > b$. Then, based on the outcome of this comparison, it determines whether it should copy one of the elements a and b to the end of the output sequence C. This determination is made based on the particular operation we are performing, be it a union, intersection, or subtraction. For example, in a union operation, we proceed as follows:

- If $a < b$, we copy a to the end of C and advance to the next element of A.
- If $a = b$, we copy a to the end of C and advance to the next elements of A and B.
- If $a > b$, we copy b to the end of C and advance to the next element of B.

Performance of Generic Merging

Let us analyze the running time of generic merging. At each iteration, we compare two elements of the input sequences A and B, possibly copy one element to the output sequence, and advance the current element of A, B, or both. Assuming that comparing and copying elements takes $O(1)$ time, the total running time is $O(n_A + n_B)$, where n_A is the size of A and n_B is the size of B; that is, generic merging takes time proportional to the number of elements. Thus, we have the following:

Proposition 11.8: *The set ADT can be implemented with an ordered sequence and a generic merge scheme that supports operations* union, intersect, *and* subtract *in $O(n)$ time, where n denotes the sum of sizes of the sets involved.*

Generic Merging as a Template Method Pattern

The generic merge algorithm is based on the ***template method pattern*** (see Section 7.3.7). The template method pattern is a software engineering design pattern describing a generic computation mechanism that can be specialized by redefining certain steps. In this case, we describe a method that merges two sequences into one and can be specialized by the behavior of three abstract methods.

Code Fragment 11.9 shows the class Merge providing a Java implementation of the generic merge algorithm.

```
/** Generic merge for sorted sequences. */
public abstract class Merge<E> {
  private E a, b;                          // current elements in A and B
  private Iterator<E> iterA, iterB;        // iterators for A and B
  /** Template method */
  public void merge(PositionList<E> A, PositionList<E> B,
        Comparator<E> comp, PositionList<E> C) {
    iterA = A.iterator();
    iterB = B.iterator();
    boolean aExists = advanceA(); // Boolean test if there is a current a
    boolean bExists = advanceB(); // Boolean test if there is a current b
    while (aExists && bExists) { // Main loop for merging a and b
      int x = comp.compare(a, b);
      if (x < 0) { aIsLess(a, C);  aExists = advanceA(); }
      else if (x == 0) {
        bothAreEqual(a, b, C); aExists = advanceA(); bExists = advanceB(); }
      else { bIsLess(b, C);  bExists = advanceB(); }
    }
    while (aExists) { aIsLess(a, C); aExists = advanceA(); }
    while (bExists) { bIsLess(b, C); bExists = advanceB(); }
  }
  // auxiliary methods to be specialized by subclasses
  protected void aIsLess(E a, PositionList<E> C) { }
  protected void bothAreEqual(E a, E b, PositionList<E> C) { }
  protected void bIsLess(E b, PositionList<E> C) { }
  // helper methods
  private boolean advanceA() {
    if (iterA.hasNext()) { a = iterA.next(); return true; }
    return false;
  }
  private boolean advanceB() {
    if (iterB.hasNext()) { b = iterB.next(); return true; }
    return false;
  }
}
```

Code Fragment 11.9: Class Merge for generic merging.

To convert the generic Merge class into useful classes, we must extend it with classes that redefine the three auxiliary methods, aIsLess, bothAreEqual, and bIsLess. We show how union, intersection, and subtraction can be easily described in terms of these methods in Code Fragment 11.10. The auxiliary methods are redefined so that the template method merge performs as follows:

- In class UnionMerge, merge copies every element from A and B into C, but does not duplicate any element.

- In class IntersectMerge, merge copies every element that is in both A and B into C, but "throws away" elements in one set but not in the other.

- In class SubtractMerge, merge copies every element that is in A and not in B into C.

```
/** Class specializing the generic merge template to union two sets */
public class UnionMerge<E> extends Merge<E> {
  protected void aIsLess(E a, PositionList<E> C) {
    C.addLast(a);        // add a
  }
  protected void bothAreEqual(E a, E b, PositionList<E> C) {
    C.addLast(a);    // add a (but not its duplicate b)
  }
  protected void bIsLess(E b, PositionList<E> C) {
    C.addLast(b);    // add b
  }
}
/** Class specializing the generic merge template to intersect two sets */
public class IntersectMerge<E> extends Merge<E> {
  protected void aIsLess(E a, PositionList<E> C) { }
  protected void bothAreEqual(E a, E b, PositionList<E> C) {
    C.addLast(a);        // add a (but not its duplicate b)
  }
  protected void bIsLess(E b, PositionList<E> C) { }
}
/** Class specializing the generic merge template to subtract two sets */
public class SubtractMerge<E> extends Merge<E> {
  protected void aIsLess(E a, PositionList<E> C) {
    C.addLast(a);        // add a
  }
  protected void bothAreEqual(E a, E b, PositionList<E> C) { }
  protected void bIsLess(E b, PositionList<E> C) { }
}
```

Code Fragment 11.10: Classes extending the Merge class by specializing the auxiliary methods to perform set union, intersection, and subtraction, respectively.

11.4.3 Partitions with Union-Find Operations

A **partition** is a collection of disjoint sets. We define the methods of the partition ADT using position objects (Section 6.2.2), each of which stores an element x. The partition ADT supports the following methods.

> makeSet(x): Create a singleton set containing the element x and return the position storing x in this set.
>
> union(A, B): Return the set $A \cup B$, destroying the old A and B.
>
> find(p): Return the set containing the element in position p.

A simple implementation of a partition with a total of n elements is with a collection of sequences, one for each set, where the sequence for a set A stores set positions as its elements. Each position object stores a variable, element, which references its associated element x and allows the execution of the element() method in $O(1)$ time. In addition, we also store a variable, set, in each position, which references the sequence storing p, since this sequence is representing the set containing p's element. (See Figure 11.16.) Thus, we can perform operation find(p) in $O(1)$ time, by following the set reference for p. Likewise, makeSet also takes $O(1)$ time. Operation union(A, B) requires that we join two sequences into one and update the set references of the positions in one of the two. We choose to implement this operation by removing all the positions from the sequence with smaller size, and inserting them in the sequence with larger size. Each time we take a position p from the smaller set s and insert it into the larger set t, we update the set reference for p to now point to t. Hence, the operation union(A, B) takes time $O(\min(|A|, |B|))$, which is $O(n)$, because, in the worst case, $|A| = |B| = n/2$. Nevertheless, as shown below, an amortized analysis shows this implementation to be much better than appears from this worst-case analysis.

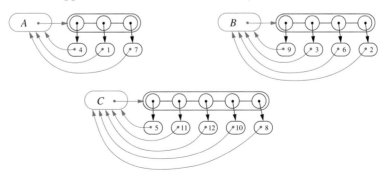

Figure 11.16: Sequence-based implementation of a partition consisting of three sets: $A = \{1, 4, 7\}$, $B = \{2, 3, 6, 9\}$, and $C = \{5, 8, 10, 11, 12\}$.

Performance of the Sequence Implementation

The sequence implementation above is simple, but it is also efficient, as the following theorem shows.

Proposition 11.9: *Performing a series of n* makeSet, union, *and* find *operations, using the sequence-based implementation above, starting from an initially empty partition takes $O(n \log n)$ time.*

Justification: We use the accounting method and assume that one cyber-dollar can pay for the time to perform a find operation, a makeSet operation, or the movement of a position object from one sequence to another in a union operation. In the case of a find or makeSet operation, we charge the operation itself 1 cyber-dollar. In the case of a union operation, however, we charge 1 cyber-dollar to each position that we move from one set to another. Note that we charge nothing to the union operations themselves. Clearly, the total charges to find and makeSet operations sum to be $O(n)$.

Consider, then, the number of charges made to positions on behalf of union operations. The important observation is that each time we move a position from one set to another, the size of the new set at least doubles. Thus, each position is moved from one set to another at most $\log n$ times; hence, each position can be charged at most $O(\log n)$ times. Since we assume that the partition is initially empty, there are $O(n)$ different elements referenced in the given series of operations, which implies that the total time for all the union operations is $O(n \log n)$.   ∎

The amortized running time of an operation in a series of makeSet, union, and find operations, is the total time taken for the series divided by the number of operations. We conclude from the proposition above that, for a partition implemented using sequences, the amortized running time of each operation is $O(\log n)$. Thus, we can summarize the performance of our simple sequence-based partition implementation as follows.

Proposition 11.10: *Using a sequence-based implementation of a partition, in a series of n* makeSet, union, *and* find *operations starting from an initially empty partition, the amortized running time of each operation is $O(\log n)$.*

Note that in this sequence-based implementation of a partition, each find operation takes worst-case $O(1)$ time. It is the running time of the union operations that is the computational bottleneck.

In the next section, we describe a tree-based implementation of a partition that does not guarantee constant-time find operations, but has amortized time much better than $O(\log n)$ per union operation.

A Tree-Based Partition Implementation ★

An alternative data structure uses a collection of trees to store the n elements in sets, where each tree is associated with a different set. (See Figure 11.17.) In particular, we implement each tree with a linked data structure whose nodes are themselves the set position objects. We still view each position p as being a node having a variable, element, referring to its element x, and a variable, set, referring to a set containing x, as before. But now we also view each position p as being of the "set" data type. Thus, the set reference of each position p can point to a position, which could even be p itself. Moreover, we implement this approach so that all the positions and their respective set references together define a collection of trees.

We associate each tree with a set. For any position p, if p's set reference points back to p, then p is the *root* of its tree, and the name of the set containing p is "p" (that is, we will be using position names as set names in this case). Otherwise, the set reference for p points to p's parent in its tree. In either case, the set containing p is the one associated with the root of the tree containing p.

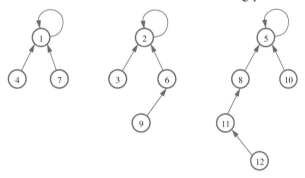

Figure 11.17: Tree-based implementation of a partition consisting of three disjoint sets: $A = \{1,4,7\}$, $B = \{2,3,6,9\}$, and $C = \{5,8,10,11,12\}$.

With this partition data structure, operation union(A,B) is called with position arguments p and q that respectively represent the sets A and B (that is, $A = p$ and $B = q$). We perform this operation by making one of the trees a subtree of the other (Figure 11.18b), which can be done in $O(1)$ time by setting the set reference of the root of one tree to point to the root of the other tree. Operation find for a position p is performed by walking up to the root of the tree containing the position p (Figure 11.18a), which takes $O(n)$ time in the worst case.

At first, this implementation may seem to be no better than the sequence-based data structure, but we add the following two simple heuristics to make it run faster.

Union-by-Size: Store, with each position node p, the size of the subtree rooted at p. In a union operation, make the tree of the smaller set become a subtree of the other tree, and update the size field of the root of the resulting tree.

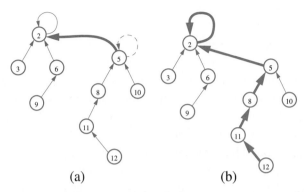

Figure 11.18: Tree-based implementation of a partition: (a) operation union(A,B); (b) operation find(p), where p denotes the position object for element 12.

Path Compression: In a find operation, for each node v that the find visits, reset the parent pointer from v to point to the root. (See Figure 11.19.)

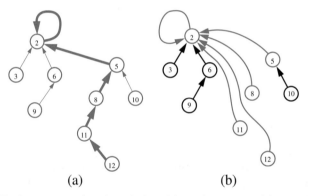

Figure 11.19: Path-compression heuristic: (a) path traversed by operation find on element 12; (b) restructured tree.

A surprising property of this data structure, when implemented using the union-by-size and path-compression heuristics, is that performing a series of n union and find operations takes $O(n\log^* n)$ time, where $\log^* n$ is the *log-star* function, which is the inverse of the *tower-of-twos* function. Intuitively, $\log^* n$ is the number of times that one can iteratively take the logarithm (base 2) of a number before getting a number smaller than 2. Table 11.1 shows a few sample values.

minimum n	2	$2^2 = 4$	$2^{2^2} = 16$	$2^{2^{2^2}} = 65,536$	$2^{2^{2^{2^2}}} = 2^{65,536}$
$\log^* n$	1	2	3	4	5

Table 11.1: Some values of $\log^* n$ and critical values for its inverse.

11.5 Selection

There are a number of applications in which we are interested in identifying a single element in terms of its rank relative to an ordering of the entire set. Examples include identifying the minimum and maximum elements, but we may also be interested in, say, identifying the *median* element, that is, the element such that half of the other elements are smaller and the remaining half are larger. In general, queries that ask for an element with a given rank are called *order statistics*.

Defining the Selection Problem

In this section, we discuss the general order-statistic problem of selecting the kth smallest element from an unsorted collection of n comparable elements. This is known as the *selection* problem. Of course, we can solve this problem by sorting the collection and then indexing into the sorted sequence at index $k - 1$. Using the best comparison-based sorting algorithms, this approach would take $O(n \log n)$ time, which is obviously an overkill for the cases where $k = 1$ or $k = n$ (or even $k = 2$, $k = 3$, $k = n - 1$, or $k = n - 5$), because we can easily solve the selection problem for these values of k in $O(n)$ time. Thus, a natural question to ask is whether we can achieve an $O(n)$ running time for all values of k (including the interesting case of finding the median, where $k = \lfloor n/2 \rfloor$).

11.5.1 Prune-and-Search

This may come as a small surprise, but we can indeed solve the selection problem in $O(n)$ time for any value of k. Moreover, the technique we use to achieve this result involves an interesting algorithmic design pattern. This design pattern is known as *prune-and-search* or *decrease-and-conquer*. In applying this design pattern, we solve a given problem that is defined on a collection of n objects by pruning away a fraction of the n objects and recursively solving the smaller problem. When we have finally reduced the problem to one defined on a constant-sized collection of objects, then we solve the problem using some brute-force method. Returning back from all the recursive calls completes the construction. In some cases, we can avoid using recursion, in which case we simply iterate the prune-and-search reduction step until we can apply a brute-force method and stop. Incidentally, the binary search method described in Section 9.3.1 is an example of the prune-and-search design pattern.

11.5.2 Randomized Quick-Select

In applying the prune-and-search pattern to the selection problem, we can design a simple and practical method, called ***randomized quick-select***, for finding the kth smallest element in an unordered sequence of n elements on which a total order relation is defined. Randomized quick-select runs in $O(n)$ ***expected*** time, taken over all possible random choices made by the algorithm, and this expectation does not depend whatsoever on any randomness assumptions about the input distribution. We note though that randomized quick-select runs in $O(n^2)$ time in the ***worst case***, the justification of which is left as an exercise (R-11.26). We also provide an exercise (C-11.32) for modifying randomized quick-select to get a ***deterministic*** selection algorithm that runs in $O(n)$ ***worst-case*** time. The existence of this deterministic algorithm is mostly of theoretical interest, however, since the constant factor hidden by the big-Oh notation is relatively large in this case.

Suppose we are given an unsorted sequence S of n comparable elements together with an integer $k \in [1,n]$. At a high level, the quick-select algorithm for finding the kth smallest element in S is similar in structure to the randomized quicksort algorithm described in Section 11.2.1. We pick an element x from S at random and use this as a "pivot" to subdivide S into three subsequences L, E, and G, storing the elements of S less than x, equal to x, and greater than x, respectively. This is the prune step. Then, based on the value of k, we then determine which of these sets to recur on. Randomized quick-select is described in Code Fragment 11.11.

Algorithm quickSelect(S,k):
    Input: Sequence S of n comparable elements, and an integer $k \in [1,n]$
    Output: The kth smallest element of S
    if $n = 1$ **then**
        return the (first) element of S.
    pick a random (pivot) element x of S and divide S into three sequences:
        • L, storing the elements in S less than x
        • E, storing the elements in S equal to x
        • G, storing the elements in S greater than x.
    if $k \leq |L|$ **then**
        quickSelect(L,k)
    else if $k \leq |L| + |E|$ **then**
        return x {each element in E is equal to x}
    else
        quickSelect($G, k - |L| - |E|$)   {note the new selection parameter}

        Code Fragment 11.11: Randomized quick-select algorithm.

11.5.3 Analyzing Randomized Quick-Select

Showing that randomized quick-select runs in $O(n)$ time requires a simple probabilistic argument. The argument is based on the *linearity of expectation*, which states that if X and Y are random variables and c is a number, then

$$E(X+Y) = E(X) + E(Y) \qquad \text{and} \qquad E(cX) = cE(X),$$

where we use $E(\mathcal{Z})$ to denote the expected value of the expression $\mathcal{Z}$.

Let $t(n)$ be the running time of randomized quick-select on a sequence of size n. Since this algorithm depends on random events, its running time, $t(n)$, is a random variable. We want to bound $E(t(n))$, the expected value of $t(n)$. Say that a recursive invocation of our algorithm is "good" if it partitions S so that the size of L and G is at most $3n/4$. Clearly, a recursive call is good with probability $1/2$. Let $g(n)$ denote the number of consecutive recursive calls we make, including the present one, before we get a good one. Then we can characterize $t(n)$ using the following *recurrence equation*:

$$t(n) \leq bn \cdot g(n) + t(3n/4),$$

where $b \geq 1$ is a constant. Applying the linearity of expectation for $n > 1$, we get

$$E(t(n)) \leq E(bn \cdot g(n) + t(3n/4)) = bn \cdot E(g(n)) + E(t(3n/4)).$$

Since a recursive call is good with probability $1/2$, and whether a recursive call is good or not is independent of its parent call being good, the expected value of $g(n)$ is the same as the expected number of times we must flip a fair coin before it comes up "heads." That is, $E(g(n)) = 2$. Thus, if we let $T(n)$ be shorthand for $E(t(n))$, then we can write the case for $n > 1$ as

$$T(n) \leq T(3n/4) + 2bn.$$

To convert this relation into a closed form, let us iteratively apply this inequality assuming n is large. So, for example, after two applications,

$$T(n) \leq T((3/4)^2 n) + 2b(3/4)n + 2bn.$$

At this point, we should see that the general case is

$$T(n) \leq 2bn \cdot \sum_{i=0}^{\lceil \log_{4/3} n \rceil} (3/4)^i.$$

In other words, the expected running time is at most $2bn$ times a geometric sum whose base is a positive number less than 1. Thus, by Proposition 4.5, $T(n)$ is $O(n)$.

Proposition 11.11: *The expected running time of randomized quick-select on a sequence S of size n is $O(n)$, assuming two elements of S can be compared in $O(1)$ time.*

11.6   Exercises

For help with exercises, please visit the web site, www.wiley.com/college/goodrich.

Reinforcement

R-11.1 What is the best algorithm for sorting each of the following: general comparable objects, long character strings, double-precision floating point numbers, 32-bit integers, and bytes? Justify your answer.

R-11.2 Suppose S is a list of n bits, that is, n 0's and 1's. How long will it take to sort S with the merge-sort algorithm? What about quick-sort?

R-11.3 Suppose S is a list of n bits, that is, n 0's and 1's. How long will it take to sort S stably with the bucket-sort algorithm?

R-11.4 Give a complete justification of Proposition 11.1.

R-11.5 In the merge-sort tree shown in Figures 11.2 through 11.4, some edges are drawn as arrows. What is the meaning of a downward arrow? How about an upward arrow?

R-11.6 Give a complete pseudo-code description of the recursive merge-sort algorithm that takes an array as its input and output.

R-11.7 Show that the running time of the merge-sort algorithm on an n-element sequence is $O(n \log n)$, even when n is not a power of 2.

R-11.8 Suppose we are given two n-element sorted sequences A and B that should not be viewed as sets (that is, A and B may contain duplicate entries). Describe an $O(n)$-time method for computing a sequence representing the set $A \cup B$ (with no duplicates).

R-11.9 Show that $(X - A) \cup (X - B) = X - (A \cap B)$, for any three sets X, A, and B.

R-11.10 Suppose we modify the deterministic version of the quick-sort algorithm so that, instead of selecting the last element in an n-element sequence as the pivot, we choose the element at index $\lfloor n/2 \rfloor$. What is the running time of this version of quick-sort on a sequence that is already sorted?

R-11.11 Consider a modification of the deterministic version of the quick-sort algorithm where we choose the element at index $\lfloor n/2 \rfloor$ as our pivot. Describe the kind of sequence that would cause this version of quick-sort to run in $\Omega(n^2)$ time.

R-11.12 Show that the best-case running time of quick-sort on a sequence of size n with distinct elements is $O(n \log n)$.

R-11.13 Describe a randomized version of in-place quick-sort in pseudo-code.

R-11.14 Show that the probability that any given input element x belongs to more than $2\log n$ subproblems in size group i, for randomized quick-sort, is at most $1/n^2$.

R-11.15 Suppose algorithm inPlaceQuickSort (Code Fragment 11.6) is executed on a sequence with duplicate elements. Show that the algorithm still correctly sorts the input sequence, but the result of the divide step may differ from the high-level description given in Section 11.2 and may result in inefficiencies. In particular, what happens in the partition step when there are elements equal to the pivot? Is the sequence E (storing the elements equal to the pivot) actually computed? Does the algorithm recur on the subsequences L and G, or on some other subsequences? What is the running time of the algorithm if all the input elements are equal?

R-11.16 Of the $n!$ possible inputs to a given comparison-based sorting algorithm, what is the absolute maximum number of inputs that could be sorted with just n comparisons?

R-11.17 Jonathan has a comparison-based sorting algorithm that sorts the first k elements in sequence of size n in $O(n)$ time. Give a big-Oh characterization of the biggest that k can be?

R-11.18 Is the merge-sort algorithm in Section 11.1 stable? Why or why not?

R-11.19 An algorithm that sorts key-value entries by key is said to be ***straggling*** if, any time two entries e_i and e_j have equal keys, but e_i appears before e_j in the input, then the algorithm places e_i after e_j in the output. Describe a change to the merge-sort algorithm in Section 11.1 to make it straggling.

R-11.20 Describe a radix-sort method for lexicographically sorting a sequence S of triplets (k,l,m), where k, l, and m are integers in the range $[0,N-1]$, for some $N \geq 2$. How could this scheme be extended to sequences of d-tuples $(k_1,k_2,\ldots,k_d)$, where each k_i is an integer in the range $[0,N-1]$?

R-11.21 Is the bucket-sort algorithm in-place? Why or why not?

R-11.22 Give an example input list that requires merge-sort and heap-sort to take $O(n\log n)$ time to sort, but insertion-sort runs in $O(n)$ time. What if you reverse this list?

R-11.23 Describe, in pseudo-code, how to perform path compression on a path of length h in $O(h)$ time in a tree-based partition union/find structure.

R-11.24 George claims he has a fast way to do path compression in a partition structure, starting at a node v. He puts v into a list L, and starts following parent pointers. Each time he encounters a new node, u, he adds u to L and updates the parent pointer of each node in L to point to u's parent. Show that George's algorithm runs in $\Omega(h^2)$ time on a path of length h.

R-11.25 Describe an in-place version of the quick-select algorithm in pseudo-code.

R-11.26 Show that the worst-case running time of quick-select on an n-element sequence is $\Omega(n^2)$.

Creativity

C-11.1 Describe an efficient algorithm for converting a dictionary D, implemented with a linked list, into a map, M, implemented with a linked list, so that each key in D has an entry in M, and the relative order of entries in M is the same as their relative order in D.

C-11.2 Linda claims to have an algorithm that takes an input sequence S and produces an output sequence T that is a sorting of the n elements in S.

    a. Give an algorithm, isSorted, for testing in $O(n)$ time if T is sorted.

    b. Explain why the algorithm isSorted is not sufficient to prove a particular output T to Linda's algorithm is a sorting of S.

    c. Describe what additional information Linda's algorithm could output so that her algorithm's correctness could be established on any given S and T in $O(n)$ time.

C-11.3 Given two sets A and B represented as sorted sequences, describe an efficient algorithm for computing $A \oplus B$, which is the set of elements that are in A or B, but not in both.

C-11.4 Suppose that we represent sets with balanced search trees. Describe and analyze algorithms for each of the methods in the set ADT, assuming that one of the two sets is much smaller than the other.

C-11.5 Describe and analyze an efficient method for removing all duplicates from a collection A of n elements.

C-11.6 Consider sets whose elements are integers in the range $[0, N-1]$. A popular scheme for representing a set A of this type is by means of a Boolean array, B, where we say that x is in A if and only if $B[x] = \textbf{true}$. Since each cell of B can be represented with a single bit, B is sometimes referred to as a **bit vector**. Describe and analyze efficient algorithms for performing the methods of the set ADT assuming this representation.

C-11.7 Consider a version of deterministic quick-sort where we pick as our pivot the median of the d last elements in the input sequence of n elements, for a fixed, constant odd number $d \geq 3$. What is the asymptotic worst-case running time of quick-sort in this case?

C-11.8 Another way to analyze randomized quick-sort is to use a **recurrence equation**. In this case, we let $T(n)$ denote the expected running time of randomized quick-sort, and we observe that, because of the worst-case partitions for good and bad splits, we can write

$$T(n) \leq \frac{1}{2}\left(T(3n/4) + T(n/4)\right) + \frac{1}{2}\left(T(n-1)\right) + bn,$$

where bn is the time needed to partition a list for a given pivot and concatenate the result sublists after the recursive calls return. Show, by induction, that $T(n)$ is $O(n \log n)$.

C-11.9 Modify inPlaceQuickSort (Code Fragment 11.6) to handle the general case efficiently when the input sequence, S, may have duplicate keys.

C-11.10 Describe a nonrecursive, in-place version of the quick-sort algorithm. The algorithm should still be based on the same divide-and-conquer approach, but use an explicit stack to process subproblems.

C-11.11 An **inverted file** is a critical data structure for implementing a search engine or the index of a book. Given a document D, which can be viewed as an unordered, numbered list of words, an inverted file is an ordered list of words, L, such that, for each w word in L, we store the indices of the places in D where w appears. Design an efficient algorithm for constructing L from D.

C-11.12 Given an array A of n entries with keys equal to 0 or 1, describe an in-place method for ordering A so that all the 0's are before every 1.

C-11.13 Suppose we are given an n-element sequence S such that each element in S represents a different vote for president, where each vote is given as an integer representing a particular candidate. Design an $O(n \log n)$-time algorithm to see who wins the election S represents, assuming the candidate with the most votes wins (even if there are $O(n)$ candidates).

C-11.14 Consider the voting problem from Exercise C-11.13, but now suppose that we know the number $k < n$ of candidates running. Describe an $O(n \log k)$-time algorithm for determining who wins the election.

C-11.15 Consider the voting problem from Exercise C-11.13, but now suppose a candidate wins only if he or she gets a majority of the votes cast. Design and analyze a fast algorithm for determining the winner if there is one.

C-11.16 Show that any comparison-based sorting algorithm can be made to be stable without affecting its asymptotic running time.

C-11.17 Suppose we are given two sequences A and B of n elements, possibly containing duplicates, on which a total order relation is defined. Describe an efficient algorithm for determining if A and B contain the same set of elements. What is the running time of this method?

C-11.18 Given an array A of n integers in the range $[0, n^2 - 1]$, describe a simple method for sorting A in $O(n)$ time.

C-11.19 Let $S_1, S_2, \ldots, S_k$ be k different sequences whose elements have integer keys in the range $[0, N - 1]$, for some parameter $N \geq 2$. Describe an algorithm running in $O(n + N)$ time for sorting all the sequences (not as a union), where n denotes the total size of all the sequences.

C-11.20 Given a sequence S of n elements, on which a total order relation is defined, describe an efficient method for determining whether there are two equal elements in S. What is the running time of your method?

C-11.21 Let S be a sequence of n elements on which a total order relation is defined. Recall that an *inversion* in S is a pair of elements x and y such that x appears before y in S but $x > y$. Describe an algorithm running in $O(n \log n)$ time for determining the *number* of inversions in S.

C-11.22 Let S be a random permutation of n distinct integers. Argue that the expected running time of insertion-sort on S is $\Omega(n^2)$. (Hint: Note that half of the elements ranked in the top half of a sorted version of S are expected to be in the first half of S.)

C-11.23 Let A and B be two sequences of n integers each. Given an integer m, describe an $O(n \log n)$-time algorithm for determining if there is an integer a in A and an integer b in B such that $m = a + b$.

C-11.24 Given a set of n integers, describe and analyze a fast method for finding the $\lceil \log n \rceil$ integers closest to the median.

C-11.25 Bob has a set A of n nuts and a set B of n bolts, such that each nut in A has a unique matching bolt in B. Unfortunately, the nuts in A all look the same, and the bolts in B all look the same as well. The only kind of a comparison that Bob can make is to take a nut-bolt pair (a, b), such that a is in A and b is in B, and test it to see if the threads of a are larger, smaller, or a perfect match with the threads of b. Describe and analyze an efficient algorithm for Bob to match up all of his nuts and bolts.

C-11.26 Show how to use a deterministic $O(n)$-time selection algorithm to sort a sequence of n elements in $O(n \log n)$ *worst-case* time.

C-11.27 Given an unsorted sequence S of n comparable elements, and an integer k, give an $O(n \log k)$ expected-time algorithm for finding the $O(k)$ elements that have rank $\lceil n/k \rceil$, $2\lceil n/k \rceil$, $3\lceil n/k \rceil$, and so on.

C-11.28 Let S be a sequence of n insert and removeMin operations, where all the keys involved are integers in the range $[0, n-1]$. Describe an algorithm running in $O(n \log^* n)$ for determining the answer to each removeMin.

C-11.29 Space aliens have given us a program, alienSplit, that can take a sequence S of n integers and partition S in $O(n)$ time into sequences $S_1, S_2, \ldots, S_k$ of size at most $\lceil n/k \rceil$ each, such that the elements in S_i are less than or equal to every element in S_{i+1}, for $i = 1, 2, \ldots, k-1$, for a fixed number, $k < n$. Show how to use alienSplit to sort S in $O(n \log n / \log k)$ time.

C-11.30 Karen has a new way to do path compression in a tree-based union/find partition data structure starting at a node v. She puts all the nodes that are on the path from v to the root in a set S. Then she scans through S and sets the parent pointer of each node in S to its parent's parent pointer (recall that the parent pointer of the root points to itself). If this pass changed the value of any node's parent pointer, then she repeats this process, and goes on repeating this process until she makes a scan through S that does not change any node's parent value. Show that Karen's algorithm is correct and analyze its running time for a path of length h.

C-11.31 Let S be a sequence of n integers. Describe a method for printing out all the pairs of inversions in S in $O(n+k)$ time, where k is the number of such inversions.

C-11.32 This problem deals with modification of the quick-select algorithm to make it deterministic yet still run in $O(n)$ time on an n-element sequence. The idea is to modify the way we choose the pivot so that it is chosen deterministically, not randomly, as follows:

> Partition the set S into $\lceil n/5 \rceil$ groups of size 5 each (except possibly for one group). Sort each little set and identify the median element in this set. From this set of $\lceil n/5 \rceil$ "baby" medians, apply the selection algorithm recursively to find the median of the baby medians. Use this element as the pivot and proceed as in the quick-select algorithm.

Show that this deterministic method runs in $O(n)$ time by answering the following questions (please ignore floor and ceiling functions if that simplifies the mathematics, for the asymptotics are the same either way):

a. How many baby medians are less than or equal to the chosen pivot? How many are greater than or equal to the pivot?

b. For each baby median less than or equal to the pivot, how many other elements are less than or equal to the pivot? Is the same true for those greater than or equal to the pivot?

c. Argue why the method for finding the deterministic pivot and using it to partition S takes $O(n)$ time.

d. Based on these estimates, write a recurrence equation to bound the worst-case running time $t(n)$ for this selection algorithm (note that in the worst case there are two recursive calls—one to find the median of the baby medians and one to recur on the larger of L and G).

e. Using this recurrence equation, show by induction that $t(n)$ is $O(n)$.

Projects

P-11.1 Design and implement two versions of the bucket-sort algorithm in Java, one for sorting an array of **byte** values and one for sorting an array of **short** values. Experimentally compare the performance of your implementations with that of the method, java.util.Arrays.sort.

P-11.2 Experimentally compare the performance of in-place quick-sort and a version of quick-sort that is not in-place.

P-11.3 Design and implement a version of the bucket-sort algorithm for sorting a linked list of n entries (for instance, a list of type java.util.LinkedList) with integer keys taken from the range $[0, N-1]$, for $N \geq 2$. The algorithm should run in $O(n+N)$ time.

P-11.4 Implement merge-sort and deterministic quick-sort and perform a series of benchmarking tests to see which one is faster. Your tests should include sequences that are "random" as well as "almost" sorted.

P-11.5 Implement deterministic and randomized versions of the quick-sort algorithm and perform a series of benchmarking tests to see which one is faster. Your tests should include sequences that are very "random" looking as well as ones that are "almost" sorted.

P-11.6 Implement an in-place version of insertion-sort and an in-place version of quick-sort. Perform benchmarking tests to determine the range of values of n where quick-sort is on average better than insertion-sort.

P-11.7 Design and implement an animation for one of the sorting algorithms described in this chapter. Your animation should illustrate the key properties of this algorithm in an intuitive manner.

P-11.8 Implement the randomized quick-sort and quick-select algorithms, and design a series of experiments to test their relative speeds.

P-11.9 Implement an extended set ADT that includes the methods union(B), intersect(B), subtract(B), size(), isEmpty(), plus the methods equals(B), contains(e), insert(e), and remove(e) with obvious meaning.

P-11.10 Implement the tree-based union/find partition data structure with both the union-by-size and path-compression heuristics.

Chapter Notes

Knuth's classic text on *Sorting and Searching* [63] contains an extensive history of the sorting problem and algorithms for solving it. Huang and Langston [52] show how to merge two sorted lists in-place in linear time. Our set ADT is derived from that of Aho, Hopcroft, and Ullman [5]. The standard quick-sort algorithm is due to Hoare [47]. More information about randomization, including Chernoff bounds, can be found in the appendix and the book by Motwani and Raghavan [79]. The quick-sort analysis given in this chapter is a combination of the analysis given in a previous edition of this book and the analysis of Kleinberg and Tardos [59]. Exercise C-11.8 is due to Littman. Gonnet and Baeza-Yates [39] analyze and compare experimentally several sorting algorithms. The term "prune-and-search" comes originally from the computational geometry literature (such as in the work of Clarkson [22] and Megiddo [72, 73]). The term "decrease-and-conquer" is from Levitin [68]. The online documentation for the java.util.Arrays.sort method states that the optimizations in its quick-sort implementation are from Bentley and McIlroy [14].

Chapter

12 Strings and Dynamic Programming

Contents

12.1 String Operations

Document processing is rapidly becoming one of the dominant functions of computers. Computers are used to edit documents, to search documents, to transport documents over the Internet, and to display documents on printers and computer screens. For example, the Internet document formats HTML and XML are primarily text formats, with added tags for multimedia content. Making sense of the many terabytes of information on the Internet requires a considerable amount of text processing.

In addition to having interesting applications, text processing algorithms also highlight some important algorithmic design patterns. In particular, the pattern matching problem gives rise to the **brute-force method**, which is often inefficient but has wide applicability. For text compression, we can apply the **greedy method**, which often allows us to approximate solutions to hard problems, and for some problems (such as in text compression) actually gives rise to optimal algorithms. Finally, in discussing text similarity, we introduce the **dynamic programming** design pattern, which can be applied in some special instances to solve a problem in polynomial time that appears at first to require exponential time to solve.

Text Processing

At the heart of algorithms for processing text are methods for dealing with character strings. Character strings can come from a wide variety of sources, including scientific, linguistic, and Internet applications. Indeed, the following are examples of such strings:

$$P = \texttt{"CGTAAACTGCTTTAATCAAACGC"}$$
$$S = \texttt{"http://www.wiley.com"}.$$

The first string, P, comes from DNA applications, and the second string, S, is the Internet address (URL) for the publisher of this book.

Several of the typical string processing operations involve breaking large strings into smaller strings. In order to be able to speak about the pieces that result from such operations, we use the term **substring** of an m-character string P to refer to a string of the form $P[i]P[i+1]P[i+2]\cdots P[j]$, for some $0 \leq i \leq j \leq m-1$, that is, the string formed by the characters in P from index i to index j, inclusive. Technically, this means that a string is actually a substring of itself (taking $i = 0$ and $j = m-1$), so if we want to rule this out as a possibility, we must restrict the definition to **proper** substrings, which require that either $i > 0$ or $j < m-1$.

To simplify the notation for referring to substrings, let us use $P[i..j]$ to denote the substring of P from index i to index j, inclusive. That is,

$$P[i..j] = P[i]P[i+1]\cdots P[j].$$

We use the convention that if $i > j$, then $P[i..j]$ is equal to the **null string**, which has length 0. In addition, in order to distinguish some special kinds of substrings, let us refer to any substring of the form $P[0..i]$, for $0 \le i \le m-1$, as a **prefix** of P, and any substring of the form $P[i..m-1]$, for $0 \le i \le m-1$, as a **suffix** of P. For example, if we again take P to be the string of DNA given above, then "CGTAA" is a prefix of P, "CGC" is a suffix of P, and "TTAATC" is a (proper) substring of P. Note that the null string is a prefix and a suffix of any other string.

To allow for fairly general notions of a character string, we typically do not restrict the characters in T and P to explicitly come from a well-known character set, like the Unicode character set. Instead, we typically use the symbol Σ to denote the character set, or **alphabet**, from which characters can come. Since most document processing algorithms are used in applications where the underlying character set is finite, we usually assume that the size of the alphabet Σ, denoted with $|\Sigma|$, is a fixed constant.

String operations come in two flavors: those that modify the string they act on and those that simply return information about the string without actually modifying it. Java makes this distinction precise by defining the String class to represent **immutable strings**, which cannot be modified, and the StringBuffer class to represent **mutable strings**, which can be modified.

12.1.1 The Java String Class

The main operations of the Java String class are listed below:

length(): Return the length, n, of S.

charAt(i): Return the character at index i in S.

startsWith(Q): Determine if Q is a prefix of S.

endsWith(Q): Determine if Q is a suffix of S.

substring(i, j): Return the substring $S[i, j]$.

concat(Q): Return the concatenation of S and Q, that is, $S + Q$.

equals(Q): Determine if Q is equal to S.

indexOf(Q): If Q is a substring of S, return the index of the beginning of the first occurrence of Q in S, else return -1.

This collection forms the typical operations for immutable strings.

Example 12.1: *Consider the following set of operations, which are performed on the string S = "abcdefghijklmnop":*

Operation	Output
length()	16
charAt(5)	'f'
concat("qrs")	"abcdefghijklmnopqrs"
endsWith("javapop")	false
indexOf("ghi")	6
startsWith("abcd")	true
substring(4,9)	"efghij"

With the exception of the indexOf(Q) method, which we discuss in Section 12.3, all the methods above are easily implemented simply by representing the string as an array of characters, which is the standard String implementation in Java.

12.1.2   The Java StringBuffer Class

The main methods of the Java StringBuffer class are listed below:

append(Q): Return $S + Q$, replacing S with $S + Q$.

insert(i, Q): Return and update S to be the string obtained by inserting Q inside S starting at index i.

reverse(): Reverse and return the string S.

setCharAt(i, ch): Set the character at index i in S to be *ch*.

charAt(i): Return the character at index i in S.

Error conditions occur when the index i is out of the bounds of the indices of the string. With the exception of the charAt method, most of the methods of the String class are not immediately available to a StringBuffer object S in Java. Fortunately, the Java StringBuffer class provides a toString() method that returns a String version of S, which can be used to access String methods.

Example 12.2: *Consider the following sequence of operations, which are performed on the mutable string that is initially S = "abcdefghijklmnop":*

Operation	S
append("qrs")	"abcdefghijklmnopqrs"
insert(3,"xyz")	"abcxyzdefghijklmnopqrs"
reverse()	"srqponmlkjihgfedzyxcba"
setCharAt(7,'W')	"srqponmWkjihgfedzyxcba"

12.2 Dynamic Programming

In this section, we discuss the ***dynamic programming*** algorithm-design technique. This technique is similar to the divide-and-conquer technique (Section 11.1.1), in that it can be applied to a wide variety of different problems. There are few algorithmic techniques that can take problems that seem to require exponential time and produce polynomial-time algorithms to solve them. Dynamic programming is one such technique. In addition, the algorithms that result from applications of the dynamic programming technique are usually quite simple—often needing little more than a few lines of code to describe some nested loops for filling in a table.

12.2.1 Matrix Chain-Product

Rather than starting out with an explanation of the general components of the dynamic programming technique, we begin by giving a classic, concrete example. Suppose we are given a collection of n two-dimensional arrays (matrices) for which we wish to compute the product

$$A = A_0 \cdot A_1 \cdot A_2 \cdots A_{n-1},$$

where A_i is a $d_i \times d_{i+1}$ matrix, for $i = 0, 1, 2, \ldots, n-1$. In the standard matrix multiplication algorithm (which is the one we will use), to multiply a $d \times e$-matrix B times an $e \times f$-matrix C, we compute the product, A, as

$$A[i][j] = \sum_{k=0}^{e-1} B[i][k] \cdot C[k][j].$$

This definition implies that matrix multiplication is associative, that is, it implies that $B \cdot (C \cdot D) = (B \cdot C) \cdot D$. Thus, we can parenthesize the expression for A any way we wish and we will end up with the same answer. We will not necessarily perform the same number of primitive (that is, scalar) multiplications in each parenthesization, however, as is illustrated in the following example.

Example 12.3: *Let B be a 2×10-matrix, let C be a 10×50-matrix, and let D be a 50×20-matrix. Computing $B \cdot (C \cdot D)$ requires $2 \cdot 10 \cdot 20 + 10 \cdot 50 \cdot 20 = 10400$ multiplications, whereas computing $(B \cdot C) \cdot D$ requires $2 \cdot 10 \cdot 50 + 2 \cdot 50 \cdot 20 = 3000$ multiplications.*

The ***matrix chain-product*** problem is to determine the parenthesization of the expression defining the product A that minimizes the total number of scalar multiplications performed. As the example above illustrates, the differences between different solutions can be dramatic, so finding a good solution can result in significant speedups.

Defining Subproblems

Of course, one way to solve the matrix chain-product problem is to simply enumerate all the possible ways of parenthesizing the expression for A and determine the number of multiplications performed by each one. Unfortunately, the set of all different parenthesizations of the expression for A is equal in number to the set of all different binary trees that have n external nodes. This number is exponential in n. Thus, this straightforward ("brute force") algorithm runs in exponential time, for there are an exponential number of ways to parenthesize an associative arithmetic expression.

We can improve the performance achieved by the brute force algorithm significantly, however, by making a few observations about the nature of the matrix chain-product problem. The first observation is that the problem can be split into **subproblems**. In this case, we can define a number of different subproblems, each of which is to compute the best parenthesization for some subexpression $A_i \cdot A_{i+1} \cdots A_j$. As a concise notation, we use $N_{i,j}$ to denote the minimum number of multiplications needed to compute this subexpression. Thus, the original matrix chain-product problem can be characterized as that of computing the value of $N_{0,n-1}$. This observation is important, but we need one more in order to apply the dynamic programming technique.

Characterizing Optimal Solutions

The other important observation we can make about the matrix chain-product problem is that it is possible to characterize an optimal solution to a particular subproblem in terms of optimal solutions to its subproblems. We call this property the **subproblem optimality** condition.

In the case of the matrix chain-product problem, we observe that, no matter how we parenthesize a subexpression, there has to be some final matrix multiplication that we perform. That is, a full parenthesization of a subexpression $A_i \cdot A_{i+1} \cdots A_j$ has to be of the form $(A_i \cdots A_k) \cdot (A_{k+1} \cdots A_j)$, for some $k \in \{i, i+1, \ldots, j-1\}$. Moreover, for whichever k is the correct one, the products $(A_i \cdots A_k)$ and $(A_{k+1} \cdots A_j)$ must also be solved optimally. If this were not so, then there would be a global optimal that had one of these subproblems solved suboptimally. But this is impossible, since we could then reduce the total number of multiplications by replacing the current subproblem solution by an optimal solution for the subproblem. This observation implies a way of explicitly defining the optimization problem for $N_{i,j}$ in terms of other optimal subproblem solutions. Namely, we can compute $N_{i,j}$ by considering each place k where we could put the final multiplication and taking the minimum over all such choices.

Designing a Dynamic Programming Algorithm

We can therefore characterize the optimal subproblem solution, $N_{i,j}$, as

$$N_{i,j} = \min_{i \leq k < j}\{N_{i,k} + N_{k+1,j} + d_i d_{k+1} d_{j+1}\},$$

where $N_{i,i} = 0$, since no work is needed for a single matrix. That is, $N_{i,j}$ is the minimum, taken over all possible places to perform the final multiplication, of the number of multiplications needed to compute each subexpression plus the number of multiplications needed to perform the final matrix multiplication.

Notice that there is a ***sharing of subproblems*** going on that prevents us from dividing the problem into completely independent subproblems (as we would need to do to apply the divide-and-conquer technique). We can, nevertheless, use the equation for $N_{i,j}$ to derive an efficient algorithm by computing $N_{i,j}$ values in a bottom-up fashion, and storing intermediate solutions in a table of $N_{i,j}$ values. We can begin simply enough by assigning $N_{i,i} = 0$ for $i = 0, 1, \ldots, n-1$. We can then apply the general equation for $N_{i,j}$ to compute $N_{i,i+1}$ values, since they depend only on $N_{i,i}$ and $N_{i+1,i+1}$ values that are available. Given the $N_{i,i+1}$ values, we can then compute the $N_{i,i+2}$ values, and so on. Therefore, we can build $N_{i,j}$ values up from previously computed values until we can finally compute the value of $N_{0,n-1}$, which is the number that we are searching for. The details of this ***dynamic programming*** solution are given in Code Fragment 12.1.

Algorithm MatrixChain($d_0, \ldots, d_n$):
    Input: Sequence $d_0, \ldots, d_n$ of integers
    Output: For $i, j = 0, \ldots, n-1$, the minimum number of multiplications $N_{i,j}$
        needed to compute the product $A_i \cdot A_{i+1} \cdots A_j$, where A_k is a $d_k \times d_{k+1}$ matrix
    for $i \leftarrow 0$ to $n-1$ **do**
        $N_{i,i} \leftarrow 0$
    for $b \leftarrow 1$ to $n-1$ **do**
        for $i \leftarrow 0$ to $n-b-1$ **do**
            $j \leftarrow i+b$
            $N_{i,j} \leftarrow +\infty$
            for $k \leftarrow i$ to $j-1$ **do**
                $N_{i,j} \leftarrow \min\{N_{i,j}, N_{i,k} + N_{k+1,j} + d_i d_{k+1} d_{j+1}\}.$

Code Fragment 12.1: Dynamic programming algorithm for the matrix chain-product problem.

Thus, we can compute $N_{0,n-1}$ with an algorithm that consists primarily of three nested for-loops. The outside loop is executed n times. The loop inside is executed at most n times. And the inner-most loop is also executed at most n times. Therefore, the total running time of this algorithm is $O(n^3)$.

12.2.2   DNA and Text Sequence Alignment

A common text processing problem, which arises in genetics and software engineering, is to test the similarity between two text strings. In a genetics application, the two strings could correspond to two strands of DNA, for which we want to compute similarities. Likewise, in a software engineering application, the two strings could come from two versions of source code for the same program, for which we want to determine changes made from one version to the next. Indeed, determining the similarity between two strings is so common that the Unix and Linux operating systems have a built-in program, `diff`, for comparing text files.

Given a string $X = x_0 x_1 x_2 \cdots x_{n-1}$, a **subsequence** of X is any string that is of the form $x_{i_1} x_{i_2} \cdots x_{i_k}$, where $i_j < i_{j+1}$; that is, it is a sequence of characters that are not necessarily contiguous but are nevertheless taken in order from X. For example, the string $AAAG$ is a subsequence of the string $CGATAATTGAGA$.

The DNA and text similarity problem we address here is the **longest common subsequence** (LCS) problem. In this problem, we are given two character strings, $X = x_0 x_1 x_2 \cdots x_{n-1}$ and $Y = y_0 y_1 y_2 \cdots y_{m-1}$, over some alphabet (such as the alphabet $\{A, C, G, T\}$ common in computational genetics) and are asked to find a longest string S that is a subsequence of both X and Y. One way to solve the longest common subsequence problem is to enumerate all subsequences of X and take the largest one that is also a subsequence of Y. Since each character of X is either in or not in a subsequence, there are potentially 2^n different subsequences of X, each of which requires $O(m)$ time to determine whether it is a subsequence of Y. Thus, this brute-force approach yields an exponential-time algorithm that runs in $O(2^n m)$ time, which is very inefficient. Fortunately, the LCS problem is efficiently solvable using **dynamic programming**.

The Components of a Dynamic Programming Solution

As mentioned above, the dynamic programming technique is used primarily for **optimization** problems, where we wish to find the "best" way of doing something. We can apply the dynamic programming technique in such situations if the problem has certain properties:

Simple Subproblems: There has to be some way of repeatedly breaking the global optimization problem into subproblems. Moreover, there should be a simple way of defining subproblems with just a few indices, like i, j, k, and so on.

Subproblem Optimization: An optimal solution to the global problem must be a composition of optimal subproblem solutions.

Subproblem Overlap: Optimal solutions to unrelated subproblems can contain subproblems in common.

Applying Dynamic Programming to the LCS Problem

Recall that in the LCS problem, we are given two character strings, X and Y, of length n and m, respectively, and are asked to find a longest string S that is a subsequence of both X and Y. Since X and Y are character strings, we have a natural set of indices with which to define subproblems—indices into the strings X and Y. Let us define a subproblem, therefore, as that of computing the value $L[i,j]$, which we will use to denote the length of a longest string that is a subsequence of both $X[0..i] = x_0 x_1 x_2 \ldots x_i$ and $Y[0..j] = y_0 y_1 y_2 \ldots y_j$. This definition allows us to rewrite $L[i,j]$ in terms of optimal subproblem solutions. This definition depends on which of two cases we are in. (See Figure 12.1.)

Figure 12.1: The two cases in the longest common subsequence algorithm: (a) $x_i = y_j$; (b) $x_i \neq y_j$. Note that the algorithm stores only the $L[i,j]$ values, not the matches.

- $x_i = y_j$. In this case, we have a match between the last character of $X[0..i]$ and the last character of $Y[0..j]$. We claim that this character belongs to a longest common subsequence of $X[0..i]$ and $Y[0..j]$. To justify this claim, let us suppose it is not true. There has to be some longest common subsequence $x_{i_1} x_{i_2} \ldots x_{i_k} = y_{j_1} y_{j_2} \ldots y_{j_k}$. If $x_{i_k} = x_i$ or $y_{j_k} = y_j$, then we get the same sequence by setting $i_k = i$ and $j_k = j$. Alternately, if $x_{j_k} \neq x_i$, then we can get an even longer common subsequence by adding x_i to the end. Thus, a longest common subsequence of $X[0..i]$ and $Y[0..j]$ ends with x_i. Therefore, we set

$$L[i,j] = L[i-1, j-1] + 1 \quad \text{if } x_i = y_j.$$

- $x_i \neq y_j$. In this case, we cannot have a common subsequence that includes both x_i and y_j. That is, we can have a common subsequence end with x_i or one that ends with y_j (or possibly neither), but certainly not both. Therefore, we set

$$L[i,j] = \max\{L[i-1, j], L[i, j-1]\} \quad \text{if } x_i \neq y_j.$$

In order to make both of these equations make sense in the boundary cases when $i = 0$ or $j = 0$, we assign $L[i, -1] = 0$ for $i = -1, 0, 1, \ldots, n-1$ and $L[-1, j] = 0$ for $j = -1, 0, 1, \ldots, m-1$.

The LCS Algorithm

The definition of $L[i,j]$ satisfies subproblem optimization, for we cannot have a longest common subsequence without also having longest common subsequences for the subproblems. Also, it uses subproblem overlap, because a subproblem solution $L[i,j]$ can be used in several other problems (namely, the problems $L[i+1,j]$, $L[i,j+1]$, and $L[i+1,j+1]$). Turning this definition of $L[i,j]$ into an algorithm is actually quite straightforward. We initialize an $(n+1) \times (m+1)$ array, L, for the boundary cases when $i = 0$ or $j = 0$. Namely, we initialize $L[i,-1] = 0$ for $i = -1,0,1,\ldots,n-1$ and $L[-1,j] = 0$ for $j = -1,0,1,\ldots,m-1$. Then, we iteratively build up values in L until we have $L[n-1,m-1]$, the length of a longest common subsequence of X and Y. We give a pseudo-code description of this algorithm in Code Fragment 12.2.

Algorithm LCS(X,Y):

   Input: Strings X and Y with n and m elements, respectively

   Output: For $i = 0,\ldots,n-1$, $j = 0,\ldots,m-1$, the length $L[i,j]$ of a longest string that is a subsequence of both the string $X[0..i] = x_0x_1x_2\cdots x_i$ and the string $Y[0..j] = y_0y_1y_2\cdots y_j$

   for $i \leftarrow -1$ to $n-1$ **do**

     $L[i,-1] \leftarrow 0$

   for $j \leftarrow 0$ to $m-1$ **do**

     $L[-1,j] \leftarrow 0$

   for $i \leftarrow 0$ to $n-1$ **do**

     for $j \leftarrow 0$ to $m-1$ **do**

       if $x_i = y_j$ **then**

         $L[i,j] \leftarrow L[i-1,j-1]+1$

       else

         $L[i,j] \leftarrow \max\{L[i-1,j], L[i,j-1]\}$

   return array L

Code Fragment 12.2: Dynamic programming algorithm for the LCS problem.

The running time of the algorithm of Code Fragment 12.2 is easy to analyze, for it is dominated by two nested **for** loops, with the outer one iterating n times and the inner one iterating m times. Since the if-statement and assignment inside the loop each requires $O(1)$ primitive operations, this algorithm runs in $O(nm)$ time. Thus, the dynamic programming technique can be applied to the longest common subsequence problem to improve significantly over the exponential-time brute-force solution to the LCS problem.

Algorithm LCS (Code Fragment 12.2) computes the length of the longest common subsequence (stored in $L[n-1, m-1]$), but not the subsequence itself. As shown in the following proposition, a simple postprocessing step can extract the longest common subsequence from the array L returned by algorithm.

Proposition 12.4: *Given a string X of n characters and a string Y of m characters, we can find the longest common subsequence of X and Y in $O(nm)$ time.*

Justification: Algorithm LCS computes $L[n-1, m-1]$, the **length** of a longest common subsequence, in $O(nm)$ time. Given the table of $L[i, j]$ values, constructing a longest common subsequence is straightforward. One method is to start from $L[n, m]$ and work back through the table, reconstructing a longest common subsequence from back to front. At any position $L[i, j]$, we can determine whether $x_i = y_j$. If this is true, then we can take x_i as the next character of the subsequence (noting that x_i is **before** the previous character we found, if any), moving next to $L[i-1, j-1]$. If $x_i \neq y_j$, then we can move to the larger of $L[i, j-1]$ and $L[i-1, j]$. (See Figure 12.2.) We stop when we reach a boundary cell (with $i = -1$ or $j = -1$). This method constructs a longest common subsequence in $O(n+m)$ additional time. ∎

L	-1	0	1	2	3	4	5	6	7	8	9	10	11
-1	0	0	0	0	0	0	0	0	0	0	0	0	0
0	0	0	1	1	1	1	1	1	1	1	1	1	1
1	0	0	1	1	2	2	2	2	2	2	2	2	2
2	0	0	1	1	2	2	2	3	3	3	3	3	3
3	0	1	1	1	2	2	2	3	3	3	3	3	3
4	0	1	1	1	2	2	2	3	3	3	3	3	3
5	0	1	1	1	2	2	2	3	4	4	4	4	4
6	0	1	1	2	2	3	3	3	4	4	5	5	5
7	0	1	1	2	2	3	4	4	4	4	5	5	6
8	0	1	1	2	3	3	4	5	5	5	5	5	6
9	0	1	1	2	3	4	4	5	5	5	6	6	6

Figure 12.2: Illustration of the algorithm for constructing a longest common subsequence from the array L.

12.3　Pattern Matching Algorithms

In the classic **pattern matching** problem on strings, we are given a **text** string T of length n and a **pattern** string P of length m, and want to find whether P is a substring of T. The notion of a "match" is that there is a substring of T starting at some index i that matches P, character by character, so that $T[i] = P[0]$, $T[i+1] = P[1]$, ..., $T[i+m-1] = P[m-1]$. That is, $P = T[i..i+m-1]$. Thus, the output from a pattern matching algorithm could either be some indication that the pattern P does not exist in T or an integer indicating the starting index in T of a substring matching P. This is exactly the computation performed by the indexOf method of the Java String interface. Alternatively, one may want to find all the indices where a substring of T matching P begins.

In this section, we present three pattern matching algorithms (with increasing levels of difficulty).

12.3.1　Brute Force

The **brute force** algorithmic design pattern is a powerful technique for algorithm design when we have something we wish to search for or when we wish to optimize some function. In applying this technique in a general situation we typically enumerate all possible configurations of the inputs involved and pick the best of all these enumerated configurations.

In applying this technique to design the **brute-force pattern matching** algorithm, we derive what is probably the first algorithm that we might think of for solving the pattern matching problem—we simply test all the possible placements of P relative to T. This algorithm, shown in Code Fragment 12.3, is quite simple.

Algorithm BruteForceMatch(T,P):

   Input: Strings T (text) with n characters and P (pattern) with m characters

   Output: Starting index of the first substring of T matching P, or an indication that P is not a substring of T

   for $i \leftarrow 0$ **to** $n - m$ {for each candidate index in T} **do**
     $j \leftarrow 0$
     while $(j < m$ **and** $T[i+j] = P[j])$ **do**
       $j \leftarrow j + 1$
     if $j = m$ **then**
       return i
   return "There is no substring of T matching P."

Code Fragment 12.3: Brute-force pattern matching.

Performance

The brute-force pattern matching algorithm could not be simpler. It consists of two nested loops, with the outer loop indexing through all possible starting indices of the pattern in the text, and the inner loop indexing through each character of the pattern, comparing it to its potentially corresponding character in the text. Thus, the correctness of the brute-force pattern matching algorithm follows immediately from this exhaustive search approach.

The running time of brute-force pattern matching in the worst case is not good, however, because, for each candidate index in T, we can perform up to m character comparisons to discover that P does not match T at the current index. Referring to Code Fragment 12.3, we see that the outer **for** loop is executed at most $n - m + 1$ times, and the inner loop is executed at most m times. Thus, the running time of the brute-force method is $O((n - m + 1)m)$, which is simplified as $O(nm)$. Note that when $m = n/2$, this algorithm has quadratic running time $O(n^2)$.

Example 12.5: *Suppose we are given the text string*

$$T = \text{"abacaabaccabacabaabb"}$$

and the pattern string

$$P = \text{"abacab"}.$$

In Figure 12.3 we illustrate the execution of the brute-force pattern matching algorithm on T and P.

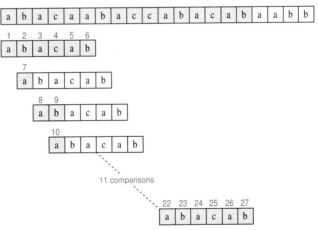

Figure 12.3: Example run of the brute-force pattern matching algorithm. The algorithm performs 27 character comparisons, indicated above with numerical labels.

12.3.2   The Boyer-Moore Algorithm

At first, we might feel that it is always necessary to examine every character in T in order to locate a pattern P as a substring. But this is not always the case, for the **Boyer-Moore** (**BM**) pattern matching algorithm, which we study in this section, can sometimes avoid comparisons between P and a sizable fraction of the characters in T. The only caveat is that, whereas the brute-force algorithm can work even with a potentially unbounded alphabet, the BM algorithm assumes the alphabet is of fixed, finite size. It works the fastest when the alphabet is moderately sized and the pattern is relatively long. Thus, the BM algorithm is ideal for searching words in documents. In this section, we describe a simplified version of the original algorithm by Boyer and Moore.

The main idea of the BM algorithm is to improve the running time of the brute-force algorithm by adding two potentially time-saving heuristics. Roughly stated, these heuristics are as follows:

Looking-Glass Heuristic: When testing a possible placement of P against T, begin the comparisons from the end of P and move backward to the front of P.

Character-Jump Heuristic: During the testing of a possible placement of P against T, a mismatch of text character $T[i] = c$ with the corresponding pattern character $P[j]$ is handled as follows. If c is not contained anywhere in P, then shift P completely past $T[i]$ (for it cannot match any character in P). Otherwise, shift P until an occurrence of character c in P gets aligned with $T[i]$.

We will formalize these heuristics shortly, but at an intuitive level, they work as an integrated team. The looking-glass heuristic sets up the other heuristic to allow us to avoid comparisons between P and whole groups of characters in T. In this case at least, we can get to the destination faster by going backwards, for if we encounter a mismatch during the consideration of P at a certain location in T, then we are likely to avoid lots of needless comparisons by significantly shifting P relative to T using the character-jump heuristic. The character-jump heuristic pays off big if it can be applied early in the testing of a potential placement of P against T.

Let us therefore get down to the business of defining how the character-jump heuristics can be integrated into a string pattern matching algorithm. To implement this heuristic, we define a function $\mathsf{last}(c)$ that takes a character c from the alphabet and characterizes how far we may shift the pattern P if a character equal to c is found in the text that does not match the pattern. In particular, we define $\mathsf{last}(c)$ as

- If c is in P, $\mathsf{last}(c)$ is the index of the last (right-most) occurrence of c in P. Otherwise, we conventionally define $\mathsf{last}(c) = -1$.

If characters can be used as indices in arrays, then the last function can be easily implemented as a look-up table. We leave the method for computing this table in $O(m + |\Sigma|)$ time, given P, as a simple exercise (R-12.8). This last function will give us all the information we need to perform the character-jump heuristic.

In Code Fragment 12.4, we show the BM pattern matching algorithm.

Algorithm BMMatch(T,P):

   Input: Strings T (text) with n characters and P (pattern) with m characters

   Output: Starting index of the first substring of T matching P, or an indication that P is not a substring of T

   compute function last

   $i \leftarrow m - 1$

   $j \leftarrow m - 1$

   repeat

     if $P[j] = T[i]$ **then**

       if $j = 0$ **then**

         return i {a match!}

       else

         $i \leftarrow i - 1$

         $j \leftarrow j - 1$

     else

       $i \leftarrow i + m - \min(j, 1 + \mathsf{last}(T[i]))$ { jump step }

       $j \leftarrow m - 1$

   until $i > n - 1$

   return "There is no substring of T matching P."

   Code Fragment 12.4: The Boyer-Moore pattern matching algorithm.

The jump step is illustrated in Figure 12.4.

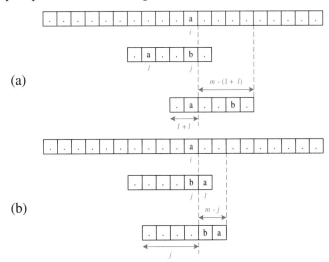

Figure 12.4: Illustration of the jump step in the algorithm of Code Fragment 12.4, where we let $l = \mathsf{last}(T[i])$. We distinguish two cases: (a) $1 + l \leq j$, where we shift the pattern by $j - l$ units; (b) $j < 1 + l$, where we shift the pattern by one unit.

In Figure 12.5, we illustrate the execution of the Boyer-Moore pattern matching algorithm on an input string similar to Example 12.5.

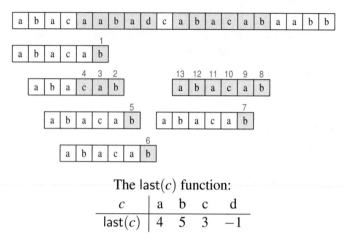

The last(c) function:

c	a	b	c	d
last(c)	4	5	3	−1

Figure 12.5: An illustration of the BM pattern matching algorithm. The algorithm performs 13 character comparisons, which are indicated with numerical labels.

The correctness of the BM pattern matching algorithm follows from the fact that each time the method makes a shift, it is guaranteed not to "skip" over any possible matches. For last(c) is the location of the *last* occurrence of c in P.

The worst-case running time of the BM algorithm is $O(nm + |\Sigma|)$. Namely, the computation of the last function takes time $O(m + |\Sigma|)$ and the actual search for the pattern takes $O(nm)$ time in the worst case, the same as the brute-force algorithm. An example of a text-pattern pair that achieves the worst case is

$$T = \overbrace{aaaaaa \cdots a}^{n}$$

$$P = b\overbrace{aa \cdots a}^{m-1}.$$

The worst-case performance, however, is unlikely to be achieved for English text, for, in this case, the BM algorithm is often able to skip large portions of text. (See Figure 12.6.) Experimental evidence on English text shows that the average number of comparisons done per character is 0.24 for a five-character pattern string.

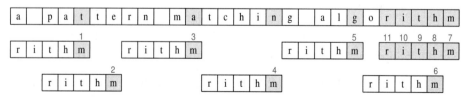

Figure 12.6: An example of a Boyer-Moore execution on English text.

A Java implementation of the BM pattern matching algorithm is shown in Code Fragment 12.5.

```java
/** Simplified version of the Boyer-Moore (BM) algorithm, which uses
  * only the looking-glass and character-jump heuristics.
  * @return Index of the beginning of the leftmost substring of the text
  * matching the pattern, or -1 if there is no match. */
public static int BMmatch (String text, String pattern) {
  int[] last = buildLastFunction(pattern);
  int n = text.length();
  int m = pattern.length();
  int i = m −1;
  if (i > n − 1)
    return −1; // no match if pattern is longer than text
  int j = m − 1;
  do {
    if (pattern.charAt(j) == text.charAt(i))
      if (j == 0)
        return i; // match
      else { // looking-glass heuristic: proceed right-to-left
        i−−;
        j−−;
      }
    else { // character jump heuristic
      i = i + m − Math.min(j, 1 + last[text.charAt(i)]);
      j = m − 1;
    }
  } while (i <= n − 1);
  return −1; // no match
}
public static int[] buildLastFunction (String pattern) {
  int[] last = new int[128]; // assume ASCII character set
  for (int i = 0; i < 128; i++) {
    last[i] = −1; // initialize array
  }
  for (int i = 0; i < pattern.length(); i++) {
    last[pattern.charAt(i)] = i; // implicit cast to integer ASCII code
  }
  return last;
}
```

Code Fragment 12.5: Java implementation of the BM pattern matching algorithm. The algorithm is expressed by two static methods: Method BMmatch performs the matching and calls the auxiliary method buildLastFunction to compute the last function, expressed by an array indexed by the ASCII code of the character. Method BMmatch indicates the absence of a match by returning the conventional value −1.

We have actually presented a simplified version of the Boyer-Moore (BM) algorithm. The original BM algorithm achieves running time $O(n+m+|\Sigma|)$ by using an alternative shift heuristic to the partially matched text string, whenever it shifts the pattern more than the character-jump heuristic. This alternative shift heuristic is based on applying the main idea from the Knuth-Morris-Pratt pattern matching algorithm, which we discuss next.

12.3.3 The Knuth-Morris-Pratt Algorithm

In studying the worst-case performance of the brute-force and BM pattern matching algorithms on specific instances of the problem, such as that given in Example 12.5, we should notice a major inefficiency. Specifically, we may perform many comparisons while testing a potential placement of the pattern against the text, yet if we discover a pattern character that does not match in the text, then we throw away all the information gained by these comparisons and start over again from scratch with the next incremental placement of the pattern. The Knuth-Morris-Pratt (or "KMP") algorithm, discussed in this section, avoids this waste of information and, in so doing, it achieves a running time of $O(n+m)$, which is optimal in the worst case. That is, in the worst case any pattern matching algorithm will have to examine all the characters of the text and all the characters of the pattern at least once.

The Failure Function

The main idea of the KMP algorithm is to preprocess the pattern string P so as to compute a ***failure function***, f, that indicates the proper shift of P so that, to the largest extent possible, we can reuse previously performed comparisons. Specifically, the failure function $f(j)$ is defined as the length of the longest prefix of P that is a suffix of $P[1..j]$ (note that we did ***not*** put $P[0..j]$ here). We also use the convention that $f(0) = 0$. Later, we will discuss how to compute the failure function efficiently. The importance of this failure function is that it "encodes" repeated substrings inside the pattern itself.

Example 12.6: *Consider the pattern string $P =$ "abacab" from Example 12.5. The Knuth-Morris-Pratt (KMP) failure function, $f(j)$, for the string P is as shown in the following table:*

j	0	1	2	3	4	5
$P[j]$	a	b	a	c	a	b
$f(j)$	0	0	1	0	1	2

The KMP pattern matching algorithm, shown in Code Fragment 12.6, incrementally processes the text string T comparing it to the pattern string P. Each time there is a match, we increment the current indices. On the other hand, if there is a mismatch and we have previously made progress in P, then we consult the failure function to determine the new index in P where we need to continue checking P against T. Otherwise (there was a mismatch and we are at the beginning of P), we simply increment the index for T (and keep the index variable for P at its beginning). We repeat this process until we find a match of P in T or the index for T reaches n, the length of T (indicating that we did not find the pattern P in T).

Algorithm KMPMatch(T, P):

    Input: Strings T (text) with n characters and P (pattern) with m characters

    Output: Starting index of the first substring of T matching P, or an indication that P is not a substring of T

    $f \leftarrow$ KMPFailureFunction(P)   {construct the failure function f for P}

    $i \leftarrow 0$

    $j \leftarrow 0$

    while $i < n$ **do**

        if $P[j] = T[i]$ **then**

            if $j = m - 1$ **then**

                return $i - m + 1$ {a match!}

            $i \leftarrow i + 1$

            $j \leftarrow j + 1$

        else if $j > 0$ {no match, but we have advanced in P} **then**

            $j \leftarrow f(j - 1)$ {j indexes just after prefix of P that must match}

        else

            $i \leftarrow i + 1$

    return "There is no substring of T matching P."

Code Fragment 12.6: The KMP pattern matching algorithm.

The main part of the KMP algorithm is the **while** loop, which performs a comparison between a character in T and a character in P each iteration. Depending upon the outcome of this comparison, the algorithm either moves on to the next characters in T and P, consults the failure function for a new candidate character in P, or starts over with the next index in T. The correctness of this algorithm follows from the definition of the failure function. Any comparisons that are skipped are actually unnecessary, for the failure function guarantees that all the ignored comparisons are redundant—they would involve comparing the same matching characters over again.

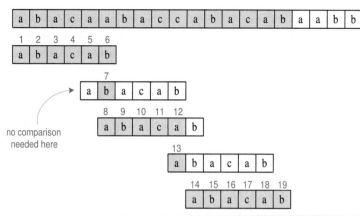

Figure 12.7: An illustration of the KMP pattern matching algorithm. The failure function f for this pattern is given in Example 12.6. The algorithm performs 19 character comparisons, which are indicated with numerical labels.

In Figure 12.7, we illustrate the execution of the KMP pattern matching algorithm on the same input strings as in Example 12.5. Note the use of the failure function to avoid redoing one of the comparisons between a character of the pattern and a character of the text. Also note that the algorithm performs fewer overall comparisons than the brute-force algorithm run on the same strings (Figure 12.3).

Performance

Excluding the computation of the failure function, the running time of the KMP algorithm is clearly proportional to the number of iterations of the **while** loop. For the sake of the analysis, let us define $k = i - j$. Intuitively, k is the total amount by which the pattern P has been shifted with respect to the text T. Note that throughout the execution of the algorithm, we have $k \leq n$. One of the following three cases occurs at each iteration of the loop.

- If $T[i] = P[j]$, then i increases by 1, and k does not change, since j also increases by 1.
- If $T[i] \neq P[j]$ and $j > 0$, then i does not change and k increases by at least 1, since in this case k changes from $i - j$ to $i - f(j-1)$, which is an addition of $j - f(j-1)$, which is positive because $f(j-1) < j$.
- If $T[i] \neq P[j]$ and $j = 0$, then i increases by 1 and k increases by 1, since j does not change.

Thus, at each iteration of the loop, either i or k increases by at least 1 (possibly both); hence, the total number of iterations of the **while** loop in the KMP pattern matching algorithm is at most $2n$. Achieving this bound, of course, assumes that we have already computed the failure function for P.

Constructing the KMP Failure Function

To construct the failure function, we use the method shown in Code Fragment 12.7, which is a "bootstrapping" process quite similar to the KMPMatch algorithm. We compare the pattern to itself as in the KMP algorithm. Each time we have two characters that match, we set $f(i) = j + 1$. Note that since we have $i > j$ throughout the execution of the algorithm, $f(j - 1)$ is always defined when we need to use it.

Algorithm KMPFailureFunction(P):

    Input: String P (pattern) with m characters

    Output: The failure function f for P, which maps j to the length of the longest prefix of P that is a suffix of $P[1..j]$

    $i \leftarrow 1$

    $j \leftarrow 0$

    $f(0) \leftarrow 0$

    while $i < m$ **do**

        if $P[j] = P[i]$ **then**

            $\{$we have matched $j + 1$ characters$\}$

            $f(i) \leftarrow j + 1$

            $i \leftarrow i + 1$

            $j \leftarrow j + 1$

        else if $j > 0$ **then**

            $\{j$ indexes just after a prefix of P that must match$\}$

            $j \leftarrow f(j - 1)$

        else

            $\{$we have no match here$\}$

            $f(i) \leftarrow 0$

            $i \leftarrow i + 1$

Code Fragment 12.7: Computation of the failure function used in the KMP pattern matching algorithm. Note how the algorithm uses the previous values of the failure function to efficiently compute new values.

Algorithm KMPFailureFunction runs in $O(m)$ time. Its analysis is analogous to that of algorithm KMPMatch. Thus, we have:

Proposition 12.7: *The Knuth-Morris-Pratt algorithm performs pattern matching on a text string of length n and a pattern string of length m in $O(n + m)$ time.*

A Java implementation of the KMP pattern matching algorithm is shown in Code Fragment 12.8.

```java
public static int KMPmatch(String text, String pattern) {
  int n = text.length();
  int m = pattern.length();
  int[] fail = computeFailFunction(pattern);
  int i = 0;
  int j = 0;
  while (i < n) {
    if (pattern.charAt(j) == text.charAt(i)) {
      if (j == m − 1)
        return i − m + 1; // match
      i++;
      j++;
    }
    else if (j > 0)
      j = fail[j − 1];
    else
      i++;
  }
  return −1; // no match
}
public static int[] computeFailFunction(String pattern) {
  int[] fail = new int[pattern.length()];
  fail[0] = 0;
  int m = pattern.length();
  int j = 0;
  int i = 1;
  while (i < m) {
    if (pattern.charAt(j) == pattern.charAt(i)) { // j + 1 characters match
      fail[i] = j + 1;
      i++;
      j++;
    }
    else if (j > 0) // j follows a matching prefix
      j = fail[j − 1];
    else { // no match
      fail[i] = 0;
      i++;
    }
  }
  return fail;
}
```

Code Fragment 12.8: Java implementation of the KMP pattern matching algorithm. The algorithm is expressed by two static methods: method KMPmatch performs the matching and calls the auxiliary method computeFailFunction to compute the failure function, expressed by an array. Method KMPmatch indicates the absence of a match by returning the conventional value −1.

12.4 Text Compression and the Greedy Method

In this section, we consider an important text processing task, ***text compression***. In this problem, we are given a string X defined over some alphabet, such as the ASCII or Unicode character sets, and we want to efficiently encode X into a small binary string Y (using only the characters 0 and 1). Text compression is useful in any situation where we are communicating over a low-bandwidth channel, such as a modem line or infrared connection, and we wish to minimize the time needed to transmit our text. Likewise, text compression is also useful for storing collections of large documents more efficiently, so as to allow for a fixed-capacity storage device to contain as many documents as possible.

The method for text compression explored in this section is the ***Huffman code***. Standard encoding schemes, such as the ASCII and Unicode systems, use fixed-length binary strings to encode characters (with 7 bits in the ASCII system and 16 in the Unicode system). A Huffman code, on the other hand, uses a variable-length encoding optimized for the string X. The optimization is based on the use of character ***frequencies***, where we have, for each character c, a count $f(c)$ of the number of times c appears in the string X. The Huffman code saves space over a fixed-length encoding by using short code-word strings to encode high-frequency characters and long code-word strings to encode low-frequency characters.

To encode the string X, we convert each character in X from its fixed-length code-word to its variable-length code-word, and we concatenate all these code words in order to produce the encoding Y for X. In order to avoid ambiguities, we insist that no code-word in our encoding is a prefix of another code-word in our encoding. Such a code is called a ***prefix code***, and it simplifies the decoding of Y in order to get back X. (See Figure 12.8.) Even with this restriction, the savings produced by a variable-length prefix code can be significant, particularly if there is a wide variance in character frequencies (as is the case for natural language text in almost every spoken language).

Huffman's algorithm for producing an optimal variable-length prefix code for X is based on the construction of a binary tree T that represents the code. Each node in T, except the root, represents a bit in a code-word, with each left child representing a "0" and each right child representing a "1." Each external node v is associated with a specific character, and the code word for that character is defined by the sequence of bits associated with the nodes in the path from the root of T to v. (See Figure 12.8.) Each external node v has a ***frequency***, $f(v)$, which is simply the frequency in X of the character associated with v. In addition, we give each internal node v in T a frequency, $f(v)$, that is the sum of the frequencies of all the external nodes in the subtree rooted at v.

(a)

Character	a	b	d	e	f	h	i	k	n	o	r	s	t	u	v
Frequency	9	5	1	3	7	3	1	1	1	4	1	5	1	2	1	1

(b)

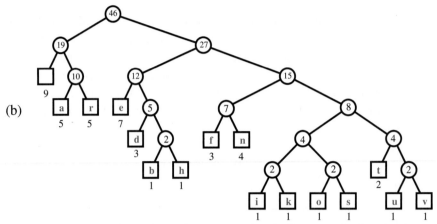

Figure 12.8: An illustration of an example Huffman code for the input string $X = $ "a fast runner need never be afraid of the dark": (a) frequency of each character of X; (b) Huffman tree T for string X. The code for a character c is obtained by tracing the path from the root of T to the external node where c is stored, and associating a left child with 0 and a right child with 1. For example, the code for "a" is 010, and the code for "f" is 1100.

12.4.1   The Huffman Coding Algorithm

The Huffman coding algorithm begins with each of the d distinct characters of the string X to encode being the root node of a single-node binary tree. The algorithm proceeds in a series of rounds. In each round, the algorithm takes the two binary trees with the smallest frequencies and merges them into a single binary tree. It repeats this process until only one tree is left. (See Code Fragment 12.9.)

Each iteration of the **while** loop in Huffman's algorithm can be implemented in $O(\log d)$ time using a priority queue represented with a heap. In addition, each iteration takes two nodes out of Q and adds one in, a process that will be repeated $d - 1$ times before exactly one node is left in Q. Thus, this algorithm runs in $O(n + d\log d)$ time. Although a full justification of this algorithm's correctness is beyond our scope here, we note that its intuition comes from a simple idea—any optimal code can be converted into an optimal code in which the code words for the two lowest-frequency characters, a and b, differ only in their last bit. Repeating the argument for a string with a and b replaced by a character c, gives the following:

Proposition 12.8: *Huffman's algorithm constructs an optimal prefix code for a string of length n with d distinct characters in $O(n + d\log d)$ time.*

Algorithm Huffman(X):

    Input: String X of length n with d distinct characters

    Output: Coding tree for X

    Compute the frequency $f(c)$ of each character c of X.

    Initialize a priority queue Q.

    for each character c in X **do**

        Create a single-node binary tree T storing c.

        Insert T into Q with key $f(c)$.

    while Q.size() > 1 **do**

        $f_1 \leftarrow Q$.min().key()

        $T_1 \leftarrow Q$.removeMin()

        $f_2 \leftarrow Q$.min().key()

        $T_2 \leftarrow Q$.removeMin()

        Create a new binary tree T with left subtree T_1 and right subtree T_2.

        Insert T into Q with key $f_1 + f_2$.

    return tree Q.removeMin()

Code Fragment 12.9: Huffman coding algorithm.

12.4.2 The Greedy Method

Huffman's algorithm for building an optimal encoding is an example application of an algorithmic design pattern called the ***greedy method***. This design pattern is applied to optimization problems, where we are trying to construct some structure while minimizing or maximizing some property of that structure.

The general formula for the greedy method pattern is almost as simple as that for the brute-force method. In order to solve a given optimization problem using the greedy method, we proceed by a sequence of choices. The sequence starts from some well-understood starting condition, and computes the cost for that initial condition. The pattern then asks that we iteratively make additional choices by identifying the decision that achieves the best cost improvement from all of the choices that are currently possible. This approach does not always lead to an optimal solution.

But there are several problems that it does work for, and such problems are said to possess the ***greedy-choice*** property. This is the property that a global optimal condition can be reached by a series of locally optimal choices (that is, choices that are each the current best from among the possibilities available at the time), starting from a well-defined starting condition. The problem of computing an optimal variable-length prefix code is just one example of a problem that possesses the greedy-choice property.

12.5   Tries

The pattern matching algorithms presented in the previous section speed up the search in a text by preprocessing the pattern (to compute the failure function in the KMP algorithm or the last function in the BM algorithm). In this section, we take a complementary approach, namely, we present string searching algorithms that preprocess the text. This approach is suitable for applications where a series of queries is performed on a fixed text, so that the initial cost of preprocessing the text is compensated by a speedup in each subsequent query (for example, a Web site that offers pattern matching in Shakespeare's *Hamlet* or a search engine that offers Web pages on the *Hamlet* topic).

A *trie* (pronounced "try") is a tree-based data structure for storing strings in order to support fast pattern matching. The main application for tries is in information retrieval. Indeed, the name "trie" comes from the word "re*trie*val." In an information retrieval application, such as a search for a certain DNA sequence in a genomic database, we are given a collection S of strings, all defined using the same alphabet. The primary query operations that tries support are pattern matching and *prefix matching*. The latter operation involves being given a string X, and looking for all the strings in S that contain X as a prefix.

12.5.1   Standard Tries

Let S be a set of s strings from alphabet Σ such that no string in S is a prefix of another string. A *standard trie* for S is an ordered tree T with the following properties (see Figure 12.9):

- Each node of T, except the root, is labeled with a character of Σ.
- The ordering of the children of an internal node of T is determined by a canonical ordering of the alphabet Σ.
- T has s external nodes, each associated with a string of S, such that the concatenation of the labels of the nodes on the path from the root to an external node v of T yields the string of S associated with v.

Thus, a trie T represents the strings of S with paths from the root to the external nodes of T. Note the importance of assuming that no string in S is a prefix of another string. This ensures that each string of S is uniquely associated with an external node of T. We can always satisfy this assumption by adding a special character that is not in the original alphabet Σ at the end of each string.

An internal node in a standard trie T can have anywhere between 1 and d children, where d is the size of the alphabet. There is an edge going from the root r to one of its children for each character that is first in some string in the collection S. In addition, a path from the root of T to an internal node v at depth i corresponds to

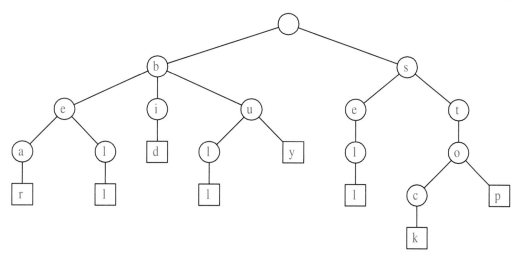

Figure 12.9: Standard trie for the strings {bear, bell, bid, bull, buy, sell, stock, stop}.

an *i*-character prefix $X[0..i-1]$ of a string X of S. In fact, for each character c that can follow the prefix $X[0..i-1]$ in a string of the set S, there is a child of v labeled with character c. In this way, a trie concisely stores the common prefixes that exist among a set of strings.

If there are only two characters in the alphabet, then the trie is essentially a binary tree, with some internal nodes possibly having only one child (that is, it may be an improper binary tree). In general, if there are d characters in the alphabet, then the trie will be a multi-way tree where each internal node has between 1 and d children. In addition, there are likely to be several internal nodes in a standard trie that have fewer than d children. For example, the trie shown in Figure 12.9 has several internal nodes with only one child. We can implement a trie with a tree storing characters at its nodes.

The following proposition provides some important structural properties of a standard trie:

Proposition 12.9: *A standard trie storing a collection S of s strings of total length n from an alphabet of size d has the following properties:*

- *Every internal node of T has at most d children.*
- *T has s external nodes.*
- *The height of T is equal to the length of the longest string in S.*
- *The number of nodes of T is $O(n)$.*

The worst case for the number of nodes of a trie occurs when no two strings share a common nonempty prefix; that is, except for the root, all internal nodes have one child.

A trie T for a set S of strings can be used to implement a dictionary whose keys are the strings of S. Namely, we perform a search in T for a string X by tracing down from the root the path indicated by the characters in X. If this path can be traced and terminates at an external node, then we know X is in the dictionary. For example, in the trie in Figure 12.9, tracing the path for "bull" ends up at an external node. If the path cannot be traced or the path can be traced but terminates at an internal node, then X is not in the dictionary. In the example in Figure 12.9, the path for "bet" cannot be traced and the path for "be" ends at an internal node. Neither such word is in the dictionary. Note that in this implementation of a dictionary, single characters are compared instead of the entire string (key). It is easy to see that the running time of the search for a string of size m is $O(dm)$, where d is the size of the alphabet. Indeed, we visit at most $m + 1$ nodes of T and we spend $O(d)$ time at each node. For some alphabets, we may be able to improve the time spent at a node to be $O(1)$ or $O(\log d)$ by using a dictionary of characters implemented in a hash table or search table. However, since d is a constant in most applications, we can stick with the simple approach that takes $O(d)$ time per node visited.

From the discussion above, it follows that we can use a trie to perform a special type of pattern matching, called **word matching**, where we want to determine whether a given pattern matches one of the words of the text exactly. (See Figure 12.10.) Word matching differs from standard pattern matching since the pattern cannot match an arbitrary substring of the text, but only one of its words. Using a trie, word matching for a pattern of length m takes $O(dm)$ time, where d is the size of the alphabet, independent of the size of the text. If the alphabet has constant size (as is the case for text in natural languages and DNA strings), a query takes $O(m)$ time, proportional to the size of the pattern. A simple extension of this scheme supports prefix matching queries. However, arbitrary occurrences of the pattern in the text (for example, the pattern is a proper suffix of a word or spans two words) cannot be efficiently performed.

To construct a standard trie for a set S of strings, we can use an incremental algorithm that inserts the strings one at a time. Recall the assumption that no string of S is a prefix of another string. To insert a string X into the current trie T, we first try to trace the path associated with X in T. Since X is not already in T and no string in S is a prefix of another string, we will stop tracing the path at an **internal** node v of T before reaching the end of X. We then create a new chain of node descendents of v to store the remaining characters of X. The time to insert X is $O(dm)$, where m is the length of X and d is the size of the alphabet. Thus, constructing the entire trie for set S takes $O(dn)$ time, where n is the total length of the strings of S.

s	e	e		a		b	e	a	r	?		s	e	l	l		s	t	o	c	k	!	
0	1	2	3	4	5	6	7	8	9	10	11	12	13	14	15	16	17	18	19	20	21	22	23

s	e	e		a		b	u	l	l	?		b	u	y		s	t	o	c	k	!	
24	25	26	27	28	29	30	31	32	33	34	35	36	37	38	39	40	41	42	43	44	45	46

b	i	d		s	t	o	c	k	!		b	i	d		s	t	o	c	k	!	
47	48	49	50	51	52	53	54	55	56	57	58	59	60	61	62	63	64	65	66	67	68

h	e	a	r		t	h	e		b	e	l	l	?		s	t	o	p	!	
69	70	71	72	73	74	75	76	77	78	79	80	81	82	83	84	85	86	87	88

(a)

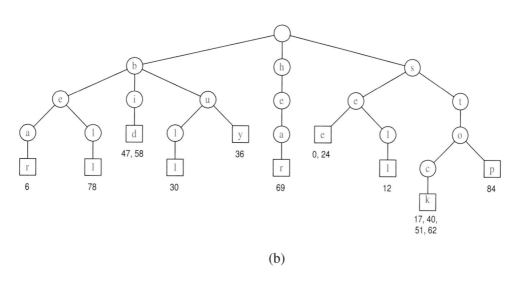

(b)

Figure 12.10: Word matching and prefix matching with a standard trie: (a) text to be searched; (b) standard trie for the words in the text (articles and prepositions, which are also known as *stop words*, excluded), with external nodes augmented with indications of the word positions.

There is a potential space inefficiency in the standard trie that has prompted the development of the ***compressed trie***, which is also known (for historical reasons) as the ***Patricia trie***. Namely, there are potentially a lot of nodes in the standard trie that have only one child, and the existence of such nodes is a waste. We discuss the compressed trie next.

12.5.2   Compressed Tries

A *compressed trie* is similar to a standard trie but it ensures that each internal node in the trie has at least two children. It enforces this rule by compressing chains of single-child nodes into individual edges. (See Figure 12.11.) Let T be a standard trie. We say that an internal node v of T is *redundant* if v has one child and is not the root. For example, the trie of Figure 12.9 has eight redundant nodes. Let us also say that a chain of $k \geq 2$ edges,

$$(v_0, v_1)(v_1, v_2) \cdots (v_{k-1}, v_k),$$

is *redundant* if:

- v_i is redundant for $i = 1, \ldots, k-1$.
- v_0 and v_k are not redundant.

We can transform T into a compressed trie by replacing each redundant chain $(v_0, v_1) \cdots (v_{k-1}, v_k)$ of $k \geq 2$ edges into a single edge (v_0, v_k), relabeling v_k with the concatenation of the labels of nodes $v_1, \ldots, v_k$.

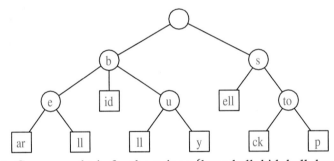

Figure 12.11: Compressed trie for the strings {bear, bell, bid, bull, buy, sell, stock, stop}. Compare this with the standard trie shown in Figure 12.9.

Thus, nodes in a compressed trie are labeled with strings, which are substrings of strings in the collection, rather than with individual characters. The advantage of a compressed trie over a standard trie is that the number of nodes of the compressed trie is proportional to the number of strings and not to their total length, as shown in the following proposition (compare with Proposition 12.9).

Proposition 12.10: *A compressed trie storing a collection S of s strings from an alphabet of size d has the following properties:*

- *Every internal node of T has at least two children and most d children.*
- *T has s external nodes.*
- *The number of nodes of T is $O(s)$.*

The attentive reader may wonder whether the compression of paths provides any significant advantage, since it is offset by a corresponding expansion of the node labels. Indeed, a compressed trie is truly advantageous only when it is used as an ***auxiliary*** index structure over a collection of strings already stored in a primary structure, and is not required to actually store all the characters of the strings in the collection.

Suppose, for example, that the collection S of strings is an array of strings $S[0]$, $S[1]$, …, $S[s-1]$. Instead of storing the label X of a node explicitly, we represent it implicitly by a triplet of integers (i, j, k), such that $X = S[i][j..k]$; that is, X is the substring of $S[i]$ consisting of the characters from the jth to the kth included. (See the example in Figure 12.12. Also compare with the standard trie of Figure 12.10.)

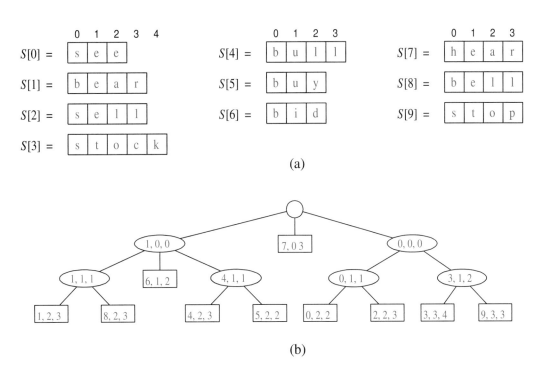

Figure 12.12: (a) Collection S of strings stored in an array. (b) Compact representation of the compressed trie for S.

This additional compression scheme allows us to reduce the total space for the trie itself from $O(n)$ for the standard trie to $O(s)$ for the compressed trie, where n is the total length of the strings in S and s is the number of strings in S. We must still store the different strings in S, of course, but we nevertheless reduce the space for the trie.

12.5.3   Suffix Tries

One of the primary applications for tries is for the case when the strings in the collection S are all the suffixes of a string X. Such a trie is called the *suffix trie* (also known as a *suffix tree* or *position tree*) of string X. For example, Figure 12.13a shows the suffix trie for the eight suffixes of string "minimize." For a suffix trie, the compact representation presented in the previous section can be further simplified. Namely, the label of each vertex is a pair (i, j) indicating the string $X[i..j]$. (See Figure 12.13b.) To satisfy the rule that no suffix of X is a prefix of another suffix, we can add a special character, denoted with $, that is not in the original alphabet Σ at the end of X (and thus to every suffix). That is, if string X has length n, we build a trie for the set of n strings $X[i..n-1]\$$, for $i = 0, \ldots, n-1$.

Saving Space

Using a suffix trie allows us to save space over a standard trie by using several space compression techniques, including those used for the compressed trie.

The advantage of the compact representation of tries now becomes apparent for suffix tries. Since the total length of the suffixes of a string X of length n is

$$1 + 2 + \cdots + n = \frac{n(n+1)}{2},$$

storing all the suffixes of X explicitly would take $O(n^2)$ space. Even so, the suffix trie represents these strings implicitly in $O(n)$ space, as formally stated in the following proposition.

Proposition 12.11: *The compact representation of a suffix trie T for a string X of length n uses $O(n)$ space.*

Construction

We can construct the suffix trie for a string of length n with an incremental algorithm like the one given in Section 12.5.1. This construction takes $O(dn^2)$ time because the total length of the suffixes is quadratic in n. However, the (compact) suffix trie for a string of length n can be constructed in $O(n)$ time with a specialized algorithm, different from the one for general tries. This linear-time construction algorithm is fairly complex, however, and is not reported here. Still, we can take advantage of the existence of this fast construction algorithm when we want to use a suffix trie to solve other problems.

Using a Suffix Trie

The suffix trie T for a string X can be used to efficiently perform pattern matching queries on text X. Namely, we can determine whether a pattern P is a substring

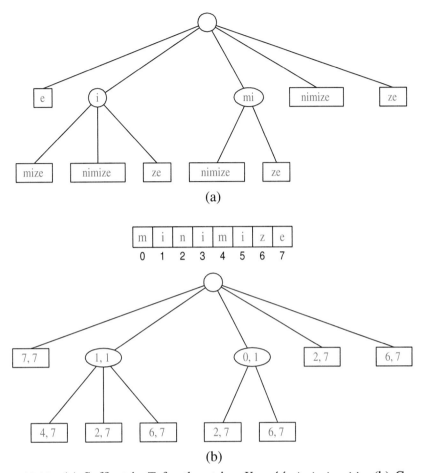

Figure 12.13: (a) Suffix trie T for the string $X =$ ''minimize''. (b) Compact representation of T, where pair (i, j) denotes $X[i..j]$.

of X by trying to trace a path associated with P in T. P is a substring of X if and only if such a path can be traced. The search down the trie T assumes that nodes in T store some additional information, with respect to the compact representation of the suffix trie:

If node v has label (i, j) and Y is the string of length y associated with the path from the root to v (included), then $X[j - y + 1..j] = Y$.

This property ensures that we can easily compute the start index of the pattern in the text when a match occurs.

12.5.4   Search Engines

The World Wide Web contains a huge collection of text documents (Web pages). Information about these pages are gathered by a program called a **Web crawler**, which then stores this information in a special dictionary database. A Web **search engine** allows users to retrieve relevant information from this database, thereby identifying relevant pages on the Web containing given keywords. In this section, we present a simplified model of a search engine.

Inverted Files

The core information stored by a search engine is a dictionary, called an **inverted index** or **inverted file**, storing key-value pairs (w, L), where w is a word and L is a collection of pages containing word w. The keys (words) in this dictionary are called **index terms** and should be a set of vocabulary entries and proper nouns as large as possible. The elements in this dictionary are called **occurrence lists** and should cover as many Web pages as possible.

We can efficiently implement an inverted index with a data structure consisting of:

1. An array storing the occurrence lists of the terms (in no particular order).
2. A compressed trie for the set of index terms, where each external node stores the index of the occurrence list of the associated term.

The reason for storing the occurrence lists outside the trie is to keep the size of the trie data structure sufficiently small to fit in internal memory. Instead, because of their large total size, the occurrence lists have to be stored on disk.

With our data structure, a query for a single keyword is similar to a word matching query (Section 12.5.1). Namely, we find the keyword in the trie and we return the associated occurrence list.

When multiple keywords are given and the desired output are the pages containing **all** the given keywords, we retrieve the occurrence list of each keyword using the trie and return their intersection. To facilitate the intersection computation, each occurrence list should be implemented with a sequence sorted by address or with a dictionary (see, for example, the generic merge computation discussed in Section 11.4).

In addition to the basic task of returning a list of pages containing given keywords, search engines provide an important additional service by **ranking** the pages returned by relevance. Devising fast and accurate ranking algorithms for search engines is a major challenge for computer researchers and electronic commerce companies.

12.6 Exercises

For help with exercises, please visit the web site, www.wiley.com/college/goodrich.

Reinforcement

R-12.1 What is the best way to multiply a chain of matrices with dimensions that are 10×5, 5×2, 2×20, 20×12, 12×4, and 4×60? Show your work.

R-12.2 Design an efficient algorithm for the matrix chain multiplication problem that outputs a fully parenthesized expression for how to multiply the matrices in the chain using the minimum number of operations.

R-12.3 List the prefixes of the string $P =$ "aaabbaaa" that are also suffixes of P.

R-12.4 Draw a figure illustrating the comparisons done by brute-force pattern matching for the text "aaabaadaabaaa" and pattern "aabaaa".

R-12.5 Repeat the previous problem for the BM pattern matching algorithm, not counting the comparisons made to compute the $\mathrm{last}(c)$ function.

R-12.6 Repeat the previous problem for the KMP pattern matching algorithm, not counting the comparisons made to compute the failure function.

R-12.7 Compute a table representing the last function used in the BM pattern matching algorithm for the pattern string

"the quick brown fox jumped over a lazy cat"

assuming the following alphabet (which starts with the space character):

$$\Sigma = \{ \text{,a,b,c,d,e,f,g,h,i,j,k,l,m,n,o,p,q,r,s,t,u,v,w,x,y,z}\}.$$

R-12.8 Assuming that the characters in alphabet Σ can be enumerated and can be used to index arrays, give an $O(m + |\Sigma|)$-time method for constructing the last function from an m-length pattern string P.

R-12.9 Compute a table representing the KMP failure function for the pattern string "cgtacgttcgtac".

R-12.10 Draw a standard trie for the following set of strings:

$$\{\text{abab, baba, ccccc, bbaaaa, caa, bbaacc, cbcc, cbca}\}.$$

R-12.11 Draw a compressed trie for the set of strings given in Exercise R-12.10.

R-12.12 Draw the compact representation of the suffix trie for the string

"minimize minime".

R-12.13 What is the longest prefix of the string "cgtacgttcgtacg" that is also a suffix of this string?

R-12.14 Draw the frequency array and Huffman tree for the following string:

"dogs do not spot hot pots or cats".

R-12.15 Show the longest common subsequence array L for the two strings

$$X = \text{"skullandbones"}$$
$$Y = \text{"lullabybabies"}.$$

What is a longest common subsequence between these strings?

Creativity

C-12.1 A native Australian named Anatjari wishes to cross a desert carrying only a single water bottle. He has a map that marks all the watering holes along the way. Assuming he can walk k miles on one bottle of water, design an efficient algorithm for determining where Anatjari should refill his bottle in order to make as few stops as possible. Argue why your algorithm is correct.

C-12.2 Describe an efficient greedy algorithm for making change for a specified value using a minimum number of coins, assuming there are four denominations of coins (called quarters, dimes, nickels, and pennies), with values 25, 10, 5, and 1, respectively. Argue why your algorithm is correct.

C-12.3 Give an example set of denominations of coins so that a greedy change making algorithm will not use the minimum number of coins.

C-12.4 In the *art gallery guarding* problem we are given a line L that represents a long hallway in an art gallery. We are also given a set $X = \{x_0, x_1, \ldots, x_{n-1}\}$ of real numbers that specify the positions of paintings in this hallway. Suppose that a single guard can protect all the paintings within distance at most 1 of his or her position (on both sides). Design an algorithm for finding a placement of guards that uses the minimum number of guards to guard all the paintings with positions in X.

C-12.5 Let P be a convex polygon, a *triangulation* of P is an addition of diagonals connecting the vertices of P so that each interior face is a triangle. The *weight* of a triangulation is the sum of the lengths of the diagonals.

Assuming that we can compute lengths and add and compare them in constant time, give an efficient algorithm for computing a minimum-weight triangulation of P.

C-12.6 Give an example of a text T of length n and a pattern P of length m that force the brute-force pattern matching algorithm to have a running time that is $\Omega(nm)$.

C-12.7 Give a justification of why the KMPFailureFunction method (Code Fragment 12.7) runs in $O(m)$ time on a pattern of length m.

C-12.8 Show how to modify the KMP string pattern matching algorithm so as to find *every* occurrence of a pattern string P that appears as a substring in T, while still running in $O(n+m)$ time. (Be sure to catch even those matches that overlap.)

C-12.9 Let T be a text of length n, and let P be a pattern of length m. Describe an $O(n+m)$-time method for finding the longest prefix of P that is a substring of T.

C-12.10 Say that a pattern P of length m is a *circular* substring of a text T of length n if there is an index $0 \le i < m$, such that $P = T[n-m+i..n-1] + T[0..i-1]$, that is, if P is a (normal) substring of T or P is equal to the concatenation of a suffix of T and a prefix of T. Give an $O(n+m)$-time algorithm for determining whether P is a circular substring of T.

C-12.11 The KMP pattern matching algorithm can be modified to run faster on binary strings by redefining the failure function as

$$f(j) = \text{the largest } k < j \text{ such that } P[0..k-2]\widehat{p}_k \text{ is a suffix of } P[1..j],$$

where $\widehat{p}_k$ denotes the complement of the kth bit of P. Describe how to modify the KMP algorithm to be able to take advantage of this new failure function and also give a method for computing this failure function. Show that this method makes at most n comparisons between the text and the pattern (as opposed to the $2n$ comparisons needed by the standard KMP algorithm given in Section 12.3.3).

C-12.12 Modify the simplified BM algorithm presented in this chapter using ideas from the KMP algorithm so that it runs in $O(n+m)$ time.

C-12.13 Given a string X of length n and a string Y of length m, describe an $O(n+m)$-time algorithm for finding the longest prefix of X that is a suffix of Y.

C-12.14 Give an efficient algorithm for deleting a string from a standard trie and analyze its running time.

C-12.15 Give an efficient algorithm for deleting a string from a compressed trie and analyze its running time.

C-12.16 Describe an algorithm for constructing the compact representation of a suffix trie, given its noncompact representation, and analyze its running time.

C-12.17 Let T be a text string of length n. Describe an $O(n)$-time method for finding the longest prefix of T that is a substring of the reversal of T.

C-12.18 Describe an efficient algorithm to find the longest palindrome that is a suffix of a string T of length n. Recall that a *palindrome* is a string that is equal to its reversal. What is the running time of your method?

C-12.19 Given a sequence $S = (x_0, x_1, x_2, \ldots, x_{n-1})$ of numbers, describe an $O(n^2)$-time algorithm for finding a longest subsequence $T = (x_{i_0}, x_{i_1}, x_{i_2}, \ldots, x_{i_{k-1}})$ of numbers, such that $i_j < i_{j+1}$ and $x_{i_j} > x_{i_{j+1}}$. That is, T is a longest decreasing subsequence of S.

C-12.20 Define the *edit distance* between two strings X and Y of length n and m, respectively, to be the number of edits that it takes to change X into Y. An edit consists of a character insertion, a character deletion, or a character replacement. For example, the strings "algorithm" and "rhythm" have edit distance 6. Design an $O(nm)$-time algorithm for computing the edit distance between X and Y.

C-12.21 Design a greedy algorithm for making change after someone buys some candy costing x cents and the customer gives the clerk $1. Your algorithm should try to minimize the number of coins returned.

  a. Show that your greedy algorithm returns the minimum number of coins if the coins have denominations $0.25, $0.10, $0.05, and $0.01.
  b. Give a set of denominations for which your algorithm may not return the minimum number of coins. Include an example where your algorithm fails.

C-12.22 Give an efficient algorithm for determining if a pattern P is a subsequence (not substring) of a text T. What is the running time of your algorithm?

C-12.23 Let x and y be strings of length n and m respectively. Define $B(i, j)$ to be the length of the longest common substring of the suffix of length i in x and the suffix of length j in y. Design an $O(nm)$-time algorithm for computing all the values of $B(i, j)$ for $i = 1, \ldots, n$ and $j = 1, \ldots, m$.

C-12.24 Anna has just won a contest that allows her to take n pieces of candy out of a candy store for free. Anna is old enough to realize that some candy is expensive, while other candy is relatively cheap, costing much less. The jars of candy are numbered $0, 1, \ldots, m-1$, so that jar j has n_j pieces in it, with a price of c_j per piece. Design an $O(n+m)$-time algorithm that allows Anna to maximize the value of the pieces of candy she takes for her winnings. Show that your algorithm produces the maximum value for Anna.

C-12.25 Let three integer arrays, A, B, and C, be given, each of size n. Given an arbitrary integer x, design an $O(n^2 \log n)$-time algorithm to determine if there exist numbers, a in A, b in B, and c in C, such that $x = a + b + c$.

C-12.26 Give an $O(n^2)$-time algorithm for the previous problem.

Projects

P-12.1 Implement the LCS algorithm and use it to compute the best sequence alignment between some DNA strings, which you can get online from GenBank.

P-12.2 Perform an experimental analysis, using documents found on the Internet, of the efficiency (number of character comparisons performed) of the brute-force and KMP pattern matching algorithms for varying-length patterns.

P-12.3 Perform an experimental analysis, using documents found on the Internet, of the efficiency (number of character comparisons performed) of the brute-force and BM pattern matching algorithms for varying-length patterns.

P-12.4 Perform an experimental comparison of the relative speeds of the brute-force, KMP, and BM pattern matching algorithms. Document the time taken for coding up each of these algorithms as well as their relative running times on documents found on the Internet that are then searched using varying-length patterns.

P-12.5 Implement a compression and decompression scheme that is based on Huffman coding.

P-12.6 Create a class that implements a standard trie for a set of ASCII strings. The class should have a constructor that takes as argument a list of strings, and the class should have a method that tests whether a given string is stored in the trie.

P-12.7 Create a class that implements a compressed trie for a set of ASCII strings. The class should have a constructor that takes as argument a list of strings, and the class should have a method that tests whether a given string is stored in the trie.

P-12.8 Create a class that implements a prefix trie for an ASCII string. The class should have a constructor that takes as argument a string and a method for pattern matching on the string.

P-12.9 Implement the simplified search engine described in Section 12.5.4 for the pages of a small Web site. Use all the words in the pages of the site as index terms, excluding stop words such as articles, prepositions, and pronouns.

P-12.10 Implement a search engine for the pages of a small Web site by adding a page-ranking feature to the simplified search engine described in Section 12.5.4. Your page-ranking feature should return the most relevant pages first. Use all the words in the pages of the site as index terms, excluding stop words, such as articles, prepositions, and pronouns.

P-12.11 Write a program that takes two character strings (which could be, for example, representations of DNA strands) and computes their edit distance, showing the corresponding pieces. (See Exercise C-12.20.)

Chapter Notes

The KMP algorithm is described by Knuth, Morris, and Pratt in their journal article [64], and Boyer and Moore describe their algorithm in a journal article published the same year [16]. In their article, however, Knuth *et al.* [64] also prove that the BM algorithm runs in linear time. More recently, Cole [23] shows that the BM algorithm makes at most $3n$ character comparisons in the worst case, and this bound is tight. All of the algorithms discussed above are also discussed in the book chapter by Aho [3], albeit in a more theoretical framework, including the methods for regular-expression pattern matching. The reader interested in further study of string pattern matching algorithms is referred to the book by Stephen [87] and the book chapters by Aho [3] and Crochemore and Lecroq [26].

The trie was invented by Morrison [78] and is discussed extensively in the classic *Sorting and Searching* book by Knuth [63]. The name "Patricia" is short for "Practical Algorithm to Retrieve Information Coded in Alphanumeric" [78]. McCreight [70] shows how to construct suffix tries in linear time. An introduction to the field of information retrieval, which includes a discussion of search engines for the Web is provided in the book by Baeza-Yates and Ribeiro-Neto [8].

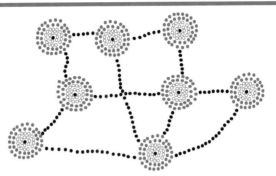

Contents

13.1   Graphs

A *graph* is a way of representing relationships that exist between pairs of objects. That is, a graph is a set of objects, called vertices, together with a collection of pairwise connections between them. By the way, this notion of a "graph" should not be confused with bar charts and function plots, as these kinds of "graphs" are unrelated to the topic of this chapter. Graphs have applications in a host of different domains, including mapping, transportation, electrical engineering, and computer networks.

Viewed abstractly, a *graph* G is simply a set V of *vertices* and a collection E of pairs of vertices from V, called *edges*. Thus, a graph is a way of representing connections or relationships between pairs of objects from some set V. Incidentally, some books use different terminology for graphs and refer to what we call vertices as *nodes* and what we call edges as *arcs*. We use the terms "vertices" and "edges."

Edges in a graph are either *directed* or *undirected*. An edge (u,v) is said to be *directed* from u to v if the pair (u,v) is ordered, with u preceding v. An edge (u,v) is said to be *undirected* if the pair (u,v) is not ordered. Undirected edges are sometimes denoted with set notation, as $\{u,v\}$, but for simplicity we use the pair notation (u,v), noting that in the undirected case (u,v) is the same as (v,u). Graphs are typically visualized by drawing the vertices as ovals or rectangles and the edges as segments or curves connecting pairs of ovals and rectangles. The following are some examples of directed and undirected graphs.

Example 13.1: *We can visualize collaborations among the researchers of a certain discipline by constructing a graph whose vertices are associated with the researchers themselves, and whose edges connect pairs of vertices associated with researchers who have coauthored a paper or book. (See Figure 13.1.) Such edges are undirected because coauthorship is a* **symmetric** *relation; that is, if A has coauthored something with B, then B necessarily has coauthored something with A.*

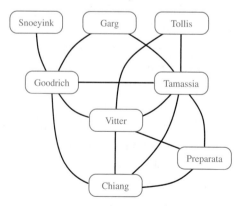

Figure 13.1: Graph of coauthorship among some authors.

Example 13.2: *We can associate with an object-oriented program a graph whose vertices represent the classes defined in the program, and whose edges indicate inheritance between classes. There is an edge from a vertex v to a vertex u if the class for v extends the class for u. Such edges are directed because the inheritance relation only goes in one direction (that is, it is* **asymmetric***).*

If all the edges in a graph are undirected, then we say the graph is an ***undirected graph***. Likewise, a ***directed graph***, also called a ***digraph***, is a graph whose edges are all directed. A graph that has both directed and undirected edges is often called a ***mixed graph***. Note that an undirected or mixed graph can be converted into a directed graph by replacing every undirected edge (u,v) by the pair of directed edges (u,v) and (v,u). It is often useful, however, to keep undirected and mixed graphs represented as they are, for such graphs have several applications, such as that of the following example.

Example 13.3: *A city map can be modeled by a graph whose vertices are intersections or dead-ends, and whose edges are stretches of streets without intersections. This graph has both undirected edges, which correspond to stretches of two-way streets, and directed edges, which correspond to stretches of one-way streets. Thus, in this way, a graph modeling a city map is a mixed graph.*

Example 13.4: *Physical examples of graphs are present in the electrical wiring and plumbing networks of a building. Such networks can be modeled as graphs, where each connector, fixture, or outlet is viewed as a vertex, and each uninterrupted stretch of wire or pipe is viewed as an edge. Such graphs are actually components of much larger graphs, namely the local power and water distribution networks. Depending on the specific aspects of these graphs that we are interested in, we may consider their edges as undirected or directed, for, in principle, water can flow in a pipe and current can flow in a wire in either direction.*

The two vertices joined by an edge are called the ***end vertices*** (or ***endpoints***) of the edge. If an edge is directed, its first endpoint is its ***origin*** and the other is the ***destination*** of the edge. Two vertices u and v are said to be ***adjacent*** if there is an edge whose end vertices are u and v. An edge is said to be ***incident*** on a vertex if the vertex is one of the edge's endpoints. The ***outgoing edges*** of a vertex are the directed edges whose origin is that vertex. The ***incoming edges*** of a vertex are the directed edges whose destination is that vertex. The ***degree*** of a vertex v, denoted $\deg(v)$, is the number of incident edges of v. The ***in-degree*** and ***out-degree*** of a vertex v are the number of the incoming and outgoing edges of v, and are denoted $\text{indeg}(v)$ and $\text{outdeg}(v)$, respectively.

Example 13.5: *We can study air transportation by constructing a graph G, called a* **flight network**, *whose vertices are associated with airports, and whose edges are associated with flights. (See Figure 13.2.) In graph G, the edges are directed because a given flight has a specific travel direction (from the origin airport to the destination airport). The endpoints of an edge e in G correspond respectively to the origin and destination for the flight corresponding to e. Two airports are adjacent in G if there is a flight that flies between them, and an edge e is incident upon a vertex v in G if the flight for e flies to or from the airport for v. The outgoing edges of a vertex v correspond to the outbound flights from v's airport, and the incoming edges correspond to the inbound flights to v's airport. Finally, the in-degree of a vertex v of G corresponds to the number of inbound flights to v's airport, and the out-degree of a vertex v in G corresponds to the number of outbound flights.*

The definition of a graph refers to the group of edges as a **collection**, not a **set**, thus allowing for two undirected edges to have the same end vertices, and for two directed edges to have the same origin and the same destination. Such edges are called **parallel edges** or **multiple edges**. Parallel edges can be in a flight network (Example 13.5), in which case multiple edges between the same pair of vertices could indicate different flights operating on the same route at different times of the day. Another special type of edge is one that connects a vertex to itself. Namely, we say that an edge (undirected or directed) is a **self-loop** if its two endpoints coincide. A self-loop may occur in a graph associated with a city map (Example 13.3), where it would correspond to a "circle" (a curving street that returns to its starting point).

With few exceptions, graphs do not have parallel edges or self-loops. Such graphs are said to be **simple**. Thus, we can usually say that the edges of a simple graph are a **set** of vertex pairs (and not just a collection). Throughout this chapter, we assume that a graph is simple unless otherwise specified.

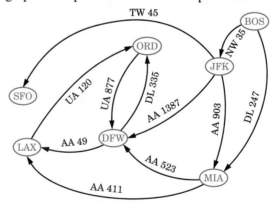

Figure 13.2: Example of a directed graph representing a flight network. The endpoints of edge UA 120 are LAX and ORD; hence, LAX and ORD are adjacent. The in-degree of DFW is 3, and the out-degree of DFW is 2.

In the propositions that follow, we explore a few important properties of graphs.

Proposition 13.6: *If G is a graph with m edges, then*

$$\sum_{v \text{ in } G} \deg(v) = 2m.$$

Justification: An edge (u, v) is counted twice in the summation above; once by its endpoint u and once by its endpoint v. Thus, the total contribution of the edges to the degrees of the vertices is twice the number of edges. ∎

Proposition 13.7: *If G is a directed graph with m edges, then*

$$\sum_{v \text{ in } G} indeg(v) = \sum_{v \text{ in } G} outdeg(v) = m.$$

Justification: In a directed graph, an edge (u, v) contributes one unit to the out-degree of its origin u and one unit to the in-degree of its destination v. Thus, the total contribution of the edges to the out-degrees of the vertices is equal to the number of edges, and similarly for the out-degrees. ∎

We next show that a simple graph with n vertices has $O(n^2)$ edges.

Proposition 13.8: *Let G be a simple graph with n vertices and m edges. If G is undirected, then $m \le n(n-1)/2$, and if G is directed, then $m \le n(n-1)$.*

Justification: Suppose that G is undirected. Since no two edges can have the same endpoints and there are no self-loops, the maximum degree of a vertex in G is $n-1$ in this case. Thus, by Proposition 13.6, $2m \le n(n-1)$. Now suppose that G is directed. Since no two edges can have the same origin and destination, and there are no self-loops, the maximum in-degree of a vertex in G is $n-1$ in this case. Thus, by Proposition 13.7, $m \le n(n-1)$. ∎

A *path* is a sequence of alternating vertices and edges that starts at a vertex and ends at a vertex such that each edge is incident to its predecessor and successor vertex. A *cycle* is a path with at least one edge that has its start and end vertices the same. We say that a path is *simple* if each vertex in the path is distinct, and we say that a cycle is *simple* if each vertex in the cycle is distinct, except for the first and last one. A *directed path* is a path such that all edges are directed and are traversed along their direction. A *directed cycle* is similarly defined. For example, in Figure 13.2, (BOS, NW 35, JFK, AA 1387, DFW) is in a directed simple path, and (LAX, UA 120, ORD, UA 877, DFW, AA 49, LAX) is a directed simple cycle. If a path P or cycle C is a simple graph, we may omit the edges in P or C, as these are well defined, in which case P is a list of adjacent vertices and C is a cycle of adjacent vertices.

Example 13.9: *Given a graph G representing a city map (see Example 13.3), we can model a couple driving to dinner at a recommended restaurant as traversing a path though G. If they know the way, and don't accidentally go through the same intersection twice, then they traverse a simple path in G. Likewise, we can model the entire trip the couple takes, from their home to the restaurant and back, as a cycle. If they go home from the restaurant in a completely different way than how they went, not even going through the same intersection twice, then their entire round trip is a simple cycle. Finally, if they travel along one-way streets for their entire trip, we can model their night out as a directed cycle.*

A ***subgraph*** of a graph G is a graph H whose vertices and edges are subsets of the vertices and edges of G, respectively. For example, in the flight network of Figure 13.2, vertices BOS, JFK, and MIA, and edges AA 903 and DL 247 form a subgraph. A ***spanning subgraph*** of G is a subgraph of G that contains all the vertices of the graph G. A graph is ***connected*** if, for any two vertices, there is a path between them. If a graph G is not connected, its maximal connected subgraphs are called the ***connected components*** of G. A ***forest*** is a graph without cycles. A ***tree*** is a connected forest, that is, a connected graph without cycles. Note that this definition of a tree is somewhat different from the one given in Chapter 7. Namely, in the context of graphs, a tree has no root. Whenever there is ambiguity, the trees of Chapter 7 should be referred to as ***rooted trees***, while the trees of this chapter should be referred to as ***free trees***. The connected components of a forest are (free) trees. A ***spanning tree*** of a graph is a spanning subgraph that is a (free) tree.

Example 13.10: *Perhaps the most talked about graph today is the Internet, which can be viewed as a graph whose vertices are computers and whose (undirected) edges are communication connections between pairs of computers on the Internet. The computers and the connections between them in a single domain, like wiley.com, form a subgraph of the Internet. If this subgraph is connected, then two users on computers in this domain can send e-mail to one another without having their information packets ever leave their domain. Suppose the edges of this subgraph form a spanning tree. This implies that, if even a single connection goes down (for example, because someone pulls a communication cable out of the back of a computer in this domain), then this subgraph will no longer be connected.*

There are a number of simple properties of trees, forests, and connected graphs.

Proposition 13.11: *Let G be an undirected graph with n vertices and m edges.*

- *If G is connected, then $m \geq n - 1$.*
- *If G is a tree, then $m = n - 1$.*
- *If G is a forest, then $m \leq n - 1$.*

13.1.1 The Graph ADT

As an abstract data type, a graph is a collection of elements that are stored at the graph's ***positions***—its vertices and edges. Hence, we can store elements in a graph at either its edges or its vertices (or both). In Java, this means we can define Vertex and Edge interfaces that each extend the Position interface. Let us then introduce the following simplified graph ADT, which is suitable for vertex and edge positions in undirected graphs, that is, graphs whose edges are all undirected. Additional methods for dealing with directed edges are discussed in Section 13.4.

vertices(): Return an iterable collection of all the vertices of the graph.

edges(): Return an iterable collection of all the edges of the graph.

incidentEdges(v): Return an iterable collection of the edges incident upon vertex v.

opposite(v, e): Return the endvertex of edge e distinct from vertex v; an error occurs if e is not incident on v.

endVertices(e): Return an array storing the end vertices of edge e.

areAdjacent(v, w): Test whether vertices v and w are adjacent.

replace(v, x): Replace the element stored at vertex v with x.

replace(e, x): Replace the element stored at edge e with x.

insertVertex(x): Insert and return a new vertex storing element x.

insertEdge(v, w, x): Insert and return a new undirected edge with end vertices v and w and storing element x.

removeVertex(v): Remove vertex v and all its incident edges and return the element stored at v.

removeEdge(e): Remove edge e and return the element stored at e.

There are several ways to realize the graph ADT. We explore three such ways in the next section.

13.2 Data Structures for Graphs

In this section, we discuss three popular ways of representing graphs, which are usually referred to as the *edge list* structure, the *adjacency list* structure, and the *adjacency matrix*. In all three representations, we use a collection to store the vertices of the graph. Regarding the edges, there is a fundamental difference between the first two structures and the latter. The edge list structure and the adjacency list structure only store the edges actually present in the graph, while the adjacency matrix stores a placeholder for every pair of vertices (whether there is an edge between them or not). As we will explain in this section, this difference implies that, for a graph G with n vertices and m edges, an edge list or adjacency list representation uses $O(n+m)$ space, whereas an adjacency matrix representation uses $O(n^2)$ space.

13.2.1 The Edge List Structure

The *edge list* structure is possibly the simplest, though not the most efficient, representation of a graph G. In this representation, a vertex v of G storing an element o is explicitly represented by a vertex object. All such vertex objects are stored in a collection V, such as an array list or node list. If V is an array list, for example, then we naturally think of the vertices as being numbered.

Vertex Objects

The vertex object for a vertex v storing element o has instance variables for:

- A reference to o.
- A reference to the position (or entry) of the vertex-object in collection V.

The distinguishing feature of the edge list structure is not how it represents vertices, however, but the way in which it represents edges. In this structure, an edge e of G storing an element o is explicitly represented by an edge object. The edge objects are stored in a collection E, which would typically be an array list or node list.

Edge Objects

The edge object for an edge e storing element o has instance variables for:

- A reference to o.
- References to the vertex objects associated with the endpoint vertices of e.
- A reference to the position (or entry) of the edge-object in collection E.

Visualizing the Edge List Structure

We illustrate an example of the edge list structure for a graph G in Figure 13.3.

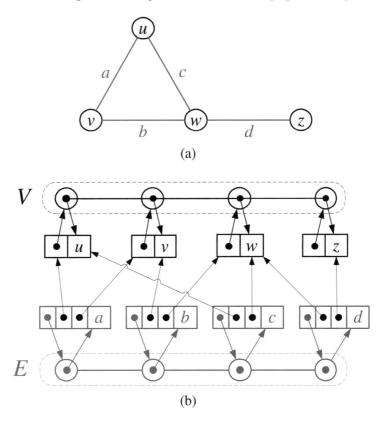

(a)

(b)

Figure 13.3: (a) A graph G; (b) schematic representation of the edge list structure for G. We visualize the elements stored in the vertex and edge objects with the element names, instead of with actual references to the element objects.

The reason this structure is called the **edge list structure** is that the simplest and most common implementation of the edge collection E is with a list. Even so, in order to be able to conveniently search for specific objects associated with edges, we may wish to implement E with a dictionary (whose entries store the element as the key and the edge as the value) in spite of our calling this the "edge list." We may also wish to implement the collection V as a dictionary for the same reason. Still, in keeping with tradition, we call this structure the edge list structure.

The main feature of the edge list structure is that it provides direct access from edges to the vertices they are incident upon. This allows us to define simple algorithms for methods endVertices(e) and opposite(v, e).

Performance of the Edge List Structure

One method that is inefficient for the edge list structure, however, is that of accessing the edges that are incident upon a vertex. Determining this set of vertices requires an exhaustive inspection of all the edge objects in the collection E. That is, in order to determine which edges are incident to a vertex v, we must examine all the edges in the edge list and check, for each one, if it happens to be incident to v. Thus, method incidentEdges(v) runs in time proportional to the number of edges in the graph, not in time proportional to the degree of vertex v. In fact, even to check if two vertices v and w are adjacent by the areAdjacent(v, w) method, requires that we search the entire edge collection looking for an edge with end vertices v and w. Moreover, since removing a vertex involves removing all of its incident edges, method removeVertex also requires a complete search of the edge collection E.

Table 13.1 summarizes the performance of the edge list structure implementation of a graph under the assumption that collections V and E are realized with doubly linked lists (Section 3.3).

Operation	Time
vertices	$O(n)$
edges	$O(m)$
endVertices, opposite	$O(1)$
incidentEdges, areAdjacent	$O(m)$
replace	$O(1)$
insertVertex, insertEdge, removeEdge,	$O(1)$
removeVertex	$O(m)$

Table 13.1: Running times of the methods of a graph implemented with the edge list structure. The space used is $O(n+m)$, where n is the number of vertices and m is the number of edges.

Details for selected methods of the graph ADT are as follows:

- Methods vertices() and edges() are implemented by calling V.iterator() and E.iterator(), respectively.

- Methods incidentEdges and areAdjacent all take $O(m)$ time, since to determine which edges are incident upon a vertex v we must inspect all edges.

- Since the collections V and E are lists implemented with a doubly linked list, we can insert vertices, and insert and remove edges, in $O(1)$ time.

- The update method removeVertex(v) takes $O(m)$ time, since it requires that we inspect all the edges to find and remove those incident upon v.

Thus, the edge list representation is simple but has significant limitations.

13.2.2 The Adjacency List Structure

The *adjacency list* structure for a graph G adds extra information to the edge list structure that supports direct access to the incident edges (and thus to the adjacent vertices) of each vertex. This approach allows us to use the adjacency list structure to implement several methods of the graph ADT much faster than what is possible with the edge list structure, even though both of these two representations use an amount of space proportional to the number of vertices and edges in the graph. The adjacency list structure includes all the structural components of the edge list structure plus the following:

- A vertex object v holds a reference to a collection $I(v)$, called the *incidence collection* of v, whose elements store references to the edges incident on v.
- The edge object for an edge e with end vertices v and w holds references to the positions (or entries) associated with edge e in the incidence collections $I(v)$ and $I(w)$.

Traditionally, the incidence collection $I(v)$ for a vertex v is a list, which is why we call this way of representing a graph the *adjacency list* structure. The adjacency list structure provides direct access both from the edges to the vertices and from the vertices to their incident edges. We illustrate the adjacency list structure of a graph in Figure 13.4.

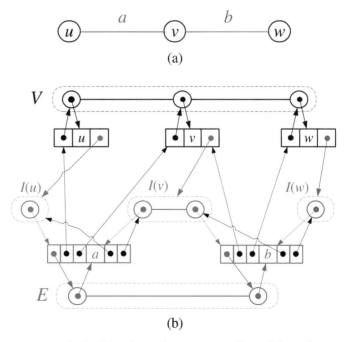

Figure 13.4: (a) A graph G; (b) schematic representation of the adjacency list structure of G. As in Figure 13.3, we visualize the elements of collections with names.

Performance of the Adjacency List Structure

All of the methods of the graph ADT that can be implemented with the edge list structure in $O(1)$ time can also be implemented in $O(1)$ time with the adjacency list structure, using essentially the same algorithms. In addition, being able to provide access between vertices and edges in both directions allows us to speed up the performance of a number of the graph methods by using an adjacency list structure instead of an edge list structure. Table 13.2 summarizes the performance of the adjacency list structure implementation of a graph, assuming that collections V and E and the incidence collections of the vertices are all implemented with doubly linked lists. For a vertex v, the space used by the incidence collection of v is proportional to the degree of v, that is, it is $O(\deg(v))$. Thus, by Proposition 13.6, the space requirement of the adjacency list structure is $O(n+m)$.

Operation	Time
vertices	$O(n)$
edges	$O(m)$
endVertices, opposite	$O(1)$
incidentEdges(v)	$O(\deg(v))$
areAdjacent(v,w)	$O(\min(\deg(v),\deg(w)))$
replace	$O(1)$
insertVertex, insertEdge, removeEdge,	$O(1)$
removeVertex	$O(\deg(v))$

Table 13.2: Running times of the methods of a graph implemented with the adjacency list structure. The space used is $O(n+m)$, where n is the number of vertices and m is the number of edges.

In contrast to the edge-list way of doing things, the adjacency list structure provides improved running times for the following methods:

- Method incidentEdges(v) takes time proportional to the number of incident vertices of v, that is, $O(\deg(v))$ time.

- Method areAdjacent(u,v) can be performed by inspecting either the incidence collection of u or that of v. By choosing the smaller of the two, we get $O(\min(\deg(u),\deg(v)))$ running time.

- Method removeVertex(v) takes $O(\deg(v))$ time.

13.2.3 The Adjacency Matrix Structure

Like the adjacency list structure, the ***adjacency matrix*** structure of a graph also extends the edge list structure with an additional component. In this case, we augment the edge list with a matrix (a two-dimensional array) A that allows us to determine adjacencies between pairs of vertices in constant time. In the adjacency matrix representation, we think of the vertices as being the integers in the set $\{0, 1, \ldots, n-1\}$ and the edges as being pairs of such integers. This allows us to store references to edges in the cells of a two-dimensional $n \times n$ array A. Specifically, the adjacency matrix representation extends the edge list structure as follows (see Figure 13.5):

- A vertex object v stores a distinct integer i in the range $0, 1, \ldots, n-1$, called the ***index*** of v.
- We keep a two-dimensional $n \times n$ array A such that the cell $A[i, j]$ holds a reference to the edge (v, w), if it exists, where v is the vertex with index i and w is the vertex with index j. If there is no such edge, then $A[i, j] = $ **null**.

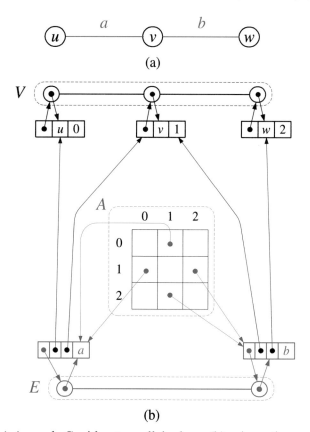

Figure 13.5: (a) A graph G without parallel edges; (b) schematic representation of the simplified adjacency matrix structure for G.

Performance of the Adjacency Matrix Structure

For graphs with parallel edges, the adjacency matrix representation must be extended so that, instead of having $A[i,j]$ storing a pointer to an associated edge (v,w), it must store a pointer to an incidence collection $I(v,w)$, which stores all the edges from v to w. Since most of the graphs we consider are simple, will not consider this complication here.

The (simple) adjacency matrix A allows us to perform method areAdjacent(v,w) in $O(1)$ time. We achieve this running time by accessing vertices v and w to determine their respective indices i and j, and then testing if $A[i,j]$ is **null** or not. The optimal performance of method areAdjacent is counteracted by an increase in space usage, however, which is now $O(n^2)$, and in the running time of other methods. For example, method incidentEdges(v) now requires that we examine an entire row or column of array A and thus runs in $O(n)$ time. Moreover, any vertex insertions or deletions now require creating a whole new array A, of larger or smaller size, respectively, which takes $O(n^2)$ time.

Table 13.3 summarizes the performance of the adjacency matrix structure implementation of a graph. From this table, we observe that the adjacency list structure is superior to the adjacency matrix in space, and is superior in time for all methods except for the areAdjacent method.

Operation	Time
vertices	$O(n)$
edges	$O(m)$
endVertices, opposite, areAdjacent	$O(1)$
incidentEdges(v)	$O(n+\deg(v))$
replace, insertEdge, removeEdge,	$O(1)$
insertVertex, removeVertex	$O(n^2)$

Table 13.3: Running times for a graph implemented with an adjacency matrix.

Historically, Boolean adjacency matrices were the first representations used for graphs (so that $A[i,j] = $ **true** if and only if (i,j) is an edge). We should not find this fact surprising, however, for the adjacency matrix has a natural appeal as a mathematical structure (for example, an undirected graph has a symmetric adjacency matrix). The adjacency list structure came later, with its natural appeal in computing due to its faster methods for most algorithms (many algorithms do not use method areAdjacent) and its space efficiency.

Most of the graph algorithms we examine will run efficiently when acting upon a graph stored using the adjacency list representation. In some cases, however, a trade-off occurs, where graphs with few edges are most efficiently processed with an adjacency list structure and graphs with many edges are most efficiently processed with an adjacency matrix structure.

13.3 Graph Traversals

Greek mythology tells of an elaborate labyrinth that was built to house the monstrous Minotaur, which was part bull and part man. This labyrinth was so complex that neither beast nor human could escape it. No human, that is, until the Greek hero, Theseus, with the help of the king's daughter, Ariadne, decided to implement a *graph traversal* algorithm. Theseus fastened a ball of thread to the door of the labyrinth and unwound it as he traversed the twisting passages in search of the monster. Theseus obviously knew about good algorithm design, for, after finding and defeating the beast, Theseus easily followed the string back out of the labyrinth to the loving arms of Ariadne. Formally, a *traversal* is a systematic procedure for exploring a graph by examining all of its vertices and edges.

13.3.1 Depth-First Search

The first traversal algorithm we consider in this section is *depth-first search* (DFS) in an undirected graph. Depth-first search is useful for testing a number of properties of graphs, including whether there is a path from one vertex to another and whether or not a graph is connected.

Depth-first search in an undirected graph G is analogous to wandering in a labyrinth with a string and a can of paint without getting lost. We begin at a specific starting vertex s in G, which we initialize by fixing one end of our string to s and painting s as "visited." The vertex s is now our "current" vertex—call our current vertex u. We then traverse G by considering an (arbitrary) edge (u,v) incident to the current vertex u. If the edge (u,v) leads us to an already visited (that is, painted) vertex v, we immediately return to vertex u. If, on the other hand, (u,v) leads to an unvisited vertex v, then we unroll our string, and go to v. We then paint v as "visited," and make it the current vertex, repeating the computation above. Eventually, we will get to a "dead-end," that is, a current vertex u such that all the edges incident on u lead to vertices already visited. Thus, taking any edge incident on u will cause us to return to u. To get out of this impasse, we roll our string back up, backtracking along the edge that brought us to u, going back to a previously visited vertex v. We then make v our current vertex and repeat the computation above for any edges incident upon v that we have not looked at before. If all of v's incident edges lead to visited vertices, then we again roll up our string and backtrack to the vertex we came from to get to v, and repeat the procedure at that vertex. Thus, we continue to backtrack along the path that we have traced so far until we find a vertex that has yet unexplored edges, take one such edge, and continue the traversal. The process terminates when our backtracking leads us back to the start vertex s, and there are no more unexplored edges incident on s.

This simple process traverses all the edges of *G*. (See Figure 13.6.)

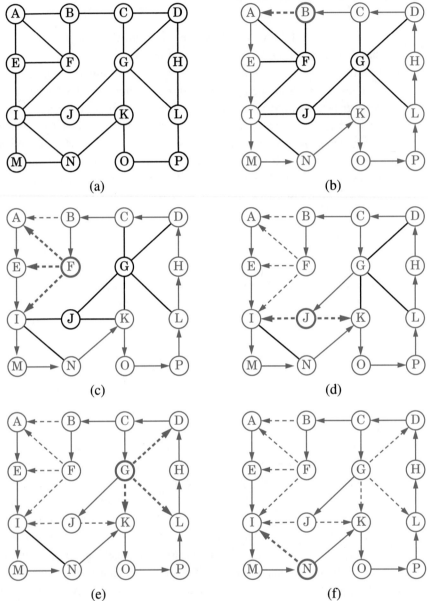

Figure 13.6: Example of depth-first search traversal on a graph starting at vertex *A*. Discovery edges are shown with solid lines and back edges are shown with dashed lines: (a) input graph; (b) path of discovery edges traced from A until back edge (B,A) is hit; (c) reaching F, which is a dead end; (d) after backtracking to C, resuming with edge (C,G), and hitting another dead end, J; (e) after backtracking to G; (f) after backtracking to N.

Discovery Edges and Back Edges

We can visualize a DFS traversal by orienting the edges along the direction in which they are explored during the traversal, distinguishing the edges used to discover new vertices, called ***discovery edges***, or ***tree edges***, from those that lead to already visited vertices, called ***back edges***. (See Figure 13.6f.) In the analogy above, discovery edges are the edges where we unroll our string when we traverse them, and back edges are the edges where we immediately return without unrolling any string. As we will see, the discovery edges form a spanning tree of the connected component of the starting vertex s. We call the edges not in this tree "back edges" because, assuming that the tree is rooted at the start vertex, each such edge leads back from a vertex in this tree to one of its ancestors in the tree.

The pseudo-code for a DFS traversal starting at a vertex v follows our analogy with string and paint. We use recursion to implement the string analogy, and we assume that we have a mechanism (the paint analogy) to determine if a vertex or edge has been explored or not, and to label the edges as discovery edges or back edges. This mechanism will require additional space and may affect the running time of the algorithm. A pseudo-code description of the recursive DFS algorithm is given in Code Fragment 13.1.

Algorithm DFS(G, v):

    Input: A graph G and a vertex v of G

    Output: A labeling of the edges in the connected component of v as discovery
        edges and back edges

  label v as visited

  for all edge e in G.incidentEdges(v) **do**

    if edge e is unvisited **then**

      $w \leftarrow G$.opposite(v, e)

      if vertex w is unexplored **then**

        label e as a discovery edge

        recursively call DFS(G, w)

    else

      label e as a back edge

Code Fragment 13.1: The DFS algorithm.

There are a number of observations that we can make about the depth-first search algorithm, many of which derive from the way the DFS algorithm partitions the edges of the undirected graph G into two groups, the discovery edges and the back edges. For example, since back edges always connect a vertex v to a previously visited vertex u, each back edge implies a cycle in G, consisting of the discovery edges from u to v plus the back edge (u, v).

Proposition 13.12: *Let G be an undirected graph on which a DFS traversal start-ing at a vertex s has been performed. Then the traversal visits all vertices in the connected component of s, and the discovery edges form a spanning tree of the connected component of s.*

Justification: Suppose there is at least one vertex v in s's connected component not visited, and let w be the first unvisited vertex on some path from s to v (we may have $v = w$). Since w is the first unvisited vertex on this path, it has a neighbor u that was visited. But when we visited u, we must have considered the edge (u, w); hence, it cannot be correct that w is unvisited. Therefore, there are no unvisited vertices in s's connected component.

Since we only mark edges when we go to unvisited vertices, we will never form a cycle with discovery edges, that is, discovery edges form a tree. Moreover, this is a spanning tree because, as we have just seen, the depth-first search visits each vertex in the connected component of s.   ■

In terms of its running time, depth-first search is an efficient method for travers-ing a graph. Note that DFS is called exactly once on each vertex, and that every edge is examined exactly twice, once from each of its end vertices. Thus, if n_s vertices and m_s edges are in the connected component of vertex s, a DFS starting at s runs in $O(n_s + m_s)$ time, provided the following conditions are satisfied:

- The graph is represented by a data structure such that creating and iterating through the incidentEdges(v) iterable collection takes $O(\text{degree}(v))$ time, and the opposite(v, e) method takes $O(1)$ time. The adjacency list structure is one such structure, but the adjacency matrix structure is not.
- We have a way to "mark" a vertex or edge as explored, and to test if a vertex or edge has been explored in $O(1)$ time. We discuss ways of implementing DFS to achieve this goal in the next section.

Given the assumptions above, we can solve a number of interesting problems.

Proposition 13.13: *Let G be a graph with n vertices and m edges represented with an adjacency list. A DFS traversal of G can be performed in $O(n + m)$ time, and can be used to solve the following problems in $O(n + m)$ time:*

- *Testing whether G is connected.*
- *Computing a spanning tree of G, if G is connected.*
- *Computing the connected components of G.*
- *Computing a path between two given vertices of G, if it exists.*
- *Computing a cycle in G, or reporting that G has no cycles.*

The justification of Proposition 13.13 is based on algorithms that use slightly modified versions of the DFS algorithm as subroutines.

13.3.2   Implementing Depth-First Search

As we have mentioned above, the data structure we use to represent a graph impacts the performance of the DFS algorithm. For example, an adjacency list can be used to yield a running time of $O(n+m)$ for traversing a graph with n vertices and m edges. Using an adjacency matrix, on the other hand, would result in a running time of $O(n^2)$, since each of the n calls to the incidentEdges method would take $O(n)$ time. If the graph is ***dense***, that is, it has close to $O(n^2)$ edges, then the difference between these two choices is minor, as they both would run in $O(n^2)$ time. But if the graph is ***sparse***, that is, it has close to $O(n)$ edges, then the adjacency matrix approach would be much slower than the adjacency list approach.

Another important implementation detail deals with the way vertices and edges are represented. In particular, we need to have a way of marking vertices and edges as visited or not. There are two simple solutions, but each has drawbacks:

- We can build our vertex and edge objects to contain an explored field, which can be used by the DFS algorithm for marking. This approach is quite simple, and supports constant-time marking and unmarking, but it assumes that we are designing our graph with DFS in mind, which will not always be valid. Furthermore, this approach needlessly restricts DFS to graphs with vertices having an explored field. Thus, if we want a generic DFS algorithm that can take any graph as input, this approach has limitations.

- We can use an auxiliary hash table to store all the explored vertices and edges during the DFS algorithm. This scheme is general, in that it does not require any special fields in the positions of the graph. But this approach does not achieve worst-case constant time for marking and unmarking of vertices edges. Instead, such a hash table only supports the mark (insert) and test (find) operations in constant ***expected*** time (see Section 9.2).

Fortunately, there is a middle ground between these two extremes.

The Decorator Pattern

Marking the explored vertices in a DFS traversal is an example of the ***decorator*** software engineering design pattern. This pattern is used to add ***decorations*** (also called ***attributes***) to existing objects. Each decoration is identified by a ***key*** identifying this decoration and by a ***value*** associated with the key. The use of decorations is motivated by the need of some algorithms and data structures to add extra variables, or temporary scratch data, to objects that do not normally have such variables. Hence, a decoration is a key-value pair that can be dynamically attached to an object. In our DFS example, we would like to have "decorable" vertices and edges with an ***explored*** decoration and a Boolean value.

Making Graph Vertices Decorable

We can realize the decorator pattern for any position by allowing it to be decorated. This allows us to add labels to vertices and edges, for example, without requiring that we know in advance the kinds of labels that we will need. We can simply require that our vertices and edges implement a ***decorable position*** ADT, which inherits from both the position ADT and the map ADT (Section 9.1). Namely, the methods of the decorable position ADT are the union of the methods of the position ADT and of the map ADT, that is, in addition to the size() and isEmpty() methods, a decorable position would support the following:

element(): Return the element stored at this position.

put(k,x): Map the decoration value x to the key k, returning the old value for k, or **null** if this is a new value for k.

get(k): Get the decoration value x assigned to k, or **null** if there is no mapping for k.

remove(k): Remove the decoration mapping for k, returning the old value, or **null** if there is none.

entrySet(): Return all the key-decoration pairs for this position.

The map methods of a decorable position p provide a simple mechanism for accessing and setting the decorations of p. For example, we use p.get(k) to obtain the value of the decoration with key k and we use p.put(k,x) to set the value of the decoration with key k to x. Moreover, the key k can be any object, including a special explored object our DFS algorithm might create. We show a Java interface defining such an ADT in Code Fragment 13.2.

We can implement a decorable position with an object that stores an element and a map. In principle, the running times of the methods of a decorable position depend on the implementation of the underlying map. However, most algorithms use a small constant number of decorations. Thus, the decorable position methods will run in $O(1)$ worst-case time no matter how we implement the embedded map.

```
public interface DecorablePosition<E>
       extends Position<E>, Map<Object,Object> {
} // no new methods needed – this is a mixture of Position and Map.
```

Code Fragment 13.2: An interface defining an ADT for decorable positions. Note that we don't use generic parameterized types for the inherited Map methods, since we don't know in advance the types of the decorations and we want to allow for objects of many different types as decorations.

Using decorable positions, the complete DFS traversal algorithm can be described in more detail, as shown in Code Fragment 13.3.

Algorithm DFS(G, v, k):

    Input: A graph G with decorable vertices and edges, a vertex v of G, and a decoration key k

    Output: A decoration of the vertices of in the connected component of v with key k and value VISITED and of the edges in the connected component of v with key k and values DISCOVERY and BACK, according to a depth-first search traversal of G

    v.put(k, VISITED)

    for all edge e in G.incidentEdges(v) **do**

        if e.get(k) = null **then**

            $w \leftarrow G$.opposite(v, e)

            if w.get(k) = null **then**

                e.put(k, DISCOVERY)

                DFS(G, w, k)

        else

            e.put(k, BACK)

Code Fragment 13.3: DFS on a graph with decorable edges and vertices.

A Generic DFS Implementation in Java

In Code Fragments 13.4 and 13.5, we show a Java implementation of a generic depth-first search traversal using a general class, DFS, which has a method, execute, which takes as input the graph, a start vertex, and any auxiliary information needed, and then initializes the graph and calls the recursive method, dfsTraversal, which activates the DFS traversal. Our implementation assumes that the vertices and edges are decorable positions, and it uses decorations to tell if vertices and edges have been visited or not. The DFS class contains the following methods to allow it to do special tasks during a DFS traversal:

- setup(): called prior to doing the DFS traversal call to dfsTraversal().
- initResult(): called at the beginning of the execution of dfsTraversal().
- startVisit(v): called at the start of the visit of v.
- traverseDiscovery(e, v): called when a discovery edge e out of v is traversed.
- traverseBack(e, v): called when a back edge e out of v is traversed.
- isDone(): called to determine whether to end the traversal early.
- finishVisit(v): called when we are finished exploring from v.
- result(): called to return the output of dfsTraversal.
- finalResult(r): called to return the output of the execute method, given the output, r, from dfsTraversal.

```
/** Generic DFS traversal of a graph using the template method pattern.
 * Parameterized types:
 *    V, the type for the elements stored at vertices
 *    E, the type for the elements stored at edges
 *    I, the type for the information object passed to the execute method
 *    R, the type for the result object returned by the DFS
 */
public class DFS<V, E, I, R> {
  protected Graph<V, E> graph;      // The graph being traversed
  protected Vertex<V> start;        // The start vertex for the DFS
  protected I info;                 // Information object passed to DFS
  protected R visitResult;          // The result of a recursive traversal call
  protected static Object STATUS = new Object(); // The status attribute
  protected static Object VISITED = new Object(); // Visited value
  protected static Object UNVISITED = new Object(); // Unvisited value
  /** Mark a position (vertex or edge) as visited. */
  protected void visit(DecorablePosition<?> p) { p.put(STATUS, VISITED); }
  /** Mark a position (vertex or edge) as unvisited. */
  protected void unVisit(DecorablePosition<?> p) { p.put(STATUS, UNVISITED); }
  /** Test if a position (vertex or edge) has been visited. */
  protected boolean isVisited(DecorablePosition<?> p) {
    return (p.get(STATUS) == VISITED);
  }
  /** Setup method that is called prior to the DFS execution. */
  protected void setup() {}
  /** Initializes result (called first, once per vertex visited). */
  protected void initResult() {}
  /** Called when we encounter a vertex (v). */
  protected void startVisit(Vertex<V> v) {}
  /** Called after we finish the visit for a vertex (v). */
  protected void finishVisit(Vertex<V> v) {}
  /** Called when we traverse a discovery edge (e) from a vertex (from). */
  protected void traverseDiscovery(Edge<E> e, Vertex<V> from) {}
  /** Called when we traverse a back edge (e) from a vertex (from). */
  protected void traverseBack(Edge<E> e, Vertex<V> from) {}
  /** Determines whether the traversal is done early. */
  protected boolean isDone() { return false; /* default value */ }
  /** Returns a result of a visit (if needed). */
  protected R result() { return null; /* default value */ }
  /** Returns the final result of the DFS execute method. */
  protected R finalResult(R r) { return r; /* default value */ }
```

Code Fragment 13.4: Instance variables and support methods of class DFS, which performs a generic DFS traversal. The methods visit, unVisit, and isVisited are implemented using decorable positions that are parameterized using the *wildcard symbol*, "?", which can match either the V or the E parameter used for decorable positions. (Continues in Code Fragment 13.5.)

```
/** Execute a depth first search traversal on graph g, starting
 * from a start vertex s, passing in an information object (in) */
public R execute(Graph<V, E> g, Vertex<V> s, I in) {
  graph = g;
  start = s;
  info = in;
  for(Vertex<V> v: graph.vertices()) unVisit(v); // mark vertices as unvisited
  for(Edge<E> e: graph.edges()) unVisit(e);    // mark edges as unvisited
  setup();            // perform any necessary setup prior to DFS traversal
  return finalResult(dfsTraversal(start));
}
/** Recursive template method for a generic DFS traversal. */
protected R dfsTraversal(Vertex<V> v) {
  initResult();
  if (!isDone())
    startVisit(v);
  if (!isDone()) {
    visit(v);
    for (Edge<E> e: graph.incidentEdges(v)) {
      if (!isVisited(e)) {
        // found an unexplored edge, explore it
        visit(e);
        Vertex<V> w = graph.opposite(v, e);
        if (!isVisited(w)) {
          // w is unexplored, this is a discovery edge
          traverseDiscovery(e, v);
          if (isDone()) break;
          visitResult = dfsTraversal(w); // get result from DFS-tree child
          if (isDone()) break;
        }
        else {
          // w is explored, this is a back edge
          traverseBack(e, v);
          if (isDone()) break;
        }
      }
    }
  }
  if(!isDone())
    finishVisit(v);
  return result();
}
} // end of DFS class
```

Code Fragment 13.5: The main template method dfsTraversal of class DFS, which performs a generic DFS traversal of a graph. (Continued from Code Fragment 13.4.)

Using the Template Method Pattern for DFS

The DFS class is based on the template method pattern (see Section 7.3.7), which describes a generic computation mechanism that can be specialized by redefining certain steps. The way we identify vertices and edges that have already been visited during the traversal is in calls to methods isVisited, visit, and unVisit. For us to do anything interesting, we must extend DFS and redefine some of its auxiliary methods. This approach conforms to the template method pattern. In Code Fragments 13.6 through 13.9, we illustrate some applications of DFS traversal.

Class ConnectivityDFS (Code Fragment 13.6) tests whether the graph is connected. It counts the vertices reachable by a DFS traversal starting at a vertex and compares this number with the total number of vertices of the graph.

```
/** This class specializes DFS to determine whether the graph is connected. */
public class ConnectivityDFS<V, E> extends DFS <V, E, Object, Boolean> {
  protected int reached;
  protected void setup() { reached = 0; }
  protected void startVisit(Vertex<V> v) { reached++; }
  protected Boolean finalResult(Boolean dfsResult) {
    return new Boolean(reached == graph.numVertices());
  }
}
```

Code Fragment 13.6: Specialization of class DFS to test if a graph is connected.

Class ComponentsDFS (Code Fragment 13.7) finds the connected components of a graph. It labels each vertex with its connected component number, using the decorator pattern, and returns the number of connected components found.

```
/** This class extends DFS to compute the connected components of a graph. */
public class ComponentsDFS<V, E> extends DFS<V, E, Object, Integer> {
  protected Integer compNumber; // Connected component number
  protected Object COMPONENT = new Object(); // Connected comp. selector
  protected void setup() { compNumber = 1; }
  protected void startVisit(Vertex<V> v) { v.put(COMPONENT, compNumber);}
  protected Integer finalResult(Integer dfsResult) {
    for (Vertex<V> v : graph.vertices()) // check for any unvisited vertices
      if (v.get(STATUS) == UNVISITED) {
        compNumber += 1; // we have found another connected component
        dfsTraversal(v);   // visit all the vertices of this component
      }
    return compNumber;
  }
}
```

Code Fragment 13.7: Specialization of DFS to compute connected components.

Class FindPathDFS (Code Fragment 13.8) finds a path between a pair of given start and target vertices. It performs a depth-first search traversal beginning at the start vertex. We maintain the path of discovery edges from the start vertex to the current vertex. When we encounter an unexplored vertex, we add it to the end of the path, and when we finish processing a vertex, we remove it from the path. The traversal is terminated when the target vertex is encountered, and the path is returned as an iterable collection of vertices and edges (both kinds of positions in a graph). Note that the path found by this class consists of discovery edges.

```java
/** Class specializing DFS to find a path between a start vertex and a target
 * vertex. It assumes the target vertex is passed as the info object to the
 * execute method. It returns an iterable list of the vertices and edges
 * comprising the path from start to info. The returned path is empty if
 * info is unreachable from start.   */
public class FindPathDFS<V, E>
    extends DFS<V, E, Vertex<V>, Iterable<Position>> {
  protected PositionList<Position> path;
  protected boolean done;
  /** Setup method to initialize the path. */
  public void setup() {
    path = new NodePositionList<Position>();
    done = false;
  }
  protected void startVisit(Vertex<V> v) {
    path.addLast(v); // add vertex v to path
    if (v == info)
      done = true;
  }
  protected void finishVisit(Vertex<V> v) {
    path.remove(path.last());   // remove v from path
    if(!path.isEmpty())         // if v is not the start vertex
      path.remove(path.last()); // remove discovery edge into v from path
  }
  protected void traverseDiscovery(Edge<E> e, Vertex<V> from) {
    path.addLast(e); // add edge e to the path
  }
  protected boolean isDone() {
    return done;
  }
  public Iterable<Position> finalResult(Iterable<Position> r) {
    return path;
  }
}
```

Code Fragment 13.8: Specialization of class DFS to find a path between start and target vertices.

Class FindCycleDFS (Code Fragment 13.9) finds a cycle in the connected component of a given vertex v, by performing a depth-first search traversal from v that terminates when a back edge is found. It returns a (possibly empty) iterable collection of the vertices and edges in the cycle formed by the found back edge.

```java
/** This class specializes DFS to find a cycle. */
public class FindCycleDFS<V, E>
  extends DFS<V, E, Object, Iterable<Position>> {
  protected PositionList<Position> cycle; // sequence of edges of the cycle
  protected boolean done;
  protected Vertex<V> cycleStart;
  public void setup() {
    cycle = new NodePositionList<Position>();
    done = false;
  }
  protected void startVisit(Vertex<V> v) { cycle.addLast(v); }
  protected void finishVisit(Vertex<V> v) {
    cycle.remove(cycle.last());  // remove v from cycle
    if (!cycle.isEmpty()) cycle.remove(cycle.last()); // remove edge into v from cycle
  }
  protected void traverseDiscovery(Edge<E> e, Vertex<V> from) {
    cycle.addLast(e);
  }
  protected void traverseBack(Edge<E> e, Vertex<V> from) {
    cycle.addLast(e);              // back edge e creates a cycle
    cycleStart = graph.opposite(from, e);
    cycle.addLast(cycleStart);   // first vertex completes the cycle
    done = true;
  }
  protected boolean isDone() { return done; }
  public Iterable<Position> finalResult(Iterable<Position> r) {
    // remove the vertices and edges from start to cycleStart
    if (!cycle.isEmpty()) {
      for (Position<Position> p: cycle.positions()) {
        if (p.element() == cycleStart)
          break;
        cycle.remove(p);                        // remove vertex from cycle
      }
    }
    return cycle; // list of the vertices and edges of the cycle
  }
}
```

Code Fragment 13.9: Specialization of class DFS to find a cycle in the connected component of the start vertex.

13.3.3 Breadth-First Search

In this section, we consider the ***breadth-first search*** (BFS) traversal algorithm. Like DFS, BFS traverses a connected component of a graph, and in so doing defines a useful spanning tree. BFS is less "adventurous" than DFS, however. Instead of wandering the graph, BFS proceeds in rounds and subdivides the vertices into *levels*. BFS can also be thought of as a traversal using a string and paint, with BFS unrolling the string in a more conservative manner.

BFS starts at vertex s, which is at level 0 and defines the "anchor" for our string. In the first round, we let out the string the length of one edge and we visit all the vertices we can reach without unrolling the string any farther. In this case, we visit, and paint as "visited," the vertices adjacent to the start vertex s—these vertices are placed into level 1. In the second round, we unroll the string the length of two edges and we visit all the new vertices we can reach without unrolling our string any farther. These new vertices, which are adjacent to level 1 vertices and not previously assigned to a level, are placed into level 2, and so on. The BFS traversal terminates when every vertex has been visited.

Pseudo-code for a BFS starting at a vertex s is shown in Code Fragment 13.10. We use auxiliary space to label edges, mark visited vertices, and store collections associated with levels. That is, the collections L_0, L_1, L_2, and so on, store the vertices that are in level 0, level 1, level 2, and so on. These collections could, for example, be implemented as queues. They also allow BFS to be nonrecursive.

Algorithm BFS(s):

    initialize collection L_0 to contain vertex s

    $i \leftarrow 0$

    while L_i is not empty **do**

        create collection L_{i+1} to initially be empty

        for all vertex v in L_i **do**

            for all edge e in G.incidentEdges(v) **do**

                if edge e is unexplored **then**

                    $w \leftarrow G$.opposite(v, e)

                    if vertex w is unexplored **then**

                        label e as a discovery edge

                        insert w into L_{i+1}

                else

                    label e as a cross edge

        $i \leftarrow i + 1$

Code Fragment 13.10: The BFS algorithm.

We illustrate a BFS traversal in Figure 13.7.

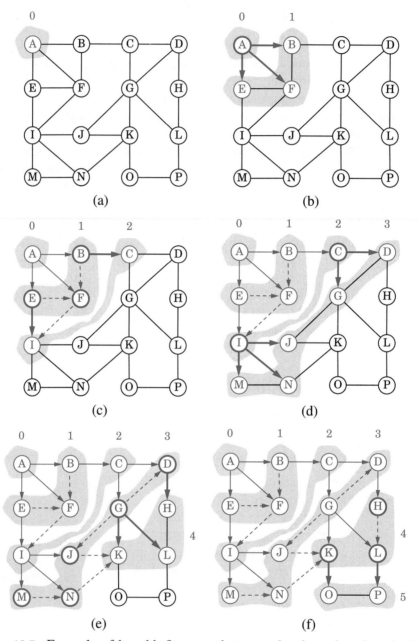

Figure 13.7: Example of breadth-first search traversal, where the edges incident on a vertex are explored by the alphabetical order of the adjacent vertices. The discovery edges are shown with solid lines and the cross edges are shown with dashed lines: (a) graph before the traversal; (b) discovery of level 1; (c) discovery of level 2; (d) discovery of level 3; (e) discovery of level 4; (f) discovery of level 5.

One of the nice properties of the BFS approach is that, in performing the BFS traversal, we can label each vertex by the length of a shortest path (in terms of the number of edges) from the start vertex s. In particular, if vertex v is placed into level i by a BFS starting at vertex s, then the length of a shortest path from s to v is i.

As with DFS, we can visualize the BFS traversal by orienting the edges along the direction in which they are explored during the traversal, and by distinguishing the edges used to discover new vertices, called *discovery edges*, from those that lead to already visited vertices, called *cross edges*. (See Figure 13.7f.) As with the DFS, the discovery edges form a spanning tree, which in this case we call the BFS tree. We do not call the nontree edges "back edges" in this case, however, for none of them connects a vertex to one of its ancestors. Every nontree edge connects a vertex v to another vertex that is neither v's ancestor nor its descendent.

The BFS traversal algorithm has a number of interesting properties, some of which we explore in the proposition that follows.

Proposition 13.14: *Let G be an undirected graph on which a BFS traversal starting at vertex s has been performed. Then*

- *The traversal visits all vertices in the connected component of s.*
- *The discovery-edges form a spanning tree T, which we call the BFS tree, of the connected component of s.*
- *For each vertex v at level i, the path of the BFS tree T between s and v has i edges, and any other path of G between s and v has at least i edges.*
- *If (u, v) is an edge that is not in the BFS tree, then the level numbers of u and v differ by at most 1.*

We leave the justification of this proposition as an exercise (C-13.13). The analysis of the running time of BFS is similar to the one of DFS, which implies the following.

Proposition 13.15: *Let G be a graph with n vertices and m edges represented with the adjacency list structure. A BFS traversal of G takes $O(n+m)$ time. Also, there exist $O(n+m)$-time algorithms based on BFS for the following problems:*

- *Testing whether G is connected.*
- *Computing a spanning tree of G, if G is connected.*
- *Computing the connected components of G.*
- *Given a start vertex s of G, computing, for every vertex v of G, a path with the minimum number of edges between s and v, or reporting that no such path exists.*
- *Computing a cycle in G, or reporting that G has no cycles.*

13.4 Directed Graphs

In this section, we consider issues that are specific to directed graphs. Recall that a directed graph (***digraph***), is a graph whose edges are all directed.

Methods Dealing with Directed Edges

When we allow for some or all the edges in a graph to be directed, we should add the following two methods to the graph ADT in order to deal with edge directions.

isDirected(e): Test whether edge e is directed.

insertDirectedEdge(v, w, o): Insert and return a new directed edge with origin v and destination w and storing element o.

Also, if an edge e is directed, the method endVertices(e) should return an array A such that $A[0]$ is the origin of e and $A[1]$ is the destination of e. The running time for the method isDirected(e) should be $O(1)$, and the running time of the method insertDirectedEdge(v, w, o) should match that of undirected edge insertion.

Reachability

One of the most fundamental issues with directed graphs is the notion of ***reachability***, which deals with determining where we can get to in a directed graph. A traversal in a directed graph always goes along directed paths, that is, paths where all the edges are traversed according to their respective directions. Given vertices u and v of a digraph $\vec{G}$, we say that u ***reaches*** v (and v is ***reachable*** from u) if $\vec{G}$ has a directed path from u to v. We also say that a vertex v reaches an edge (w, z) if v reaches the origin vertex w of the edge.

A digraph $\vec{G}$ is ***strongly connected*** if for any two vertices u and v of $\vec{G}$, u reaches v and v reaches u. A ***directed cycle*** of $\vec{G}$ is a cycle where all the edges are traversed according to their respective directions. (Note that $\vec{G}$ may have a cycle consisting of two edges with opposite direction between the same pair of vertices.) A digraph $\vec{G}$ is ***acyclic*** if it has no directed cycles. (See Figure 13.8 for some examples.)

The ***transitive closure*** of a digraph $\vec{G}$ is the digraph $\vec{G}^*$ such that the vertices of $\vec{G}^*$ are the same as the vertices of $\vec{G}$, and $\vec{G}^*$ has an edge (u, v), whenever $\vec{G}$ has a directed path from u to v. That is, we define $\vec{G}^*$ by starting with the digraph $\vec{G}$ and adding in an extra edge (u, v) for each u and v such that v is reachable from u (and there isn't already an edge (u, v) in $\vec{G}$).

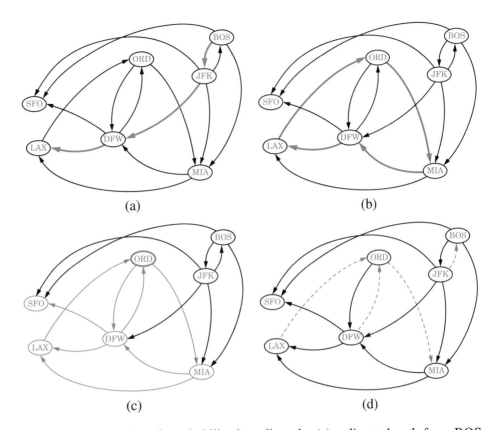

(a) (b)

(c) (d)

Figure 13.8: Examples of reachability in a digraph: (a) a directed path from BOS to LAX is drawn in blue; (b) a directed cycle (ORD, MIA, DFW, LAX, ORD) is shown in blue; its vertices induce a strongly connected subgraph; (c) the subgraph of the vertices and edges reachable from ORD is shown in blue; (d) removing the dashed blue edges gives an acyclic digraph.

Interesting problems that deal with reachability in a digraph $\vec{G}$ include the following:

- Given vertices u and v, determine whether u reaches v.
- Find all the vertices of $\vec{G}$ that are reachable from a given vertex s.
- Determine whether $\vec{G}$ is strongly connected.
- Determine whether $\vec{G}$ is acyclic.
- Compute the transitive closure $\vec{G}^*$ of $\vec{G}$.

In the remainder of this section, we explore some efficient algorithms for solving these problems.

13.4.1   Traversing a Digraph

As with undirected graphs, we can explore a digraph in a systematic way with methods akin to the depth-first search (DFS) and breadth-first search (BFS) algorithms defined previously for undirected graphs (Sections 13.3.1 and 13.3.3). Such explorations can be used, for example, to answer reachability questions. The directed depth-first search and breadth-first search methods we develop in this section for performing such explorations are very similar to their undirected counterparts. In fact, the only real difference is that the directed depth-first search and breadth-first search methods only traverse edges according to their respective directions.

The directed version of DFS starting at a vertex v can be described by the recursive algorithm in Code Fragment 13.11. (See Figure 13.9.)

Algorithm DirectedDFS(v):

    Mark vertex v as visited.

    for each outgoing edge (v,w) of v **do**

        if vertex w has not been visited **then**

            Recursively call DirectedDFS(w).

Code Fragment 13.11: The DirectedDFS algorithm.

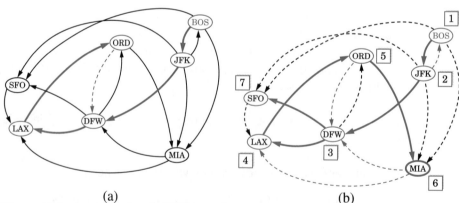

(a)   (b)

Figure 13.9: An example of a DFS in a digraph: (a) intermediate step, where, for the first time, an already visited vertex (DFW) is reached; (b) the completed DFS. The tree edges are shown with solid blue lines, the back edges are shown with dashed blue lines, and the forward and cross edges are shown with dashed black lines. The order in which the vertices are visited is indicated by a label next to each vertex. The edge (ORD,DFW) is a back edge, but (DFW,ORD) is a forward edge. Edge (BOS,SFO) is a forward edge, and (SFO,LAX) is a cross edge.

A DFS on a digraph $\vec{G}$ partitions the edges of $\vec{G}$ reachable from the starting vertex into **tree edges** or **discovery edges**, which lead us to discover a new vertex, and **nontree edges**, which take us to a previously visited vertex. The tree edges form a tree rooted at the starting vertex, called the **depth-first search** tree, and there are three kinds of nontree edges:

- **back edges**, which connect a vertex to an ancestor in the DFS tree

- **forward edges**, which connect a vertex to a descendent in the DFS tree

- **cross edges**, which connect a vertex to a vertex that is neither its ancestor nor its descendent.

Refer back to Figure 13.9b to see an example of each type of nontree edge.

Proposition 13.16: *Let $\vec{G}$ be a digraph. Depth-first search on $\vec{G}$ starting at a vertex s visits all the vertices of $\vec{G}$ that are reachable from s. Also, the DFS tree contains directed paths from s to every vertex reachable from s.*

Justification: Let V_s be the subset of vertices of $\vec{G}$ visited by DFS starting at vertex s. We want to show that V_s contains s and every vertex reachable from s belongs to V_s. Suppose now, for the sake of a contradiction, that there is a vertex w reachable from s that is not in V_s. Consider a directed path from s to w, and let (u,v) be the first edge on such a path taking us out of V_s, that is, u is in V_s but v is not in V_s. When DFS reaches u, it explores all the outgoing edges of u, and thus must reach also vertex v via edge (u,v). Hence, v should be in V_s, and we have obtained a contradiction. Therefore, V_s must contain every vertex reachable from s. ∎

Analyzing the running time of the directed DFS method is analogous to that for its undirected counterpart. In particular, a recursive call is made for each vertex exactly once, and each edge is traversed exactly once (from its origin). Hence, if n_s vertices and m_s edges are reachable from vertex s, a directed DFS starting at s runs in $O(n_s + m_s)$ time, provided the digraph is represented with a data structure that supports constant-time vertex and edge methods. The adjacency list structure satisfies this requirement, for example.

By Proposition 13.16, we can use DFS to find all the vertices reachable from a given vertex, and hence to find the transitive closure of $\vec{G}$. That is, we can perform a DFS, starting from each vertex v of $\vec{G}$, to see which vertices w are reachable from v, adding an edge (v,w) to the transitive closure for each such w. Likewise, by repeatedly traversing digraph $\vec{G}$ with a DFS, starting in turn at each vertex, we can easily test whether $\vec{G}$ is strongly connected. Namely, $\vec{G}$ is strongly connected if each DFS visits all the vertices of $\vec{G}$.

Thus, we may immediately derive the proposition that follows.

Proposition 13.17: *Let $\vec{G}$ be a digraph with n vertices and m edges. The following problems can be solved by an algorithm that traverses $\vec{G}$ n times using DFS, runs in $O(n(n+m))$ time, and uses $O(n)$ auxiliary space:*

- *Computing, for each vertex v of $\vec{G}$, the subgraph reachable from v*
- *Testing whether $\vec{G}$ is strongly connected*
- *Computing the transitive closure $\vec{G}^*$ of $\vec{G}$.*

Testing for Strong Connectivity

Actually, we can determine if a directed graph $\vec{G}$ is strongly connected much faster than this, just using two depth-first searches. We begin by performing a DFS of our directed graph $\vec{G}$ starting at an arbitrary vertex s. If there is any vertex of $\vec{G}$ that is not visited by this DFS, and is not reachable from s, then the graph is not strongly connected. So, if this first DFS visits each vertex of $\vec{G}$, then we reverse all the edges of $\vec{G}$ (using the reverseDirection method) and perform another DFS starting at s in this "reverse" graph. If every vertex of $\vec{G}$ is visited by this second DFS, then the graph is strongly connected, for each of the vertices visited in this DFS can reach s. Since this algorithm makes just two DFS traversals of $\vec{G}$, it runs in $O(n+m)$ time.

Directed Breadth-First Search

As with DFS, we can extend breadth-first search (BFS) to work for directed graphs. The algorithm still visits vertices level by level and partitions the set of edges into *tree edges* (or *discovery edges*), which together form a directed *breadth-first search tree* rooted at the start vertex, and *nontree edges*. Unlike the directed DFS method, however, the directed BFS method only leaves two kinds of nontree edges: *back edges*, which connect a vertex to one of its ancestors, and *cross edges*, which connect a vertex to another vertex that is neither its ancestor nor its descendent. There are no forward edges, which is a fact we explore in an exercise (C-13.9).

13.4.2 Transitive Closure

In this section, we explore an alternative technique for computing the transitive closure of a digraph. Let $\vec{G}$ be a digraph with n vertices and m edges. We compute the transitive closure of $\vec{G}$ in a series of rounds. We initialize $\vec{G}_0 = \vec{G}$. We also arbitrarily number the vertices of $\vec{G}$ as $v_1, v_2, \ldots, v_n$. We then begin the computation of the rounds, beginning with round 1. In a generic round k, we construct digraph $\vec{G}_k$ starting with $\vec{G}_k = \vec{G}_{k-1}$ and adding to $\vec{G}_k$ the directed edge (v_i, v_j) if digraph $\vec{G}_{k-1}$ contains both the edges (v_i, v_k) and (v_k, v_j). In this way, we will enforce a simple rule embodied in the proposition that follows.

Proposition 13.18: *For $i = 1, \ldots, n$, digraph $\vec{G}_k$ has an edge (v_i, v_j) if and only if digraph $\vec{G}$ has a directed path from v_i to v_j, whose intermediate vertices (if any) are in the set $\{v_1, \ldots, v_k\}$. In particular, $\vec{G}_n$ is equal to $\vec{G}^*$, the transitive closure of $\vec{G}$.*

Proposition 13.18 suggests a simple algorithm for computing the transitive closure of $\vec{G}$ that is based on the series of rounds we described above. This algorithm is known as the ***Floyd-Warshall algorithm***, and its pseudo-code is given in Code Fragment 13.12. From this pseudo-code, we can easily analyze the running time of the Floyd-Warshall algorithm assuming that the data structure representing G supports methods areAdjacent and insertDirectedEdge in $O(1)$ time. The main loop is executed n times and the inner loop considers each of $O(n^2)$ pairs of vertices, performing a constant-time computation for each one. Thus, the total running time of the Floyd-Warshall algorithm is $O(n^3)$.

Algorithm FloydWarshall($\vec{G}$):

    Input: A digraph $\vec{G}$ with n vertices
    Output: The transitive closure $\vec{G}^*$ of $\vec{G}$

    let $v_1, v_2, \ldots, v_n$ be an arbitrary numbering of the vertices of $\vec{G}$
    $\vec{G}_0 \leftarrow \vec{G}$
    for $k \leftarrow 1$ **to** n **do**
        $\vec{G}_k \leftarrow \vec{G}_{k-1}$
        for all i, j in $\{1, \ldots, n\}$ with $i \neq j$ and $i, j \neq k$ **do**
            if both edges (v_i, v_k) and (v_k, v_j) are in $\vec{G}_{k-1}$ **then**
                add edge (v_i, v_j) to $\vec{G}_k$ (if it is not already present)
    return $\vec{G}_n$

Code Fragment 13.12: Pseudo-code for the Floyd-Warshall algorithm. This algorithm computes the transitive closure $\vec{G}^*$ of G by incrementally computing a series of digraphs $\vec{G}_0, \vec{G}_1, \ldots, \vec{G}_n$, where for $k = 1, \ldots, n$.

This description is actually an example of an algorithmic design pattern known as dynamic programming, which is discussed in more detail in Section 12.2. From the description and analysis above we may immediately derive the following proposition.

Proposition 13.19: *Let $\vec{G}$ be a digraph with n vertices, and let $\vec{G}$ be represented by a data structure that supports lookup and update of adjacency information in $O(1)$ time. Then the Floyd-Warshall algorithm computes the transitive closure $\vec{G}^*$ of $\vec{G}$ in $O(n^3)$ time.*

We illustrate an example run of the Floyd-Warshall algorithm in Figure 13.10.

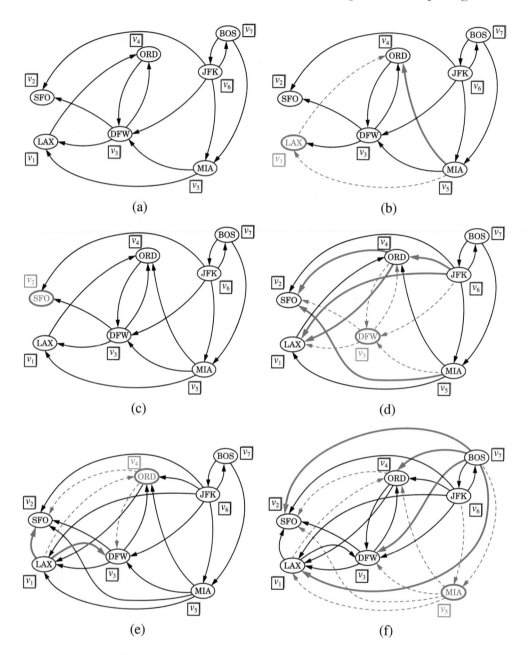

Figure 13.10: Sequence of digraphs computed by the Floyd-Warshall algorithm: (a) initial digraph $\vec{G} = \vec{G}_0$ and numbering of the vertices; (b) digraph $\vec{G}_1$; (c) $\vec{G}_2$; (d) $\vec{G}_3$; (e) $\vec{G}_4$; (f) $\vec{G}_5$. Note that $\vec{G}_5 = \vec{G}_6 = \vec{G}_7$. If digraph $\vec{G}_{k-1}$ has the edges (v_i, v_k) and (v_k, v_j), but not the edge (v_i, v_j), in the drawing of digraph $\vec{G}_k$, we show edges (v_i, v_k) and (v_k, v_j) with dashed blue lines, and edge (v_i, v_j) with a thick blue line.

Performance of the Floyd-Warshall Algorithm

The running time of the Floyd-Warshall algorithm might appear to be slower than performing a DFS of a directed graph from each of its vertices, but this depends upon the representation of the graph. If a graph is represented using an adjacency matrix, then running the DFS method once on a directed graph $\vec{G}$ takes $O(n^2)$ time (we explore the reason for this in Exercise R-13.9). Thus, running DFS n times takes $O(n^3)$ time, which is no better than a single execution of the Floyd-Warshall algorithm, but the Floyd-Warshall algorithm would be much simpler to implement. Nevertheless, if the graph is represented using an adjacency list structure, then running the DFS algorithm n times would take $O(n(n+m))$ time to compute the transitive closure. Even so, if the graph is *dense*, that is, if it has $\Omega(n^2)$ edges, then this approach still runs in $O(n^3)$ time and is more complicated than a single instance of the Floyd-Warshall algorithm. The only case where repeatedly calling the DFS method is better is when the graph is not dense and is represented using an adjacency list structure.

13.4.3 Directed Acyclic Graphs

Directed graphs without directed cycles are encountered in many applications. Such a digraph is often referred to as a ***directed acyclic graph***, or ***DAG***, for short. Applications of such graphs include the following:

- Inheritance between classes of a Java program.
- Prerequisites between courses of a degree program.
- Scheduling constraints between the tasks of a project.

Example 13.20: *In order to manage a large project, it is convenient to break it up into a collection of smaller tasks. The tasks, however, are rarely independent, because scheduling constraints exist between them. (For example, in a house building project, the task of ordering nails obviously precedes the task of nailing shingles to the roof deck.) Clearly, scheduling constraints cannot have circularities, because they would make the project impossible. (For example, in order to get a job you need to have work experience, but in order to get work experience you need to have a job.) The scheduling constraints impose restrictions on the order in which the tasks can be executed. Namely, if a constraint says that task a must be completed before task b is started, then a must precede b in the order of execution of the tasks. Thus, if we model a feasible set of tasks as vertices of a directed graph, and we place a directed edge from v to w whenever the task for v must be executed before the task for w, then we define a directed acyclic graph.*

The example above motivates the following definition. Let $\vec{G}$ be a digraph with n vertices. A ***topological ordering*** of $\vec{G}$ is an ordering $v_1, \ldots, v_n$ of the vertices of $\vec{G}$ such that for every edge (v_i, v_j) of $\vec{G}$, $i < j$. That is, a topological ordering is an ordering such that any directed path in $\vec{G}$ traverses vertices in increasing order. (See Figure 13.11.) Note that a digraph may have more than one topological ordering.

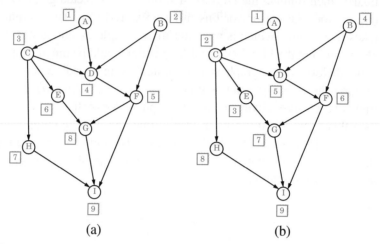

(a)   (b)

Figure 13.11: Two topological orderings of the same acyclic digraph.

Proposition 13.21: *$\vec{G}$ has a topological ordering if and only if it is acyclic.*

Justification: The necessity (the "only if" part of the statement) is easy to demonstrate. Suppose $\vec{G}$ is topologically ordered. Assume, for the sake of a contradiction, that $\vec{G}$ has a cycle consisting of edges $(v_{i_0}, v_{i_1}), (v_{i_1}, v_{i_2}), \ldots, (v_{i_{k-1}}, v_{i_0})$. Because of the topological ordering, we must have $i_0 < i_1 < \cdots < i_{k-1} < i_0$, which is clearly impossible. Thus, $\vec{G}$ must be acyclic.

We now argue the sufficiency of the condition (the "if" part). Suppose $\vec{G}$ is acyclic. We will give an algorithmic description of how to build a topological ordering for $\vec{G}$. Since $\vec{G}$ is acyclic, $\vec{G}$ must have a vertex with no incoming edges (that is, with in-degree 0). Let v_1 be such a vertex. Indeed, if v_1 did not exist, then in tracing a directed path from an arbitrary start vertex we would eventually encounter a previously visited vertex, thus contradicting the acyclicity of $\vec{G}$. If we remove v_1 from $\vec{G}$, together with its outgoing edges, the resulting digraph is still acyclic. Hence, the resulting digraph also has a vertex with no incoming edges, and we let v_2 be such a vertex. By repeating this process until the digraph becomes empty, we obtain an ordering $v_1, \ldots, v_n$ of the vertices of $\vec{G}$. Because of the construction above, if (v_i, v_j) is an edge of $\vec{G}$, then v_i must be deleted before v_j can be deleted, and thus $i < j$. Thus, $v_1, \ldots, v_n$ is a topological ordering.   ∎

Proposition 13.21's justification suggests an algorithm (Code Fragment 13.13), called ***topological sorting***, for computing a topological ordering of a digraph.

Algorithm TopologicalSort($\vec{G}$):

    Input: A digraph $\vec{G}$ with n vertices.

    Output: A topological ordering $v_1, \ldots, v_n$ of $\vec{G}$.

    $S \leftarrow$ an initially empty stack.

    for all u in $\vec{G}$.vertices() **do**

        Let incounter(u) be the in-degree of u.

        if incounter(u) $= 0$ **then**

           S.push(u)

    $i \leftarrow 1$

    while !S.isEmpty() **do**

        $u \leftarrow S$.pop()

        Let u be vertex number i in the topological ordering.

        $i \leftarrow i + 1$

        for all outgoing edge (u, w) of u **do**

           incounter(w) $\leftarrow$ incounter(w) $- 1$

           if incounter(w) $= 0$ **then**

               S.push(w)

Code Fragment 13.13: Pseudo-code for the topological sorting algorithm. (We show an example application of this algorithm in Figure 13.12.)

Proposition 13.22: *Let $\vec{G}$ be a digraph with n vertices and m edges. The topological sorting algorithm runs in $O(n + m)$ time using $O(n)$ auxiliary space, and either computes a topological ordering of $\vec{G}$ or fails to number some vertices, which indicates that $\vec{G}$ has a directed cycle.*

Justification: The initial computation of in-degrees and setup of the incounter variables can be done with a simple traversal of the graph, which takes $O(n + m)$ time. We use the decorator pattern to associate counter attributes with the vertices. Say that a vertex u is *visited* by the topological sorting algorithm when u is removed from the stack S. A vertex u can be visited only when incounter(u) $= 0$, which implies that all its predecessors (vertices with outgoing edges into u) were previously visited. As a consequence, any vertex that is on a directed cycle will never be visited, and any other vertex will be visited exactly once. The algorithm traverses all the outgoing edges of each visited vertex once, so its running time is proportional to the number of outgoing edges of the visited vertices. Therefore, the algorithm runs in $O(n + m)$ time. Regarding the space usage, observe that the stack S and the incounter variables attached to the vertices use $O(n)$ space. ∎

As a side effect, the topological sorting algorithm of Code Fragment 13.13 also tests whether the input digraph $\vec{G}$ is acyclic. Indeed, if the algorithm terminates without ordering all the vertices, then the subgraph of the vertices that have not been ordered must contain a directed cycle.

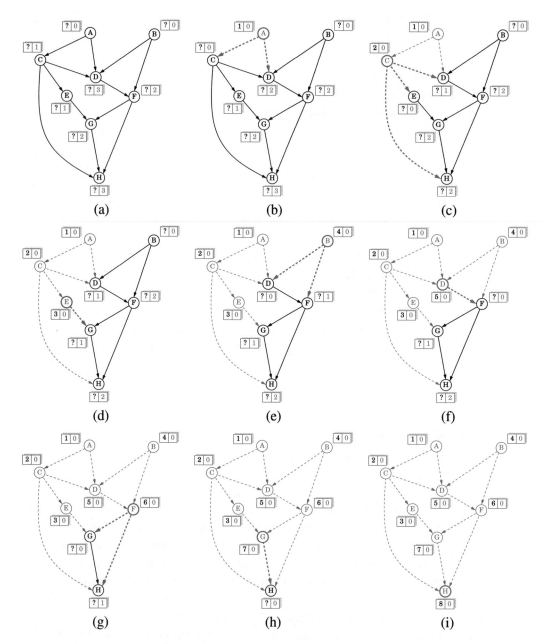

Figure 13.12: Example of a run of algorithm TopologicalSort (Code Fragment 13.13): (a) initial configuration; (b–i) after each while-loop iteration. The vertex labels show the vertex number and the current incounter value. The edges traversed are shown with dashed blue arrows. Thick lines denote the vertex and edges examined in the current iteration.

13.5   Shortest Paths

As we saw in Section 13.3.3, the breadth-first search strategy can be used to find a shortest path from some starting vertex to every other vertex in a connected graph. This approach makes sense in cases where each edge is as good as any other, but there are many situations where this approach is not appropriate. For example, we might be using a graph to represent a computer network (such as the Internet), and we might be interested in finding the fastest way to route a data packet between two computers. In this case, it is probably not appropriate for all the edges to be equal to each other, for some connections in a computer network are typically much faster than others (for example, some edges might represent slow phone-line connections while others might represent high-speed, fiber-optic connections). Likewise, we might want to use a graph to represent the roads between cities, and we might be interested in finding the fastest way to travel cross-country. In this case, it is again probably not appropriate for all the edges to be equal to each other, for some inter-city distances will likely be much larger than others. Thus, it is natural to consider graphs whose edges are not weighted equally.

13.5.1   Weighted Graphs

A **weighted graph** is a graph that has a numeric (for example, integer) label $w(e)$ associated with each edge e, called the **weight** of edge e. We show an example of a weighted graph in Figure 13.13.

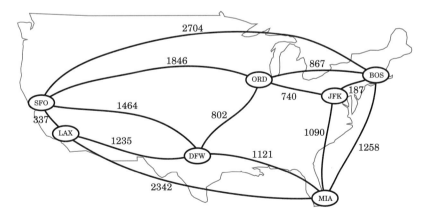

Figure 13.13: A weighted graph whose vertices represent major U.S. airports and whose edge weights represent distances in miles. This graph has a path from JFK to LAX of total weight 2,777 (going through ORD and DFW). This is the minimum weight path in the graph from JFK to LAX.

Defining Shortest Paths in a Weighted Graph

Let G be a weighted graph. The *length* (or weight) of a path is the sum of the weights of the edges of P. That is, if $P = ((v_0, v_1), (v_1, v_2), \ldots, (v_{k-1}, v_k))$, then the length of P, denoted $w(P)$, is defined as

$$w(P) = \sum_{i=0}^{k-1} w((v_i, v_{i+1})).$$

The *distance* from a vertex v to a vertex u in G, denoted $d(v, u)$, is the length of a minimum length path (also called *shortest path*) from v to u, if such a path exists.

People often use the convention that $d(v, u) = +\infty$ if there is no path at all from v to u in G. Even if there is a path from v to u in G, the distance from v to u may not be defined, however, if there is a cycle in G whose total weight is negative. For example, suppose vertices in G represent cities, and the weights of edges in G represent how much money it costs to go from one city to another. If someone were willing to actually pay us to go from say JFK to ORD, then the "cost" of the edge (JFK,ORD) would be negative. If someone else were willing to pay us to go from ORD to JFK, then there would be a negative-weight cycle in G and distances would no longer be defined. That is, anyone could now build a path (with cycles) in G from any city A to another city B that first goes to JFK and then cycles as many times as he or she likes from JFK to ORD and back, before going on to B. The existence of such paths would allow us to build arbitrarily low negative-cost paths (and, in this case, make a fortune in the process). But distances cannot be arbitrarily low negative numbers. Thus, any time we use edge weights to represent distances, we must be careful not to introduce any negative-weight cycles.

Suppose we are given a weighted graph G, and we are asked to find a shortest path from some vertex v to each other vertex in G, viewing the weights on the edges as distances. In this section, we explore efficient ways of finding all such shortest paths, if they exist. The first algorithm we discuss is for the simple, yet common, case when all the edge weights in G are nonnegative (that is, $w(e) \geq 0$ for each edge e of G); hence, we know in advance that there are no negative-weight cycles in G. Recall that the special case of computing a shortest path when all weights are equal to one was solved with the BFS traversal algorithm presented in Section 13.3.3.

There is an interesting approach for solving this *single-source* problem based on the *greedy method* design pattern (Section 12.4.2). Recall that in this pattern we solve the problem at hand by repeatedly selecting the best choice from among those available in each iteration. This paradigm can often be used in situations where we are trying to optimize some cost function over a collection of objects. We can add objects to our collection, one at a time, always picking the next one that optimizes the function from among those yet to be chosen.

13.5.2 Dijkstra's Algorithm

The main idea in applying the greedy method pattern to the single-source shortest-path problem is to perform a "weighted" breadth-first search starting at v. In particular, we can use the greedy method to develop an algorithm that iteratively grows a "cloud" of vertices out of v, with the vertices entering the cloud in order of their distances from v. Thus, in each iteration, the next vertex chosen is the vertex outside the cloud that is closest to v. The algorithm terminates when no more vertices are outside the cloud, at which point we have a shortest path from v to every other vertex of G. This approach is a simple, but nevertheless powerful, example of the greedy method design pattern.

A Greedy Method for Finding Shortest Paths

Applying the greedy method to the single-source, shortest-path problem, results in an algorithm known as ***Dijkstra's algorithm***. When applied to other graph problems, however, the greedy method may not necessarily find the best solution (such as in the so-called ***traveling salesman problem***, in which we wish to find the shortest path that visits all the vertices in a graph exactly once). Nevertheless, there are a number of situations in which the greedy method allows us to compute the best solution. In this chapter, we discuss two such situations: computing shortest paths and constructing a minimum spanning tree.

In order to simplify the description of Dijkstra's algorithm, we assume, in the following, that the input graph G is undirected (that is, all its edges are undirected) and simple (that is, it has no self-loops and no parallel edges). Hence, we denote the edges of G as unordered vertex pairs (u, z).

In Dijkstra's algorithm for finding shortest paths, the cost function we are trying to optimize in our application of the greedy method is also the function that we are trying to compute—the shortest path distance. This may at first seem like circular reasoning until we realize that we can actually implement this approach by using a "bootstrapping" trick, consisting of using an approximation to the distance function we are trying to compute, which in the end will be equal to the true distance.

Edge Relaxation

Let us define a label $D[u]$ for each vertex u in V, which we use to approximate the distance in G from v to u. The meaning of these labels is that $D[u]$ will always store the length of the best path we have found ***so far*** from v to u. Initially, $D[v] = 0$ and $D[u] = +\infty$ for each $u \neq v$, and we define the set C, which is our "***cloud***" of vertices, to initially be the empty set $\emptyset$. At each iteration of the algorithm, we select a vertex u not in C with smallest $D[u]$ label, and we pull u into C. In the very first iteration we will, of course, pull v into C. Once a new vertex u is pulled into C, we then update the label $D[z]$ of each vertex z that is adjacent to u and is outside of C, to reflect the fact that there may be a new and better way to get to z via u. This update operation is known as a ***relaxation*** procedure, for it takes an old estimate and checks if it can be improved to get closer to its true value. (A metaphor for why we call this a relaxation comes from a spring that is stretched out and then "relaxed" back to its true resting shape.) In the case of Dijkstra's algorithm, the relaxation is performed for an edge (u,z) such that we have computed a new value of $D[u]$ and wish to see if there is a better value for $D[z]$ using the edge (u,z). The specific edge relaxation operation is as follows:

Edge Relaxation:

$$\textbf{if } D[u] + w((u,z)) < D[z] \textbf{ then}$$
$$D[z] \leftarrow D[u] + w((u,z))$$

We give the pseudo-code for Dijkstra's algorithm in Code Fragment 13.14. Note that we use a priority queue Q to store the vertices outside of the cloud C.

Algorithm ShortestPath(G,v):

    Input: A simple undirected weighted graph G with nonnegative edge weights, and a distinguished vertex v of G.

    Output: A label $D[u]$, for each vertex u of G, such that $D[u]$ is the length of a shortest path from v to u in G

    Initialize $D[v] \leftarrow 0$ and $D[u] \leftarrow +\infty$ for each vertex $u \neq v$.

    Let a priority queue Q contain all the vertices of G using the D labels as keys.

    while Q is not empty **do**

        {pull a new vertex u into the cloud}

        $u \leftarrow Q.\text{removeMin}()$

        for each vertex z adjacent to u such that z is in Q **do**

            {perform the ***relaxation*** procedure on edge (u,z)}

            if $D[u] + w((u,z)) < D[z]$ **then**

                $D[z] \leftarrow D[u] + w((u,z))$

                Change to $D[z]$ the key of vertex z in Q.

    return the label $D[u]$ of each vertex u

Code Fragment 13.14: Dijkstra's algorithm for the single-source shortest path problem.

We illustrate several iterations of Dijkstra's algorithm in Figures 13.14 and 13.15.

Figure 13.14: An execution of Dijkstra's algorithm on a weighted graph. The start vertex is BWI. A box next to each vertex v stores the label $D[v]$. The symbol • is used instead of $+\infty$. The edges of the shortest-path tree are drawn as thick blue arrows, and for each vertex u outside the "cloud" we show the current best edge for pulling in u with a solid blue line. (Continues in Figure 13.15.)

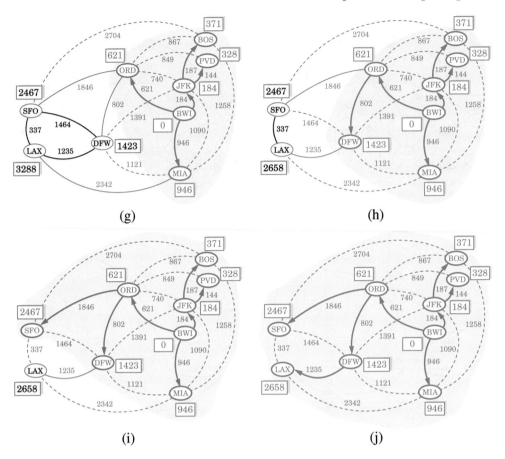

Figure 13.15: An example execution of Dijkstra's algorithm. (Continued from Figure 13.14.)

Why It Works

The interesting, and possibly even a little surprising, aspect of the Dijkstra algorithm is that, at the moment a vertex u is pulled into C, its label $D[u]$ stores the correct length of a shortest path from v to u. Thus, when the algorithm terminates, it will have computed the shortest-path distance from v to every vertex of G. That is, it will have solved the single-source shortest path problem.

It is probably not immediately clear why Dijkstra's algorithm correctly finds the shortest path from the start vertex v to each other vertex u in the graph. Why is it that the distance from v to u is equal to the value of the label $D[u]$ at the time vertex u is pulled into the cloud C (which is also the time u is removed from the priority queue Q)? The answer to this question depends on there being no negative-weight edges in the graph, for it allows the greedy method to work correctly, as we show in the proposition that follows.

Proposition 13.23: *In Dijkstra's algorithm, whenever a vertex u is pulled into the cloud, the label $D[u]$ is equal to $d(v,u)$, the length of a shortest path from v to u.*

Justification: Suppose that $D[t] > d(v,t)$ for some vertex t in V, and let u be the *first* vertex the algorithm pulled into the cloud C (that is, removed from Q) such that $D[u] > d(v,u)$. There is a shortest path P from v to u (for otherwise $d(v,u) = +\infty = D[u]$). Let us therefore consider the moment when u is pulled into C, and let z be the first vertex of P (when going from v to u) that is not in C at this moment. Let y be the predecessor of z in path P (note that we could have $y = v$). (See Figure 13.16.) We know, by our choice of z, that y is already in C at this point. Moreover, $D[y] = d(v,y)$, since u is the *first* incorrect vertex. When y was pulled into C, we tested (and possibly updated) $D[z]$ so that we had at that point

$$D[z] \le D[y] + w((y,z)) = d(v,y) + w((y,z)).$$

But since z is the next vertex on the shortest path from v to u, this implies that

$$D[z] = d(v,z).$$

But we are now at the moment when we are picking u, not z, to join C; hence,

$$D[u] \le D[z].$$

It should be clear that a subpath of a shortest path is itself a shortest path. Hence, since z is on the shortest path from v to u,

$$d(v,z) + d(z,u) = d(v,u).$$

Moreover, $d(z,u) \ge 0$ because there are no negative-weight edges. Therefore,

$$D[u] \le D[z] = d(v,z) \le d(v,z) + d(z,u) = d(v,u).$$

But this contradicts the definition of u; hence, there can be no such vertex u. ∎

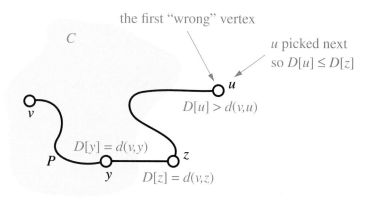

Figure 13.16: A schematic illustration for the justification of Proposition 13.23.

The Running Time of Dijkstra's Algorithm

In this section, we analyze the time complexity of Dijkstra's algorithm. We denote with n and m, the number of vertices and edges of the input graph G, respectively. We assume that the edge weights can be added and compared in constant time. Because of the high level of the description we gave for Dijkstra's algorithm in Code Fragment 13.14, analyzing its running time requires that we give more details on its implementation. Specifically, we should indicate the data structures used and how they are implemented.

Let us first assume that we are representing the graph G using an adjacency list structure. This data structure allows us to step through the vertices adjacent to u during the relaxation step in time proportional to their number. It still does not settle all the details for the algorithm, however, for we must say more about how to implement the other principle data structure in the algorithm—the priority queue Q.

An efficient implementation of the priority queue Q uses a heap (Section 8.3). This allows us to extract the vertex u with smallest D label (call to the removeMin method) in $O(\log n)$ time. As noted in the pseudo-code, each time we update a $D[z]$ label we need to update the key of z in the priority queue. Thus, we actually need a heap implementation of an adaptable priority queue (Section 8.4). If Q is an adaptable priority queue implemented as a heap, then this key update can, for example, be done using the replaceKey(e,k), where e is the entry storing the key for the vertex z. If e is location-aware, then we can easily implement such key updates in $O(\log n)$ time, since a location-aware entry for vertex z would allow Q to have immediate access to the entry e storing z in the heap (see Section 8.4.2). Assuming this implementation of Q, Dijkstra's algorithm runs in $O((n+m)\log n)$ time.

Referring back to Code Fragment 13.14, the details of the running-time analysis are as follows:

- Inserting all the vertices in Q with their initial key value can be done in $O(n\log n)$ time by repeated insertions, or in $O(n)$ time using bottom-up heap construction (see Section 8.3.6).

- At each iteration of the **while** loop, we spend $O(\log n)$ time to remove vertex u from Q, and $O(\mathrm{degree}(v)\log n)$ time to perform the relaxation procedure on the edges incident on u.

- The overall running time of the **while** loop is

$$\sum_{v \text{ in } G} (1+\mathrm{degree}(v))\log n,$$

which is $O((n+m)\log n)$ by Proposition 13.6.

Note that if we wish to express the running time as a function of n only, then it is $O(n^2 \log n)$ in the worst case.

13.5.3   Implementations of Dijkstra's Algorithm

Let us now consider an alternative implementation for the adaptable priority queue Q using an unsorted sequence. This, of course, requires that we spend $O(n)$ time to extract the minimum element, but it allows for very fast key updates, provided Q supports location-aware entries (Section 8.4.2). Specifically, we can implement each key update done in a relaxation step in $O(1)$ time—we simply change the key value once we locate the entry in Q to update. Hence, this implementation results in a running time that is $O(n^2 + m)$, which can be simplified to $O(n^2)$ since G is simple.

Comparing the Two Implementations

We have two choices for implementing the adaptable priority queue with location-aware entries in Dijkstra's algorithm: a heap implementation, which yields a running time of $O((n+m)\log n)$, and an unsorted sequence implementation, which yields a running time of $O(n^2)$. Since both implementations would be fairly simple to code up, they are about equal in terms of the programming sophistication needed. These two implementations are also about equal in terms of the constant factors in their worst-case running times. Looking only at these worst-case times, we prefer the heap implementation when the number of edges in the graph is small (that is, when $m < n^2/\log n$), and we prefer the sequence implementation when the number of edges is large (that is, when $m > n^2/\log n$).

Proposition 13.24: *Given a simple undirected weighted graph G with n vertices and m edges, such that the weight of each edge is nonnegative, and a vertex v of G, Dijkstra's algorithm computes the distance from v to all other vertices of G in $O((n+m)\log n)$ worst-case time, or, alternatively, in $O(n^2)$ worst-case time.*

In Exercise R-13.16, we explore how to modify Dijkstra's algorithm to output a tree T rooted at v, such that the path in T from v to a vertex u is a shortest path in G from v to u.

Programming Dijkstra's Algorithm in Java

Having given a pseudo-code description of Dijkstra's algorithm, let us now present Java code for performing Dijkstra's algorithm, assuming we are given an undirected graph with positive integer weights. We express the algorithm by means of class Dijkstra (Code Fragments 13.15 and 13.16), which uses a weight decoration for each edge e to extract e's weight. Class Dijkstra assumes that each edge has a *weight* decoration.

```
/* Dijkstra's algorithm for the single-source shortest path problem
 * in an undirected graph whose edges have non-negative integer weights. */
public class Dijkstra<V, E> {
  /** Infinity value. */
  protected static final Integer INFINITE = Integer.MAX_VALUE;
  /** Input graph. */
  protected Graph<V, E> graph;
  /** Decoration key for edge weights */
  protected Object WEIGHT;
  /** Decoration key for vertex distances */
  protected Object DIST = new Object();
  /** Decoration key for entries in the priority queue */
  protected Object ENTRY = new Object();
  /** Auxiliary priority queue. */
  protected AdaptablePriorityQueue<Integer, Vertex<V>> Q;
  /** Executes Dijkstra's algorithm.
   * @param g Input graph
   * @param s Source vertex
   * @param w Weight decoration object */
  public void execute(Graph<V, E> g, Vertex<V> s, Object w) {
    graph = g;
    WEIGHT = w;
    DefaultComparator dc = new DefaultComparator();
    Q = new HeapAdaptablePriorityQueue<Integer, Vertex<V>>(dc);
    dijkstraVisit(s);
  }
  /** Get the distance of a vertex from the source vertex.
   * @param u Start vertex for the shortest path tree */
  public int getDist(Vertex<V> u) {
    return (Integer) u.get(DIST);
  }
}
```

Code Fragment 13.15: Class Dijkstra implementing Dijkstra's algorithm. (Continues in Code Fragment 13.16.)

The main computation of Dijkstra's algorithm is performed by method dijkstraVisit. An adaptable priority queue Q supporting location-aware entries (Section 8.4.2) is used. We insert a vertex u into Q with method insert, which returns the location-aware entry of u in Q. We "attach" to u its entry in Q by means of method setEntry, and we retrieve the entry of u by means of method getEntry. Note that associating entries to the vertices is an instance of the decorator design pattern (Section 13.3.2). Instead of using an additional data structure for the labels $D[u]$, we exploit the fact that $D[u]$ is the key of vertex u in Q, and thus $D[u]$ can be retrieved given the entry for u in Q. Changing the label of a vertex z to d in the relaxation procedure corresponds to calling method replaceKey(e, d), where e is the location-aware entry for z in Q.

```
/** The actual execution of Dijkstra's algorithm.
 * @param v source vertex.
 */
protected void dijkstraVisit (Vertex<V> v) {
  // store all the vertices in priority queue Q
  for (Vertex<V> u: graph.vertices()) {
    int u_dist;
    if (u==v)
      u_dist = 0;
    else
      u_dist = INFINITE;
    Entry<Integer, Vertex<V>> u_entry = Q.insert(u_dist, u); // autoboxing
    u.put(ENTRY, u_entry);
  }
  // grow the cloud, one vertex at a time
  while (!Q.isEmpty()) {
    // remove from Q and insert into cloud a vertex with minimum distance
    Entry<Integer, Vertex<V>> u_entry = Q.min();
    Vertex<V> u = u_entry.getValue();
    int u_dist = u_entry.getKey();
    Q.remove(u_entry); // remove u from the priority queue
    u.put(DIST,u_dist); // the distance of u is final
    u.remove(ENTRY); // remove the entry decoration of u
    if (u_dist == INFINITE)
      continue; // unreachable vertices are not processed
    // examine all the neighbors of u and update their distances
    for (Edge<E> e: graph.incidentEdges(u)) {
      Vertex<V> z = graph.opposite(u,e);
      Entry<Integer, Vertex<V>> z_entry
                          = (Entry<Integer, Vertex<V>>) z.get(ENTRY);
      if (z_entry != null) { // check that z is in Q, i.e., not in the cloud
        int e_weight = (Integer) e.get(WEIGHT);
        int z_dist = z_entry.getKey();
        if ( u_dist + e_weight < z_dist ) // relaxation of edge e = (u,z)
          Q.replaceKey(z_entry, u_dist + e_weight);
      }
    }
  }
}
```

Code Fragment 13.16: Method dijkstraVisit of class Dijkstra. (Continued from Code Fragment 13.15.)

13.6   Minimum Spanning Trees

Suppose we wish to connect all the computers in a new office building using the least amount of cable. We can model this problem using a weighted graph G whose vertices represent the computers, and whose edges represent all the possible pairs (u, v) of computers, where the weight $w((v, u))$ of edge (v, u) is equal to the amount of cable needed to connect computer v to computer u. Rather than computing a shortest path tree from some particular vertex v, we are interested instead in finding a (free) tree T that contains all the vertices of G and has the minimum total weight over all such trees. Methods for finding such a tree are the focus of this section.

Problem Definition

Given a weighted undirected graph G, we are interested in finding a tree T that contains all the vertices in G and minimizes the sum

$$w(T) = \sum_{(v,u) \text{ in } T} w((v,u)).$$

A tree, such as this, that contains every vertex of a connected graph G is said to be a ***spanning tree***, and the problem of computing a spanning tree T with smallest total weight is known as the ***minimum spanning tree*** (or ***MST***) problem.

The development of efficient algorithms for the minimum spanning tree problem predates the modern notion of computer science itself. In this section, we discuss two classic algorithms for solving the MST problem. These algorithms are both applications of the ***greedy method***, which, as was discussed briefly in the previous section, is based on choosing objects to join a growing collection by iteratively picking an object that minimizes some cost function. The first algorithm we discuss is Kruskal's algorithm, which "grows" the MST in clusters by considering edges in order of their weights. The second algorithm we discuss is the Prim-Jarník algorithm, which grows the MST from a single root vertex, much in the same way as Dijkstra's shortest-path algorithm.

As in Section 13.5.2, in order to simplify the description of the algorithms, we assume, in the following, that the input graph G is undirected (that is, all its edges are undirected) and simple (that is, it has no self-loops and no parallel edges). Hence, we denote the edges of G as unordered vertex pairs (u, z).

Before we discuss the details of these algorithms, however, let us give a crucial fact about minimum spanning trees that forms the basis of the algorithms.

A Crucial Fact about Minimum Spanning Trees

The two MST algorithms we discuss are based on the greedy method, which in this case depends crucially on the following fact. (See Figure 13.17.)

e Belongs to a Minimum Spanning Tree

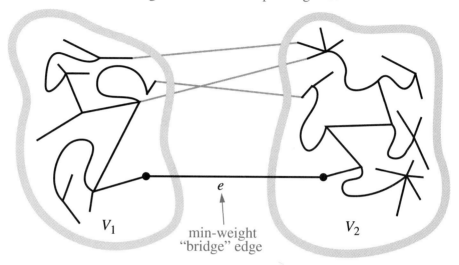

Figure 13.17: An illustration of the crucial fact about minimum spanning trees.

Proposition 13.25: *Let G be a weighted connected graph, and let V_1 and V_2 be a partition of the vertices of G into two disjoint nonempty sets. Furthermore, let e be an edge in G with minimum weight from among those with one endpoint in V_1 and the other in V_2. There is a minimum spanning tree T that has e as one of its edges.*

Justification: Let T be a minimum spanning tree of G. If T does not contain edge e, the addition of e to T must create a cycle. Therefore, there is some edge f of this cycle that has one endpoint in V_1 and the other in V_2. Moreover, by the choice of e, $w(e) \leq w(f)$. If we remove f from $T \cup \{e\}$, we obtain a spanning tree whose total weight is no more than before. Since T was a minimum spanning tree, this new tree must also be a minimum spanning tree. ∎

In fact, if the weights in G are distinct, then the minimum spanning tree is unique; we leave the justification of this less crucial fact as an exercise (C-13.17). In addition, note that Proposition 13.25 remains valid even if the graph G contains negative-weight edges or negative-weight cycles, unlike the algorithms we presented for shortest paths.

13.6.1 Kruskal's Algorithm

The reason Proposition 13.25 is so important is that it can be used as the basis for building a minimum spanning tree. In Kruskal's algorithm, it is used to build the minimum spanning tree in clusters. Initially, each vertex is in its own cluster all by itself. The algorithm then considers each edge in turn, ordered by increasing weight. If an edge e connects two different clusters, then e is added to the set of edges of the minimum spanning tree, and the two clusters connected by e are merged into a single cluster. If, on the other hand, e connects two vertices that are already in the same cluster, then e is discarded. Once the algorithm has added enough edges to form a spanning tree, it terminates and outputs this tree as the minimum spanning tree.

We give pseudo-code for Kruskal's MST algorithm in Code Fragment 13.17 and we show the working of this algorithm in Figures 13.18, 13.19, and 13.20.

Algorithm Kruskal(G):

    Input: A simple connected weighted graph G with n vertices and m edges

    Output: A minimum spanning tree T for G

  for each vertex v in G **do**

    Define an elementary cluster $C(v) \leftarrow \{v\}$.

  Initialize a priority queue Q to contain all edges in G, using the weights as keys.

  $T \leftarrow \emptyset$ {T will ultimately contain the edges of the MST}

  while T has fewer than $n-1$ edges **do**

    $(u,v) \leftarrow Q.\mathsf{removeMin}()$

    Let $C(v)$ be the cluster containing v, and let $C(u)$ be the cluster containing u.

    if $C(v) \neq C(u)$ **then**

      Add edge (v,u) to T.

      Merge $C(v)$ and $C(u)$ into one cluster, that is, union $C(v)$ and $C(u)$.

  return tree T

      Code Fragment 13.17: Kruskal's algorithm for the MST problem.

As mentioned before, the correctness of Kruskal's algorithm follows from the crucial fact about minimum spanning trees, Proposition 13.25. Each time Kruskal's algorithm adds an edge (v,u) to the minimum spanning tree T, we can define a partitioning of the set of vertices V (as in the proposition) by letting V_1 be the cluster containing v and letting V_2 contain the rest of the vertices in V. This clearly defines a disjoint partitioning of the vertices of V and, more importantly, since we are extracting edges from Q in order by their weights, e must be a minimum-weight edge with one vertex in V_1 and the other in V_2. Thus, Kruskal's algorithm always adds a valid minimum spanning tree edge.

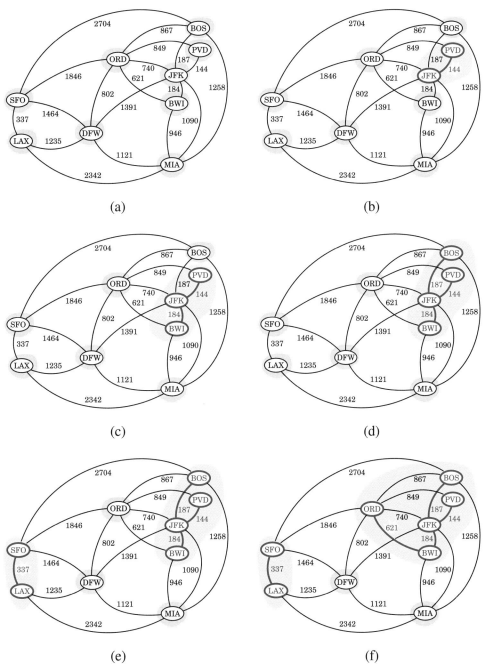

(a) (b)

(c) (d)

(e) (f)

Figure 13.18: Example of an execution of Kruskal's MST algorithm on a graph with integer weights. We show the clusters as shaded regions and we highlight the edge being considered in each iteration. (Continues in Figure 13.19.)

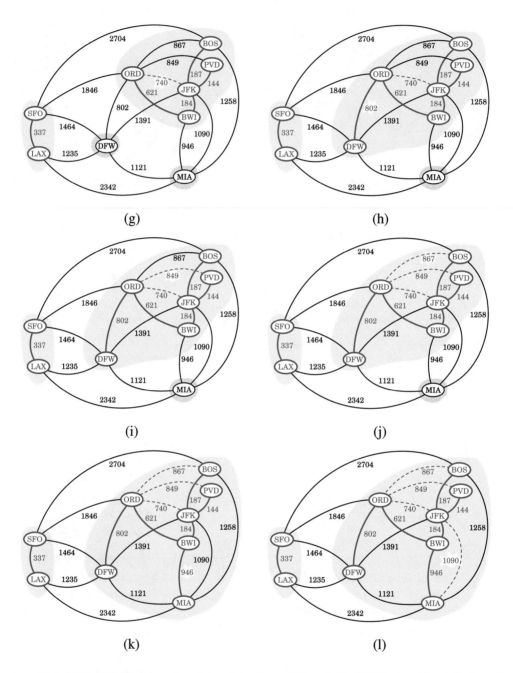

Figure 13.19: An example of an execution of Kruskal's MST algorithm. Rejected edges are shown dashed. (Continues in Figure 13.20.)

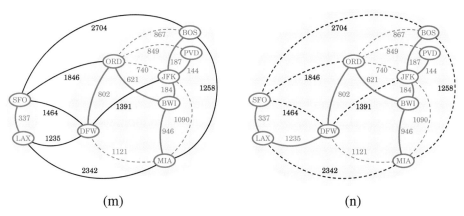

(m)   (n)

Figure 13.20: Example of an execution of Kruskal's MST algorithm (continued). The edge considered in (n) merges the last two clusters, which concludes this execution of Kruskal's algorithm. (Continued from Figure 13.19.)

The Running Time of Kruskal's Algorithm

We denote the number of vertices and edges of the input graph G with n and m, respectively. Because of the high level of the description we gave for Kruskal's algorithm in Code Fragment 13.17, analyzing its running time requires that we give more details on its implementation. Specifically, we should indicate the data structures used and how they are implemented.

We can implement the priority queue Q using a heap. Thus, we can initialize Q in $O(m \log m)$ time by repeated insertions, or in $O(m)$ time using bottom-up heap construction (see Section 8.3.6). In addition, at each iteration of the **while** loop, we can remove a minimum-weight edge in $O(\log m)$ time, which actually is $O(\log n)$, since G is simple. Thus, the total time spent performing priority queue operations is no more than $O(m \log n)$.

We can represent each cluster C using one of the union-find partition data structures discussed in Section 11.4.3. Recall that the sequence-based union-find structure allows us to perform a series of N union and find operations in $O(N \log N)$ time, and the tree-based version can implement such a series of operations in $O(N \log^* N)$ time. Thus, since we perform $n - 1$ calls to method union and at most m calls to find, the total time spent on merging clusters and determining the clusters that vertices belong to is no more than $O(m \log n)$ using the sequence-based approach or $O(m \log^* n)$ using the tree-based approach.

Therefore, using arguments similar to those used for Dijkstra's algorithm, we conclude that the running time of Kruskal's algorithm is $O((n+m) \log n)$, which can be simplified as $O(m \log n)$, since G is simple and connected.

13.6.2   The Prim-Jarník Algorithm

In the Prim-Jarník algorithm, we grow a minimum spanning tree from a single cluster starting from some "root" vertex v. The main idea is similar to that of Dijkstra's algorithm. We begin with some vertex v, defining the initial "cloud" of vertices C. Then, in each iteration, we choose a minimum-weight edge $e = (v, u)$, connecting a vertex v in the cloud C to a vertex u outside of C. The vertex u is then brought into the cloud C and the process is repeated until a spanning tree is formed. Again, the crucial fact about minimum spanning trees comes to play, for by always choosing the smallest-weight edge joining a vertex inside C to one outside C, we are assured of always adding a valid edge to the MST.

To efficiently implement this approach, we can take another cue from Dijkstra's algorithm. We maintain a label $D[u]$ for each vertex u outside the cloud C, so that $D[u]$ stores the weight of the best current edge for joining u to the cloud C. These labels allow us to reduce the number of edges that we must consider in deciding which vertex is next to join the cloud. We give the pseudo-code in Code Fragment 13.18.

Algorithm PrimJarnik(G):
  Input: A weighted connected graph G with n vertices and m edges
  Output: A minimum spanning tree T for G
  Pick any vertex v of G
  $D[v] \leftarrow 0$
  for each vertex $u \neq v$ **do**
    $D[u] \leftarrow +\infty$
  Initialize $T \leftarrow \emptyset$.
  Initialize a priority queue Q with an entry $((u, \text{null}), D[u])$ for each vertex u, where (u, null) is the element and $D[u]$ is the key.
  while Q is not empty **do**
    $(u, e) \leftarrow Q.\text{removeMin}()$
    Add vertex u and edge e to T.
    for each vertex z adjacent to u such that z is in Q **do**
      {perform the relaxation procedure on edge (u, z)}
      if $w((u, z)) < D[z]$ **then**
        $D[z] \leftarrow w((u, z))$
        Change to $(z, (u, z))$ the element of vertex z in Q.
        Change to $D[z]$ the key of vertex z in Q.
  return the tree T

Code Fragment 13.18: The Prim-Jarník algorithm for the MST problem.

Analyzing the Prim-Jarník Algorithm

Let n and m denote the number of vertices and edges of the input graph G, respectively. The implementation issues for the Prim-Jarník algorithm are similar to those for Dijkstra's algorithm. If we implement the adaptable priority queue Q as a heap that supports location-aware entries (Section 8.4.2), then we can extract the vertex u in each iteration in $O(\log n)$ time. In addition, we can update each $D[z]$ value in $O(\log n)$ time, as well, which is a computation considered at most once for each edge (u,z). The other steps in each iteration can be implemented in constant time. Thus, the total running time is $O((n+m)\log n)$, which is $O(m\log n)$.

Illustrating the Prim-Jarník Algorithm

We illustrate the Prim-Jarník algorithm in Figures 13.21 through 13.22.

(a) (b)

(c) (d)

Figure 13.21: An illustration of the Prim-Jarník MST algorithm. (Continues in Figure 13.22.)

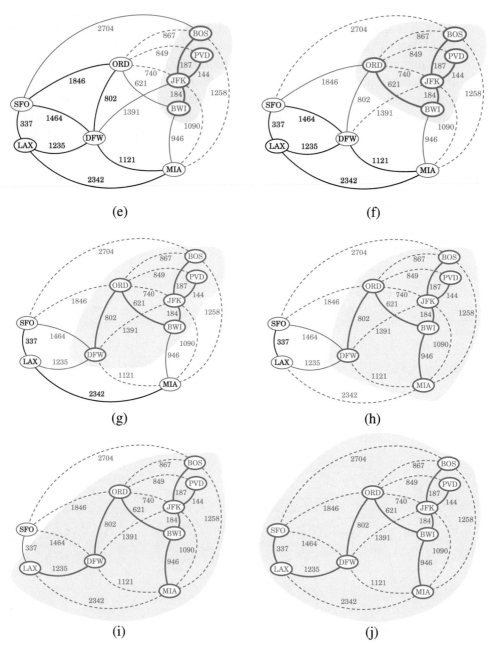

Figure 13.22: An illustration of the Prim-Jarník MST algorithm. (Continued from Figure 13.21.)

13.7 Exercises

For help with exercises, please visit the web site, www.wiley.com/college/goodrich.

Reinforcement

R-13.1 Draw a simple undirected graph G that has 12 vertices, 18 edges, and 3 connected components. Why would it be impossible to draw G with 3 connected components if G had 66 edges?

R-13.2 Draw an adjacency list and adjacency matrix representation of the undirected graph shown in Figure 13.1.

R-13.3 Draw a simple connected directed graph with 8 vertices and 16 edges such that the in-degree and out-degree of each vertex is 2. Show that there is a single (nonsimple) cycle that includes all the edges of your graph, that is, you can trace all the edges in their respective directions without ever lifting your pencil. (Such a cycle is called an *Euler tour*.)

R-13.4 Repeat the previous problem and then remove one edge from the graph. Show that now there is a single (nonsimple) path that includes all the edges of your graph. (Such a path is called an *Euler path*.)

R-13.5 Bob loves foreign languages and wants to plan his course schedule for the following years. He is interested in the following nine language courses: LA15, LA16, LA22, LA31, LA32, LA126, LA127, LA141, and LA169. The course prerequisites are:

- LA15: (none)
- LA16: LA15
- LA22: (none)
- LA31: LA15
- LA32: LA16, LA31
- LA126: LA22, LA32
- LA127: LA16
- LA141: LA22, LA16
- LA169: LA32.

Find the sequence of courses that allows Bob to satisfy all the prerequisites.

R-13.6 Suppose we represent a graph G having n vertices and m edges with the edge list structure. Why, in this case, does the insertVertex method run in $O(1)$ time while the removeVertex method runs in $O(m)$ time?

R-13.7 Let *G* be a graph whose vertices are the integers 1 through 8, and let the adjacent vertices of each vertex be given by the table below:

vertex	adjacent vertices
1	(2, 3, 4)
2	(1, 3, 4)
3	(1, 2, 4)
4	(1, 2, 3, 6)
5	(6, 7, 8)
6	(4, 5, 7)
7	(5, 6, 8)
8	(5, 7)

Assume that, in a traversal of *G*, the adjacent vertices of a given vertex are returned in the same order as they are listed in the table above.

a. Draw *G*.

b. Give the sequence of vertices of *G* visited using a DFS traversal starting at vertex 1.

c. Give the sequence of vertices visited using a BFS traversal starting at vertex 1.

R-13.8 Would you use the adjacency list structure or the adjacency matrix structure in each of the following cases? Justify your choice.

a. The graph has 10,000 vertices and 20,000 edges, and it is important to use as little space as possible.

b. The graph has 10,000 vertices and 20,000,000 edges, and it is important to use as little space as possible.

c. You need to answer the query areAdjacent as fast as possible, no matter how much space you use.

R-13.9 Explain why the DFS traversal runs in $O(n^2)$ time on an *n*-vertex simple graph that is represented with the adjacency matrix structure.

R-13.10 Draw the transitive closure of the directed graph shown in Figure 13.2.

R-13.11 Compute a topological ordering for the directed graph drawn with solid edges in Figure 13.8d.

R-13.12 Can we use a queue instead of a stack as an auxiliary data structure in the topological sorting algorithm shown in Code Fragment 13.13? Why or why not?

R-13.13 Draw a simple, connected, weighted graph with 8 vertices and 16 edges, each with unique edge weights. Identify one vertex as a "start" vertex and illustrate a running of Dijkstra's algorithm on this graph.

R-13.14 Show how to modify the pseudo-code for Dijkstra's algorithm for the case when the graph may contain parallel edges and self-loops.

R-13.15 Show how to modify the pseudo-code for Dijkstra's algorithm for the case when the graph is directed and we we want to compute shortest directed paths from the source vertex to all the other vertices.

R-13.16 Show how to modify Dijkstra's algorithm to not only output the distance from v to each vertex in G, but also to output a tree T rooted at v such that the path in T from v to a vertex u is a shortest path in G from v to u.

R-13.17 There are eight small islands in a lake, and the state wants to build seven bridges to connect them so that each island can be reached from any other one via one or more bridges. The cost of constructing a bridge is proportional to its length. The distances between pairs of islands are given in the following table.

	1	2	3	4	5	6	7	8
1	-	240	210	340	280	200	345	120
2	-	-	265	175	215	180	185	155
3	-	-	-	260	115	350	435	195
4	-	-	-	-	160	330	295	230
5	-	-	-	-	-	360	400	170
6	-	-	-	-	-	-	175	205
7	-	-	-	-	-	-	-	305
8	-	-	-	-	-	-	-	-

Find which bridges to build to minimize the total construction cost.

R-13.18 Draw a simple, connected, undirected, weighted graph with 8 vertices and 16 edges, each with unique edge weights. Illustrate the execution of Kruskal's algorithm on this graph. (Note that there is only one minimum spanning tree for this graph.)

R-13.19 Repeat the previous problem for the Prim-Jarník algorithm.

R-13.20 Consider the unsorted sequence implementation of the priority queue Q used in Dijkstra's algorithm. In this case, why is this the best-case running time of Dijkstra's algorithm $O(n^2)$ on an n-vertex graph?

R-13.21 Describe the meaning of the graphical conventions used in Figure 13.6 illustrating a DFS traversal. What do the colors blue and black refer to? What do the arrows signify? How about thick lines and dashed lines?

R-13.22 Repeat Exercise R-13.21 for Figure 13.7 illustrating a BFS traversal.

R-13.23 Repeat Exercise R-13.21 for Figure 13.9 illustrating a directed DFS traversal.

R-13.24 Repeat Exercise R-13.21 for Figure 13.10 illustrating the Floyd-Warshall algorithm.

R-13.25 Repeat Exercise R-13.21 for Figure 13.12 illustrating the topological sorting algorithm.

R-13.26 Repeat Exercise R-13.21 for Figures 13.14 and 13.15 illustrating Dijkstra's algorithm.

R-13.27 Repeat Exercise R-13.21 for Figures 13.18 and 13.20 illustrating Kruskal's algorithm.

R-13.28 Repeat Exercise R-13.21 for Figures 13.21 and 13.22 illustrating the Prim-Jarník algorithm.

R-13.29 How many edges are in the transitive closure of a graph that consists of a simple directed path of n vertices?

R-13.30 Given a complete binary tree T with n nodes, consider a directed graph $\vec{G}$ having the nodes of T as its vertices. For each parent-child pair in T, create a directed edge in $\vec{G}$ from the parent to the child. Show that the transitive closure of $\vec{G}$ has $O(n \log n)$ edges.

R-13.31 A simple undirected graph is **complete** if it contains an edge between every pair of distinct vertices. What does a depth-first search tree of a complete graph look like?

R-13.32 Recalling the definition of a complete graph from Exercise R-13.31, what does a breadth-first search tree of a complete graph look like?

R-13.33 Say that a maze is **constructed correctly** if there is one path from the start to the finish, the entire maze is reachable from the start, and there are no loops around any portions of the maze. Given a maze drawn in an $n \times n$ grid, how can we determine if it is constructed correctly? What is the running time of this algorithm?

Creativity

C-13.1 Say that an n-vertex directed acyclic graph $\vec{G}$ is **compact** if there is some way of numbering the vertices of $\vec{G}$ with the integers from 0 to $n-1$ such that $\vec{G}$ contains the edge (i, j) if and only if $i < j$, for all i, j in $[0, n-1]$. Give an $O(n^2)$-time algorithm for detecting if $\vec{G}$ is compact.

C-13.2 Describe, in pseudo-code, an $O(n+m)$-time algorithm for computing **all** the connected components of an undirected graph G with n vertices and m edges.

C-13.3 Let T be the spanning tree rooted at the start vertex produced by the depth-first search of a connected, undirected graph G. Argue why every edge of G not in T goes from a vertex in T to one of its ancestors, that is, it is a **back edge**.

C-13.4 Suppose we wish to represent an n-vertex graph G using the edge list structure, assuming that we identify the vertices with the integers in the set $\{0, 1, \ldots, n-1\}$. Describe how to implement the collection E to support $O(\log n)$-time performance for the areAdjacent method. How are you implementing the method in this case?

C-13.5 Tamarindo University and many other schools worldwide are doing a joint project on multimedia. A computer network is built to connect these schools using communication links that form a free tree. The schools decide to install a file server at one of the schools to share data among all the schools. Since the transmission time on a link is dominated by the link setup and synchronization, the cost of a data transfer is proportional to the number of links used. Hence, it is desirable to choose a "central" location for the file server. Given a free tree T and a node v of T, the *eccentricity* of v is the length of a longest path from v to any other node of T. A node of T with minimum eccentricity is called a *center* of T.

    a. Design an efficient algorithm that, given an n-node free tree T, computes a center of T.

    b. Is the center unique? If not, how many distinct centers can a free tree have?

C-13.6 Show that, if T is a BFS tree produced for a connected graph G, then, for each vertex v at level i, the path of T between s and v has i edges, and any other path of G between s and v has at least i edges.

C-13.7 The time delay of a long-distance call can be determined by multiplying a small fixed constant by the number of communication links on the telephone network between the caller and callee. Suppose the telephone network of a company named RT&T is a free tree. The engineers of RT&T want to compute the maximum possible time delay that may be experienced in a long-distance call. Given a free tree T, the *diameter* of T is the length of a longest path between two nodes of T. Give an efficient algorithm for computing the diameter of T.

C-13.8 A company named RT&T has a network of n switching stations connected by m high-speed communication links. Each customer's phone is directly connected to one station in his or her area. The engineers of RT&T have developed a prototype video-phone system that allows two customers to see each other during a phone call. In order to have acceptable image quality, however, the number of links used to transmit video signals between the two parties cannot exceed 4. Suppose that RT&T's network is represented by a graph. Design an efficient algorithm that computes, for each station, the set of stations it can reach using no more than 4 links.

C-13.9 Explain why there are no forward nontree edges with respect to a BFS tree constructed for a directed graph.

C-13.10 An **Euler tour** of a directed graph $\vec{G}$ with n vertices and m edges is a cycle that traverses each edge of $\vec{G}$ exactly once according to its direction. Such a tour always exists if $\vec{G}$ is connected and the in-degree equals the out-degree of each vertex in $\vec{G}$. Describe an $O(n+m)$-time algorithm for finding an Euler tour of such a digraph $\vec{G}$.

C-13.11 An independent set of an undirected graph $G = (V, E)$ is a subset I of V such that no two vertices in I are adjacent. That is, if u and v are in I, then (u, v) is not in E. A ***maximal independent set*** M is an independent set such that, if we were to add any additional vertex to M, then it would not be independent any more. Every graph has a maximal independent set. (Can you see this? This question is not part of the exercise, but it is worth thinking about.) Give an efficient algorithm that computes a maximal independent set for a graph G. What is this method's running time?

C-13.12 Let G be an undirected graph G with n vertices and m edges. Describe an $O(n + m)$-time algorithm for traversing each edge of G exactly once in each direction.

C-13.13 Justify Proposition 13.14.

C-13.14 Give an example of an n-vertex simple graph G that causes Dijkstra's algorithm to run in $\Omega(n^2 \log n)$ time when its implemented with a heap.

C-13.15 Give an example of a weighted directed graph $\vec{G}$ with negative-weight edges, but no negative-weight cycle, such that Dijkstra's algorithm incorrectly computes the shortest-path distances from some start vertex v.

C-13.16 Consider the following greedy strategy for finding a shortest path from vertex *start* to vertex *goal* in a given connected graph.

    1: Initialize *path* to *start*.
    2: Initialize *VisitedVertices* to {*start*}.
    3: If *start*=*goal*, return *path* and exit. Otherwise, continue.
    4: Find the edge (*start*,*v*) of minimum weight such that *v* is adjacent to *start* and *v* is not in *VisitedVertices*.
    5: Add *v* to *path*.
    6: Add *v* to *VisitedVertices*.
    7: Set *start* equal to *v* and go to step 3.

Does this greedy strategy always find a shortest path from *start* to *goal*? Either explain intuitively why it works, or give a counter example.

C-13.17 Show that if all the weights in a connected weighted graph G are distinct, then there is exactly one minimum spanning tree for G.

C-13.18 Design an efficient algorithm for finding a ***longest*** directed path from a vertex s to a vertex t of an acyclic weighted digraph $\vec{G}$. Specify the graph representation used and any auxiliary data structures used. Also, analyze the time complexity of your algorithm.

C-13.19 Consider a diagram of a telephone network, which is a graph G whose vertices represent switching centers, and whose edges represent communication lines joining pairs of centers. Edges are marked by their bandwidth, and the bandwidth of a path is the bandwidth of its lowest bandwidth edge. Give an algorithm that, given a diagram and two switching centers a and b, outputs the maximum bandwidth of a path between a and b.

C-13.20 Computer networks should avoid single points of failure, that is, network nodes that can disconnect the network if they fail. We say a connected graph G is **biconnected** if it contains no vertex whose removal would divide G into two or more connected components. Give an $O(n+m)$-time algorithm for adding at most n edges to a connected graph G, with $n \geq 3$ vertices and $m \geq n - 1$ edges, to guarantee that G is biconnected.

C-13.21 NASA wants to link n stations spread over the country using communication channels. Each pair of stations has a different bandwidth available, which is known a priori. NASA wants to select $n - 1$ channels (the minimum possible) in such a way that all the stations are linked by the channels and the total bandwidth (defined as the sum of the individual bandwidths of the channels) is maximum. Give an efficient algorithm for this problem and determine its worst-case time complexity. Consider the weighted graph $G = (V, E)$, where V is the set of stations and E is the set of channels between the stations. Define the weight $w(e)$ of an edge e in E as the bandwidth of the corresponding channel.

C-13.22 Suppose you are given a *timetable*, which consists of:
- A set $\mathcal{A}$ of n airports, and for each airport a in $\mathcal{A}$, a minimum connecting time $c(a)$.
- A set $\mathcal{F}$ of m flights, and the following, for each flight f in $\mathcal{F}$:
  - Origin airport $a_1(f)$ in $\mathcal{A}$
  - Destination airport $a_2(f)$ in $\mathcal{A}$
  - Departure time $t_1(f)$
  - Arrival time $t_2(f)$.

Describe an efficient algorithm for the flight scheduling problem. In this problem, we are given airports a and b, and a time t, and we wish to compute a sequence of flights that allows one to arrive at the earliest possible time in b when departing from a at or after time t. Minimum connecting times at intermediate airports should be observed. What is the running time of your algorithm as a function of n and m?

C-13.23 Inside the Castle of Asymptopia there is a maze, and along each corridor of the maze there is a bag of gold coins. The amount of gold in each bag varies. A noble knight, named Sir Paul, will be given the opportunity to walk through the maze, picking up bags of gold. He may enter the maze only through a door marked "ENTER" and exit through another door marked "EXIT." While in the maze he may not retrace his steps. Each corridor of the maze has an arrow painted on the wall. Sir Paul may only go down the corridor in the direction of the arrow. There is no way to traverse a "loop" in the maze. Given a map of the maze, including the amount of gold in and the direction of each corridor, describe an algorithm to help Sir Paul pick up the most gold.

C-13.24 Let $\vec{G}$ be a weighted digraph with n vertices. Design a variation of Floyd-Warshall's algorithm for computing the lengths of the shortest paths from each vertex to every other vertex in $O(n^3)$ time.

C-13.25 Suppose we are given a directed graph $\vec{G}$ with n vertices, and let M be the $n \times n$ adjacency matrix corresponding to $\vec{G}$.

    a. Let the product of M with itself (M^2) be defined, for $1 \le i, j \le n$, as follows:

$$M^2(i, j) = M(i, 1) \odot M(1, j) \oplus \cdots \oplus M(i, n) \odot M(n, j),$$

where "$\oplus$" is the Boolean **or** operator and "$\odot$" is Boolean **and**. Given this definition, what does $M^2(i, j) = 1$ imply about the vertices i and j? What if $M^2(i, j) = 0$?

    b. Suppose M^4 is the product of M^2 with itself. What do the entries of M^4 signify? How about the entries of $M^5 = (M^4)(M)$? In general, what information is contained in the matrix M^p?

    c. Now suppose that $\vec{G}$ is weighted and assume the following:

        1: for $1 \le i \le n$, $M(i, i) = 0$.
        2: for $1 \le i, j \le n$, $M(i, j) = weight(i, j)$ if (i, j) is in E.
        3: for $1 \le i, j \le n$, $M(i, j) = \infty$ if (i, j) is not in E.

Also, let M^2 be defined, for $1 \le i, j \le n$, as follows:

$$M^2(i, j) = \min\{M(i, 1) + M(1, j), \ldots, M(i, n) + M(n, j)\}.$$

If $M^2(i, j) = k$, what may we conclude about the relationship between vertices i and j?

C-13.26 A graph G is **bipartite** if its vertices can be partitioned into two sets X and Y such that every edge in G has one end vertex in X and the other in Y. Design and analyze an efficient algorithm for determining if an undirected graph G is bipartite (without knowing the sets X and Y in advance).

C-13.27 An old MST method, called **Barůvka's algorithm**, works as follows on a graph G having n vertices and m edges with distinct weights:

    Let T be a subgraph of G initially containing just the vertices in V.
    while T has fewer than $n - 1$ edges **do**
        for each connected component C_i of T **do**
            Find the lowest-weight edge (v, u) in E with v in C_i and u not in C_i.
            Add (v, u) to T (unless it is already in T).
    return T

Argue why this algorithm is correct and why it runs in $O(m \log n)$ time.

C-13.28 Let G be a graph with n vertices and m edges such that all the edge weights in G are integers in the range $[1, n]$. Give an algorithm for finding a minimum spanning tree for G in $O(m \log^* n)$ time.

Projects

P-13.1 Write a class implementing a simplified graph ADT that has only methods relevant to undirected graphs and does not include update methods, using the adjacency matrix structure. Your class should include a constructor method that takes two collections (for example, sequences)—a collection V of vertex elements and a collection E of pairs of vertex elements—and produces the graph G that these two collections represent.

P-13.2 Implement the simplified graph ADT described in Project P-13.1, using the adjacency list structure.

P-13.3 Implement the simplified graph ADT described in Project P-13.1, using the edge list structure.

P-13.4 Extend the class of Project P-13.2 to support all the methods of the graph ADT (including methods for directed edges).

P-13.5 Implement a generic BFS traversal using the template method pattern.

P-13.6 Implement the topological sorting algorithm.

P-13.7 Implement the Floyd-Warshall transitive closure algorithm.

P-13.8 Design an experimental comparison of repeated DFS traversals versus the Floyd-Warshall algorithm for computing the transitive closure of a digraph.

P-13.9 Implement Kruskal's algorithm assuming that the edge weights are integers.

P-13.10 Implement the Prim-Jarník algorithm assuming that the edge weights are integers.

P-13.11 Perform an experimental comparison of two of the minimum spanning tree algorithms discussed in this chapter (Kruskal and Prim-Jarník). Develop an extensive set of experiments to test the running times of these algorithms using randomly generated graphs.

P-13.12 One way to construct a *maze* starts with an $n \times n$ grid such that each grid cell is bounded by four unit-length walls. We then remove two boundary unit-length walls, to represent the start and finish. For each remaining unit-length wall not on the boundary, we assign a random value and create a graph G, called the *dual*, such that each grid cell is a vertex in G and there is an edge joining the vertices for two cells if and only if the cells share a common wall. The weight of each edge is the weight of the corresponding wall. We construct the maze by finding a minimum spanning tree T for G and removing all the walls corresponding to edges in T. Write a program that uses this algorithm to generate mazes and then solves them. Minimally, your program should draw the maze and, ideally, it should visualize the solution as well.

P-13.13 Write a program that builds the routing tables for the nodes in a computer network, based on shortest-path routing, where path distance is measured by hop count, that is, the number of edges in a path. The input for this problem is the connectivity information for all the nodes in the network, as in the following example:

241.12.31.14:   241.12.31.15 241.12.31.18 241.12.31.19

which indicates three network nodes that are connected to 241.12.31.14, that is, three nodes that are one hop away. The routing table for the node at address A is a set of pairs (B,C), which indicates that, to route a message from A to B, the next node to send to (on the shortest path from A to B) is C. Your program should output the routing table for each node in the network, given an input list of node connectivity lists, each of which is input in the syntax as shown above, one per line.

Chapter Notes

The depth-first search method is a part of the "folklore" of computer science, but Hopcroft and Tarjan [48, 90] are the ones who showed how useful this algorithm is for solving several different graph problems. Knuth [62] discusses the topological sorting problem. The simple linear-time algorithm that we describe for determining if a directed graph is strongly connected is due to Kosaraju. The Floyd-Warshall algorithm appears in a paper by Floyd [33] and is based upon a theorem of Warshall [98]. The mark-sweep garbage collection method we describe is one of many different algorithms for performing garbage collection. We encourage the reader interested in further study of garbage collection to examine the book by Jones [55]. To learn about different algorithms for drawing graphs, please see the book chapter by Tamassia and Liotta [88] and the book by Di Battista, Eades, Tamassia and Tollis [28]. The first known minimum spanning tree algorithm is due to Barůvka [9], and was published in 1926. The Prim-Jarník algorithm was first published in Czech by Jarník [54] in 1930 and in English in 1957 by Prim [82]. Kruskal published his minimum spanning tree algorithm in 1956 [65]. The reader interested in further study of the history of the minimum spanning tree problem is referred to the paper by Graham and Hell [43]. The current asymptotically fastest minimum spanning tree algorithm is a randomized method of Karger, Klein, and Tarjan [56] that runs in $O(m)$ expected time.

Dijkstra [29] published his single-source, shortest path algorithm in 1959. The reader interested in further study of graph algorithms is referred to the books by Ahuja, Magnanti, and Orlin [6], Cormen, Leiserson, and Rivest [25], Even [31], Gibbons [37], Mehlhorn [75], and Tarjan [91], and the book chapter by van Leeuwen [94]. Incidentally, the running time for the Prim-Jarník algorithm, and also that of Dijkstra's algorithm, can actually be improved to be $O(n \log n + m)$ by implementing the queue Q with either of two more sophisticated data structures, the "Fibonacci Heap" [35] or the "Relaxed Heap" [30].

Chapter

14 Memory Management and B-Trees

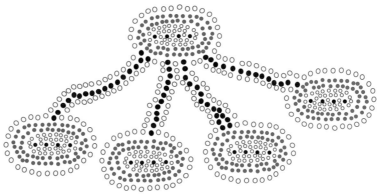

Contents

14.1   Memory Management

In order to implement any data structure on an actual computer, we need to use computer memory. Computer memory is simply a sequence of memory **words**, each of which usually consists of 4, 8, or 16 bytes (depending on the computer). These memory words are numbered from 0 to $N - 1$, where N is the number of memory words available to the computer. The number associated with each memory word is known as its **address**. Thus, the memory in a computer can be viewed as basically one giant array of memory words. Using this memory to construct data structures (and run programs) requires that we **manage** the computer's memory to provide the space needed for data—including variables, nodes, pointers, arrays, and character strings—and the programs the computer is to run. We discuss the basics of memory management in this section.

14.1.1   Stacks in the Java Virtual Machine

A Java program is typically compiled into a sequence of byte codes that are defined as "machine" instructions for a well-defined model—the **Java Virtual Machine** (**JVM**). The definition of the JVM is at the heart of the definition of the Java language itself. By compiling Java code into the JVM byte codes, rather than the machine language of a specific CPU, a Java program can be run on any computer, such as a personal computer or a server, that has a program that can emulate the JVM. Interestingly, the stack data structure plays a central role in the definition of the JVM.

The Java Method Stack

Stacks have an important application to the run-time environment of Java programs. A running Java program (more precisely, a running Java thread) has a private stack, called the **Java method stack** or just **Java stack** for short, which is used to keep track of local variables and other important information on methods as they are invoked during execution. (See Figure 14.1.)

More specifically, during the execution of a Java program, the Java Virtual Machine (JVM) maintains a stack whose elements are descriptors of the currently active (that is, nonterminated) invocations of methods. These descriptors are called **frames**. A frame for some invocation of method "fool" stores the current values of the local variables and parameters of method fool, as well as information on method "cool" that called fool and on what needs to be returned to method "cool".

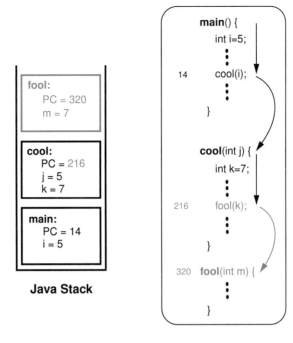

Java Stack

Java Program

Figure 14.1: An example of a Java method stack: method fool has just been called by method cool, which itself was previously called by method main. Note the values of the program counter, parameters, and local variables stored in the stack frames. When the invocation of method fool terminates, the invocation of method cool will resume its execution at instruction 217, which is obtained by incrementing the value of the program counter stored in the stack frame.

Keeping Track of the Program Counter

The JVM keeps a special variable, called the **program counter**, to maintain the address of the statement the JVM is currently executing in the program. When a method "cool" invokes another method "fool", the current value of the program counter is recorded in the frame of the current invocation of cool (so the JVM will know where to return to when method fool is done). At the top of the Java stack is the frame of the **running method**, that is, the method that currently has control of the execution. The remaining elements of the stack are frames of the **suspended methods**, that is, methods that have invoked another method and are currently waiting for it to return control to them upon its termination. The order of the elements in the stack corresponds to the chain of invocations of the currently active methods. When a new method is invoked, a frame for this method is pushed onto the stack. When it terminates, its frame is popped from the stack and the JVM resumes the processing of the previously suspended method.

Understanding Call-by-Value Parameter Passing

The JVM uses the Java stack to perform parameter passing to methods. Specifically, Java uses the ***call-by-value*** parameter passing protocol. This means that the current ***value*** of a variable (or expression) is what is passed as an argument to a called method.

In the case of a variable x of a primitive type, such as an int or float, the current value of x is simply the number that is associated with x. When such a value is passed to the called method, it is assigned to a local variable in the called method's frame. (This simple assignment is also illustrated in Figure 14.1.) Note that if the called method changes the value of this local variable, it will ***not*** change the value of the variable in the calling method.

In the case of a variable x that refers to an object, however, the current value of x is the memory address of object x. (We will say more about where this address actually is in Section 14.1.2.) Thus, when object x is passed as a parameter to some method, the address of x is actually passed. When this address is assigned to some local variable y in the called method, y will refer to the same object that x refers to.

Therefore, if the called method changes the internal state of the object that y refers to, it will simultaneously be changing the internal state of the object that x refers to (which is the same object). Nevertheless, if the called program changes y to refer to some other object, x will remain unchanged—it will still refer to the same object it was referencing before.

Thus, the Java method stack is used by the JVM to implement method calls and parameter passing. Incidentally, method stacks are not a specific feature of Java. They are used in the run-time environment of most modern programming languages, including C and C++.

The Operand Stack

Interestingly, there is actually another place where the JVM uses a stack. Arithmetic expressions, such as $((a+b)*(c+d))/e$, are evaluated by the JVM using an ***operand stack***. A simple binary operation, such as $a+b$, is computed by pushing a on the stack, pushing b on the stack, and then calling an instruction that pops the top two items from the stack, performs the binary operation on them, and pushes the result back onto the stack. Likewise, instructions for writing and reading elements to and from memory involve the use of pop and push methods for the operand stack. Thus, the JVM uses a stack to evaluate arithmetic expressions in Java.

In Section 7.3.6 we described how to evaluate an arithmetic expression using a postorder traversal, which is exactly the algorithm the JVM uses. We described that algorithm in a recursive way, however, not in a way that explicitly uses an operand stack. Nevertheless, this recursive description is equivalent to a nonrecursive version based on using an operand stack.

Implementing Recursion

One of the benefits of using a stack to implement method invocation is that it allows programs to use **recursion**. That is, it allows a method to call itself, as discussed in Section 3.5. Interestingly, early programming languages, such as Cobol and Fortran, did not originally use run-time stacks to implement method and procedure calls. But because of the elegance and efficiency that recursion allows, all modern programming languages, including the modern versions of classic languages like Cobol and Fortran, utilize a run-time stack for method and procedure calls.

In the execution of a recursive method, each box of the recursion trace corresponds to a frame of the Java method stack. Also, the content of the Java method stack corresponds to the chain of boxes from the initial method invocation to the current one.

To better illustrate how a run-time stack allows for recursive methods, let us consider a Java implementation of the classic recursive definition of the factorial function,

$$n! = n(n-1)(n-2)\cdots 1,$$

as shown in Code Fragment 14.1.

```java
public static long factorial(long n) {
  if (n <= 1)
    return 1;
  else
    return n*factorial(n-1);
}
```

Code Fragment 14.1: Recursive method factorial.

The first time we call method factorial, its stack frame includes a local variable storing the value n. Method factorial() recursively calls itself to compute $(n-1)!$, which pushes a new frame on the Java run-time stack. In turn, this recursive invocation calls itself to compute $(n-2)!$, etc. The chain of recursive invocations, and thus the run-time stack, only grows up to size n, because calling factorial(1) returns 1 immediately without invoking itself recursively. The run-time stack allows for method factorial() to exist simultaneously in several active frames (as many as n at some point). Each frame stores the value of its parameter n as well as the value to be returned. Eventually, when the first recursive call terminates, it returns $(n-1)!$, which is then multiplied by n to compute $n!$ for the original call of the factorial method.

14.1.2   Allocating Space in the Memory Heap

We have already discussed (in Section 14.1.1) how the Java Virtual Machine allocates a method's local variables in that method's frame on the Java run-time stack. The Java stack is not the only kind of memory available for program data in Java, however.

Dynamic Memory Allocation

Memory for an object can also be allocated dynamically during a method's execution, by having that method utilize the special **new** operator built into Java. For example, the following Java statement creates an array of integers whose size is given by the value of variable k:

> int[] items = **new** int[k];

The size of the array above is known only at runtime. Moreover, the array may continue to exist even after the method that created it terminates. Thus, the memory for this array cannot be allocated on the Java stack.

The Memory Heap

Instead of using the Java stack for this object's memory, Java uses memory from another area of storage—the ***memory heap*** (which should not be confused with the "heap" data structure presented in Chapter 8). We illustrate this memory area, together with the other memory areas, in a Java Virtual Machine in Figure 14.2. The storage available in the memory heap is divided into ***blocks***, which are contiguous array-like "chunks" of memory that may be of variable or fixed sizes.

   To simplify the discussion, let us assume that blocks in the memory heap are of a fixed size, say, 1,024 bytes, and that one block is big enough for any object we might want to create. (Efficiently handling the more general case is actually an interesting research problem.)

Figure 14.2: A schematic view of the layout of memory addresses in the Java Virtual Machine.

Memory Allocation Algorithms

The Java Virtual Machine definition requires that the memory heap be able to quickly allocate memory for new objects, but it does not specify the data structure that we should use to do this. One popular method is to keep contiguous "holes" of available free memory in a doubly linked list, called the *free list*. The links joining these holes are stored inside the holes themselves, since their memory is not being used. As memory is allocated and deallocated, the collection of holes in the free lists changes, with the unused memory being separated into disjoint holes divided by blocks of used memory. This separation of unused memory into separate holes is known as *fragmentation*. Of course, we would like to minimize fragmentation as much as possible.

There are two kinds of fragmentation that can occur. *Internal fragmentation* occurs when a portion of an allocated memory block is not actually used. For example, a program may request an array of size 1000, but only use the first 100 cells of this array. There isn't much that a run-time environment can do to reduce internal fragmentation. *External fragmentation*, on the other hand, occurs when the there is a significant amount of unused memory between several contiguous blocks of allocated memory. Since the run-time environment has control over where to allocate memory when it is requested (for example, when the **new** keyword is used in Java), the run-time environment should allocate memory in a way that tries to reduce external fragmentation as much as reasonably possible.

Several heuristics have been suggested for allocating memory from the heap so as to minimize external fragmentation. The *best-fit algorithm* searches the entire free list to find the hole whose size is closest to the amount of memory being requested. The *first-fit algorithm* searches from the beginning of the free list for the first hole that is large enough. The *next-fit algorithm* is similar, in that it also searches the free list for the first hole that is large enough, but it begins its search from where it left off previously, viewing the free list as a circularly linked list (Section 3.4.1). The *worst-fit algorithm* searches the free list to find the largest hole of available memory, which might be done faster than a search of the entire free list if this list were maintained as a priority queue (Chapter 8). In each algorithm, the requested amount of memory is subtracted from the chosen memory hole and the leftover part of that hole is returned to the free list.

Although it might sound good at first, the best-fit algorithm tends to produce the worst external fragmentation, since the leftover parts of the chosen holes tend to be small. The first-fit algorithm is fast, but it tends to produce a lot of external fragmentation at the front of the free list, which slows down future searches. The next-fit algorithm spreads fragmentation more evenly throughout the memory heap, thus keeping search times low. This spreading also makes it more difficult to allocate large blocks, however. The worst-fit algorithm attempts to avoid this problem by keeping contiguous sections of free memory as large as possible.

14.1.3   Garbage Collection

In some languages, like C and C++, the memory space for objects must be explicitly deallocated by the programmer, which is a duty often overlooked by beginning programmers and is the source of frustrating programming errors even for experienced programmers. Instead, the designers of Java placed the burden of memory management entirely on the run-time environment.

As mentioned above, memory for objects is allocated from the memory heap and the space for the instance variables of a running Java program are placed in its method stacks, one for each running thread (for the simple programs discussed in this book there is typically just one running thread). Since instance variables in a method stack can refer to objects in the memory heap, all the variables and objects in the method stacks of running threads are called ***root objects***. All those objects that can be reached by following object references that start from a root object are called ***live objects***. The live objects are the active objects currently being used by the running program; these objects should ***not*** be deallocated. For example, a running Java program may store, in a variable, a reference to a sequence S that is implemented using a doubly linked list. The reference variable to S is a root object, while the object for S is a live object, as are all the node objects that are referenced from this object and all the elements that are referenced from these node objects.

From time to time, the Java virtual machine (JVM) may notice that available space in the memory heap is becoming scarce. At such times, the JVM can elect to reclaim the space that is being used for objects that are no longer live, and return the reclaimed memory to the free list. This reclamation process is known as ***garbage collection***. There are several different algorithms for garbage collection, but one of the most used is the ***mark-sweep algorithm***.

In the mark-sweep garbage collection algorithm, we associate a "mark" bit with each object that identifies if that object is live or not. When we determine at some point that garbage collection is needed, we suspend all other running threads and clear the mark bits of all the objects currently allocated in the memory heap. We then trace through the Java stacks of the currently running threads and we mark all the (root) objects in these stacks as "live." We must then determine all the other live objects—the ones that are reachable from the root objects. To do this efficiently, we can use the directed-graph version of the depth-first search traversal (Section 13.3.1). In this case, each object in the memory heap is viewed as a vertex in a directed graph, and the reference from one object to another is viewed as a directed edge. By performing a directed DFS from each root object, we can correctly identify and mark each live object. This process is known as the "mark" phase. Once this process has completed, we then scan through the memory heap and reclaim any space that is being used for an object that has not been marked. At this time, we can also optionally coalesce all the allocated space in the memory heap into a single block, thereby eliminating external fragmentation for the time being. This scanning and reclamation process is known as the "sweep" phase, and when it completes, we resume running the suspended threads. Thus, the mark-sweep garbage collection algorithm will reclaim unused space in time proportional to the number of live objects and their references plus the size of the memory heap.

Performing DFS In-place

The mark-sweep algorithm correctly reclaims unused space in the memory heap, but there is an important issue we must face during the mark phase. Since we are reclaiming memory space at a time when available memory is scarce, we must take care not to use extra space during the garbage collection itself. The trouble is that the DFS algorithm, in the recursive way we have described it in Section 13.3.1, can use space proportional to the number of vertices in the graph. In the case of garbage collection, the vertices in our graph are the objects in the memory heap; hence, we probably don't have this much memory to use. So our only alternative is to find a way to perform DFS in-place rather than recursively, that is, we must perform DFS using only a constant amount of additional storage.

The main idea for performing DFS in-place is to simulate the recursion stack using the edges of the graph (which in the case of garbage collection correspond to object references). When we traverse an edge from a visited vertex v to a new vertex w, we change the edge (v, w) stored in v's adjacency list to point back to v's parent in the DFS tree. When we return back to v (simulating the return from the "recursive" call at w), we can now switch the edge we modified to point back to w. Of course, we need to have some way of identifying which edge we need to change back. One possibility is to number the references going out of v as 1, 2, and so on, and store, in addition to the mark bit (which we are using for the "visited" tag in our DFS), a count identifier that tells us which edges we have modified.

Using a count identifier requires an extra word of storage per object. This extra word can be avoided in some implementations, however. For example, many implementations of the Java virtual machine represent an object as a composition of a reference with a type identifier (which indicates if this object is an Integer or some other type) and as a reference to the other objects or data fields for this object. Since the type reference is always supposed to be the first element of the composition in such implementations, we can use this reference to "mark" the edge we changed when leaving an object v and going to some object w. We simply swap the reference at v that refers to the type of v with the reference at v that refers to w. When we return to v, we can quickly identify the edge (v, w) we changed, because it will be the first reference in the composition for v, and the position of the reference to v's type will tell us the place where this edge belongs in v's adjacency list. Thus, whether we use this edge-swapping trick or a count identifier, we can implement DFS in-place without affecting its asymptotic running time.

14.2 External Memory and Caching

There are several computer applications that must deal with a large amount of data. Examples include the analysis of scientific data sets, the processing of financial transactions, and the organization and maintenance of databases (such as telephone directories). In fact, the amount of data that must be dealt with is often too large to fit entirely in the internal memory of a computer.

14.2.1 The Memory Hierarchy

In order to accommodate large data sets, computers have a *hierarchy* of different kinds of memories, which vary in terms of their size and distance from the CPU. Closest to the CPU are the internal registers that the CPU itself uses. Access to such locations is very fast, but there are relatively few such locations. At the second level in the hierarchy is the *cache* memory. This memory is considerably larger than the register set of a CPU, but accessing it takes longer (and there may even be multiple caches with progressively slower access times). At the third level in the hierarchy is the *internal memory*, which is also known as *main memory* or *core memory*. The internal memory is considerably larger than the cache memory, but also requires more time to access. Finally, at the highest level in the hierarchy is the *external memory*, which usually consists of disks, CD drives, DVD drives, and/or tapes. This memory is very large, but it is also very slow. Thus, the memory hierarchy for computers can be viewed as consisting of four levels, each of which is larger and slower than the previous level. (See Figure 14.3.)

In most applications, however, only two levels really matter—the one that can hold all data items and the level just below that one. Bringing data items in and out of the higher memory that can hold all items will typically be the computational bottleneck in this case.

Figure 14.3: The memory hierarchy.

Caches and Disks

Specifically, the two levels that matter most depend on the size of the problem we are trying to solve. For a problem that can fit entirely in main memory, the two most important levels are the cache memory and the internal memory. Access times for internal memory can be as much as 10 to 100 times longer than those for cache memory. It is desirable, therefore, to be able to perform most memory accesses in cache memory. For a problem that does not fit entirely in main memory, on the other hand, the two most important levels are the internal memory and the external memory. Here the differences are even more dramatic, for access times for disks, the usual general-purpose external-memory device, are typically as much as 100 000 to 1 000 000 times longer than those for internal memory.

To put this latter figure into perspective, imagine there is a student in Baltimore who wants to send a request-for-money message to his parents in Chicago. If the student sends his parents an e-mail message, it can arrive at their home computer in about five seconds. Think of this mode of communication as corresponding to an internal-memory access by a CPU. A mode of communication corresponding to an external-memory access that is 500 000 times slower would be for the student to walk to Chicago and deliver his message in person, which would take about a month if he can average 20 miles per day. Thus, we should make as few accesses to external memory as possible.

14.2.2 Caching Strategies

Most algorithms are not designed with the memory hierarchy in mind, in spite of the great variance between access times for the different levels. Indeed, all of the algorithm analyses described in this book so far have assumed that all memory accesses are equal. This assumption might seem, at first, to be a great oversight—and one we are only addressing now in the final chapter—but there are good reasons why it is actually a reasonable assumption to make.

One justification for this assumption is that it is often necessary to assume that all memory accesses take the same amount of time, since specific device-dependent information about memory sizes is often hard to come by. In fact, information about memory size may be impossible to get. For example, a Java program that is designed to run on many different computer platforms cannot be defined in terms of a specific computer architecture configuration. We can certainly use architecture-specific information, if we have it (and we will show how to exploit such information later in this chapter). But once we have optimized our software for a certain architecture configuration, our software will no longer be device-independent. Fortunately, such optimizations are not always necessary, primarily because of the second justification for the equal-time memory-access assumption.

Caching and Blocking

Another justification for the memory-access equality assumption is that operating system designers have developed general mechanisms that allow for most memory accesses to be fast. These mechanisms are based on two important *locality-of-reference* properties that most software possesses:

- **Temporal locality**: If a program accesses a certain memory location, then it is likely to access this location again in the near future. For example, it is quite common to use the value of a counter variable in several different expressions, including one to increment the counter's value. In fact, a common adage among computer architects is that "a program spends ninety percent of its time in ten percent of its code."

- **Spatial locality**: If a program accesses a certain memory location, then it is likely to access other locations that are near this one. For example, a program using an array is likely to access the locations of this array in a sequential or near-sequential manner.

Computer scientists and engineers have performed extensive software profiling experiments to justify the claim that most software possesses both of these kinds of locality-of-reference. For example, a for-loop used to scan through an array will exhibit both kinds of locality.

Temporal and spatial localities have, in turn, given rise to two fundamental design choices for two-level computer memory systems (which are present in the interface between cache memory and internal memory, and also in the interface between internal memory and external memory).

The first design choice is called *virtual memory*. This concept consists of providing an address space as large as the capacity of the secondary-level memory, and of transferring data located in the secondary level, into the primary level, when they are addressed. Virtual memory does not limit the programmer to the constraint of the internal memory size. The concept of bringing data into primary memory is called *caching*, and it is motivated by temporal locality. For, by bringing data into primary memory, we are hoping that it will be accessed again soon, and we will be able to respond quickly to all the requests for this data that come in the near future.

The second design choice is motivated by spatial locality. Specifically, if data stored at a secondary-level memory location l is accessed, then we bring into primary-level memory, a large block of contiguous locations that include the location l. (See Figure 14.4.) This concept is known as *blocking*, and it is motivated by the expectation that other secondary-level memory locations close to l will soon be accessed. In the interface between cache memory and internal memory, such blocks are often called *cache lines*, and in the interface between internal memory and external memory, such blocks are often called *pages*.

A block on disk

A block in the external memory address space

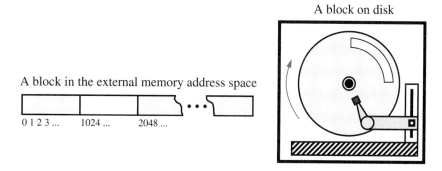

0 1 2 3 ...   1024 ...   2048 ...

Figure 14.4: Blocks in external memory.

When implemented with caching and blocking, virtual memory often allows us to perceive secondary-level memory as being faster than it really is. There is still a problem, however. Primary-level memory is much smaller than secondary-level memory. Moreover, because memory systems use blocking, any program of substance will likely reach a point where it requests data from secondary-level memory, but the primary memory is already full of blocks. In order to fulfill the request and maintain our use of caching and blocking, we must remove some block from primary memory to make room for a new block from secondary memory in this case. Deciding how to do this eviction brings up a number of interesting data structure and algorithm design issues.

Caching Algorithms

There are several web applications that must deal with revisiting information presented in web pages. These revisits have been shown to exhibit localities of reference, both in time and in space. To exploit these localities of reference, it is often advantageous to store copies of web pages in a *cache* memory, so these pages can be quickly retrieved when requested again. In particular, suppose we have a cache memory that has m "slots" that can contain web pages. We assume that a web page can be placed in any slot of the cache. This is known as a *fully associative* cache.

As a browser executes, it requests different web pages. Each time the browser requests such a web page l, the browser determines (using a quick test) if l is unchanged and currently contained in the cache. If l is contained in the cache, then the browser satisfies the request using the cached copy. If l is not in the cache, however, the page for l is requested over the Internet and transferred into the cache. If one of the m slots in the cache is available, then the browser assigns l to one of the empty slots. But if all the m cells of the cache are occupied, then the computer must determine which previously viewed web page to evict before bringing in l to take its place. There are, of course, many different policies that can be used to determine the page to evict.

Page Replacement Algorithms

Some of the better-known page replacement policies include the following (see Figure 14.5):

- **First-in, first-out (FIFO)**: Evict the page that has been in the cache the longest, that is, the page that was transferred to the cache furthest in the past.
- **Least recently used (LRU)**: Evict the page whose last request occurred furthest in the past.

In addition, we can consider a simple and purely random strategy:

- **Random**: Choose a page at random to evict from the cache.

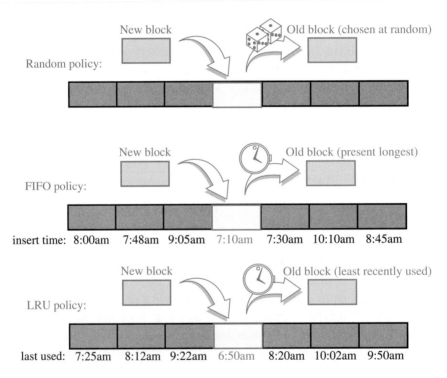

Figure 14.5: The Random, FIFO, and LRU page replacement policies.

The Random strategy is one of the easiest policies to implement, for it only requires a random or pseudo-random number generator. The overhead involved in implementing this policy is an $O(1)$ additional amount of work per page replacement. Moreover, there is no additional overhead for each page request, other than to determine whether a page request is in the cache or not. Still, this policy makes no attempt to take advantage of any temporal or spatial localities that a user's browsing exhibits.

The FIFO strategy is quite simple to implement, as it only requires a queue Q to store references to the pages in the cache. Pages are enqueued in Q when they are referenced by a browser, and then are brought into the cache. When a page needs to be evicted, the computer simply performs a dequeue operation on Q to determine which page to evict. Thus, this policy also requires $O(1)$ additional work per page replacement. Also, the FIFO policy incurs no additional overhead for page requests. Moreover, it tries to take some advantage of temporal locality.

The LRU strategy goes a step further than the FIFO strategy, for the LRU strategy explicitly takes advantage of temporal locality as much as possible, by always evicting the page that was least-recently used. From a policy point of view, this is an excellent approach, but it is costly from an implementation point of view. That is, its way of optimizing temporal and spatial locality is fairly costly. Implementing the LRU strategy requires the use of a priority queue Q that supports searching for existing pages, for example, using special pointers or "locators." If Q is implemented with a sorted sequence based on a linked list, then the overhead for each page request and page replacement is $O(1)$. When we insert a page in Q or update its key, the page is assigned the highest key in Q and is placed at the end of the list, which can also be done in $O(1)$ time. Even though the LRU strategy has constant-time overhead, using the implementation above, the constant factors involved, in terms of the additional time overhead and the extra space for the priority queue Q, make this policy less attractive from a practical point of view.

Since these different page replacement policies have different trade-offs between implementation difficulty and the degree to which they seem to take advantage of localities, it is natural for us to ask for some kind of comparative analysis of these methods to see which one, if any, is the best.

From a worst-case point of view, the FIFO and LRU strategies have fairly unattractive competitive behavior. For example, suppose we have a cache containing m pages, and consider the FIFO and LRU methods for performing page replacement for a program that has a loop that repeatedly requests $m+1$ pages in a cyclic order. Both the FIFO and LRU policies perform badly on such a sequence of page requests, because they perform a page replacement on every page request. Thus, from a worst-case point of view, these policies are almost the worst we can imagine—they require a page replacement on every page request.

This worst-case analysis is a little too pessimistic, however, for it focuses on each protocol's behavior for one bad sequence of page requests. An ideal analysis would be to compare these methods over all possible page-request sequences. Of course, this is impossible to do exhaustively, but there have been a great number of experimental simulations done on page-request sequences derived from real programs. Based on these experimental comparisons, the LRU strategy has been shown to be usually superior to the FIFO strategy, which is usually better than the Random strategy.

14.3   External Searching and B-Trees

Consider the problem of implementing the map ADT for a large collection of items that do not fit in main memory. Since one of the main uses of a large map is in a database, we refer to the secondary-memory blocks as ***disk blocks***. Likewise, we refer to the transfer of a block between secondary memory and primary memory as a ***disk transfer***. Recalling the great time difference that exists between main memory accesses and disk accesses, the main goal of maintaining a map in external memory is to minimize the number of disk transfers needed to perform a query or update. In fact, the difference in speed between disk and internal memory is so great that we should be willing to perform a considerable number of internal-memory accesses if they allow us to avoid a few disk transfers. Let us, therefore, analyze the performance of map implementations by counting the number of disk transfers each would require to perform the standard map search and update operations. We refer to this count as the ***I/O complexity*** of the algorithms involved.

Some Inefficient External-Memory Dictionaries

Let us first consider the simple map implementations that use a list to store n entries. If the list is implemented as an unsorted, doubly linked list, then insert and remove operations can be performed with $O(1)$ transfers each, but removals and searches require n transfers in the worst case, since each link hop we perform could access a different block. This search time can be improved to $O(n/B)$ transfers (see Exercise C-14.2), where B denotes the number of nodes of the list that can fit into a block, but this is still poor performance. We could alternately implement the sequence using a sorted array. In this case, a search performs $O(\log_2 n)$ transfers, via binary search, which is a nice improvement. But this solution requires $\Theta(n/B)$ transfers to implement an insert or remove operation in the worst case, for we may have to access all blocks to move elements up or down. Thus, list-based map implementations are not efficient in external memory.

Since these simple implementations are I/O inefficient, we should consider the logarithmic-time internal-memory strategies that use balanced binary trees (for example, AVL trees or red-black trees) or other search structures with logarithmic average-case query and update times (for example, skip lists or splay trees). These methods store the map items at the nodes of a binary tree or of a graph. Typically, each node accessed for a query or update in one of these structures will be in a different block. Thus, these methods all require $O(\log_2 n)$ transfers in the worst case to perform a query or update operation. This performance is good, but we can do better. In particular, we can perform map queries and updates using only $O(\log_B n) = O(\log n / \log B)$ transfers.

14.3.1 (a,b) Trees

To reduce the importance of the performance difference between internal-memory accesses and external-memory accesses for searching, we can represent our map using a multi-way search tree (Section 10.4.1). This approach gives rise to a generalization of the $(2,4)$ tree data structure known as the (a,b) tree.

An (a,b) tree is a multi-way search tree such that each node has between a and b children and stores between $a-1$ and $b-1$ entries. The algorithms for searching, inserting, and removing entries in an (a,b) tree are straightforward generalizations of the corresponding ones for $(2,4)$ trees. The advantage of generalizing $(2,4)$ trees to (a,b) trees is that a generalized class of trees provides a flexible search structure, where the size of the nodes and the running time of the various map operations depends on the parameters a and b. By setting the parameters a and b appropriately with respect to the size of disk blocks, we can derive a data structure that achieves good external-memory performance.

Definition of an (a,b) Tree

An (a,b) **tree**, where a and b are integers, such that $2 \le a \le (b+1)/2$, is a multi-way search tree T with the following additional restrictions:

Size Property: Each internal node has at least a children, unless it is the root, and has at most b children.

Depth Property: All the external nodes have the same depth.

Proposition 14.1: *The height of an (a,b) tree storing n entries is $\Omega(\log n/\log b)$ and $O(\log n/\log a)$.*

Justification: Let T be an (a,b) tree storing n entries, and let h be the height of T. We justify the proposition by establishing the following bounds on h:

$$\frac{1}{\log b}\log(n+1) \le h \le \frac{1}{\log a}\log\frac{n+1}{2}+1.$$

By the size and depth properties, the number n'' of external nodes of T is at least $2a^{h-1}$ and at most b^h. By Proposition 10.7, $n'' = n+1$. Thus

$$2a^{h-1} \le n+1 \le b^h.$$

Taking the logarithm in base 2 of each term, we get

$$(h-1)\log a + 1 \le \log(n+1) \le h\log b. \qquad \blacksquare$$

Search and Update Operations

We recall that in a multi-way search tree T, each node v of T holds a secondary structure $M(v)$, which is itself a map (Section 10.4.1). If T is an (a,b) tree, then $M(v)$ stores at most b entries. Let $f(b)$ denote the time for performing a search in a map, $M(v)$. The search algorithm in an (a,b) tree is exactly like the one for multi-way search trees given in Section 10.4.1. Hence, searching in an (a,b) tree T with n entries takes $O(\frac{f(b)}{\log a}\log n)$ time. Note that if b is a constant (and thus a is also), then the search time is $O(\log n)$.

The main application of (a,b) trees is for maps stored in external memory. Namely, to minimize disk accesses, we select the parameters a and b so that each tree node occupies a single disk block (so that $f(b) = 1$ if we wish to simply count block transfers). Providing the right a and b values in this context gives rise to a data structure known as the B-tree, which we will describe shortly. Before we describe this structure, however, let us discuss how insertions and removals are handled in (a,b) trees.

The insertion algorithm for an (a,b) tree is similar to that for a $(2,4)$ tree. An overflow occurs when an entry is inserted into a b-node v, which becomes an illegal $(b+1)$-node. (Recall that a node in a multi-way tree is a d-node if it has d children.) To remedy an overflow, we split node v by moving the median entry of v into the parent of v and replacing v with a $\lceil (b+1)/2\rceil$-node v' and a $\lfloor (b+1)/2\rfloor$-node v''. We can now see the reason for requiring $a \le (b+1)/2$ in the definition of an (a,b) tree. Note that as a consequence of the split, we need to build the secondary structures $M(v')$ and $M(v'')$.

Removing an entry from an (a,b) tree is similar to what was done for $(2,4)$ trees. An underflow occurs when a key is removed from an a-node v, distinct from the root, which causes v to become an illegal $(a-1)$-node. To remedy an underflow, we perform a transfer with a sibling of v that is not an a-node or we perform a fusion of v with a sibling that is an a-node. The new node w resulting from the fusion is a $(2a - 1)$-node, which is another reason for requiring $a \le (b+1)/2$.

Table 14.1 shows the performance of a map realized with an (a,b) tree.

Method	Time
get	$O\left(\dfrac{f(b)}{\log a}\log n\right)$
put	$O\left(\dfrac{g(b)}{\log a}\log n\right)$
remove	$O\left(\dfrac{g(b)}{\log a}\log n\right)$

Table 14.1: Time bounds for an n-entry map realized by an (a,b) tree T. We assume the secondary structure of the nodes of T support search in $f(b)$ time, and split and fusion operations in $g(b)$ time, for some functions $f(b)$ and $g(b)$, which can be made to be $O(1)$ when we are only counting disk transfers.

14.3.2 B-Trees

A version of the (a,b) tree data structure, which is the best known method for maintaining a map in external memory, is called the "B-tree." (See Figure 14.6.) A ***B-tree of order*** d is an (a,b) tree with $a = \lceil d/2 \rceil$ and $b = d$. Since we discussed the standard map query and update methods for (a,b) trees above, we restrict our discussion here to the I/O complexity of B-trees.

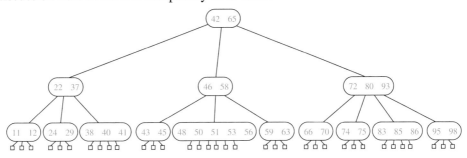

Figure 14.6: A B-tree of order 6.

An important property of B-trees is that we can choose d so that the d children references and the $d-1$ keys stored at a node can all fit into a single disk block, implying that d is proportional to B. This choice allows us to assume that a and b are also proportional to B in the analysis of the search and update operations on (a,b) trees. Thus, $f(b)$ and $g(b)$ are both $O(1)$, for each time we access a node to perform a search or an update operation, we need only perform a single disk transfer.

As we have already observed above, each search or update requires that we examine at most $O(1)$ nodes for each level of the tree. Therefore, any map search or update operation on a B-tree requires only $O(\log_{\lceil d/2 \rceil} n)$, that is, $O(\log n / \log B)$, disk transfers. For example, an insert operation proceeds down the B-tree to locate the node in which to insert the new entry. If the node would ***overflow*** (to have $d+1$ children) because of this addition, then this node is ***split*** into two nodes that have $\lfloor (d+1)/2 \rfloor$ and $\lceil (d+1)/2 \rceil$ children, respectively. This process is then repeated at the next level up, and will continue for at most $O(\log_B n)$ levels.

Likewise, if a remove operation results in a node ***underflow*** (to have $\lceil d/2 \rceil - 1$ children), then we move references from a sibling node with at least $\lceil d/2 \rceil + 1$ children or we need to perform a ***fusion*** operation of this node with its sibling (and repeat this computation at the parent). As with the insert operation, this will continue up the B-tree for at most $O(\log_B n)$ levels. The requirement that each internal node have at least $\lceil d/2 \rceil$ children implies that each disk block used to support a B-tree is at least half full. Thus, we have the following:

Proposition 14.2: *A B-tree with n entries has I/O complexity $O(\log_B n)$ for search or update operation, and uses $O(n/B)$ blocks, where B is the size of a block.*

14.4 External-Memory Sorting

In addition to data structures, such as maps, that need to be implemented in external memory, there are many algorithms that must also operate on input sets that are too large to fit entirely into internal memory. In this case, the objective is to solve the algorithmic problem using as few block transfers as possible. The most classic domain for such external-memory algorithms is the sorting problem.

Multi-way Merge-Sort

An efficient way to sort a set S of n objects in external memory amounts to a simple external-memory variation on the familiar merge-sort algorithm. The main idea behind this variation is to merge many recursively sorted lists at a time, thereby reducing the number of levels of recursion. Specifically, a high-level description of this *multi-way merge-sort* method is to divide S into d subsets S_1, S_2, ..., S_d of roughly equal size, recursively sort each subset S_i, and then simultaneously merge all d sorted lists into a sorted representation of S. If we can perform the merge process using only $O(n/B)$ disk transfers, then, for large enough values of n, the total number of transfers performed by this algorithm satisfies the following recurrence:

$$t(n) = d \cdot t(n/d) + cn/B,$$

for some constant $c \geq 1$. We can stop the recursion when $n \leq B$, since we can perform a single block transfer at this point, getting all of the objects into internal memory, and then sort the set with an efficient internal-memory algorithm. Thus, the stopping criterion for $t(n)$ is

$$t(n) = 1 \quad \text{if } n/B \leq 1.$$

This implies a closed-form solution that $t(n)$ is $O((n/B)\log_d(n/B))$, which is

$$O((n/B)\log(n/B)/\log d).$$

Thus, if we can choose d to be $\Theta(M/B)$, then the worst-case number of block transfers performed by this multi-way merge-sort algorithm will be quite low. We choose

$$d = (1/2)M/B.$$

The only aspect of this algorithm left to specify, then, is how to perform the d-way merge using only $O(n/B)$ block transfers.

14.4.1 Multi-way Merging

We perform the *d*-way merge by running a "tournament." We let *T* be a complete binary tree with *d* external nodes, and we keep *T* entirely in internal memory. We associate each external node *i* of *T* with a different sorted list S_i. We initialize *T* by reading into each external node *i*, the first object in S_i. This has the effect of reading into internal memory the first block of each sorted list S_i. For each internal-node parent *v* of two external nodes, we then compare the objects stored at *v*'s children and we associate the smaller of the two with *v*. We repeat this comparison test at the next level up in *T*, and the next, and so on. When we reach the root *r* of *T*, we will associate the smallest object from among all the lists with *r*. This completes the initialization for the *d*-way merge. (See Figure 14.7.)

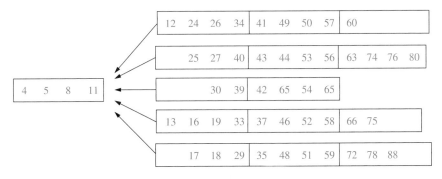

Figure 14.7: A *d*-way merge. We show a five-way merge with $B = 4$.

In a general step of the *d*-way merge, we move the object *o* associated with the root *r* of *T* into an array we are building for the merged list S'. We then trace down *T*, following the path to the external node *i* that *o* came from. We then read into *i* the next object in the list S_i. If *o* was not the last element in its block, then this next object is already in internal memory. Otherwise, we read in the next block of S_i to access this new object (if S_i is now empty, associate the node *i* with a pseudo-object with key $+\infty$). We then repeat the minimum computations for each of the internal nodes from *i* to the root of *T*. This again gives us the complete tree *T*. We then repeat this process of moving the object from the root of *T* to the merged list S', and rebuilding *T*, until *T* is empty of objects. Each step in the merge takes $O(\log d)$ time; hence, the internal time for the *d*-way merge is $O(n \log d)$. The number of transfers performed in a merge is $O(n/B)$, since we scan each list S_i in order once, and we write out the merged list S' once. Thus, we have:

Proposition 14.3: *Given an array-based sequence S of n elements stored in external memory, we can sort S using $O((n/B)\log(n/B)/\log(M/B))$ transfers and $O(n \log n)$ internal CPU time, where M is the size of the internal memory and B is the size of a block.*

14.5   Exercises

For help with exercises, please visit the web site, www.wiley.com/college/goodrich.

Reinforcement

R-14.1 Julia just bought a new computer that uses 64-bit integers to address memory cells. Argue why Julia will never in her life be able to upgrade the main memory of her computer so that it is the maximum-size possible, assuming that you have to have distinct atoms to represent different bits.

R-14.2 Describe, in detail, add and remove algorithms for an (a,b) tree.

R-14.3 Suppose T is a multi-way tree in which each internal node has at least five and at most eight children. For what values of a and b is T a valid (a,b) tree?

R-14.4 For what values of d is the tree T of the previous exercise an order-d B-tree?

R-14.5 Show each level of recursion in performing a four-way, external-memory merge-sort of the sequence given in the previous exercise.

R-14.6 Consider an initially empty memory cache consisting of four pages. How many page misses does the LRU algorithm incur on the following page request sequence: $(2,3,4,1,2,5,1,3,5,4,1,2,3)$?

R-14.7 Consider an initially empty memory cache consisting of four pages. How many page misses does the FIFO algorithm incur on the following page request sequence: $(2,3,4,1,2,5,1,3,5,4,1,2,3)$?

R-14.8 Consider an initially empty memory cache consisting of four pages. How many page misses can the random algorithm incur on the following page request sequence: $(2,3,4,1,2,5,1,3,5,4,1,2,3)$? Show all of the random choices your algorithm made in this case.

R-14.9 Draw the result of inserting, into an initially empty order-7 B-tree, entries with keys (4,40,23,50,11,34,62,78,66,22,90,59,25,72,64,77,39,12), in this order.

R-14.10 Show each level of recursion in performing a four-way merge-sort of the sequence given in the previous exercise.

Creativity

C-14.1 Describe an efficient external-memory algorithm for removing all the duplicate entries in an array list of size n.

C-14.2 Show how to implement a map in external memory, using an unordered sequence so that insertions require only $O(1)$ transfers and searches require $O(n/B)$ transfers in the worst case, where n is the number of elements and B is the number of list nodes that can fit into a disk block.

C-14.3 Change the rules that define red-black trees so that each red-black tree T has a corresponding $(4,8)$ tree, and vice versa.

C-14.4 Describe a modified version of the B-tree insertion algorithm so that each time we create an overflow because of a split of a node v, we redistribute keys among all of v's siblings, so that each sibling holds roughly the same number of keys (possibly cascading the split up to the parent of v). What is the minimum fraction of each block that will always be filled using this scheme?

C-14.5 Another possible external-memory map implementation is to use a skip list, but to collect consecutive groups of $O(B)$ nodes, in individual blocks, on any level in the skip list. In particular, we define an ***order-d B-skip list*** to be such a representation of a skip-list structure, where each block contains at least $\lceil d/2 \rceil$ list nodes and at most d list nodes. Let us also choose d in this case to be the maximum number of list nodes from a level of a skip list that can fit into one block. Describe how we should modify the skip-list insertion and removal algorithms for a B-skip list so that the expected height of the structure is $O(\log n / \log B)$.

C-14.6 Describe an external-memory data structure to implement the queue ADT so that the total number of disk transfers needed to process a sequence of n enqueue and dequeue operations is $O(n/B)$.

C-14.7 Solve the previous problem for the deque ADT.

C-14.8 Describe how to use a B-tree to implement the partition (union-find) ADT (from Section 11.4.3) so that the union and find operations each use at most $O(\log n / \log B)$ disk transfers.

C-14.9 Suppose we are given a sequence S of n elements with integer keys such that some elements in S are colored "blue" and some elements in S are colored "red." In addition, say that a red element e ***pairs*** with a blue element f if they have the same key value. Describe an efficient external-memory algorithm for finding all the red-blue pairs in S. How many disk transfers does your algorithm perform?

C-14.10 Consider the page caching problem where the memory cache can hold m pages, and we are given a sequence P of n requests taken from a pool of $m+1$ possible pages. Describe the optimal strategy for the offline algorithm and show that it causes at most $m+n/m$ page misses in total, starting from an empty cache.

C-14.11 Consider the page caching strategy based on the **least frequently used** (LFU) rule, where the page in the cache that has been accessed the least often is the one that is evicted when a new page is requested. If there are ties, LFU evicts the least frequently used page that has been in the cache the longest. Show that there is a sequence P of n requests that causes LFU to miss $\Omega(n)$ times for a cache of m pages, whereas the optimal algorithm will miss only $O(m)$ times.

C-14.12 Suppose that instead of having the node-search function $f(d) = 1$ in an order-d B-tree T, we have $f(d) = \log d$. What does the asymptotic running time of performing a search in T now become?

C-14.13 Describe an efficient external-memory algorithm that determines whether an array of n integers contains a value occurring more than $n/2$ times.

Projects

P-14.1 Write a Java class that simulates the best-fit, worst-fit, first-fit, and next-fit algorithms for memory management. Determine experimentally which method is the best under various sequences of memory requests.

P-14.2 Write a Java class that implements all the methods of the ordered map ADT by means of an (a,b) tree, where a and b are integer constants passed as parameters to a constructor.

P-14.3 Implement the B-tree data structure, assuming a block size of $1,024$ and integer keys. Test the number of "disk transfers" needed to process a sequence of map operations.

P-14.4 Implement an external-memory sorting algorithm and compare it experimentally to any internal-memory sorting algorithm.

Chapter Notes

Knuth [60] has very nice discussions about external-memory sorting and searching, and Ullman [93] discusses external memory structures for database systems. The reader interested in the study of the architecture of hierarchical memory systems is referred to the book chapter by Burger *et al.* [19] or the book by Hennessy and Patterson [46]. The handbook by Gonnet and Baeza-Yates [39] compares the performance of a number of different sorting algorithms, many of which are external-memory algorithms. B-trees were invented by Bayer and McCreight [11] and Comer [24] provides a very nice overview of this data structure. The books by Mehlhorn [74] and Samet [84] also have nice discussions about B-trees and their variants. Aggarwal and Vitter [2] study the I/O complexity of sorting and related problems, establishing upper and lower bounds, including the lower bound for sorting given in this chapter. Goodrich *et al.* [42] study the I/O complexity of several computational geometry problems. The reader interested in further study of I/O-efficient algorithms is encouraged to examine the survey paper of Vitter [95].

Useful Mathematical Facts

In this appendix we give several useful mathematical facts. We begin with some combinatorial definitions and facts.

Logarithms and Exponents

The logarithm function is defined as

$$\log_b a = c \quad \text{if} \quad a = b^c.$$

The following identities hold for logarithms and exponents:

1. $\log_b ac = \log_b a + \log_b c$
2. $\log_b a/c = \log_b a - \log_b c$
3. $\log_b a^c = c \log_b a$
4. $\log_b a = (\log_c a)/\log_c b$
5. $b^{\log_c a} = a^{\log_c b}$
6. $(b^a)^c = b^{ac}$
7. $b^a b^c = b^{a+c}$
8. $b^a/b^c = b^{a-c}$

In addition, we have the following:

Proposition A.1: If $a > 0$, $b > 0$, and $c > a + b$, then

$$\log a + \log b \leq 2\log c - 2.$$

Justification: It is enough to show that $ab < c^2/4$. We can write

$$
\begin{aligned}
ab &= \frac{a^2 + 2ab + b^2 - a^2 + 2ab - b^2}{4} \\
&= \frac{(a+b)^2 - (a-b)^2}{4} \leq \frac{(a+b)^2}{4} < \frac{c^2}{4}.
\end{aligned}
$$

∎

The **_natural logarithm_** function $\ln x = \log_e x$, where $e = 2.71828\ldots$, is the value of the following progression:

$$e = 1 + \frac{1}{1!} + \frac{1}{2!} + \frac{1}{3!} + \cdots.$$

In addition,

$$e^x = 1 + \frac{x}{1!} + \frac{x^2}{2!} + \frac{x^3}{3!} + \cdots$$

$$\ln(1+x) = x - \frac{x^2}{2!} + \frac{x^3}{3!} - \frac{x^4}{4!} + \cdots.$$

There are a number of useful inequalities relating to these functions (which derive from these definitions).

Proposition A.2: *If $x > -1$,*

$$\frac{x}{1+x} \leq \ln(1+x) \leq x.$$

Proposition A.3: *For $0 \leq x < 1$,*

$$1 + x \leq e^x \leq \frac{1}{1-x}.$$

Proposition A.4: *For any two positive real numbers x and n,*

$$\left(1 + \frac{x}{n}\right)^n \leq e^x \leq \left(1 + \frac{x}{n}\right)^{n+x/2}.$$

Integer Functions and Relations

The "floor" and "ceiling" functions are defined respectively as follows:
1. $\lfloor x \rfloor$ = the largest integer less than or equal to x.
2. $\lceil x \rceil$ = the smallest integer greater than or equal to x.

The *modulo* operator is defined for integers $a \geq 0$ and $b > 0$ as

$$a \bmod b = a - \left\lfloor \frac{a}{b} \right\rfloor b.$$

The *factorial* function is defined as

$$n! = 1 \cdot 2 \cdot 3 \cdot \cdots \cdot (n-1)n.$$

The binomial coefficient is

$$\binom{n}{k} = \frac{n!}{k!(n-k)!},$$

which is equal to the number of different **combinations** one can define by choosing k different items from a collection of n items (where the order does not matter). The name "binomial coefficient" derives from the **binomial expansion**:

$$(a+b)^n = \sum_{k=0}^{n} \binom{n}{k} a^k b^{n-k}.$$

We also have the following relationships.

Proposition A.5: *If* $0 \le k \le n$, *then*

$$\left(\frac{n}{k}\right)^k \le \binom{n}{k} \le \frac{n^k}{k!}.$$

Proposition A.6 (Stirling's Approximation):

$$n! = \sqrt{2\pi n} \left(\frac{n}{e}\right)^n \left(1 + \frac{1}{12n} + \varepsilon(n)\right),$$

where $\varepsilon(n)$ *is* $O(1/n^2)$.

The **Fibonacci progression** is a numeric progression such that $F_0 = 0$, $F_1 = 1$, and $F_n = F_{n-1} + F_{n-2}$ for $n \ge 2$.

Proposition A.7: *If* F_n *is defined by the Fibonacci progression, then* F_n *is* $\Theta(g^n)$, *where* $g = (1 + \sqrt{5})/2$ *is the so-called* **golden ratio**.

Summations

There are a number of useful facts about summations.

Proposition A.8: *Factoring summations:*

$$\sum_{i=1}^{n} af(i) = a \sum_{i=1}^{n} f(i),$$

provided a *does not depend upon* i.

Proposition A.9: *Reversing the order:*

$$\sum_{i=1}^{n} \sum_{j=1}^{m} f(i, j) = \sum_{j=1}^{m} \sum_{i=1}^{n} f(i, j).$$

One special form of summation is a **telescoping sum**:

$$\sum_{i=1}^{n} (f(i) - f(i-1)) = f(n) - f(0),$$

which arises often in the amortized analysis of a data structure or algorithm.

The following are some other facts about summations that arise often in the analysis of data structures and algorithms.

Proposition A.10: $\sum_{i=1}^{n} i = n(n+1)/2$.

Proposition A.11: $\sum_{i=1}^{n} i^2 = n(n+1)(2n+1)/6$.

Proposition A.12: *If $k \geq 1$ is an integer constant, then*

$$\sum_{i=1}^{n} i^k \text{ is } \Theta(n^{k+1}).$$

Another common summation is the **geometric sum**, $\sum_{i=0}^{n} a^i$, for any fixed real number $0 < a \neq 1$.

Proposition A.13:

$$\sum_{i=0}^{n} a^i = \frac{a^{n+1} - 1}{a - 1},$$

for any real number $0 < a \neq 1$.

Proposition A.14:

$$\sum_{i=0}^{\infty} a^i = \frac{1}{1 - a}$$

for any real number $0 < a < 1$.

There is also a combination of the two common forms, called the **linear exponential** summation, which has the following expansion:

Proposition A.15: *For $0 < a \neq 1$, and $n \geq 2$,*

$$\sum_{i=1}^{n} i a^i = \frac{a - (n+1)a^{(n+1)} + na^{(n+2)}}{(1 - a)^2}.$$

The nth **Harmonic number** H_n is defined as

$$H_n = \sum_{i=1}^{n} \frac{1}{i}.$$

Proposition A.16: *If H_n is the nth harmonic number, then H_n is $\ln n + \Theta(1)$.*

Basic Probability

We review some basic facts from probability theory. The most basic is that any statement about a probability is defined upon a **sample space** S, which is defined as the set of all possible outcomes from some experiment. We leave the terms "outcomes" and "experiment" undefined in any formal sense.

Example A.17: *Consider an experiment that consists of the outcome from flipping a coin five times. This sample space has 2^5 different outcomes, one for each different ordering of possible flips that can occur.*

Sample spaces can also be infinite, as the following example illustrates.

Example A.18: *Consider an experiment that consists of flipping a coin until it comes up heads. This sample space is infinite, with each outcome being a sequence of i tails followed by a single flip that comes up heads, for $i = 1, 2, 3, \ldots$.*

A *probability space* is a sample space S together with a probability function Pr that maps subsets of S to real numbers in the interval $[0, 1]$. It captures mathematically the notion of the probability of certain "events" occurring. Formally, each subset A of S is called an *event*, and the probability function Pr is assumed to possess the following basic properties with respect to events defined from S:

1. $\Pr(\emptyset) = 0$.
2. $\Pr(S) = 1$.
3. $0 \leq \Pr(A) \leq 1$, for any $A \subseteq S$.
4. If $A, B \subseteq S$ and $A \cap B = \emptyset$, then $\Pr(A \cup B) = \Pr(A) + \Pr(B)$.

Two events A and B are *independent* if

$$\Pr(A \cap B) = \Pr(A) \cdot \Pr(B).$$

A collection of events $\{A_1, A_2, \ldots, A_n\}$ is *mutually independent* if

$$\Pr(A_{i_1} \cap A_{i_2} \cap \cdots \cap A_{i_k}) = \Pr(A_{i_1}) \Pr(A_{i_2}) \cdots \Pr(A_{i_k}).$$

for any subset $\{A_{i_1}, A_{i_2}, \ldots, A_{i_k}\}$.

The *conditional probability* that an event A occurs, given an event B, is denoted as $\Pr(A|B)$, and is defined as the ratio

$$\frac{\Pr(A \cap B)}{\Pr(B)},$$

assuming that $\Pr(B) > 0$.

An elegant way for dealing with events is in terms of *random variables*. Intuitively, random variables are variables whose values depend upon the outcome of some experiment. Formally, a *random variable* is a function X that maps outcomes from some sample space S to real numbers. An *indicator random variable* is a random variable that maps outcomes to the set $\{0, 1\}$. Often in data structure and algorithm analysis we use a random variable X to characterize the running time of a randomized algorithm. In this case, the sample space S is defined by all possible outcomes of the random sources used in the algorithm.

We are most interested in the typical, average, or "expected" value of such a random variable. The *expected value* of a random variable X is defined as

$$\mathbf{E}(X) = \sum_x x \Pr(X = x),$$

where the summation is defined over the range of X (which in this case is assumed to be discrete).

Proposition A.19 (The Linearity of Expectation): *Let* X *and* Y *be two random variables and let* c *be a number. Then*

$$E(X+Y) = E(X) + E(Y) \quad \text{and} \quad E(cX) = cE(X).$$

Example A.20: *Let* X *be a random variable that assigns the outcome of the roll of two fair dice to the sum of the number of dots showing. Then* $E(X) = 7$.

Justification: *To justify this claim, let* X_1 *and* X_2 *be random variables corresponding to the number of dots on each die. Thus,* $X_1 = X_2$ *(i.e., they are two instances of the same function) and* $E(X) = E(X_1 + X_2) = E(X_1) + E(X_2)$. *Each outcome of the roll of a fair die occurs with probability* $1/6$. *Thus*

$$E(X_i) = \frac{1}{6} + \frac{2}{6} + \frac{3}{6} + \frac{4}{6} + \frac{5}{6} + \frac{6}{6} = \frac{7}{2},$$

for $i = 1, 2$. *Therefore,* $E(X) = 7$. ∎

Two random variables X and Y are ***independent*** if

$$\Pr(X = x | Y = y) = \Pr(X = x),$$

for all real numbers x and y.

Proposition A.21: *If two random variables* X *and* Y *are independent, then*

$$E(XY) = E(X)E(Y).$$

Example A.22: *Let* X *be a random variable that assigns the outcome of a roll of two fair dice to the product of the number of dots showing. Then* $E(X) = 49/4$.

Justification: *Let* X_1 *and* X_2 *be random variables denoting the number of dots on each die. The variables* X_1 *and* X_2 *are clearly independent; hence*

$$E(X) = E(X_1 X_2) = E(X_1)E(X_2) = (7/2)^2 = 49/4.$$ ∎

The following bound and corollaries that follow from it are known as ***Chernoff bounds***.

Proposition A.23: *Let* X *be the sum of a finite number of independent* $0/1$ *random variables and let* $\mu > 0$ *be the expected value of* X. *Then, for* $\delta > 0$,

$$\Pr(X > (1+\delta)\mu) < \left[\frac{e^{\delta}}{(1+\delta)^{(1+\delta)}} \right]^{\mu}.$$

Useful Mathematical Techniques

To compare the growth rates of different functions, it is sometimes helpful to apply the following rule.

Proposition A.24 (L'Hôpital's Rule): *If we have $\lim_{n\to\infty} f(n) = +\infty$ and we have $\lim_{n\to\infty} g(n) = +\infty$, then $\lim_{n\to\infty} f(n)/g(n) = \lim_{n\to\infty} f'(n)/g'(n)$, where $f'(n)$ and $g'(n)$ respectively denote the derivatives of $f(n)$ and $g(n)$.*

In deriving an upper or lower bound for a summation, it is often useful to *split a summation* as follows:

$$\sum_{i=1}^{n} f(i) = \sum_{i=1}^{j} f(i) + \sum_{i=j+1}^{n} f(i).$$

Another useful technique is to *bound a sum by an integral*. If f is a nondecreasing function, then, assuming the following terms are defined,

$$\int_{a-1}^{b} f(x)\,dx \le \sum_{i=a}^{b} f(i) \le \int_{a}^{b+1} f(x)\,dx.$$

There is a general form of recurrence relation that arises in the analysis of divide-and-conquer algorithms:

$$T(n) = aT(n/b) + f(n),$$

for constants $a \ge 1$ and $b > 1$.

Proposition A.25: *Let $T(n)$ be defined as above. Then*

1. *If $f(n)$ is $O(n^{\log_b a - \varepsilon})$, for some constant $\varepsilon > 0$, then $T(n)$ is $\Theta(n^{\log_b a})$.*
2. *If $f(n)$ is $\Theta(n^{\log_b a} \log^k n)$, for a fixed nonnegative integer $k \ge 0$, then $T(n)$ is $\Theta(n^{\log_b a} \log^{k+1} n)$.*
3. *If $f(n)$ is $\Omega(n^{\log_b a + \varepsilon})$, for some constant $\varepsilon > 0$, and if $af(n/b) \le cf(n)$, then $T(n)$ is $\Theta(f(n))$.*

This proposition is known as the *master method* for characterizing divide-and-conquer recurrence relations asymptotically.

Bibliography

[1] G. M. Adel'son-Vel'skii and Y. M. Landis, "An algorithm for the organization of information," *Doklady Akademii Nauk SSSR*, vol. 146, pp. 263–266, 1962. English translation in *Soviet Math. Dokl.*, **3**, 1259–1262.

[2] A. Aggarwal and J. S. Vitter, "The input/output complexity of sorting and related problems," *Commun. ACM*, vol. 31, pp. 1116–1127, 1988.

[3] A. V. Aho, "Algorithms for finding patterns in strings," in *Handbook of Theoretical Computer Science* (J. van Leeuwen, ed.), vol. A. Algorithms and Complexity, pp. 255–300, Amsterdam: Elsevier, 1990.

[4] A. V. Aho, J. E. Hopcroft, and J. D. Ullman, *The Design and Analysis of Computer Algorithms*. Reading, MA: Addison-Wesley, 1974.

[5] A. V. Aho, J. E. Hopcroft, and J. D. Ullman, *Data Structures and Algorithms*. Reading, MA: Addison-Wesley, 1983.

[6] R. K. Ahuja, T. L. Magnanti, and J. B. Orlin, *Network Flows: Theory, Algorithms, and Applications*. Englewood Cliffs, NJ: Prentice Hall, 1993.

[7] K. Arnold, J. Gosling, and D. Holmes, *The Java Programming Language*. The Java Series, Upper Saddle River, NJ: Prentice Hall, 4th ed., 2006.

[8] R. Baeza-Yates and B. Ribeiro-Neto, *Modern Information Retrieval*. Reading, Mass.: Addison-Wesley, 1999.

[9] O. Baruvka, "O jistem problemu minimalnim," *Praca Moravske Prirodovedecke Spolecnosti*, vol. 3, pp. 37–58, 1926. (in Czech).

[10] R. Bayer, "Symmetric binary B-trees: Data structure and maintenance," *Acta Informatica*, vol. 1, no. 4, pp. 290–306, 1972.

[11] R. Bayer and McCreight, "Organization of large ordered indexes," *Acta Inform.*, vol. 1, pp. 173–189, 1972.

[12] J. L. Bentley, "Programming pearls: Writing correct programs," *Communications of the ACM*, vol. 26, pp. 1040–1045, 1983.

[13] J. L. Bentley, "Programming pearls: Thanks, heaps," *Communications of the ACM*, vol. 28, pp. 245–250, 1985.

[14] J. L. Bentley and M. D. McIlroy, "Engineering a sort function," *Software—Practice and Experience*, vol. 23, no. 11, pp. 1249–1265, 1993.

[15] G. Booch, *Object-Oriented Analysis and Design with Applications*. Redwood City, CA: Benjamin/Cummings, 1994.

[16] R. S. Boyer and J. S. Moore, "A fast string searching algorithm," *Communications of the ACM*, vol. 20, no. 10, pp. 762–772, 1977.

[17] G. Brassard, "Crusade for a better notation," *SIGACT News*, vol. 17, no. 1, pp. 60–64, 1985.

[18] T. Budd, *An Introduction to Object-Oriented Programming*.   Reading, Mass.: Addison-Wesley, 1991.

[19] D. Burger, J. R. Goodman, and G. S. Sohi, "Memory systems," in *The Computer Science and Engineering Handbook* (A. B. Tucker, Jr., ed.), ch. 18, pp. 447–461, CRC Press, 1997.

[20] L. Cardelli and P. Wegner, "On understanding types, data abstraction and polymorphism," *ACM Computing Surveys*, vol. 17, no. 4, pp. 471–522, 1985.

[21] S. Carlsson, "Average case results on heapsort," *BIT*, vol. 27, pp. 2–17, 1987.

[22] K. L. Clarkson, "Linear programming in $O(n3^{d^2})$ time," *Inform. Process. Lett.*, vol. 22, pp. 21–24, 1986.

[23] R. Cole, "Tight bounds on the complexity of the Boyer-Moore pattern matching algorithm," *SIAM Journal on Computing*, vol. 23, no. 5, pp. 1075–1091, 1994.

[24] D. Comer, "The ubiquitous B-tree," *ACM Comput. Surv.*, vol. 11, pp. 121–137, 1979.

[25] T. H. Cormen, C. E. Leiserson, and R. L. Rivest, *Introduction to Algorithms*. Cambridge, MA: MIT Press, 1990.

[26] M. Crochemore and T. Lecroq, "Pattern matching and text compression algorithms," in *The Computer Science and Engineering Handbook* (A. B. Tucker, Jr., ed.), ch. 8, pp. 162–202, CRC Press, 1997.

[27] S. A. Demurjian, Sr., "Software design," in *The Computer Science and Engineering Handbook* (A. B. Tucker, Jr., ed.), ch. 108, pp. 2323–2351, CRC Press, 1997.

[28] G. Di Battista, P. Eades, R. Tamassia, and I. G. Tollis, *Graph Drawing*. Upper Saddle River, NJ: Prentice Hall, 1999.

[29] E. W. Dijkstra, "A note on two problems in connexion with graphs," *Numerische Mathematik*, vol. 1, pp. 269–271, 1959.

[30] J. R. Driscoll, H. N. Gabow, R. Shrairaman, and R. E. Tarjan, "Relaxed heaps: An alternative to Fibonacci heaps with applications to parallel computation.," *Commun. ACM*, vol. 31, pp. 1343–1354, 1988.

[31] S. Even, *Graph Algorithms*. Potomac, Maryland: Computer Science Press, 1979.

[32] D. Flanagan, *Java in a Nutshell*. O'Reilly, 5th ed., 2005.

[33] R. W. Floyd, "Algorithm 97: Shortest path," *Communications of the ACM*, vol. 5, no. 6, p. 345, 1962.

[34] R. W. Floyd, "Algorithm 245: Treesort 3," *Communications of the ACM*, vol. 7, no. 12, p. 701, 1964.

[35] M. L. Fredman and R. E. Tarjan, "Fibonacci heaps and their uses in improved network optimization algorithms," *J. ACM*, vol. 34, pp. 596–615, 1987.

[36] E. Gamma, R. Helm, R. Johnson, and J. Vlissides, *Design Patterns: Elements of Reusable Object-Oriented Software*. Reading, Mass.: Addison-Wesley, 1995.

[37] A. M. Gibbons, *Algorithmic Graph Theory*. Cambridge, UK: Cambridge University Press, 1985.

[38] A. Goldberg and D. Robson, *Smalltalk-80: The Language*.   Reading, Mass.: Addison-Wesley, 1989.

[39] G. H. Gonnet and R. Baeza-Yates, *Handbook of Algorithms and Data Structures in Pascal and C*. Reading, Mass.: Addison-Wesley, 1991.

[40] G. H. Gonnet and J. I. Munro, "Heaps on heaps," *SIAM Journal on Computing*, vol. 15, no. 4, pp. 964–971, 1986.

[41] M. T. Goodrich, M. Handy, B. Hudson, and R. Tamassia, "Accessing the internal organization of data structures in the JDSL library," in *Proc. Workshop on Algorithm Engineering and Experimentation* (M. T. Goodrich and C. C. McGeoch, eds.), vol. 1619 of *Lecture Notes Comput. Sci.*, pp. 124–139, Springer-Verlag, 1999.

[42] M. T. Goodrich, J.-J. Tsay, D. E. Vengroff, and J. S. Vitter, "External-memory computational geometry," in *Proc. 34th Annu. IEEE Sympos. Found. Comput. Sci.*, pp. 714–723, 1993.

[43] R. L. Graham and P. Hell, "On the history of the minimum spanning tree problem," *Annals of the History of Computing*, vol. 7, no. 1, pp. 43–57, 1985.

[44] L. J. Guibas and R. Sedgewick, "A dichromatic framework for balanced trees," in *Proc. 19th Annu. IEEE Sympos. Found. Comput. Sci.*, Lecture Notes Comput. Sci., pp. 8–21, Springer-Verlag, 1978.

[45] Y. Gurevich, "What does $O(n)$ mean?," *SIGACT News*, vol. 17, no. 4, pp. 61–63, 1986.

[46] J. Hennessy and D. Patterson, *Computer Architecture: A Quantitative Approach*. San Francisco: Morgan Kaufmann, 2nd ed., 1996.

[47] C. A. R. Hoare, "Quicksort," *The Computer Journal*, vol. 5, pp. 10–15, 1962.

[48] J. E. Hopcroft and R. E. Tarjan, "Efficient algorithms for graph manipulation," *Communications of the ACM*, vol. 16, no. 6, pp. 372–378, 1973.

[49] C. S. Horstmann, *Java Concepts for Java 5 and 6*. New York: John Wiley & Sons, 2008.

[50] C. S. Horstmann and G. Cornell, *Core Java*, vol. I–Fundamentals. Upper Saddle River, NJ: Prentice Hall, 8th ed., 2008.

[51] C. S. Horstmann and G. Cornell, *Core Java*, vol. II–Advanced Features. Upper Saddle River, NJ: Prentice Hall, 8th ed., 2008.

[52] B. Huang and M. Langston, "Practical in-place merging," *Communications of the ACM*, vol. 31, no. 3, pp. 348–352, 1988.

[53] J. JáJá, *An Introduction to Parallel Algorithms*. Reading, Mass.: Addison-Wesley, 1992.

[54] V. Jarnik, "O jistem problemu minimalnim," *Praca Moravske Prirodovedecke Spolecnosti*, vol. 6, pp. 57–63, 1930. (in Czech).

[55] R. E. Jones, *Garbage Collection: Algorithms for Automatic Dynamic Memory Management*. John Wiley and Sons, 1996.

[56] D. R. Karger, P. Klein, and R. E. Tarjan, "A randomized linear-time algorithm to find minimum spanning trees," *Journal of the ACM*, vol. 42, pp. 321–328, 1995.

[57] R. M. Karp and V. Ramachandran, "Parallel algorithms for shared memory machines," in *Handbook of Theoretical Computer Science* (J. van Leeuwen, ed.), pp. 869–941, Amsterdam: Elsevier/The MIT Press, 1990.

[58] P. Kirschenhofer and H. Prodinger, "The path length of random skip lists," *Acta Informatica*, vol. 31, pp. 775–792, 1994.

[59] J. Kleinberg and É. Tardos, *Algorithm Design*. Reading, MA: Addison-Wesley, 2006.

[60] D. E. Knuth, *Sorting and Searching*, vol. 3 of *The Art of Computer Programming*. Reading, MA: Addison-Wesley, 1973.

[61] D. E. Knuth, "Big omicron and big omega and big theta," in *SIGACT News*, vol. 8, pp. 18–24, 1976.

[62] D. E. Knuth, *Fundamental Algorithms*, vol. 1 of *The Art of Computer Programming*. Reading, MA: Addison-Wesley, 3rd ed., 1997.

[63] D. E. Knuth, *Sorting and Searching*, vol. 3 of *The Art of Computer Programming*. Reading, MA: Addison-Wesley, 2nd ed., 1998.

[64] D. E. Knuth, J. H. Morris, Jr., and V. R. Pratt, "Fast pattern matching in strings," *SIAM Journal on Computing*, vol. 6, no. 1, pp. 323–350, 1977.

[65] J. B. Kruskal, Jr., "On the shortest spanning subtree of a graph and the traveling salesman problem," *Proc. Amer. Math. Soc.*, vol. 7, pp. 48–50, 1956.

[66] N. G. Leveson and C. S. Turner, "An investigation of the Therac-25 accidents," *IEEE Computer*, vol. 26, no. 7, pp. 18–41, 1993.

[67] R. Levisse, "Some lessons drawn from the history of the binary search algorithm," *The Computer Journal*, vol. 26, pp. 154–163, 1983.

[68] A. Levitin, "Do we teach the right algorithm design techniques?," in *30th ACM SIGCSE Symp. on Computer Science Education*, pp. 179–183, 1999.

[69] B. Liskov and J. Guttag, *Abstraction and Specification in Program Development*. Cambridge, Mass./New York: The MIT Press/McGraw-Hill, 1986.

[70] E. M. McCreight, "A space-economical suffix tree construction algorithm," *Journal of Algorithms*, vol. 23, no. 2, pp. 262–272, 1976.

[71] C. J. H. McDiarmid and B. A. Reed, "Building heaps fast," *Journal of Algorithms*, vol. 10, no. 3, pp. 352–365, 1989.

[72] N. Megiddo, "Linear-time algorithms for linear programming in R^3 and related problems," *SIAM J. Comput.*, vol. 12, pp. 759–776, 1983.

[73] N. Megiddo, "Linear programming in linear time when the dimension is fixed," *J. ACM*, vol. 31, pp. 114–127, 1984.

[74] K. Mehlhorn, *Data Structures and Algorithms 1: Sorting and Searching*, vol. 1 of *EATCS Monographs on Theoretical Computer Science*. Heidelberg, Germany: Springer-Verlag, 1984.

[75] K. Mehlhorn, *Data Structures and Algorithms 2: Graph Algorithms and NP-Completeness*, vol. 2 of *EATCS Monographs on Theoretical Computer Science*. Heidelberg, Germany: Springer-Verlag, 1984.

[76] K. Mehlhorn and A. Tsakalidis, "Data structures," in *Handbook of Theoretical Computer Science* (J. van Leeuwen, ed.), vol. A. Algorithms and Complexity, pp. 301–341, Amsterdam: Elsevier, 1990.

[77] M. H. Morgan, *Vitruvius: The Ten Books on Architecture*. New York: Dover Publications, Inc., 1960.

[78] D. R. Morrison, "PATRICIA—practical algorithm to retrieve information coded in alphanumeric," *Journal of the ACM*, vol. 15, no. 4, pp. 514–534, 1968.

[79] R. Motwani and P. Raghavan, *Randomized Algorithms*. New York, NY: Cambridge University Press, 1995.

[80] T. Papadakis, J. I. Munro, and P. V. Poblete, "Average search and update costs in skip lists," *BIT*, vol. 32, pp. 316–332, 1992.

[81] P. V. Poblete, J. I. Munro, and T. Papadakis, "The binomial transform and its application to the analysis of skip lists," in *Proceedings of the European Symposium on Algorithms (ESA)*, pp. 554–569, 1995.

[82] R. C. Prim, "Shortest connection networks and some generalizations," *Bell Syst. Tech. J.*, vol. 36, pp. 1389–1401, 1957.

[83] W. Pugh, "Skip lists: a probabilistic alternative to balanced trees," *Commun. ACM*, vol. 33, no. 6, pp. 668–676, 1990.

[84] H. Samet, *The Design and Analysis of Spatial Data Structures*. Reading, MA: Addison-Wesley, 1990.

[85] R. Schaffer and R. Sedgewick, "The analysis of heapsort," *Journal of Algorithms*, vol. 15, no. 1, pp. 76–100, 1993.

[86] D. D. Sleator and R. E. Tarjan, "Self-adjusting binary search trees," *J. ACM*, vol. 32, no. 3, pp. 652–686, 1985.

[87] G. A. Stephen, *String Searching Algorithms*. World Scientific Press, 1994.

[88] R. Tamassia and G. Liotta, "Graph drawing," in *Handbook of Discrete and Computational Geometry* (J. E. Goodman and J. O'Rourke, eds.), ch. 52, pp. 1163–1186, CRC Press LLC, 2nd ed., 2004.

[89] R. Tarjan and U. Vishkin, "An efficient parallel biconnectivity algorithm," *SIAM J. Comput.*, vol. 14, pp. 862–874, 1985.

[90] R. E. Tarjan, "Depth first search and linear graph algorithms," *SIAM Journal on Computing*, vol. 1, no. 2, pp. 146–160, 1972.

[91] R. E. Tarjan, *Data Structures and Network Algorithms*, vol. 44 of *CBMS-NSF Regional Conference Series in Applied Mathematics*. Philadelphia, PA: Society for Industrial and Applied Mathematics, 1983.

[92] A. B. Tucker, Jr., *The Computer Science and Engineering Handbook*. CRC Press, 1997.

[93] J. D. Ullman, *Principles of Database Systems*. Potomac, MD: Computer Science Press, 1983.

[94] J. van Leeuwen, "Graph algorithms," in *Handbook of Theoretical Computer Science* (J. van Leeuwen, ed.), vol. A. Algorithms and Complexity, pp. 525–632, Amsterdam: Elsevier, 1990.

[95] J. S. Vitter, "Efficient memory access in large-scale computation," in *Proc. 8th Sympos. Theoret. Aspects Comput. Sci.*, Lecture Notes Comput. Sci., Springer-Verlag, 1991.

[96] J. S. Vitter and W. C. Chen, *Design and Analysis of Coalesced Hashing*. New York: Oxford University Press, 1987.

[97] J. S. Vitter and P. Flajolet, "Average-case analysis of algorithms and data structures," in *Algorithms and Complexity* (J. van Leeuwen, ed.), vol. A of *Handbook of Theoretical Computer Science*, pp. 431–524, Amsterdam: Elsevier, 1990.

[98] S. Warshall, "A theorem on boolean matrices," *Journal of the ACM*, vol. 9, no. 1, pp. 11–12, 1962.

[99] J. W. J. Williams, "Algorithm 232: Heapsort," *Communications of the ACM*, vol. 7, no. 6, pp. 347–348, 1964.

[100] D. Wood, *Data Structures, Algorithms, and Performance*. Reading, Mass.: Addison-Wesley, 1993.

Index

abstract data type, viii, 62
    array list, 238–239
    deque, 227
    dictionary, 424–425
    graph, 598–603
    list, 248–251
    map, 386–389
    ordered map, 407
    partition, 543–546
    priority queue, 338–342
    queue, 218–220
    sequence, 268
    set, 538–546
    stack, 203–204
    string, 8–9, 558–560
    tree, 288–289
abstraction, 62
(a, b) tree, 683–685
    depth property, 683
    size property, 683
acyclic, 626
adaptability, 60, 61
adaptable priority queue, 372
adapter, 239
Adel'son-Vel'skii, 504
adjacency list, 604, 607
adjacency matrix, 604, 609
adjacent, 599
ADT, *see* abstract data type
Aggarwal, 690
Aho, 236, 282, 504, 556, 596
Ahuja, 666
algorithm, 170
algorithm analysis, 170–188
    average case, 173–174
    worst case, 174
alphabet, 8, 559
amortization, 245–246, 543–546
ancestor, 286, 625

antisymmetric, 339
API, 82, 204
arc, 598
Archimedes, 170, 200
Ariadne, 611
arithmetic, 21
Arnold, 58
array, 34–38, 100–120
    capacity, 35
    length, 34
array list, 238–246, 408
    abstract data type, 238–239
    implementation, 240–246
associative stores, 386
asymmetric, 599
asymptotic analysis, 178–188
asymptotic notation, 174–178
    big-Oh, 175–177, 180–188
    big-Omega, 178
    big-Theta, 178
attribute, 615
autoboxing, 26
AVL tree, 447–458
    balance factor, 455
    height-balance property, 447

back edge, 613, 629, 630, 660
Baeza-Yates, 504, 556, 596, 690
bag, 433
balance factor, 455
balanced search tree, 472
Barůvka, 664, 666
base class, 65
base type, 5, 11, 19
Bayer, 504, 690
Bentley, 384, 434, 556
best-fit algorithm, 673
BFS, *see* breadth-first search
biconnected graph, 663